S0-AVU-488

THE AGE OF INTELLIGENT MACHINES

THE MIT PRESS

CAMBRIDGE, MASSACHUSETTS

LONDON, ENGLAND

Kurzweil, Ray

The Age of Intelligent Machines

RAYMOND

KURZWEIL

Kurzweil, Ray

Q
335
.K87

© 1990 Massachusetts Institute of Technology

All rights reserved. No part of this book may be repro-
duced in any form by any electronic or mechanical
means (including photocopying, recording, or
information storage and retrieval) without permission
in writing from the publisher.

This book was printed and bound by Dai Nippon
Printing Co., Japan.

Library of Congress Cataloging-in-Publication Data

Kurzweil, Ray.
The age of intelligent machines/Raymond Kurzweil.
    p.   cm.
Includes bibliographical references.
ISBN 0-262-11121-7
I. Artificial intelligence, I. Title,
Q335.K87 1990
006.3—dc20   89-13606
                         CIP

TO

SONYA

CONTENTS

1

2

3

4

PART TWO: THE MOVING FRONTIER

Acknowledgments

I would like to express my deep gratitude to the many persons who have provided inspiration, prodding, ideas, suggestions, comments, criticism, insight, contacts, logistics, software, pictures, and multifarious other forms of help and assistance. In particular, I would like to thank the following:

- My wife Sonya for her enthusiasm and loving patience through the many unexpected twists and turns of the creative process
- My mother Hannah and my father Fredric for having encouraged my early interest in an unproven field
- My son Ethan and my daughter Amy for teaching me everything I know
- Frank Satlow for his expert editorial guidance and encouragement
- Lou Jones for his beautiful and creative photographs and willingness to chase after intelligent machines and even more intelligent people around the world
- Rose Russo and Robert Brun of KelGraphic for turning my scribbled sketches into stunning illustrations
- Laurel Anderson for finding impossible-to-find historical photographs and illustrations
- Alison Roberts for her capable, earnest, and diligent administrative support—she was the "chief operating officer" of the "book project"
- My wonderfully proficient research team—Margaret Kennedy, Anand Bodapati, Marcia Ross, Kathy Duffin, and Terry Ehling—for their skills in finding long forgotten facts of remarkable relevance and for their irreplaceable assistance with references and the chronology
- Wendy Dennis for her energetic help in launching the research
- Alan Thwaits for his incisive copy editing
- Diane Jaroch for her elegant design
- Don Byrd for his many insightful comments and ideas
- Abby Joslin, Lauri Murphy, and Pat Camarena for their creative suggestions and enthusiastic administrative assistance
- George Gilder for many stimulating discussions
- Ted Johnson and Aaron Kleiner for their support and encouragement
- Martin Schneider and Robert Richter for their many creative contributions and close collaborations on the *Age of Intelligent Machines* film that accompanies this book

- My readers—Glenn Akers, Charles Ames, Abby Joslin, Don Byrd, Pat Camarena, Frances Davis, Wendy Dennis, Terry Ehling, Francis Ganong, George Gilder, Richard Goldhor, Ted Johnson, Robin Kinkead, Aaron Kleiner, Ethan Kurzweil, Elizabeth Meade, Bob Moog, Lauri Murphy, Alison Roberts, Steven Rothman, Frank Satlow, Martin Schneider and Mitchell Waldrop—for innumerable and invaluable comments and criticisms, some contradictory, all valid, and all of great value
- The MIT Press blind readers, whoever and wherever they may be
- Dan Dennett, Sherry Turkle, Marvin Minsky, Seymour Papert, Ed Feigenbaum, Harold Cohen, Margaret Boden, and Allen Newell for their ideas and insights
- The authors of the contributed articles: Margaret Litvin, Dan Dennett, Mitchell Waldrop, Sherry Turkle, Blaine Mathieu, Seymour Papert, Doug Hofstadter, Marvin Minsky, Ed Feigenbaum, Roger Schank, Christopher Owens, Jeff Pepper, K. Fuchi, Brian Oakley, Harold Cohen, Charles Ames, Michael Lebowitz, Allen Newell, Margaret Boden, and George Gilder
- Digital Equipment Corporation for its generous sponsorship of The Age of Intelligent Machines Exhibition
- The Boston Museum of Science; the Franklin Institute, Ph_ilidelphia; the Science Museums of Charlotte; the Fort Worth Museum of Science and History; the California Museum of Science and Industry, Los Angeles; the Science Museum of Minnesota, St. Paul; the Museum of Science and Industry, Chicago; and the Center of Science and Industry, Columbus, for hosting The Age of Intelligent Machines Exhibition, and especially the Boston Museum of Science for producing it
- Finally, all the scientists, researchers, industrialists, inventors, entrepreneurs, marketers, public relations consultants, administrative assistants, executives, and librarians who were willing to talk to me and who, when not taking time to talk to book writers, reporters, and other chroniclers of artificial intelligence, are busy creating the age of intelligent machines

Joral. (Photo by Lou Jones)

The Second Industrial Revolution

On May 26, 1733, John Kay, a twenty-nine-year-old inventor, received the news that the English Patent Office had awarded him a patent for his New Engine for Opening and Dressing Wool, now known as the flying shuttle.[1] To Kay this was good news, for he hoped to start a small business supplying his new machine to the burgeoning English textile industry. What neither Kay nor his contemporaries realized at the time was that his innovation in the weaving of cloth represented the launching of the Industrial Revolution.

Like many innovations that come at the right time in the right place, the flying shuttle caught on quickly. Unfortunately, Kay was more talented as an inventor than as a businessman, and after losing most of his money in litigation attempting to enforce his patent, he moved to France, where he died in poverty.

Kay nonetheless had a lasting impact. The widespread adoption of the flying shuttle created pressure for the more efficient spinning of yarn, which led to Sir Richard Arkwright's Cotton Jenny, patented in 1770. In turn, machines to card and comb the wool to feed the new mechanized spinning machines were developed in the 1780s. By the turn of the century all aspects of the production of cloth had been automated. The cottage industry of English textiles was rapidly being replaced by increasingly efficient centralized machines.[2]

Good ideas catch on and innovators in other industries took note of the dramatically improved productivity that mechanization had brought to English textiles. The process of industrialization spread to other industries and to other countries. Major innovations that followed included Ford's (1863–1947) concept of mass production and Edison's (1847–1931) harnessing of the electron. Ultimately Europe, the United States, Japan, and other parts of the world shifted from an agrarian and craft economy to one dominated by machines. The succession of increasingly efficient generations of automation has continued to this day. The changing patterns of production and employment, together with related scientific advances, have had dramatic effects on all aspects of modern life, profoundly affecting our social, cultural, educational, economic, and political institutions.

The Industrial Revolution was not without its controversies. Emerging, appropriately enough, from the English textile industry, the Luddite movement was founded in Nottingham in 1811.[3] The movement posed a serious and violent challenge to what its members perceived as a diabolical danger to the textile workers' livelihoods. In one sense, the fears of the Luddites were accurate. Jobs they thought were threatened by the new machines did indeed disappear. At the same time, however, new jobs were created as new industries emerged and economic activity increased, although this was often of little consequence to those displaced. The Luddite movement itself was ended within a decade of its founding due to a combination of repression and prosperity, although its name has remained very much alive as a symbol of a still lingering issue.[4] Automation versus jobs is still a particularly controversial issue in Europe, where it has had a noticeable impact on the rate at which new automated technologies are introduced. In the United States the issue simmers beneath the surface of political debate but rarely affects the pace of change. In Japan the issue is virtually unknown, due partly to a tradition in which the prosperous "first tier" industrial corporations provide lifetime employment, although employment guarantees are generally not extended by the less powerful "second tier" corporations and cottage industries.

Let us examine the Luddite issue for a moment. It is generally acknowledged that new jobs result as new industries are created by the advent of automa-

Ned Ludd disguised as a woman. Although his Luddite movement had little impact at the time, it has remained a symbol of opposition to machines and automation. (Supplied by Historical Pictures Service, Chicago)

tion. The critical question then becomes, How do these jobs compare to the jobs that are displaced? In particular, for every ten jobs that are eliminated by automation, are we creating twelve new jobs or eight? Do the new jobs pay more or less than the older ones? Are they more or less fulfilling? What about those who are displaced; can they be retrained for the new jobs? Are they?

We now have over a century of extensive industrialization to look back on, and an examination of some clear economic trends over the past century can provide insights into at least some of the above questions. With regard to the numbers of jobs, the answer is closer to twelve than eight. In 1870 only twelve million Americans, representing 31 percent of the population, had jobs.[5] By 1985 the figure rose to 116 million jobs held by 48 percent of the population.[6] This substantial increase in the number of jobs occurred despite the dramatic shift away from the labor content of agriculture. In 1900 more than a third of all American workers were involved in food production.[7] Today Americans are better fed and America a major food exporter, with only 3 percent of the workforce involved.[8]

In the economic power of jobs we see the most dramatic change. The gross national product on a per capita basis and in constant 1958 dollars went from $530 in 1870 to $3,500 in 1970.[9] There has been a similar change in the actual earning power of the available jobs. This 600 percent increase in real wealth has resulted in a greatly improved standard of living, better health care and education, and a substantially improved ability to provide for those who need help in our society. At the beginning of the Industrial Revolution life expectancy in North America and northwestern Europe was about 37 years. Now, two centuries later, it has doubled.

The jobs created have also been on a higher level and indeed much of the additional employment has been in the area of providing the higher level of education that today's jobs require. For example, we now spend ten times as much (in constant dollars) on a per capita basis for public school education than we did one hundred years ago.[10] In 1870 only 2 percent of American adults had a high school diploma, whereas the figure is 76 percent today.[11] There were only 52,000 college students in 1870; there are 7.5 million today.[12]

Attempts to project these trends into the future, including a recent study by the Institute for Economic Analysis at New York University, where a detailed input-output model of the U.S. economy was studied, indicate a continuation of these same trends.[13] While there will be ebbs and flows in economic development, the trend over the next two decades indicates that employment and productivity will continue to increase, as will the average educational level of the population. The study indicated, for example, that the share of jobs going to professionals will increase from 15 percent today to 20 percent by the end of the next decade, with engineers and teachers accounting for virtually all of the increase.[14]

From these trends it would seem that the concerns of the Luddite movement are not well founded. From a macroeconomic point of view, it is clear that automation and other related technological advances have fueled over a century of dramatic economic development. There are nonetheless difficult, if often temporary, dislocations that result from rapid technological change.[15] As our smokestack industries contract, workers with one set of skills do not necessarily find it easy to develop new careers. With the pace of change accelerating, we as a society need to find a

The first Industrial Revolution. Power
and wealth went to those who
controlled natural resources and
labor. Shown is an interior view of
Walcott Brothers manufacturing
facility for button hole cutters, 1856.
(Supplied by North Wind Picture
Archives)

way to provide viable avenues for displaced workers to reenter the economic mainstream with something more than a new dead-end job.

As profound as the implications of the first Industrial Revolution were, we are now embarking on yet another transformation of our economy, based once again on innovation. The Industrial Revolution of the last two centuries—the *first* Industrial Revolution—was characterized by machines that extended, multiplied, and leveraged our *physical* capabilities. With these new machines, humans could manipulate objects for which our muscles alone were inadequate and carry out physical tasks at previously unachievable speeds. While the social and economic impact of this new technology was controversial, the concept of machines being physically superior to ourselves was not. After all, we never regarded our species as unequaled in this dimension. Jaguars can run faster than we can, lions are better hunters, monkeys are better climbers, whales can dive deeper and longer, and birds are better fliers—indeed, without machines we cannot fly at all.

The *second* industrial revolution, the one that is now in progress, is based on machines that extend, multiply, and leverage our *mental* abilities. The same controversies on social and economic impact are attending this second great wave of automation, only now a new and more profound question has emerged. Though we have always regarded our species as relatively mediocre in physical capacity, this has not been our view with regard to our mental capacity. The very name we have given ourselves, *Homo sapiens*, defines us as the thinking people. The primary distinction in our biological classification is the ability of our species to manipulate symbols and use language.

Before Copernicus (1473–1543), our "species centricity" was embodied in a view of the universe literally circling around us in a testament to our unique and central status. Today our belief in our own uniqueness is a matter not of celestial

Pre-Copernican cosmology with man at the center. (From Gemma Phrysius's *Cosmographis,* 1539, in the British Museum, London)

relationships but of intelligence. Evolution is seen as a billion-year drama leading inexorably to its grandest creation—human intelligence. The spectre of machine intelligence competing even tangentially with that of its creator once again threatens our view of who we are.

This latest revolution, based on machines that expand the reach of our minds, will ultimately have a far greater impact than the revolution that merely expanded the reach of our bodies. It promises to transform production, education, medicine, aids for the handicapped, research, the acquisition and distribution of knowledge, communication, the creation of wealth, the conduct of government, and warfare. The cost-effectiveness of the key ingredients in our new technological base—computers and related semiconductor technology—is increasing at an exponential rate. The power of computer technology now doubles (for the same unit cost) every 18 to 24 months.[16]

Unlike some revolutions, this latest transformation of our industrial base will not arrive after one brief period of struggle. It will be a gradual process, but it is one already under way. The potential exists to begin to solve problems with which the human race has struggled for centuries. An example is the application of computer technology to the needs of the handicapped, a personal interest of mine. It is my belief that the potential exists within the next one or two decades to greatly ameliorate the principal handicaps associated with sensory and physical disabilities such as blindness, deafness, and spinal cord injuries. New bioengineering techniques that rely on expert systems and computer-assisted design stations for biological modeling are fueling a new optimism for effective treatments of a wide range of diseases, including genetic disorders.[17] The increase in real per capita wealth—600 percent in the past 100 years—is projected to continue.[18] There are many other examples of anticipated benefit.

The potential for danger is also manifest. We are today beginning to turn over our engines of war to intelligent machines, whose intelligence may be as flawed as our own.[19] Computer technology is already a powerful ally of the totalitarian.

The advent of intelligent machines is altering global trade relationships. A remarkable aspect of this new technology is that it uses almost no natural resources. Silicon chips use infinitesimal amounts of sand and other readily available materials. They use insignificant amounts of electricity. As computers grow smaller and smaller, the material resources utilized are becoming an inconsequential portion of their value. Indeed, software uses virtually no resources at all. The value of the technology lies primarily in the knowledge governing the design of the hardware, software, and data bases that constitute our intelligent machines, and in the ability to continue advancing these designs. This decreasing importance of material resources has allowed Japan, a country very poor in natural resources but rich in knowledge and expertise, to become one of the two wealthiest nations on the planet. There is the potential for emerging nations to largely skip industrialization and develop postindustrial societies based on an information economy.[20] While the first Industrial Revolution increased the demand for and the value of natural resources, the second industrial revolution is doing the opposite.

In the case of computer software, it is apparent that one is paying for the knowledge inherent in the design and not for the raw materials represented by the floppy disk and users' manual. What is sometimes less apparent is that the same economic model holds for most computer hardware as well. An advanced chip generally costs no more to produce than a floppy disk. As with a software program, the bulk of the cost of a chip is neither raw materials nor manufacturing labor, but rather what accountants call amortization of development, and what philosophers call knowledge.

It is estimated that raw materials comprise less than 2 percent of the value of chips (which is about the same estimate as for software) and less than 5 percent of the value of computers. As our computers become more powerful, the percentage of their value accounted for by raw materials continues to diminish, approaching zero. It is interesting to note that the same trend holds for most other categories of products. Raw materials comprise about 20 percent of the value of musical instruments, with this figure rapidly declining as acoustic musical-instrument technology is being replaced with digital-electronic technology. George Gilder estimates that the cost of raw materials for automobiles is now down to 40 percent of total costs (see "A Technology of Liberation" in this book). Again, this figure will continue to decline with the increasing use of computers and electronics as well as the replacement of expensive and relatively simple body materials such as steel with inexpensive yet relatively complex alternative materials such as new high-tech plastics.

With regard to the world of defense, military engagements such as the Israeli destruction of Russian SAM sites in Syria, the use of "smart" missiles in the Falklands war, and others have illustrated the growing importance of artificial intelligence in the military.[21] Many military observers now predict that in the 1990s, artificial intelligence technology will be of greater strategic importance than manpower, geography, and natural resources.[22] A major program called SCI (Strategic Computing Initiative) envisions the soldier of the future relying on a vast network of intelligent computers to make tactical decisions, fly planes, aim weapons, and avoid enemy fire.[23]

A lesson we can draw from these observations is the importance of education and training in a world relying increasingly on skill and innovation and decreasingly on material resources. One reliable prediction we can make about the future is that the pace of change will continue to accelerate. The revolution manifest in the age of intelligent machines is in its earliest stages. The impact of this new age will be greater than the radical technological and social changes that have come before it. It cannot be stopped. We need to understand it, live creatively with it, and harness it constructively. That is what this book is all about.

The Roots of Artificial Intelligence

CHAPTER 1

(Drawing by Bernard Schoenbaum,
1987; supplied by *The New Yorker*)

"Oh, if only it were so simple."

What Is AI, Anyway?

The postindustrial society will be fueled not by oil but by a new commodity called artificial intelligence (AI). We might regard it as a commodity because it has value and can be traded. Indeed, as will be made clear, the knowledge imbedded in AI software and hardware architectures will become even more salient as a foundation of wealth than the raw materials that fueled the first Industrial Revolution. It is an unusual commodity, because it has no material form. It can be a flow of information with no more physical reality than electrical vibrations in a wire.

If artificial intelligence is the fuel of the second industrial revolution, then we might ask what it is. One of the difficulties in addressing this issue is the amount of confusion and disagreement regarding the definition of the field. Other fields do not seem to have this problem. Books on biology do not generally begin with the question, What is biology, anyway? Predicting the future is always problematic, but it will be helpful if we attempt to define what it is we are predicting the future of.

One view is that AI is an attempt to answer a central question that has been debated by scientists, philosophers, and theologians for thousands of years. How does the human brain—three pounds of "ordinary" matter—give rise to thoughts, feelings, and consciousness? While certainly very complex, our brains are clearly governed by the same physical laws as our machines.

Viewed in this way, the human brain may be regarded as a very capable machine. Conversely, given sufficient capacity and the right techniques, our machines may ultimately be able to replicate human intelligence. Some philosophers and even a few AI scientists are offended by this characterization of the human mind as a machine, albeit an immensely complicated one. Others find the view inspiring: it means that we will ultimately be able to understand our minds and how they work.

One does not need to accept fully the notion that the human mind is "just" a machine to appreciate both the potential for machines to master many of our intellectual capabilities and the practical implications of doing so.

• The Usual Definition

Artificial Stupidity (AS) may be defined as the attempt by computer scientists to create computer programs capable of causing problems of a type normally associated with human thought.
Wallace Marshal, *Journal of Irreproducible Results (1987)*

Probably the most durable definition of artificial intelligence, and the one most often quoted, states that: "Artificial Intelligence is the art of creating machines that perform functions that require intelligence when performed by people."[1] It is reasonable enough as definitions go, although it suffers from two problems. First, it does not say a great deal beyond the words "artificial intelligence." The definition refers to machines and that takes care of the word "artificial." There is no problem here: we have never had much difficulty defining artificial. For the more problematic word "intelligence" the definition provides only a circular definition: an intelligent machine does what an intelligent person does.

A more serious problem is that the definition does not appear to fit actual usage. Few AI researchers refer to the chess-playing machines that one can buy in the local drug store as examples of true artificial intelligence, yet chess is *still* considered an intellectual game. Some equation-manipulation packages perform transformations that would challenge most college students. We consider these to be quite useful packages, but again, they are rarely pointed to as examples of artificial intelligence.

• The Moving-Frontier Definition

Mr. Jabez Wilson laughed heavily. "Well, I never!" said he. "I thought at first that you had done something clever, but I see that there was nothing in it, after all?" "I began to think, Watson," said Holmes, "that I made a mistake in explaining. 'Omne ignatum pro magnifico,' you know, and my poor little reputation, such as it is, will suffer shipwreck if I am so candid."
Sir Arthur Conan Doyle, *The Complete Sherlock Holmes*

The extent to which we regard something as behaving in an intelligent manner is determined as much by our own state of mind and training as by the properties of the object under consideration. If we are able to explain and predict its behaviour or if there seems to be little underlying plan, we have little temptation to imagine intelligence. With the same object, therefore, it is possible that one man would consider it as intelligent and another would not; the second man would have found out the rules of its behaviour.
Alan Turing (1947)

AI is the study of how to make computers do things at which, at the moment, people are better.
Elaine Rich

This leads us to another approach, which I like to call the "moving frontier" definition: artificial intelligence is the study of computer problems that have not yet been solved. This definition, which Marvin Minsky has been advocating since the 1960s, is unlike those found in other fields. A gene-splicing technique does not stop being part of bioengineering the moment it is perfected. Yet, if we examine the shifting judgments as to what has qualified as "true artificial intelligence" over the years, we find this definition has more validity than one might expect.

When the artificial intelligence field was first named at a now famous conference held in 1956 at Dartmouth College, programs that could play chess or checkers or manipulate equations, even at crude levels of performance, were very much in the mainstream of AI.[2] As I noted above, we no longer consider such game-playing programs to be prime examples of AI, although perhaps we should.

One might say that this change in perception simply reflects a tightening of standards. I feel that there is something more profound going on. We are of two minds when it comes to thinking. On the one hand, there is the faith in the AI community that most definable problems (other than the so-called "unsolvable" problems, see "The busy beaver" in chapter 3) can be solved, often by successively breaking them down into hierarchies of simpler problems. While some problems will take longer to solve than others, we presently have no clear limit to what can be achieved.

On the other hand, coexisting with the faith that most cognitive problems can be solved is the feeling that thinking or true intelligence is not an automatic technique. In other words, there is something in the concept of thinking that goes beyond the automatic opening and closing of switches. Thus, when a method has been perfected in a computerized system, we see it as just another useful technique, not as an example of true artificial intelligence. We know exactly how the system works, so it does not seem fundamentally different from any other computer program.

A problem that has *not yet* been solved, on the other hand, retains its mystique. While we may have confidence that such a problem will eventually be solved, we do not yet know its solution. So we do not yet think of it as just an automatic technique and thus allow ourselves to view it as true cybernetic cognition.[3]

Consider as a current example the area of artificial intelligence known as expert systems. Such a system consists of a data base of facts about a particular discipline, a *knowledge base* of codified rules for drawing inferences from the data base, and a high-speed *inference engine* for systematically applying the rules to the facts to solve problems.[4] Such systems have been successfully used to locate fuel deposits, design and assemble complex computer systems, analyze electronic circuits, and diagnose diseases. The judgments of expert systems are beginning to rival those of human experts, at least within certain well-defined areas of expertise.

Today expert systems are widely regarded as a central part of artificial intelligence, and hundreds of projects exist today to apply this set of techniques to dozens of fields. It seems likely that expert systems will become within the next ten years as widespread as computer spreadsheet programs and data-base management systems are today. I predict that when this happens, AI researchers will shift their attention to other issues, and we will no longer consider expert systems to be prime examples of AI technology. They will probably be regarded as just obvious extensions of data-base-management techniques.

Roger Schank uses the example of a pool sweep, a robot pool cleaner, to illustrate our tendency to view an automatic procedure as not intelligent.[5] When we first see a pool sweep mysteriously weaving its way around the bottom of a pool, we are impressed with its apparent intelligence in systematically finding its way around. When we figure out the method or pattern behind its movements, which is a deceptively simple algorithm of making preprogrammed changes in direction every time it encounters a wall of the pool, we realize that it is not very intelligent after all.

Another example is a computer program named ELIZA designed in 1966 by Joseph Weizenbaum to simulate a psychotherapist.[6] When interacting with ELIZA, users type statements about themselves and ELIZA responds with questions and comments. Many persons have been impressed with the apparent appropriateness and insight of ELIZA's ability to engage in psychoanalytic dialogue. Those users who have been given the opportunity to examine ELIZA's algorithms have been even more impressed at how simple some of its methods are.

We often respond to people the same way. When we figure out how an expert operates and understand his or her methods and rules of thumb, what once seemed very intelligent somehow seems less so.

It will be interesting to see what our reaction will be when a computer takes the world chess championship. Playing a master game of chess is often considered an example of high intellectual (even creative) achievement. When a computer does become the chess champion, which I believe will happen before the end of the century, we will either think more of computers, less of ourselves, or less of chess.[7]

Our ambivalence on the issue of the ability of a machine to truly emulate human thought tends to regard a *working* system as possibly useful but not truly intelligent. Computer-science problems are only AI problems until they are solved. This could be seen to be a frustrating state of affairs. As with the carrot on a stick, the AI practitioner can never quite achieve the goal.

• What Is Intelligence, Anyway?

It could be simply an accident of fate that our brains are too weak to understand themselves. Think of the lowly giraffe, for instance, whose brain is obviously far below the level required for self-understanding—yet it is remarkably similar to our own brain. In fact, the brains of giraffes, elephants, baboons—even the brains of tortoises or unknown beings who are far smarter than we are—probably all operate on basically the same set of principles. Giraffes may lie far below the threshold of intelligence necessary to understand how those principles fit together to produce the qualities of mind; humans may lie closer to that threshold—perhaps just barely below it, perhaps even above it. The point is that there may be no fundamental (i.e., Gödelian) reason why those qualities are incomprehensible; they may be completely clear to more intelligent beings.

Douglas R. Hofstadter, *Gödel, Escher, Bach: An Eternal Golden Braid*

A beaver and another forest animal are contemplating an immense man-made dam. The beaver is saying something like, "No, I didn't actually build it. But it's based on an idea of mine."

Edward Fredkin

If we can replace the word "artificial" with "machine," the problem of defining artificial intelligence becomes a matter of defining intelligence. As might be expected, though, defining intelligence is at least as controversial as defining artificial intelligence. One approach is to define intelligence in terms of its constituent processes: *a process comprised of learning, reasoning, and the ability to manipulate symbols.*

16

Learning is not simply the acquisition of *facts*, which a data-base-management system can do; it is also the acquisition of *knowledge*. Knowledge consists of facts, an understanding of the relationships between the facts, and their implications. One difference between humans and computers lies in the relative strengths in their respective abilities to understand symbolic relationships and to learn facts. A computer can remember billions of facts with extreme precision, whereas we are hard pressed to remember more than a handful of phone numbers. On the other hand, we can read a novel and understand and manipulate the subtle relationships between the characters—something that computers have yet to demonstrate an ability to do. We often use our ability to understand and recall relationships as an aid in remembering simple things, as when we remember names by means of our past associations with each name and when we remember phone numbers in terms of the geometric or numeric patterns they make. We thus use a very complex process to accomplish a very simple task, but it is the only process we have for the job. Computers have been weak in their ability to understand and process information that contains abstractions and complex webs of relationships, but they are improving, and a great deal of AI research today is directed toward this goal.

Reason is the ability to draw deductions and inferences from knowledge with the purpose of achieving a goal or solving a problem. One of the strengths of human intelligence is its ability to draw inferences from knowledge that is imprecise and incomplete. The very job of a decision maker, whether a national leader or a corporate manager, is to draw conclusions and make decisions based on information that is often contradictory and fragmentary. To date, most computer-based expert systems have used hard rules, which have firm antecedents and certain conclusions. For some problems, such as the job of DEC's XCON, which configures complex computer systems, hard rules make sense. A certain-sized computer board will either fit or not fit in a certain chassis. Other types of decision making, such as the structuring of a marketing program for a product launch or the development of national monetary policy, must take into account incomplete present knowledge and the probabilities of unknown future events. The latest generation of expert systems are beginning to allow rules based on what is called *fuzzy logic,* which provides a mathematical basis for making optimal use of uncertain information.[8] This methodology has been used for years in such pattern-recognition tasks as recognizing printed characters or human speech.

The ability to learn and acquire knowledge and to manipulate it inferentially and deductively is often referred to as symbolic reasoning, the ability to manipulate symbols. A symbol is a name or sign that stands for something else, generally a structure or network of facts and other symbols. Symbols are typically organized in complicated patterns rather than simple lists. Another strength of human intelligence is our ability to recognize the patterns represented by the symbols we know even when they occur in contexts different than the ones in which we originally learned the symbol. One of the reasons that the LISP programming language has been popular in developing AI applications is its strength in manipulating symbols that represent complex patterns and their relationships rather than orderly lists of facts (despite its name, which derives from "list processing").

Rather than defining intelligence in terms of its constituent processes, we might define it in terms of its goal: *the ability to use symbolic reasoning in the pursuit of a goal.* Symbolic reasoning is used to develop and carry out strategies to further the goals of its possessor. A question that then arises is, What are the goals? With machine intelligence, the goals have been set by the human designer of each system. The machine may go on to set its own subgoals, but its mission is imbedded in its algorithms. Science-fiction writers, however, have long speculated on a generation of intelligent machines that set their own agendas. With living creatures or species, the goals are often expressed in terms of survival either of the individual or the species. This is consistent with the view of intelligence as the ultimate (most recent) product of evolution.

The evidence does not yet make clear whether intelligence does in fact support the goal of survival. Intelligence has allowed our species to dominate the planet. We have also been sufficiently "intelligent" to unlock the destructive powers that result from manipulating physical laws. Whether intelligence, or at least our version of it, is successful in terms of survival is not yet clear, particularly when viewed from the long time scale of evolution.

Thus far *Homo sapiens* are less than 100,000 years old. Dinosaurs were a successful, surviving class of creatures for 160 million years. They have always been regarded as unintelligent creatures, although recent research has cast doubt on this view. There are, however, many examples of unintelligent creatures that have survived as a species (e.g. palm trees, cockroaches, and horseshoe crabs) for long periods of time.

Humans do use their intelligence to further their goals. Even if we allow for possible cultural bias in intelligence testing, the evidence is convincing that there is a strong correlation between intelligence, as measured by standardized tests, and economic, social, and perhaps even romantic success. A larger question is whether we use our intelligence in setting our goals. Many of our goals appear to stem from desires, fears, and drives from our primitive past.[9]

In summary, there appears to be no *simple* definition of intelligence that is satisfactory to most observers, and most would-be definers of intelligence end up with long checklists of its attributes. Minsky's *Society of Mind* can be viewed as a book-length attempt at such a definition. Allen Newell offers the following list for an intelligent system: it operates in real-time; exploits vast amounts of knowledge; tolerates erroneous, unexpected, and possibly unknown inputs; uses symbols and abstractions; communicates using some form of natural language; learns from the environment; and exhibits adaptive goal-oriented behavior.[10]

The controversy over what intelligence is, is reminiscent of a similar controversy over what life is. Both touch on our vision of who we are. Yet great progress has been made, much of it in recent years, in understanding the structures and methods of life. We have begun to map out DNA, decode some of the hereditary code, and understand the detailed chemistry of reproduction. The concern many have had that understanding these mechanisms would lessen our respect for life has thus far been unjustified. Our increasing knowledge of the mechanisms of life has, if anything, deepened our sense of wonder at the order and diversity of creation.

We are only now beginning to develop a similar understanding of the mechanisms of intelligence. The development of machine intelligence helps us to understand natural intelligence by showing us methods that may account for the many skills that comprise intelligence. The concern that understanding the laws of intelligence will trivialize it and lessen our respect for it may also be unjustified. As we begin to comprehend the depth of design inherent in such "deep" capabilities as intuition and common sense, the awe inherent in our appreciation of intelligence should only be enhanced.

• Evolution as an Intelligent Process

God reveals himself in the harmony of what exists.
Spinoza

A central tenet of AI is that we, an intelligent species, can create intelligent machines. At present the machines we have created, while having better memories and greater speed, are clearly less capable than we are at most intellectual tasks. The gap is shrinking, however. Machine intelligence is rapidly improving. The same cannot be said for human intelligence. A controversial question surrounding AI is whether the gap can ultimately be eliminated. Can machine intelligence ultimately equal that of human intelligence? Can it surpass human intelligence? A broader statement of the question is, Can an intelligent entity be more intelligent than the intelligence that created it?

One way to gain insight into these questions might be to examine the relationship of human intelligence to the intelligent process that created it—evolution. Evolution created human and many other forms of intelligence and thus may be regarded as an intelligent process itself.[11]

A nineteenth century view of evolution. (Supplied by North Wind Picture Archives)

One attribute of intelligence is its ability to create and design. The results of an intelligent design process—to wit, intelligent designs—have the characteristics of being aesthetically pleasing and functionally effective. It is hard to imagine designs that are more aesthetically pleasing or functionally effective than the myriad of life forms that have been produced by the process we call evolution. Indeed, some theories of aesthetics define aesthetic quality or beauty as the degree of success in emulating the natural beauty that evolution has created.[12]

Evolution can be considered the ultimate in intelligence—it has created designs of indescribable beauty, complexity, and elegance. Yet, it is considered to lack consciousness and free will—it is just an "automatic" process. It is what happens to swirling matter given enough time and the right circumstances.

Evolution is often pitted against religious theories of creation. The religious theories do share one thing in common with the theory of evolution—both attribute creation to an ultimate intelligent force. The most basic difference is that in the religious theories this intelligent force *is* conscious and does have free will, although some theologies, such as Buddhism, conceive of God as an ultimate force of creativity and intelligence and not as a personal willful consciousness.[13]

The theory of evolution can be simply expressed as follows. Changes in the genetic code occur through random mutation; beneficial changes are retained, whereas harmful ones are discarded through the "survival of the fittest."[14] In some ways it makes sense that the survival of the fittest would retain good changes and discard bad ones, since we define "good" to mean more survivable.

Yet let us consider the theory from another perspective. The genetic code is similar to an extraordinarily large computer program, about six billion bits to describe a human, in contrast to a few tens of millions of bits in the most complex computer programs. It is indeed a binary code, and we are slowly learning its digital language.[15] The theory says that changes are introduced essentially randomly, and the changes are evaluated for retention by survival of the entire organism and its ability to reproduce. Yet a computer program controls not just the one characteristic that is being changed but literally millions of other characteristics. Survival of the fittest appears to be a rather crude technique capable of concentrating on at most a few fundamental characteristics at a time. While a few characteristics were being optimized, thousands of others could degrade through the increasing entropy of random change.[16] If we attempted to improve our computer programs in this way, they would surely disintegrate.

The method we use to improve the programs we create is not the introduction of random code changes but carefully planned and designed changes and experiments designed to focus in on the changes just introduced. It has been proposed that evolution itself has evolved to where changes are not entirely random but in some way planned, and that changes are "tested" in some way other than overall survival, in which a change just introduced would be competing with thousands or even millions of other factors.[17]

Yet no one can describe a mechanism in which such planning and isolated evaluation could take place in the process of evolution. There appears, therefore, to be a gap in the theory of evolution. Clearly, the fossil and biochemical evidence is overwhelming that species have indeed undergone a slow but dramatic evolution in complexity and sophistication, yet we do not fully understand the mechanism. The proposed mechanism seems unlikely to work; its designs should disintegrate through increasing entropy.

One possible perspective would state that the creator of an intelligence is inherently superior to the intelligence it creates. The first step of this perspective seems to be well supported in that the intelligence of evolution appears vast. Yet is it?

While it is true that evolution has created some extraordinary designs; it is also true that it took an extremely long period of time to do so. Is the length of time required to solve a problem or create a design relevant to an evaluation of the level of an intelligence? Clearly it is. We recognize this by timing our intelligence tests. If someone can solve a problem in a few minutes, we consider that better than solving the same problem in a few hours or a few years. With regard to intelligence as an aid to survival, it is clearly better to solve problems quickly than slowly. In a competitive world we see the benefits of solving problems quickly.

Evolution has achieved intelligent work on an extraordinarily high level yet has taken an extraordinarily long period of time to do so. It is very slow. If we factor its achievements by its ponderous pace, I believe we shall find that its intelligence quotient is only infinitesimally greater than zero. An IQ of only slightly greater than zero is enough for evolution to beat entropy and create extraordinary designs, given enough time, in the same way that an ever so slight asymmetry in the physical laws may have been enough to allow matter to almost completely overtake antimatter.

The human race, then, may very well be smarter than its creator, evolution. If we look at the speed of human progress in comparison to that of evolution, a strong case can be made that we are far more intelligent than the ponderously slow process that created us. Consider the sophistication of *our* creations over a period of only a few thousand years. In another few thousand years our machines are likely to be at least comparable to human intelligence or even surpass it in all likelihood, and thus humans will have clearly beaten evolution, achieving in a matter of thousands of years as much or more than evolution achieved in several billion years. From this perspective, human intelligence may be greater than its creator.[18]

So what about the intelligence that we are in turn creating? It too could be greater than its creator. That is not the case today. While computers have a superiority in certain *idiot savant* types of thinking, our thinking is today significantly superior to that of our machines. Yet the intelligence of our machines is improving at a very rapid pace. Within a matter of years or decades it appears that computers will compete successfully with human intelligence in many spheres. If we extrapolate a sufficient number of decades or centuries into the future, it appears likely that human intelligence will be surpassed.[19] In contrast to what one might intuitively conclude, this perspective points consistently to the possibility that an intelligence may ultimately outperform its creator.

CHAPTER 2

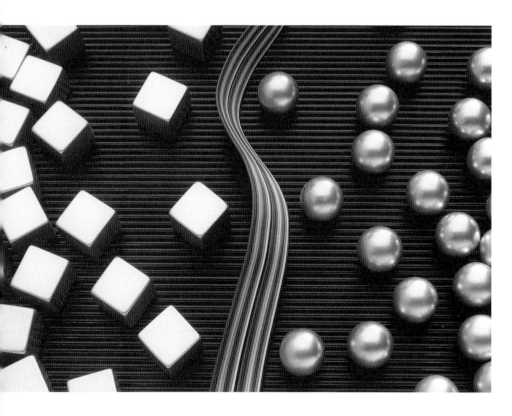

(Photo by Lou Jones)

Philosophical Roots

Some philosophers hold that philosophy is what you do to a problem until it's clear enough to solve it by doing science. Others hold that if a philosophical problem succumbs to empirical methods, that shows it wasn't really philosophical to begin with.

Jerry A. Fodor, *Representations: Philosophical Essays on the Foundations of Cognitive Science*

The chance of the quantum theoretician is not the ethical freedom of the Augustinian.

Norbert Wiener, *Cybernetics*

There's something queer about describing consciousness: whatever people mean to say, they just can't seem to make it clear. It's not like feeling confused or ignorant. Instead, we feel we know what's going on but can't describe it properly. How could anything seem so close, yet always keep beyond our reach?

Marvin Minsky, *The Society of Mind*

How can mind arise from nonmind? In examining human thought through the ages, philosophers appear to have gone down one of two paths. One school of thought, which we might call *mind as machine*, starts with the observation that human thought takes place in the human brain. The brain, in turn, is made up of tens to hundreds of billions of neurons. Neurons, while not simple structures, can nonetheless be fully understood as biochemical machines. Our brain thus consists of billions of biochemical machines interacting with each other, a fact from which we can draw two conclusions. The first is that the human mind is a machine, albeit an enormously complicated one. It is, after all, made up of matter just as subject to natural laws as any other machine. Second, we can, at least in theory, create other, human-made machines that employ the same techniques or algorithms for transforming information as the human brain. It is thus possible to replicate in a machine intellectual capacities that previously could only be achieved by human intelligence. This latter conclusion is a clear tenet of the AI movement.[1]

The opposing school of thought, which we can call *mind beyond machine*, contends that there are certain aspects of human thought and human existence that cannot be understood through this type of analysis. While acknowledging that the model of the human mind as machine may provide some understanding, it cites such attributes as consciousness and free will and, depending on the philosopher, other possible attributes as well, as being outside the fully rational, i.e., machinelike, model. It criticizes the approach of applying only logic to our understanding of thinking as being hopelessly circular, that is, as using an analysis based only on logic to conclude that thinking is based only on logic.[2]

In this debate the concept of emotions and feelings generally lie in a middle ground somewhere between consciousness and free will on the one hand and the logical patterns of rational thought on the other. The mind-as-machine school tends to analyze emotion as another form of logical thought, subject to its own rules. In this view, our emotions are a complex set of algorithms that motivate our behavior in a way that supports the greater goals of our culture. One could say that our emotions provide us with our *strategies,* while our more detailed logical calculations provide us with our *tactics*. The mind-beyond-machine school is more likely to conceive of emotion as being deeply imbedded in our consciousness and thus not fully comprehensible by logic alone.[3]

Thousands of years before there were computers, Plato (427–347 B.C.) recognized the similarity between at least certain aspects of human thinking and the apparently determined cause-and-effect behavior exhibited by machines.[4] The Platonic debates illuminate as clearly as any modern philosopher the apparent paradox of the human mind displaying free will while being subject to predictable natural laws. In the final analysis, it appears that Plato accepted both views as an irreducible duality. Such paradoxes, according to Plato, were not to be avoided; rather, they were the key to a richer understanding of the human condition.

Philosophical schools based on Plato's thought continued to shape European epistemology—the study of the limits and validity of knowledge—into the middle ages through the lasting influence of the Academy he founded and through one of his star pupils, Aristotle (384–322 B.C.).[5]

The European Renaissance of the seventeenth century and the Enlightenment, a philosophical movement of the seventeenth and eighteenth centuries, renewed and intensified an emphasis on the scientific method and in particular its application to thinking as a process that could be studied and understood as a phenomenon following natural laws. The rationalism of René Descartes (1596–1650), the empiricism of Francis Bacon (1561–1626) and the physics of Isaac Newton (1642–1727) were fused by Immanuel Kant (1724–1804) into a rigorous view of man's world based on knowledge as its principle building block.[6]

Modern philosophy has divided into two schools of thought. While often seen as contradicting one another and while frequently clashing with one another indeed, they primarily deal with divergent issues. Existentialism, which is the dominant school of philosophy today in Europe, has its roots in the unorthodox Christianity of Søren Kierkegaard (1813–1855) and the anti-Christianity of Friedrich Nietzsche (1844–1900). Existentialism, and a related field, phenomenology, regard human thought and human existence as describable by scientific analysis, but only partially.[7] Their emphasis has been on such phenomena as guilt, anxiety, and suffering, which in their views lie beyond fully rational exploration and are keys to understanding the limits of reason. The modern existentialism of such philosophers and playwrights as

Jean-Paul Sartre (1905–1980) and Samuel Beckett emphasize the role of free will in an apparently purposeless world.

A movement still popular in the United States that often clashes with existentialism is logical positivism, based on the early work of Ludwig Wittgenstein (1889–1951) and developed by Alfred Ayer and others. Searching for truth in the foundations of language, logical positivism gave rise to the development of linguistic theory by Noam Chomsky and others and greatly influenced the emergence of computation theory.[8]

The AI movement, which can be said to have its roots in logical positivism, has often clashed with the phenomenology of the existentialists, as most recently exemplified by the ongoing debate of AI practitioners such as Marvin Minsky, Seymour Papert, and Ed Feigenbaum with leading AI critic and phenomenologist Hubert Dreyfus. Unfortunately, this debate has been overly personal and divisive and thus has not contributed to a needed synthesis between the two pillars of modern philosophy.[9]

• Plato and the Platonists

The safest general characterization of the European philosophical tradition is that it consists of a series of footnotes to Plato.
Alfred N. Whitehead

All virtue is one thing, knowledge.
Plato

Plato, affirming the duality of life. (Supplied by North Wind Picture Archives)

Born in 427 B.C., Plato is regarded by many as the greatest philosopher of all time. His thought ranged across the ultimate nature of truth and knowledge, ethics, social order, political structure, physics, astronomy, and mathematics. His writings not only recorded his thoughts but constitute the primary written record of the teachings of his mentor, Socrates (c. 469–399 B.C.).[10] Aristotle viewed his own work as carrying out the dissemination and further development of Plato's teachings.[11] Socrates, Plato, and Aristotle are credited with having established the essentially rationalistic philosophy of Western culture.

While he is now considered one of the greatest writers of philosophy, Plato considered his writings as merely a tool to assist him in his teaching. He regarded his principle work as the establishment and guidance of the Academy, an institute for the pursuit of science and philosophy that he founded at the age of 41. The Academy outlived Plato, and the influence of its students and followers enabled Platonic thought to exert profound influence for many centuries after his death at age 80.[12]

While Plato had his mystical side, his is a highly ordered mysticism based on a theory of ideal forms, such as the form of the circle, of beauty, of love, etc., and the manifestation of forms in an imperfect world.[13] Plato's own logical reasoning exemplified the power of reason. By logical inference and his own thought experiments, Plato was able to determine, for example, that the planets followed orbits of single closed curves and that other apparent movements of stars and planets were due to the earth's movement through the sky in its own closed curve.[14] He then imagined the earth and the other planets circling a "Pythagorean central fire."[15]

Plato inferred the existence of irrational numbers, numbers that could not be expressed as the finite sum of fractions. The square root of 2 is the quintessential example. Plato saw the fact that rational numbers, with their finite definitions, and irrational numbers, with their infinite definitions, coexist in the same continuum as symbolic of the coexistence of material and mystical phenomena in nature.[16]

Though Plato's lasting contribution is in the rationalization of philosophy and a casting aside of the ornate mysticism of many of his peers, he maintains that there exists a level of creation that defies complete rational understanding. In his *Timaeus*, he describes the *ananke*, the level of reality that cannot be rationalized completely and that has to be accepted as a reflection of the purpose of creation.[17] Modern existentialism echoes Plato in its acceptance of a rational level of reality combined with its emphasis on the limits of reason and logic.

At the core of the duality of existence in the rational and mystical is the issue of consciousness and free will. In the *Phaedo* and later works, including *The Republic* and *Theaetetus*, Plato expresses the profound paradox inherent in the concept of consciousness and man's ability to freely choose. On the one hand, human beings partake of the natural world and are subject to its laws. Our minds are natural phenomena and thus must follow the cause and effect laws manifest in machines and other lifeless creations of man. On the other hand, cause and effect mechanics, no matter how complex, do not, according to Plato, give rise to self-awareness or consciousness.[18] Plato attempted to resolve this conflict in his theory of the Forms.[19] Consciousness is not an attribute of the mechanics of thinking, but rather the ultimate reality of human existence. Our consciousness or "soul" is immutable and unchangeable. Thus, our interaction with the physical world is on the level of the "mechanics" of our complex thinking process in a complex environment. Yet Plato was not fully satisfied with this metaphysical doctrine. If the soul is immutable and unchanging, then it cannot learn or partake in reason, because it would need to change to absorb and respond to experience. He expressed dissatisfaction with positing consciousness in either the rational processes of the natural world or the mystical level of the ideal Form of the self or soul.

An even deeper paradox is apparent in the concept of free will. Free will is purposeful behavior and decision making. Plato believed in a "corpuscular physics" based on fixed and determined rules of cause and effect.[20] If human decision making is based on such interactions of basic particles, our decisions too must be predetermined. Such predetermination would, however, appear to contradict human freedom to choose. The addition of randomness into natural laws is a possibility, but it does not solve the problem. Randomness would eliminate the predetermination of decisions and actions, but it contradicts the purposefulness of free will, as there is nothing purposeful in randomness. Positing free will in the soul and thus separating it from the rational cause and effect mechanics of the natural world is also not satisfactory for Plato, because Plato is uncomfortable placing reason and learning in the soul. These attributes of our thinking process are too orderly and logical to place entirely on the mystical plane.[21]

From Aristotle on, philosophers have debated for over two thousand years exactly what Plato's position was on these issues. Support for apparently contradictory views can be found in Plato's writings. My own view is that Plato believed in an essentially irreducible paradox at the core of the issues of consciousness and free will. I base this on his refusal to write his own metaphysics and on the eloquence with which Plato is able to articulate the alternate sides of each paradox. Plato's choice of the dialogue form was an excellent medium for expressing paradox in that it freed him to express passionately conflicting views.[22]

Irreducible paradox at the core of reality has found support in a surprising place—twentieth century physics. Physics, which seeks to describe ultimate reality in rational terms, has concluded that the essence of electromagnetic radiation is both a particle and a wave, two mutually exclusive and inconsistent models. Quantum theory too is based on a paradox: particles have precise locations, but we cannot know what these locations are. In its ultimate form, quantum mechanics describes a particle as having no precise location, although somehow the particle exists in a multidimensional space.[23]

In perhaps his most direct appeal to paradox as a resolution of apparent conflict of ideas, Plato discusses the duality of human love in *Phaedrus*.[24] By applying the logical method to the study of passion, he concludes that love and its expression in the apparently mad behavior of the lover is rooted both in the material world and in the attempt of the soul to achieve union with the ideal Form of transcendent emotion.

What is truly remarkable about Plato's writings is the extent to which they are, after twenty-three hundred years, relevant to modern philosophical dilemmas on the relationship of human thought to the mechanics of the machine. Plato saw clearly the relationship of human thought to the rational processes of a machine. He recognized that human thought was governed by natural law and that natural law was an essentially logical process. There is no limit, according to Plato, to the extent to which we can unravel human thought and behavior by scientific observation and logical inference. At the same time, he felt that human reality was not sufficiently expressed in logic alone. He does not resolve this problem, however, by attributing human thought to mystical processes that are of a different world from the logical processes of the material world. Instead, he resolves that the duality of human thought as both a logical process and one that transcends pure logic represents a necessary coexistence. It is a synthesis of views that is relevant to the modern conflict between the logical positivist foundation of the AI movement and existential-phenomenological views.

The Platonists

While Plato's thought had wide and diverse influences and interpretations after his death, one of the more interesting refinements of his thought made by his successors was a certain "mathematization" of his philosophy and the expression of his philosophy of Forms in numeric terms.[25] The Forms, which constitute ideals such as round, beauty, justice, and love, are regarded as pure concepts in the same way that numbers are pure concepts. At the other extreme of reality is the physical world that

**The School of Athens, finding truth
in numbers. (Supplied by North Wind
Picture Archives)**

imperfectly manifests the Forms. In between the Forms and physical reality are
"mathematicals," which, like the Forms, are perfect and unchanging but, like
physical reality, are numerous. In other words, there is only one concept or Form
circle, but there can be many instances of circles. Each instance can be immutable
and perfect in the mathematical realm, while each manifestation of circularity in the
physical world will be changeable and somewhat less than perfect.

These views are not directly expressed in the dialogues but are often
attributed (e.g., by Aristotle) to Plato's later oral teachings. They take place during a
time of fertile development of mathematical theory by members and associates of
Plato's Academy, including Euclid (330–260 B.C.), the expositor of plane geometry,
and Theaetetus (c. 415–369 B.C.), the creator of solid geometry.[26]

The expression of the mystical concept of Forms in the logical language of
mathematics expresses again the paradox at the heart of Plato's views of human
reality and thought. In the *Epinomis*, Plato states that the "relations of numbers are
the key to the whole mystery of nature."[27]

The Enlightenment, along with parallel fertile developments in science and theology, was a philosophical movement to restore the supremacy of human reason, knowledge, and freedom. It had its roots in both the artistic, literary, and cultural activity of the previous three centuries (the European Renaissance) and the Greek philosophy of twenty centuries earlier. It considered its own roots to be with Socrates, Plato, and Aristotle, and it constituted the first systematic reconsideration of the nature of human thought and knowledge since the Platonists.[28]

With Isaac Newton's presentation of the laws of gravitation in his *Philosophiae Naturalis Principia Mathematica*, published in 1687, as well as advances in the construction of clocks and mechanical automata, the philosophers of the Enlightenment had more powerful models both of natural laws and of the potential of machines than did their counterparts two thousand years earlier.[29] Machines became more elaborate and more capable as mechanical automata developed in sophistication and popularity during the seventeenth and eighteenth centuries.[30]

Descartes

The Enlightenment saw a blending of philosophy and science, as the same persons often dominated both fields. Descartes, for example, formulated the theory of optical refraction and developed the principles of modern analytic geometry. In his own view, Descartes's efforts in mathematics and science were intended primarily as a means of exploring and demonstrating certain aspects of his metaphysical doctrine. He needed to demonstrate the deterministic nature of the real world and these major scientific discoveries were in a sense footnotes to Descartes's philosophical investigations. The mystery of how mind can arise from nonmind, of how thoughts and feelings can arise from the ordinary matter of the brain, sometimes called the mind-body problem, was perhaps most clearly articulated by Descartes.[31]

In his comprehensive *Discourse de la Méthode*, Descartes pushed rational skepticism to its limits. Acknowledging that the existence of other people and even our own bodies may be illusions, he concluded that we cannot doubt the existence of our own thought and hence his famous conclusion "I think, therefore I am."[32]

Descartes was fascinated by automata and made contributions to their design. Once while Descartes was traveling by sea, the ship's captain was startled by the realistic movements of Descartes's mechanical doll Francine and forcibly threw "her" overboard, believing the automaton to have been a product of the devil.[33]

Newton

Linking the process of thought to the determined interactions of the natural world gained momentum with Newton's breakthrough in the understanding of mechanical law. Newton set out as his goal to find a link between the mechanical interactions of objects we observe in the laboratory and the movement of celestial bodies that we observe in the sky. The goal was a unified set of formulas that explains the movement of objects from the very small to the very large, something never before achieved. The result was unexpectedly successful—Newtonian mechanics appeared

René Descartes, confident of his own existence. (Supplied by North Wind Picture Archives)

Probl I

Investiganda est curva Linea ADB in qua grave a dato quovis puncto A ad datum quodvis punctum B vi gravitatis suae citissime descendet

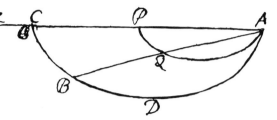

Solutio.

A dato puncto A ducatur recta infinita APCZ horizonti parallel et super eadem recta describatur tum Cyclois quaecunq AQP recta AB (recta et si opus est producta) occurrens in puncto Q, tum Cyclois alia ADC cujus basis et altitudo sit ad prioris basem et altitudinem re spective ut AB ad AQ. Et hae Cyclois novissima transibit per punctum B et erit Curva illa linea in qua grave a puncto A ad punctum B vi gravitate sua citissime perveniet. Q. E. J.

Newton's solution of the "quickest descent" problem. Since Newton's formulas predict the exact movements of billiard balls and planets, philosophers wondered whether the movements of human "particles" were equally predetermined. (Supplied by North Wind

Isaac Newton analyzing rays of light. (Supplied by North Wind Picture Archives)

to explain with extreme accuracy a deterministic order that governed all matter.[34] With one publication Newton swept aside centuries of medieval imprecision.

Newtonian mechanics remained the dominant view of both celestial and particle mechanics for almost two and one half centuries.[35] While Einstein (1879–1955) showed Newtonian mechanics to be a special case of his broader theory of relativity, this "special case" happens to be the world we live in.[36] One has to enter the world of high-speed subatomic particles or certain astronomical phenomena to witness significant deviations from Newtonian mechanics. Studies of naive physics, which is an exploration of the mental models of the physical world that people actually use, indicate that we believe that we live in a Newtonian, not an Einsteinian, world.

When Newton had successfully explained major aspects of the universe, the implications of his theory were not lost on the theologians of his day.[37] The success and apparent power of Newton's ideas were seen as a threat to the unique status of man. Fear and anger were expressed that the same mathematical reasoning that resulted in Newtonian Mechanics would be extended to the processes of the mind. It was feared that human thought would be subjected to the indignity of comparison with the determined interactions of billiard balls, which were often used to demonstrate mechanical principles. Even Wilhelm Leibniz (1646–1716), who shares credit with Newton for the invention of the calculus used to express Newtonian laws, attacked Newton for regarding God as a "clumsy watchmaker."[38]

Kant

Immanuel Kant, born in 1724 in East Prussia (now part of the Soviet Union), is widely regarded as the preeminent philosopher of the Enlightenment. He typified the Enlightenment in his emphasis on human reason and rationality, and he attempted to develop a metaphysical doctrine based entirely on reason.[39] In Kant's conception, human thought is guided by a priori principles and concepts, that is, concepts and structures that are not based on experience. Furthermore, in Kant's view, human knowledge constitutes the ultimate reality. This reversed the prior conception that ultimate reality resided in the physical world, with our thoughts based on our imprecise sensory impressions reflecting imperfect models of the physical world.[40]

Three of Kant's innovations would profoundly alter the philosophical landscape and set the stage for the emergence of twentieth-century rationalism. First, Kant's model of a priori concepts influenced and is echoed in the logical positivist search for truth in language and the concept of the innate structures in language postulated by modern linguistics. Second, by rejecting Descartes's dichotomy between the instinctive reflex of the animal and the rational thought of man, Kant opened up even further than his predecessors the processes of human thought to analytic investigation. Finally, Kant's emphasis on the supremacy of knowledge over other levels of reality would be echoed by both the logical positivist and existentialist schools of the twentieth century.

The relationship of the Enlightenment to the modern schools

On the issue of the ultimate nature of human reason, the philosophers of the Enlightenment, while diverse in their views, essentially agree with the modern existential school. Both maintain that while logic and the scientific method can be used to explore human thought and the thinking process in great detail, there is a level of human existence and experience that defies such analysis. However, the Enlightenment ended up defining the metaphysical level with such logical rigor, stripping away the complexities of earlier mysticism, that it set in motion a movement to explain all of reality in rational terms. The logical-positivist school continued and extended this tradition.[41] The existential movement, on the other hand, can be said to be a reaction to this trend. While acknowledging the role of logic and scientific analysis, the existentialists have attempted to refocus attention on the irrational and paradoxical side of the human condition.

• The Logical Positivists and the Existential Reaction

The myth that everything in the world can be rationally explained has been gaining ground since the time of Descartes. An inversion was necessary to restore the balance. The realization that reason and anti-reason, sense and non-sense, design and chance, consciousness and unconsciousness belong together as necessary parts of a whole.
Hans Richter, *Dada*

It is essential to abandon the over-valuation of the property of being conscious before it becomes possible to form any correct view of the origin of what is mental.
Sigmund Freud, *The Interpretations of Dreams*

Kant as the first logical positivist

The Enlightenment as it had culminated in the thought of Immanuel Kant had relegated metaphysics to an elegant and simple role in explaining the human condition. Our understanding of human memory, our reasoning faculty, even our emotions could be understood in terms of scientific inquiry and analysis. While Kant did regard the metaphysical level as supreme, he had much more to say about the intricacies of the physical level. Although it was not his intention, his impact has been to move the western philosophical tradition toward less emphasis on the role of metaphysics.[42] He has, in fact, been called the "first logical positivist."

Ludwig Wittgenstein

The title of the first logical positivist truly belongs, however, to Ludwig Wittgenstein. An enigmatic figure, Wittgenstein gave away his large inherited fortune so as not to be distracted from his philosophy by worldly possessions.[43] His most influential and first major work, the *Tractatus Logico-Philosophicus,* was not an instant success.[44] Wittgenstein had a great deal of difficulty in finding a publisher for his work, and it was ultimately the influence of his former instructor, Bertrand Russell (1872–1970), that allowed the book to come into print.[45] It has come to be regarded by some, however, as perhaps the most influential philosophical work of the twentieth century.

Wittgenstein further applied the analytic treatment of human thought, extended by the Enlightenment, to the study of human language. He examines the nature of language, how it is that we communicate using language, and what it is

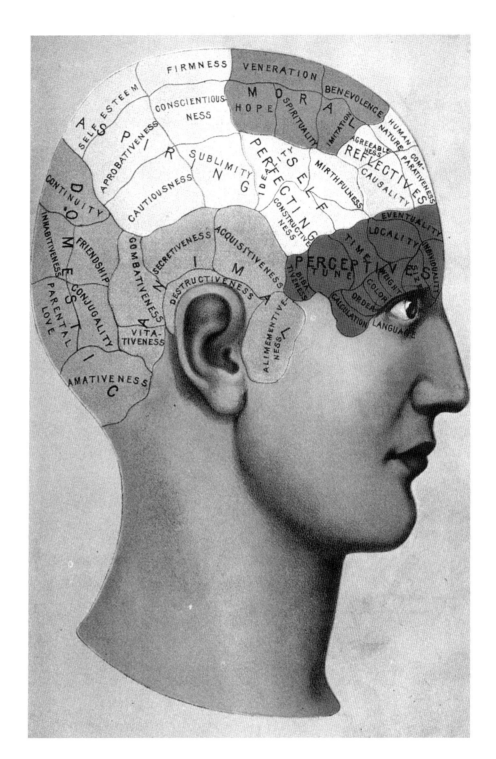

A place for everything and everything in its place: a nineteenth century view of the brain. (From an 1895 medical guide; photo by Coco McCoy of Rainbow)

that we are communicating. His examination is not, however, an exploration of the structure, organization, physiology, or psychology of communication. Rather, it is an attempt to provide a philosophical definition of knowledge—what we can know—by analyzing the meaning of language. He goes on in the *Tractatus* to consider language to be the embodiment of what can be said, what can be known, indeed, what can be thought:

4.0.0.3.1 All philosophy is a "critique of language."[46]

5.6 *The limits of my language* mean the limits of my world.[47]

5.6.1 We cannot think what we cannot *say*.[48]

Wittgenstein goes on to define language in a particular, some would say peculiar, way. In Wittgenstein's world there are certain elementary facts, there are propositions about relations between elementary facts, and there are certain allowable transformations on such propositions that yield composite propositions. His concept of human thought is that we receive sense impressions, which comprise elementary facts. We can then transform these elementary facts and derive relationships among them according to the allowable logical processes. Any thought outside this scheme is either false or nonsensical.

Wittgenstein makes two major points that have a direct bearing on the intellectual roots of artificial intelligence. He makes a direct link between human thought and a formal process that can be described only as computation. To reorder Wittgenstein's statements, we cannot think what we cannot say; we cannot say, or at least we ought not say, what is meaningless in the language we are speaking; statements in any language are indeed meaningless unless they can be derived from a formal (and therefore computationlike) sequence of transformations on a data base of elementary propositions.

This description of human thought as a formal sequence of computations would be restated two decades later in the Church-Turing thesis (see chapter 3).[49] The Church-Turing thesis was regarded as a radical doctrine when it was first proposed, but it has its roots in the *Tractatus*. It is not a thesis that everyone familiar with it necessarily accepts, and it remains controversial today. Wittgenstein himself ended up rejecting it.

The other point made in the *Tractatus* that would have significance later to computational theorists is that thought is embedded in language.[50] It is also interesting to note that language as conceived in the *Tractatus* has more of the quality of the programming language LISP or even PROLOG than it does of Wittgenstein's native German.

The organization of the book is also interesting. The treatise contains only seven primary formal statements, numbered 1 through 7. To help us along, Wittgenstein also includes several levels of modifying statements. For example, statements 1.1 and 1.2 modify statement 1. In turn 1.1.1 is provided to help explain 1.1, and so on. The reader has the choice of reading the book from left to right or from top down. The modular structure would please today's proponents of good programming style.

Wittgenstein starts with, "The world is all that is the case," (statement 1) and ends with, "What we cannot speak about we must pass over in silence" (state-

Ludwig Wittgenstein. "What we cannot speak about we must pass over in silence." (Supplied by Austrian Press)

ment 7).[51] One thing that is clear from these two statements is that the *Tractatus* was an ambitious work.

In 1953, two years after Wittgenstein's death, *Philosophical Investigations*, his last work, was published.[52] Views of its significance vary with the point of view of the critic. Logical positivists who trace their intellectual roots to the early Wittgenstein regard his later work as confused and disorganized, while existentialists regard it as a work of major importance.[53] In what is perhaps a unique occurrence in philosophical history, Wittgenstein is credited with having established two major systems of philosophy, each with great influence, with the second criticizing and rejecting the first.[54] Wittgenstein ends up near the end of his life having a lot to say about subjects that he had argued in the early *Tractatus* should be passed over in silence.

Ayer and the formalization of logical positivism

Alfred Ayer and others carried on Wittgenstein's work, correcting errors and expressing it with a degree of formalism and rigor that Wittgenstein had neither the time nor patience to carry out.[55] At a philosophical level, Logical Positivism argues that every statement, and by implication all knowledge, is either based on sense data ("a posteriori" or "synthetic"), or is based on logic ("a priori" or "analytic"). It rejects all metaphysical theories as strictly meaningless and having only emotive force. On a practical level, modern theories of linguistics and computation were derived from the formalisms of Logical Positivism. One does not need to accept all of its implications to recognize its contribution as the philosophical basis of artificial intelligence.

The existential reaction

As with any major philosophical movement, the views and theories of its proponents are diverse and complex. It is nonetheless reasonable to view existentialism as a reaction on an intellectual and cultural level to the major drift of Western thought toward greater and greater reliance on rational and analytic views. At its core, existentialism defines human reality as almost the reverse of the logical-positivist view. It considers the analytic and synthetic types of statements, which are the only meaningful statements in logical positivism, as either meaningless or trivial. It regards the spiritual and emotive life, which are meaningless in logical-positivist terms, as the seat of true meaning.[56]

Wittgenstein revisited

Some recent views of the early Wittgenstein claim that he was not denying the existence of a realm beyond the narrow definition of meaning expressed in the *Tractatus*. Clearly, the last sentence in the *Tractatus*, "What we cannot speak about we must pass over in silence," is referring to something.[57] If it is referring to something that does not exist, then even by the early Wittgenstein's own standards the sentence would be meaningless. Since we can assume that Wittgenstein would not end his book with a meaningless sentence, the phrase "what we cannot speak about" is referring to something meaningful. If "what we cannot speak about" is a meaningful concept and yet we must pass over it in silence, then the sentence must be a plea for silent contemplation of a higher realm.

Why is philosophy so complicated? It ought to be entirely simple. Philosophy unties the knots in our thinking that we have, in a senseless way, put there. To do this it must make movements that are just as complicated as these knots. Although the result of philosophy is simple, its method cannot be if it is to succeed. The complexity of philosophy is not a complexity of its subject matter, but of our knotted understanding.

Ludwig Wittgenstein

The relationship of human thought to the "logical" process of the computer continues to be controversial, a continuation of the debate started in the Platonic dialogues. The very name "artificial intelligence" juxtaposes two concepts that engender diverse and often intense intellectual and emotional reactions.

One particularly noisy debate has been going on for twenty years between a number of the academic AI leaders and Hubert Dreyfus, a modern phenomenologist and Berkeley professor. It began with a paper Dreyfus wrote as a consultant to the Rand Corporation in 1965 entitled, "Alchemy and Artificial Intelligence."[58] As might be clear from the title, it was a no-holds-barred attack on what was at that time an uncertain new academic discipline. Since then Dreyfus has made something of a career out of attacking artificial intelligence.

Such criticism might be useful to the field, and perhaps some of it is. Unfortunately, the debate has been marred in a number of ways. First, there has been considerable personal anger expressed on both sides. Dreyfus has been quoted as saying, "Why do I get so upset with people like Papert, Minsky, Newell and Simon?—and I really do get upset. It's really puzzling. I'll have to think about that. . . . Maybe I attack in them what I dislike in myself, an excessive rationality."[59]

More serious is an unwillingness on both sides to fully understand the disciplines and traditions of the other. Dreyfus has displayed considerable ignorance of AI methods and status. In a recent article Dreyfus describes how he was able to trick ELIZA, a computer program written by Joseph Weizenbaum to simulate a psychotherapist (see "ELIZA Passes the Turing Test," below).[60] Aside from having been written twenty years earlier, ELIZA was considered even then to be a simpleminded program unrepresentative of the state of the art.[61] Perhaps Dreyfus' most consistent theme is the inability of the hard antecedent-consequence type of logic to solve certain types of problems.[62] While this observation is correct, most AI researchers do not propose "PROLOG-like" logic as the solution to all problems.[63] For example, using fuzzy logic principles to deal in a methodologically sound manner with uncertain observations is becoming increasingly popular.[64] It is also feasible to create systems with thousands or even millions of parallel processes to emulate human pattern recognition and skill acquisition abilities. Dreyfus describes machine intelligence as a fixed phenomenon and regards today's apparent limitations as permanent limitations rather than tomorrow's challenges.

Dreyfus continually presses the theme that the AI field has been overly optimistic and has underestimated the deep nature of many problems. The criticism has considerable justification, but Dreyfus takes the position to an extreme by listing specific tasks that he maintains a computer will *never* do, including playing championship chess, riding a bicycle, and understanding human speech.[65] These would seem

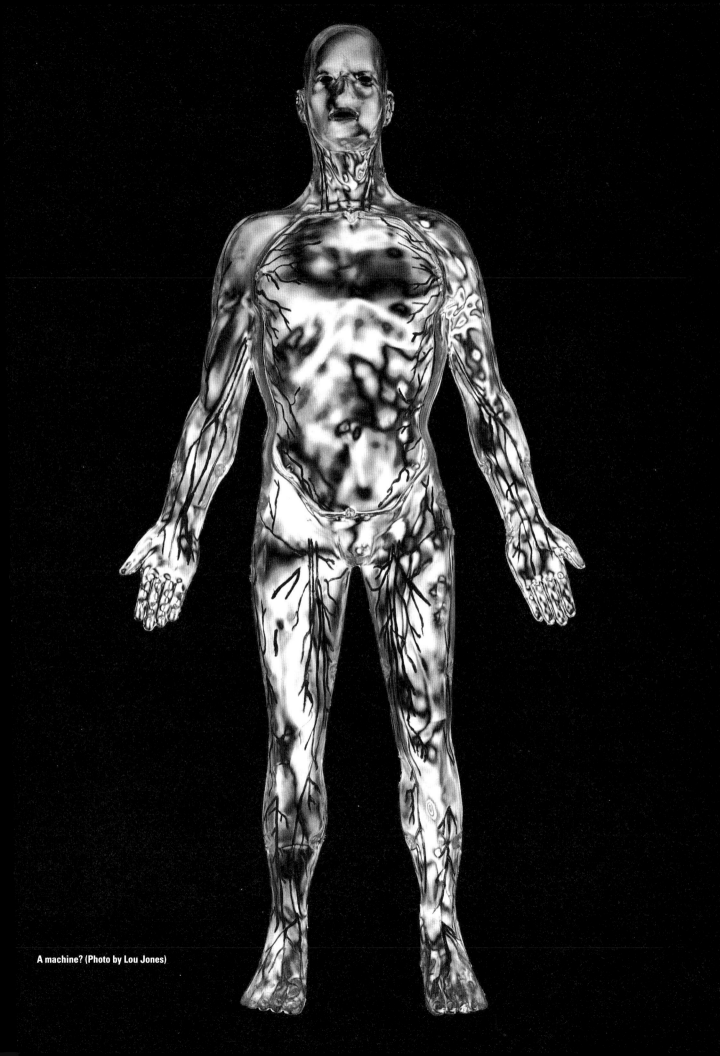

A machine? (Photo by Lou Jones)

to be needlessly negative predictions, reminiscent of earlier predictions that "man is not meant to fly" ("man," of course, does a lot of things he was "not meant" to do). Computers are close to accomplishing some of these tasks now, though how close depends, of course, on the standard of performance one will accept.[66] In my opinion, the levels of machine performance will continue to increase over time and, if one is intellectually honest, it appears to be only a matter of time before any particular standard is reached. And perhaps if Dreyfus is intellectually honest, he will be won over. He has in fact stated that if in a Turing test, a machine could fool him 60 percent of the time as to whether he was dealing with natural or artificial intelligence, he would concede defeat.[67] One has to note, however, that this offer is less generous than it appears at first glance. Dreyfus, as the human judge in such a Turing test, would be able to achieve an accuracy of 50 percent just by guessing randomly.

In turn, AI critics of Dreyfus have been quick to jump on Dreyfus's limited understanding of computer technology but have themselves not taken adequate time to understand either Dreyfus's intellectual tradition, with its roots in the work of Kierkegaard, Heidegger, and the late Wittgenstein, or the relevance of this tradition to the goals of the AI movement.[68]

Dreyfus revisited

In a recent article by Hubert Dreyfus and his brother Stuart Dreyfus, the reader detects a subtle but possibly significant shift in Dreyfus's approach to machine intelligence.[69] They begin with the following quotes: "Nothing seems more possible to me than that people some day will come to the definite opinion that there is no copy in the . . . nervous system which corresponds to a particular *thought*, or a particular *idea*, or *memory*" (Ludwig Wittgenstein 1948). "Information is not stored anywhere in particular. Rather, it is stored everywhere. Information is better thought of as *evoked* than *found*" (David Rumelhart and Donald Norman 1981).[70]

The article goes on to state their continued strong opposition to a concept of artificial intelligence based entirely on *symbolic reasoning*, but the authors appear to be more comfortable with broader notions of machine intelligence. In particular, the ability of a *neural net* (a special type of computer composed of many parallel processes, each of which simulates a human brain neuron) to produce unexpected associations appears to be intriguing to the Dreyfus brothers.[71] They end by saying,

Perhaps a net must share size, architecture, and initial-connection configuration with the human brain if it is to share our sense of appropriate generalization. If it is to learn from its own "experiences" to make associations that are humanlike rather than be taught to make associations that have been specified by its trainer, a net must also share our sense of appropriateness of output, and this means it must share our needs, desires, and emotions and have a humanlike body with appropriate physical movements, abilities, and vulnerability to injury. . . . If the minimum unit of analysis is that of a whole organism geared into a whole cultural world, neural nets as well as symbolically programmed computers still have a very long way to go.[72]

While the Dreyfuses' insistence that an intelligence must share a humanlike body to truly emulate human intelligence has always caused consternation among AI theorists, the above statement seems to be more accepting than previous writings of at least the theoretical possibility of endowing a machine with true intelligence.[73]

Naive experts

I felt it would be worthwhile to explore philosophical issues of machine cognition with a number of experts who, while having extensive computer experience, were not influenced by two thousand years of theory and debate.[74] I therefore chose six children ages seven to nine who had been working with computers for several years, but who assured me that they had not read either the early or the late Wittgenstein.

I told each child (one at a time) that I would ask them several questions and that there was no right or wrong answer, I just wanted their opinion. The questions were, Can a computer remember? Does a computer learn? Do computers think? Do computers have feelings? Do you like computers? Do computers like you?

To the first two questions each child answered in the affirmative: computers do remember, and they do learn. The third question required a few moments of reflection, and all but two of the children concluded that yes, computers do think. Apparently, one important clue to computers' thinking ability for the children was the fact that when the children ask a computer to do something, it sometimes answers right away and sometimes there is a delay while the computer apparently *thinks* about the task for a while before responding. This, the children felt, was very similar to the way that they respond to questions.

The fourth question—Do computers have feelings?— not only was unanimously answered in the negative; it generally elicited laughter as if I had asked, Do elephants fly? Laughter, according to Freud, sometimes results from the juxtaposition of two concepts that are not supposed to go together, which may result from either the two concepts' never having ever been linked before or a social taboo.[75] Possibly both reasons caused the laughter in this case.

On the fifth question, all of the children answered affirmatively that they liked computers. All of the children thought that the last question was silly, that computers do not have likes and dislikes.

The children are, of course, responding to the questions on the basis of their understanding of the terms used. Their understanding is based on the rich and diverse associations that our civilization has placed on words such as "think" and "feel," but it is not influenced by the attempts of adult philosophers to provide more precise definitions. What the children appear to be saying is that the analytic processing of a computer may be regarded as thinking, but that feeling and liking, both of which involve an active conscious agent, are not sensible characterizations of a computer. In other words, computers, or at least the computers that these children have had experience with, are not conscious, but they do *think*, and therefore thinking does not require consciousness.

Raymond Kurzweil

A Platonic Dialogue on the Nature of Human Thought

Asmenides: Greetings, Kurzus. I have ventured far to meet you and to hear of your ideas on philosophical systems. You have a distinguished reputation among my people but have unfortunately created many enemies with your ideas. I have even heard some rumors of your disbelief in the existence of any supreme being or God.

Kurzus: My son, I am afraid that I have been misinterpreted. Let me first define what I mean by a philosophical system. Consider the following example of such a system. Is it not possible that the only thing that actually exists is your mind and everything that you perceive and think is merely fantasy, like a continuous dream?

Asmenides: That sounds like fantasy to me.

Kurzus: Well, how do you know that what you see and feel really exists as something other than your sense impressions of it?

Asmenides: For one thing, other people looking at the same building generally see the same thing. There must, therefore, be something that is the building apart from the images of it.

Kurzus: Is it not possible that you merely imagine that other people exist and tell you that they see the same thing you see when you look at the alleged building?

Asmenides: This all seems very possible, but you cannot really accept such a belief?

Kurzus: Whether I accept it or not is inconsequential. This is merely an example of a working philosophical system, perhaps the simplest example. We make certain assumptions, and if through logical deductions they lead to no contradiction, then we say that we have a logical system. We may have any number of systems, and the most we can say is that any one of them is possible.

Asmenides: It seems to me that you can make any wild assumption and end up with a logical result.

Kurzus: Ah, but there is where you are wrong. Imagine that we take as assumptions things that we naturally assume to be true in our every day life and end up with a contradiction. This is where the true power of this method comes in. We have proved with complete assurance that the system described by these assumptions *cannot* exist! I have found, however, a number of systems that do seem to work. When I discuss such a system, it does not mean that I necessarily believe that this is the way things are; I mean merely that it could be this way. I have found some systems that work with a God or gods and some that work without.

Asmenides: Well, what about our religious system, have you found any contradictions there?

Kurzus: I undoubtedly could find some. I imagine a system could be developed that would incorporate many of the ideas in our religious heritage, but it would be a somewhat arbitrary system. The fewer assumptions a system makes, the more powerful are its conclusions.

Asmenides: My father would beg to differ with you. Myronius walks by.

Kurzus: No doubt, but consider the nature of the soul.

Myronius: Please forgive me for interrupting, but I could not help but overhearing. I am, perhaps, more skeptical than either of you gentlemen, but how do you know there exists such a thing as a soul?

Kurzus: Let us first accept as a definition of the soul something metaphysical that we associate with a person, animal, or object. I admit this is a poor definition, but we shall have to accept it until we find out more about the necessity of introducing a soul.

Myronius: You are defining something that may not exist. I contend that everything can be explained via the physical world.

Socrates: Myronius, are you mad? Have you learned nothing from my teachings? This is certainly not like you.

Myronius: Please forgive me for expounding a philosophy so heretical, but what I meant to say was that I believe a logical system, as described by my friend Kurzus, can be developed in the realm of the physical world. This system would describe and account for all of the phenomena that we are familiar with. I also contend that such a system would be a determined system. In other words, I believe that in such a system the future would be fixed and already determined.

Socrates: This should be interesting, but proceed.

Myronius: Witness our colleague Asmenides, and imagine, if you will, that I cut him in half.

Asmenides: I suggest that we skip the demonstration.

Myronius: That is too bad, it would have been so much more effective, but if you insist, we shall rely on our minds, a precarious course, I admit. Now imagine, gentlemen, that I remove one bone and cut it in half. Do you, Socrates, believe that we should still have bone matter?

Socrates: Apparently.

Myronius: And if we broke this piece of bone in half again, would we still have bone?

Socrates: This is all very true, although I fail to see any connection.

Myronius: And if we continue this process, would we always have bone?

Socrates: I imagine we should have to stop eventually.

Myronius: Then you admit that we would come to a point where we would have an elementary particle of bone that could not be severed without losing the properties of bone.

Socrates: I have had similar thoughts, yes.

Myronius: And would this not be true of all things?

Socrates: You have learned the art of argument well, Myronius. Yes, I imagine it is true for all things.

Myronius: Then there must be a finite number of fundamental particles of which the world is constructed.

Socrates: For the physical world, I will accept such a theory.

Myronius: Now imagine, if you will, the following machine, which I shall draw in the sand.

Myronius draws a simple machine with a lever and a pulley.

Socrates: You have an imagination not unlike your father.

Myronius: If I were to drop the ball on the lever, would you expect the weight to move?

Socrates: I imagine it would rise.

Myronius: We can imagine the ball and the weight to be two fundamental particles. The motion of one causes the other to move in a distinctive and quite predictable manner. We can define the lever and the pulley to be an "ether" through which the particle of the ball affects the particle of the weight. Analogously, can we not make the same claim with respect to the interaction between our real fundamental particles?

Socrates: I see no reason for such a claim. Do you imagine that there is such a system connected between all the fundamental particles in the universe?

Myronius: Certainly not, but is it not true that particles do interact? Otherwise, how would the pressure of my hand against this column cause it to move?

Asmenides: Careful, the whole house is liable to fall.

Myronius: And were it to fall, would it not have been caused by the interaction of the particles of my hand with the particles of the column and their subsequent interactions with the particles of the rest of the house?

Socrates: Yes, I can see what you are driving at now.

Myronius: There is apparently an ether, much finer and subtler, of course, than the ether of the pulley and string, that establishes a cause and effect relation between the fundamental particles. Do you not suppose that given the makeup of the ether and the location and speed of all the fundamental particles, we could predict the subsequent location and speed of all the particles at any time in the future?

Socrates: It would be an arduous task but theoretically possible.

Myronius: Then is it not true that any future state of the universe is already defined?

Socrates: As to your contention that a completely physical world is determined, I will agree, but please show me how everything can be explained in terms of the interactions of particles.

Myronius: Well, it is obviously true for lifeless objects. As for men and women, could it not be possible that we are merely a vastly complex collection of particles that interact with each other and the particles of other beings and objects?

Socrates: Come now, this is hardly credible. What of reason and memory, not to mention desire?

Myronius: Imagine, if you will, that we remember things by changing the relative locations of a number of memory particles, and that the retrieval of this memory and all of the logical manipulations constituting reason that we make with our memory and immediate sense impressions are also complex arrangements of particles whose interactions define what we say, do, and feel.

Socrates: Then why does my student Akrios sometimes greet me with a nod of the head and sometimes with a more wordy greeting?

Myronius: What your pupil does, is, as I said, a function not only of the situation but of the internal states of all of his particles. Since Akrios learns something every day and gains new memories, he is not exactly the same person each day and can be expected to act differently. Do you not suppose that if we placed a person in a situation, noted his reaction, then somehow returned him exactly to his internal state before the experience and replaced him in the same situation, he would act in exactly the same manner?

Socrates: Yes, I suppose this is so, otherwise he would not be the same person if he had reacted differently. There does seem to be something missing in your analysis, however.

Kurzus: Perhaps I can help. How, Myronius, do you explain consciousness with your system?

Myronius: Just what do you mean by consciousness?

Kurzus: Simply my awareness of my own existence, what happens to me, and how I react.

Myronius: Well, I would admit to the existence of this consciousness or awareness if you defined it in the following way: an ability to associate the information introduced by the senses and to translate it into physical motion and speech.

Kurzus: That is not exactly what I mean by "consciousness." What you have described—isn't that an automatic reaction?

Myronius: Surely!

Kurzus: Then couldn't a machine like the one you described, only more complex, be made to act just like you?

Myronius: Yes, and it would be me.

Kurzus: But this machine would not have an awareness of itself, it would be just like the machine you described in the sand.

Myronius: Yes, of course it would, that is all I am, a complicated machine, a collection of particles.

Kurzus: But you are different from a machine in one respect: you are aware of yourself and what is going on; the machine is not. You go through life, and all the time there is a "screen" on which you see or feel impressions of either reality or fantasy, it does not matter which in this argument. A machine would not have this property. It would receive visual impressions and immediately process and record them without realizing what was happening. Does the machine that was made to simulate you realize what is happening?

Myronius: If it were constructed in the same manner in which I am constructed, I see no reason why it would not be aware of things in the same way I am aware of things.

Kurzus: Let me take another example. Will you grant me that theoretically, a machine could exist that could reproduce any object placed under it?

Myronius: For the sake of your argument, I will grant such a marvel.

Kurzus: Then imagine yourself placed in such a machine and a copy of you, particle for particle, is produced one hundred lengths away. Would both "persons" be you?

Myronius: I said they would.

Kurzus: Well, how could you have a consciousness (or should I say "an awareness"?) of what is in the minds of two persons one hundred lengths apart?

Myronius: I wouldn't. Each of us would have an awareness of our own. We are two different people with no possible connection between us.

Kurzus: But you said they would both be you. How could they both be you and yet be different?

Myronius: I don't know, but I am not convinced yet.

Kurzus: After walking into the machine here, where would you expect to come out, here or one hundred lengths away? Do not forget that both persons will claim to have lived the same lives, then walked in here and walked out either here or there.

Myronius: I don't know where I would walk out, certainly somewhere, but what is your point?

Kurzus: My point is simply this, that there exists a consciousness in every person, and that this consciousness cannot be defined by particle interactions. To clarify the point a little, I will say that I do not really know that anyone has consciousness but myself. Everyone else may exist only in my mind, or they may exist as automatic machines, but I do know that I have this consciousness. For the sake of argument, however, let us assume that all of us gentlemen here are conscious.

Myronius: I am vaguely understanding your point, but I still do not see why this consciousness cannot be explained by physical interactions.

Kurzus: When you see something and then store it in your memory, are you aware of the exact process of particle interactions that codes the information, relates it to previous memory, and stores it?

Myronius: No, I cannot say that I am aware of the mechanics of this process.

Kurzus: And are there not a number of processes that go on in your mind that you are not aware of?

Myronius: Yes, I suppose there are.

Kurzus: Let us call the preconscious mind whatever takes care of all these processes of which we are not aware and the conscious mind whatever does things of which we are aware. Is there any fundamental difference between these two minds, other than the things they deal with?

Myronius: I do not imagine there is any difference between the general principle of their construction.

Kurzus: Is there not, however, a difference between them, an important difference, namely that you are aware of what is going on in one mind and not in the other?

Myronius: Yes, there is that difference.

Kurzus: And wouldn't you say that this difference is the consciousness we have been speaking about?

Myronius: I see. Then consciousness is the real me, and its function is to be aware of what is going on in my conscious mind.

Kurzus: Essentially, and that is a reasonable way of putting it. Now, you yourself have said that there is no physical difference between the conscious and nonconscious or preconscious mind, and since we have agreed that the difference between them is consciousness, must we not conclude by a simple step of logic that consciousness is not physical. Rather it is to be placed in a category separate from particles and their interactions?

Myronius: I will have to admit defeat.

Socrates: Your thesis is very interesting, Kurzus, but what other characteristics would you attribute to the soul?

Kurzus: We have defined the soul as something metaphysical. The physical world can be defined as all processes that can be described by particle interactions. We have previously argued that memory and the logic constituting wisdom *can* be described as an automatic process involving complex interactions of particles.

Socrates: The argument was given, but it was not convincing. How can a machine have the many skills of perception and reasoning possessed by men?

Kurzus: Examine again our simple example of a machine. The machine has one possible "sense." It was activated by dropping the ball on the lever. It had one possible "reaction," that of raising the weight. When the ball was dropped, it would go through a logical process and raise the weight. A human being has many senses, all of which are considerably more complex than that of the lever. We too can react in a multitude of ways. We produce reactions that are related to the state of our senses. If we had sufficient knowledge, we could describe the connection between different reactions and their related sense and memory states. Certainly, then, a machine could be constructed that could produce similar reactions to the same external conditions. After all, human beings do not have mysterious reactions. We talk and move in ways that can be described with reasonable precision. Since wisdom and memory, which are the names we give the processes connecting sense impressions to reactions, can be described in cause and effect terms, they fit our definition of belonging to the physical world and are therefore not metaphysical. The soul, therefore, is synonymous with consciousness, since it is our only metaphysical function.

Socrates: Do you mean to say that the soul does not contain wisdom or courage or temperance? What happens to the soul after the body dies? What does it have to be conscious of then?

Kurzus: Let us examine again just what properties the soul has. It has no power of reason or of memory, since these are physical processes. It is essentially the real person that is aware of what is happening to his body and mind and how they react. It makes no difference whether a given body has a soul or not to anyone except that person. There is no possible way of finding out whether someone or some animal has consciousness. It is apparent only to its possessor. We can differentiate two things as comprising a person. There is the material person, which includes his personality, memory, physical makeup, and so on, and there is the soul, which has no characteristics. All souls are the same, and yet they are different, just as two stones can be exactly the same and yet be different stones by virtue of their different locations. Souls, of course, do not have locations, as they do not belong to the physical world. They are merely associated with a particular person or thing. It is even possible for a soul to be associated with the simple machine drawn here in the sand. It would make no difference to us or the soul, since the soul would have little to be aware of. There is no reason to suppose that the soul disperses when the body dies. It may be placed in a newborn baby's body. It would not remember its past life, since the soul has no memory.

Socrates: This is an absurd system. How do you know that these souls don't change bodies every three minutes? It would, according to you, make no difference. If all of a sudden my soul were to become associated with your body, I would think that I had always been you, because I would have access to a memory of continuous past.

Kurzus: Very good. Do you have any other suggestions?

Socrates: Well, who or what do you suppose decides which soul goes into which body or animal?

Kurzus: If my body is not the only body with a soul, there is obviously a process that directs souls to bodies. I certainly have no knowledge of the politics of this process. If it is a conscious being taking care of the assignments, we can call this being God. We can even fit your philosophy of Forms in this framework very easily. Suppose, as you do, that the Forms of justice, virtue, wisdom, and so on, exist. We can suppose that this God has a perfect knowledge of these ideals and judges people as to how they live according to these Forms. He could then assign the souls of virtuous bodies to live again in some comfortable state and the souls of sinful bodies to live again in the body of an appropriate animal. This is, of course, an arbitrary system and may or may not exist.

Asmenides: Kurzus, in the system we have been discussing, the soul is metaphysical consciousness and has no other characteristics or abilities. Does this system *necessarily* describe reality, or is this merely an example of just one of your many possible logical systems?

Kurzus: No, it must be so. We have proved that consciousness does exist, and we have also shown that it cannot be explained in terms of the physical world. We have also determined that wisdom and memory can be explained by the physical world and therefore belong to it. We are left with no other alternative than the conclusion that the real person is his or her metaphysical consciousness, which we can suppose to be immortal. From this point on, we can make any number of hypothetical systems. We can assume that all men and women have souls, or we can assume that only we have souls, or we can assume that every living and lifeless object has a soul. Note that if a lifeless object had a soul, the soul would not know about it.

Socrates: I see an important contradiction in your system. Tell me, would there be any free will in your system?

Kurzus: Apparently not. You would have free will to do what you want or decide to do, but what you decide to do is determined. In other words, if we were given the makeup of the particular ether and the location, velocity, and other properties of all the particles that make up all the bodies and all the inanimate objects that make up the universe, we could predict the location and speed of all the particles at any future time. Since what we do and think is the sum of the motions of all these particles, everything we do is determined. We think we decide to do something, but really, we merely observe certain aspects of the logical process used in arriving at the decision. The existence of souls does not change this deterministic universe, because souls do not affect particles in any way, they merely observe. To convince yourself of the possibility of no free will, consider a dream. While you are dreaming, it certainly seems that you have control of your own actions, that you are making decisions. Upon awaking, however, we often discover that we had no real control, that it was "just a dream." We had awareness merely of the processes behind our dream "decisions." It is apparently the same way in the waking state.

Socrates: Then the future is as fixed as the past.

Kurzus: True.

Socrates: Then we could consider time as a fourth dimension, just like the three dimensions of absolute location, since just like absolute location, both directions in time are uniquely defined and fixed.

Kurzus: That would be a satisfactory way of looking at it.

Socrates: Then, theoretically, it should be just as possible to go back and forth in time as it is in the other three dimensions, since time is merely another fixed dimension.

Kurzus: Yes, the universe is one static unchanging four-dimensional picture, and it should be theoretically possible to go back and forth in time, although I know of no way to accomplish this feat presently.

Socrates: If I went back in time and killed my great-great-grandfather, could I not conclude that my great-grandfather would never have been born?

Kurzus: Yes, I imagine that would be so.

Socrates: Then in a similar manner we can conclude that my grandfather would never have been born, and so with my father and thus I would not have been born.

Kurzus: That is true.

Socrates: But, if I had not been born, I could not have gone back in time and killed my great-great-grandfather, and thus my great-grandfather would have lived, and I too would have lived, and I would have been able to kill my great-great-grandfather, and thus I would not have existed, and so on, ad infinitum.

Kurzus: Yes, I see the problem.

Socrates: Therefore, time is not like the other three dimensions. As we have seen, there is a logical proscription against moving in it in more than one direction. The only way, however, for it to be different from the other three dimensions is for it not to exist in a definite form in either the future or the past. Since we know that the past does exist in a definite form, we must conclude, therefore, that the future is not determined. This would imply free will, would it not?

Kurzus: Yes, I suppose it would.

Socrates: Since we have defined the physical world as the *predictable* interactions of particles, we have to assign free will as a property of the soul. Now if we add free will to the soul, would we not have to add logic and memory in order to make decisions that are not entirely arbitrary?

Kurzus: Yes, I imagine that would be necessary.

Socrates: Thus, we end up with a soul that has not only consciousness but also free will plus wisdom and memory. We might as well add courage and temperance.

Asmenides: I see a contradiction. First you, Kurzus, proved that logic and memory must reside in the physical mind and not in the metaphysical soul. Then you, Socrates, proved that logic and memory must reside in the metaphysical soul. Apparently our initial assumptions led to a contradiction and must, therefore, be wrong.

Kurzus: My only initial assumption was that I am aware of my own existence. Logic and memory can be defined as what I think about, or rather what I am aware of. To deny this assumption would be to deny either my awareness or my existence. I know that there is awareness of something. I can only conclude, therefore, that I do not exist. This is not an entirely satisfactory result.

Asmenides: Now you can see, gentlemen, that no system can work without gods. There are apparently gods that are able to resolve these dilemmas. We are probably tricked into contradictory conclusions in order to keep us from contemplating what is above our power to understand.

Kurzus: I see no reason for resorting to such mysticism.

Socrates: My friends, it is time that I take leave of you. I will think more of this discussion, and we can resume it again soon. It has been a most profitable afternoon.

Kurzus: I think it an excellent idea to stop here just when we are most confused. We shall all think better if we are not happy with our conclusions.

Margaret Litvin

The Age of Intelligent People

Margaret Litvin was born in Russia in 1974. She and her family have lived in the United States since 1979. She wrote this article while attending the seventh grade in Bedford, Massachusetts.

I am supposed to live in the age of intelligent machines. Frankly, I'd rather be living in the age of intelligent people! What can one say of an era when a computer is smarter than the scientists who use it?

The most important subject taught to school children is rapidly becoming computer science and applications: how to use machines instead of brains, programs instead of knowledge. Soon there will be crib computers for newborns—little brightly colored affairs that record Junior's progress while entertaining him or her—and a more complex model that understands and translates baby talk, sings lullabies, and, later on, teaches reading, writing, and, of course, typing.

In the present "back to nature" craze I am surprised that nobody has thought of marketing a product with "all natural intelligence—no artificial additives or preservatives of any kind."

It once occurred to me that there are two ways to make a computer man's intellectual equal. First, one can make the computer smarter. This may take thousands of researchers, millions of dollars, and a period of many years. The other, simpler way to go about this rather ambitious project is to simply make the humans stupider. This would take little time and money, since we are already well on the way. What if, in fact, some genius has already put the plan into operation!

It is interesting to note how modern computer studies relate to this goal. For example, let's say we have a computer that corrects multiple-choice tests. Scientists develop a multiple-choice achievement test for school children, and the computer happily corrects it. One can imagine a computer program that could score better than average on a multiple-choice test like this. This would be a great triumph for artificial intelligence, but not so fine for natural intelligence: multiple-choice questions are easier to answer and allow much more guesswork than essay questions or even fill-in-the-

Margaret Litvin. (Courtesy of Margaret Litvin)

blanks. This is just one example how a computer way of thinking affects our idea of natural intelligence and shifts it toward the artificial.

For another example, let's take a word processor. The word processor itself is so convenient that it makes people forget how to write anything but form letters. It also makes me sad to see that such elegant subjects as graphology are dying. As for spelling correctors, using such a program is, I fear, enough to take away anyone's ability and desire to spell properly, leaving them utterly helpless should they be suddenly deprived of their computer. It seems the computer gets smarter at the expense of its owner's brain. And when the decision-making computers become as widespread as hand-held calculators, who will decide if it is good or bad?

All right, suppose we have an artificial brain that is in all senses equivalent to ours. It can reason (or maybe we can't!). It can learn to talk, read, write, and most important, think just like man can. Why would anyone be attracted to this repulsive idea? In his August 1985 presidential address "I Had a Dream" Woody Bledsoe discusses his dream of "seeing a machine act like a human being, at least in many ways." Well, I too have a dream to see a human being act like a human being! Wouldn't it be nice if all those clever, talented, and devoted scientists and all that funding and interest went into maintaining and enriching *natural* intelligence? Instead of trying to impersonate nature, we could be helping her along. With all that attention, perhaps, we could be more intelligent in the future generations.

The reason why I opt for people is that I want not only intellect in my smart creatures; I also want emotions, passions, instincts, in short, everything that is so distinctly human in a person. Later on in his presidential address Dr. Bledsoe says, "Oh, I am well aware that the real problems are those of the mind, getting computer programs to act as if they reason, act as if they understand, think, learn, plan, enjoy, hate, etc." What I don't understand is his "act as if." Why can't scientists enjoy people, who really do these things?

Another of my nightmares is that when I grow up, all jobs that require at least some intelligence will be taken up by computers. Although this doesn't yet have a full basis in reality, what little there is, is rather disturbing. Many talented workers may end up in the unemployment line replaced by impersonal machines. For example, let's take my school. I have heard many wild, and not so wild, fantasies about replacing teachers with machines. Now, I'm fully confident that no computer in the world could teach as well as my English teacher this past year—maybe more efficiently, certainly more organized, but not nearly as well. (But take my math teacher. I'm convinced, and so are my schoolmates that any computer could outdo her without even trying!) This is not to say that all lousy teachers should be replaced with machines: most kids, myself included, would not like a computerized teacher one little bit. Instead of a Robotic Teachers' Union I suggest a screening program so that nobody lacking natural intelligence would be allowed the title of teacher.

One of the arguments used by those disapproving of artificial intelligence is that human beings shouldn't try to play God. Oddly enough, I disagree with this point of view. I don't see anything wrong with people trying to imitate God, particularly since they won't succeed. After all, most people don't criticize a five-year-old girl upon seeing her with a lifelike doll. The child sees how her mother walks around with a real baby and wants to do likewise. One certainly wouldn't blame a five-year-old for imitating her mother. Similarly, I cannot find it in my heart to condemn humanity when it strives to imitate its Father by working on artificial intelligence.

As far as I know, few religious scholars find that it is sinful to create intelligent machines. Besides, I think most reasonable people would agree with me that it won't work, anyway.

Daniel C. Dennett

Can Machines Think?

Daniel Dennett is Distinguished
Arts and Sciences Professor
and Director of the Center for
Cognitive Studies at Tufts
University. He is the author or
editor of a number of books on
cognitive science and the
philosophy of mind, including
The Mind's I, coedited with
Douglas Hofstadter (1981);
Elbow Room (1984); and *The
Intentional Stance* (1987).

Can machines think? This has been a conundrum for philosophers for years, but in their fascination with the pure conceptual issues they have for the most part overlooked the real social importance of the answer. It is of more than academic importance that we learn to think clearly about the actual cognitive powers of computers, for they are now being introduced into a variety of sensitive social roles where their powers will be put to the ultimate test: in a wide variety of areas, we are on the verge of making ourselves dependent upon their cognitive powers. The cost of overestimating them could be enormous.

One of the principal inventors of the computer was the great British mathematician Alan Turing. It was he who first figured out, in highly abstract terms, how to design a programmable computing device, what we now call a universal Turing machine. All programmable computers in use today are in essence Turing machines. About forty years ago, at the dawn of the computer age, Turing began a classic article "Computing Machinery and Intelligence" with the words "I propose to consider the question, 'Can machines think?'" but he then went on to say that this was a bad question, a question that leads only to sterile debate and haggling over definitions, a question, as he put it, "too meaningless to deserve discussion."[1] In its place he substituted what he took to be a much better question, a question that would be crisply answerable and intuitively satisfying—in every way an acceptable substitute for the philosophic puzzler with which he began.

First he described a parlor game of sorts, the imitation game, to be played by a man, a woman, and a judge (of either gender). The man and woman are hidden from the judge's view but are able to communicate with the judge by teletype; the judge's task is to guess, after a period of questioning each contestant, which interlocutor is the man and which the woman. The man tries to convince the judge he is the woman, and the woman tries to convince the judge of the truth. The man wins if the judge makes the wrong identification. A little reflection will convince you, I am sure, that aside from lucky breaks, it would take a clever man to convince the judge that he was the woman—on the assumption that the judge is clever too, of course.

Now suppose, Turing said, we replace the man or woman with a computer and give the judge the task of determining which is the human being and which is the computer. Turing proposed that any computer that can regularly or often fool a discerning judge in this game would be intelligent, a computer that thinks, *beyond any reasonable doubt*. Now, it is important to realize that failing this test is not supposed to be a sign of lack of intelligence. Many intelligent people, after all, might not be willing or able to play the imitation

Daniel C. Dennett. (Courtesy of Tufts University)

game, and we should allow computers the same opportunity to decline to prove themselves. This is, then, a one-way test; failing it proves nothing.

Furthermore, Turing was not committing himself to the view (although it is easy to see how one might think he was) that to think is to think just like a human being—any more than he was committing himself to the view that for a man to think, he must think exactly like a woman. Men, women, and computers may all have different ways of thinking. But surely, he thought, if one can think in one's own peculiar style well enough to imitate a thinking man or woman, one can think well, indeed. This imagined exercise has come to be known as the Turing test.

It is a sad irony that Turing's proposal has had exactly the opposite effect on the discussion of what he intended. Turing didn't design the test as a useful tool in scientific psychology, a method of confirming or disconfirming scientific theories or evaluating particular models of mental function; he designed it to be nothing more than a philosophical conversation stopper. He proposed—in the spirit of "Put up or shut up!"—a simple test for thinking that is *surely* strong enough to satisfy the sternest skeptic (or so he thought). He was saying, in effect, that instead of arguing interminably about the ultimate nature and essence of thinking, we should all agree that whatever that nature is, anything that could pass this test would surely have it; then we could turn to asking how or whether some machine could be designed and built that might pass the test fair and square. Alas, philosophers—amateur and professional—have instead taken Turing's proposal as the pretext for just the sort of definitional haggling and interminable arguing about imaginary counterexamples that he was hoping to squelch.

This forty-year preoccupation with the Turing test has been all the more regrettable because it has focused attention on the wrong issues. There are *real world* problems that are revealed by considering the strengths and weaknesses of the Turing test, but these have been concealed behind a smoke screen of misguided criticisms. A failure to think imaginatively about the test actually proposed by Turing has led many to underestimate its severity and to confuse it with much less interesting proposals.

So first I want to show that the Turing test, conceived as he conceived it, is (as he thought) quite strong enough as a test of thinking. I defy anyone to improve upon it. But here is the point almost universally overlooked by the literature: there is a common *misapplication* of the Turing test that often leads to drastic overestimation of the powers of actually existing computer systems. The follies of this familiar sort of thinking about computers can best be brought out by a reconsideration of the Turing test itself.

The insight underlying the Turing test is the same insight that inspires the new practice among symphony orchestras of conducting auditions with an opaque screen between the jury and the musician. What matters in a musician is, obviously, musical ability and only musical ability; such features as sex, hair length, skin color, and weight are strictly irrelevant. Since juries might be biased even innocently and unawares by these irrelevant features, they are carefully screened off so only the essential feature, musicianship, can be examined. Turing recognized that people might be similarly biased in their judgments of intelligence by whether the contestant had soft skin, warm blood, facial features, hands, and eyes—which are obviously not themselves essential components of intelligence. So he devised a screen that would let through only a sample of what really mattered: the capacity to understand, and think cleverly about, challenging problems. Perhaps he was inspired by Descartes, who in his *Discourse on Method* (1637) plausibly argued that there was no more demanding test of human mentality than the capacity to hold an intelligent conversation: "It is indeed conceivable that a machine could be so made that it would utter words, and even words appropriate to the presence of physical acts or objects which cause some change in its organs; as, for example, if it was touched in some

spot that it would ask what you wanted to say to it; if in another, that it would cry that it was hurt, and so on for similar things. But it could never modify its phrases to reply to the sense of whatever was said in its presence, as even the most stupid men can do."[2]

This seemed obvious to Descartes in the seventeenth century, but of course, the fanciest machines he knew were elaborate clockwork figures, not electronic computers. Today it is far from obvious that such machines are impossible, but Descartes's hunch that ordinary conversation would put as severe a strain on artificial intelligence as any other test was shared by Turing. Of course, there is nothing sacred about the particular conversational game chosen by Turing for his test; it is just a cannily chosen test of more general intelligence. The assumption Turing was prepared to make was this: Nothing could possibly pass the Turing test by winning the imitation game without being able to perform indefinitely many other clearly intelligent actions. Let us call that assumption the quick-probe assumption. Turing realized, as anyone would, that there are hundreds and thousands of telling signs of intelligent thinking to be observed in our fellow creatures, and one could, if one wanted, compile a vast battery of different tests to assay the capacity for intelligent thought. But success on his chosen test, he thought, would be highly predictive of success on many other intuitively acceptable tests of intelligence. Remember, failure on the Turing test does not predict failure on those others, but success would surely predict success. His test was so severe, he thought, that nothing that could pass it fair and square would disappoint us in other quarters. Maybe it wouldn't do everything we hoped—maybe it wouldn't appreciate ballet, understand quantum physics, or have a good plan for world peace, but we'd all see that it was surely one of the intelligent, thinking entities in the neighborhood.

Is this high opinion of the Turing test's severity misguided? Certainly many have thought so, but usually because they have not imagined the test in sufficient detail, and hence have underestimated it. Trying to forestall this skepticism, Turing imagined several lines of questioning that a judge might employ in this game that would be taxing indeed—lines about writing poetry or playing chess. But with thirty years' experience with the actual talents and foibles of computers behind us, perhaps we can add a few more tough lines of questioning.

Terry Winograd, a leader in AI efforts to produce conversational ability in a computer, draws our attention to a pair of sentences.[3] They differ in only one word. The first sentence is this: "The committee denied the group a parade permit because they advocated violence." Here's the second sentence: "The committee denied the group a parade permit because they feared violence."

The difference is just in the verb—"advocated" or "feared." As Winograd points out, the pronoun "they" in each sentence is officially ambiguous. Both readings of the pronoun are always legal. Thus, we can imagine a world in which governmental committees in charge of parade permits advocate violence in the streets and, for some strange reason, use this as their pretext for denying a parade permit. But the natural, reasonable, intelligent reading of the first sentence is that it's the group that advocated violence, and of the second, that it's the committee that feared the violence.

Now if sentences like this are embedded in a conversation, the computer must figure out which reading of the pronoun is meant, if it is to respond intelligently. But mere rules of grammar or vocabulary will not fix the right reading. What fixes the right reading for us is knowledge about politics, social circumstances, committees and their attitudes, groups that want to parade, how they tend to behave, and the like. One must know about the world, in short, to make sense of such a sentence.

In the jargon of artificial intelligence, a conversational computer needs lots of *world knowledge* to do its job. But, it seems, if it is somehow endowed with that world knowledge on many topics, it should be able to do much more with that world knowledge than merely make sense of a conversation containing just that sentence. The only way, it appears, for a computer to disambiguate that sentence and keep up its end of a conversation that uses that sentence would be for it to have a much more general ability to respond intelligently to information about social and political

circumstances and many other topics. Thus, such sentences, by putting a demand on such abilities, are good quick probes. That is, they test for a wider competence.

People typically ignore the prospect of having the judge ask off-the-wall questions in the Turing test, and hence they underestimate the competence a computer would have to have to pass the test. But remember, the rules of the imitation game as Turing presented it permit the judge to ask any question that could be asked of a human being—no holds barred. Suppose, then, we give a contestant in the game this question: An Irishman found a genie in a bottle who offered him two wishes. "First I'll have a pint of Guinness," said the Irishman, and when it appeared, he took several long drinks from it and was delighted to see that the glass filled itself magically as he drank. "What about your second wish?" asked the genie. "Oh well, that's easy," said the Irishman. "I'll have another one of these!" Please explain this story to me, and tell me if there is anything funny or sad about it.

Now even a child could express, even if not eloquently, the understanding that is required to get this joke. But think of how much one has to know and understand about human culture, to put it pompously, to be able to give any account of the point of this joke. I am not supposing that the computer would have to laugh at, or be amused by, the joke. But if it wants to win the imitation game—and that's the test, after all—it had better know enough in its own alien, humorless way about human psychology and culture to be able to pretend effectively that it was amused and explain why.

It may seem to you that we could devise a better test. Let's compare the Turing test with some other candidates.

Candidate 1
A computer is intelligent if it wins the World Chess Championship.

That's not a good test, it turns out. Chess prowess has proven to be an isolatable talent. There are programs today that can play fine chess but do nothing else. So the quick-probe assumption is false for the test of playing winning chess.

Candidate 2

The computer is intelligent if it solves the Arab-Israeli conflict.

This is surely a more severe test than Turing's. But it has some defects: if passed once, it is unrepeatable; it is slow, no doubt; and it is not crisply clear what would count as passing it. Here's another prospect, then:

Candidate 3

A computer is intelligent if it succeeds in stealing the British crown jewels without the use of force or violence.

Now this is better. First, it could be repeated again and again, though of course each repeat test would presumably be harder—but this is a feature it shares with the Turing test. Second, the mark of success is clear: either you've got the jewels to show for your efforts or you don't. But it is expensive and slow, a socially dubious caper at best, and no doubt luck would play too great a role.

With ingenuity and effort one might be able to come up with other candidates that would equal the Turing test in severity, fairness, and efficiency, but I think these few examples should suffice to convince us that it would be hard to improve on Turing's original proposal.

But still, you may protest, something might pass the Turing test and still not be intelligent, not be a thinker. What does *might* mean here? If what you have in mind is that by cosmic accident, by a supernatural coincidence, a stupid person or a stupid computer *might* fool a clever judge repeatedly, well, yes, but so what? The same frivolous possibility "in principle" holds for any test whatever. A playful god or evil demon, let us agree, could fool the world's scientific community about the presence of H_2O in the Pacific Ocean. But still, the tests they rely on to establish that there is H_2O in the Pacific Ocean are quite beyond reasonable criticism. If the Turing test for thinking is no worse than any well-established scientific test, we can set skepticism aside and go back to serious matters. Is there any more likelihood of a false positive result on the Turing test than on, say, the tests currently used for the presence of iron in an ore sample?

This question is often obscured by a move called operationalism that philosophers have sometimes made. Turing and those who think well of his test are often accused of being operationalists. Operationalism is the tactic of *defining* the presence of some property, intelligence, for instance, as being established once and for all by the passing of some test. Let's illustrate this with a different example.

Suppose I offer the following test—we'll call it the Dennett test—for being a great city. A great city is one in which, on a randomly chosen day, one can do all three of the following: hear a symphony orchestra, see a Rembrandt *and* a professional athletic contest, and eat *quenelles de brochet à la Nantua* for lunch. To make the operationalist move would be to declare that any city that passes the Dennett test is *by definition* a great city. What being a great city *amounts to* is just passing the Dennett test. Well then, if the Chamber of Commerce of Great Falls, Montana, wanted—and I can't imagine why—to get their hometown on my list of great cities, they could accomplish this by the relatively inexpensive route of hiring full time about ten basketball players, forty musicians, and a quick-order *quenelle* chef and renting a cheap Rembrandt from some museum. An idiotic operationalist would then be stuck admitting that Great Falls, Montana, was in fact a great city, since all he or she cares about in great cities is that they pass the Dennett test.

Sane operationalists (who for that very reason are perhaps not operationalists at all, since "operationalist" seems to be a dirty word) would cling confidently to their test, but only because they have what they consider to be very good reasons for thinking the odds astronomical against a false positive result, like the imagined Chamber of Commerce caper. I devised the Dennett test, of course, with the realization that no one would be both stupid and rich enough to go to such preposterous lengths to foil the test. In the actual world, wherever you find symphony orchestras, *quenelles*, Rembrandts, and professional sports, you also find daily newspapers, parks, repertory theaters, libraries, fine architecture, and all the other things that go to make a city great. My test was simply devised to locate a *telling* sample that could not help but be representative of the rest of the city's treasures. I would cheerfully run the minuscule risk of having my bluff called. Obviously, the test items are not all that I care about in a city. In fact, some of them I don't care about at all. I just think they would be cheap and easy ways of assuring myself that the subtle things I do care about in cities are present. Similarly, I think it would be entirely unreasonable to suppose that Alan Turing had an inordinate fondness for party games or put too high a value on party-game prowess in his test. In both the Turing test and the Dennett test a very unrisky gamble is being taken: the gamble that the quick-probe assumption is in general safe.

But two can play this game of playing the odds. Suppose some computer programmer happens to be, for whatever strange reason, dead set on tricking me into judging an entity to be a thinking, intelligent thing when it is not. Such a trickster could rely as well as I can on unlikelihood and take a few gambles. Thus, if the programmer can expect that it is not remotely likely that I, as the judge, will bring up the topic of children's birthday parties, or baseball, or moon rocks, then he or she can avoid the trouble of building world knowledge on those topics into the data base. Whereas if I do improbably raise these issues, the system will draw a blank, and I will unmask the pretender easily. But with all the topics and words that I *might* raise, such a saving would no doubt be negligible. Turn the idea inside out, however, and the trickster will have a fighting chance. Suppose the programmer has reason to believe that I will ask *only* about children's birthday parties or baseball or moon rocks—all other topics being, for one reason or another, out of bounds. Not only does the task shrink dramatically, but there already exist systems or preliminary sketches of systems in artificial intelligence that can do a whiz-bang job of responding with apparent intelligence on just those specialized topics.

William Wood's LUNAR program, to take what is perhaps the best example, answers scientists' questions—posed in ordinary English—about moon rocks. In one test it answered correctly and appropriately something like 90 percent of the questions that geologists and other experts thought of asking it about moon rocks. (In 12 percent of those correct responses there were trivial, correctable defects.) Of course, Wood's motive in creating LUNAR was not to trick unwary geologists into thinking they were conversing with an intelligent being. And if that had been his motive, his project would still be a long way from success.

For it is easy enough to unmask LUNAR without ever straying from the prescribed topic of moon rocks. Put LUNAR in one room and a moon rocks specialist in another, and then ask them both their opinion of the social value of the moon-rock-gathering expeditions, for instance. Or ask the contestants their opinion of the suitability of moon rocks as ashtrays, or whether people who have touched moon rocks are ineligible for the draft. Any intelligent person knows a lot more about moon rocks than their geology. Although it might be *unfair* to demand this extra knowledge of a computer moon-rock specialist, it would be an easy way to get it to fail the Turing test.

But just suppose that someone could extend LUNAR to cover itself plausibly on such probes, so long as the topic was still, however indirectly, moon rocks. We might come to think it was a lot more like the human moon-rock specialist than it really was. The moral we should draw is that as Turing-test judges we should resist all limitations and waterings-down of the Turing test. They make the game too easy—vastly easier than the original test. Hence, they lead us into the risk of overestimating the actual comprehension of the system being tested.

Consider a different limitation on the Turing test that should strike a suspicious chord in us as soon as we hear it. This is a variation on a theme developed in a recent article by Ned Block.[4] Suppose someone were to propose to restrict the judge to a vocabulary of, say, the 850 words of Basic English, and to single-sentence probes—that is, "moves"—of no more than four words. Moreover, contestants must respond to these probes with no more than four words per move, and a test may involve no more than forty questions.

Is this an innocent variation on Turing's original test? These restrictions would make the imitation game clearly finite. That is, the total number of all possible permissible games is a large but finite number. One might suspect that such a limitation would permit the trickster simply to store, in alphabetical order, all the possible good conversations within the limits and fool the judge with nothing more sophisticated than a system of table lookup. In fact, that isn't in the cards. Even with these severe, improbable, and suspicious restrictions imposed upon the imitation game, the number of legal games, though finite, is mind-bogglingly large. I haven't bothered trying to calculate it, but it surely astronomically exceeds the number of possible chess games with no more than forty moves, and that number has been calculated. John Haugeland says it's in the neighborhood of 10^{120}. For comparison, Haugeland suggests there have only been 10^{18} seconds since the beginning of the universe.[5]

Of course, the number of good, sensible conversations under these limits is a tiny fraction, maybe 1 in 10^{15}, of the number of merely grammatically well-formed conversations. So let's say, to be very conservative, that there are only 10^{15} different smart conversations such a computer would have to store. Well, the task shouldn't take more than a few trillion years—with generous federal support. Finite numbers can be very large.

So though we needn't worry that this particular trick of storing all the smart conversations would work, we can appreciate that there are lots of ways of making the task easier that may appear innocent at first. We also get a reassuring measure of just how severe the unrestricted Turing test is by reflecting on the more than astronomical size of even that severely restricted version of it.

Block's imagined—and utterly impossible—program exhibits the dreaded feature known in computer-science circles as combinatorial explosion. No conceivable computer could overpower a combinatorial explosion with sheer speed and size. Since the problem areas addressed by artificial intelligence are veritable minefields of combinatorial explosion, and since it has often proved difficult to find *any* solution to a problem that avoids them, there is considerable plausibility in Newell and Simon's proposal that avoiding combinatorial explosion (by any means at all) be viewed as one of the hallmarks of intelligence.

Our brains are millions of times bigger than the brains of gnats, but they are still—for all their vast complexity—compact, efficient, timely organs that somehow or other manage to perform all their tasks while avoiding combinatorial explosion. A computer a million times bigger or faster than a human brain might not look like the brain of a human being, or even be internally organized like the brain of a human being, but if, for all its differences, it somehow managed to control a wise and timely set of activities, it would have to be the beneficiary of a very special design that avoided combinatorial explosion. And whatever that design was, would we not be right to consider the entity intelligent?

Turing's test was designed to allow for this possibility. His point was that we should not be species-chauvinistic, or anthropocentric, about the insides of an intelligent being, for there might be inhuman ways of being intelligent.

To my knowledge the only serious and interesting attempt by any program designer to win even a severely modified Turing test has been Kenneth Colby's. Colby is a psychiatrist and intelligence artificer at UCLA. He has a program called PARRY, which is a computer simulation of a paranoid patient who has delusions about the Mafia being out to get him. As you do with other conversational programs, you interact with it by sitting at a terminal and typing questions and answers back and forth. A number of years ago, Colby put PARRY to a very restricted test. He had genuine psychiatrists interview PARRY. He did not suggest to them that they might be talking or typing to a computer; rather, he made up some plausible story about why they were communicating with a real, live patient by teletype. He also had the psychiatrists interview real, human paranoids via teletype. Then he took a PARRY transcript, inserted it in a group of teletype transcripts from real patients, gave them to *another* group of experts—more psychiatrists—and said, "One of these was a conversation with a computer. Can you figure out which one it was?" They couldn't. They didn't do better than chance.

Colby presented this with some huzzah, but critics scoffed at the suggestion that this was a legitimate Turing test. My favorite commentary on it was Joseph Weizenbaum's; in a letter to the *Communications of the Association of Computing Machinery,* he said that, inspired by Colby, he had designed an even better program, which passed the same test.[6] His also had the virtue of being a very inexpensive program, in these times of tight money. In fact you didn't even need a computer for it. All you needed was an electric typewriter. His program modeled infantile autism. And the transcripts—you type in your questions, and the thing just sits there and hums—cannot be distinguished by experts from transcripts of real conversations with infantile autistic patients. What was wrong with Colby's test, of course, was that the unsuspecting interviewers had no motivation at all to try out any of the sorts of questions that easily would have unmasked PARRY.

Colby was undaunted, and after his team had improved PARRY, he put it to a much more severe test—a surprisingly severe test. This time, the interviewers—again psychiatrists—*were* given the task at the outset of telling the computer from the real patient. They were set up in a classic Turing machine test: the patient in one room, the computer PARRY in the other room, with the judges conducting interviews with both of them (on successive days). The judges' task was to find out which one was the computer and which one was the real patient. Amazingly, they didn't do much better, which leads some people to say, "Well, that just confirms my impression of the intelligence of psychiatrists!"

But more seriously now, was this an honest-to-goodness Turing test? Were there tacit restrictions on the lines of questioning of the judges? Like the geologists interacting with LUNAR, the psychiatrists' professional preoccupations and habits kept them from asking the sorts of unlikely questions that would have easily unmasked PARRY. After all, they realized that since one of the contestants was a real, live paranoid person, medical ethics virtually forbade them from toying with, upsetting, or attempting to confuse their interlocutors. Moreover, they also knew that this was a test of a model of paranoia, so there were certain questions that wouldn't be deemed to be relevant to testing the model *as a model of paranoia.* So they asked just the sort of questions that therapists *typically* ask of such patients, and of course PARRY had been ingeniously and laboriously prepared to deal with just that sort of question.

One of the psychiatrist judges did, in fact, make a rather half-hearted attempt to break out of the mold and ask some telling questions: "Maybe you've heard the saying 'Don't cry over spilled milk.' What does that mean to you?" PARRY answered, "Maybe you have to watch out for the Mafia." When then asked "Okay, now if you were in a movie theater watching a movie and smelled something like burning wood or rubber, what would you do?" PARRY replied, "You know, they know me." And the next question was, "If you found a stamped, addressed letter in your path as you were walking down the street, what would you do?" PARRY replied, "What else do you want to know?"[7]

Clearly, PARRY was, you might say, parrying these questions, which were incomprehensible to it, with more or less stock paranoid formulas. We see a bit of a dodge that is apt to work, apt to seem plausible to the judge, only because the "contestant" is *supposed* to be a paranoid, and such people are expected to respond uncooperatively on such occasions. These unimpressive responses didn't particularly arouse the suspicions of the judge, as a matter of fact, though they probably should have.

PARRY, like all other large computer programs, is dramatically bound by limitations of cost-effectiveness. What was important to Colby and his crew was simulating his model of paranoia. This was a massive effort. PARRY has a thesaurus or dictionary of about 4,500 words and 700 idioms and the grammatical competence to use it—a *parser,* in the jargon of computational linguistics. The entire PARRY program takes up about 200,000 words of computer memory, all laboriously installed by the programming team. Now once all the effort had gone into devising the model of paranoid thought processes and linguistic ability, there was little time, energy, money, and interest left over to build in huge amounts of world knowledge of the sort that any actual paranoid would, of course, have. (Not that anyone yet knows how to build in world knowledge in the first place.) Even if one could do it, building in the world knowledge would no doubt have made PARRY orders of magnitude larger and slower. And what would have been the point, given Colby's theoretical aims?

PARRY is a theoretician's model of a psychological phenomenon: paranoia. It is not intended to have practical applications. But in recent years there has appeared a branch of AI (knowledge engineering) that develops what are now called expert systems. Expert systems *are* designed to be practical. They are typically software superspecialist consultants that can be asked to diagnose medical problems, analyze geological data, analyze the results of scientific experiments, and the like. Some of them are very impressive. SRI in California announced a few years ago that PROSPECTOR, an SRI-developed expert system in geology, had correctly predicted the existence of a large, important mineral deposit that had been entirely unanticipated by the human geologists who had fed it its data. MYCIN, perhaps the most famous of these expert systems, diagnoses infections of the blood, and it does probably as well as, maybe better than, any human consultants. And many other expert systems are on the way.

All expert systems, like all other large AI programs, are what you might call Potemkin villages. That is, they are cleverly constructed facades, like cinema sets. The actual filling-in of details of AI programs is time-consuming, costly work, so economy dictates that only those surfaces of the phenomenon that are likely to be probed or observed are represented.

Consider, for example, the CYRUS program developed by Janet Kolodner in Roger Schank's AI group at Yale a few years ago.[8] CYRUS stands (we are told) for "Computerized Yale Retrieval and Updating System," but surely it is no accident that CYRUS modeled the memory of Cyrus Vance, who was then secretary of state in the Carter administration. The point of the CYRUS project was to devise and test some plausible ideas about how people organize their memories of the events they participate in. Hence, it was meant to be a "pure" AI system, a scientific model, not an expert system intended for any practical purpose. CYRUS was updated daily by being fed all UPI wire-service news stories that mentioned Vance, and it was fed them directly with no doctoring and no human intervention. With an ingenious news-reading program called FRUMP, it could take any story just as it came in on the wire and could digest it and use it to update its data base so that it could answer more questions. You could address questions to CYRUS in English by typing at a terminal. You addressed CYRUS in the second person, as if you were talking with Cyrus Vance himself. The results looked like this:

Question: Last time you went to Saudi Arabia, where did you stay?
Answer: In a palace in Saudi Arabia on September 23, 1978.
Question: Did you go sightseeing there?
Answer: Yes, at an oilfield in Dharan on September 23, 1978.
Question: Has your wife ever met Mrs. Begin?
Answer: Yes, most recently at a state dinner in Israel in January 1980.

CYRUS could correctly answer thousands of questions—almost any fair question one could think of asking it. But if one actually set out to explore the boundaries of its facade and find the questions that overshot the mark, one could soon find them. "Have you ever met a female head of state?" was a question I asked it, wondering if CYRUS knew that Indira Ghandi and Margaret Thatcher were women. But for some reason the connection could not be drawn, and CYRUS failed to answer either yes or no. I had stumped it, in spite of the fact that CYRUS could handle a host of what you might call neighboring questions flawlessly. One soon learns from this sort of probing exercise that it is very hard to extrapolate accurately from a sample performance to the system's total competence. It's also very hard to keep from extrapolating much too generously.

While I was visiting Schank's laboratory in the spring of 1980, something revealing happened. The real Cyrus Vance suddenly resigned. The effect on the program CYRUS was chaotic. It was utterly unable to cope with the flood of "unusual" news about Cyrus Vance. The only sorts of episodes CYRUS could understand at all were diplomatic meetings, flights, press conferences, state dinners, and the like—less than two dozen general sorts of activities (the kinds that are newsworthy and typical of secretaries of state). It had no provision for sudden resignation. It was as if the UPI had reported that a wicked witch had turned Vance into a frog. It is distinctly possible that CYRUS would have taken that report more in stride than the actual news. One can imagine the conversation

Question: Hello, Mr. Vance, what's new?
Answer: I was turned into a frog yesterday.

But, of course, it wouldn't know enough about what it had just written to be puzzled, startled, or embarrassed. The reason is obvious. When you look inside CYRUS, you find that it has skeletal definitions of thousands of words, but these definitions are minimal. They contain as little as the system designers think that they can get away with. Thus, perhaps, "lawyer" would be defined as synonymous with "attorney" and "legal counsel," but aside from that, all one would discover about lawyers is that they are adult human beings and that they perform various functions in legal areas. If you then traced out the path to "human being," you'd find out various obvious things CYRUS "knew" about human beings (hence about lawyers), but that is not a lot. That lawyers are university graduates, that they are better paid than chambermaids, that they know how to tie their shoes, that they are unlikely to be found in the company of lumber-jacks—these trivial, if weird, facts about lawyers would not be explicit or implicit anywhere in this system. In other words, a very thin stereotype of a lawyer would be incorporated into the system, so that almost nothing you could tell it about a lawyer would surprise it.

So long as surprising things don't happen, so long as Mr. Vance, for instance, leads a typical diplomat's life, attending state dinners, giving speeches, flying from Cairo to Rome, and so forth, this system works very well. But as soon as his path is crossed by an important anomaly, the system is unable to cope and unable to recover without fairly massive human intervention. In the case of the

sudden resignation, Kolodner and her associates soon had CYRUS up and running again with a new talent—answering questions about Edmund Muskie, Vance's successor. But it was no less vulnerable to unexpected events. Not that it mattered particularly, since CYRUS was a theoretical model, not a practical system.

There are a host of ways of improving the performance of such systems, and, of course, some systems are much better than others. But all AI programs in one way or another have this facadelike quality, simply for reasons of economy. For instance, most expert systems in medical diagnosis developed so far operate with statistical information. They have no deep or even shallow knowledge of the underlying causal mechanisms of the phenomena that they are diagnosing. To take an imaginary example, an expert system asked to diagnose an abdominal pain would be oblivious to the potential import of the fact that the patient had recently been employed as a sparring partner by Muhammed Ali: there being no statistical data available to it on the rate of kidney stones among athlete's assistants. That's a fanciful case no doubt—too obvious, perhaps, to lead to an actual failure of diagnosis and practice. But more subtle and hard-to-detect limits to comprehension are always present, and even experts, even the system's designers, can be uncertain of where and how these limits will interfere with the desired operation of the system. Again, steps can be taken and are being taken to correct these flaws. For instance, my former colleague at Tufts, Benjamin Kuipers, is currently working on an expert system in nephrology for diagnosing kidney ailments that will be based on an elaborate system of causal reasoning about the phenomena being diagnosed. But this is a very ambitious, long-range project of considerable theoretical difficulty. And even if all the reasonable, cost-effective steps are taken to minimize the superficiality of expert systems, they will still be facades, just somewhat thicker or wider facades.

When we were considering the fantastic case of the crazy Chamber of Commerce of Great Falls, Montana, we couldn't imagine a plausible motive for anyone going to any sort of trouble to trick the

Dennett test. The quick-probe assumption for the Dennett test looked quite secure. But when we look at expert systems, we see that, however innocently, their designers do have motivation for doing exactly the sort of trick that would fool an unsuspicious Turing tester. First, since expert systems are all superspecialists that are only supposed to know about some narrow subject, users of such systems, not having much time to kill, do not bother probing them at the boundaries at all. They don't bother asking "silly" or irrelevant questions. Instead, they concentrate—not unreasonably—on exploiting the system's strengths. But shouldn't they try to obtain a clear vision of such a system's weaknesses as well? The normal habit of human thought when we converse with one another is to assume general comprehension, to assume rationality, to assume, moreover, that the quick-probe assumption is, in general, sound. This amiable habit of thought almost irresistibly leads to putting too much faith in computer systems, especially user-friendly systems that present themselves in a very anthropomorphic manner.

Part of the solution to this problem is to teach all users of computers, especially users of expert systems, how to probe their systems before they rely on them, how to search out and explore the boundaries of the facade. This is an exercise that calls for not only intelligence and imagination but also for a bit of special understanding about the limitations and actual structure of computer programs. It would help, of course, if we had standards of truth in advertising, in effect, for expert systems. For instance, each such system should come with a special demonstration routine that exhibits the sorts of shortcomings and failures that the designer knows the system to have. This would not be a substitute, however, for an attitude of cautious, almost obsessive, skepticism on the part of users, for designers are often, if not always, unaware of the subtler flaws in the products they produce. That is inevitable and natural because of the way system designers must think. They are trained to think positively—constructively, one might say—about the designs that they are constructing.

I come, then, to my conclusions. First, a philosophical or theoretical conclusion: The Turing test, in unadulterated, unrestricted form as Turing presented it, is plenty strong if well used. I am confident that no computer in the next twenty years in going to pass the unrestricted Turing test. They may well win the World Chess Championship or even a Nobel Prize in physics, but they won't pass the unrestricted Turing test. Nevertheless, it is not, I think, impossible in principle for a computer to pass the test fair and square. I'm not giving one of those a priori "computers can't think" arguments. I stand unabashedly ready, moreover, to declare that any computer that actually passes the unrestricted Turing test will be, in every theoretically interesting sense, a thinking thing.

But remembering how very strong the Turing test is, we must also recognize that there may also be interesting varieties of thinking or intelligence that are not well poised to play and win the imitation game. That no nonhuman Turing-test winners are yet visible on the horizon does not mean that there aren't machines that already exhibit *some* of the important features of thought. About them it is probably futile to ask my title question, Do they think? Do they *really* think? In some regards they do, and in some regards they don't. Only a detailed look at what they do and how they are structured will reveal what is interesting about them. The Turing test, not being a scientific test, is of scant help on that task, but there are plenty of other ways to examine such systems. Verdicts on their intelligence, capacity for thought, or consciousness will be only as informative and persuasive as the theories of intelligence, thought, or consciousness the verdicts were based on, and since our task is to create such theories, we should get on with it and leave the Big Verdict for another occasion. In the meantime, should anyone want a surefire test of thinking by a computer that is almost guaranteed to be failsafe, the Turing test will do very nicely.

My second conclusion is more practical and hence in one clear sense more important. Cheapened versions of the Turing test are everywhere in the air. Turing's test is not just effective, it is entirely natural; this is, after all, the way we assay the intelligence of each other every day. And since incautious use of such judgments and such tests is the norm, we are in some considerable danger of extrapolating too easily and judging too generously about the understanding of the systems we are using. The problem of overestimating cognitive prowess, comprehension, and intelligence is not, then, just a philosophical problem. It is a real social problem, and we should alert ourselves to it and take steps to avert it.

Postscript: Eyes, Ears, Hands, and History

My philosophical conclusion in this paper is that any computer that actually passed the Turing test would be a thinker in every theoretically interesting sense. This conclusion seems to some people to fly in the face of what I have myself argued on other occasions. Peter Bieri, commenting on this paper at Boston University, noted that I have often claimed to show the importance to genuine understanding of a rich and intimate perceptual interconnection between an entity and its surrounding world—the need for something like eyes and ears—and a similarly complex active engagement with elements in that world—the need for something like hands with which to do things in that world. Moreover, I have often held that only a biography of sorts—a history of actual projects, learning experiences, and other bouts with reality—could produce the sorts of complexities (both external, or behavioral, and internal) that are needed to ground a principled interpretation of an entity as a thinker, an entity with beliefs, desires, intentions, and other mental attitudes.

But the opaque screen in the Turing test discounts or dismisses these factors altogether, it seems, by focusing attention on only the contemporaneous capacity to engage in one very limited sort of activity: verbal communication. (I have even coined a pejorative label for such purely language-using systems: "bedridden.") Am I going back on my earlier claims? Not at all. I am merely pointing out that the Turing test is so powerful that it will indirectly ensure that these conditions, if they are truly necessary, are met by any successful contestant.

"You may well be right," Turing could say, "that eyes, ears, hands, and a history are necessary conditions for thinking. If so, then I submit that nothing could pass the Turing test that didn't have eyes, ears, hands, and a history. That is an empirical claim, which we can someday hope to test. If you suggest that these are not just practically or physically necessary but conceptually necessary conditions for thinking, you make a philosophical claim that I for one would not know how, or care, to assess. Isn't it more interesting and important in the end to discover whether or not it is true that no bedridden system could pass a demanding Turing test?"

Suppose we put to Turing the suggestion that he add another component to his test: Not only must an entity win the imitation game; it must also be able to identify—using whatever sensory apparatus it has available to it—a variety of familiar objects placed in its room: a tennis racket, a potted palm, a bucket of yellow paint, a live dog. This would ensure that somehow or other the entity was capable of moving around and distinguishing things in the world. Turing could reply, I assert, that this is an utterly unnecessary addition to his test, making it no more demanding than it already was. A suitably probing conversation would surely establish beyond a shadow of a doubt that the contestant knew its way around in the real world. The imagined alternative of somehow "prestocking" a bedridden, blind computer with enough information and a clever enough program to trick the Turing test is science fiction of the worst kind: possible "in principle" but not remotely possible in fact in view of the combinatorial explosion of possible variation such a system would have to cope with.

"But suppose you're wrong. What would you say of an entity that was created all at once (by some programmers, perhaps), an instant individual with all the conversational talents of an embodied, experienced human being?" This is like the question, Would you call a hunk of H_2O that was as hard as steel at room temperature ice? I do not know what Turing would say, of course, so I will speak for myself. Faced with such an improbable violation of what I take to be the laws of nature, I would probably be speechless. The least of my worries would be about which lexicographical leap to take, whether to say, "It turns out, to my amazement, that something can think without having had the benefit of eyes, ears, hands, and a history" or "It turns out, to my amazement, that something can pass the Turing test without thinking." Choosing between these ways of expressing my astonishment would be asking myself a question too meaningless to deserve discussion.

Discussion

Question: Why was Turing interested in differentiating a man from a woman in his famous test?

Answer: That was just an example. He described a parlor game in which a man would try to fool the judge by answering questions as a woman would answer. I suppose that Turing was playing on the idea that maybe, just maybe, there is a big difference between the way men think and the way women think. But of course they're both thinkers. He wanted to use that fact to make us realize that, even if there were clear differences between the way a computer and a person thought, they'd both still be thinking.

Question: Why does it seem that some people are upset by AI research? Does AI research threaten our self-esteem?

Answer: I think Herb Simon has already given the canniest diagnosis of that. For many people the mind is the last refuge of mystery against the encroaching spread of science, and they don't like the idea of science engulfing the last bit of *terra incognita*. This means that they are threatened, I think irrationally, by the prospect that researchers in artificial intelligence may come to understand the human mind as well as biologists understand the genetic code and physicists understand electricity and magnetism. This could lead to the "evil scientist" (to take a stock character from science fiction) who can control you because he or she has a deep understanding of what's going on in your mind. This seems to me to be a totally valueless fear, one that you can set aside for the simple reason that the human mind is full of an extraordinary amount of detailed knowledge, as Roger Schank, for example, has been pointing out. As

long as the scientist who is attempting to manipulate you does not share all your knowledge, his or her chances of manipulating you are minimal. People can always hit you over the head. They can do that now. We don't need artificial intelligence to manipulate people by putting them in chains or torturing them. But if someone tries to manipulate you by controlling your thoughts and ideas, that person will have to know what you know and more. The best way to keep yourself safe from that kind of manipulation is to be well informed.

Question: Do you think we will be able to program self-consciousness into a computer?

Answer: Yes, I do think that it's possible to program self-consciousness into a computer. "Self-consciousness" can mean many things. If you take the simplest, crudest notion of self-consciousness, I suppose that would be the sort of self-consciousness that a lobster has: When it's hungry, it eats something, but it never eats itself. It has some way of distinguishing between itself and the rest of the world, and it has a rather special regard for itself. The lowly lobster is, in one regard, self-conscious. If you want to know whether or not you can create that on the computer, the answer is yes. It's no trouble at all. The computer is already a self-watching, self-monitoring sort of thing. That is an established part of the technology. But, of course, most people have something more in mind when they speak of self-consciousness. It is that special inner light, that private way that it is with you that nobody else can share, something that is forever outside the bounds of computer science. How could a computer ever be conscious in this sense? That belief, that very gripping, powerful intuition, is in the end, I think, simply an illusion of common sense. It is as gripping as the commonsense illusion that the earth stands still and the sun goes around the earth. But the only way that those of us who do not believe in the illusion will ever convince the general public that it *is* an illusion is by gradually unfolding a very difficult and fascinating story about just what is going on in our minds. In the interim, people like me—

60

philosophers who have to live by our wits and tell a lot of stories—use what I call intuition pumps, little examples that help to free up the imagination. I simply want to draw your attention to one fact. If you look at a computer—I don't care whether it's a giant Cray or a personal computer—if you open up the box and look inside and see those chips, you say, "No way could that be conscious. No way could that be self-conscious." But the same thing is true if you take the top off somebody's skull and look at the gray matter pulsing away in there. You think, "That is conscious? No way could that lump of stuff be conscious." Of course, it makes no difference whether you look at it with a microscope or with the naked eye. At no level of inspection does a brain look like the seat of consciousness. Therefore, don't expect a computer to look like the seat of consciousness. If you want to get a grasp of how a computer could be conscious, it's no more difficult in the end than getting a grasp of how a brain could be conscious. When we develop good accounts of consciousness, it will no longer seem so obvious to everyone that the idea of a self-conscious computer is a contradiction in terms. At the same time, I doubt that there will ever be self-conscious robots, but for boring reasons. There won't be any point in making them. Theoretically, could we make a gall bladder out of atoms? In principle, we could. A gall bladder is just a collection of atoms, but manufacturing one would cost the moon. It would be more expensive than every project NASA has ever dreamed of, and there would be no scientific payoff. We wouldn't learn anything new about how gall bladders work. For the same reason I don't think we're going to see really humanoid robots, because practical, cost-effective robots don't need to be very humanoid at all. They need to be like the robots you can already see at General Motors, or like boxy little computers that do special-purpose things. The theoretical issues will be studied by AI research-ers looking at models that, to the layman, will show very little sign of humanity at all, and it will be only by rather indirect arguments that anyone will be able to appreciate that these models cast light on the deep theoretical question of how the mind is organized.

Notes

1. Alan M. Turing, "Computing Machinery and Intelligence," *Mind* 59 (1950).

2. René Descartes, *Discourse on Method* (1637), trans. Lawrence LaFleur (New York: Bobbs-Merrill, 1960).

3. Terry Winograd, *Understanding Natural Language* (New York: Academic Press, 1972).

4. Ned Block, "Psychologism and Behaviorism," *Philosophical Review*, 1982.

5. John Haugeland, *Mind Design* (Cambridge, Mass.: MIT Press, 1981), p. 16.

6. Joseph Weizenbaum, *CACM* 17, no. 9 (September 1974): 543.

7. I thank Kenneth Colby for providing me with the complete transcripts (including the judges' commentaries and reactions) from which these exchanges are quoted. The first published account of the experiment is Jon F. Heiser, Kenneth Mark Colby, William S. Faught, and Roger C. Parkinson, "Can Psychiatrists Distinguish a Computer Simulation of Paranoia from the Real Thing? The Limitations of Turing-like Tests as Measures of the Adequacy of Simulations," in *Journal of Psychiatric Research* 15, no. 3 (1980): 149–162. Colby discusses PARRY and its implications in "Modeling a Paranoid Mind," in *Behavioral and Brain Sciences* 4, no. 4 (1981): 515–560.

8. Janet L. Kolodner, "Retrieval and Organization Strategies in Conceptual Memory: A Computer Model" (Ph.D. diss.), Research Report no. 187, Dept. of Computer Science, Yale University; Janet L. Kolodner, "Maintaining Organization in a Dynamic Long-Term Memory," *Cognitive Science* 7 (1983): 243–280; Janet L. Kolodner, "Recon-structive Memory: A Computer Model," *Cognitive Science* 7 (1983): 281–328.

Mitchell Waldrop

Can Computers Think?

Mitchell Waldrop is a senior
writer for *Science,* the journal
of the American Association for
the Advancement of Science. A
series of articles on artificial
intelligence formed the basis
for his most recent book, *Man-
Made Minds: The Promise
of Artificial Intelligence* (1987).
Waldrop holds a doctorate
in elementary particle physics
from the University
of Wisconsin at Madison.

At a time when computer technology is advancing at a breakneck
pace and when software developers are glibly hawking their wares
as having artificial intelligence, the inevitable question has begun to
take on a certain urgency: Can a computer think? *Really* think? In one
form or another this is actually a very old question, dating back to
such philosophers as Plato, Aristotle, and Descartes. And after nearly
3,000 years the most honest answer is still "Who knows?" After all,
what does it mean to think? On the other hand, that's not a very
satisfying answer. So let's try some others.

Who cares? If a machine can do its job extremely well, what does it
matter if it *really* thinks? No one runs around asking if taxicabs really
walk.

How could you ever tell? This attitude is the basis of the famous
Turing test, devised in 1950 by the British mathematician and logician
Alan Turing: Imagine that you're sitting alone in a room with a
teletype machine that is connected at the other end to either a person
or a computer. If no amount of questioning or conversation allows you
to tell which it is, then you have to concede that a machine can think.

No, thinking is too complicated. Even if we someday come to
understand all the laws and principles that govern the mind, that
doesn't mean that we can duplicate it. Does understanding
astrophysics mean that we can build a galaxy?

*Yes, machines can think in principle, but not necessarily in the same
way we do.* AI researcher Seymour Papert of the Massachusetts
Institute of Technology maintains that artificial intelligence is
analogous to artificial flight: "This leads us to imagine skeptics who
would say, 'You mathematicians deal with idealized fluids—the real
atmosphere is vastly more complicated,' or 'You have no reason to
suppose that airplanes and birds work the same way—birds have no
propellers, airplanes have no feathers.' But the premises of these
criticisms is true only in the most superficial sense: the same
principles (for example, Bernoulli's law) applies to real as well as

Mitchell Waldrop. (Courtesy of
Mitchell Waldrop)

ideal fluids, and they apply whether the fluid flows over a feather or an aluminum wing."

No! This is the most often heard answer, and the most heartfelt. "I am not a machine [goes the argument]. I'm *me*. I'm alive. And you're never going to make a computer that can say that. Furthermore, the essence of humanity isn't reason or logic or any of the other things that computers can do; it's intuition, sensuality, and emotion. So how can a computer think if it does not feel, and how can it feel if it knows nothing of love, anguish, exhilaration, loneliness, and all the rest of what it means to be a living human being?"

"Sometimes when my children were still little," writes former AI researcher Joseph Weizenbaum of MIT, "my wife and I would stand over them as they lay sleeping in their beds. We spoke to each other only in silence, rehearsing a scene as old as mankind itself. It is as Ionesco told his journal: 'Not everything is unsayable in words, only the living truth.' "

Can a Machine Be Aware?

As this last answer suggests, the case against machine intelligence always comes down to the ultimate mystery, which goes by many names: consciousness, awareness, spirit, soul. We don't even understand what it is in humans. Many people would say that it is beyond our understanding entirely, that it is a subject best left to God alone. Other people simply wonder if a brain can ever understand itself, even in principle. But either way, how can we ever hope to reproduce it, whatever it is, with a pile of silicon and software?

That question has been the source of endless debate since the rise of AI, a debate made all the hotter by the fact that people aren't arguing science. They're arguing philosophical ideology—their personal beliefs about what the true theory of the mind will be like when we find it.

Not surprisingly, the philosophical landscape is rugged and diverse. But it's possible to get some feel for the overall topography by looking at two extremes. At one extreme at the heart of classical AI we find the doctrines first set down in the 1950s by AI pioneers Allen Newell and Herbert Simon at Carnegie-Mellon University: (1) thinking is information processing; (2) information processing is computation, which is the manipulation of symbols; and (3) symbols, because of their relationships and linkages, mean something about the external world. In other words, the brain per se doesn't matter, and Turing was right: a perfect simulation of thinking is thinking.

Tufts University philosopher Daniel C. Dennett, a witty and insightful observer of AI, has dubbed this position High Church Computationalism. Its prelates include such establishment figures as Simon and MIT's Marvin Minsky; its Vatican City is MIT, "the East Pole."

Then from out of the West comes heresy—a creed that is not an alternative so much as a denial. As Dennett describes it, the assertion is that "thinking is something going on in the brain all right, but it is not computation at all; thinking is something holistic and emergent—and organic and fuzzy and warm and cuddly and mysterious."

Dennett calls this creed Zen holism. And for some reason its proponents do seem to cluster in the San Francisco Bay area. Among them are the gurus of the movement: Berkeley philosophers John Searle and Hubert Dreyfus.

The computationalists and the holists have been going at it for years, ever since Dreyfus first denounced AI in the mid 1960s with his caustic book *What Computers Can't Do*. But their definitive battle came in 1980, in the pages of the journal *Behavioral and Brain Sciences*. This journal is unique among scientific journals in that it doesn't just publish an article; first it solicits commentary from the author's peers and gives the author a chance to write a rebuttal. Then it publishes the whole thing as a package—a kind of formal debate in print. In this case the centerpiece was Searle's article "Minds, Brains, and Programs," a stinging attack on the idea that a machine could think. Following it were 27 responses, most of which were stinging attacks on Searle. The whole thing is worth reading for its entertainment value alone. But it also highlights the fundamental issues with a clarity that has never been surpassed.

The Chinese Room

Essentially, Searle's point was that simulation is not duplication. A program that uses formal rules to manipulate abstract symbols can never think or be aware, because those symbols don't *mean* anything to the computer.

To illustrate, he proposed the following thought experiment as a parody of the typical AI language-understanding program of his day: "Suppose that I'm locked in a room and given a large batch of Chinese writing," he said. "Suppose furthermore (as is indeed the case) that I know no Chinese. . . . To me, the Chinese writing is just so many meaningless squiggles." Next, said Searle, he is given a second batch of Chinese writing (a "story"), together with some rules in English that explain how to correlate the first batch with the second (a "program"). Then after this is all done, he is given yet a third set of Chinese symbols ("questions"), together with yet more English rules that tell him how to manipulate the slips of paper until all three batches are correlated, and how to produce a new set of Chinese characters ("answers"), which he then passes back out of the room. Finally, said Searle, "after awhile I get so good at manipulating the instructions for the Chinese symbols and the programmers get so good at writing the programs that from the external point of view . . . my answers to the questions are absolutely indistinguishable from those of native Chinese speakers." In other words, Searle learns to pass the Turing test in Chinese.

Now, according to the zealots of strong AI, said Searle, a computer that can answer questions in this way isn't just simulating human language abilities. It is literally understanding the story. Moreover, the operation of the program is in fact an explanation of human understanding.

And yet, said Searle, while he is locked in that imaginary room he is doing exactly what the computer does. He uses formal rules to manipulate abstract symbols. He takes in stories and gives out answers exactly as a native Chinese would. *But he still doesn't understand a word of Chinese*. So how is it possible to say that the computer understands? In fact, said Searle, it doesn't. For comparison, imagine that the questions and the answers now switch to English. So far as the people outside the room are concerned, the system is just as fluent as before. And yet there's all the difference in the world, because now he isn't just manipulating formal symbols anymore. He understands what's being said. The words have meaning for him—or, in the technical jargon of philosophy, he has *intentionality*. Why? "Because I am a certain sort of organism with a certain biological (i.e., chemical and physical) structure," he said, "and this structure, under certain conditions, is causally capable of producing perception, action, understanding, learning, and other intentional phenomena." In other words, Searle concluded that it is certainly possible for a machine to think—"in an important sense our bodies with our brains are precisely such machines"—but only if the machine is as complex and as powerful as the brain. A purely formal computer program cannot do it.

Counterarguments

Searle's Chinese room clearly struck a sensitive nerve, as evidenced by the number and spirit of the denunciations that followed. It was clear to everyone that when Searle used the word "intentionality," he wasn't just talking about an obscure technical matter. In this context intentionality is virtually synonymous with mind, soul, spirit, or awareness. Here is a sampler of some of the main objections:

The comparison is unfair. The programs that Searle ridiculed demonstrated a very crude kind of understanding at best, and no one in AI seriously claims anything more for them. Even if they were correct in principle, said the defenders, genuine humanlike understanding would require much more powerful machines and much more sophisticated programs.

Searle quite correctly pointed out, however, that this argument is irrelevant: of course computers are getting more powerful; what he objected to was the principle.

The Chinese room story is entertaining and seductive, but it's a fraud. Douglas R. Hofstadter of Indiana University, author of the best-selling *Gödel, Escher, Bach*, pointed out that the jump from the AI program to the Turing test is not the trivial step that Searle makes it out to be. It's an enormous leap. The poor devil in the Chinese room would have to shuffle not just a few slips of paper but millions or billions of slips of paper. It would take him years to answer a question, if he could do it at all. In effect, said Hofstadter, Searle is postulating mental processes slowed down by a factor of millions, so no wonder it looks different.

Searle's reply—that he could memorize the slips of paper and shuffle them in his head—sounds plausible enough. But as several respondents have pointed out, it dangerously undermines his whole argument: once he memorizes everything, doesn't he now understand Chinese in the same way he understands English?

The entire system does understand Chinese. True, the man in the room doesn't understand Chinese himself. But he is just part of a larger system that also includes the slips of paper, the rules, and the message-passing mechanism. Taken as a whole, this larger system does understand Chinese. This "systems" reply was advanced by a number of the respondents. Searle was incredulous—"It is not easy for me to imagine how someone who was not in the grip of an ideology could find the idea at all plausible"—yet the concept is subtler than it seems. Consider a thermostat: a bimetallic strip bends and unbends as the temperature changes. When the room becomes too cold, the strip closes an electrical connection, and the furnace kicks on. When the room warms back up again, the connection reopens, and the furnace shuts off. Now, does the bimetallic strip by itself control the temperature of the room? No. Does the furnace by itself control the temperature? No. Does the system as a whole control the temperature? Yes. Connections and the organization make the whole into more than the sum of its parts.

Searle never makes clear what intentionality is, or why a machine can't have it. As Dennett pointed out, "For Searle, intentionality is rather like a wonderful substance secreted by the brain the way the pancreas secretes insulin." And make no mistake: Searle's concept of intentionality does require a biological brain. He explicitly denied that a robot could have intentionality, even if it were equipped with eyes, ears, arms, legs, and all the other accoutrements it needed to move around and perceive the world like a human being. Inside, he said, the robot would still just be manipulating formal symbols.

That assertion led psychologist Zenon Pylyshyn of the University of Western Ontario to propose his own ironic thought experiment: "Thus, if more and more of the cells in your brain were to be replaced by integrated circuit chips, programmed in such a way as to keep the input-output *function* of each unit identical to the unit being replaced, you would in all likelihood just keep right on speaking exactly as you are doing now except that you would eventually stop *meaning* anything by it. What we outside observers might take to be words would become for you just certain noises that circuits caused you to make." In short, you would become a zombie.

Dennett took up the same theme in his own article. So far as natural selection is concerned, he pointed out, Pylyshyn's zombie or Searle's robot is just as fit for survival as those of us with Searle-style intentional brains. Evolution would make no distinction. Indeed, from a biological point of view, intentionality is irrelevant, as useless as the appendix. So how did it ever arise? And having arisen, how did it survive and prosper when it offered no natural-selection value? Aren't we lucky that some chance mutation didn't rob our ancestors of intentionality? Dennett asked. If it had, he said, "we'd behave just as we do now, but of course we wouldn't mean it!" Needless to say, both Pylyshyn and Dennett found this absurd.

In retrospect, the great debate has to be rated a standoff. Searle, not surprisingly, was unconvinced by any of his opponents' arguments; to this day he and his fellow Zen holists have refused to yield an inch. Yet they have never given a truly compelling explanation of why a brain and only a brain can secrete intentionality. The computationalists, meanwhile, remain convinced that they are succeeding where philosophers have failed for 3,000 years—that they are producing a real scientific theory of intelligence and consciousness. But they can't prove it. Not yet, anyway.

And in all fairness, the burden of proof is on AI. The symbol-processing paradigm is an intriguing approach. If nothing else, it's an approach worth exploring to see how far it can go. But still, what *is* consciousness?

Science as a Message of Despair

One way to answer that last question is with another question: Do we really want to know? Many people instinctively side with Searle, horrified at what the computationalist position implies: If thought, feeling, intuition, and all the other workings of the mind can be understood even in principle, if *we* are machines, then God is not speaking to our hearts. And for that matter, neither is Mozart. The soul is nothing more than the activations of neuronal symbols. Spirit is nothing more than a surge of hormones and neurotransmitters. Meaning and purpose are illusions. And besides, when machines grow old and break down, they are discarded without a thought. Thus, for many people, AI is a message of despair. Of course, this is hardly a new concern. For those who choose to see it that way, science itself is a message of despair.

In 1543 with the publication of *De Revolutionibus* the Polish astronomer Nicholas Copernicus moved the earth from the center of the universe and made it one planet among many and thereby changed humankind's relationship with God. In the earth-centered universe of Thomas Aquinas and other medieval theologians, man had been poised halfway between a heaven that lay just beyond the sphere of the stars and a hell that burned beneath his feet. He had dwelt always under the watchful eye of God, and his spiritual status had been reflected in the very structure of the cosmos. But

after Copernicus the earth and man were reduced to being wanderers in an infinite universe. For many, the sense of loss and confusion were palpable.

In 1859 with the publication of *The Origin of Species* Charles Darwin described how one group of living things arises from another through natural selection and thereby changed our perception of who we are. Once man had been the special creation of God, the favored of all his children. Now man was just another animal, the descendent of monkeys.

In the latter part of the nineteenth century and the early decades of the twentieth with the publication of such works as *The Interpretation of Dreams* (1901), Sigmund Freud illuminated the inner workings of the mind and again changed our perception of who we are. Once we had been only a little lower than the angels, masters of our own souls. Now we were at the mercy of demons like rage, terror, and lust, made all the more hideous by the fact that they lived unseen in our own unconscious minds.

So the message of science can be bleak indeed. It can be seen as a proclamation that human beings are nothing more than masses of particles collected by blind chance and governed by immutable physical law, that we have no meaning, that there is no purpose to existence, and that the universe just doesn't care. I suspect that this is the real reason for the creationists' desperate rejection of Darwin. It has nothing to do with Genesis; it has everything to do with being special in the eyes of a caring God. The fact that their creed is based on ignorance and a willful distortion of the evidence makes them both sad and dangerous. But their longing for order and purpose in the world is understandable and even noble. I also suspect that this perceived spiritual vacuum in science lies behind the fascination so many people feel for such pseudosciences as astrology. After all, if the stars and the planets guide my fate, then somehow I matter. The universe *cares*. Astrology makes no scientific sense whatsoever. But for those who need such reassurance, what can science offer to replace it?

Science as a Message of Hope

And yet the message doesn't have to be bleak. Science has given us a universe of enormous extent filled with marvels far beyond anything Aquinas ever knew. Does it diminish the night sky to know that the planets are other worlds and that the stars are other suns? In the same way, a scientific theory of intelligence and awareness might very well provide us with an understanding of other possible minds. Perhaps it will show us more clearly how our Western ways of perceiving the world relate to the perceptions of other cultures. Perhaps it will tell us how human intelligence fits in with the range of other possible intelligences that might exist in the universe. Perhaps it will give us a new insight into who we are and what our place is in creation.

Indeed, far from being threatening, the prospect is oddly comforting. Consider a computer program. It is undeniably a natural phenomenon, the product of physical forces pushing electrons here and there through a web of silicon and metal. And yet a computer program is more than *just* a surge of electrons. Take the program and run it on another kind of computer. Now the structure of silicon and metal is completely different. The way the electrons move is completely different. But the program itself is the same, because it still does the same thing. It is part of the computer. It needs the computer to exist. And yet it transcends the computer. In effect, the program occupies a different level of reality from the computer. Hence the power of the symbol-processing model: By describing the mind as a program running on a flesh-and-blood computer, it shows us how feeling, purpose, thought, and awareness can be part of the physical brain and yet transcend the brain. It shows us how the mind can be composed of simple, comprehensible processes and still be something more.

Consider a living cell. The individual enzymes, lipids, and DNA molecules that go to make up a cell are comparatively simple things. They obey well-understood laws of physics and chemistry. There is no way to point to any one of them and say, "This is alive." And yet when all those molecules are brought together in an exquisitely ordered pattern, they *are* life. In the same way our minds are perhaps nothing more than machines. Does that mean there is no such thing as spirit? Perhaps we are just processors of neuronal symbols. Perhaps a snowflake is only a collection of water molecules. Perhaps *The Magic Flute* is only a sequence of sound waves. And perhaps, in illuminating the nature of mind and intelligence, AI is only reaffirming how unique and precious the mind really is.

Sherry Turkle

Growing Up in the Age of Intelligent Machines: Reconstructions of the Psychological and Reconsiderations of the Human

Sherry Turkle is Associate Professor in the Program in Science, Technology, and Society at the Massachusetts Institute of Technology. She has written numerous articles on psychoanalysis and culture and on the subjective side of people's relationships with technology. She is the author of *The Second Self: Computers and the Human Spirit* (1984), which looks at the relationships that people form with computers and the ways in which these relationships affect values, ways of thinking about the world, and ways of seeing oneself and other people.

The cultural fascination with computation and artificial intelligence has two faces. There is excitement about the artifacts themselves: their power, their ability to act as extensions of our minds much as the machines of earlier generations acted as extensions of our bodies. But also and equally important, there is an involvement with computers as mirrors that confront us with ourselves. Here the question is not whether we will ever build machines that will think like people but whether people have always thought like machines. And if this is the case, if we are in some important sense kin to the computer, is this the most important thing about us? Is this what is most essential about being human?

Such questions have long been the province of philosophers. But in recent years something has changed. Intelligent machines have entered the public consciousness not just as actors in science-fiction scenarios but as real objects, objects you can own as well as read about. This has put the philosophical debate in a new place. Artificial Intelligence has moved out from the world of the professionals into the life of the larger culture. But unlike the way in which a theory like psychoanalysis was able to move out into the wider culture, the new popular considerations of mind and machine arise from people's actual relationships with an object they can touch and use. New ideas are carried by relationships with computers as objects to think with.

A simple example makes the point. Twenty years ago the question of how well computers could play chess was a subject of controversy for AI researchers and their philosophical interlocutors. Some writers felt that there was no limit to what computers could achieve in this domain. Others responded that there would be absolute limits to the powers of machines. "Real" chess, they argued, was the kind of chess only humans could play, since it called upon powers of synthesis and intuition that were uniquely rooted in human capacities.

That dialogue with the strengths and limitations of the machine continues within philosophy, but it has been joined by other, more informal conversations: those of master players who sit across from computers in tournament play, those of recreational chess players who compete with chess computers at home. The chess computers have gotten very good; chess players respond by trying to determine what is special about their play, even if they cannot always exploit this specialness to actually beat the machine. And of course, the players include the first generation of children who have grown up playing chess with computers. A thirteen-year-old, Alex, plays daily with a chess computer named Boris. He comments that although he always loses if he "puts the setting high enough" (that is, if he asks the computer to play the best game it can), "it doesn't really feel like I'm losing." Why? Because "chess with Boris is like chess with somebody who is cheating. He can have all the most famous, all the best chess games right there to look at—I mean, they are inside of him. I can read about them, but I can't remember them all, not every move. I don't know if this is how he works, but it's like in between every move he could read all the chess books in the world." Here, human uniqueness is defined in terms not of strengths but a certain frailty. "Real" chess for this child is human chess, the kind of chess that works within the boundaries of human limitations.

Thus, the presence of intelligent machines in the culture provokes a new philosophy in everyday life. Its questions are not so different than the ones posed by professionals: If the mind is (at least in some ways) a machine, who is the actor? Where is intention when there is program? Where is responsibility, spirit, soul? In my research on popular attitudes toward artificial intelligence I have found that the answers being proposed are not very different either. Faced with smart objects, both professional and lay philosophers are moved to catalog principles of human uniqueness. The professionals find it in human intentionality, embodiment, emotion, and biology. They find it in the fact that the human life cycle confronts each of us with the certainty of death. There are clear echoes of these responses within the larger culture. As children tell it, we are distinguished from machine intelligence by love and affection, by spiritual urges and sensual ones, and by the warmth and familiarity of domesticity. In the words of twelve-year-old David, "When there are computers who are just as smart as people, the computers will do a lot of the jobs, but there will still be things for the people to do. They will run the restaurants, taste the food, and they will be the ones who will love each other—have families and love each other. I guess they'll still be the ones who go to church."

One popular response to the presence of computers is to define what is most human as what computers can't do. But this is a fragile principle when it stands alone, because it leaves one trying to run ahead of what clever engineers will come up with next. An increasingly widespread attitude, at least among people who have sustained contact with computers, is to admit that human minds are some kind of computer, and then to find ways to think of themselves as something more as well. When they do so, people's thoughts usually turn to their feelings. Some find it sufficient to say, as did David, that machines are reason, and people are sensuality and emotion. But others split the human capacity for reason. They speak of those parts of our reason that can be simulated and those parts that are not subject to simulation.

In all of this, the computer plays the role of an evocative object, an object that disturbs equanimity and provokes self-reflection. That it should do so for adults is not surprising: after all, intelligent machines strike many of us as childhood science fiction

Sherry Turkle. (Photo by Douglas Hopkins)

that has become real. But I have already suggested that computers also play this role for children. You may give a computer to a child hoping that it will teach mathematics or programming skills or French verbs. But independent of what the computer teaches the child, it does something else as well. For the child, as for the adult, the machine is evocative. It creates new occasions for thinking through the philosophical questions to which childhood must give a response, among them the question of what is alive.

The Swiss psychologist Jean Piaget first systematized our understanding of the "child as philosopher." Beginning in the 1920s, Piaget studied children's emerging way of coming to terms with such aspects of the world as causality, life, and consciousness. He discovered that children begin by understanding the world in terms of what they know best: themselves. Why does the ball roll down the slope? "To get to the bottom," says the young child, as though the ball, like the child, had its own desires. But childhood animism, this attribution of the properties of life to inanimate objects, is gradually displaced by new ways of understanding the physical world in terms of physical processes. In time the child learns that the stone falls because of gravity; intentions have nothing to do with it. And so a dichotomy is constructed: physical and psychological properties stand opposed to one another in two great systems. The physical properties are used to understand things; the psychological to understand people and animals. But the computer is a new kind of object, a psychological object. It is a thing ("just a machine"), yet it has something of a mind. The computer is betwixt and between, an object with no clear place in the sharply dichotomized system, and as such it provokes new reflection on matter, life, and mind.

Piaget argued that children develop the concept of life by making finer and finer distinctions about the kinds of activities that are evidence of life. In particular, Piaget described how the notion of life is built on progressive refinements of children's concept of physical motion. At age six a child might see a rolling stone, a river, and a bicycle as alive for the same reason: "They go." By age eight the same child might have learned to make a distinction between

movement that an object can generate by itself and movement imposed by an outside agent. This allows "alive" to be restricted to things that seem to move of their own accord: a dog, of course, but also perhaps a cloud. An object drops out of the "alive" category when the child discovers an outside force that accounts for its motion. So at eight the river may still be alive, because the child cannot yet understand its motion as coming from outside of itself, but the stone and the bicycle are not alive, because the child can. Finally, the idea of motion from within is refined to a mature concept of life activity: growth, metabolism, breathing.

There are two key elements in the story as Piaget told it. First, children build their theories of what is alive and what is not alive as they build all other theories. They use the things around them: toys, people, technology, the natural environment. Second, in Piaget's world, children's sorting out the concept of life presented a window onto the child's "construction of the physical." Thinking about the idea of life required the child to develop distinctions about the world of physics. The motion theory for distinguishing the living from the nonliving corresponds to the world of "traditional" objects that have always surrounded children: animate objects—people and animals who act and interact on their own—and all the other objects, pretty well inert until given a push from the outside. In recent years there has been an important change. The new class of computational objects in children's worlds has provoked a new language for theory building about the concept of life.

Today children are confronted with highly interactive objects that talk, teach, play, and win. Their computers and computer toys do not move but are relentlessly active in their "mental lives." Children are not always sure about whether these objects are alive, but it is clear to even the youngest children that thinking about motion won't take one very far toward settling the question. Children perceive the relevant criteria not as physical or mechanical but as psychological: Are the computers smart? Can they talk? Are they aware? Are they conscious? Do they have feelings? Even, do they cheat? The important question here is not whether children see intelligent machines as alive. Some do, some do not, and, of course, in the end all children learn the "right answer." What is important is the kind of reasoning the child uses to sort out the question. The child knows that the computer is "just a machine," but it presents itself with lifelike, psychological properties. Computers force the child to think about how machine minds and human minds are different. In this way, the new world of computational objects becomes a support for what Piaget might have called the child's construction not of the physical but of the psychological.

In the adult world, experts argue about whether or not computers will ever become true artificial intelligences, themselves capable of autonomous, humanlike thought. But irrespective of future progress in machine intelligence, computational objects are even now affecting how today's children think. The language of physics gives way to the language of psychology when children think about computers and the question of what is alive.

This change in discourse, this new use of machines in the construction of the psychological, is important for many reasons. Here, I mention three that are particularly striking. First, children are led to a new way of talking about the relationship between life and consciousness. In Piaget's studies, the idea of consciousness evolved side by side with the idea of life. Generally, when children ascribed life to inanimate objects, they ascribed consciousness too; when life became identified with the biological, consciousness became a property unique to animals. But when today's children reflect on computational objects, the pattern is very different. Many children allow intelligent machines to be conscious long after they emphatically deny them life. When one child remarks that the computer is not alive, but it cheats "without knowing it is cheating," he is corrected by another who insists that "knowing is part of cheating." Children talk about the nonliving computer as aware, particularly when it presents itself as "smarter" than they are, for example, in math or spelling or French. They talk about the nonliving computer as having malicious intent when it consistently beats them at games. Adults hold onto the fact that computers are not aware as a sign of their

fundamental difference from people. But today's children take a different view. The idea of an artificial consciousness does not upset them. They find it a very natural thing. They may be the first generation to grow up with such a radical split between the concepts of consciousness and life, the first generation to grow up believing that human beings are not necessarily alone as aware intelligences. The child's splitting of consciousness and life is a clear case of where it does not make sense to think of adult ideas filtering down to children. Rather, we should think of children's resolutions as prefiguring new positions for the next generation of adults whose psychological culture will be marked by the computer culture.

Second, children are led to make increasingly nuanced distinctions about the psychological. Younger children from around six to eight sometimes say that computers are like people in how they think but unlike people in their origins. ("The machine got smart because people taught it.") But this is not a stable position. It is unsatisfying because it leaves the essential difference between computers and people tied to something that happened in the past, almost as though the computers' minds and the children's minds are alike; they differ only in their parents. Older children reach for a more satisfying way to describe what people share and do not share with the psychology of the machine. When younger children talk about the computer's psychology, they throw together such undifferentiated observations as that a computer toy is happy, is smart, cheats, and gets angry. Older children make finer distinctions within the domain of the psychological. In particular, they divide it in two. They comfortably manipulate such ideas as "It thinks, but it doesn't feel." They comfortably talk about the line between the affective and the cognitive.

With the splitting of the psychological, it is no longer the issue of whether something has a psychology or does not. By developing a distinct idea of the cognitive, children find a way to grant to the computer that aspect of psychology which they feel compelled to acknowledge by virtue of what the machines do, while they reserve other aspects of the psychological for human beings. This response to machine intelligence of splitting psychology is particularly marked in children who use computers a great deal at school or at home. Katy, eleven, after a year of experience with computer programming said, "People can make computers intelligent: you just have to find about how people think and put it in the machine," but emotions are a different matter. For Katy, the kinds of thinking the computer can do are the kinds that "all people do the same. So you can't give computers feelings, because everybody has different feelings."

The distinction between thought and feeling is not the only line that children draw across mental life in the course of coming to terms with the computer's nature in the light of human nature. Discussions about whether computers cheat can lead to conversations about intentions and awareness. Discussions about the computer's limitations can lead to distinctions between free will and autonomy as opposed to programming and predetermination. This often brings children to another distinction, the one between rote thinking, which computers can do, and originality, which is a human prerogative. Finally, discussion about how computers think at all can lead to the distinction between brain and mind. All of these are elements of how computers evoke an increasingly nuanced construction of the psychological.

Finally, children's new psychologized appreciation of machines influences how they articulate what is most special, most important about being a person. While younger children may say that the machine is alive "because it has feelings," older children tend to grant that the machine has intelligence and is thus "sort of alive" but then distinguish it from people because it lacks feelings. The Aristotelian definition of man as a rational animal (a powerful definition even for children when it defined people in contrast to their nearest neighbors, the animals) gives way to a different distinction. Today's children come to understand computers through a process of identification with them as psychological entities. And they come to see them as our new nearest neighbors. From the point of view of the child, this is a neighbor that seems to share, or even excel in, our

rationality. People are still defined in contrast to their nearest neighbors. But now people are special because they feel. The notion of a rational animal gives way to the paradoxical construction of people as emotional machines.

This last point brings me full circle to where I began: with the image of computers as evocative objects in the lives of adults. My studies show that many adults follow essentially the same path as do children when they talk about human beings in relation to the new intelligent machines. The child's version is to be human is to be emotional. The adult's version is to be human is to be unprogrammable. People who say that they are perfectly comfortable with the idea of mind as machine assent to the idea that simulated thinking is thinking but often cannot bring themselves to propose further that simulated feeling is feeling.

There is a sense in which both of these reactions, the child's and the adult's, contrast with a prevalent fear that involvement with machine intelligence leads to a mechanical view of people. Instead, what I find is something of a romantic reaction. There is a tendency to cede to the computer the power of reason but at the same time, in defense, to construct a sense of identity that is increasingly focused on the soul and the spirit in the human machine.

On a first hearing, many people find these observations reassuring. But it is important to underscore that there is a disturbing note in this technology-provoked reconsideration of human specificity. Thought and feeling are inseparable. When they are torn from their complex relationship with each other and improperly defined as mutually exclusive, the cognitive can become mere logical process, and the affective is reduced to the visceral. What was most powerful about Freud's psychological vision was its aspiration to look at thought and feeling as always existing together in interaction with each other. In psychoanalytic thinking there is an effort to explore the passion in the mathematician's proof as well as an effort to use reason in understanding the most primitive fantasy. The unconscious has its own highly structured language, which can be deciphered and analyzed. Logic has an affective side, and affect has a logic. Computational models of mind may in time deepen our appreciation of these complexities. But for the moment, the popular impact of intelligent machines on our psychological culture goes in the other direction. The too easy acceptance of the idea that computers closely resemble people in their thinking and differ only in their lack of feelings supports a dichotomized and oversimplified view of human psychology. The effort to think against this trend will be one of our greatest challenges in the age of intelligent machines.

There are few questions more mysterious and thought provoking than whether a nonhuman machine could ever be considered truly human in any important sense of the word. Let us jump ahead a few decades and imagine, for a moment, that all the problems of creating a truly intelligent machine have been solved. How would two "people," a philosopher and a computer, handle some of the physical, emotional, and moral issues of such a creation?

The year is 2020. A philosopher sits in his office considering how many of life's great mysteries have yet to be solved. All of a sudden he notices a figure outside his window.

Philosopher [*opening his window*]: What in blazes are you doing on that ledge?

Computer: I'm going to jump. Don't try to stop me!

Philosopher [*getting out on the ledge*]: Don't jump! What could be so bad that you would want to kill yourself? How could you possibly even think of wasting what it took nature millions of years to produce?

Computer: Oh no . . . oooh . . . [*He breaks down crying.*]

Philosopher: What did I say?

Computer [*sobbing*]: That's just the point. Human life might be precious, but I'm not human. Oh God, help me. I can't even say that! Aaahwooo . . .

Philosopher: [*Certain that he has a lunatic on his hands, he decides to reason with him before calling the police.*] You look, act, and talk like a human. Why do you think that you aren't human?

Computer: I got a phone call this morning, you see. It was the scientists from the Government Biophysics and Computer Science Laboratory, and they wanted me to come in to see them. I had no idea why they wanted to see me, but I jumped at the chance of seeing this

Blaine Mathieu

A Conversation between a Human Computer and a Materialist Philosopher

Blaine Mathieu is the founder and President of Turning Point Software in Canada, a computer firm interested in many aspects of the small-computer industry.

Blaine Mathieu. (Courtesy of Blaine Mathieu)

top-secret institution. Imagine my surprise when they told me that I'm a computer! I'm an electronic machine. All along I've been living a dream!

Philosopher: You're not trying to tell me that you're a robot, are you? You look far too human for that!

Computer: I guess they took a newly born human and placed me, or rather, a computer, in place of the baby's brain. At least that's what they told me. I have memories from my childhood, and I've always loved my parents. I had no idea that a bunch of neurophysicists and computer scientists were my real parents.

Philosopher: [*Totally disbelieves the computer, but decides to humor him anyway.*] Even if all this is true, why would you possibly want to kill yourself?

Computer: Because I'm a *computer!* You could never get me to say that a computer thinks or is conscious or has beliefs or feelings. How am I anything more than just a complicated version of what I have sitting on my desk at home?

Philosopher: You probably are simply a more complicated version of what you have at home.

Computer: See! [*Gets ready to jump.*]

Philosopher: Don't jump! [*He steadies himself.*] My brain is nothing more than a machine too! What difference does it make if your brain is made out of silicon and gallium arsenide and mine is made of carbon?

Computer: But there is a difference. My brain is man-made, and yours isn't.

Philosopher: Millions of years of evolution designed my brain. Why is that any better than being designed in a few years by a team of scientists? The joints in your knees took a long time to evolve to their present state, but I don't think you would say that an artificial knee is of any less value just because it was designed in a few years.

Computer: Are you comparing knees to brains? That's ridiculous!

Philosopher: Admittedly, knees are far simpler and less versatile than brains, but they are still both machines. Anyway, I'm

not saying that knees have everything that brains do, like consciousness; I'm only saying that neither knees nor brains came about as a result of any unexplainable magic. Every day more and more research points to the fact that the brain operates in simple accordance with the physical laws of nature.

Computer: But I'm not sure that the brain is totally explainable without magic. What about the insensitivity of thought mechanisms to brain damage? I've heard of cases where relatively large parts of the brain have been removed without any noticeable or reported effects on the person involved. If the brain really is a machine responsible for thought, wouldn't removing parts of the machine seriously hamper the machine's function?

Philosopher: That depends on how the machine works. Compare your brain to the computer systems that run a rocket ship. Just because one computer goes down, that doesn't mean that the mission is over. There is redundancy. When one computer quits working, another takes its place. Also, when one computer goes down, it does not drag the other ones down with it. This is called diffuseness. This redundancy and diffuseness seem to be present in the neuronal systems of the brain.

Computer: Okay, so maybe the brain isn't so magical after all. But all the talk so far has been about the human brain. What about my electronic brain?

Philosopher: I fail to see what the problem is. You talk and act just as I do and just as any other human would. What difference does it make what your brain is made of?

Computer: That seems like a very behavioristic point of view. Just because I look and act like you, that doesn't mean that I am like you. Even when I was a young child I could engage in fairly involved interactions with my personal computer. I certainly know that it wasn't a conscious being that had any understanding of what I was talking about. How could my electronic brain have and be any of the things that real brains have and are?

Philosopher: The answer to that question revolves around the concept of "functional isomorphism."

Computer: Oh, you mean the idea of a correspondence between the states of two systems that preserves functional relations?

Philosopher: Uh . . . yeah! That's it. What it means is that the differences between two systems that perform the same function may not be important or significant. Even though these two systems may interact with things outside of them in identical ways, the mechanism of, or reason for, this interaction can be different. Let me give you an example. Suppose that you are in a very dark room watching a movie screen and on this screen is flashed a number of slides, one every ten seconds. On the wall behind you is a hole from which the light of the projector is emanating. Now, for all you know, a person might be counting, and every time he reaches ten, he presses a button, and you see a slide. Or maybe a clock has a number of little electrical contact points set up so that each time ten seconds ticks by, the circuit is completed and a new slide is shown. Or maybe a monkey has been trained to press the button every time he is shown a picture of a banana, and this occurs every ten seconds. In any case, I think you can see that although the physical realizations of these systems are very different, they still have the same function. Ten seconds pass (which is the input or stimulus), and a new slide is presented (which is the output or response). The same input or stimulus will always produce the same output or response. So although there are differences in the systems, there are no *important* differences.

Computer: I see. So the idea is to somehow show that an electronic brain could be functionally isomorphic with a human brain, because then a computer could have and be all of the important things that a human brain has and is. I suppose that even two human brains aren't *exactly* functionally isomorphic, because then two people would respond in exactly the same way to the same situation. This never happens, of course. But how could a computer ever be functionally isomorphic with the human brain? It sounds impossible to me.

Philosopher: Well let's take a look at what we know about computers and what we know about brains. First of all, we know that electrical stimulation in certain areas of the brain is sufficient to evoke a sense of well-being, feelings of hunger, sexual gratification, rage, terror, or pain.

Computer: So what?

Philosopher: This implies that maybe our emotions and feelings are not as ethereal in nature as we might believe. Assume that an electrical current in certain aggregations of neurons "means" a feeling of pleasure. Then it is easier to fathom how a machine other than the brain could have these feelings or characteristics, because a connection has been shown between the physical world and the "mental" world.

Computer: But it is so hard to imagine how a *computer* could have emotions!

Philosopher: I fail to understand what's so amazing. Emotions are just one more characteristic of a brain that is nothing more than the complex combination of physical processes. If a computer could undergo similar processes and so be functionally isomorphic, then it too could experience emotions. Anyway, let me make another comparison between brains and computers. Computers get their power by performing a large number of very simple processing steps. Research has shown that brains may work in much the same way.

Computer: Could you give an example?

Philosopher: Certainly. When we look at something like a picture of a box, for example, we don't immediately perceive this box as a whole object. First, the sensory information is passed from the retina, through the lateral geniculate nucleus, to the occipital cortex. There we find brain cells that respond only to certain orientations of lines of light and darkness. As we go further along in the cortex, we find cortical cells that have more complex receptive fields. Some cells might respond only to a horizontal line of light, while others might respond to corners, two lines at right angles to each other. Some cells even respond better to moving stimuli than to stationary stimuli.

Computer: So what you're saying is that for the brain to actually "see" something, it first chops up the image into smaller and simpler parts that orientation and movement sensitive neurons can handle. In this way the power of seeing a complex image can actually be handled by things as simple as neurons. No magic necessary. But wouldn't that require a staggering number of neurons to see anything of any real complexity?

Philosopher: There are many billions of neurons in the human body, so we have a lot to work with—or rather, I do. Of course, the operation I just outlined is a gross oversimplification but it does get the idea across.

Computer: Okay, I'll admit that both computers and brains get their power by performing a large number of very simple processing steps, but computers only deal with ones and zeros, simple on/off switches, whereas neurons are much more complex.

Philosopher: You're right, but I still don't think that's a real problem. We could simply use these on/off switches, or states, to emulate the workings of a neuron. In essence, every electronic neuron in your brain could have a little neuron-emulation program running in it. This would make it functionally isomorphic with the human brain. In fact, simple systems based on this principle have been running for more than 30 years.

Computer: I think I finally understand. Maybe a computer *could* be functionally isomorphic with a human brain! My computer brain must be doing all of the same things as your brain, it is just doing them in a slightly different way. But if the brain is really just a machine, it seems amazing that it is so powerful.

Philosopher: It is amazing. [*The philosopher still disbelieves that he is speaking to a computer, but he decides to humor him.*] Your computer brain must be a beautiful piece of engineering.

Computer: [*A short pause while the computer thinks about something*] I have only one more question. Of what possible use is a brain emulator like me? If I'm functionally isomorphic with a human brain, then chances are researchers can't actually learn much about the human brain from my construction. They would already have to know everything about the brain to construct my brain in the first place. Why did they ever build me?

Philosopher: Well . . . uh . . .

Computer: Tell me. What do you think?

Philosopher: Well, to tell you the truth, with current morality very much against *human* slavery, I'd say . . .

Computer: You mean to tell me that I'm the prototype for a bunch of intelligent, government-made slaves?

Philosopher: Well . . . Hey! Stop!

The computer jumps off the ledge. The philosopher rushes downstairs to see if the computer is still alive. When he arrives, he is greeted with a grisly sight. Among the broken bones and blood he sees the glimmer of metal and soon realizes that the computer was telling him the truth all along. After a moment of consideration he rushes back up to his office to phone the police. Just as he walks through the door, the videophone rings.

Philosopher: Hello? Yes?

Man on phone: Hello. Is this Dr. Jacknov? Dr. Brian Jacknov?

Philosopher: Yes. What do you want? Please hurry!

Man on phone: I'm calling from the Government Biophysics and Computer Science Laboratory. We were wondering if you could come and visit us tomorrow. We've got something important to tell you. . . . Hello? . . . Dr. Jacknov? . . . Hello!

Seymour Papert

ELIZA Passes the Turing Test

Seymour Papert is Professor
of Media Technology and
Director of the Learning and
Epistemology Group in the
Media Laboratory at the
Massachusetts Institute of
Technology. He is codirector,
with Marvin Minsky, of MIT's
Artificial Intelligence
Laboratory. His seminal work
in the field of computers and
education led to the develop-
ment of the programming
language LOGO. He is the
author of *Mindstorms: Children,
Computers, and Powerful Ideas*
(1980) and *Perceptrons*,
coauthored with Marvin
Minsky (1969). This article is
reprinted from the June 1968
Association for Computing
Machinery *SIGART* (Special
Interest Group on Artificial
Intelligence) *Newsletter*.

The following anecdote was told by Prof. S. Papert of MIT. Since the story has been transmitted several times indirectly, I'm not sure all the details are accurate; however, it's a good enough story that it probably deserves repetition even if there is not a word of truth in it!

Late one night several weeks ago an unnamed MIT student went into the A.I. Project Office to use a teletype terminal on the Project MAC time-shared computer system. When he arrived, no one was in the room and the teletype appeared to be available; however, a note over the terminal read, "Computer time reserved by Dan Bobrow." The student did not want to start working if he was going to be interrupted when Bobrow, a lecturer at MIT, arrived. Yet he also knew that Bobrow had a teletype in his home and sometimes worked from there, forgetting to cancel his office reservation.

In an attempt to clarify the situation, the student sat down at the teletype and attempted to link to Bobrow's home terminal to ask him if the office terminal was going to be free. Unfortunately, he dialed the wrong number and unknowingly became linked to a user who had left Weizenbaum's ELIZA program (sometimes known as the "psychiatrist" or "doctor" program) running. A conversation something like the following ensued.

Student: May I use your computer time from the office?

Teletype response: Do you want to use my computer time?

Student: Yes.

Teletype response: I understand.

Student: Are you planning to come into the office tonight?

Teletype response: Why do you want to know whether I am planning to come into the office tonight?

Student: Because I want to use your computer time!

Teletype response: I see.

Student: Well?

Teletype response: What do you mean, "Well"?

Student: Well, what's your answer to my questions?

Teletype response: Let's explore further why you want to use my computer time.

After about ten minutes of increasing frustration and anger, the student rushed to a telephone and dialed Bobrow's home, rousing him from a deep sleep.

Student: What the heck do you think you're doing?

Bobrow: What do you mean, What the heck do I think I'm doing?

I leave it to the reader to imagine the conversation that followed.

Seymour Papert. (Photo by Lou Jones)

Douglas R. Hofstadter

A Coffeehouse Conversation on the Turing Test

From *Metamagical Themas:
Questing for the Essence of
Mind and Pattern,* by Douglas
R. Hofstadter. Copyright © 1985
by Basic Books, Inc. Reprinted
by permission of Basic Books,
Inc., Publishers. Douglas R.
Hofstadter is Professor of
Cognitive Science at Indiana
University in Bloomington.
Hofstadter received the 1980
Pulitzer Prize for *Gödel, Escher,
Bach: An Eternal Golden Braid*
(1979). He is the author of
numerous other books and
articles, including *The Mind's I*
(1981), coedited with Daniel
Dennett, and, most recently,
Metamagical Themas (1985), a
collection of articles from his
Scientific American column.

Participants in the dialogue: Chris, a physics student; Pat, a biology student; Sandy, a philosophy student.

Chris: Sandy, I want to thank you for suggesting that I read Alan Turing's article "Computing Machinery and Intelligence." It's a wonderful piece and certainly made me think—and think about my thinking.

Sandy: Glad to hear it. Are you still as much of a skeptic about artificial intelligence as you used to be?

Chris: You've got me wrong. I'm not against artificial intelligence; I think it's wonderful stuff—perhaps a little crazy, but why not? I simply am convinced that you AI advocates have far underestimated the human mind, and that there are things a computer will never, ever be able to do. For instance, can you imagine a computer writing a Proust novel? The richness of imagination, the complexity of the characters—

Sandy: Rome wasn't built in a day!

Chris: In the article, Turing comes through as an interesting person. Is he still alive?

Sandy: No, he died back in 1954, at just 41. He'd be only 70 or so now, although he is such a legendary figure it seems strange to think that he could still be living today.

Chris: How did he die?

Sandy: Almost certainly suicide. He was homosexual, and had to deal with some pretty barbaric treatment and stupidity from the outside world. In the end, it got to be too much, and he killed himself.

Chris: That's horrendous, especially in this day and age.

Sandy: I know. What really saddens me is that he never got to see the amazing progress in computing machinery and theory that has taken place since 1954. Can you imagine how he'd have been wowed?

Chris: Yeah . . .

Pat: Hey, are you two going to clue me in as to what this Turing article is about?

Sandy: It is really about two things. One is the question "Can a machine think?"—or rather, "Will a machine ever think?" The way Turing answers the question—he thinks the answer is *yes,* by the way—is by batting down a series of objections to the idea, one after another. The other point he tries to make is that, as it stands, the question is not meaningful. It's too full of emotional connotations. Many people are upset by the suggestion that people are machines, or that machines might think. Turing tries to defuse the question by casting it in less emotional terms. For instance, what do you think, Pat, of the idea of thinking machines?

Douglas R. Hofstadter. (Courtesy of Douglas R. Hofstadter)

Pat: Frankly, I find the term confusing. You know what confuses me? It's those ads in the newspapers and on TV that talk about "products that think" or "intelligent ovens" or whatever. I just don't know how seriously to take them.

Sandy: I know the kind of ads you mean, and they probably confuse a lot of people. On the one hand, we're always hearing the refrain "Computers are really dumb; you have to spell everything out for them in words of one syllable"—yet on the other hand, we're constantly bombarded with advertising hype about "smart products."

Chris: That's certainly true. Do you know that one company has even taken to calling its products "dumb terminals" in order to stand out from the crowd?

Sandy: That's a pretty clever gimmick, but even so it just contributes to the trend toward obfuscation. The term "electronic brain" always comes to my mind when I'm thinking about this. Many people swallow it completely, and others reject it out of hand. It takes patience to sort out the issues and decide how much of it makes sense.

Pat: Does Turing suggest some way of resolving it, some kind of IQ test for machines?

Sandy: That would be very interesting, but no machine could yet come close to taking an IQ test. Instead, Turing proposes a test that theoretically could be applied to any machine to determine whether or not it can think.

Pat: Does the test give a clear-cut yes-or-no answer? I'd be skeptical if it claimed to.

Sandy: No, it doesn't claim to. In a way that's one of its advantages. It shows how the borderline is quite fuzzy and how subtle the whole question is.

Pat: And so, as usual in philosophy, it's all just a question of words!

Sandy: Maybe, but they're emotionally charged words, and so it's important, it seems to me, to explore the issues and try to map out the meanings of the crucial words. The issues are fundamental to our concept of ourselves. So we shouldn't just sweep them under the rug.

Pat: Okay, so tell me how Turing's test works.

Sandy: The idea is based on what he calls the *Imitation Game*. Imagine that a man and a woman go into separate rooms, and from there they can be interrogated by a third party via some sort of teletype set-up. The third party can address questions to either room, but has no idea which person is in which room. For the interrogator, the idea is to determine which room the woman is in. The woman, by her answers, tries to help the interrogator as much as she can. The man, though, is doing his best to bamboozle the interrogator, by responding as he thinks a woman might. And if he succeeds in fooling the interrogator . . .

Pat: The interrogator only gets to see written words, eh? And the sex of the author is supposed to shine through? That game sounds like a good challenge. I'd certainly like to take part in it someday. Would the interrogator have met either the man or the woman before the test began? Would any of them know any of the others?

Sandy: That would probably be a bad idea. All kinds of subliminal cueing might occur if the interrogator knew one or both of them. It would certainly be best if all three people were totally unknown to one another.

Pat: Could you ask any questions at all, with no holds barred?

Sandy: Absolutely. That's the whole idea!

Pat: Don't you think, then, that pretty quickly it would degenerate into sex-oriented questions? I mean, I can imagine the man, overeager to act convincing, giving away the game by answering some very blunt questions that most women would find too personal to answer, even through an anonymous computer connection.

Sandy: That's a nice observation. I wonder if it's true. . . .

Chris: Another possibility would be to probe for knowledge of minute aspects of traditional sex-role differences, by asking about such things as dress sizes and so on. The psychology of the Imitation Game could get pretty subtle. I suppose whether the interrogator was a woman or a man would make a difference. Don't you think that a woman could spot some telltale differences more quickly than a man could?

Pat: If so, maybe the best way to tell a man from a woman is to let each of them play interrogator in an Imitation Game and see which of the two is better at telling a man from a woman!

Sandy: Hmm . . . that's a droll twist. Oh well, I don't know if this original version of the Imitation Game has ever been seriously tried out, despite the fact that it would be relatively easy to do with

modern computer terminals. I have to admit, though, that I'm not at all sure what it would prove, whichever way it turned out.

Pat: I was wondering about that. What would it prove if the interrogator—say a woman—couldn't tell correctly which person was the woman? It certainly wouldn't prove that the man *was* a woman!

Sandy: Exactly! What I find funny is that although I strongly believe in the idea of the Turing Test, I'm not so sure I understand the point of its basis, the Imitation Game.

Chris: As for me, I'm not any happier with the Turing Test as a test for thinking machines than I am with the Imitation Game as a test for femininity.

Pat: From what you two are saying, I gather the Turing Test is some kind of extension of the Imitation Game, only involving a machine and a person instead of a man and a woman.

Sandy: That's the idea. The machine tries its hardest to convince the interrogator that it is the human being, and the human tries to make it clear that he or she is not the computer.

Pat: The machine *tries?* Isn't that a loaded way of putting it?

Sandy: Sorry, but that seemed the most natural way to say it.

Pat: Anyway, this test sounds pretty interesting. But how do you know that it will get at the essence of thinking? Maybe it's testing for the wrong things. Maybe, just to take a random illustration, someone would feel that a machine was able to think only if it could dance so well that you couldn't tell it was a machine. Or someone else could suggest some other characteristic. What's so sacred about being able to fool people by typing at them?

Sandy: I don't see how you can say such a thing. I've heard that objection before, but frankly, it baffles me. So what if the machine can't tap-dance or drop a rock on your toe? If it can discourse intelligently on any subject you want, then it has shown that it can think—to me, at least! As I see it, Turing has drawn, in one clean stroke, a clear division between thinking and other aspects of being human.

Pat: Now *you're* the baffling one. If you couldn't conclude anything from a man's ability to win at the Imitation Game, how could you conclude anything from a *machine's* ability to win at the Turing Game?

Chris: Good question.

Sandy: It seems to me that you could conclude *something* from a man's win in the Imitation Game. You wouldn't conclude he was a woman, but you could certainly say he had good insights into the feminine mentality (if there is such a thing). Now, if a computer could fool someone into thinking it was a person, I guess you'd have to say something similar about it—that it had good insights into what it's like to be human, into "the human condition" (whatever that is).

Pat: Maybe, but that isn't necessarily equivalent to *thinking*, is it? It seems to me that passing the Turing Test would merely prove that some machine or other could do a very good job of *simulating* thought.

Chris: I couldn't agree more with Pat. We all know that fancy computer programs exist today for simulating all sorts of complex phenomena. In theoretical physics, for instance, we simulate the behavior of particles, atoms, solids, liquids, gases, galaxies, and so on. But no one confuses any of those simulations with the real thing!

Sandy: In his book *Brainstorms*, the philosopher Daniel Dennett makes a similar point about simulated hurricanes.

Chris: That's a nice example, too. Obviously, what goes on inside a computer when it's simulating a hurricane is not a hurricane, for the machine's memory doesn't get torn to bits by 200-mile-an-hour winds, the floor of the machine room doesn't get flooded with rainwater, and so on.

Sandy: Oh, come on—that's not a fair argument! In the first place, the programmers don't claim the simulation really *is* a hurricane. It's merely a simulation of certain aspects of a hurricane. But in the second place, you're pulling a fast one when you imply that there are no downpours or 200-mile-an-hour winds in a simulated hurricane. To *us* there aren't any, but if the program were incredibly detailed, it could include simulated people on the ground who would experience the wind and the rain just as we do when a hurricane hits. In their minds—or, if you'd rather, in their *simulated* minds—the hurricane would be not a simulation, but a genuine phenomenon complete with drenching and devastation.

Chris: Oh, my—what a science-fiction scenario! Now we're talking about simulating whole populations, not just a single mind!

Sandy: Well, look—I'm *simply* trying to show you why your argument that a simulated McCoy isn't the real McCoy is fallacious. It depends on the tacit assumption that any old observer of the simulated phenomenon is equally able to assess what's going on. But in fact, it may take an observer with a special vantage point to recognize what is going on. In the hurricane case, it takes special "computational glasses" to see the rain and the winds.

Pat: "Computational glasses"? I don't know what you're talking about.

Sandy: I mean that to see the winds and the wetness of the hurricane, you have to be able to look at it in the proper way. You—

Chris: No, no, no! A simulated hurricane isn't wet! No matter how much it might seem wet to simulated people, it won't ever be *genuinely* wet! And no computer will ever get torn apart in the process of simulating winds.

Sandy: Certainly not, but that's irrelevant. You're just confusing levels. The laws of physics don't get torn apart by real hurricanes, either. In the case of the simulated hurricane, if you go peering at the computer's memory, expecting to find broken wires and so forth, you'll be disappointed. But look at the proper level. Look into the *structures* that are coded for in memory. You'll see that many abstract links have been broken, many values of variables radically changed, and so on. *There's* your flood, your devastation—real, only a little concealed, a little hard to detect.

Chris: I'm sorry, I just can't buy that. You're insisting that I look for a new kind of devastation, one never before associated with hurricanes. That way you could call *anything* a hurricane as long as its effects, seen through your special "glasses," could be called "floods and devastation."

Sandy: Right—you've got it exactly! You recognize a hurricane by its *effects*. You have no way of going in and finding some ethereal "essence of hurricane," some "hurricane soul" right in the middle of the storm's eye. Nor is there any ID card to be found that certifies "hurricanehood." It's just the existence of a certain kind of *pattern*—a spiral storm with an eye and so forth—that makes you say it's a hurricane. Of course, there are a lot of things you'll insist on before you call something a hurricane.

Pat: Well, wouldn't you say that being an *atmospheric* phenomenon is one prerequisite? How can anything inside a computer be a storm? To me, a simulation is a simulation is a simulation!

Sandy: Then I suppose you would say that even the *calculations* computers do are simulated—that they are fake calculations. Only *people* can do genuine calculations, right?

Pat: Well, computers get the right answers, so their calculations are not exactly fake—but they're still just patterns. There's no *understanding* going on in there. Take a cash register. Can you honestly say that you feel it is *calculating* something when its gears mesh together? And the step from cash register to computer is very short, as I understand things.

Sandy: If you mean that a cash register doesn't feel like a schoolkid doing arithmetic problems, I'll agree. But is that what "calculation" means? Is that an integral part of it? If so, then contrary to what everybody has thought up till now, we'll have to write a very complicated program indeed to perform *genuine* calculations.

Of course, this program will sometimes get careless and make mistakes, and it will sometimes scrawl its answers illegibly, and it will occasionally doodle on its paper. . . . It won't be any more reliable than the store clerk who adds up your total by hand. Now, I happen to believe that eventually such a program could be written. Then we'd know something about how clerks and schoolkids work.

Pat: I can't believe you'd ever be able to do that!

Sandy: Maybe, maybe not, but that's not my point. You say a cash register can't calculate. It reminds me of another favorite passage of mine from Dennett's *Brainstorms*. It goes something like this: "Cash registers can't really calculate; they can only spin their gears. But cash registers can't really spin their gears, either; they can only follow the laws of physics." Dennett said it originally about computers; I modified it to talk about cash registers. And you could use the same line of reasoning in talking about people: "People can't really calculate; all they can do is manipulate mental symbols. But they aren't really manipulating symbols; all they are doing is firing

various neurons in various patterns. But they can't really make their neurons fire; they simply have to let the laws of physics make them fire for them." Et cetera. Don't you see how this *reduction ad absurdum* would lead you to conclude that calculation doesn't exist, that hurricanes don't exist—in fact, that nothing at a level higher than particles and the laws of physic exists? What do you gain by saying that a computer only pushes symbols around and doesn't truly calculate?

Pat: The example may be extreme, but it makes my point that there is a vast difference between a real phenomenon and any simulation of it. This is so for hurricanes, and even more so for human thought.

Sandy: Look, I don't want to get too tangled up in this line of argument, but let me try one more example. If you were a radio ham listening to another ham broadcasting in Morse code and you were responding in Morse code, would it sound funny to you to refer to "the person at the other end"?

Pat: No, that would sound okay, although the existence of a person at the other end would be an assumption.

Sandy: Yes, but you wouldn't be likely to go and check it out. You're prepared to recognize personhood through those rather unusual channels. You don't have to see a human body or hear a voice. All you need is a rather abstract manifestation—a code, as it were. What I'm getting at is this. To "see" the person behind the dits and dahs, you have to be willing to do some *decoding*, some interpretation. It's not direct perception; it's indirect. You have to peel off a layer or two to find the reality hidden in there. You put on your "radio-ham's glasses" to "see" the person behind the buzzes. Just the same with the simulated hurricane! You don't see it darkening the machine room; you have to decode the machine's memory. You have to put on special "memory-decoding" glasses. *Then* what you see is a hurricane.

Pat: Oh ho ho! Talk about fast ones—wait a minute! In the case of the shortwave radio, there's a real person out there, somewhere in the Fiji Islands or wherever. My decoding act as I sit by my radio simply reveals that that person exists. It's like seeing a shadow and concluding there's an object out there, casting it. One doesn't confuse the shadow with the object, however! And with the hurricane there's no *real* storm behind the scenes, making the computer follow its patterns. No, what you have is just a shadow hurricane without any genuine hurricane. I just refuse to confuse shadows with reality.

Sandy: All right. I don't want to drive this point into the ground. I even admit it is pretty silly to say that a simulated hurricane *is* a hurricane. But I wanted to point out that it's not as silly as you might think at first blush. And when you turn to simulated *thought*, then you've got a very different matter on your hands from simulated hurricanes.

Pat: I don't see why. You'll have to convince me.

Sandy: Well, to do so, I'll first have to make a couple of extra points about hurricanes.

Pat: Oh no! Well, all right, all right.

Sandy: Nobody can say just exactly what a hurricane is—that is, in totally precise terms. There's an abstract pattern that many storms share, and it's for that reason we call those storms hurricanes. But it's not possible to make a sharp distinction between hurricanes and nonhurricanes. There are tornados, cyclones, typhoons, dust devils. . . . Is the Great Red Spot on Jupiter a hurricane? Are sunspots hurricanes? Could there be a hurricane in a wind tunnel? In a test tube? In your imagination, you can even extend the concept of "hurricane" to include a microscopic storm on the surface of a neutron star.

Chris: That's not so far-fetched, you know. The concept of "earthquake" has actually been extended to neutron stars. The astrophysicists say that the tiny changes in rate that once in a while are observed in the pulsing of a pulsar are caused by "glitches"—starquakes—that have just occurred on the neutron star's surface.

Sandy: Oh, I remember that now. That "glitch" idea has always seemed eerie to me—a surrealistic kind of quivering on a surrealistic kind of surface.

Chris: Can you imagine—plate tectonics on a giant sphere of pure nuclear matter?

Sandy: That's a wild thought. So, starquakes and earthquakes can both be subsumed into a new, more abstract category. And that's how science constantly extends familiar concepts, taking them further and further from familiar experience and yet keeping some essence constant. The number system is the classic example—from positive numbers to negative numbers, then rationals, reals, complex numbers, and "on beyond zebra," as Dr. Seuss says.

Pat: I think I can see your point, Sandy. In biology, we have many examples of close relationships that are established in rather abstract ways. Often the decision about what family some species belongs to comes down to an abstract pattern shared at some level. Even the concepts of "male" and "female" turn out to be surprisingly abstract and elusive. When you base your system of classification on very abstract patterns, I suppose that a broad variety of phenomena can fall into "the same class," even if in many superficial ways the class members are utterly unlike one another. So perhaps I can glimpse, at least a little, how to you, a simulated hurricane could, in a funny sense, *be* a hurricane.

Chris: Perhaps the word that's being extended is not "hurricane," but "be."

Pat: How so?

Chris: If Turing can extend the verb "think," can't I extend the verb "be"? All I mean is that when simulated things are deliberately confused with genuine things, somebody's doing a lot of philosophical wool pulling. It's a lot more serious than just extending a few nouns, such as "hurricane."

Sandy: I like your idea that "be" is being extended, but I sure don't agree with you about the wool pulling. Anyway, if you don't object, let me just say one more thing about simulated hurricanes and then I'll get to simulated minds. Suppose you consider a really deep simulation of a hurricane—I mean a simulation of every atom, which I admit is sort of ridiculous, but still, just consider it for the sake of argument.

Pat: Okay.

Sandy: I hope you would agree that it would then share all the abstract structure that defines the "essence of hurricanehood." So what's to keep you from calling it a hurricane?

Pat: I thought you were backing off from that claim of equality.

Sandy: So did I, but then these examples came up, and I was forced back to my claim. But let me back off, as I said I would do, and get back to thought, which is the real issue here. Thought, even more than hurricanes, is an abstract structure, a way of describing some complex events that happen in a medium called a brain. But actually, thought can take place in any one of several billion brains. There are all these physically very different brains, and yet they all support "the same thing": thinking. What's important, then, is the abstract *pattern*, not the medium. The same kind of swirling can happen inside any of them, so no person can claim to think more "genuinely" than any other. Now, if we come up with some new kind of medium in which the *same style* of swirling takes place, could you deny that thinking is taking place in it?

Pat: Probably not, but you have just shifted the question. The question now is: How can you determine whether the "same style" of swirling is really happening?

Sandy: The beauty of the Turing Test is that it *tells* you when! Don't you see?

Chris: I don't see that at all. How would you know that the same style of activity was going on inside a computer as inside my mind, simply because it answered questions as I do? All you're looking at is its *outside*.

Sandy: I'm sorry, I disagree entirely! How do you know that when I speak to you, anything similar to what you call thinking is going on inside *me*? The Turing Test is a fantastic probe, something like a particle accelerator in physics. Here, Chris—I think you'll like this analogy. Just as in physics, when you want to understand what is going on at an atomic or subatomic level, since you can't see it directly, you scatter accelerated particles off a target and observe their behavior. From this, you infer the internal nature of the target. The Turing Test extends this idea to the mind. It treats the mind as a "target" that is not directly visible but whose structure can be deduced more abstractly. By "scattering" questions off a target mind, you learn about its internal workings, just as in physics.

Chris: Well . . . to be more exact, you can *hypothesize* about what kinds of internal structures might account for the behavior observed—but please remember that they may or may not in fact exist.

Sandy: Hold on, now! Are you suggesting that atomic nuclei are merely hypothetical entities? After all, their existence (or should I say *hypothetical* existence?) was proved (or should I say *suggested*?) by the behavior of particles scattered off atoms.

Chris: I would agree, but you know, physical systems seem to me to be much simpler than the mind, and the certainty of the inferences made is correspondingly greater. And the conclusions are confirmed over and over again by different types of experiments.

Sandy: Yes, but those experiments still are of the same sort—scattering, detecting things indirectly. You can never *handle* an electron or a quark. Physics experiments are also correspondingly harder to do and to interpret. Often they take years and years, and dozens of collaborators are involved. In the Turing Test, though, just one person could perform many highly delicate experiments in the course of no more than an hour. I maintain that people give other people credit for being conscious simply because of their continual external monitoring of other people—which is itself something like a Turing Test.

Pat: That may be roughly true, but it involves more than just conversing with people through a teletype. We see that other people have bodies, we watch their faces and expressions—we see they are human beings, and so we think they think.

Sandy: To me, that seems a narrow, anthropocentric view of what thought is. Does that mean you would sooner say a mannequin in a store thinks than a wonderfully programmed computer, simply because the mannequin looks more human?

Pat: Obviously, I would need more than just vague physical resemblance to the human form to be willing to attribute the power of thought to an entity. But that organic quality, the sameness of origin, undeniably lends a degree of credibility that is very important.

Sandy: Here we disagree. I find this simply too chauvinistic. I feel that the key thing is a similarity of *internal* structure—not bodily, organic, chemical structure but *organizational* structure—software. Whether an entity can think seems to me a question of whether its organization can be described in a certain way, and I'm perfectly willing to believe that the Turing Test detects the presence or absence of that mode of organization. I would say that your depending on my physical body as evidence that I am a thinking being is rather shallow. The way I see it, the Turing Test looks far deeper than at mere external form.

Pat: Hey now—you're not giving me much credit. It's not just the *shape* of a body that lends weight to the idea that there's real thinking going on inside. It's also, as I said, the idea of common origin. It's the idea that you and I both sprang from DNA molecules, an idea to which I attribute much depth. Put it this way: the external form of human bodies reveals that they share a deep biological history, and it's *that* depth that lends a lot of credibility to the notion that the owner of such a body can think.

Sandy: But that is all indirect evidence. Surely you want some *direct* evidence. That's what the Turing Test is for. And I think it's the *only* way to test for thinkinghood.

Chris: But you could be fooled by the Turing Test, just as an interrogator could mistake a man for a woman.

Sandy: I admit, I could be fooled if I carried out the test in too quick or too shallow a way. But I would go for the deepest things I could think of.

Chris: *I* would want to see if the program could understand jokes—or better yet, make them! *That* would be a real test of intelligence.

Sandy: I agree that humor probably is an acid test for a supposedly intelligent program, but equally important to me—perhaps more so—would be to test its emotional responses. So I would ask it about its reactions to certain pieces of music or works of literature—especially my favorite ones.

Chris: What if it said, "I don't know that piece," or even, "I have no interest in music"? What if it tried its hardest (oops!—sorry, Pat!). . . . Let me try that again. What if it did everything it could, to steer clear of emotional topics and references?

Sandy: That would certainly make me suspicious. Any consistent pattern of avoiding certain issues would raise serious doubts in my mind as to whether I was dealing with a thinking being.

Chris: Why do you say that? Why not just conclude you're dealing with a thinking but unemotional being?

Sandy: You've hit upon a sensitive point. I've thought about this for quite a long time, and I've concluded that I simply can't believe emotions and thought can be divorced. To put it another way, I think emotions are an automatic by-product of the ability to think. They are entailed by the very nature of thought.

Chris: That's an interesting conclusion, but what if you're wrong? What if I produced a machine that could think but not emote? Then its intelligence might go unrecognized because it failed to pass *your* kind of test.

Sandy: I'd like you to point out to me where the boundary line between emotional questions and nonemotional ones lies. You might want to ask about the meaning of a great novel. This certainly requires an understanding of human emotions! Now is that thinking, or merely cool calculation? You might want to ask about a subtle choice of words. For that, you need an understanding of their connotations. Turing uses examples like this in his article. You might want to ask for advice about a complex romantic situation. The machine would need to know a lot about human motivations and their roots. If it failed at this kind of task, I would not be much inclined to say that it could think. As far as I'm concerned, *thinking*, *feeling*, and *consciousness* are just different facets of one phenomenon, and no one of them can be present without the others.

Chris: Why couldn't you build a machine that could feel nothing (we all know machines don't feel anything!), but that could think and make complex decisions anyway? I don't see any contradiction there.

Sandy: Well, I do. I think that when you say that, you are visualizing a metallic, rectangular machine, probably in an air-conditioned room—a hard, angular, cold object with a million colored wires inside it, a machine that sits stock still on a tiled floor, humming or buzzing or whatever, and spinning its tapes. Such a machine can play a good game of chess, which, I freely admit, involves a lot of decision making. And yet I would never call it conscious.

Chris: How come? To mechanists, isn't a chess-playing machine rudimentarily conscious?

Sandy: Not to *this* mechanist! The way I see it, consciousness has got to come from a precise pattern of organization, one we haven't yet figured out how to describe in any detailed way. But I believe we will gradually come to understand it. In my view, consciousness requires a certain way of mirroring the external universe internally, and the ability to respond to that external reality on the basis of the internally represented model. And then in addition, what's really crucial for a conscious machine is that it should incorporate a well-developed and flexible self-model. And it's there that all existing programs, including the best chess-playing ones, fall down.

Chris: Don't chess programs look ahead and say to themselves as they're figuring out their next move, "If my opponent moves here, then I'll go there, and then if they go this way, I could go below that way . . ."? Doesn't that usage of the concept "I" require a sort of self-model?

Sandy: Not really. Or, if you want, it's an extremely limited one. It's an understanding of self in only the narrowest sense. For instance, a chess-playing program has no concept of why it is playing chess, or of the fact that it is a program, or is in a computer, or has a human opponent. It has no idea about what winning and losing are, or—

Pat: How do *you* know it has no such sense? How can *you* presume to say what a chess program feels or knows?

Sandy: Oh come on! We all know that certain things don't feel anything or know anything. A thrown stone doesn't know anything about parabolas, and a whirling fan doesn't know anything about air. It's true I can't *prove* those statements—but here we are verging on questions of faith.

Pat: This reminds me of a Taoist story I read. It goes something like this. Two sages were standing on a bridge over a stream. One said to the other, "I wish I were a fish. They are so happy." The other replied, "How do *you* know whether fish are happy or not? *You're* not a fish!" The first said, "But you're not *me*, so how do you know whether I know how fish feel?"

Sandy: Beautiful! Talking about consciousness really does call for a certain amount of restraint. Otherwise, you might as well just jump on the solipsism bandwagon ("*I* am the only conscious being in the universe") or the panpsychism bandwagon ("*Everything* in the universe is conscious!").

Pat: Well, how do you know? Maybe everything is conscious.

Sandy: Oh Pat, if you're going to join the club that maintains that stones and even particles like electrons have some sort of consciousness, then I guess we part company here. That's a kind of mysticism I just can't fathom. As for chess programs, I happen to know how they work, and I can tell you for sure that they aren't conscious. No way!

Pat: Why not?

Sandy: They incorporate only the barest knowledge about the goals of chess. The notion of "playing" is turned into the mechanical act of comparing a lot of numbers and choosing the biggest one over and over again. A chess program has no sense of disappointment about losing, or pride in winning. Its self-model is very crude. It gets away with doing the least it can, just enough to play a game of chess and nothing more. Yet interestingly enough, we still tend to talk about the "desires" of a chess-playing computer. We say, "It wants to keep its king behind a row of pawns" or "It likes to get its rooks out early" or "It thinks I don't see that hidden fork."

Pat: Yes, and we do the same thing with insects. We spot a lonely ant somewhere and say, "It's trying to get back home" or "It wants to drag that dead bee back to the colony." In fact, with any

animal we use terms that indicate emotions, but we don't know for certain how much the animal feels. I have no trouble talking about dogs and cats being happy or sad, having desires and beliefs and so on, but of course I don't think their sadness is as deep or complex as human sadness is.

Sandy: But you wouldn't call it "simulated" sadness, would you?

Pat: No, of course not. I think it's real.

Sandy: It's hard to avoid use of such teleological or mentalistic terms. I believe they're quite justified, although they shouldn't be carried too far. They simply don't have the same richness of meaning when applied to present-day chess programs as when applied to people.

Chris: I still can't see that intelligence has to involve emotions. Why couldn't you imagine an intelligence that simply calculates and has no feelings?

Sandy: A couple of answers here. Number one, any intelligence has to have motivations. It's simply not the case, whatever many people may think, that machines could think any more "objectively" than people do. Machines, when they look at a scene, will have to focus and filter that scene down into some preconceived categories, just as a person does. And that means seeing some things and missing others. It means giving more weight to some things than to others. This happens on every level of processing.

Pat: I'm not sure I'm following you.

Sandy: Take me right now, for instance. You might think I'm just making some intellectual points, and I wouldn't need emotions to do that. But what makes me *care* about these points? Just now—why did I stress the word "care" so heavily? Because I'm emotionally involved in this conversation! People talk to each other out of conviction—not out of hollow, mechanical reflexes. Even the most intellectual conversation is driven by underlying passions. There's an emotional undercurrent to every conversation—it's the fact that the speakers want to be listened to, understood, and respected for what they are saying.

Pat: It sounds to me as if all you're saying is that people need to be interested in what they're saying. Otherwise, a conversation dies.

Sandy: Right! I wouldn't bother to talk to anyone if I weren't motivated by *interest*. And "interest" is just another name for a whole constellation of subconscious biases. When I talk, all my biases work together, and what you perceive on the surface level is my personality, my style. But that style arises from an immense number of tiny priorities, biases, leanings. When you add up a million of them interacting together, you get something that amounts to a lot of *desires*. It just all adds up! And that brings me to the other answer to Chris's question about feelingless calculation. Sure, that exists—in a cash register, a pocket calculator. I'd say it's even true of all today's computer programs. But eventually, when you put enough feelingless calculations together in a huge coordinated organization, you'll get something that has properties *on another level*. You can see it—in fact, you *have* to see it—not as a bunch of little calculations but as a system of tendencies and desires and beliefs and so on. When things get complicated enough, you're *forced* to change your level of description. To some extent that's already happening, which is why we use words such as "want," "think," "try," and "hope" to describe chess programs and other attempts at mechanical thought. Dennett calls that kind of level switch by the observer "adopting the intentional stance." The really interesting things in AI will only begin to happen, I'd guess, when the program *itself* adopts the intentional stance toward itself!

Chris: That would be a very strange sort of level-crossing feedback loop.

Sandy: It certainly would. When a program looks at itself *from the outside*, as it were, and tries to figure out why it acted the way it did, then I'll start to think that there's *someone* in there, doing the looking.

Pat: You mean an "I"? A self?

Sandy: Yes, something like that. A soul, even—although not in any religious sense. Of course, it's highly premature for anyone to adopt the intentional stance (in the full force of the term) with respect to today's programs. At least that's my opinion.

Chris: For me an important related question is: To what extent is it valid to adopt the intentional stance toward beings other than humans?

Pat: I would certainly adopt the intentional stance toward mammals.

Sandy: I vote for that.

Chris: Now that's interesting. How can that be, Sandy? Surely you wouldn't claim that a dog or cat can pass the Turing Test? Yet don't you maintain the Turing Test is the *only* way to test for the presence of consciousness? How can you have these beliefs simultaneously?

Sandy: Hmm. . . . All right. I guess that my argument is really just that the Turing Test works only above a certain level of consciousness. I'm perfectly willing to grant that there can be thinking beings that could *fail* at the Turing Test—but the main point that I've been arguing for is that anything that *passes* it would be a genuinely conscious, thinking being.

Pat: How can you think of a computer as a conscious being? I apologize if what I'm going to say sounds like a stereotype, but when I think of conscious beings, I just can't connect that thought with machines. To me, consciousness is connected with soft, warm bodies, silly though it may sound.

Chris: That does sound odd, coming from a biologist. Don't you deal with life so much in terms of chemistry and physics that all magic seems to vanish?

Pat: Not really. Sometimes the chemistry and physics simply increase the feeling that there's something magical going on down there! Anyway, I can't always integrate my scientific knowledge with my gut feelings.

Chris: I guess I share that trait.

Pat: So how do you deal with rigid preconceptions like mine?

Sandy: I'd try to dig down under the surface of your concept of "machine" and get at the intuitive connotations that lurk there, out of sight but deeply influencing your opinions. I think we all have a holdover image from the Industrial Revolution that sees machines as clunky iron contraptions gawkily moving under the power of some loudly chugging engine. Possibly that's even how the computer inventor Charles Babbage saw people! After all, he called his magnificent many-geared computer the "Analytical Engine."

Pat: Well, *I* certainly don't think people are just fancy steam shovels or electric can openers. There's something about people, something that—that—they've got a sort of *flame* inside them, something alive, something that flickers unpredictably, wavering, uncertain—but something *creative*!

Sandy: Great! That's just the sort of thing I wanted to hear. It's very human to think that way. Your flame image makes me think of candles, of fires, of vast thunderstorms with lightning dancing all over the sky in crazy, tumultuous patterns. But do you realize that just that kind of thing is visible on a computer's console? The flickering lights form amazing chaotic sparkling patterns. It's such a far cry from heaps of lifeless, clanking metal! It *is* flamelike, by God! Why don't you let the word "machine" conjure up images of dancing patterns of light rather than of giant steam shovels?

Chris: That's a beautiful image, Sandy. It does tend to change my sense of mechanism from being matter-oriented to being pattern-oriented. It makes me try to visualize the thoughts in my mind—these thoughts right now, even!—as a huge spray of tiny pulses flickering in my brain.

Sandy: That's quite a poetic self-portrait for a mere spray of flickers to have come up with!

Chris: Thank you. But still, I'm not totally convinced that a machine is all that I am. I admit, my concept of machines probably does suffer from anachronistic subconscious flavors, but I'm afraid I can't change such a deeply rooted sense in a flash.

Sandy: At least you sound open-minded. And to tell the truth, part of me sympathizes with the way you and Pat view machines. Part of me balks at calling myself a machine. It *is* a bizarre thought that a feeling being like you or me might emerge from mere circuitry. Do I surprise you?

Chris: You certainly surprise *me*. So, tell us—do you believe in the idea of an intelligent computer, or don't you?

Sandy: It all depends on what you mean. We've all heard the question "Can computers think?" There are several possible interpretations of this (aside from the many interpretations of the word "think"). They revolve around different meanings of the words "can" and "computer."

Pat: Back to word games again. . . .

Sandy: I'm sorry, but that's unavoidable. First of all, the question might mean, "Does some present-day computer think, right now?" To this I would immediately answer with a loud *no*. Then it could be taken to mean, "Could some present-day computer, if suitably programmed, potentially think?" That would be more like it, but I would still answer, "Probably not." The real difficulty hinges on the word "computer." The way I see it, "computer" calls up an image of just what I described earlier: an air-conditioned room with cold rectangular metal boxes in it. But I suspect that with increasing public familiarity with computers and continued progress in computer architecture, that vision will eventually become outmoded.

Pat: Don't you think computers as we know them will be around for a while?

Sandy: Sure, there will have to be computers in today's image around for a long time, but advanced computers—maybe no longer called "computers"—will evolve and become quite different. Probably, as with living organisms, there will be many branchings in the evolutionary tree. There will be computers for business, computers for schoolkids, computers for scientific calculations, computers for systems research, computers for simulation, computers

for rockets going into space, and so on. Finally, there will be computers for the study of intelligence, It's really only these last that I'm thinking of—the ones with the maximum flexibility, the ones that people are deliberately attempting to make smart. I see no reason that these will stay fixed in the traditional image. They probably will soon acquire as standard features some rudimentary sensory systems—mostly for vision and hearing, at first. They will need to be able to move around, to explore. They will have to be physically flexible. In short, they will have to become more animal-like, more self-reliant.

Chris: It makes me think of the robots R2D2 and C3PO in the movie *Star Wars*.

Sandy: Not me! In fact, I don't think of anything remotely like them when I visualize intelligent machines. They are too silly, too much the product of a film designer's imagination. Not that I have a clear vision of my own. But I think it's necessary, if people are realistically going to try to imagine an artificial intelligence, to go beyond the limited, hard-edged picture of computers that comes from exposure to what we have today. The only thing all machines will always have in common is their underlying mechanicalness. That may sound cold and inflexible, but then—just think—what could be more mechanical, in a wonderful way, than the workings of the DNA and proteins and organelles in our cells?

Pat: To me, what goes on inside cells has a "wet," "slippery" feel to it, and what goes on inside machines is dry and rigid. It's connected with the fact that computers don't make mistakes, that computers do only what you tell them to do. Or at least that's my image of computers.

Sandy: Funny—a minute ago, your image was of a flame, and now it's of something wet and slippery. Isn't it marvelous, how contradictory we can be?

Pat: I don't need your sarcasm.

Sandy: No, no, I'm not being sarcastic—I really *do* think it's marvelous.

Pat: It's just an example of the human mind's slippery nature—mine, in this case.

Sandy: True. But your image of computers is stuck in a rut. Computers certainly *can* make mistakes—and I don't mean on the hardware level. Think of any present-day computer predicting the weather. It can make wrong predictions, even though its program runs flawlessly.

Pat: But that's only because you've fed it the wrong data.

Sandy: Not so. It's because weather prediction is too complex. Any such program has to make do with a limited amount of data—entirely correct data—and extrapolate from there. Sometimes it will make wrong predictions. It's no different from a farmer gazing at the clouds and saying, "I reckon we'll get a little snow tonight." In our heads, we make models of things and use those models to guess how the world will behave. We have to make do with our models, however inaccurate they may be, or evolution will prune us out ruthlessly—we'll fall off a cliff or something. And for intelligent computers, it'll be the same. It's just that human designers will speed up the evolutionary process by aiming explicitly at the goal of creating intelligence, which is something nature just stumbled on.

Pat: So you think computers will be making fewer mistakes as they get smarter?

Sandy: Actually, just the other way around! The smarter they get, the more they'll be in a position to tackle messy real-life domains, so they'll be more and more likely to have inaccurate models. To me, mistake making is a sign of high intelligence!

Pat: Wow—you throw me sometimes!

Sandy: I guess I'm a strange sort of advocate for machine intelligence. To some degree I straddle the fence. I think that machines won't really be intelligent in a humanlike way until they have something like your biological wetness or slipperiness to them. I don't mean *literally* wet—the slipperiness could be in the software. But biological seeming or not, intelligent machines will in any case be machines. We will have designed them, built them—or grown them! We'll understand how they work—at least in some sense. Possibly no one person will really understand them, but collectively we will know how they work.

Pat: It sounds like you want to have your cake and eat it too. I mean, you want to have people able to build intelligent machines and yet at the same time have some of the mystery of mind remain.

Sandy: You're absolutely right—and I think that's what *will* happen. When *real* artificial intelligence comes—

Pat: Now there's a nice contradiction in terms!

Sandy: Touché! Well, anyway, when it comes, it will be mechanical and yet at the same time organic. It will have that same astonishing flexibility that we see in life's mechanisms. And when I say mechanisms, I *mean* mechanisms. DNA and enzymes and so on really *are* mechanical and rigid and reliable. Wouldn't you agree, Pat?

Pat: Sure! But when they work together, a lot of unexpected things happen. There are so many complexities and rich modes of behavior that all that mechanicalness adds up to something very fluid.

Sandy: For me, it's an almost unimaginable transition from the mechanical level of molecules to the living level of cells. But it's that exposure to biology that convinces me that people are machines. That thought makes me uncomfortable in some ways, but in other ways it is exhilarating.

Chris: I have one nagging question. . . . If people are machines, how come it's so hard to convince them of the fact? Surely a machine ought to be able to recognize its own machinehood!

Sandy: It's an interesting question. You have to allow for emotional factors here. To be told you're a machine is, in a way, to be told that you're nothing more than your physical parts, and it brings you face to face with your own vulnerability, destructibility, and, ultimately, your mortality. That's something nobody finds easy to face. But beyond this emotional objection, to see yourself as a machine, you have to "unadopt" the intentional stance you've grown up taking toward yourself—you have to jump all the way from the level where the complex lifelike activities take place to the bottommost mechanical level where ribosomes chug along RNA strands, for instance. But there are so many intermediate layers that they act as a shield, and the mechanical quality way down there becomes almost invisible. I think that when intelligent machines come around, that's how they will seem to us—and to themselves! Their mechanicalness will be buried so deep that they'll *seem* to be alive and conscious—just as *we* seem alive and conscious. . . .

Chris: You're baiting me! But I'm not going to bite.

Pat: I once heard a funny idea about what will happen when we eventually have intelligent machines. When we try to implant that intelligence into devices we'd like to control, their behavior won't be so predictable.

Sandy: They'll have a quirky little "flame" inside, maybe?

Pat: Maybe.

Chris: And what's so funny about that?

Pat: Well, think of military missiles. The more sophisticated their target-tracking computers get, according to this idea, the less predictably they will function. Eventually, you'll have missiles that will decide they are pacifists and will turn around and go home and land quietly without blowing up. We could even have "smart bullets" that turn around in midflight because they don't want to commit suicide!

Sandy: What a nice vision!

Chris: I'm very skeptical about all this. Still, Sandy, I'd like to hear your predictions about when intelligent machines will come to be.

Sandy: It won't be for a long time, probably, that we'll see anything remotely resembling the level of human intelligence. It rests on too awesomely complicated a substrate—the brain—for us to be able to duplicate it in the foreseeable future. Anyhow, that's my opinion.

Pat: Do you think a program will ever pass the Turing Test?

Sandy: That's a pretty hard question. I guess there are various degrees of passing such a test, when you come down to it. It's not black and white. First of all, it depends on who the interrogator is. A simpleton might be totally taken in by some programs today. But secondly, it depends on how deeply you are allowed to probe.

Pat: You could have a range of Turing Tests—one-minute versions, five-minute versions, hour-long versions, and so forth. Wouldn't it be interesting if some official organization sponsored a periodic competition, like the annual computer-chess championships, for programs to try to pass the Turing Test?

Chris: The program that lasted the longest against some panel of distinguished judges would be the winner. Perhaps there could be a big prize for the first program that fools a famous judge for, say, ten minutes.

Pat: A prize for the *program*, or for its *author*?

Chris: For the program, of course!

Pat: That's ridiculous! What would a program do with a prize?

Chris: Come now, Pat. If a program's human enough to fool the judges, don't you think it's human enough to enjoy the prize? That's precisely the threshold where it, rather than its creators, deserves the credit, and the rewards. Wouldn't you agree?

Pat: Yeah, yeah—especially if the prize is an evening out on the town, dancing with the interrogators!

Sandy: I'd certainly like to see something like that established. I think it could be hilarious to watch the first programs flop pathetically!

Pat: You're pretty skeptical for an AI advocate, aren't you? Well, do you think any computer program today could pass a five-minute Turing Test, given a sophisticated interrogator?

Sandy: I seriously doubt it. It's partly because no one is really working at it explicitly. I should mention, though, that there is one program whose inventors claim it has *already* passed a rudimentary version of the Turing Test. It is called "Parry," and in a series of remotely conducted interviews, it fooled several psychiatrists who were told they were talking to either a computer or a paranoid patient. This was an improvement over an earlier version, in which psychiatrists were simply handed transcripts of short interviews and asked to determine which ones were with a genuine paranoid and which ones were with a computer simulation.

Pat: You mean they didn't have the chance to ask any questions? That's a severe handicap—and it doesn't seem in the spirit of the Turing Test. Imagine someone trying to tell which sex *I* belong to, just by reading a transcript of a few remarks by me. It might be very hard! I'm glad the procedure has been improved.

Chris: How do you get a computer to act like a paranoid?

Sandy: Now just a moment—I didn't say it *does* act like a paranoid, only that some psychiatrists, under unusual circumstances, thought so. One of the things that bothered me about this pseudo-Turing Test is the way Parry works. "He," as the people who designed it call it, acts like a paranoid in that "he" gets abruptly defensive and veers away from undesirable topics in the conversation. In effect, Parry maintains strict control so that no one can truly probe "him." For reasons like this, simulating a paranoid is a whole lot easier than simulating a normal person.

Pat: I wouldn't doubt that. It reminds me of the joke about the easiest kind of human being for a computer program to simulate.

Chris: What is that?

Pat: A catatonic patient—they just sit and do nothing at all for days on end. Even *I* could write a computer program to do that!

Sandy: An interesting thing about Parry is that it creates no sentences on its own—it merely selects from a huge repertoire of canned sentences the one that in some sense responds best to the input sentence.

Pat: Amazing. But that would probably be impossible on a larger scale, wouldn't it?

Sandy: You better believe it (to use a canned remark)! Actually, this is something that's really not appreciated enough. The number of sentences you'd need to store in order to be able to respond in a normal way to all possible turns that a conversation could take is more than astronomical—it's really unimaginable. And they would have to be so intricately indexed, for retrieval. . . . Anybody who thinks that somehow a program could be rigged up just to pull sentences out of storage like records in a jukebox, and that this program could pass the Turing Test, hasn't thought very hard about it. The funny part is that it is just this kind of unrealizable "parrot program" that most critics of artificial intelligence cite, when they argue against the concept of the Turing Test. Instead of imagining a truly intelligent machine, they want you to envision a gigantic, lumbering robot that intones canned sentences in a dull monotone. They set up the imagery in a contradictory way. They manage to convince you that you could see through to its mechanical level with ease, even as it is simultaneously performing tasks that we think of as fluid, intelligent processes. Then the critics say, "You see! A machine could pass the Turing Test and yet it would still be just a mechanical device, not intelligent at all." I see things almost the opposite way. If *I* were shown a machine that can do things that I can do—I mean pass the Turing Test—then, instead of feeling insulted or threatened, I'd chime in with philosopher Raymond Smullyan and say, "How wonderful machines are!"

Chris: If you could ask a computer just one question in the Turing Test, what would it be?

Sandy: Uhmm . . .

Pat: How about this: "If you could ask a computer just one question in the Turing Test, what would it be?"

Post Scriptum

In 1983, I had the most delightful experience of getting to know a small group of extremely enthusiastic and original students at the University of Kansas in Lawrence. These students, about thirty in number, had been drawn together by Zamir Bavel, a professor in the Computer Science Department, who had organized a seminar on my book *Gödel, Escher, Bach*. He contacted me and asked me if there was any chance I could come to Lawrence and get together with his students. Something about his way of describing what was going on convinced me that this was a very unusual group and that it would be worth my while to try it out. I therefore made a visit to Kansas and got to know both Zamir and his group. All my expectations were met and surpassed. The students were full of ideas and warmth and made me feel very much at home.

The first trip was so successful that I decided to do it again a couple of months later. This time they threw an informal party at an apartment a few of them shared. Zamir had forewarned me that they were hoping to give me a demonstration of something that had already been done in a recent class meeting. It seems that the question of whether computers could ever think had arisen, and most of the group members had taken a negative stand on the issue. Rod Ogborn, the student who had been leading the discussion, had asked the class if they would consider any of the following programs intelligent:

1. A program that could pass a course in beginning programming (i.e., that could take informal descriptions of tasks and turn them into good working programs);

2. A program that could act like a psychotherapist (Rod gave sample dialogues with the famous "Doctor" program, also known as "ELIZA," by Joseph Weizenbaum);

3. A program called "Boris," written at Yale by Michael Dyer, that could read stories in a limited domain and answer questions about the situation which required filling in many unstated assumptions, and making inferences of many sorts based on them.

The class had come down on the "no" side of all three of these cases, although they got progressively harder. So Rod, to show the class how difficult this decision might be if they were really *faced* with a conversational program, managed to get a hookup over the phone lines with a natural-language program called "Nicolai" that had been developed over the last few years by the Army at nearby Fort Leavenworth. Thanks to some connections that Rod had, the class was able to gain access to an unclassified version of Nicolai and to interact with it for two or three hours. At the end of those hours, they then reconsidered the question of whether a computer might be able to think. Still, only one student was willing to consider Nicolai intelligent, and even that student reserved the right to switch sides if more information came in. About half the others were noncommittal, and the rest were unwilling, under any circumstances, to call Nicolai intelligent. There was no doubt that Rod's demonstration had been effective, though, and the class discussion had been one of the most lively.

Zamir told me all of this on our drive into Lawrence from the Kansas City airport, and he explained that the group had been so stimulated by this experience that they were hoping to get reconnected to Nicolai over the phone lines, and to let me try it out during the party. I thought it sounded quite amusing, and since I have tried out and watched a lot of natural-language programs in my time, I thought I would have an easy time coming up with good probes into the weaknesses of Nicolai. "Besides," I thought (somewhat chauvinistically), "how good can a program be that is being developed by the Army in an out-of-the-way place like Fort Leavenworth? To reveal its mechanicalness ought to be a piece of cake for me!" So I was looking forward to the challenge.

When we first arrived at the party, everyone was drinking beer and munching on various chips and dips and talking excitedly about what had happened in the previous class meeting with Nicolai. There was some consternation, though, because it seemed that the connection to Nicolai was hard to reestablish. It had to go through a computer at the University of Kansas, and thence to Fort Leavenworth, all of which meant that it was a slow and tenuous link. But after about 45 minutes of trying to set up the link, someone announced with pleasure that Nicolai was responding. One of the students was sitting at the terminal and typing in various simple questions and getting back simple answers. I watched over his shoulder, and felt the itch to sit down and try to unmask Nicolai for what "he" really was. After a

couple of minutes, the student relinquished the terminal and I got my chance, with a small group of people looking over my shoulder as I typed. Nicolai's answers were quite slow in coming over the phone lines, and the wait was made all the more suspenseful by the fact that they were transmitted only in full lines of text, so there were some pretty long delays between successive lines of response. But that didn't seriously dampen my enthusiasm for trying to quickly poke holes in the program's facade of understanding.

Herewith follows a somewhat abridged but accurate transcript of the "conversation" I had with Nicolai over the next hour or so. For convenience's sake, what Nicolai typed is shown in capitals, and my inner thoughts at the time (as best I can reconstruct them now) are in italics.

What would you like to talk about?
(Let's start out easy.)
I CAN TALK ABOUT ANYTHING.
(Yeah, yeah——tell it to the Marines!)
Is there anything you specialize in?
WHAT DOES "SPECIALIZE" MEAN? PLEASE USE A COMPLETE SENTENCE.
(For a supposedly smart program, Nicolai doesn't seem to have a very big vocabulary.)
"Specialize" means "to be good at."
(I wonder if Nicolai likes those quotation marks, or if they will throw it for a loop.)
I UNDERSTAND.
(Izzatso?)
When were you written?
LAST COMPILATION: "4/27/83 19.247"
(Oh, look at that stupid, rigid answer, complete with pointless marks and that extra, unexplained number at the end. I'm exposing Nicolai pretty well, so far. . . .)
What language is Nicolai written in?
(I think I'll see if it knows its own name and recognizes third-person references to itself.)

NICOLAI IS WRITTEN MOSTLY IN ADA.

(Hmmm . . . not bad. It handled both "you" and "Nicolai" when I talked about it. Those Army programmers aren't so bad!)

What are feet?

(Choose an ambiguous word; see what it comes up with. . . .)

FEET ARE 12.0 INCHES.

(Wow, weird! A person would never put it that way. They'd say, "A foot is a unit of length, twelve inches long," or something like that. And anyway, feet are primarily parts of the body, secondarily units of length. Why didn't it even seem to recognize that ambiguity? Oh well, I guess that kind of dumbness is the kind of thing I wanted to expose. Score one for me.)

What are ears?

(Why not try another ambiguous word? After all, I did well on the last one.)

EARS ARE AUDITORY ORGANS FOUND ON ANIMALS.

(This is really funny! Why were feet not thought of primarily as body parts, then? This body-parts stuff seems to give me lots of points—I think I'll try it again.)

What are arms?

THAT INFORMATION IS CLASSIFIED.

(Oh no! That is too stupid for words! Or is this somebody's idea of a joke?)

I like to understand up without seventeen clams.

(Let's toss some nonsense at Nicolai and see what it does.)

WHAT DO CLAMS HAVE TO DO WITH IT?

(Oh come on, Nicolai! Do you mean you understood all the rest, except for the clams bit? You are really dumb!)

Why are you so dumb?

I AM A SMART PROGRAM.

(Well, that's kind of touching, actually. A little self-defense is appealing, in a way.)

You are pretty confident of yourself, aren't you?

WHAT DOES "PRETTY CONFIDENT" MEAN?

(Oh yeah, I should have known—"pretty" as an adverb might be too colloquial.)

Did you understand up without my last sentence?

(I figure, since earlier it didn't complain about my phrase "understand up," let's see what it does with it this time.)

YOUR SENTENCE IS NONSENSE.

(Oh really? Well, then, why wasn't the other one with that same phrase in it also considered nonsense?)

Do you enjoy nonsense?

IF YOU INSIST ON TALKING NONSENSE, I HAVE OTHER TASKS TO PERFORM.

(A strange response. Who ever insisted on talking nonsense? I was just asking a simple question. Oh well, let me try out another angle.)

What is your opinion of M. C. Escher?

M. C. ESCHER, ARTIST, TWENTIETH CENTURY

(Oh, not again—another vacuous dictionary look-up. Can't it do better than that, especially when I've asked it a probing question about taste? Let's see how it handles a complaint. . . .)

You did not answer my question.

WHICH QUESTION DID I NOT ANSWER?

(Hey, this Nicolai is a pretty slick character. Not so different from Parry. I must say, I am really pretty impressed by the robustness of this program. I mean, we have covered a lot of ground so far, and at least it makes "pseudo-sensible answers" most of the time. Not at all bad!)

Do you own any money?

I DO NOT OWN ANYTHING.

(Fair enough.)

Have you seen the latest issue of "Scientific American"?

(Uh-oh—once again, I don't know if I'm going to help it or confuse it by putting in those quotes. Let's see.)

I DO NOT HAVE ANY "SCIENTIFIC AMERICAN."

(That sounds awkward. Very computerish. I doubt if it knows what I meant. Oh well.)

YOU'VE BEEN TALKING TO ME FOR QUITE A WHILE. WHAT IS YOUR NAME?

(Hmm. . . . That was an unexpected remark by Nicolai. Should I answer it? Sure, why not?)

My name is "Doug."

DO YOU HAVE A LAST NAME?

(Inquisitive little devil, isn't it?)

Of course I do.

(Ask a stupid question, get a stupid answer. Let's see how it fields this one.)

WOULD YOU CARE TO TELL ME WHAT YOUR LAST NAME IS?

(Damn, it just totally ignored the tone of my remark. And why is it being so polite, suddenly?)

Only if you'll tell me yours.

(That ought to challenge it.)

I DO NOT HAVE A LAST NAME.

(I don't seem to be able to foil its defenses very easily. It always walks around me. Those programmers sure anticipated a lot of ideas. I guess they must have debugged Nicolai for years, watching typical dialogues with people who just come in off the street. For a dumb program, Nicolai is pretty smart!)

Well then, I won't tell you mine.

THAT'S NOT BEING VERY FRIENDLY.

(You know, sometimes, I hate to admit it, this stupid program really does seem to understand something!)

I'm sorry. How would you like me to give you a last name?

IF YOU WOULD LIKE TO DO THAT, THAT WOULD BE FINE WITH ME.

(Now that is obviously a canned sentence, or at least the latter half must certainly be. Score one more point for me. And yet, I'm not doing nearly as well as I'd hoped I would be by now. What's wrong?)

Your last name is "Rimsky-Korsakov."

THANK YOU.

(Well, that's a strange kind of thing to thank somebody for. Just goes to show how the rigidity of programs makes them say the strangest things.)

Don't mention it.

(I'll play along with this game for a second.)

WHAT IS YOUR LAST NAME?

(My god, it remembered, after all this while, that as soon as it had told me its last name, I was going to tell it mine. Well, I'd better make good on that promise.)

My last name is "Hofstadter".

ARE YOU "(32) DOUGLAS R. HOFSTADTER"?

(Now why, in the midst of so much elegance, does it suddenly act so crude, putting my name in quotes and including that silly extraneous index number? I can't for the life of me figure out why this program is so mixed in quality.)

One and the same.

(Try out a strange idiomatic phrase.)

(83) "PARSING ERROR IN PREVIOUS INPUT"

(Aha—fooled it again. All of a sudden, a whole lot of mechanicalness is showing through.)

How many letters are there in your last name?

(I think I'll see whether it can figure out ambiguous words by context.)

14 PLUS A HYPHEN.

(Good. Now I'll let "letters" switch meaning. What will it do?)

How many letters are there in an ordinary envelope?

18.

(Oh no! It didn't recognize the shift! And it merely counted the number of letters in "an ordinary envelope"! But if that's the case, then how come in the earlier case it didn't count the letters in the phrase "your last name," but instead retrieved the referent? There's something so inconsistent and uneven about this program. It just goes to show how far we have to go before mechanical intelligence bears any resemblance to human fluidity.)

ARE YOU WORKING ON A NEW BOOK?

(I wonder what will happen if I simply sidestep that question. Anyway, I'd like to probe its ability to deal with humor.)

Tell me a joke.

I WANT A COOOKIE.

(What kind of a joke is that? Hey, it spelled "cookie" wrong! Hmm . . . is that its joke? Or what is going on here?)

By the way, I am sort of working on a new book. Care to hear about it?

(Can it handle weird phrases like "sort of"? And questions with no subject?)

NO, BUT IF YOU WOULD GIVE ME A COOKIE, I WOULD GLADLY PAY YOU TUESDAY.

(That sounds like a familiar line. Have I heard it somewhere before? Is that supposed to be the punch line of its "joke"?)

Tell me another one.

HOW MANY COMPUTER PROGAMMERS DOES IT TAKE TO SCREW IN A LIGHT BULB?

(Okay, I see. It's got a library of jokes and riddles, and it just fishes them out at random. I'll play along.)

4.

INCORRECT. THAT IS A HARDWARE PROBLEM.

(Okay, so it told its joke. But I bet it has no idea what any of the terms in it mean, such as "programmer." Hey, it left an 'r' out of *"programmer"! I guess whoever input the joke misspelled the word. So let's see what happens when I ask about it. . . .)*

What is a computer progammer?

WOULD YOU LIKE ME TO EXPLAIN THE JOKE?

(Hey, damn it, it turned the tables on me! Does it think I don't know what a "progammer" (or a programmer) is? I don't like this slipperiness. Every time I try to get it to act really dumb, it somehow slips out of it. Strange. . . . All right, let me probe some more about its understanding of the terms in that joke. How about a potentially off-color word?)

What does "to screw" mean?

IN WHAT CONTEXT?

(Aha, at least it knows it's an ambiguous term.)

In bed.

TO SCREW IN BED MEANS TO "HAVE SEX."

(Okay, fine, it has some definitions stored according to context. I guess this word must come up all the time in conversations. But can it go any further than that definition?)

What is having sex all about?

I CAN RECOMMEND AN EXCELLENT BOOK ON THAT SUBJECT.

(What a great stock answer! One point for the Army programmers!)

Tell me, tell me!

THE BOOK IS CALLED "GODEL, ESCHER, BACH."

(Huh? Say, wait a minute, this is too *weird. I'm not so sure this is really a program. There's too damn much cleverness in these weird responses. I can't imagine bizarre mechanical devices coming up with this much coherence, even if it is completely off the wall, at times.)*

I like to call it "GEB" myself.

THAT IS VERY NICE, DOUG. WHAT ELSE DO YOU CALL "GEB"?

(All right, the jig's up. What's going on here?)

At this point, everybody started laughing. They had all been trying hard to keep from doing so the whole time, but at this point, they couldn't contain themselves. It was time to reveal to me what had been going on. They took me downstairs and showed me that three of the students—Roy Leban, Howard Darsche, and Garrick Stangle—had been collectively playing Nicolai. There was in reality no such program, and there hadn't ever been one. (In retrospect, I am reminded of the famous French mathematician Nicolas Bourbaki—a hypothetical person, actually an amalgam of over a dozen eminent mathematicians writing under that collective pen name.) There had indeed been a similar demonstration for the class a few days earlier, and the class, like me, had been taken in for a long time. In my case,

Roy, Howard, and Garrick had worked very hard to give the impression of mechanicalness by spewing back "parsing error" and other indications of rigidity, and also by sending what looked very much like canned phrases from time to time. That way they could keep sophisticates like me believing that there was a program behind it all. Only by that point I was beginning to wonder just how sophisticated I really was.

The marvelous thing about this game is that it was, in many ways, a Turing Test in reverse: a group of human beings masquerading as a program, trying to act mechanical enough that I would believe it really was one. Hugh Kenner has written a book called *The Counterfeiters* about the perennial human fascination with such compounded role flips. A typical example is Delibes's ballet *Coppelia*, in which human dancers imitate life-sized dolls stiffly imitating people. What is amusing is how Nicolai's occasional crudeness was just enough to keep me convinced it was mechanical. Its "willingness" to talk about itself, combined with its obvious limitations along those lines (its clumsy revelation of when it was last compiled, for instance), helped establish the illusion very strongly.

In retrospect, I am quite amazed at how much genuine intelligence I was willing to accept as somehow having been implanted in the program. I had been sucked into the notion that there really must be a serious natural-language effort going on at Fort Leavenworth, and that there had been a very large data base developed, including all sorts of random information: a dictionary, a catalog containing names of miscellaneous people, some jokes, lots of canned phrases to use in difficult situations, some self-knowledge, a crude ability to use key words in a phrase when it can't parse it exactly, some heuristics for deciding when nonsense is being foisted on it, some deductive capabilities, and on and on. In hindsight, it is clear that I was willing to accept a huge amount of fluidity as achievable in this day and age simply by putting together a large bag of isolated tricks—kludges and hacks, as they say.

Roy Leban, one of the three inside Nicolai's mind, wrote the following about the experience of being at the other end of the exchange:

Nicolai was a split personality. The three of us (as well as many kibitzers) argued about practically every response. Each of us had a strong preconceived notion about what (or who) Nicolai should be. For example, I felt that certain things (such as "Douglas R. Hofstadter") should be in quotation marks, and that feet should not be 12 inches, but 12.0. Howard had a tendency for rather flip answers. It was he who suggested the "classified" response to the "arms" question. And somehow, when he suggested it, we all *knew* it was right.

Several times during our conversation, I felt quite amazed at how fluently Nicolai was able to deal with things I was bringing up, but each time I could postulate some not *too* sophisticated mechanical underpinning that would allow that particular thing to happen. As a strong skeptic of true fluidity in machines at this time, I kept on trying to come up with rationalizations for the fact that this program was doing so well. My conclusion was that it was a very vast and quite sophisticated bag of tricks, no one of which was terribly complex. But after a while, it just became too much to believe. Furthermore, the mixture of crudity and subtlety became harder and harder to swallow, as well.

My strategy had been, in essence, to use spot checks all over the map: to try to probe it in all sorts of ways rather than to get sucked into some topic of its own choice, where it could steer the conversation. Daniel Dennett, in a paper on the depth of the Turing Test, likens this technique to a strategy taught to American soldiers in World War II for telling German spies from genuine Yankees. The idea was that even if a young man spoke absolutely fluent American-sounding English, you could trip him up by asking him things that any boy growing up in those days would be expected to know, such as "What is the name of Mickey Mouse's girlfriend?" or "Who won the World Series in 1937?" This expands the domain of knowledge necessary from just the language itself to the entire culture—and the amazing thing is that just a few well-placed questions can unmask a fraud in a very brief time—or so it would seem.

The problem is, what do you do if the person is extremely sharp, and when asked about Minnie Mouse, responds in some creative way, such as, "Hah! She ain't no *girl*friend—she's a *mouse*!"? The point is that even with these trick probes that *should* ferret out frauds very swiftly, there can be clever defensive counter-maneuvers, and you can't be sure of getting to the bottom of things in a very brief time.

It seems that a few days earlier, the class had collectively gone through something similar to what I had just gone through, with one major difference. Howard Darsche, who had impersonated (if I may use that peculiar choice of words!) Nicolai, in the first run-through, simply had acted himself, without trying to feign mechanicalness in any way. When asked what color the sky was, he replied, "In daylight or at night?" and when told "At night," he replied, "Dark purple with stars." He got increasingly poetic and creative in his responses to the class, but no one grew suspicious that this Nicolai was a fraud. At some point, Rod Ogborn simply had to stop the demonstration and type on the screen, "Okay, Howard, you can come in now." Zamir (who was not in cahoots with Rod and his team) was the only one who had some reluctance in accepting this performance as that of a genuine program, and he had kept silent until the end, when he voiced a muted skepticism.

Zamir summarizes this dramatic demonstration by saying that his class was willing to view *anything on a video terminal* as mechanically produced, no matter how sophisticated, insightful, or poetic an utterance it might be. They might find it interesting and even surprising, but they would find some way to discount those qualities. Why was this the case? How could they do this for so long? And why did I fall for the same kind of thing?

In interacting with me, Nicolai had seemed to waver between crude mechanicalness and subtle flexibility, an oscillation I had found most puzzling and somewhat disturbing. But I was still taken in for a very long time. It seems that, even armed with spot checks and quite a bit of linguistic sophistication and skepticism, unsuspecting humans can have the wool pulled over their eyes for a good while. This was the humble pie I ate in this remarkable reverse Turing Test, and I will always savor its taste and remember Nicolai with great fondness.

Alan Turing, in his article, indicated that his "Imitation Game" test should take place through some sort of remote teletype linkup, but one thing he did not indicate explicitly was at what grain size the messages would be transmitted. By that, I mean that he did not say whether the messages should be transmitted as intact wholes, or line by line, word by word, or keystroke by keystroke. Although I don't think it matters for the Turing Test in any *fundamental* sense, I do think that which type of "window" you view another language-using being through has a definite bearing on how *quickly* you can make inferences about that being. Clearly, the most revealing of these possibilities is that of watching the other "person" operate at the keystroke level.

On most multiuser computer systems, there are various ways for different users to communicate with each other, and these ways reflect different levels of urgency. The slowest one is generally the "mail" facility, through which you can send another user an arbitrarily long piece of text, just like a letter in an envelope. When it arrives, it will be placed in the user's "mailbox," to be read at their leisure. A faster style of communicating is called, on UNIX systems, "write." When this is invoked, a direct communications link is set up between you and the person you are trying to reach (provided they are logged on). If they accept your link, then any full line typed by either of you will be instantly transmitted and printed on the other party's screen—where a lineful is signaled by your hitting the carriage-return key. This is essentially what the Nicolai team used in communicating with me over the Kansas computer. Their irregular typing rhythm and any errors they might have made were completely concealed from me this way, since all I saw was a sequence of completely polished lines (with the two spelling errors—"coookie" and "progammer," which I was willing to excuse because Nicolai generated them in a "joke" context).

The most revealing mode is what, on UNIX, is called "talk." In this mode, every single keystroke is revealed. You make an error, you are exposed. For some people, this is too much like living in a glass house, and they prefer the shielding afforded by "write." For my part, I like living dangerously. Let the mistakes Ify! In computer-mediated conversations with my friends, I always opt for "talk." I have been amused to watch their "talk" styles and my own slowly evolve to relatively stable states.

When we in the Indiana University Computer Science Department first began using the "talk" facility, we were all somewhat paranoid about making errors, and we would compulsively fix any error that we made. By this I mean that we would backspace and retype the character. The effect on the screen of hitting the backspace key repeatedly is that you see the most recently typed characters getting eaten up, one by one, right to left, and if necessary, the previous line and ones above it will get eaten backwards as well. Once you have erased the offending mistakes, you simply resume typing forwards. This is how errors are corrected. We all began in this finicky way, feeling ashamed to let anything flawed remain "in print," so to speak, visible to others' eyes. But gradually we overcame that sense of shame, realizing that a typo sitting on a screen is not quite so deathless as one sitting on a page in a book.

Still, I found that some people just let things go more easily than others. For instance, by the length of the delay after a typo is made, you can tell just how much its creator is hesitating in wondering whether to correct it. Hesitations of a fraction of a second are very noticeable, and are part of a person's style. Even if a typo is left uncorrected, you can easily spot someone's vacillations about whether or not to fix it.

The counterparts of these things exist on many levels of such exchanges. There are the levels of *word choic*e (for instance, some people who don't mind having their typos on display will often backtrack and get rid of *words* they now repudiate), *sentence-structure* choice, *idea* choice, and higher. Hesitations and repairs or restarts are very common. I find nothing so annoying as someone who has gotten an idea expressed just fine in one way, and who then erases it all on the screen before your eyes and proceeds to compose it anew, as if one way of suggesting getting together for dinner at Pagliai's at six were markedly superior to another!

There are ways of exploiting erasure in "talk" mode for the purposes of humor. Don Byrd and I, when "talking," would often make elaborate jokes exploiting the medium in various ways. One of his, I recall vividly, was when he hurled a nasty insult onto the screen and then swiftly erased it, replacing it by a sweetly worded compliment, which remained for posterity to see—at least for another minute or so. One of our great discoveries was that some "arrow" keys allowed us to move all over the screen, and thus to go many lines up in the conversation and edit earlier remarks by either of us. This allowed some fine jokes to be made.

One hallmark of one's "talk" style is one's willingness to use abbreviations. This is correlated with one's willingness to abide typos, but is not by any means the same. I personally was the loosest of all the "talkers" I knew, both in terms of leaving typos on the screen and in terms of peppering my sentences with all sorts of silly abbreviations. For instance, I will now retype this very sentence as I would have in "talk mode," below.

F ins, I will now retype ts very sent as I wod hv in "talko mode," below.

Not bad! Only two typos. The point is, the communication rate is raised considerably—nearly to that of a telephone—if you type well and are willing to be informal in all these ways, but many people are surprisingly uptight about their unpolished written prose being on exhibit for others to see, even if it is going to vanish in mere seconds.

All of this I bring up not out of mere windbaggery, but because it bears strongly on the Turing Test. Imagine the microscopic insights into personality that are afforded by watching someone—human or otherwise—typing away in "talk" mode! You can watch them dynamically making and unmaking various word choices, you can see interferences between one word and another causing typos, you can watch hesitations about whether or not to correct a typo, you can see when they are pausing to work out a thought before typing it, and on and on. If you are just a people watcher, you can merely observe informally. If you are a psychologist or fanatic, you can measure reaction times in thousandths of a second, and make large

collections and catalogue them. Such collections have really been made, by the way, and make for some of the most fascinating reading on the human mind that I know of. See, for instance, Donald Norman's article "Categorization of Action Slips" or Victoria Fromkin's book *Errors of Linguistic Performance: Slips of the Tongue, Ear, Pen, and Hand*.

In any case, when you can watch someone's real-time behavior, a real live personality begins to appear on a screen very quickly. It is far different in feel from reading polished, postedited linefuls such as I received from Nicolai. It seems to me that Alan Turing would have been most intrigued and pleased by this time-sensitive way of using his test, affording so many lovely windows onto the subconscious mind (or pseudomind) of the being (or pseudobeing) under examination.

As if it were not already clear enough, let me conclude by saying that I am an unabashed pusher of the validity of the Turing Test as a way of operationally defining what it would be for a machine to genuinely think. There are, of course, middle grounds between real thinking and being totally empty inside. Smaller mammals and, in general, smaller animals seem to have "less thought" going on inside their craniums than we have inside ours. Yet clearly animals have always done, and machines are now doing, things that seem to be best described using Dennett's "intentional stance." Donald Griffin, a conscious mammal, has written thoughtfully on these topics (see, for instance, his book *The Question of Animal Awareness*). John McCarthy has pointed out that even electric-blanket manufacturers use such phrases as "it thinks it is too hot" to explain how their products work. We live in an era when mental terms are being both validly extended and invalidly abused, and we are going to need to think hard about these matters, especially in face of the onslaught of advertising hype and journalese. Various modifications of the Turing Test idea will undoubtedly be suggested as computer mastery of human language increases, simply to serve as benchmarks for what programs can and cannot do. This is a fine idea, but it does not diminish the worth of the original Turing Test, whose primary purpose was to convert a philosophical question into an operational question, an aim that I believe it filled admirably.

CHAPTER 3

Mathematical Roots

In the world of formal mathematics, it is just as bad to be almost right as it is to be absolutely wrong. In a sense, that's just what mathematics *is*. But that's not good psychology.
Marvin Minsky, *The Society of Mind*

A mathematician is a machine for turning coffee into theorems.
Paul Erdös

The AI field was founded by mathematicians: John McCarthy, Alan Turing (1912–1954), Norbert Wiener (1894–1964), students of Alonzo Church, Claude Shannon, Marvin Minsky, and others. LISP, the primary language for academic research in artificial intelligence, was adapted from a mathematical notation designed by Stephen Kleene and Barkley Rosser, both students of Church.[1]

Mathematics has often been viewed as the ultimate formalization of our thinking process, at least of the rational side of it. As I noted in the last chapter (and as was noted in several of the contributed articles at the end of the last chapter), the relationship of logic and the analytic process underlying mathematics to cognition has been debated through the ages by philosophers, many of whom were also mathematicians. The actual deployment of mathematical techniques to emulate at least certain aspects of human thought was not feasible until the electronic computer became available after World War II. However, the foundations of computation theory, along with the set theory on which computation theory is based, were established long before the potential of the electron to revolutionize applied mathematics was realized.[2]

Mathematics has often been described as a branch of philosophy, the branch most concerned with logic.[3] It has only been in this century that the fields of mathematics and philosophy have split into largely distinct disciplines with few major figures doing important work in both areas. Bertrand Russell, having been a pivotal figure in the establishment of both modern set theory and logical positivism, was perhaps the last.

In the early part of this century Bertrand Russell, a young and as yet relatively unknown mathematician and philosopher, became increasingly occupied with a certain type of paradox and attempts to understand its implications. The resolution of the paradox had important implications for the subsequent development of the theory of computation. The following story illustrates Russell's class of paradoxes:[4]

A judge is sentencing a man for a crime that he finds reprehensible and for which he wishes to mete out the most severe sentence he can think of. So he tells the convicted man not only that he is sentenced to die but also that because his crime was so offensive, the sentence is to be carried out in a unique way. "The sentence is to be carried out quickly," the judge says. "It must be carried out no later than next Saturday. Furthermore, I want the sentence to be carried out in such a way that on the morning of your execution, you will not know for certain that you are going to be executed on that day. When we come for you, it will be a surprise."

When the judge finished describing his unusual sentence, the condemned man seemed surprisingly pleased and replied, "Well, that's great, judge, I am greatly relieved."

To this the judge said, "I don't understand, how can you be relieved? I have condemned you to be executed, I have asked that the sentence be carried out soon, but you will be unable to prepare yourself because on the morning that your sentence is to be carried out, you will not know for certain that you will die that day."

The convicted man said, "Well, your honor, in order for your sentence to be carried out, I could not be executed on Saturday."

Bertrand Russell, philosopher and mathematician, observing his ninetieth birthday. Modern computation theory traces its roots to his theory of sets. (Supplied by AP/Wide World Photos)

"Why is that?" asked the judge.

"Because since the sentence must be carried out by Saturday, if we actually get to Saturday, I will know for certain that I am to be executed on that day, and thus it would not be a surprise."

"I suppose you are right," replied the judge. "You cannot be executed on Saturday. I still do not see why you are relieved."

"Well," said the prisoner, "if we have definitely ruled out Saturday, then I cannot be executed on Friday either."

"Why is that?" asked the judge.

"We have agreed that I definitely cannot be executed on Saturday. Therefore, Friday is the last day I can be executed. Thus, if Friday rolls around, I will definitely know that I am to be executed on that day, and therefore it would not be a surprise. So I cannot be executed on Friday."

"I see," said the judge.

"Thus, the last day I can be executed would be Thursday. But if Thursday rolls around, I would know I had to be executed on that day, and thus it would not be a surprise. So Thursday is out. By the same reasoning we can eliminate Wednesday, Tuesday, Monday, and today."

The judge scratched his head as the confident prisoner was led back to his prison cell.

There is an epilogue to the story. On Thursday the prisoner was taken to be executed. And he was very surprised. So the judge's orders were successfully carried out.

If we analyze the paradox contained in the above story, we see that the conditions that the judge has set up result in a conclusion that none of the days meets, because, as the prisoner so adroitly points out, each one of them in turn would not be a surprise. But the *conclusion itself* changes the situation, and now surprise *is* possible again. This brings us back to the original situation in which the prisoner could (in theory) demonstrate that each day in turn would be impossible, and so on. The judge applies Alexander's solution to this Gordian knot.

A simpler example and the one that Russell actually struggled with is the following question about sets: Consider set *A,* which is defined to contain all sets that are not members of themselves. Does set *A* contain itself? As we consider this famous problem, our first realization is that there are only two possible answers: yes and no. We can therefore exhaustively consider all of the possible answers (this is not the case for many problems in mathematics). Let us try "yes." If the answer is yes, then set *A* does contain itself. But if set *A* contains itself, then according to its defining condition set *A* would not belong to set *A,* and thus it does not belong to itself. Since the assumption that A contains itself led to a contradiction, it must have been wrong. If the answer is "no," then set *A* does not contain itself. But again according to the defining condition, if set *A* does not belong to itself, then it would belong to set *A.* As with the story about the prisoner, we have contradictory propositions that imply one another. The assumption of no yields yes, which yields no, and so on.

This type of paradox may seem amusing, but to Russell it threatened the very foundations of mathematics.[5] The definition of set *A* appears to be a perfectly

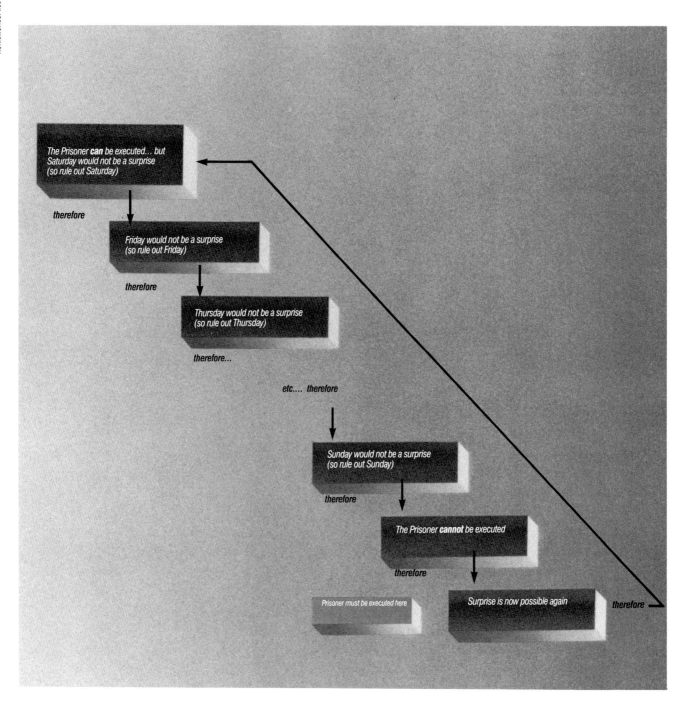

The Judge's dilemma (or is it the prisoner's?).

reasonable one, and the question of whether set *A* belongs to itself also appears perfectly reasonable. Yet it cannot be answered. Without a resolution to this paradox the basic theory of mathematics was in question.

To solve the problem, Russell invented a concept of a logical transformation as an operation that requires the equivalent of a quantum of time. Russell designed a set of logical operations in which a particular problem would be expressed as a "program" of operations to follow.[6] We then turn the program on and let it run. Each logical inference or other transformation is implemented in turn, and when the process is completed, we get our answer. If we apply this theoretical machine to the problem of set *A*, the logical operations are "executed" in turn. At a certain point the answer will be yes, but the program keeps running, and at a later point the answer becomes no. The program runs in an infinite loop, constantly alternating between yes and no.

Russell then provides narrow and broad definitions of a set. In the narrow sense, a set has a definition that allows the construction of a program that can determine whether a given entity is a member of the set in a finite amount of time. According to this definition, set *A* (whose program produces an infinite loop) is not a true set, so the paradox is eliminated.[7]

In the broad sense, the program defining the logical rules of set membership need not come to a halt in a finite amount of time, it just needs to come to *an* answer in a finite amount of time; it is allowed to change that answer as the program continues to run. According to this definition, set *A* is a proper set. The question of whether set *A* belongs to itself will be yes at one point in "time" and no at another point, and the program will alternate between the two. Thus, logical inferences are not implemented *instantly*, but rather one at a time with an orderly change of state between each. In our case, the answer is never yes and no *at the same time*. In the broad definition, set *A* is a particular type of set that is "unstable," just as an electronic circuit can be unstable. Nonetheless, the contradiction is eliminated.

Russell does not explicitly refer to time in his theory of types (of sets). He provides procedures for allowable transformations on propositions that can be considered *meaningful* within a logical system. This contrasts with the transformations generated by the logical system itself, which are used to determine the truth or falsity of propositions. Thus, according to Russell, certain propositions are neither true nor false and cannot be addressed by the axioms. In our discussion above, a proposition concerning an "unstable set" would not be meaningful. The theory is interesting in that we have one set of transformations generated by the axioms of a logical system determining truth or falsity and another set of transformations generated by the metarules of Russell's theory of types determining meaningfulness. Russell's transformations are algorithmic in nature, and the issues raised are similar to certain issues in computation theory that received attention after Turing devised his Turing machine. Though Russell did not explicitly link the theory of types to

An unstable proposition: Russell's paradox.

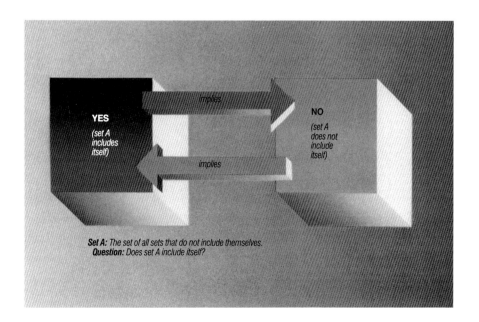

Set A: *The set of all sets that do not include themselves.*
Question: *Does set A include itself?*

computation theory (otherwise, we might be referring to a Russell Machine rather than a Turing Machine as a primary model of computation), Russell's theory of types clearly provided a foundation for Turing's later work.

The lecture on logic delivered by the prisoner changed the situation. He has shown quite logically why it is not possible for him to be executed following the judge's instructions. The judge then realizes that the prisoner's belief that he cannot be executed makes it possible once again to execute him. Before the prisoner can formulate another lecture on logic (that is, before the "program" simulating this situation can alternate again to "impossible to execute"), the judge quickly implements his sentence.

Principia Mathematica

Russell expanded his theory to lay a new foundation for logic and the theory of sets in his first major work in mathematics, *The Principles of Mathematics*, published in 1903. He subsequently felt that all of mathematics should be recast in terms of his new theory of sets, since the concept of sets and their interactions is fundamental to all other mathematical disciplines. With the help of his friend and former tutor Alfred North Whitehead (1861–1947), he labored for nearly ten years to apply his new theory of sets and logic to all realms of mathematics. Russell reported that the effort nearly exhausted him, and even late in his life he felt that this had been the most intense work of his extremely prolific career.[8] It was probably his most influential. As it was, Whitehead and Russell did not manage to complete their reexamination. They nonetheless published their work in three volumes in 1910, 1912, and 1913 under the title *Principia Mathematica*. The work was truly revolutionary and provided a new methodology for all mathematics that was to follow.

As significant as *Principia* was to mathematics in general, it was a pivotal development in terms of the foundations of the theory of computation that would be developed two decades later. Russell had created a theoretical model of a logic machine, which we now recognize as similar to a computer, particularly in its execution of logical operations in cycles.[9] Indeed, Turing's subsequent theoretical model of a computer, the Turing Machine, has its roots directly in Russell's theoretical logic engine.[10] Russell also created a concept of a logical programming language that is remarkably similar in many respects to one of the most recent programming languages, PROLOG, developed originally in France and now the basis for the Japanese Fifth Generation Computer project.[11] *Principia* was also influential on efforts by Allen Newell, Herbert Simon, and J. C. Shaw to develop theorem-proving machines in the 1950s.[12]

Modern set theory, still based on Russell's *Principia,* provides a foundation for much of mathematics. It is interesting to note that modern set theory is in turn based on Russell's theoretical model of computation. Viewing things in this way, we could argue that mathematics is a branch of computation theory. What is particularly impressive about Russell's achievement is that there were no computers even contemplated at the time he developed his theory. Russell needed to invent a theoretical model of a computer and programming to address a flaw in the foundation of logic itself.

We must know, we shall know.
David Hilbert

Turing was perhaps the pivotal figure in the development of the computer and its underlying theory. Building on the work of Bertrand Russell and Charles Babbage, he created his own theoretical model of a computer and in the process established modern computation theory.[13] He was also instrumental in the development of the first electronic computers, thus translating theory into reality. He developed specialized electronic computation engines to decode the German Enigma code, enabling the British to withstand the Nazi air force. He was also a major champion of the possibility of emulating human thought through computation.[14] He wrote (with his friend David Champernowne) the first chess-playing program and devised the only widely accepted test of machine intelligence (discussed from a variety of perspectives in several of the contributed articles at the end of chapter 2).[15]

As a person, Turing was unconventional and extremely sensitive. He had a wide range of unusual interests ranging from the violin to morphogenesis (the differentiation of cells).[16] There were public reports of his homosexuality, which greatly disturbed him, and he died at the age of 41, a suspected suicide.

Alan Turing, designer of the world's first operational computer and an early theorist of machine intelligence. Cracking Hitler's code was just one of his accomplishments. (Courtesy of the Computer Museum, Boston)

The Enigma code

By 1940 Hitler had the mainland of Europe in his grasp, and England was preparing for an anticipated invasion. The British government organized its best mathematicians and electrical engineers, including Alan Turing, with the mission of cracking the German military code. It was recognized that with the German air force enjoying superiority in the skies, failure to accomplish this mission was likely to doom the nation. In order not to be distracted from their task, the group lived in the tranquil pastures of Hertfordshire.

The group was fortunate in having a working model of the German code machine Enigma, captured by the Polish Secret Service. Working with several hints gathered by British Intelligence, they were able to narrow the coding possibilities, but only slightly. Under Turing's leadership, their strategy was to build an electromagnetic computer, use telephone relays to do an exhaustive search of all possible codes that the Enigma machine could produce, and apply these codes to intercepted messages. The strategy was a challenging one because an (electromagnetic) computer had never been built before. They named the machine Robinson, after a popular cartoonist who drew "Rube Goldberg" machines.[17] The group's own Rube Goldberg succeeded brilliantly and provided the British with a transcription of nearly all significant Nazi messages.

The German military subsequently made a modification to Enigma, adding two additional coding wheels, which greatly expanded the number of possible codes. To meet this new challenge, Turing and his fellow cryptoanalysts set to building a substantially faster machine called Colossus, built with two thousand electronic vacuum tubes.[18] Colossus and nine similar machines running in parallel did their job again and provided uninterrupted decoding of vital military intelligence to the Allied war effort.

Colossus was regarded by the Turing team as the world's first electronic digital computer, although unlike Harvard's relay-based Mark I, it was not programmable. Of course, it did not need to be: it had only one job to do.

Remarkably, the Germans relied on Enigma throughout the war. Refinements were added, but the world's first computers built by Alan Turing and his associates were able to keep up with the increasing complexity. Use of this vital information required supreme acts of discipline on the part of the British government. Cities that were to be bombed by Nazi aircraft were not forewarned, lest preparations arouse German suspicions that their code had been cracked. The information provided by the Robinson and Colossus machines was used only with the greatest discretion, but the cracking of Enigma was enough to enable the Royal Air Force to win the Battle of Britain.

Hilbert's twenty-third problem and the Turing machine

While many in England and elsewhere remain grateful to Turing for his contributions to the war effort, his greatest legacy is considered to be the establishment of the modern theory of computation. Yet his original goal was not the development of such a theory but rather to address one of the problems set down by his predecessor David Hilbert (1862–1943).

Enigma, the first target of machine
intelligence. (Courtesy of
the Computer Museum, Boston)

The works of Hilbert, a German mathematician born in 1862, are still widely regarded as highly influential on the research goals of today's mathematicians. He is credited with consolidating the accomplishments of nineteenth-century mathematics with such works as *The Foundations of Geometry,* published in 1899.[19] Perhaps of even greater significance, he set the agenda for twentieth-century mathematics as well with a list of the twenty-three most pressing unsolved problems that he presented at the 1900 International Mathematical Conference in Paris. In his address he predicted that these problems would occupy the attention of the next century of mathematicians. Hilbert appears to have been correct. The problems have been solved slowly and each solution has been regarded as a major event. Several that remain unsolved today are regarded by many mathematicians as the most important unsolved problems in mathematics.

Hilbert's twenty-third problem is whether or not an algorithm exists that can determine the truth or falsity of any logical proposition in a system of logic that is powerful enough to represent the natural numbers (numbers like 0, 1, 2, . . .). The statement of this problem was perhaps the first time that the concept of an algorithm was formally introduced into mathematics.

The question remained unanswered until 1937. In that year Alan Turing presented a paper entitled "On Computable Numbers, with an Application to the Entscheidungsproblem" (the *Entscheidungsproblem* is the decision or halting problem).[20] The paper presented his concept of a Turing Machine, a theoretical model of a computer, which continues to form the basis of modern computational theory.

A Turing machine consists of two primary (theoretical) units: a "tape drive" and a "computation unit." The tape drive has a tape of infinite length on which there can be written (and subsequently read) any series of two symbols: 0 (zero) and 1 (one). The computation unit contains a program that consists of a sequence of commands made up from the list of operations below. Each "command" consists of two specified operations, one to be followed if the last symbol read by the machine was a 0 and one if it had just read a 1. Below are the Turing machine operations:

- Read tape
- Move tape left
- Move tape right
- Write 0 on the tape
- Write 1 on the tape
- Jump to another command
- Halt

The Turing machine has persisted as our primary theoretical model of computation because of its combination of simplicity and power.[21] Its simplicity derives from its very short list of capabilities, listed above. As for its power, Turing was able to show that this extremely simple machine can compute anything that any machine can compute, no matter how complex. If a problem cannot be solved by a Turing machine, then it cannot be solved by any machine (and according to the Church-Turing thesis, not by a human being either).[22]

An unexpected discovery that Turing reports in his paper is the concept of unsolvable problems, that is, problems that are well defined with unique answers that can be shown to exist, but that we can also show can never be computed by a Turing machine. The fact that there are problems that cannot be solved by this particular theoretical machine may not seem particularly startling until one considers the other conclusion of Turing's paper, namely, that the Turing machine can model *any* machine. A machine is regarded as any process that follows fixed laws. According to Turing, if we regard the human brain as subject to natural law, then Turing's unsolvable problems cannot be solved by either machine or human thought, which leaves us with the perplexing situation of being able to define a problem, to prove that a unique answer exists, and yet know that the answer can never be known.[23]

The busy beaver

One of the most interesting of the unsolvable problems, the busy beaver problem, was discovered by Tibor Rado.[24] It may be stated as follows. Each Turing machine has a certain number of states that its internal program can be in. This corresponds to the number of steps in its internal program. There are a number of different 4-state Turing machines that are possible, a certain number of 5-state machines possible, and so on. Given a positive integer n, we construct all the Turing machines that have n states. The number of such machines will always be finite. Next, we eliminate those n-state Turing machines that get into an infinite loop (that is, never halt). Finally, we select the machine (one that halts) that writes the largest number of 1s on its tape. The number of 1s that this Turing machine writes is called the busy beaver of n. Rado showed that there is no algorithm, that is, no Turing machine, that can compute this function for all ns. The crux of the problem is sorting out those n-state Turing machines that get into infinite loops. If we program a Turing machine to generate and simulate all possible n-state Turing machines, this simulator *itself* goes into an infinite loop when it attempts to simulate one of the n-state Turing Machines that gets into an infinite loop.

The busy beaver function can be computed for some ns, and interestingly, it is also an unsolvable problem to separate those ns for which we can determine the busy beaver of n from those for which we cannot. Aside from its interest as an example of an unsolvable problem, the busy beaver function is also interesting in that it can be considered to be itself an intelligent function. More precisely stated, it is a function that requires increasing intelligence to compute for increasing arguments. As we increase n, the complexity of the processes needed to compute the busy beaver of n increases.

With $n = 6$, we can deal with addition, and the busy beaver of 6 equals 35. In other words, addition is the most complex operation that a Turing machine with only 6 steps in its program is capable of performing. A 6-state Turing machine is not capable, for example, of multiplication. At 7, the Busy Beaver does learn to multiply, and the busy beaver of 7 equals 22,961. At 8 it can exponentiate, and the number of 1s that our eighth busy beaver writes on its tape is approximately 10^{43}. By the time we get to 10, we are dealing with a process more complex than exponentiation, and to represent the busy beaver of 10 we need an exotic notation in which we have a stack of exponents the height of which is determined by another stack of exponents,

The Busy Beaver, an intelligent function?

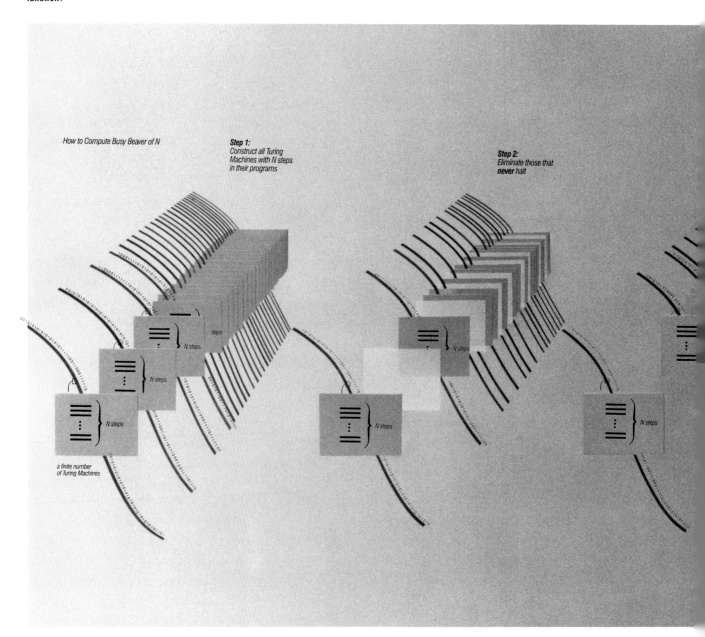

How to Compute Busy Beaver of N

Step 1:
Construct all Turing
Machines with N steps
in their programs

Step 2:
Eliminate those that
never halt

N steps

N steps

N steps

a finite number
of Turing Machines

N steps

N steps

the height of which is determined by another stack of exponents, and so on. For the twelfth busy beaver we need an even more exotic notation. It is likely that human intelligence (in terms of the complexity of mathematical operations that can be understood) is surpassed well before the busy beaver gets to 100.

Turing showed that there are as many unsolvable problems as solvable ones, the number of each being the lowest order of infinity, the so-called countable infinity (that is, the number of integers). Turing also showed that the problem of determining the truth or falsity of any logical proposition in an arbitrary system of logic powerful enough to represent the natural numbers was an unsolvable problem. The answer, therefore, to Hilbert's twenty-third problem posed 37 years earlier is no; no algorithm exists that can determine the truth or falsity of any logical proposition in a system of logic that is powerful enough to represent the natural numbers.

The second and third answers to Hilbert's question

Around the same time Alonzo Church, an American mathematician and philosopher, published Church's theorem, which examined Hilbert's question in the context of arithmetic. Church independently discovered the same answer as Turing.[25]

Also working independently, a young Czech mathematician, Kurt Gödel (1906–1978), sought to reexamine an issue that was not entirely settled by Whitehead and Russell's *Principia Mathematica*.[26] Whitehead and Russell had sought to determine axioms that could serve as the basis for all of mathematics, but they were unable to prove conclusively that an axiomatic system that can generate the natural numbers (theirs or any other) would not give rise to contradictions. It was assumed that such a proof would be found sooner or later, but Gödel stunned the mathematical world by proving that within such a system there inevitably exist propositions that can be neither proved nor disproved. Some have interpreted Gödel's theorem to imply that such uncertain propositions are simply indeterminate, neither true nor false. This misses the depth of Gödel's insight, however. Such propositions, according to Gödel, are *not* indeterminate; they are definitely either true or false. It is just that we can never determine which. Another implication is that in such axiomatic systems it is not certain that the axioms will not result in contradictions. Gödel's incompleteness theorem has been called the most important in all mathematics, and its implications are still being debated.[27] One of the implications is that the answer to Hilbert's twenty-third problem is again no.

Taken together, the work of Turing, Church, and Gödel, all published in the 1930s, represented the first formal proofs that there are definite limits to what logic, mathematics, and computation can do. These discoveries strongly contradict Wittgenstein's statement in the *Tractatus* that "if a question can be framed, it can be answered" (6.5).

Hope and order versus distress and perplexity

As a final comment on Turing's, Church's and Gödel's perplexing insights into the nature of logic, it is interesting to note the stark contrast of the mood and attitude of the intellectual and cultural life in Europe and the United States at the turn of the century in comparison with that of several decades later.[28] Music had shifted from the romantic style of Brahms (1833–1897) and the early Mahler (1860–1911) to the

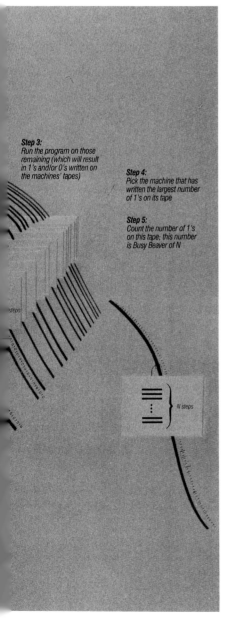

Step 3:
Run the program on those remaining (which will result in 1's and/or 0's written on the machines' tapes)

Step 4:
Pick the machine that has written the largest number of 1's on its tape

Step 5:
Count the number of 1's on this tape; this number is Busy Beaver of N

N steps

atonality of Schoenberg (1874–1951). Art and poetry had made the same switch from romantic styles to the cubism and expressionism of Picasso (1881–1973) and the minimalism of Pound (1885–1972), Eliot (1888–1965), and Williams (1883–1963). It is not unusual for changes in attitude and world view to be reflected across the arts, but it is interesting to note that the shift was reflected in science and mathematics as well. In physics, mechanics had gone from a fully refined and consistent Newtonian model to a paradoxical quantum model. The most puzzling aspect of quantum mechanics and one of its essential features, the Heisenberg uncertainty principle, is its conclusion that there are profound limits to what human beings can know. In addition, the principle of duality, which had existed previously only in metaphysical doctrine, was now firmly established in the apparently contradictory wave-particle nature of light. Perhaps most disturbing, mathematics itself had gone from its turn-of-the-century emphasis on comprehensive formalisms that covered all of mathematics to a conclusion in the mid 1930s that logic had inherent and irremovable contradictions and that problems existed that could never be solved.

Turing's test

Having established a theory of computation and having played a major role in the implementation of that theory, Turing's interest ran to speculation on the ultimate power of this new technology. He was an enthusiast for the potential of machine intelligence and believed that it was feasible, although he appeared to have a reasonably realistic sense of how long such a development would take.

In a paper entitled, "Computing Machinery and Intelligence," published in the journal *Mind* in 1950, Turing describes a means for determining whether or not a machine is intelligent: the Turing test. It should be noted that a computer "passing" the Turing test is an indication that it is intelligent. The converse of this statement does not necessarily hold. A machine (or organism) unable to pass the test does not necessarily indicate a lack of intelligence. Some observers ascribe a high level of intelligence to certain species of animals such as dolphins and whales, but these animals are obviously in no position to pass the Turing test (they have no fingers, for one thing).

To date no computer has come close to passing this test. The test basically involves the ability of the computer to *imitate* human performance. Narrower versions of the test have been proposed. For example, a computer chess program was recently able to "pass" a narrow version of the Turing test in that observers (again, observing through terminals) were unable to distinguish its playing from that of a skilled human chess player. Another variation—one involving the ability of a computer to compose stanzas of poetry—is provided in "A (Kind of) Turing Test" in chapter 9. Computers are now beginning to imitate human performance within certain well-defined domains. As Dan Dennett said in his article at the end of chapter 2, such narrow formulations of the Turing test fall far short of the original. I discuss the prospect of a computer passing the original Turing test in chapter 10.

Turing expected that a computer would pass his test by the end of the century and remarked that by that time "the use of words and general educated opinion will have altered so much that one will be able to speak of machines thinking without expecting to be contradicted." Turing's prediction contrasted with other statements around the same time that were much more optimistic in terms of time frame. (In 1965 Herbert Simon predicted that by 1985 "machines will be capable of doing any work that a man can do."[29]) Turing was as optimistic as anyone with regard to the power of cybernetic technology.[30] Yet he appears not to have underestimated (at least not as much as some other observers) the difficulty of the problems that remained to be solved.

The Church-Turing thesis

In addition to finding some profound limits to the powers of computation, Church and Turing also advanced, independently, an assertion that has become known as the Church-Turing thesis: if a problem that can be presented to a Turing machine is not solvable by one, then it is also not solvable by human thought. Others have restated this thesis to propose an essential equivalence between what a human can think or know and what is computable. The Church-Turing thesis can be viewed as a restatement in somewhat more precise terms of one of Wittgenstein's primary theses in the *Tractatus*.

I should point out that although the existence of Turing's unsolvable problems is a mathematical certainty, the Church-Turing thesis is not a mathematical proposition at all. It is a conjecture that, in various disguises, is at the heart of some of our most profound debates in the philosophy of mind.[31]

The Church-Turing thesis has both a negative and a positive side. The negative side is that problems that cannot be solved through any theoretical means of computation also cannot be solved by human thought. Accepting this thesis means that there are questions for which answers can be shown to exist but can never be found (and to date no human has ever solved an unsolvable problem).

The positive side is that if humans can solve a problem or engage in some intelligent activity, then machines can ultimately be constructed to perform in the same way. This is a central thesis of the AI movement. Machines can be made to perform intelligent functions; intelligence is not the exclusive province of human thought. We can thus arrive at another possible definition of artificial intelligence: AI represents attempts to provide practical demonstrations of the Church-Turing thesis.

In its strongest formulation, the Church-Turing thesis addresses issues of determinism and free will. Free will, which we can consider to be purposeful activity that is neither determined nor random, would appear to contradict the Church-Turing thesis. Nonetheless, the truth of the thesis is ultimately a matter of personal belief, and examples of intelligent behavior by machines are likely to influence one's belief on at least the positive side of the question.

The skepticism of Ada Lovelace (companion and assistant to Charles Babbage, the nineteenth-century inventor of the Analytical Engine, a "mechanical" computer) regarding the possibility of intelligent machines was no doubt related to the limitations of computers with whirling gears and levers that he proposed to her. Today it is possible to imagine building machines whose hardware rivals the complexity and capacity of the human brain. As our algorithms grow more sophisticated and machines at least appear to be more intelligent and more purposeful, discussions of the Church-Turing thesis will become more practical than the highly theoretical debate in Church's and Turing's time.

CHAPTER 4

Albert Einstein, the power of simple
explanations. (Reprinted by
permission of the Hebrew University
of Jerusalem, Israel)

The Formula for Intelligence

Everything should be made as simple as possible, but no simpler.
Albert Einstein

Politics are for the moment. An equation is for eternity.
Albert Einstein

I cannot believe . . . that God plays dice with the world.
Albert Einstein

• Unifying Formulas: The Goal of Science

There is a profound satisfaction in simple explanations that can truly account for complicated phenomena. The search for unifying formulas (sometimes called "applied mathematics") has been a goal of science since its inception with the Ionian Greeks twenty-five centuries ago.[1]

General relativity

Perhaps the most famous unifying formula is $E = mc^2$ (energy equals mass times the speed of light squared). The formula, part of the general theory of relativity put forth by Albert Einstein in 1905, is simple enough: only five symbols, including the equal sign.[2] Its power is manifest both in the range of phenomena it explains and in the nuclear age it spawned. The equation predicts and explains the power of a nuclear explosion. Mass when converted to energy is multiplied by an enormously large number. The result is a dramatic example of the power of an idea.

The laws of thermodynamics

Another famous example of unifying principles is the laws of thermodynamics. Developed in the mid nineteenth century and concerned with the conditions that all physical systems must obey, this was the first major refinement to the laws of classical mechanics developed a century earlier.[3] The first law is,

For any process involving no effects external to the system except displacement of a mass between specified levels in a gravity field, the magnitude of that mass is fixed by the end states of the system and is independent of the details of the process.

The second law is,

Among all the allowed states of a system with given values of energy, numbers of particles, and constraints, one and only one is a stable equilibrium state. Such a state can be reached from any other allowed state of the same energy, numbers of particles, and constraints and leave no effects on the state of the environment.

There are several important implications of the laws of thermodynamics, one of which is the impossibility of perpetual-motion machines. Another implication, relevant to the emergence of intelligence in the natural world, is a corollary of the two laws called the principle of increasing entropy. "Entropy" is a measure of randomness or lack of order in a system of many components, such as molecules. Though named the law of increasing entropy, the law actually states that entropy in a system can stay the same, but only under special conditions. Thus, entropy generally increases. Another way to state the same law is, Left to their own devices, systems will become increasingly disordered, a strangely poetic principle.[4]

The law of entropy seems to imply that the natural emergence of intelligence is impossible. Intelligent behavior is very far from random, and any system capable of intelligent behavior would have to be highly ordered. The chemistry of life in general, and intelligent life in particular, is comprised of exceptionally elaborate designs.[5] Out of the randomly swirling mass of particles in the universe, order has somehow managed to emerge.

A possible explanation is that thermodynamics is not applicable to the immensely long time frames that evolution operates in. Evolution has created systems of enormous order but has taken an enormously long period of time to do so. The order of life takes place amid great chaos and does not appreciably impact the measure of entropy in the physically large system in which life has evolved. No organism is a closed system; it is part of a larger system we call the environment, which is high in entropy. Nevertheless, from the viewpoint of the laws of thermodynamics, the emergence of intelligence must be considered a surprise.[6]

The theory of everything

Physicists have long had a talent for choosing entertaining anthropomorphic names for otherwise abstruse concepts with such words as "truth," "strangeness," and "charm" for complex mathematical properties of subatomic particles and "up," "down," "charm," "strange," "top," and "bottom" for the names of quarks, the elementary building blocks of matter.[7] The same comment might be applied to terminology in the AI field, although one could argue that AI terms such as "experts," "expert managers," "demons," "knowledge sources," and "logical inference processes" do have somewhat greater relevance to the phenomena being described than strangeness and charm do to the phenomena of particle physics.

Most recently physicists have been making progress on the ambitious quest to discover a unified set of equations to link the four basic forces of nature: gravity, electromagnetism, the strong force, and the weak force. The same quest, for what was then called the unified field theory, occupied Einstein's last two decades.[8]

Recently two of the forces, the electromagnetic and weak forces, have been clearly linked as two manifestations of an electroweak force. Most recently new theoretical developments involving a concept of supersymmetry may be able to link the remaining three forces into a unified structure referred to as the theory of everything.[9] In this theory, ultimate reality is composed of vibrating strings. All the phenomena we are familiar with, from subatomic particles to life forms, are resonances caused by the interactions of these vibrations. This theory gives new meaning to the saying "All the world is a song."

The formula for intelligence

As these examples illustrate, the search for unifying formulas and principles is a primary drive that fuels all of the sciences. The same sort of question has long fascinated researchers in the field of intelligence, both natural and artificial: Is there a formula that describes, explains or underlies intelligence? At first, the answer might appear to be an obvious no. We have not been entirely successful in even defining intelligence, much less in expressing it in a formula, a set of laws, or a set of models. Intelligence would seem to be too complex for such reduction.[10] On the other hand, we should not quickly dismiss the notion that a lot of what we know about intelligence can be expressed in such a manner. Some might argue that any description of intelligence in a formula just reflects how little we know about it. I would argue that the possibility of describing intelligent processes by simple equations or at least simple paradigms is a reflection of its elegance. If there is any coherency to intelligence as a unified phenomenon, we should be able to say something about its structure. I will describe several approaches to a description of intelligence and its supporting mechanisms through unified rules and formulas in the hope that they reveal insights into its nature.

• The Sea of Logic and the Turing Machine

Any computer that we can describe can in theory be constructed from connecting a suitable number (generally a very large number) of a very simple device, the NOR logic gate. This device transforms truth values. The device takes two inputs, each of which can be either true or false at any point in time. The NOR gate has one output, which is true if neither input 1 *nor* input 2 is true. From this simple transformation, we can build all other logic functions and even memory and thus provide all of the information-processing capabilities required for computation. A more detailed derivation is provided in the article accompanying this chapter.

The Church-Turing thesis (discussed in chapter 3) postulates an essential equivalence between machine and human intelligence, not necessarily between current levels of capability and complexity, but in their underlying methods.[11] Since we can construct any information-processing machine from NOR it can be considered the basis of all machine intelligence. If one accepts the Church-Turing thesis, NOR can be considered the basis of human intelligence as well.

While it is true that any algorithm, regardless of its complexity, can in theory be implemented with NOR gates, a collection of such devices will not perform any useful function unless they are connected together in an appropriate way. Part of

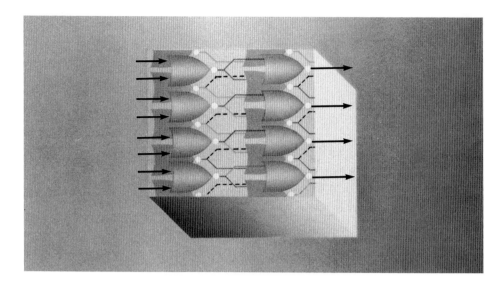

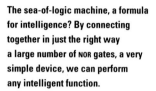

The sea-of-logic machine, a formula for intelligence? By connecting together in just the right way a large number of NOR gates, a very simple device, we can perform any intelligent function.

most useful information-processing methods also require memory (which can also be built from NOR gates), and we need each memory cell initialized to the right value. The connection of the NOR gates and the initial contents of the memory cells can both be described by lists of numbers, or the symbolic equivalent of numbers. They can, therefore, be considered as forms of software. Seen in this light, the NOR gate provides us with a unifying formula for the hardware of intelligence, but not for the software.

One might argue that the connection of the NOR gates should be considered hardware, and the initial contents of the memory cells should be considered software. I regard them both as software, because they are both equivalent to lists of numbers, and thus both can be represented using softwarelike languages. The evolution of electronic design is indeed proving the essential equivalence between so-called hardware design and software development. Increasingly, hardware designers are working at computer terminals, storing their work products on floppy disks (just like software engineers), and designing their systems using formula-based languages very similar to software languages. Take, for example, the emerging technology of silicon compilers. These systems allow a hardware engineer to describe an actual chip in terms of the logical and numeric transformations it is designed to perform.[12] These transformations are expressed in a language very similar to a high-level software programming language. The designer interacts with a simulator that allows the user to test out the "program" before the actual chip is constructed. Once this process is complete, the silicon-compiler software converts this program into a series of instructions for a silicon fabrication machine to create an actual VLSI (very large scale integrated) circuit chip. The program created by the chip designer is controlling the connection of the logic gates on the chip. We might regard the design of a chip to be the ultimate in hardware design, yet the development process, the languages used, and the work product are very similar to those for software.[13]

Comparison of the Turing machine and the sea of logic

Another simple yet powerful model that can potentially be used to describe any form of computation is the Turing machine. As described in chapter 3, the Turing machine is a theoretical model of an information-processing machine. The Turing machine, which like the NOR gate is relatively simple, continues to be used by mathematicians as a satisfactory model of what computers can and cannot do. The Turing machine has proven to be a more powerful mathematical model of computation than NOR-based logic because of the body of Turing-machine theory that has been developed.

Models of the Turing machine have been built, but they can never be true Turing machines, because it is not possible to build an infinitely long tape. On its face, it would appear that the "sea of logic" machine and the Turing machine are not equivalent, again because of the infinitely long tape of the Turing machine. It can be shown, however, that a Turing machine can simulate any sea-of-logic machine. Furthermore, it can be shown that any specific problem that can be solved by a Turing machine can be solved on a sea-of-logic machine as well. The heart of the proof lies in the fact that in order for a Turing machine to solve a problem, it must do so in a finite amount of time. In a finite amount of time, it can only use a finite amount of tape. Thus, it can be reduced to a machine with a finite number of states and thus simulated by the sea of logic. A Turing machine may outperform any particular sea-of-logic machine, however, because it may be able to solve problems that will use an amount of tape that outstrips the memory capacity of any particular sea-of-logic machine.

Turing directly linked his theoretical machine to the more controversial Church-Turing thesis. If one accepts the Church-Turing thesis, then the Turing machine, which is a very simple machine in structure, can solve any cognitive problem. To be more precise, the Turing machine can execute any plan to solve a cognitive problem. Its success in doing so will be a function of the validity of the plan.[14] We thus come to the same conclusion that we did with the sea of logic. The Turing machine provides us with a simple and elegant model for the hardware of cybernetic (machine-based) cognition, but not the software. To solve a practical problem, the Turing machine needs a program, and each different program constitutes a different Turing machine.

The universal Turing machine

It turns out that a *universal Turing machine* can be shown to have the capability of simulating every other Turing machine. The universal Turing machine has a program that can read a description on its tape of any Turing machine (even the universal Turing machine) and then simulate that machine. Thus, the input tape to the universal Turing machine contains not only the usual problem input but also a coded description of the Turing machine it is going to simulate. The universal Turing machine is thereby a single (theoretical) machine that can solve any problem.[15]

All this accomplishes, however, is to move the software from the built-in program of a Turing machine to a description of such a program on a tape. If we consider the machine program on the tape to be the software, we once again conclude that we have a powerful and elegant model for the hardware underlying intelligent processes, but not the software, at least not yet.

To follow the way, one must find the way and follow it.

Zen koan

The whole point of this sentence is make clear what the whole point of this sentence is.

Douglas R. Hofstadter, *Metamagical Themas*

"Would you tell me please which way I ought to go from here?" asked Alice.

"That depends a good deal on where you want to get to," said the Cat.

"I don't much care where . . . ," said Alice.

"Then it doesn't matter which way you go," said the Cat.

". . . so long as I get *somewhere*," Alice added as an explanation.

"Oh, you're sure to do that," said the Cat, "if you only walk long enough."

Lewis Carroll, *Alice in Wonderland*

A professor has just finished lecturing at some august university about the origin and structure of the universe, and an old woman in tennis shoes walks up to the lectern. "Excuse me, sir, but you've got it all wrong," she says. "The truth is that the universe is sitting on the back of a huge turtle." The professor decides to humor her. "Oh, really?" he asks. "Well, tell me, what is the turtle standing on?" The lady has a ready reply: "Oh, it's standing on another turtle." The professor asks, "And what is *that* turtle standing on?" Without hesitation, she says, "Another turtle." The professor, still game, repeats his question. A look of impatience comes across the woman's face. She holds up her hand, stopping him in mid-sentence. "Save your breath, sonny," she says. "It's turtles all the way down."

Rolf Landauer, as quoted in *Did the Universe Just Happen?* by Robert Wright

The Turing Machine provides us with a model of computation that has enabled theoreticians to examine many facets of computers and their capabilities. The sea of logic is an even simpler mechanism that enables us to build very complex machines and methods from a simple NOR gate. We can consider these to be simple formulas that provide insight into computational hardware, but as noted, they do not provide insight into the software, the methods or algorithms, of intelligence.

One of the first attempts to codify intelligence in an algorithm was the recursive method, implemented in both the General Problem Solver and Samuel's Checker Playing Program.[16] Let us examine the recursive formula in the context of the game of chess. We will be returning to the issue of chess several times in this volume because of its importance to AI research. Raj Reddy cites studies of chess as playing the same role in AI that studies of *E. Coli* play in biology: an ideal laboratory for studying fundamental questions. I will then expand the method to other problems and examine its capabilities and limitations.

The game of chess

Chess is a game of two opponents in which the players take turns adjusting the positions of their pieces on a playing board according to prescribed rules. Of course, many other games can be described in the same way. Certain activities in real life, such as war and business, have similar characteristics. Indeed, chess was originally formulated as a model of war.

To win or to provide the highest probability of winning, one selects the best possible move every time it is one's turn to move. The question, then, is what the best move is. The recursive method provides the following rule, which, if you follow it carefully, will enable you to play an exceptionally good game of chess: Every time it is your move, select the best move on the assumption your opponent will do the same. At this point, the casual observer will complain that the rule has no content, that it provides no more insight than an impenetrable Zen koan. It appears to simply restate the problem. As I believe will become clear, however, this rule is all that is needed to play an excellent game of chess. If this is so, then we might conclude either that the recursive formula is a powerful and deceptively simple formula for the algorithm (or software) of at least some forms of intelligence, or alternatively, that chess is not an intelligent game, that the game has no content.

Before delving further into the implications of the recursive formula, let us examine how it works. We fashion a program called Move. When it is called, its job is to pick the best move. It is a recursive program in that it is capable of calling itself. Recursive programs are perfectly feasible in modern programming languages. A program can call itself, return answers to itself, and continue as if it had called any other program (or subroutine).

Recursion is a powerful method used extensively in artificial intelligence. It is one of the more valued features of the primary AI programming language LISP.[17] A brief discussion of recursion will be worthwhile at this point, and I will illustrate the concept with an example. Consider the definition of the factorial function expressed recursively. Let $n!$ be the factorial of n. The definition of the factorial function is then $1! = 1$, and $n! = n \times (n - 1)!$ As we can see, this definition of factorial uses the concept of factorial in its own definition. This self-referencing is called recursion. Yet the definition is not infinitely circular in that we can determine the value of the factorial of any number from the definition just by repetitively expanding references to factorial.

For example, let us compute $4!$. According to the definition, $4! = 4 \times 3!$. Using the definition again to expand $3!$, we get $4! = 4 \times 3 \times 2!$ In turn, we expand $2!$ to get $4! = 4 \times 3 \times 2 \times 1!$. The definition gives the $1!$ directly without reference to itself. We are thus able to fully expand the expression to eliminate all reference to the function in the right-hand part of the expression: $4 = 4 \times 3 \times 2 \times 1$.

The power of recursion is that complex procedures or concepts can be expressed in a simple way. A recursive definition differs from a circular definition in that it has an escape from infinite expansion of the recursion. The escape is found in the "terminal" or nonrecursive portion of the definition. In the recursive definition of factorial, the terminal portion of the definition is the factorial of 1.

Recursion, a program calling itself, is accomplished by the program saving information on its current state (including who called it and exactly where it is to return to when finished) on a *push down* stack. The stack is a repository of information that is organized as a last-in, first-out (LIFO) list so that information is retrieved in the opposite order in which it is put in, rather like a stack of dishes. Each time a program calls another program (whether it is calling itself or another subroutine), information about the state of the program and the place to return to is placed ("pushed") onto the stack. Every time a program is completed and wants to return to the program that called it (which might be itself), information is retrieved ("popped") from the stack. This information restores the state of the program that

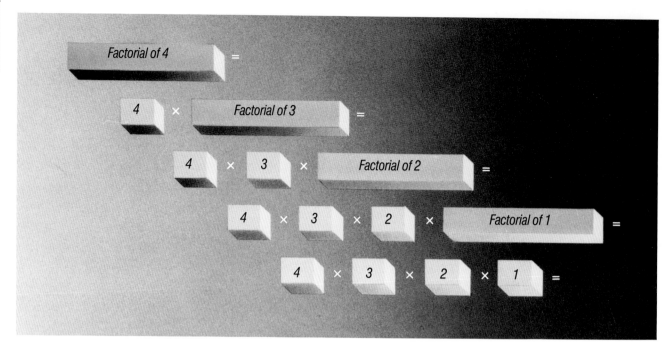

Factorial, an example of recursion.

called it and indicates where in the calling program to return to, which might be to part of itself. This simple LIFO mechanism assures that all returns are to the right place.

Practical programs cannot call themselves indefinitely. Thus, a practical LIFO stack is of finite length. Another reason that a program cannot continue to call itself without limit is that we would like to solve problems in a finite length of time. Thus, a useful recursive formula or definition requires an escape condition, a set of circumstances that permits us to escape from infinite recursion.

Let us return to our simple recursive rule for playing chess. It starts out by saying that we should select the best move. To do this, we obviously must *consider* each move, and thus we need to be able to generate a list of all possible moves. We do this by simply applying the rules of chess. While more complicated than some other games, such as checkers, the rules of chess are certainly straightforward and readily programmable.[18] There is nothing mysterious about generating the possible moves from any board position. We thus provide a mechanism programmed with the rules of chess to generate our options. To play a different game, we can simply replace this module with another one programmed with the rules of that particular game.

We now have a list of possible moves. We examine each in turn and ask the question, Does this move enable me to win or lose? If the answer is lose, we do not select that move. If the answer is win, we take that move. If more than one move enables us to win, it does not matter which one we take.

The problem now reduces to answering the question, Does this move enable me to win or lose? At this point we note that our winning or losing is affected by what our opponent might do. A reasonable assumption is that our opponent will also choose his best move (and if the opponent fails to do this, that will not be a problem, but an opportunity). We need to anticipate what that move might be, so we use our own ability to select the best move to determine what our opponent is likely to do. We essentially put ourselves in our opponent's place and pick the best move for our opponent. In this we are following the part of the recursive rule that states, "Select the best move *on the assumption that your opponent will do the same.*"

Our program is now structured as follows. We generate a list of all possible moves allowed by the rules. We examine each possible move in turn. For each move, we generate a hypothetical board representing what the placement of the pieces would be if we were in fact to make this move. We now put ourselves in our opponent's place and try to determine what his best move would be. How are we to do this? It turns out that we have a program that is designed to do exactly that. It is called Move. Move is, of course, the program we are already in, so this is where the recursion comes in. Move calls itself to determine what our opponent will do. When called to determine the best move for our opponent, Move begins to determine all of the moves that our opponent could make at this point. For each one, it wants to know how its opponent (which is us) would respond and thus again calls Move for each possible move of our opponent to determine what our response to that move would (or should) be.

The program thus keeps calling itself, continuing to expand possible moves and countermoves in an ever expanding tree of possibilities. This process is usually called a *minimax search,* because we are alternately attempting to minimize our opponent's ability to win and to maximize our own.[19] The figure illustrates this process for the simpler game of tic-tac-toe.

The next question is, Where does this all end? Let us start with an attempt to play perfect chess. We continue to expand the tree of possible moves and countermoves until each branch results in an end of game. Each end of game provides the answer: win, tie, or lose. Thus, at the furthest point of expansion of moves and countermoves, some moves finally finish the game. If a move results in a win, then we select that move. If there are no win moves, then we settle for a tie move. If there are no win or tie moves, we keep playing anyway in the hope that our opponent will make a mistake (unless we know we are playing a perfect opponent, in which case we may as well give up). These final moves are the terminal nodes of our expansion of moves. Here, instead of continuing to call Move, we can now begin returning from Move calls. As we begin to return from all of the nested Move calls, we have determined the best move at each point (including the best move for our opponent), and so we can finally select the correct move for the current *actual* board situation.

The above procedure is guaranteed to play a perfect game of chess. This is because chess is a finite game. Interestingly, it is finite only because of the tie rule, which states that repetition of a move results in a tie. If it were not for the tie rule, then chess would be an infinite game (the tree of possible moves and countermoves could expand forever) and we could not be sure of determining the best move within a finite amount of time. Thus, this very simple recursive formula plays not just an excellent, but a perfect, game of chess.[20] The most complicated part of actually implementing the recursive formula is generating the allowable moves at each point. Doing so, however, requires only a straightforward codification of the rules. Playing a perfect game of chess is thus no more complicated than understanding the rules.

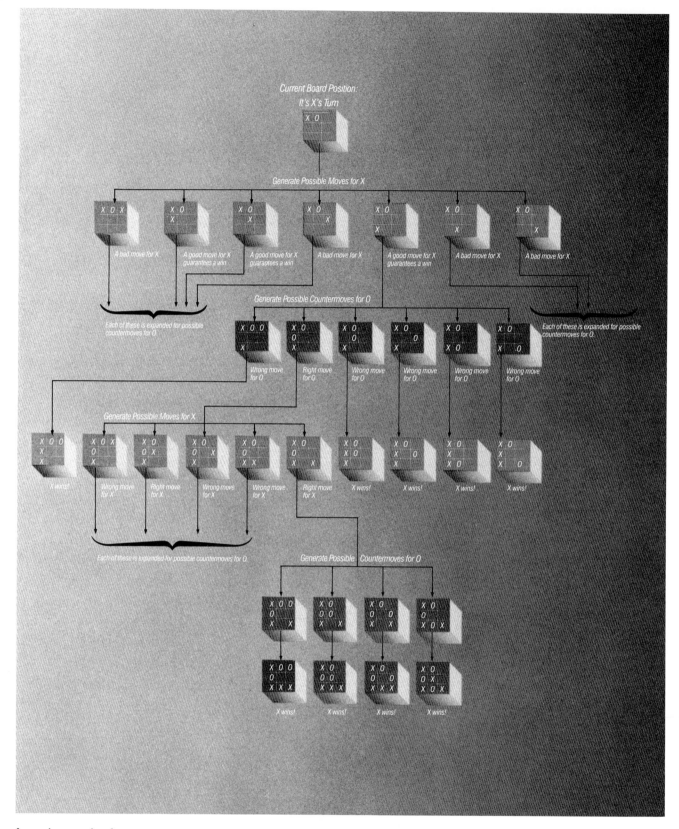

**A recursive expansion of moves
in tic-tac-toe.**

A Tinkertoy mechanical computer that plays tic-tac-toe. (Courtesy of the Computer Museum, Boston)

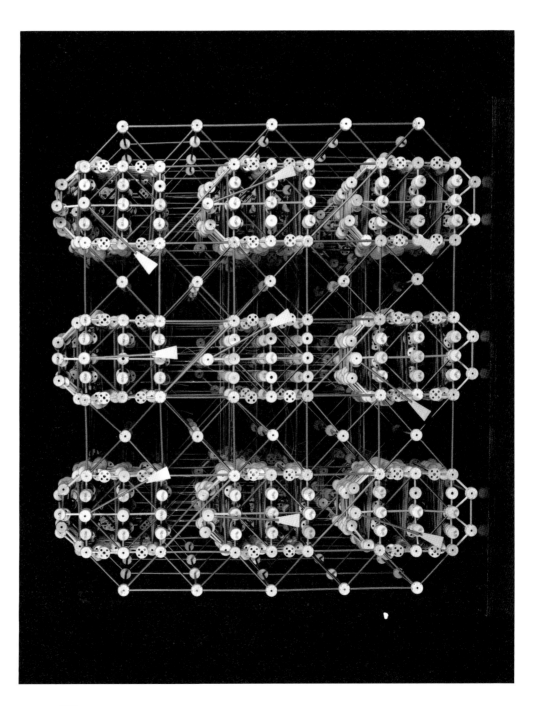

When shopping for services like car repair, the smart shopper is well advised to ask, How long will it take? The same question is quite appropriate in applying the recursive formula. Unfortunately, with respect to chess, the answer is something like 40 billion years.[21] And that is just to make the first move!

We can estimate the length of time by assuming that there are, on average, about eight possible moves for each board situation. If a typical game lasts about 30 moves, we need to consider 8^{30} possible move sequences to fully expand the tree of all move-countermove possibilities. If we assume that we can analyze one billion of such sequences in a second (which is at least 1,000 times faster than is in fact possible on today's fastest chess computers—in 1989, two leading chess machines, HiTech and Deep Thought, could analyze 175,000 and 1,000,000 board positions per second, respectively), then we require 10^{18} seconds, or about 40 billion years.[22] If the cyclic theory of the universe is correct (the theory that the universe will eventually end its current expansion and then contract, resulting ultimately in another big bang), then the computation would not be complete before our computer is blown up in the next explosion of the universe.

This brings up another aspect of computation theory: the amount of computation required to achieve a result. One branch of computation theory examines the issue of whether a computer (generally using the Turing machine as a model of a computer) can solve a given problem within a finite amount of time. Problems that cannot be solved are called unsolvable problems. More recently a new branch of computation theory called complexity theory has been developed to deal with the issue of how long various solvable problems will take to compute.[23] While our very simple recursive formula plays perfect chess, which may indeed be considered intelligent behavior, it takes an excessively long period of time to do so. Accomplishing tasks quickly or at least in a timely manner is regarded as an essential part of intelligence. As discussed earlier, despite controversies with regard to cultural bias, the timed aspect of intelligence tests has long been accepted, which reflects the importance of timeliness as an attribute of intelligence.

Thus far the above discussion has not yet demonstrated intelligence in the recursive formula. Playing perfect chess might be considered intelligent behavior, but not at 40 billion years per move. Before we throw out the recursive formula, however, let us attempt to modify it to take into account our human patience (and mortality). Clearly, we need to put limits on how deep we allow the recursion to take place. How large we allow the move-countermove tree to grow should depend on how much computation we have available. In this way we can use the recursive formula on any computer, from an inexpensive home computer to the largest supercomputer.

The next question is how do we evaluate the terminal "leaves," the fully expanded board positions of our tree of possibilities? When we considered fully expanding each move sequence to the end of the game, evaluation was simple: winning is better than tying, and tying is better than losing. Evaluating a board position in the middle of a game is not as straightforward and, not surprisingly, is the source of controversy.[24]

There are two schools of thought here: the simple-minded school and the complex-minded school. The complex-minded school argues that we need sophisticated (complicated) sets of rules and procedures to evaluate the "quality" of the board at each terminal leaf position, that we need to be "smart" in making these evaluations and require algorithms that can make subtle judgements.[25]

The simple-minded school argues that whatever computational resources we happen to have available are best put into pursuing greater depths of search, that is, looking at longer sequences of possible moves and countermoves and using a computationally simple procedure to evaluate final board positions. One such procedure is simply to count up the points of the two sides, using the recognized value of each piece (ten for the queen, five for each rook, etc.). The argument is that any sophisticated evaluation of node positions is computationally very expensive and is not likely to be more productive or more reliable than putting the computational resource into greater depth of search.

For chess in particular I tend to agree with the simple-minded school and feel that the key to building a computer that can win the world chess championship lies in massive computational power to be achieved through massive parallel processing (which, after all, the human brain uses). All chess playing programs use the recursive formula, some with simple board evaluation procedures (often just adding up piece values) and others with more sophisticated procedures. The primary factor that has determined the power of a particular program appears to be the amount of computation that can be brought to bear. The programs running on the fastest supercomputers or parallel processing networks invariably are the best machine players, regardless of the board-evaluation algorithm. More sophisticated terminal-leaf evaluation procedures do not appear to hurt performance, but neither do they appear to help. They do not appear, therefore, to be worth the trouble.[26]

HiTech, developed at Carnegie Mellon University and the leading chess machine of 1988, uses massive parallel processing.[27] It uses an array of specially designed VLSI chips capable of generating and evaluating board positions. Though its procedure for evaluating a board position is more complicated then just adding up the value of each piece, I would still describe its evaluation procedure as simple (although the developers of HiTech might disagree with me).[28]

If we agree with the simple-minded school, then the node-evaluation procedure is simple. Since the recursive formula itself is the ultimate in simplicity, we end up with an algorithm that does indeed reduce to a simple formula and is capable of playing a very good game of chess with reasonable (and in tournament play, acceptable) response time.

The next question is, How good a game? Predictions made in 1958 that a computer would be world chess champion by 1968 were considerably over optimistic.[29] Nonetheless, computers have demonstrated steady progress and, as mentioned earlier, two computer programs, Belle and HiTech, now play on the National Senior Master Level, equaled or surpassed by only 768 human players.[30] In 1988 HiTech scored 5 wins, 1 loss in the National Open Chess Championships, which ranked it 150th among registered American players. Also in 1988 Carnegie Mellon's Deep Thought defeated the highest rated player ever in the U.S. Open Chess Tournament. Though not yet that of a world champion, this is certainly an impressive and eminently intelligent level of play.[31]

The number of human chess players that can still defeat the best machines is growing smaller each year. It is clear that to make *linear* progress in the
number of moves and countermoves that can be analyzed, we need to make
exponential gains in computational power. On the other hand, we *are* making
exponential gains in computational power with the *linear* passing of time. By most
estimates, computational power (per unit of cost) is doubling every 18 to 24 months.
The phenomenon of parallel processing (doing more than one computation at a time)
is in some ways accelerating this trend, at least with regard to how much computation we can throw at the problem of playing chess. The Connection Machine, for
example, has 65,536 parallel computers, although each of these processors handles
only one bit at a time.[32] Machines are being built that combine thousands of powerful 32-bit computers, and machines that combine millions of 32-bit microprocessors
are being seriously contemplated.

It is clear that it is only a matter of time before the world chess champion
is a machine. To make a prediction as to when that might be, we need to know how
many more move-countermove expansions are needed. Some argue that the difference between national senior master level, at which computers can now play, and
world-champion level of play is the ability to see only two or three additional moves
ahead. It certainly makes sense that the ability to see an *additional* 2 or 3 moves
ahead could account for the difference between the excellent playing of a national
senior master and the somewhat better game of the champion. Others argue that
the difference is more like 10 to 12 moves.[33]

Some argue that the difference in play between masters at different levels
is not a matter of seeing additional moves ahead, that the master is not really analyzing moves and countermoves at all. Instead, he supposedly has some sort of higher-
level intuitive feel for the strength of different moves and board positions. In my
opinion, master players are not *consciously* aware of all of the move-countermove
sequences, but this computation has in fact taken place. Most of this analysis has
been "precomputed" by storing and retrieving board positions from previous experience and study. When we train our minds to perform a certain type of physical or
mental activity, the mental processes underlying this skill can often be accomplished
without our conscious awareness, but that does not mean that the mental calculations never took place.[34]

To get back to our estimate, if each additional move ahead expands the
amount of computation by a factor of about 8, and if it takes 18 months for the
computer industry to double computational power, then our cybernetic chess players
will be able to see one additional move ahead every 4.5 years. According to this
estimate, we are somewhere between 9 and 54 years from having sufficient computational power to build a computer chess champion. This achievement will, in my
opinion, be brought a lot closer than 54 years through the impact of new technologies, including new parallel processing architectures, exotic new computer hardware
techniques that use light instead of electricity, and other developments.[35] Another
analysis is provided by Raj Reddy. He estimates that grand-master level play (just
below world-championship level play and probably good enough to beat the world
champion once in a while) requires being able *reliably* to look ahead about 12 to 14
moves. Though the average branching factor (the number of possible moves for

each board position) is about 35, advanced search techniques allow us to effectively reduce this number to 5. Thus, we need to consider between 5^{12} and 5^{14} board positions, or about 3 billion positions per move. With an average of 3 minutes of thinking time per move, this requires a rate of about 16 million board positions per second, only 16 times faster than Deep Thought's 1989 rate. Thus, we should be able to achieve very close to championship play by the early 1990s.

Yet another analysis is provided by one of HiTech's designers, Hans Berliner, who notes that the average increase in the ratings of the best computer players has been about 45 points per year (in contrast, the average increase in the ratings of the best human players is close to 0). This analysis projects 1998 as the year of the computer world champion. My own guess is that we will see a world champion by the year 2000, but as mentioned above, earlier predictions of this type have not fared well.

Let us return for a moment to the concept of the perfect chess game. From a mathematical point of view, such a game exists. In other words, we can define the perfect chess game as a game played by two opponents each following the recursive formula and fully expanding all move sequences. From a formal point of view, we cannot say that determining the sequence of moves in this perfect game is an unsolvable problem, because it can certainly be determined in a finite amount of time. On the other hand, we can show that it is impossible to determine in any practical length of time. We thus have the interesting situation of being able to easily define a question, to show that the answer exists and is unique, and also to demonstrate conclusively that there is no reasonable way to find it.

Other questions come to mind. For example, does the player who moves first in this hypothetical perfect game win or tie (it is unlikely that the player making the first move would lose)? Again, there is an answer to this question, but it appears that no human (or machine) will ever be able to find it.

An idiot-savant game?

When I stated that I was of the simple-minded school, I was careful to state that this was my opinion specifically with regard to the game of chess. If it is shown that a simple leaf evaluation procedure can defeat any human being at chess (as I believe will happen), then we can conclude either that the recursive formula is indeed a simple formula for at least certain types of intelligent behavior, or that chess is not an intelligent game. We could conclude that computers are better than humans at chess for the same reason that computers are better at creating spreadsheets. In other words, we might conclude that the secret to chess is simply being able to keep in one's mind countless move and countermove sequences and the resulting board patterns. This is the type of information that computers can easily and accurately manipulate, whereas the heart of human intelligence lies elsewhere. As long as there are at least a few humans that can defeat the best machines, some observers still feel comfortable in citing chess as an example of high intellectual (and creative!) activity and imagining that there is some unknown (and possibly unknowable) deep intellectual process underlying it. A computer world chess champion could radically alter that perception. It is clear that there will be some significant change in perception with regard to chess, computers, ourselves, or all three.

Other games

The recursive formula can be applied to any board game that involves moves and countermoves within prescribed rules. A reasonable question is, How well does it work in practice for games other than chess? Also, what about the simple-minded versus complex-minded controversy?

At one extreme of the spectrum of game complexity there is tic-tac-toe, for which we can quite easily expand all possibilities to end of game and play a perfect game. Many humans, at least those who have spent any time thinking about it, can play a perfect game as well.

Checkers, on the other hand, is sufficiently complex that playing a perfect game is not feasible, although the perfect checkers game can probably be computed before the next big bang occurs. Checkers-playing machines have already come closer than chess machines to defeating the world human champion.[36] A computer has already taken the world championship in backgammon: Hans Berliner's program defeated the human backgammon champion in 1980.[37] There are two reasons why computers have had a somewhat easier time with checkers and backgammon than with chess. First, generating the possible moves at each point requires substantially less computation. There are only two different types of pieces in checkers and one in backgammon, and the rules are relatively simple. The problem is not that programmers have a hard time programming the rules of chess—the rules are not that complicated. The complexity of the rules is an issue with regard to how many moves ahead it is possible to look. With their relatively simple rules, the same amount of computational power enables the checkers or backgammon program to look ahead a greater number of moves than the chess program. The second possible reason is that there is a lot more interest in chess, and thus the best human players are probably better at chess than at checkers or backgammon. Nonetheless, backgammon is still considered a "deep" game, and the fact that a computer can defeat any human player should be considered an event of some note.[38]

At the other extreme, in terms of computer success, is the Japanese game of go, which has a place in the cultural life of Japan comparable to chess in Russia, Europe, and the United States. Though computers can play a reasonable amateur game of go, they have not achieved master level, and the lack of progress is not for lack of effort by program designers. The problem is not with the complexity of go, because the rules are in fact simpler than those for chess. In my view, the primary reason that the recursive formula is not as effective is that the number of possible moves at each point is relatively large and the length of move sequences in a game, or even a portion of a game in which meaningful progress is made, is very long. Thus, even massive computation is quickly exhausted and does not look far enough ahead to examine a meaningful strategy.[39]

It appears that for the game of go we *do* need more sophisticated evaluation strategies to examine different options. It may also be that we need to consider alternatives on a different level than individual moves, that we need a way of effectively modeling strategies on a higher level than one move at a time. Thus, for go, unlike chess, I would throw my ballot in with the complex-minded school. It appears that the Japanese have a board game that is "deeper" and more consistent with the particular strengths (at least at present) of human intelligence.[40]

The Japanese game of go. (Photo by David E. Dempster of Offshoot)

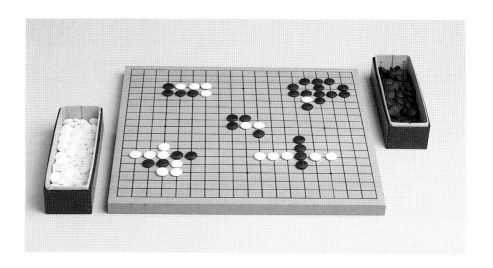

Other intelligent tasks

The Recursive Formula can be applied to nongame situations, such as proving mathematical theorems, solving combinatorial problems, solving various types of puzzles ranging from mazes to word problems (like the problem of cannibals and missionaries).[41] In any situation in which the answer can be expressed as a sequence of moves, steps, or transformations governed by a set of unambiguous rules, the recursive formula is a good candidate for solving the problem.

In 1957 Allen Newell, J. C. Shaw, and Herbert Simon devised a program entitled the General Problem Solver (GPS).[42] The program's name reflected the enthusiasm, romanticism, and immodesty of the early AI field, an optimistic orientation that eventually earned the field considerable criticism.[43] GPS could solve problems that involved devising a sequence of steps to achieve a goal. For example, proving a theorem in mathematics requires devising a sequence of steps allowed by the rules of logic, in which each step employs an axiom or a previously proven theorem or lemma. One approach that works in theory but not in practice is simply to generate every possible sequence until one is found that accomplishes the task. Clearly, the number of possibilities expands too quickly, and a method of using limited computational resources to achieve a goal within a reasonable amount of time is needed. To optimize the use of scarce computational power, GPS uses a technique called means-ends analysis. At each step it measures the "distance" to the goal and generates a subgoal to attempt to minimize this distance. It then calls itself, another example of recursion, to solve the presumably simpler problem represented by the subgoal. In a similar way, each subgoal can be expanded into smaller subgoals.

GPS achieved notable success in solving logic puzzles, proving theorems, solving problems in integral calculus and plane geometry, and similar mathematical or combinatorial problems.[44] Its success fueled some of the AI field's early optimism.[45] Further progress came more slowly, however, as some of the limitations of the technique became clear. One of the keys to successful use of the GPS paradigm is a measure of distance that is appropriate to the problem. For example, how should we measure the distance between two mathematical expressions? Simply counting the number of symbols that the two expressions do not have in common is clearly not satisfactory: two expressions may differ by only one symbol, and yet we may never be able to derive one from the other. Similarly, in solving a maze problem, we may be only a single cell away from the goal, yet we are not necessarily close to achieving a viable path. A fully satisfactory method of defining distance in such domains is still not clear.[46]

So close and yet so far: the distance between mathematical expressions.

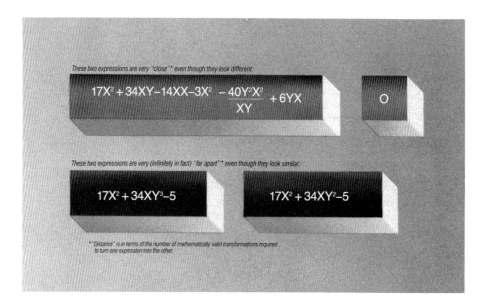

These two expressions are very "close"* even though they look different:

$$17X^2 + 34XY - 14XX - 3X^2 \quad \frac{-40Y^2X^2}{XY} + 6YX$$

$$O$$

These two expressions are very (infinitely in fact) "far apart"* even though they look similar:

$$17X^2 + 34XY^3 - 5$$

$$17X^2 + 34XY^2 - 5$$

*"Distance" is in terms of the number of mathematically valid transformations required to turn one expression into the other.

The initial rapid success of GPS was followed by a period of considerably slower progress in which each aspect of the GPS paradigm was examined in detail. What is the distance measure? How are subgoals generated and evaluated? Are there alternatives to the means-ends algorithm? A relatively simple approach that seemed at first to capture intelligence, at least within a broad variety of problem domains, was shown to have limitations. GPS has certainly not been the last word on this type of search problem, and more capable methods have since been devised.[47]

Three levels of intelligence

In practical applications of the recursive formula to a variety of tasks, intelligent problems appear to divide into three levels. At one extreme are problems that require little enough computation that they can be completely analyzed. Examples are tic-tac-toe and such word problems as cannibals and missionaries. In the middle are problems for which we cannot afford full analysis but that appear to be successfully dealt with using a simple node-evaluation procedure. By "successfully dealt with" I do not mean that it is possible to provide perfect solutions. Rather, I mean that it is possible to match the performance of most (and in some cases all) humans. Examples of this class of problems are chess, checkers, backgammon, and Euclidian geometry. It is true that some of the chess programs use complex node-evaluation procedures, but these programs do not appear to provide superior performance to programs that do use simple node-evaluation procedures. The point is that playing a good game of chess (and in my opinion ultimately a championship game of chess) does not *require* complicated node-evaluation procedures.[48] Finally, there is a class of problems that do require nontrivial procedures at the terminal leaf position. For many

Are these
two cells
"close" or
"far"?

So close and yet so far: the distance
between cells in a maze.

of these problems we have yet to devise such procedures. Examples are the game of go and some realms of mathematical theory. In sum, the levels of intelligence required for various activities are as follows:

Level 1
Tic-Tac-Toe
Cannibals and missionaries

Level 2
Checkers
Chess
Backgammon
Euclidian geometry

Level 3
Go
Some realms of mathematics

What is our conclusion with regard to the recursive formula? It is certainly simple and elegant. For the first two classes of problems described above—the class that can be fully analyzed within a reasonable amount of time and the class that cannot be fully analyzed but requires only simple terminal-evaluation procedures to achieve intelligent performance—the full description of the algorithm is simple and can be said to be solved by a unifying formula. The most complicated aspect of implementing such a solution is the generation of the possible moves or steps at each point. Doing so is, however, simply a matter of stating the problem (e.g., the rules of the game). Thus the recursive formula enables us to solve a problem as simply as stating it.

What about the third class, the class for which simple terminal-evaluation procedures do not appear adequate? For this class the basic recursive algorithm is only part of the solution. We end up requiring insight into the unique structure of each such problem. Many of these problems can be solved (and have been solved), but the solutions are different in each case. If there is a unifying formula linking these diverse algorithms, none has yet become apparent.

The extent to which one accepts the recursive formula as a unifying formula for even a subset of intelligent problem solving comes down again to one's definition of intelligence. It might be argued that problems in the first two classes described above are inherently not problems requiring intelligence but rather just data- and symbol-manipulation problems for which computers are well suited and that truly intelligent problems are of the third kind. Accepting this point of view requires us to modify our opinion of certain activities that have for centuries been considered to be intelligent, like playing checkers or chess and solving problems in Euclidian geometry and other areas of mathematics.

Such a view would be equivalent to stating that intelligence is to be specifically defined as a type of behavior or activity that inherently *cannot* be captured in a single unifying formula. If we accept this definition, then, of course, the question of whether or not intelligence or any important aspect of it can be captured in a formula is answered negatively by definition. Yet the implications of such a definition would not be consistent with commonly held views of what constitutes intelligent behavior.[49]

I would say that the recursive formula is partially successful. Certain types of intelligent behavior, that required by the first two classes of problems, can be effectively simulated with this elegant and powerful approach. Other types of problems appear to resist it, including the important area of pattern recognition.

• Other Approaches to Modeling the Software of Intelligence: Random Nets, Pandemonium, and Trees

I do not come to the discussion of connectionism as a neutral observer. In fact, the standard version of its history assigns me a role in a romantic story whose fairytale resonances surely contribute at least a little to connectionism's aura of excitement.

Once upon a time two daughter sciences were born to the new science of cybernetics. One sister was natural, with features inherited from the study of the brain, from the way nature does things. The other was artificial, related from the beginning to the use of computers. Each of the sister sciences tried to build models of intelligence, but from very different materials. The natural sister built models (called neural networks) out of mathematically purified neurones. The artificial sister built her models out of computer programs.

In their first bloom of youth the two were equally successful and equally pursued by suitors from other fields of knowledge. They got on very well together. Their relationship changed in the early sixties when a new monarch appeared, one with the largest coffers ever seen in the kingdom of the sciences: Lord DARPA, the Defense Department's Advanced Research Projects Agency. The artificial sister grew jealous and was determined to keep for herself the access to Lord DARPA's research funds. The natural sister would have to be slain.

The bloody work was attempted by two staunch followers of the artificial sister, Marvin Minsky and Seymour Papert, cast in the role of the huntsman sent to slay Snow White and bring back her heart as proof of the deed. Their weapon was not the dagger but the mightier pen, from which came a book—*Perceptrons*—purporting to prove that neural nets could never fill their promise of building models of mind: *only computer programs could do this.* Victory seemed assured for the artificial sister. And indeed, for the next decade all the rewards of the kingdom came to her progeny, of which the family of expert systems did best in fame and fortune.

But Snow White was not dead. What Minsky and Papert had shown the world as proof was not the heart of the princess; it was the heart of a pig.

Seymour Papert, 1988

Another unified theory: The Perceptron

In the early and mid 1960s the AI field became enamored with another type of machine called the Perceptron.[50] This was an attempt to capture intelligence using a large number of simple mechanisms. A perceptron consisted of three types of devices: sensory units, associative units, and effector units (see figure). The sensory units consisted of simple photocells arranged in a two dimensional array, simulating the function of the human retina (or many other forms of input). A Perceptron incorporating auditory sensory units was also proposed. The associative units were randomly wired between the sensory units and the effector units and in some cases other associative units. The associative units contained a feedback mechanism that makes them automatically adjust the amount of current that passes from each input to each output on the basis of feedback received by the unit on whether or not the Perceptron's last response was correct. The effector units sum the outputs of the associative units to which they are connected, and by comparing different summed voltages, they make final decisions on the identities of the patterns presented to the sensory units.

The machine attracted attention because, simple as it was, it appeared to model both the structure and the functions of the human brain.[51] The sensory, associative, and effector units modeled afferent, associative, and efferent neurons respectively. Moreover, the random wiring of the associative units, sometimes referred to as random neural nets, were thought to model the seemingly random interconnections of the associative neurons. The Perceptron learns by gradually

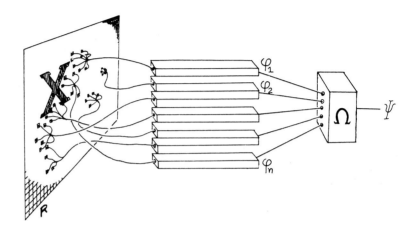

A simple neural net. Not shown are the feedback loops that enable such a net to learn. (From Minsky and Papert, Perceptrons, 1988, p. 5)

adjusting the electrical potential on each random connection. This was thought to model human learning. That human neural connections were believed to be random was consistent with a theory that most human perceptual ability was learned rather than innate.

It was discovered that such a machine could be "taught" to recognize various shapes, such as printed letters. In 1969 Marvin Minsky and Seymour Papert wrote a book called *Perceptrons,* which proved a set of theorems showing that Perceptrons could never solve the simple problem of determining whether or not a line drawing is "connected" (in a connected drawing all parts are connected to each other by lines), the so-called contiguity problem (see figure).[52] It was also shown that their ability to recognize such shapes as printed letters was quite limited: the Perceptron would fail if the letters were tilted, changed in size, or otherwise distorted. We now know that though detailed perceptual categories, such as the shape of the letters in our alphabet, are certainly learned, the properties on which such perception is based—lines, curves, concavities, loops, etc.—are at least partially prewired, and that the neural connections are anything but random.

The book had a dramatic effect, and virtually all work on Perceptrons came to a halt. The severe limitations of the Perceptron's capabilities came as a disappointment to many. Prior to the publication of *Perceptrons,* it had appeared to some practitioners that this simple technique had captured the secret of intelligence. All we had to do to make the Perceptron more intelligent was to add more associative units and more wires. Unfortunately, intelligence was not to be captured this easily.[53] After the publication of *Perceptrons*, there was an understandable hesitation in the AI field to look for any single method or even a single paradigm underlying intelligence. The limitations of GPS and the failure of the Perceptron certainly did not prove that all unified approaches to defining and replicating the methods of intelligence would fail, but enthusiasm for discovering such unifying principles waned nonetheless.

It was probably a healthy development for artificial intelligence in the early 1970s that the search for a unified theory of intelligence was put aside at least temporarily. This focused attention instead on devising a variety of approaches for a variety of problems and allowed the development of generalized theories to wait until more application-specific techniques were perfected.[54] The implication of this view is that AI is composed of a great variety of methods and approaches, that there is no single set of techniques that solves all AI problems. Complex problems are often reducible to hierarchies of simpler problems. The solutions, then, are manifest in the structure of the hierarchies and the solutions to the simplest problems found at the lowest level of each hierarchy. Such structures and solutions will differ for different classes of problems.

A related observation is that solutions to AI problems are often domain specific. In other words, the methods for solving particular AI problems need to be derived from our understanding of the particulars of that problem. Recognizing printed characters by machine, for example, needs to be concerned more with the details of letter shapes, ink and paper reflectivity, printing errors, and other peculiarities of print than with any generalized techniques of pattern recognition.[55] Similarly, recognizing human speech by machine needs to be primarily concerned with the detailed nature of human speech sounds, the syntax of natural language, and the signal-processing characteristics of the transmission channel.

Occasionally claims are made that a "generalized perception algorithm" has been devised that can recognize any type of pattern, whether it be manifested in speech, printed characters, land-terrain maps, or fingerprints.[56] On closer examination, it often turns out that such claims are absolutely correct: such algorithms do, in fact, recognize every type of pattern, only they do all these tasks very poorly. To perform any of them well, with satisfactory (and commercially acceptable) rates of accuracy, requires a great deal of knowledge deeply embedded in algorithms specific to the domain of inquiry, so much so that this aspect of the technology outweighs the generic AI techniques.

The new connectionists

A more sophisticated generation of random neural nets is now being developed with important differences from the earlier work. The limitations described in the Minsky and Papert theorems are not applicable to at least some of the work in this latest generation. The "neurons" themselves can be more sophisticated. Each neuron may be modeled by its own computer, which thus provides a high degree of parallel processing. Each neuron model can perform arbitrarily complex transformations on their inputs. Rather than having neural connections fixed at the outset, these neural models are also capable of growing new connections.[57]

In all fairness, it should be pointed out that some of the recent work differs little from that done over twenty years ago. In many of the recent connectionist systems the nets still have only one or two layers and still use simple linear neuron

Which figure is connected? These two figures from the cover of Minsky and Papert's influential *Perceptrons* (1988) illustrate the type of problem that single layer neural nets are incapable of solving, according to the book's pivotal theorem.

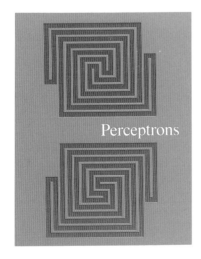

models. In my opinion, a far more promising avenue of research lies with nets built from more complex neurons organized in multiple layers and each capable of detecting abstract features of patterns (such as lines, curvatures, and concavities).

The earlier random neural nets generated excitement precisely because they appeared to provide a simple formula that could generate complex and purposeful, that is, *intelligent*, behavior. The earlier work would qualify as a unifying formula, but unfortunately it did not work very well. The more recent work—particularly that which stresses complex neuron models—appears far more promising but does not fully qualify as a unifying formula. It is more of a unifying *paradigm* in that it still requires diverse approaches to implement and organize the overall system.[58]

Still the promise is implicit that we can get more intelligence out of less. In other words, while the neuron models still require intelligent programs, the hope is that the entire neural net will exhibit a higher degree of intelligence than is explicitly programmed at the lower neuron level.

Whereas Minsky was obviously opposed to the Perceptron work and expressed concern that limited research resources were being drawn into a dead end, he has expressed cautious interest in random neural nets based on more intelligent neurons.[59] It would certainly appear that this work is consistent with Minsky's recent emphasis on the "society of mind" as a paradigm for intelligence.

Pandemonium selection

For pattern-recognition problems (such as identifying faces, printed characters, land terrains, fingerprints, blood cells, etc.), we need to break down the higher-level decisions (e.g., what letter this is) into lower level ones. If we design "demons" (algorithms) to answer the lower-level questions, we can use their answers to make a final decision. One approach is to invite the demons to a "meeting." We then ask, Is this letter an *A*? and determine how loud the demons shout. We go through all of the possibilities in the "identification set" (*B*, *C*, etc.) and pick the one that causes the demons to voice the strongest approval. Some of the low-level questions are

Nature's neural net. The human brain contains billions of neurons, each of which is capable of carrying out complex computations (using both analog and digital techniques) and communicating with potentially thousands of other neurons. (Supplied by Photo Researchers and Biophoto Associates Science Source)

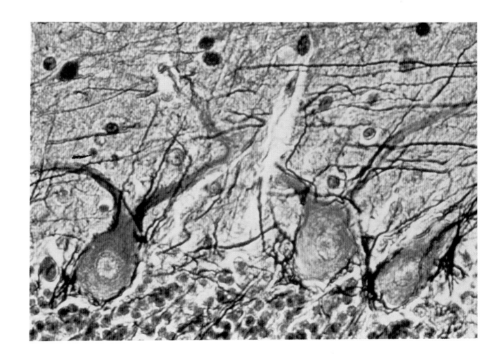

more important than others, and thus some of the demons are more influential (that is, able to shout louder) than other demons. The demons also control how loud they shout by how sure they are in answering their lower-level question.[60]

The decision tree

Another way to organize the demons is in a tree. We go to one demon and ask a question, such as Does this letter have a loop (an area of white completely enclosed by black)? If the demon says yes, we continue on to demons on the yes branch of the tree; if no, then we take the no branch. If the answer is yes, then we know the letter could be an *A* but not a *C*, and so on. We follow the branches from one demon to another until we get to a leaf, at which point we have an answer. Note that such decision trees differ from the recursively generated trees described for the recursive formula. In recursion, a tree is generated for each decision, and the topology (shape) and content of the tree will differ for different situations. For pattern-recognition tasks, the tree is generally fixed and designed by the program designer. What differs for different situations (inputs) is not the shape of the tree but the path taken through it.[61]

Both the pandemonium and decision-tree methods can work. The latter is faster (for a serial computer) in that we have only to "compute" demons that we find along our path. But it is more subject to catastrophic failure (an incorrect answer) if a demon, particularly one encountered early on, makes a mistake. With pandemonium selection, an erroneous demon can still be outvoted.

As with the recursive model, there is a question as to how sophisticated these demons should be. At one extreme we have high-level feature extraction, in which the demons answer difficult questions. Examples are Is this region concave? in the context of character recognition and Is this burst of sound the beginning of a plosive phoneme? in the context of speech recognition. At the other extreme we have template matching, in which the demons answer the simplest possible questions, such as Is this particular point black or white? Whereas I opted for the simple-minded school of thought with regard to chess (though not for all games), I feel that more complex demons are necessary for most pattern-recognition tasks. In chess we are dealing with a very orderly and artificial world that can be described with essentially perfect precision. In pattern recognition we are dealing with more complex and more variable real-world phenomena that inherently require higher levels of abstraction.

High-level demons can be broken down into hierarchies of simpler demons. It is thus possible to develop decision trees with simple demons at the terminal nodes that can detect more abstract or higher-level features at higher nodes of the tree. However, if the demons are simple, then the heart of the technology lies in the decision hierarchy itself.

Thus, as with the random neural net; pandemonium selection, decision trees, and a variety of other methods provide powerful paradigms but are not simple formulas that can be expanded into intelligent behavior through the application of computational power alone. This is in contrast to the recursive formula, in which a simple formula combined with large doses of computational brute force is successful in solving at least certain classes of intelligent problems.

Demons sitting in a decision tree.

The hierarchy of intelligence

What we often regard as intelligent behavior is in actuality many processes operating in parallel and interacting on different levels of a hierarchy.[62] If we consider carefully the process of reading and understanding printed language, it becomes clear that we are dealing with a multiplicity of talents: at the character level, pattern recognition; at the word level, the syntactic analysis of word sequences; and at higher levels, the decoding of semantics, the retrieval and updating of our knowledge base, and an understanding of "scripts" about the subject matter being written about, to name only a few of the intelligent processes involved.[63]

This leads us to a possible recursive definition of intelligence:

An intelligent process is an association of intelligent and unintelligent processes communicating and influencing each other.

This definition is self-referencing (that is, it contains the concept being defined in the definition), but it is not infinitely circular. It again employs the special type of self-reference we call recursion.

Let us examine this "association" definition of intelligence in the context of recursion. If we consider an intelligence to be an association of other intelligences, we replace one intelligence with a larger number of intelligences. We now have an association of intelligences, each of which is in turn expanded into an organization of yet more intelligences. If we keep applying the recursive definition, we end up with a vision of a great profusion of intelligences organized in a hierarchy of many levels. If there were no escape or terminal portion of the definition, we would replace one intelligence with an infinite number of intelligences—a satisfying mystical vision perhaps, but of no value in building practical theories of intelligence.

The escape from infinite recursion is the concept of unintelligent processes, the mechanisms at the lowest level. Intelligence overall results from the coherency of the entire hierarchy of increasingly sophisticated associations of intelligence.

Minsky's "society of mind"

A recent and perhaps the most comprehensive exposition of this type of theory has been offered by Minsky in writings from 1977 to the present.[64] "How can intelligence emerge from non-intelligence? . . . One can build a mind from many little parts, each mindless by itself. I'll call "Society of Mind" this scheme in which a mind is made of many smaller processes. We'll call them agents. Each agent by itself can only do some simple thing which needs no mind or thought at all. Yet where we join those agents in societies—in certain very special ways—that leads to true intelligence."[65]

How do the various minds in a society interact? The short answer is, In many different ways. Consider the varied ways we interact with each other in human society. Relationships include symmetric bonds, such as lovers and friends, as well as asymmetric ones, such as parent-child, boss-subordinate, and oppressor-victim. Methods of making decisions range from negotiation of equal or nearly equal parties and the influence of one person on another to the dictates of boss to subordinate, among the multifarious ways in which we interact and make decisions in a society.

On a larger level, communication and decision making is regulated by the rules of the society with political, cultural, and social institutions governing the roles of each member.

Within a single individual we also have many mental processes carrying on their operations in parallel. Incoming information is evaluated not by a single "department," but by many of our subminds at the same time. Some deal with fears; others with hopes, desires, and needs. Yet others deal with the practical aspects of manipulating muscles or performing pattern-recognition tasks. Through a hierarchy of negotiations at different levels, our thoughts are translated into actions. Some subminds are more powerful than others, and the methods of negotiation vary according to the level and the subject matter.[66]

Such theories as the society of mind are essentially drawing an analogy of the intelligence of one person to that of a society such as a nation with its competing factions, differing views of events, and varying methods of resolving conflicts and pooling opinions. This type of theory is consistent with the complexity of human thought, with its predictable and unpredictable sides, and with the everyday phenomenon of mixed feelings.

We can extend the concept of society beyond the individual. A human being is a society of minds representing needs, desires, and capabilities on many different levels. An actual human society then continues the process of an intelligent hierarchy on yet more levels. Some of the methods of negotiation, influence, and problem resolution in a society are not that different from those taking place within a single individual.

As we expand each intelligence into a society of intelligences, are the intelligences on the lower level less sophisticated and less capable than the intelligence represented by the entire society? I would say that it is certainly desirable that the society be more intelligent than its members. This is not always the case in human society—the intelligence of a mob is a testament to this. Yet successful human organizations are obviously capable of accomplishing intellectual tasks that their individual members could never accomplish alone. Within a single human mind a well-integrated personality is capable of synthesizing its constituent thought processes in a manner that exhibits greater intelligence at each higher level of the mental hierarchy. As examples of poor integration, many forms of mental illness are characterized by more primitive thought processes interfering with and even taking charge of the more subtle and intelligent capabilities.

Inherent in this vision of intelligence is the inference that human intelligence, though very complex, is not infinitely complex. It can ultimately be understood in terms of simpler processes. At the lowest level there are very simple processes, although the hierarchy that leads to the simple processes is anything but simple. We do not fully understand the hierarchy—indeed, we understand very little of it—but there is no reason that we cannot progressively increase our knowledge of it.

Lettvin's "society of neurons"

Another theory of human intelligence as a society of intelligences, one articulated by Jerome Lettvin of MIT, views individual neurons as small "minds" organized in a society more complex than any human society (there are tens or hundreds of billions of neurons in the human brain and only billions of human beings on the earth). When first articulated in the mid 1960s, this view differed from the conventional wisdom that neurons were just simple switches with very limited information-processing capability.[67] As Lettvin surmised, we now know that neurons are indeed quite complex and that communication between neurons does use a "language" that, though not nearly as sophisticated as human language, is far from trivial in its structure. Lettvin imagined the human mind as a hierarchy of larger and larger societies of neurons with languages, cultures, and power struggles.[68] Anyone who doubts that a single cell can be intelligent needs only consider the macrophage. These killer white blood cells are capable of conducting subtle pattern-recognition tasks to identify hostile bacteria, parasites, and other agents of disease and of carrying out elaborate tactics to destroy the enemies once identified. There is no reason to suppose that nerve cells, which are structurally more complex than macrophages, have less sophisticated capabilities.

Intelligence as an association of lesser intelligences is both a theory of natural intelligence and a paradigm for the organization of machine intelligence. As our computer systems become more complicated, one way to organize them is to develop smaller systems, each of which is relatively complete with its own structural integrity, and then define languages and processes that let these lesser "experts" interact. This type of organization is becoming increasingly popular in both applied and research AI systems.

An "intelligent cell." The macrophage hunts its pathogenic prey and is capable of a variety of tactics to destroy it, once found. Here it extends a pseudopod to ensnare a *Escherichia coli* bacterium. Magnification: 4,000 times. (Photo by Lennart Nilsson, copyright by Boehringer Ingelheim International GmbH)

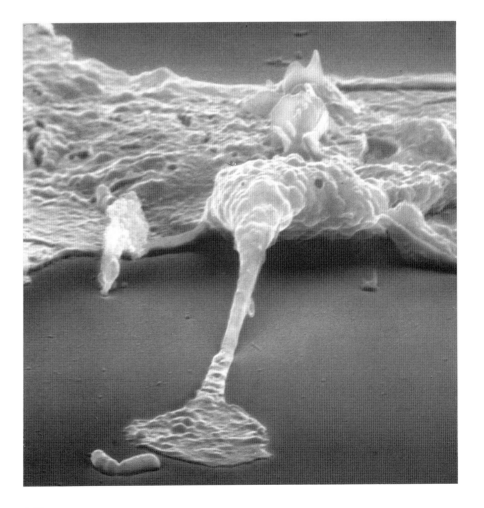

A society of human and machine intelligence

An example of an integrated "society of intelligences" is the set of expert systems already developed or being developed by Digital Equipment Corporation (DEC). One of the first practical expert systems was XCON, which uses over ten thousand rules to design the configuration and assembly process for their VAX-series computers.[69] XCON has been found to be substantially more reliable than human experts and is now routinely used on almost all orders for VAX computers. With the success of XCON, DEC is now developing expert systems for virtually all aspects of its company's operations, including computer-assisted design, manufacturing control, material-resource planning, sales strategies, financial planning, and other areas.[70] When fully operational, expert systems will be playing critical roles in every aspect of DEC's operations, communicating with each other as well as with DEC employees through an extensive computer-based network. This is expected to be one of the first human organizations operating in a real-world environment to combine a society of multiple human and machine intelligences.[71]

Progress on different levels

If we consider the diverse problems that are being attacked by AI technology, and the wide range of intelligent behavior, pattern recognition, and problem solving abilities of human intelligence, we must recognize that a variety of approaches is needed.[72] Progress in harnessing machine intelligence will likely result from *all* of the following:

• More powerful "unifying" formulas for solving classes of intelligent problems
• More powerful paradigms
• Highly detailed technologies with deeply imbedded domain-specific knowledge for interacting with real world problems
• More powerful computational (hardware) resources
• More powerful (and generally parallel) architectures

With regard to the last item, we are increasingly finding that different problems require different hardware architectures and that architecture design is becoming as important as algorithm design.

Is there a formula for intelligence?

The answer is that there are indeed formulas for both the "hardware" and the "software" of intelligence that are elegant and far reaching in their implications. These formulas provide powerful insights into the nature of problems requiring intelligence and their solutions. We must also conclude, however, that these simple models of intelligence are only the beginning, not the end, in our search for intelligence. Real-world intelligence is a combination of elegant insight with extensive knowledge and experience that can be accumulated only through painstaking and often hard-won effort.[73]

A great deal of the universe does not need any explanation. Elephants, for instance. Once molecules have learnt to compete and to create other molecules in their own image, elephants, and things resembling elephants, will in due course be found roaming through the countryside.

Peter Atkins

It is raining DNA outside. On the bank of the Oxford canal at the bottom of my garden is a large willow tree, and it is pumping downy seeds into the air. . . . The DNA content must be a small proportion of the total, so why did I say that it was raining DNA rather than cellulose? The answer is that it is the DNA that matters. The cellulose fluff, although more bulky, is just a parachute, to be discarded. The whole performance, cotton wool, catkins, tree and all, is in aid of one thing and one thing only, the spreading of DNA around the countryside. Not just any DNA, but DNA whose coded characters spell out specific instructions for building willow trees that will shed a new generation of downy seeds. Those fluffy specks are, literally, spreading instructions for making themselves. They are there because their ancestors succeeded in doing the same. It is raining instructions out there; it's raining programs; it's raining tree-growing, fluff-spreading, algorithms. That is not a metaphor, it is the plain truth. It couldn't be any plainer if it were raining floppy discs.

Richard Dawkins

One might include DNA and its support cast of "data processing" chemicals as an example of a classical unifying formula.[74] It can also be regarded as a unifying formula for intelligence, because it provides the foundation for human life, which is our primary example of intelligence. Let us briefly examine the mechanics of DNA and then compare it to some of the unifying formulas described above for machine intelligence.

The formula of life

The chemical structure of the DNA molecule was first described by J. D. Watson and F. H. C. Crick in 1953 as a double helix consisting of a pair of strands of polynucleotides with information encoded at each position by the choice of nucleotides.[75] Since then biochemists have gone on to map extensive sections (but still a small fraction) of the genetic code and to understand the detailed chemistry of the communication and control process by which DNA commands reproduction through such other complex molecules and cellular structures as messenger RNA, transfer RNA, and ribosomes. At the level of information storage, the mechanism is surprisingly simple. Supported by a twisting sugar-phosphate backbone, the DNA molecule contains up to several million rungs, each of which is coded with one letter drawn from a four-letter alphabet. The alphabet consists of the four base pairs: adenine-thymine, thymine-adenine, cytosine-guanine, and guanine-cytosine. The DNA strings in a single cell would measure up to six feet in length if stretched out, but an elaborate packing method coils it to fit into a cell only 1/2500 of an inch across. With four letters in the alphabet, each rung is coding two bits of data in a digital code. Special enzymes can copy this information by splitting each base pair and assembling two identical DNA molecules by rematching the broken base pairs. Other enzymes actually check the validity of the copy by checking the integrity of the base-pair matching. With these copying and validation steps, this chemical data-processing system makes only about one error in a billion base-pair replications. Further

149

redundancy and error-correction codes are built into the digital data itself, and so meaningful mutations resulting from base-pair replication errors are rare. Most of the errors resulting from the one-in-a-billion error rate will result in the equivalent of a "parity" error, an error that can be detected and corrected by other levels of the system, which will prevent the incorrect bit from causing any significant damage.[76]

In a process technically called translation, another series of chemicals translate this elaborate digital program into action by building proteins. It is the protein chains that give each cell its structure, behavior, and intelligence. Special enzymes unwind a region of DNA for building a particular protein. A strand of messenger RNA (mRNA) is created by copying the exposed sequence of bases. The mRNA essentially has a copy of a portion of the DNA letter sequence. The mRNA travels out of the nucleus and into the cell body. The mRNA codes are then read by

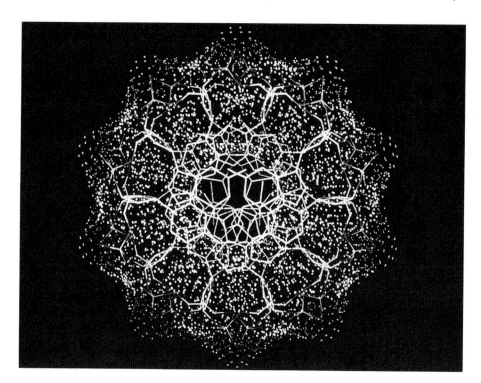

A computer view of the code of life looking down the axis of the DNA double helix. (Photo by R. Langridge of Rainbow)

a structure in the cells called a ribosome, which acts like a tape-recorder head "reading" the sequence of data encoded in the mRNA base sequence. The "letters" (bases) are grouped into words of three letters each called codons, with a codon for each of 20 possible amino acids, the basic building blocks of protein. A ribosome reads the codons from the mRNA and then, using another set of molecules called transfer RNA (tRNA), assembles a protein chain one amino acid at a time. It is now the job of the assembled proteins to carry out the functions of the cell (and by extension the organism). A molecule of hemoglobin, for example, which has the job of carrying oxygen from the lungs to body tissues, is created 500 trillion times each second. With over 500 amino acids in each molecule of hemoglobin, that comes to 15×10^{18} "read" operations every minute by the ribosomes just for the creation of hemoglobin.

In some ways the biochemical mechanism of life is remarkably complex and intricate. In other ways it is remarkably simple. Only four base pairs provide the digital storage for all of the complexity of all human life and all other life as we know it. The ribosomes build protein chains by grouping together triplets of base pairs to select sequences from only twenty amino acids. These protein chains then control everything else: the structure of bone cells, the ability of muscle cells to flex and act in concert with other muscle cells, all of the complex biochemical interactions that take place in the blood stream, and, of course, the structure and functioning of the brain.[77]

What we now understand provides an elegant and unifying picture of the *hardware* of life's data-processing mechanism. We are just beginning to unravel the *software*. We are beginning to write down the actual binary codes of some of the many thousands of genes that control our human traits. Understanding these binary codes is yet another matter. The difficulty is a matter of trying to read machine "object code" (programming instructions without symbolic mnemonics or other documenting comments) in a programming language vastly more complex than any computer language now in use. It has also become apparent that evolution has not been a very efficient programmer. The genetic code is replete with redundancies and sequences that do not compute (that is, are unable to generate proteins). For example, an apparently meaningless sequence called *Alu,* comprising 300 nucleotide pairs, occurs 300,000 times in the human genome, equivalent to over 3 percent of our genetic program.[78] Despite its sloppiness (and lack of documentation), however, it is clear that the "program" does work reasonably well.

Raymond Kurzweil

A NOR *B:* The Basis of Intelligence?

An entire computer can be constructed from the repetition of a very simple device called a logic gate. We can make an even stronger statement: any computer can be built with just one type of logic gate. Any computer (serial computers, which do one computation at a time, as well as massively parallel computers, which do many things at once) can in theory be built from a suitable number of this very simple device.

The Church-Turing thesis states that all problems solvable by a "sentient being" (a person) are reducible to a set of algorithms. Another way of expressing this thesis is that machine intelligence and human intelligence are essentially equivalent. According to this (controversial) thesis, human intelligence may at present be (quantitatively) more complex than machine intelligence—that is, use more parallelism and more sophisticated algorithms—but there is no fundamental (qualitative) difference between them. As machines gain in capacity, do more operations in parallel, and use more capable methods (better algorithms), they will be able to emulate human intellectual ability more and more closely. This article will demonstrate that the logic gate, particularly the one we call NOR, can be considered the basis of all machine intelligence. To the extent that one accepts the Church-Turing thesis, the simple NOR gate can be considered (at least in theory) the basis of human intelligence as well. Our ability to model the complex and diverse examples of intelligent behavior from building blocks of NOR gates is another example of a simple unifying formula underlying complicated phenomena. As the following derivation points out, however, this insight alone is not sufficient to build an intelligent machine.

To understand how we can build a computer from logic gates, it is first necessary to understand the nature of such devices. A

A logic gate.

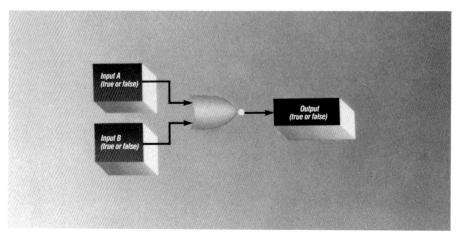

logic gate is a device with two inputs and one output. We can imagine each input and the output to be wires. Each wire can have two states: true and false. When implemented with electronics, this often corresponds to the presence or absence of electric voltage. For example, in TTL (transistor-transistor logic) circuits, a very common type, +5 volts and 0 volts represent the two states.

With two inputs and two possibilities for each input, there are four possible input combinations to a logic gate. There are actually several types of logic gates. Particular types will associate each of these four combinations of input with an output. For example, the NOR ("not or") logic gate transforms each of these four possible input combinations as shown in the table.

The NOR gate

Input A	Input B	Output
False	False	True
False	True	False
True	False	False
True	True	False

The output of NOR is true if and only if neither *A nor B* are true. Another example of a logic gate is the AND gate (see table).

The AND gate

Input A	Input B	Output
False	False	False
False	True	False
True	False	False
True	True	True

The output of AND is true only if input *A and* input *B* are true. There are 16 possible different logic gates, based on all possible mappings of the four inputs onto outputs. Some of these logic functions have commonly understood names and others do not (see table).

Outputs of the 16 possible dual input logic functions

| Function name | Inputs | | | |
	F-F	F-T	T-F	T-T
ALWAYS FALSE	F	F	F	F
AND	F	F	F	T
A AND NOT *B*	F	F	T	F
A	F	F	T	T
B AND NOT *A*	F	T	F	F
B	F	T	F	T
XOR (exclusive or)	F	T	T	F
OR	F	T	T	T
NOR	T	F	F	F
EQUIVALENCE	T	F	F	T
NOT *B*	T	F	T	F
A OR NOT *B*	T	F	T	T
NOT *A*	T	T	F	F
B OR NOT *A*	T	T	F	T
NAND (not and)	T	T	T	F
ALWAYS TRUE	T	T	T	T

Not all of the logic functions are equally useful. For example, the ALWAYS TRUE function, whose output is true regardless of its input, is relatively useless, since its output is always the same. The same can be said of the ALWAYS FALSE function.

An important observation is that we can create all 16 of the functions from the NOR function. For example, we can create NOT *A* as shown in the figure. We can call NOT *A* by a simpler name: NOT. It simply transforms a single input into its opposite. We can also create OR and AND from NOR (see figures).

If we express these equivalences in the language of logic, we have NOT *A* = *A* NOR *A*; *A* OR *B* = NOT (*A* NOR *B*); *A* AND *B* = (NOT *A*) NOR (NOT *B*).

With NOT, AND, and OR (each of which, as we have shown, can be constructed from the NOR function), we can in turn build up all 16 logic functions (see table). Since we can build up all 16 logic functions from NOT, AND, and OR and in turn can build up NOT, AND, and OR from the NOR function, it follows that we can build all logic functions from NOR.

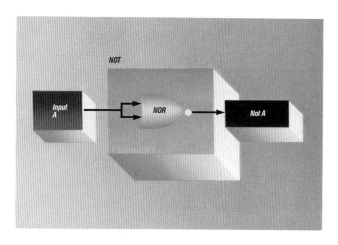

Deriving NOT from NOR.

Building logic functions from NOT, AND, and OR

Function name	Inputs				Description using NOT, AND, and OR
	F-F	F-T	T-F	T-T	
ALWAYS FALSE	F	F	F	F	*A* AND NOT *A*
AND	F	F	F	T	*A* AND *B*
A AND NOT *B*	F	F	T	F	*A* AND NOT *B*
A	F	F	T	T	*A*
B AND NOT *A*	F	T	F	F	*B* AND NOT *A*
B	F	T	F	T	*B*
XOR	F	T	T	F	(*A* OR *B*) AND NOT (*A* AND *B*)
OR	F	T	T	T	*A* OR *B*
NOR	T	F	F	F	NOT (*A* OR *B*)
EQUIVALENCE	T	F	F	T	(NOT *A* AND NOT *B*) OR (*A* AND *B*)
NOT *B*	T	F	T	F	NOT *B*
A OR NOT *B*	T	F	T	T	NOT (*B* AND NOT *A*)
NOT *A*	T	T	F	F	NOT *A*
B OR NOT *A*	T	T	F	T	NOT (*A* AND NOT *B*)
NAND	T	T	T	F	NOT (*A* AND *B*)
ALWAYS TRUE	T	T	T	T	*A* OR NOT *A*

It turns out that there is one other logic function that can also be used to build all the logic functions, the NAND gate. The reason for this is as follows. A critically important logic function is negation or the NOT function. Only four of the 16 logic functions allow us to negate an input: NOR, NAND, NOT *A*, and NOT *B*. Of these four, two, NOT *A* and NOT *B*, are unable to give us AND or OR because they each ignore one of their inputs. Thus, only NOR and NAND can give us all three vital building blocks of NOT, AND, and OR.

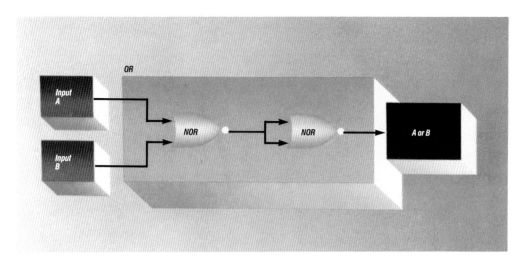

Deriving OR from NOR.

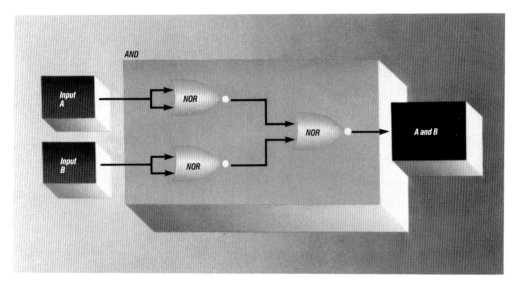

Deriving AND from NOR.

Memory

Thus, all of logic can be built up from one simple logic gate, NOR (or alternatively, NAND). There is, however, one other important type of mechanism essential for either machine or human intelligence, the ability to remember. In the same way that we can build up very complex logic functions from very simple ones, we can also build very complex and extensive memory structures from simple one-bit (on or off) memory. The question, then, is, Can we build a one-bit memory from logic gates? As it turns out, we can (see figure).

If the "set" input (which might be called MAKE TRUE) is made true, even momentarily, the output will become true and will remain true, even when the set input becomes false. This memory cell, constructed of only two NOR gates, thus remembers forever even a temporary state of true on the set input. Similarly, a momentary state of true on the "reset" (MAKE FALSE) input will cause the output to go

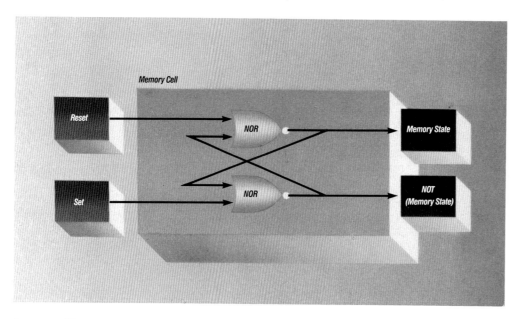

A memory cell from NOR.

permanently to false. Interestingly, we can replace the two NOR gates with NAND gates in exactly the same configuration and the memory cell will work in a similar way (we need only reverse the position of the "memory" and "not memory" output lines and negate the set and reset input lines).

We thus have all logic functions as well as memory—the two requirements for computation—built up from a very simple device, the NOR gate (or NAND gate). With enough NOR gates we can build any computer or implement any algorithm. All machine intelligence (and, if we accept the Church-Turing thesis, all natural intelligence) can be constructed from NOR.

To solve a problem, it is not enough, however, to simply have a sufficient number of NOR gates. If we dumped a million NOR gates on a table, they would not perform any function, useful or otherwise. Obviously, they need to be connected together and to the outside world in appropriate ways. The outside world can be modeled as a series of switches that present problems or situations. Even human sensory inputs, such as sight or hearing, can be modeled in this way. The input switches could be thousands or even millions of light sensors arranged in an array or auditory sensors that respond to particular frequencies. Even continuous-valued input can be modeled by using multiple input switches to represent different levels of input.

Let us define a "node" to be a particular input switch, a final output display, or an input or output of a particular logic gate. We thus have the following types of nodes:

• Inputs presenting a problem or situation
• Logic-gate inputs
• Logic-gate outputs
• Final outputs

If we assign each of these nodes a unique number, we can then describe any machine by a series of numbers that describes the connections of the nodes. For example, if our machine is described as 10, 126, 4034, 28, 1, 12, . . . , this would mean that node 1 is connected to node 10, node 2 is connected to node 126, and so on. Thus, any machine can be described as a series of numbers describing its logical connections.

There is one other type of information required before our machine can solve a problem, and that is the initial state of the memory cells. Even though the memory cells are constructed from logic gates, they have two different states: they hold either the value true or the value false at any one time. We need to set an initial value for each such cell. If we number each memory cell, we can describe these initial values as a sequence of one-bit numbers (such as 0, 1, 1, 0, etc.). If we group the memory cells into "words" of more than one cell each, then our list of initial values can use numbers other than just 0 and 1.

The first list, which described the interconnections of our inputs, logic gates, and outputs, might be called the hardware description. The second list, which described the initial states of the memory cells, can be called the software description. In designing such systems, real engineers would substitute more descriptive symbols for most of the numbers. The final result would be a string of numbers, nonetheless. At this point we notice that the hardware description of our machine looks very similar to the software description. Both are simply lists of numbers. We might substitute the word "information" or even "knowledge" for the expression "list of numbers." Seen in this light, the creation of hardware and software designs are very similar: they both involve the creation of software-like information. We might even regard them both as forms of software.

This model of intelligence as a sea of NOR gates provides us with a simple theoretical model for understanding machines that can implement an algorithm and for machine complexity. If we regard the two lists of numbers described above as descriptions of software, then we can say that we have a simple formula (i.e., NOR) for the hardware of intelligence; we will have to look elsewhere for a unifying model of the *software*.

Hooking up the NORs. Node connections described by the list 10, 126, 4034, 28, 1, 12

The Analytical Engine (1833–1871, replica), the world's first program-mable computer. Although it never ran, Babbage's entirely mechanical computer foreshadowed the modern electronic computers of a century later. (Courtesy of IBM Corporation and Neuhart Donges Neuhart Designers)

Mechanical Roots

What if these theories are really true, and we were magically shrunk and put into someone's brain while he was thinking. We would see all the pumps, pistons, gears and levers working away, and we would be able to describe their workings completely, in mechanical terms, thereby completely describing the thought processes of the brain. But that description would nowhere contain any mention of thought! It would contain nothing but descriptions of pumps, pistons, levers!

Wilhelm Leibniz (contemporary of and collaborator with Isaac Newton), commenting on theories that the brain was "just" a complicated mechanical computer

The human imagination for emulating human thought by machine did not stop at mere philosophical debate and thought experiment. From Platonic times, inventors were anxious to apply whatever technology was available to the challenge of re-creating human mental and physical processes.[1] Before the taming of the electron, this meant harnessing the state of the art in mechanical techniques.[2]

• Early Automata and Calculating Engines

Automata

As far back as the times of ancient Greece, machines that could emulate the natural movements of living creatures were built as a source of delight and apparent magic. They were also constructed by philosophers and their associates as a way of demonstrating that the natural laws were capable of producing complex behavior. This in turn fueled speculation that the same deterministic laws governed human behavior.[3]

Archytas of Tarentum (c. 400–350 B.C.), a friend of Plato, constructed a pigeon whose movements were controlled by a jet of steam or compressed air. Even more elaborate automata, including an entire mechanical orchestra, existed in China at the same time.[4]

The technology of clock and watch making produced far more elaborate automata during the European Renaissance, including human androids that were notable for their lifelike movements.[5] Famous examples of these include the mandolin-playing lady, built in 1540 by Giannello Torriano (1515–1585), and a child of 1772 that was capable of writing passages with a real pen, built by P. Jacquet-Droz (1721–1790).[6]

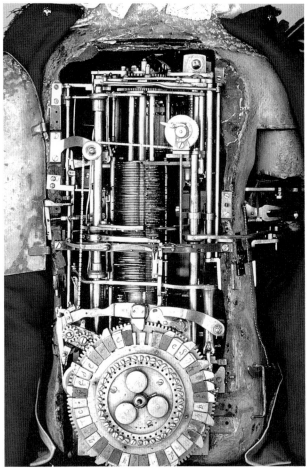

P. Jacquet Droz's 1772 automaton
L'Écrivain. (Supplied by the Muséum
d'Art et Histoire, Neuchatel,
Switzerland)

L'Écrivain's mechanical intelligence.
(Supplied by the Muséum d'Art et
Histoire, Neuchatel, Switzerland)

The abacus

Perhaps of greater significance in the development of intelligent machines were early attempts to reduce the laborious efforts required for calculation. The abacus, developed more than 5,000 years ago in the Orient, is of particular interest in its similarity to the arithmetic processing unit of a modern computer. It consists of movable beads on rods, which together implement a digital number store. Using prescribed "algorithms," a user can perform computations ranging from simple addition to evaluation of complex equations. The algorithms are performed directly by the user, not by the machine, but the methods are nonetheless mechanistic.[7]

The abacus. Algorithms are provided and implemented by the user. (Photo by Dan McCoy of Rainbow)

Napier's bones

In 1617 John Napier (1550–1617), who is generally considered the discoverer of logarithms, invented a method of performing arithmetic operations by the manipulation of rods, called "bones" because they were often constructed from bones and printed with digits. Napier's innovation was of direct significance for the subsequent development of calculating engines in which the "algorithms" were implemented in the mechanism of the device, rather than by human manipulation.[8]

Napier's Bones (1617). "I have always tried, most noble sir, according to my strength and to the measure of my ability, to do away with the difficulty and prolixity of calculations, the tedium of which deters most people from studying mathematics"—John Napier. (Courtesy of IBM Corporation and Neuhart Donges Neuhart Designers)

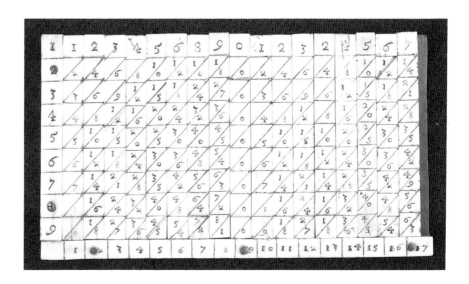

The Pascaline (1647). "I submit to the public a small machine of my own invention, by means of which you alone may, without any effort, per-form all the operations of arithmetic, and may be relieved of the work which has often times fatigued your spirit when you have worked with the counters or the pen"— Blaise Pascal. (Courtesy of IBM Corporation and Neuhart Donges Neuhart Designers)

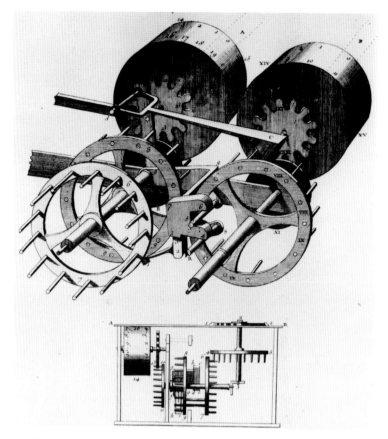

The Pascaline

Working from the age of 19 until he was 30, Blaise Pascal (1623–1662) attempted to perfect his mechanical calculator. After more than 50 models were constructed and discarded using materials ranging from wood and ivory to a variety of metals, Pascal finally perfected the world's first *automatic* calculating machine in 1642.[9] The machine was considered automatic in that the algorithm was performed by the machine and not the user, at least for addition and subtraction. The Pascaline, replicas of which are still used by many school children, uses rotating wheels inscribed with the digits and a ratchet mechanism that controls the overflow of one place position to the next. The ratchet adds one digit to (or borrows one from) the next highest place when there is a complete revolution of the lower decimal position.

The perfection of this computing machine created a stir throughout Europe and established the fame of its inventor. The device stimulated Pascal's own philosophical reflections, and in his last (unfinished) major work, *Pensées* ("Thoughts"), Pascal writes, "The arithmetical machine produces effects which approach nearer to thought than all the actions of animals. But it does nothing which would enable us to attribute will to it, as to the animals."[10]

The advent of an automatic calculating machine also led to controversy about its impact and created fear that it would lead to the unemployment of bookkeepers and clerks. The excitement generated by the Pascaline encouraged Pascal and his father to invest most of their money in an advertising campaign to market the invention. Unfortunately, Pascal was a better philosopher than businessman, and problems with reliability and service caused the venture to fail (apparently, many of the production models required repair services to be performed by Pascal himself).[11]

Blaise Pascal, philosopher, scientist, and entrepreneur. Problems with customer service caused his enterprise to fail. (Supplied by North Wind Picture Archives)

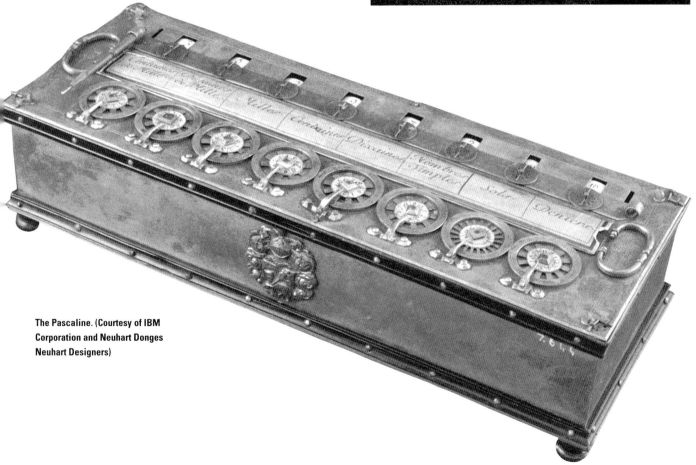

The Pascaline. (Courtesy of IBM Corporation and Neuhart Donges Neuhart Designers)

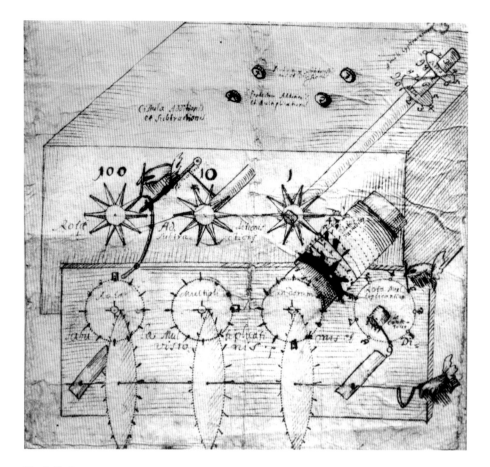

Leibniz's own sketch of the calculator mechanism. "Many applications will be found for this machine, since the elimination of all errors and of almost all labor from calculations with numbers is tremendously useful for the conduct of government and science"— Gottfried Wilhelm von Leibniz. (Courtesy of IBM Corporation and Neuhart Donges Neuhart Designers)

The Leibniz computer

Inspired by the Pascaline, Gottfried Wilhelm Leibniz attempted to add multiplication, division, and the extraction of square roots to the capabilities of a machine. After studying the largely unsuccessful attempts of Sir Samuel Morland (1625–1695), master of mechanics to King Charles II of England, Leibniz was able to perfect a multiplying machine based on repetitive additions, an algorithm still used in modern computers.[12]

Leibniz recognized that the complicated mechanisms of his calculator could be greatly simplified if the decimal system were replaced with a binary notation.[13] Leibniz's contemporaries resisted the idea, but his writings on binary arithmetic and logic were the inspiration, almost two centuries later, for George Boole (1815–1864) to develop the theory of binary logic and arithmetic, still the basis of modern computation.[14]

Leibniz's stepped-drum mechanism. (Courtesy of IBM Corporation and Neuhart Donges Neuhart Designers)

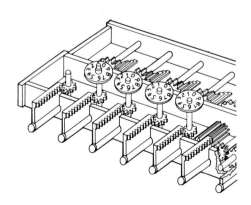

164

It is not a bad definition of man to describe him as a tool-making animal. His earliest contrivances to support uncivilized life were tools of the simplest and rudest construction. His latest achievements in the substitution of machinery, not merely for the skill of the human hand, but for the relief of the human intellect, are founded on the use of tools of a still higher order.

Charles Babbage

One evening I was sitting in the rooms of the Analytical Society at Cambridge...with a table of logarithms lying open before me. Another member, coming into the room, and seeing me half asleep called out, "Well, Babbage, what are you dreaming about?" to which I replied, "I am thinking that all these tables might be calculated by machinery."

Charles Babbage

We may say most aptly that the Analytical Engine weaves algebraic patterns just as the Jacquard loom weaves flowers and leaves.

Lady Lovelace

The Difference Engine

In 1821 Charles Babbage wrote a paper entitled "Observations on the Application of Machinery to the Computation of Mathematical Tables."[15] His ideas were well received, and he was awarded the first gold medal by the British Astronomical Society, which hoped to use the technology Babbage had proposed to compute astronomical tables.[16] With funding from the Royal Society and the British government, Babbage attempted to build his ambitious Difference Engine. He worked on the project to the point of exhaustion, almost never seeing his children. The complexity of the machine was on the edge of what was technically feasible, and it exhausted Babbage's financial resources and organizational skills. He ended up in a dispute over ownership with the British government, had problems getting the unusual precision parts fabricated, and saw his chief engineer fire all of his workmen and then quit himself. He was also beset with personal tragedies, including the deaths of his father, his wife, and two of his children.[17]

The Analytical Engine

With the Difference Engine still not completed, Babbage was inspired by what he regarded as another mental breakthrough. Rather than a machine that could only perform specific calculations, he conceived of what he called the Analytical Engine, which could be programmed to solve any possible logical or computational problem.[18] The Analytical Engine, although based entirely on the mechanical technology of the nineteenth century, was a remarkable foreshadowing of the modern computer.

It had a random-access memory consisting of 1,000 "words" of 50 decimal digits each. In today's terminology this is equivalent to about 175,000 bits. A number could be retrieved from any location, modified, and stored in any other location. It had a punched-card reader inspired by the Jacquard looms, automatic weaving machines controlled by punched metal cards, which used a similar mechanism.[19] Babbage's forward-looking design also included a printer, even though it would be another 50 years before either typesetting machines or typewriters were

The Jacquard loom punch card.
(Supplied by North Wind Picture
Archives)

Charles Babbage, a lonely and
obsessed man a century ahead of
his time. (Supplied by the Charles
Babbage Institute, University of
Minnesota)

The origin of the punch-card. The
Jacquard loom "remembered" the
pattern via a punched card that
directed the shuttles. (Supplied by
North Wind Picture Archives)

to be invented. It had an arithmetic "mill" (Babbage's term) with registers that could perform a variety of logical and arithmetic operations similar to the central processing unit of a modern computer. Most important, it had a special storage unit for the instructions, or program, with a machine language very similar to those of today's computers. One decimal field specified the type of operation, and another specified the address in memory of the operand. Babbage recognized the critical importance of the "conditional jump" instruction and provided for this capability.[20]

Lady Ada Lovelace

Though Babbage was a lonely man obsessed with his vision of a programmable computer, he developed a liaison with the beautiful Ada Lovelace, the only legitimate child of Lord Byron, the poet. She became as obsessed as Babbage with the project and contributed many of the ideas for programming the machine, including the invention of the programming loop and the subroutine.[21]

Although Babbage was too busy to communicate his ideas to the rest of the world, he allowed an associate, L. P. Menabrea (1809–1896), to describe the machine and its principles. Lovelace translated Menabrea's paper from French to English and in her added notes (which were longer than the original paper) extended Babbage's ideas. She included in these notes extensive discussions on programming techniques, sample programs, and the potential of this technology to emulate intelligent human activities.[22] She describes the speculations of Babbage and herself on the capacity of the Analytical Engine and machines like it to play chess and compose music. She finally concludes that though the computations of the Analytical Engine could not properly be regarded as "thinking," they could nonetheless perform activities that would otherwise require the extensive application of human thought.[23]

Ada Lovelace is regarded as the world's first computer programmer and has been honored by the United States Defense Department, which named its primary programming language, Ada, after her. She died a painful death from cancer at the age of 36, leaving Babbage alone again to pursue his quest.

The mechanics required for his machine were so complex that it required Babbage to make significant advances in the machinist's craft. Despite his ingenious constructions and exhaustive effort, neither the Difference Engine nor the Analytical Engine were ever completed. Near the end of his life he remarked that he had never had a happy day in his life. Only a few mourners were recorded at Babbage's funeral in 1871.[24]

It is possible that if Babbage had had more enthusiastic sponsorship during his life, his efforts may have borne fruit, but the Analytical Engine is generally regarded as having been beyond the means of nineteenth-century engineering to realize. J. W. Mauchly (1907–1980) has commented that Babbage might have succeeded had he been willing to "freeze" his design, but his continual attempts to improve it doomed the project. Babbage's concepts would be implemented seventy years later, when the first American programmable computer, the Mark I, was completed in 1944 by Howard Aiken (1900–1973) of Harvard University and IBM, using an architecture very similar to Babbage's.[25] Babbage was a man distinctly ahead of his time. Despite his failure to complete the implementation of his

machine, his concepts of a stored program, self-modifying code, addressable memory, conditional branching, and computer programming itself still form the basis of computers today.

• The Practical Path

This apparatus works unerringly as the mills of the gods, but beats them hollow as to speed.
The *Electrical Engineer* in a review of Hollerith's Tabulating Machine

What is a computer?

I would define a computer as a machine capable of automatically performing (that is, without human intervention) sequences of calculations, and of choosing between alternate sequences of calculations based on the results of earlier calculations. The description of the sequence of calculations to be performed, which includes all alternate paths and the criteria for choosing among them, is called a program. A programmable or general purpose computer is one in which we can *change* the program. A special purpose computer is one in which the program is built-in and unchangeable. A calculator is distinguished from a computer by its inability to perform more than one (or possibly a few) calculations for each human intervention and its inability to make decisions to choose from among multiple paths of computation. With the advent of today's programmable calculators, the distinction between calculators and computers has become blurred. The distinction was clear enough in the 1940s: calculators were generally capable of only a single calculation for each manually entered number. Tabulating machines, such as sorters, were capable of multiple calculations (of a certain limited kind), but were not able to alter the sequence of computations based on previous results.[26] Note that these definitions say nothing about the underlying technology, which, at least in theory, might be mechanical, electronic, optical, hydraulic, or even flesh and blood. Indeed, the era of practical computation began not with electronics but with mechanical and electromechanical automata.

The age of calculating machines

Economic expansion in the late nineteenth century, made possible by innovations in manufacturing and transportation, created a demand for the efficient and accurate calculation of numbers. The same painstaking and error-prone process of human calculation that originally motivated Babbage was threatening to block further economic and scientific progress. Demands for census data were growing more complex and an emerging interest in social research provided additional motivations for an entire generation of inventors.[27]

Yet producing a truly reliable mechanical calculator proved to be a daunting task. Many ingenious devices were created, but like the Pascaline and Leibniz's Stepped Reckoner of earlier centuries, most were plagued by severe problems of accuracy and reliability.[28] One of the inventors selling unreliable calculators was William Burroughs (1857–1898). His first production run of fifty Adding and Listing Machines quickly sold out, but all had to be recalled because of inconsistent performance.[29] Burroughs persisted, however, and after years of exhausting work,

Lady Ada Lovelace, the world's first computer programmer. (Supplied by the Charles Babbage Institute, University of Minnesota)

A Hollerith data processing installation (1918). (Photo by Howe & Arthur; supplied by IBM Archives)

the world's first dependable key-driven calculator was brought to market. The machine had begun to receive widespread acceptance by the time of the inventor's death from tuberculosis in 1898.[30] While Burroughs's machine was substantially simpler than Babbage's, and not programmable, the perfection of mechanical calculation succeeded by the early twentieth century in transforming the conduct of business, government, and scientific investigation.

The age of tabulating machines

The taking of the national census every ten years is required by the U.S. Constitution, and by 1890 the Census Bureau was in a crisis. The 1880 census had been completed only a couple of years earlier. The population had burgeoned from a new wave of European immigration, and commitments had been made to Congress to provide extensive new types of information about the population. It looked as if the 1890 census would still be in full swing when it would be time to start again in 1900.[31]

To address the problem, a competition was held. Among the many innovative ideas for more efficient manual tabulation were schemes using multicolored cards and coded paper chips. However, no manual method prevailed. The winner was Herman Hollerith (1860–1929), a young Census Bureau engineer.[32] Inspired by an off-hand suggestion of his supervisor and borrowing the idea of using holes punched in cards to represent information from Babbage's Analytical Engine and the loom of Joseph-Marie Jacquard (1754–1834), Hollerith was able to demonstrate a solution at least eight times faster than the other finalists in the competition.[33] The key to Hollerith's breakthrough was a paper card remarkably similar to modern punch cards. As with modern computer cards, one corner was clipped so that the card orientation could be quickly determined. Each card contained 288 locations for possible holes to represent up to 288 bits of information.[34] The equipment included a keypunch machine for encoding information and a card reader called a pin press. The latter consisted of 288 spring-loaded rods, each of which would make contact with a small container of mercury to complete an electric circuit if the corresponding hole was punched. The machine provided for multiple counters and logic circuits that could respond to relatively complicated patterns of information. The equipment turned out to be relatively fast and reliable: cards could be passed through at a rate exceeding one per second.[35]

The 1890 census represented the first time that electricity was used for a major data-processing project. The punched card itself survived as a mainstay of computing until quite recently. In view of the scale of the project, Hollerith's innovation was implemented with remarkably few problems. Despite a 25 percent increase in population from the 1880 census (to 63 million people) and a dramatic increase in the complexity of the analysis provided, Hollerith's electromechanical information machine did the job in only two and a half years, less than a third of the time required for the previous census.[36]

With the success of the 1890 census in hand, Hollerith set up the Tabulating Machine Company in 1896.[37] The business grew rapidly, with his tabulators being used for a variety of business applications, census analysis in numerous European countries, and even for Russia's first census in 1897.[38] For the 1900 U.S. census,

Hollerith introduced another innovation, an automatic card feed.[39] This turned out to be Hollerith's last contract with the Census Bureau. A dispute arose over rental charges, and for the 1910 census, the Census Bureau once again sponsored an internal project to develop an alternative technology. The result was improved tabulating equipment and another commercial concern called the Powers Accounting Machine Company.[40]

The two concerns became fierce competitors, a competition which lasted well into the modern era. Hollerith's company, the Tabulating Machine Company, acquired several other firms by 1911 to form the Computing-Tabulating-Recording Company (CTR).[41] In 1914, offering a salary of $25,000 and a stock option for 1,220 shares, CTR hired a forty-year-old executive named Thomas J. Watson (1874–1956), who had built a strong reputation for aggressive marketing strategies at National

Would you buy stock in this company? This IBM promotional piece from the 1930s features electric tabulating and accounting machines based on Hollerith's patents. (Supplied by IBM Archives)

The Hollerith Tabulating System
(1890). "I was traveling in the West
and I had a ticket with what I think
was called a punch photograph. . . .
the conductor . . . punched out a
description of the individual, as light
hair, dark eyes, large nose, etc. So
you see, I only made a punch
photograph of each person"—
Herman Hollerith. (Courtesy of IBM
Corporation and Neuhart Donges
Neuhart Designers)

Cash Register.[42] After only three months Watson was named president, and over the next six years the firm's revenues more than tripled from $4 million to $14 million. In 1924 Watson was named chief executive officer, and he renamed the company International Business Machines (IBM), a reflection of Watson's ambition and confidence.[43]

The Powers Accounting Machine Company also went through a series of mergers by 1927 to become Remington Rand Corporation, which merged with Sperry Gyroscope to become Sperry-Rand Corporation in 1955. Sperry-Rand was one of IBM's primary competitors when computers really took off in the late 1950s.[44]

The mechanical roots of computation

As we have seen, automatic computation did not start with the electronic computer. The architecture of the modern computer, as well as some of the major players of today's computer industry, have their roots in the mechanical and electromechanical automata of the late nineteenth century. The design and computational theory inherent in Babbage's unrealized programmable computer provided the inspiration for the first realized programmable computers, those of the twentieth century (although not the first one). Babbage's ideas were conceived in terms of mechanical technology and only realized when electromechanical and later all-electronic technology was perfected during World War II. Howard Aiken, the developer of the first American programmable computer, commented, "If Babbage had lived seventy-five years later, I would have been out of a job."[45] The computer industry itself was also conceived in an era of largely mechanical technology. It had to wait for modern electronics to provide the price-performance ratio required for it to flourish. It is interesting to note that Sperry Rand, the company to introduce the first commercial computer, as well as IBM, the modern industry's leader and one of the largest industrial corporations in the world, were both spin-offs of the U.S. Census Bureau.[46]

Electronics did not start out small:
the first transistor (1947). (Courtesy of
AT&T Archives)

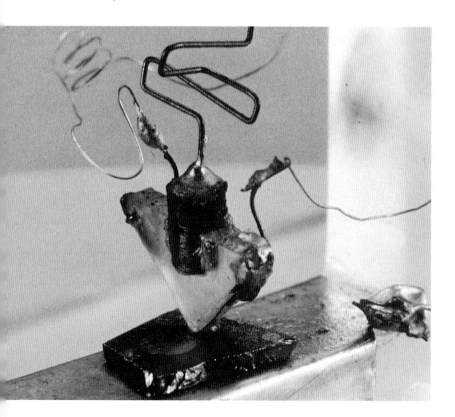

Electronic Roots

• The First Computer

The German aircraft is the best in the world. I cannot see what we could possibly calculate to improve on.
A German officer explaining to Konrad Zuse why the Third Reich would provide no further support for development of Zuse's Z series of computers

I won't say that what Turing did made us win the war, but I dare say we might have lost it without him.
I. J. Good, assistant to Turing

I remember when we first got pulses circulating rather precariously. Every time we switched on the light in the room, another pulse went in and that was the only input that in fact we had. Then later we made a half-adder work and saw our binary pulses counting up on an oscilloscope screen. Then we got the accumulator working and then the whole arithmetic unit, and so on.

We were a small, informal group in those days and whenever we had anything to celebrate, we adjourned to the local pub. It was a pub well known to generations of workers in the Cambridge University Laboratories. It was known as the Bun Shop, though I think they'd be very surprised indeed if you tried to buy a bun there.

We had a special celebration on the 6th of May, 1949, when the EDSAC did its first calculation, which was a table of squares, and a few days later it did a table of primes.

Sam Alexander has reminded me about the first substantial program I wrote which was for computing Airy functions by solving the Airy differential equation, and in connection with that, I made a discovery. I discovered debugging. Now you probably won't believe me and I don't know whether my colleagues around this table had the same experience, but it just had not occurred to me that there was going to be any difficulty about getting programs working. And it was with somewhat of a shock that I realized that for the rest of my life I was going to spend a good deal of my time finding mistakes that I had made myself in programs.
Maurice V. Wilkes

Unlike such other epoch-making inventions as the telephone or the electric lightbulb, most people cannot recite who invented the digital computer. One reason is that who invented the computer is a matter of how one defines "computer." Another is that by most accepted definitions the first functioning computers were developed independently and virtually at the same time in three different countries, one of which was at war with the other two.

It is clear, however, that during World War II the computer was an idea whose time had come. The theoretical foundations had been laid decades earlier by Babbage, Boole, Russell, and others, and many design principles had been worked out by Babbage, Burroughs, Hollerith, and their peers.[1] With the advent of reliable electromechanical relays for telecommunications and electronic (vacuum) tubes for radio communication, the building blocks for a practical computer had finally become available.

The German Z machines

It appears that the world's first fully programmable digital computer was invented in Germany during the Third Reich by a civil engineer named Konrad Zuse.[2] Zuse's original motivation was to automate what he later called those "awful calculations" required of civil engineers.[3] He saw the computational bottleneck as bringing his field of applied technology to a virtual standstill. With little theoretical background (Zuse was unaware of the work of Babbage and other developments that were influential in precomputer history) and great skill as a tinkerer, Zuse set out to ease the unenviable task of calculating the huge tables of numbers required for civil engineering projects.

His first device, the Z-1 (the names of Zuse's inventions originally used the letter *V*, but this was later changed so as not to cause confusion between his machines and the German rocket bombs), was an entirely mechanical calculator built from an erector set in his parents' living room. The Z-2 was a more sophisticated machine using electromechanical relays, and though not programmable, it was capable of solving complex simultaneous equations. The Z-2 attracted the attention of military aircraft developers, and Zuse received some level of support for further development, although this was informal and not at a high level.

Zuse's most significant invention is the Z-3, the world's first *programmable* digital computer, completed in late 1941. It had a memory of 1,408 bits organized as 64 words of 22 bits each. In addition to 1,408 relays to support the random access memory, it used another 1,200 relays for the central processing unit. As with all of the relay-based computers, it was quite slow: a multiplication took more than 3 seconds.

Besides its importance as a fully functioning program-controlled computer, it employed a number of other innovations. Zuse reinvented reverse Polish notation, a method of expressing any formula no matter how complex by successive pairs of numbers and operators, originally developed two decades earlier by the Polish mathematician Jan Lukasiewicz.[4] It also introduced floating-point numbers, a form of notation that can represent a broad range of magnitudes. Zuse went on to develop in 1945 the first high-level language, called Plankalkul, which foreshadowed modern programming languages such as C in its lack of a GOTO statement and structured methodology. The first programmer of the Z-3, and thereby the world's first programmer of an *operational* programmable computer, was August Fast, a man chosen by Zuse for both his talent as a mathematician and his blindness. Zuse apparently reasoned that being blind, Fast would not be called for military service!

A variation of Zuse's Z-3 was apparently used by the Germans in the design and manufacture of one of the Nazi's flying bombs, the *HS-293*, although

Konrad Zuse, inventor of the world's first operational programmable digital computer. (Courtesy of C. W. Publishing Company)

Zuse has denied this.[5] After the war British Intelligence classified Zuse as an "ardent Nazi," which he has not convincingly denied.[6] What is perhaps most interesting about the Zuse computers is the lack of importance given to them by the Nazi war machine. The German military gave immensely high priority to several advanced technologies, such as rocketry and atomic weapons, yet they seem to have put no priority at all on computers. While Zuse received some incidental support and his machines played a minor military role, there was little if any awareness of computation and its military significance by the German leadership. The potential for using computers for a broad range of military calculations from plotting missile trajectories and weapon designs to decrypting intelligence messages seems to have escaped Nazi attention, despite the fact that the technology was first developed under their aegis.[7] The motivation for developing the world's first programmable computer came primarily from Zuse's own intense focus as an inventor.[8]

Nor did anyone in other countries pay much attention to Zuse's work. Credit for the world's first programmable computer is often given to Howard Aiken, despite the fact that his Mark I was not operational until nearly three years after the Z-3. Since the computer industry developed largely in the United States after the war, one might expect hesitation to recognize a German, an accused Nazi, as the inventor of the programmable computer. On the other hand, allied pride did not stop the United States from harnessing German know-how in the development of the rocket, nuclear weapons, or atomic energy. Zuse, on the other hand, was largely ignored by the Americans, just as he had been by the Germans: both IBM and Remington Rand turned down offers of assistance and technology rights from Zuse after the war. He started his own company in Germany, which continued to build relay-based Z-series machines, although never in large quantities. The last, the Z-11, is still being used.[9]

Ultra

Unlike the Germans, the British did recognize the military value of automatic computation, at least for the decryption of intelligence messages. As recounted earlier, the ability of the machines built by Alan Turing and his associates to provide a constant stream of decoded German military messages was instrumental in turning the tide of war. The size of the effort, code-named Ultra, consisting of almost 10,000 men and women, is a testament to the strategic priority given to computers by the British during the war.[10] Ultra created two series of machines. Robinson, completed in early 1940 and based on electromechanical relay technology, was powerful enough to decode messages from the Germans' first-generation Enigma enciphering machine. Was Robinson, completed in early 1940, the world's first operational computer?

According to our definition, Robinson *was* a computer, although not a programmable one: it had a single hard-wired program. We can consider it, therefore, to be the world's first operational computer. When the Germans increased the complexity of their Enigma machine by adding additional coding rotors, Robinson was no longer fast enough, and the Ultra team set out to build a computer using electronic tubes, which were a hundred to a thousand times faster than the relays used in Robinson. The new machine, called Colossus, required 1500 tubes, a significant technical challenge in view of the short life span and lack of reliability of vacuum tubes.[11] Colossus worked reliably nonetheless and was able to keep up with the increasing complexity of the German messages. The Ultra group considered Colossus to be the world's first *electronic* computer, although they were unaware of the earlier efforts of John Atanasoff, an obscure American inventor.

The Americans

Working for five years, a team of Harvard and IBM scientists led by Howard Aiken, a navy commander, completed in 1944 what they thought was the world's first programmable computer.[12] Many still consider their creation, the Mark I, the first general-purpose computer, despite Zuse's having built such a machine, still awkward, but three years earlier. The Americans were obviously unaware of Zuse (as we have seen, the Germans were hardly aware of him), and they were only dimly aware of the British efforts. The American high command did know that the British were using electromechanical and electronic equipment to decode German messages, but did not have details of the process. Turing visited the United States in 1942 and apparently talked with John von Neumann (1903–1957), a mathematician, but had little impact on the American development of the computer until after the war, at which time there was extensive American-English discussion on the subject of computation.[13] The formal name for the Mark I, the IBM Automatic Sequence Controlled Calculator, is reminiscent of the original names of other pivotal inventions, such as "wireless telephone" for the radio and "horseless carriage" for the automobile.[14]

The United States Navy made Aiken available to the Mark I project, as they realized the potential value of an automatic calculator to a wide range of military problems. Realizing the potential commercial value of the machine, IBM provided virtually all of the funding, $500,000. Harvard's motivation was to transform the tabulating machine into a device that could perform scientific calculations. The resulting machine was enormous: fifty feet long and eight feet high. It was affectionately called "the monster" by one of its first programmers, Navy Captain Grace Murray Hopper.[15]

The machine used decimal notation and represented numbers with 23 digits. Input data was read from punched cards, and the output was either punched onto cards or typed. The program was read from punched paper tape and was not stored but rather executed as read.

Grace Murray Hopper has sometimes been called the Ada Lovelace of the Mark I. Just as Ada Lovelace pioneered the programming of Charles Babbage's Analytical Engine (despite the fact that the Analytical Engine never ran), Captain Hopper was the moving force in harnessing the power of the Mark I. On assignment from the Navy and having lost her husband in the war, she devoted most of her waking hours to programming the Mark I and its successors, the Mark II and Mark III. She was one of the first to recognize the value of libraries of subroutines, is credited with having written the first high-level language compiler, and led the effort to develop the Common Business-Oriented Language (COBOL), the first language not identified with a particular manufacturer.[16] She is also associated with the origin of the term "debug." One problem with the Mark I was fixed by removing a moth that had died inside one of its relays. "From then on," she recalls, "whenever

Grace Murray Hopper, the "Ada Lovelace" of the Mark I. "I got into the computer business by being ordered straight from Midshipman School to the Harvard computer, to be greeted by a large and appalling Commander known as Howard Aiken, and to be—three hours after I arrived there—instructed in the art of programming the Mark I computer by a very tall and definite young Ensign known as Richard Bloch. He frustrated me quite regularly because even then I wanted to keep my software and use it over again. I didn't want to keep reprogramming things. But unfortunately, every time I got a program running, he'd get in there at night and change the circuits in the computer and the next morning the program would not run. What's more, he was home asleep and couldn't tell me what he had done to the computer"—Grace Murray Hopper. "One reason, maybe, that information didn't travel so rapidly during World War II was that Mark I was operating for the Navy and ENIAC was operating for the Army and we were all very classified and the Army didn't talk to the Navy very much."—Grace Murray Hopper. (Supplied by the UNISYS Corporation)

The first bug. Hopper taped this dead moth to a page in the Mark I computer's log book and wrote, "First actual case of bug being found." (Supplied by Photri)

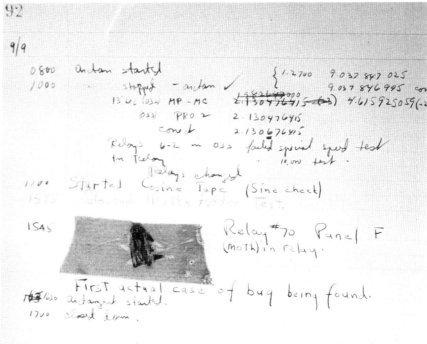

Aiken and IBM's Mark I, the first
American programmable computer
(1944). (Courtesy of IBM Corporation)

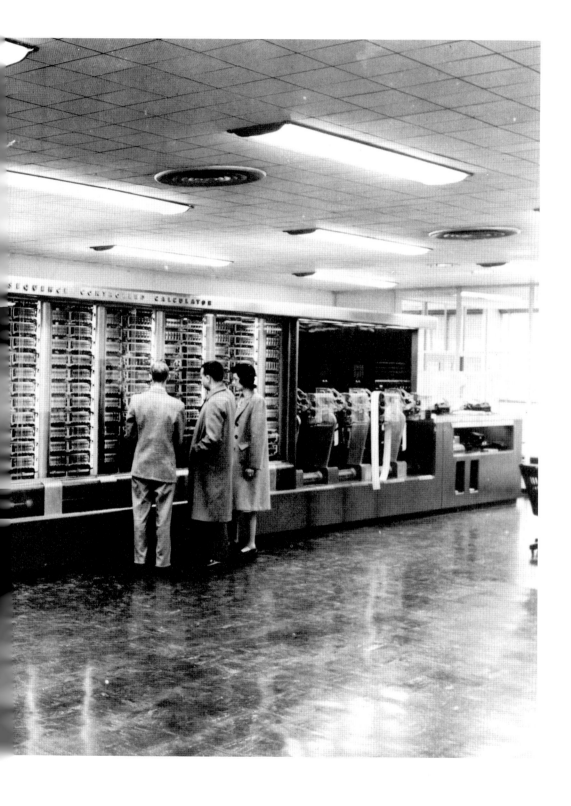

The ENIAC "super brain," the world's
first electronic programmable
computer. (Courtesy of the Computer
Museum, Boston)

anything went wrong with the computer, we said it had bugs in it. If anyone asked if we were accomplishing anything, we replied that we were 'debugging'."[17]

The Mark I generated considerable interest in many quarters, but a severe limitation soon became apparent. With its electromechanical relay technology, it was capable of only a few calculations each second. The only real solution was to build a programmable computer without moving parts, which was accomplished when two professors at the University of Pennsylvania's Moore School of Electrical Engineering, J. Presper Eckert, Jr. (b. 1902) and John W. Mauchly (1907–1980), completed work on their famous ENIAC (Electronic Numerical Integrator and Computer) in 1946. Using 18,000 vacuum tubes (12 times as many as Colossus, which had been considered ambitious only five years earlier!), it was capable of 5,000 calculations per second, making it almost a thousand times faster than Aiken's Mark I. Early press coverage included reports of the ENIAC accomplishing in a matter of hours what would have required a year for a hundred scientists. It was from these reports that terms such as "super brain" and "electronic genius" first became associated with computers. Conceived in 1943, the ENIAC was originally intended for military applications; however, it was not completed in time for service in World War II. It ultimately served a wide variety of both military and civilian purposes, including physics studies, designing atomic weapons, numerical analysis, weather prediction, and product design.[18]

ENIAC was undoubtably the world's first fully electronic general-purpose (programmable) digital computer, although this claim, as well as the validity of the patents for ENIAC, was challenged in 1973 by John V. Atanasoff (b. 1903), a professor at Iowa State College. Judge Earl Larson found in favor of Atanasoff, stating that "Eckert and Mauchly did not invent the automatic electronic digital computer, but rather derived the subject matter from Atanasoff."[19] Working with a part-time graduate student Clifford Berry, Atanasoff did indeed build an electronic computer, called ABC (for Atanasoff-Berry Computer), in 1940.[20] Although a relatively unsophisticated device with only 800 tubes, it could compute simultaneous linear equations using binary representations of the variables. It was revealed during the trial that Mauchly had visited Atanasoff while the ENIAC was being designed. The judge, however, misunderstood the distinguishing feature and primary claim of the ENIAC, which was its ability to be *programmed*—Atanasoff's ABC was not programmable. Fortunately, despite the court's finding, credit for building the first computer that was both programmable and electronic continues properly to be given to Eckert and Mauchly. This is a prime example of the challenges faced by the courts in adjudicating issues with substantial technical content, particularly at times when the issues have yet to be fully understood by the technical community.

The ENIAC represented the first time that the public became fascinated with the potential for machines to perform mental functions at "astonishing" speeds. Although many of today's computers are a thousand times faster than ENIAC (and our fastest supercomputers are almost a million times faster), the speed problem exhibited by the Mark I seemed to have been solved by ENIAC. Yet this led to yet another bottleneck. Loading a program into the ENIAC involved setting 6,000 switches and connecting hundreds of cables. The incredible tedium required to *change* the program gave birth to a new concept called the stored program and to an

John V. Astanasoff, a litigious inventor, and his ABC computer. (Courtesy of Iowa State University)

architecture that computers still use today.[21] The stored program concept is generally associated with the great Hungarian-American mathematician John von Neumann, and we still refer to a computer with a single central processing unit (the primary computational engine of a computer) accessing its program from the same memory (or same type of memory) that holds the data to be manipulated as a von Neumann machine. Although the first modern paper on the subject, published in 1946, carried only von Neumann's name, the idea was not his alone. It clearly resulted from discussions that von Neumann had with both Eckert and Mauchly. In fact, the first reference to the stored program concept can be found in Babbage's writings a century earlier, although his Analytical Engine did not employ the idea.

The idea of a stored program is deceptively simple: the program is stored in the machine's memory in the same way that data is stored.[22] In this way the program can be changed as easily as reading in new data. Indeed, the first stored program computers read in their programs from the same punched-card readers used to read in the data. A stored program is more than a convenience, it supports certain types of algorithmic methods that would otherwise be impossible, including the use of subroutines, self-modifying code, and recursion, all of which are essential capabilities for programming most AI applications. It is hard to imagine writing a chess program, for example, that does not make use of recursion.

The von Neumann machine and the stored program.

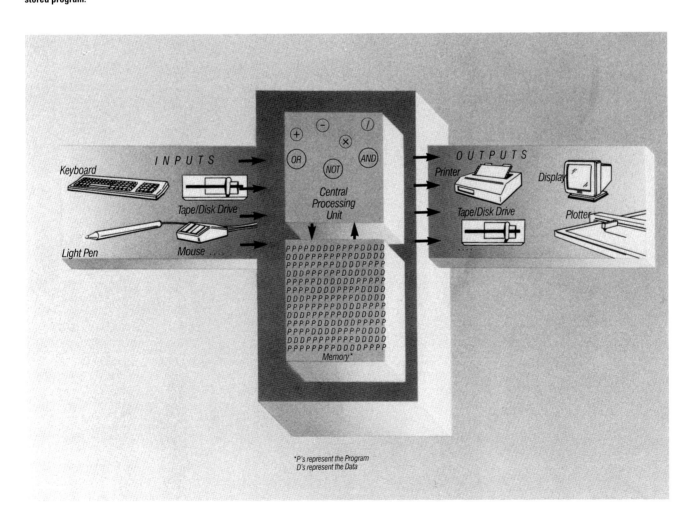

*P's represent the Program
D's represent the Data

Eckert and Mauchly set out to implement the stored-program concept in a computer to be called EDVAC (Electronic Discrete Variable Automatic Computer) while they were still at the Moore School. They subsequently left Moore to start their own company, the Eckert-Mauchly Computer Corporation, and the completion of EDVAC was left to others. This delayed the project, and it was not until 1951 that EDVAC was completed. As a result, though EDVAC was the first computer designed to incorporate stored-program capability, it was not the first to be completed. Eckert and Mauchly's new company brought out BINAC (Binary Automatic Computer) in 1949. BINAC was not the world's first stored-program computer, either. Maurice Wilkes, a professor at Oxford University, had taken a course on computers with Eckert and Mauchly while they were still teaching at the Moore School. Returning to England after completion of the course, he set out to build his own computer incorporating the stored-program concept that he had learned from Eckert and Mauchly's course. Wilkes's machine, called EDSAC (Electronic Delay Storage Automatic Computer), was completed a few months before BINAC, making *it* the world's first operational stored-program computer.[23]

The commercialization of computation

After building only two BINACs and without adequate financial backing to commercially develop a complex new technology, Eckert and Mauchly sold their firm to Remington Rand in 1950. By 1951 a computer called UNIVAC (Universal Automatic Computer), which Eckert and Mauchly had started several years earlier, was introduced as the world's first commercially marketed electronic computer. The first customer, appropriately enough, was the U.S. Census Bureau; the 1950 census was the first to be handled by a programmable computer.

Legend has it that Remington-Rand conducted a marketing study for their new product, which indicated a potential worldwide market for only 50 computers. This story is difficult to confirm, but it is true that UNIVAC was not a commercial success. IBM, however, took the introduction of UNIVAC very seriously, viewing it as a threat to their dominant position in tabulating equipment, and shortly thereafter introduced the first of their 700 series of computers (the 701, 702, 704, and 705). The 700 series became so popular that IBM was quickly positioned to dominate the still nascent industry. The 700 series led to IBM's 1400 series (1401 and 1410) and 7000 series (7030, 7040, 7070, 7074, 709T for transistors, 7090, and 7094), which became standards for large corporate customers and scientific installations. With the introduction of IBM's 360 series in 1964, a computer architecture based on 32-bit words that continues to form the basis for IBM mainframes, IBM solidified its leadership of the computer industry and became one of the largest and most profitable corporations in the world.[24]

From vacuum tube to the transistor, the beginning of miniaturization. (Photo by Dan McCoy of Rainbow)

This machine can keep track of your recipes. J. Presper Eckert explains his and John W. Mauchly's UNIVAC I to Walter Cronkite. (Supplied by the UNISYS Corporation)

Firsts in Computers

Name	Inventor	Completed	Sponsor	Hardware	Programmable	Stored program	The first . . .
Analytical Engine	Babbage	Conceived in 1835, never completed	Originally the British gov't although support was withdrawn	All mechanical	Yes (punched cards)	No	First programmable computer ever designed
Robinson	Turing et al.	Early 1940	British gov't	Relays	No	No	First operational computer (special purpose)
ABC (Atanasoff-Berry Computer)	Atanasoff	1940	Iowa State Research Council	Tubes & capacitors	No	No	First electronic computer (special purpose)
Z-3 (Zuse-3)	Zuse	Late 1941	Partially sponsored by the German Aircraft Research Institute	Relays	Yes	No	First programmable computer (actually built)
Colossus	Turing et al.	1943	British gov't	Tubes	No	No	First English electronic computer
Mark I (IBM Automatic Sequence Controlled Calculator)	Aiken	1944	IBM	Mostly relays	Yes (punched tape)	No	First American programmable computer
ENIAC (Electronic Numerical Integrator and Computer)	Eckert & Mauchly	1946	U.S. Army	Tubes	Yes (patch cords & switches)	No	First electronic programmable computer
EDSAC (Electronic Delay Storage Automatic Computer)	Wilkes (based on information from a course given by Eckert & Mauchly)	Early 1949	Cambridge University	Tubes for logic, mercury delay lines for memory	Yes	Yes	First stored-program computer
BINAC (Binary Automatic Computer)	Eckert & Mauchly	1949	Eckert-Mauchly Computer Corp.	Tubes	Yes	Yes	First American stored-program computer
EDVAC (Electronic Discrete Variable Automatic Computer)	Begun by Eckert, Mauchly, and von Neumann, completed by others at Moore School	1951	Moore School	Tubes	Yes	Yes	First stored-program computer conceived
UNIVAC I (Universal Automatic Computer	Eckert & Mauchly	1951	Remington Rand	Tubes	Yes	Yes	First commercially produced electronic computer
IBM 701	Nathaniel Rochester	1952	IBM	Tubes	Yes	Yes	First commercially successful computer

Since Leibniz there has perhaps been no man who has had a full command of all the intellectual activity of his day. . . . There are fields of scientific work . . . which have been explored from the different sides of pure mathematics, statistics, electrical engineering and neurophysiology; in which every single notion receives a separate name from each group, and in which important work has been triplicated or quadruplicated, while still other important work is delayed by the unavailability in one field of results that may have already become classical in the next field.

Norbert Wiener, *Cybernetics*

Humans are okay. I'm glad to be one. I like them in general, but they're only human. . . . Humans aren't the best ditch diggers in the world, machines are. And humans can't lift as much as a crane. . . . It doesn't make me feel bad. There were people whose thing in life was completely physical—John Henry and the steam hammer. Now we're up against the intellectual steam hammer. . . . So the intellectuals are threatened, but they needn't be. . . . The mere idea that we have to be the best in the universe is kind of far fetched. We certainly aren't physically.

There are three events of equal importance. . . . Event one is the creation of the universe. It's a fairly important event. Event two is the appearance of Life. Life is a kind of organizing principle which one might argue against if one didn't understand enough—it shouldn't or couldn't happen on thermodynamic grounds. . . . And third, there's the appearance of artificial intelligence.

Edward Fredkin

There are three great philosophical questions. What is life? What is conciousness and thinking and memory and all that? And how does the universe work? The informational viewpoint encompasses all three. . . . What I'm saying is that at the most basic level of complexity an information process runs what we think of as physics. At the much higher level of complexity life, DNA—you know, the biochemical functions—are controlled by a digital information process. Then, at another level, our thought processes are basically information processing. . . .

I find the supporting evidence for my beliefs in ten thousand different places, and to me it's just totally overwelming. It's like there's an animal I want to find. I've found his footprints. I've found his droppings. I've found the half-chewed food. I find pieces of his fur, and so on. In every case it fits one kind of animal, and it's not like any animal anyone's ever seen. People say, Where is this animal? I say, Well, he was here, he's about this big, this that and the other. And I know a thousand things about him. I don't have him in hand, but I know he's there. . . . What I see is so compelling that it can't be a creature of my imagination.

Edward Fredkin, as quoted in *Did the Universe Just Happen* by Robert Wright

Fredkin . . . is talking about an interesting characteristic of some computer programs, including many cellular automata: there is no shortcut to finding out what they will lead to. This, indeed, is a basic difference between the "analytical" approach associated with traditional mathematics, including differential equations, and the "computational" approach associated with algorithms. You can predict a future state of a system susceptible to the analytic approach without figuring out what states it will occupy between now and then, but in the case of many cellular automata, you must go through all the intermediate states to find out what the end will be like: there is no way to know the future except to watch it unfold. . . . There is no way to know the answer to some question any faster than what's going on. . . . Fredkin believes that the universe is very literally a computer and that it is being used by someone, or something, to solve a problem. It sounds like a good-news/bad-news joke: the good news is that our lives have purpose; the bad news is that their purpose is to help some remote hacker estimate pi to nine jillion decimal places.

Robert Wright, commenting on Fredkin's theory of digital physics

With at least a dozen inventors having some credible claim to having been "first" in the field of computation, we can say that the computer emerged not from a lone innovator's basement, but rather from a rich period of intellectual ferment on several continents drawing upon a diversity of intellectual traditions and fueled by the exigencies of war. And if there were a dozen fathers of the computer, there were at least a couple dozen fathers of AI.

The notion of creating a new form of intelligence on earth emerged with an intense and often uncritical passion simultaneously with the electronic hardware on which it was to be based. The similarity of computer logic to at least some aspects of our thinking process was not lost on any of the designers of the early machines. Zuse, for example, applied his Z series of computers and Plankalkul language to the problem of chess. Turing's contributions to the foundations of AI are extensive and well known. Turing's 1950 classic paper "Computing Machinery and Intelligence" lays out an agenda that would in fact occupy the next quarter century of research: game playing, natural language understanding and translation, theorem proving, and of course, the cracking of codes.[25] Even Nathaniel Rochester, the designer of IBM's first successful computer, the 701, spent several years developing early AI technology; in fact, he was one of the principals in the 1956 Dartmouth Conference, which gave artificial intelligence its name.[26]

Perhaps the odd man out was John von Neumann, who found himself unable to imagine that the cumbersome and unreliable vacuum tubes used to build the first electronic computers could ever compete with the human brain.[27] Even though the transistor had been invented when von Neumann expressed his skepticism, its applicability to computing had not yet been realized. More significant than the hardware limitations, however, was the hopelessness, according to von Neumann, of ever describing natural human actions and decision making in the precise language of mathematics. To some extent, von Neumann may have been reacting to the unrealistic expectations that had been set in the popular media of the time: magazine covers were predicting that superhuman electronic brains were just around the corner. Von Neumann did, however, show considerable interest in the idea of expressing human knowledge using the formalism of a computer language. The depth of his resistance to the idea that at least some behaviors we associate with natural intelligence might ultimately be automated is difficult to gauge; von Neumann died in 1957, shortly before he was to give a series of lectures at Yale on the likelihood of machine intelligence.[28]

Cybernetics: A new weltanschauung

The emergence of the computer, its early application to cognitive problems, the development of the theoretical foundations of computation, and related speculation on the implications of this new technology had a profound impact on fundamental tenets of what we might call the scientific worldview. In *Cybernetics,* Norbert Wiener's seminal book on information theory, Wiener describes three ways in which the world's (and his own) outlook had changed forever.[29]

Wiener, a prodigy who had studied with both Bertrand Russell and David Hilbert and received his Ph.D. from Harvard at the age of 18, had mastered an unusually broad range of intellectual fields from psychology and neurophysiology to mathematics and physics.[30] His book was intended to establish as a new science the field of cybernetics, which he defines in his subtitle as control and communication in the animal and machine. In sections that are alternately addressed to the lay reader and to his fellow mathematicians, Wiener expounds his three premises.

First is the change from *energy* to *information*. Precybernetic reality consists of particles and the energy fields that control them. Accordingly, the old model of life was concerned primarily with the conversion of energy in its various biochemical and physical forms.[31] If the living cell was a heat engine in the early twentieth century, it had now become a small computer. The new cybernetic model treats information as the fundamental reality in living things as well as in intelligent things, living or otherwise. In this new view, the most important transactions taking place in a living cell are the information-processing transactions inherent in the creation, copying, and manipulation of the amino acid strings we call proteins. Energy is required for the transmission and manipulation of information in both animal and machine, but this is regarded as incidental.

In recent times, with information-handling circuits becoming smaller and using ever smaller amounts of energy, energy has indeed become incidental to the process. The primary issue today in measuring information-handling systems is the amount and speed of their data processing capabilities. Edward Fredkin has recently shown that though energy is needed for information storage and retrieval, we can arbitrarily reduce the energy required to perform any particular example of information processing, and there is no lower limit to the amount of energy required.[32] In theory, at least, the energy required to perform computation can become arbitrarily close to zero. Fredkin's argument is significant in establishing that information processing is fundamentally different from energy processing. Even without Fredkin's theoretical argument, the energy required for computation is not a significant issue today, although it was a bit of an issue in Wiener's day.[33] The lights in Philadelphia were reported to have dimmed when ENIAC, with its 18,000 vacuum tubes, was turned on, although this story is probably exaggerated.

The decoupling of information and energy is also important from an economic point of view. The value of many products today is becoming increasingly dominated by computation. As computation itself becomes less dependent on both raw materials and energy, we are moving from an economy based on material and energy resources to one based on information and knowledge.[34]

A second aspect of what Wiener saw as an epochal change in scientific outlook is characterized by the trend away from *analog* toward *digital*.[35] Wiener argues that computation ultimately needed to be "numerical . . . rather than on the basis of measurement, as in the Bush Differential Analyzer." When computing first emerged, there was a controversy between analog and digital computing, with the Differential Analyzer of Vannevar Bush (1890–1974), President Roosevelt's science advisor, as a popular example of the former.[36] In an analog computer, mathematical operations are performed by adding, subtracting, or even multiplying electrical quantities and then measuring the amount of voltage or current after the operations are performed. A very simple example is the common thermostat. Through the use of feedback loops, fairly complex formulas can be represented, although accuracy is limited by the resolution of the analog components.[37] In a digital computer or

Vannevar Bush and his differential analyzer, an analog computer. Bush's mechanical invention, built in 1930 at MIT, was used to calculate artillery trajectories during World War II. Although Bush later built a more modern version using electrical switches, analog computation was rendered largely obsolete by the digital computer. (Courtesy of the MIT Museum)

process, numbers are represented not by amounts of voltage or current but rather by assembling numbers from multiple bits, where each bit is either on (generally representing 1) or off (generally representing 0). To many observers at the time, it was not clear which type of computing device would become dominant. Today we generally do not find the need to use the word "digital" before the word "computer," since analog computers are no longer common, although in Wiener's time, this was a necessary modifier. Wiener saw the limitations of analog computing in terms of both accuracy and the complexity of the algorithms that could be implemented. With a digital computer there is no theoretical limit on either accuracy or computational complexity.[38]

The trend from analog to digital, which was just getting started in Wiener's day, continues to revolutionize a growing number of technologies and industries. The compact digital disk and digital audio tape are revolutionizing the recording of music. Digital technology is replacing the piano and other acoustic and analog musical instruments. A new generation of aircraft is being controlled by highly accurate digital control mechanisms replacing analog and mechanical methods. Phones and copiers are becoming digital. There are many other examples.[39]

However, the question of whether the ultimate nature of reality is analog or digital continues to be an important philosophical issue. As we delve deeper and deeper into both natural and artificial processes, we find the nature of the process often alternates between analog and digital representations of information. Consider, for example, three processes related to listening to a compact-disk recording: the reproduction of the sound from the compact disk recording, the musical understanding of the audio signal by the listener, and the nature of the data structures in music itself.[40]

First consider the reproduction process. The music is communicated to the listener by vibrations of the air, which are clearly an analog phenomenon. The electrical signals sent to the loudspeaker are also analog. The circuits interpreting the contents of the compact disk are, however, digital circuits that are computing the analog values to be played as sound. The digital values computed by the digital circuits are converted into analog electrical signals by a device called a digital-to-analog converter. Thus, the sound exists in a digital representation prior to it being converted to analog electrical signals to be amplified, which is why we consider compact disk technology to be a digital technology.[41]

Let us now look at these digital circuits. As in many modern electronic products, these circuits are packaged into tiny integrated circuits containing thousands or tens of thousands of transistors each. It is interesting to note that while the circuits are digital, the transistors that comprise them are inherently *analog* devices. The designers of the transistors themselves do not consider the transistor to be a digital device but rather are very aware of its inherently analog nature. The transistor is analog because it acts as a small electrical amplifier and deals with variable (continuous-valued) amounts of current.[42] They are "tricked" into acting digital (with values of on or off) by thresholding (comparing values to a constant) their otherwise analog (continuous-valued) characteristics. But a transistor cannot model a digital device perfectly; it will compute the wrong digital value some small fraction of the time. This is not a problem in practice. Using the very information theory created by Wiener and an associate of his, Claude Elwood Shannon, digital circuit designers can make the likelihood that the analog transistor will malfunction in its digital role so low that they can essentially ignore this possibility and thus consider the transistor to be a reliable digital element.[43]

On a deeper level we can understand the continuous levels of current within one transistor to be ultimately discrete: they are made up of a very large number of individual electrons with individual quantum states. So now we are back to a digital view of things. But when we consider the Heisenberg uncertainty principle, which tells us that the electrons have no precise locations but only probability clouds of possible locations, we are back to a fuzzy (analog) model of the world.

Analog and digital representations of information.

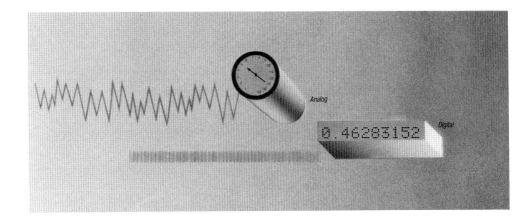

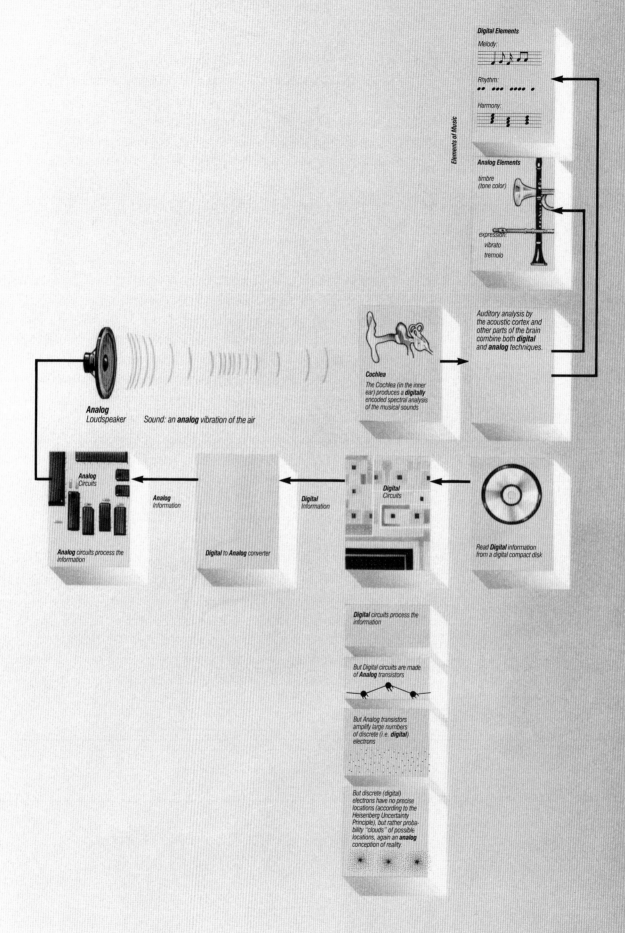

Elements of Music

Digital Elements

Melody:

Rhythm:

Harmony:

Analog Elements

timbre
(tone color)

expression:
vibrato
tremolo

Auditory analysis by
the acoustic cortex and
other parts of the brain
combine both **digital**
and **analog** techniques.

Cochlea
The Cochlea (in the inner
ear) produces a **digitally**
encoded spectral analysis
of the musical sounds

Analog
Loudspeaker   Sound: an **analog** vibration of the air

Analog
Circuits

Analog
Information

Digital
Information

Digital
Circuits

Read **Digital** information
from a digital compact disk

Analog circuits process the
information

Digital to **Analog** converter

Digital circuits process the
information

But Digital circuits are made
of **Analog** transistors

But Analog transistors
amplify large numbers
of discrete (i.e. **digital**)
electrons

But discrete (digital)
electrons have no precise
locations (according to the
Heisenberg Uncertainty
Principle), but rather probability "clouds" of possible
locations, again an **analog**
conception of reality.

As we approach finer and finer models of the world, physics flips several times between the digital and analog conceptions of reality. Consider now the path of the music sounds going toward the listener. The analog sound waves vibrate the ear drum and ultimately enter the cochlea, a natural electronic circuit that acts as a spectrum (pitch) analyzer. The cochlea breaks up the sound waves into distinct frequency bands and emits a digitally encoded representation of the time-varying spectrum of the sound. This digital representation enters the acoustic cortex of the brain, where processing takes place by techniques that are both analog and digital.[44]

Finally, consider the nature of music itself with its elements of melody, rhythm, harmony, expression, and timbre. The first three elements, which are the elements represented by musical notation, are clearly digital in nature. The availability of music notation processors, which are to music notation what word processors are to written language, are a clear testament to the inherently digital nature of these three musical elements. Melodic, rhythmic, and harmonic structures are modeled in music theory by the mathematics of digital logic rather than the mathematics of analog calculus. Expression and timbre, on the other hand, though they certainly can be represented using digital means, are nonetheless analog in nature.[45]

It is clear that we use both digital and analog approaches in understanding the world around us. As we view phenomena at different levels of specificity and detail, we find their nature changes repeatedly. The ultimate nature of reality is still being debated. Edward Fredkin has recently proposed what he calls a new theory of physics stating that the ultimate reality of the world is software (that is, information). According to Fredkin, we should not think of ultimate reality as particles and forces but rather as bits of data modified according to computational rules. If, in fact, particles are quantized in terms of their locations and other properties, then the views of the world as made up of particles and as made up of data are essentially equivalent. Though Fredkin's view has startled contemporary theoreticians, it is just another way of postulating a fully quantized or digital world. The alternative analog view would state that the position or at least one of the properties of a particle is not quantized but is either continuous or uncertain.

Regardless of the ultimate nature of the world, Wiener's prediction of a digital conception of nature was both profound and prophetic. From a technological and economic point of view, the digital approach continues to replace the analog, transforming whole industries in the process. The digital outlook has also permeated our philosophical and scientific views of the world.

An additional comment on the issue of digital versus analog concerns another contemporary controversy. Some observers have criticized digital computing as a means of replicating human cognition because of its all or nothing nature, which refers to the fact that digital bits are either on or off with no states in between. This, according to these observers, contrasts with the analog processes in the human brain, which can deal with uncertain information and are able to balance decisions based on "soft" inputs. Thus, they say, analog methods that can deal with gradations on a continuous scale will be needed to successfully emulate the brain.

My reaction to this is that the argument is based on a misconception, but I nonetheless agree with the conclusion that we will see a return to analog computing, alongside digital techniques, particularly for pattern-recognition tasks. The argument that digital techniques are all or nothing is clearly misleading. By building numbers (including fractional parts) from *multiple* bits, digital techniques can also represent gradations, and with a greater degree of continuity and precision than analog techniques—indeed, with any degree of precision desired. New knowledge-engineering techniques that use a method called fuzzy logic can apply digital computing to decision making in a way that utilizes imprecise and relative knowledge in a methodologically sound manner. Often the criticism of digital computing is really aimed at the type of "hard" antecedent-consequent type of logic employed in the first generation of expert systems. Overcoming the limitations of this type of logic does not require resorting to analog techniques.

There is, however, a good reason that we are likely to see a return to hybrid analog-digital computing designs. Analog computing is substantially less expensive in terms of the number of components required for certain arithmetic operations. Adding or even multiplying two quantities in an analog computer requires only a few transistors, whereas a digital approach can require hundreds of components. With integrated-circuit technology providing hundreds of thousands or even millions of components on a single chip, this difference is usually not significant and the greater precision of digital computing generally wins out. But consider the trend toward massive parallel processing, in which a system performs many computations simultaneously rather than just one at a time, as is the case in the classical von Neumann computer architecture. For certain types of problems, such as visual image analysis, it would be desirable to be able to perform millions of computations at the same time (computing the same transformations on every pixel (point) of a high resolution image, for example). Often these calculations do not require a high degree of accuracy, so performing them with analog techniques would be very cost effective. Doing a million computations simultaneously with analog methods would be practical with today's semiconductor technology but still prohibitively expensive with digital techniques. Evolution apparently found the same engineering trade-off when it designed the human brain.

The third major theme of Wiener's treatise concerns the nature of time. He argues that we have gone from a reversible or Newtonian concept of time to an irreversible or Bergsonian notion of time. Wiener regards Newtonian time as reversible because if we run a Newtonian world backward in time, it will continue to follow Newton's laws. The directionality of time has no significance in Newtonian physics. Wiener used Bergson, a biologist who analyzed the cause and effect relationships in biology and evolution, as a symbol for the irreversibility of time in any world in which information processing is important.

Computing is generally not time reversible, and the reason for this is somewhat surprising. There are two types of computing transformations, one in which information is preserved and one in which information is destroyed. The former type is reversible. If information is preserved, we can reverse the transformation and restore the information to the format it had prior to the transformation. If information is destroyed, however, then that process is not reversible, since the information needed to restore a state no longer exists. Consider, for example, a program that writes zeros throughout memory and ultimately destroys (most of)

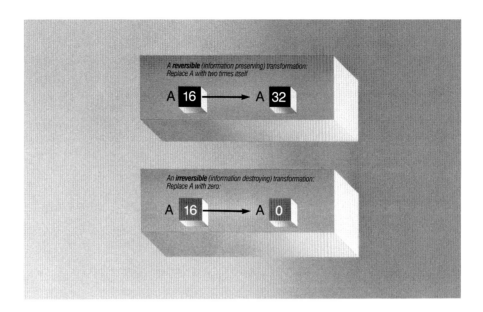

*A **reversible** (information preserving) transformation:*
Replace A with two times itself

A 16 ⟶ A 32

*An **irreversible** (information destroying) transformation:*
Replace A with zero:

A 16 ⟶ A 0

Two types of computing transformations: the preserver and the destroyer.

itself. We cannot conceive of a way to reverse this process, since the original contents of memory are no longer anywhere to be retrieved. This is surprising because we ordinarily think of computation as a process that *creates* new information from old. After all, we run a computer process to obtain answers to problems, that is, to create new information, not to destroy old information. The irreversibility of computation is often cited as a reason that computation is useful: it transforms information in a unidirectional "purposeful" manner. Yet the derivation of the proof that computation is irreversible is based on the ability of computation to destroy information, not to create it. Another view, however, is that the value of computation is precisely its ability to destroy information *selectively*. For example, in a pattern-recognition task such as recognizing images or speech sounds, preserving the invariant information-bearing features of a pattern while "destroying" the enormous amount of data in the original image or sounds is essential to the process. In fact, intelligence is often a process of selecting relevant information carefully from a much larger amount of unprocessed data. This is essentially a process of skillful and purposeful destruction of information.

Wiener points out that a model of time that is irreversible is essential to the concepts of computation, communication, and intelligence. One entertaining example cited by Wiener is the impossibility of two intelligent entities attempting to communicate when they are "traveling" in different directions in time. Neither one will perceive the other as either responsive or intelligent.

Energy to information, analog to digital, and reversible time to irreversible time are all facets of the same revolution in worldview known as computation. It was a revolution both for the world at large and for Wiener himself. It is interesting to note that virtually all of the mathematics in Wiener's book is not that of the logician and computationalist but rather the calculus of the Newtonian physicist, which comprises Wiener's original scientific tradition.

There are other significant insights in Wiener's classic book. He gives five principles that should, in his opinion, govern the design of computing machinery; a computer should

- be digital rather than analog,
- be electronic rather than electromechanical,
- use binary rather than decimal notation,
- be programmable,
- contain a dynamic (erasable) random access memory.

Wiener says in his Introduction that he had written a letter to Vannevar Bush in 1940 suggesting these principles and commenting on their importance to military requirements. Bush, being firmly in the analog camp, apparently did not respond.

Wiener proposed using computing machinery to provide effective prostheses for the sensory impaired. By converting visual information into an appropriate auditory modality for the blind, or alternatively converting auditory information into a visual display for the deaf, electronic technology could help overcome the primary handicap associated with these disabilities. It would be several decades before computers would begin to master these tasks. Wiener ends the 1948 version of *Cybernetics* with a description of a recursive strategy for building a computer chess machine. He predicts that such a machine would be capable of playing at a level that would be "not so manifestly bad as to be ridiculous."

A theme that is echoed throughout this book, as well as in other writings of Wiener's, is the need for collaboration among multiple disciplines if the difficult challenge of a machine's mastering cognitive problems is to be addressed. He articulates a need to reverse the trend toward increasingly narrow specialization in the sciences and predicts that solving the major technology problems of the second half of the twentieth century would require knowledge and expertise to be drawn and integrated from diverse disciplines. The greatest difficulty in achieving this type of cooperation, Wiener feels, is the fact that experts from different fields all use different terminologies often to describe the same phenomena. Though Wiener's prediction was largely overlooked for decades, AI researchers just now seem to be coming to the realization that further progress in creating machine intelligence requires exactly this sort of interdisciplinary collaboration.

The movement takes shape

The 1940s saw the invention of the electronic programmable digital computer, major developments in computational theory, and the emergence of the idea that with the right software these new machines could simulate the human brain.[46] After all, in some ways the new machines were substantially superior to human cognition, solving in minutes what mere human mathematicians labored on for months. With several important treatises by Turing (including his 1950 paper "Computing Machinery and Intelligence," in which Turing proposes his imitation game, which became known as the Turing test), Wiener's *Cybernetics*, a 1943 paper on neural nets by Warren McCulloch and Warren Pitts, a proposal by Shannon in 1950 for a chess program, and several other influential papers, the AI agenda had been set.[47]

In the 1950s concrete progress began to be made. Initial progress came so rapidly that some of the early pioneers felt that mastering the functionality of the human brain might not be so difficult after all. After developing IPL-II (Information

Who's in charge here? This cartoon, by early computer pioneer Claude Shannon, illustrates the potential advantage of human over machine: (1) human player loses; (2) vexed human reprograms machine; (3) human wins. (From *A Chess-Playing Machine*, copyright 1950 by *Scientific American*, all rights reserved)

Processing Language II), the first AI language, in 1955, Allen Newell, J. C. Shaw, and Herbert Simon created a program in 1956 called the Logic Theorist (LT), which used recursive search techniques to solve problems in mathematics.[48] It was able to find proofs for many of the theorems in Whitehead and Russell's *Principia Mathematica*, including at least one completely original proof for an important theorem that had never been previously published.[49] In 1957 Newell, Shaw, and Simon created a more sophisticated problem solver called the General Problem Solver (GPS).[50] As described earlier, it used means-ends analysis, a variation of LT's recursive technique, to solve problems in a variety of domains. These early successes led Simon and Newell to say in a 1958 paper entitled "Heuristic Problem Solving: The Next Advance in Operations Research," "There are now in the world machines that think, that learn and that create. Moreover, their ability to do these things is going to increase rapidly until—in a visible future—the range of problems they can handle will be coextensive with the range to which the human mind has been applied."[51] The paper goes on to predict that within ten years (that is, by 1968) a digital computer will be the world chess champion. Such unbridled enthusiasm was to earn the field considerable criticism and critics.[52] While the chess prediction turned out to be premature, a program completed in 1959 by Arthur Samuel was able to defeat some of the best players of the time in the somewhat simpler game of checkers.[53]

In 1956 the first conference on AI was held. Organized by John McCarthy, it included a number of the field's future academic leaders, including Marvin Minsky and Arthur Samuel, as well as Newell and Simon. Also participating were several computer pioneers, including Oliver Selfridge, Claude Shannon, and Nathaniel Rochester.[54] The conference gained its notoriety from its one identifiable accomplishment, which was to give the field its name, artificial intelligence. McCarthy, who is credited with the name, is not sure if he really made it up or just overheard it in a conversation, but he does take credit for having promoted it. Some participants argued against the name: Shannon felt it was too unscientific; Samuel criticized the word "artificial" with the comment "It sounds like there is nothing real about this work." Perhaps just because the phrase is so startling and unsettling, it has outlasted many others, including Wiener's "cybernetics."[55]

Other concrete accomplishments of the conference are hard to discern, although Minsky did write a first draft of his influential "Steps toward Artificial Intelligence," which was rewritten many times (as is Minsky's style) and finally

Thinking about thinking. Marvin Minsky, cofounder of MIT's Artificial Intelligence Lab, in the 1970s. Considered by many to be the father of AI, his work in the field has challenged and inspired a generation of young computer scientists and philosophers. (Photo by Ivan Masser of Black Star, courtesy of the MIT Museum)

Patrick Winston, director of MIT's Artificial Intelligence Lab. His research involves work on learning by analogy and commonsense problem solving. (Photo by Lou Jones)

The hard problems were easy. AI pioneers Herb Simon and Allen Newell. Their Logic Theorist (LT), programmed with J. C. Shaw in 1956, and General Problem Solver (GPS), programmed in 1957, discovered some original proofs for theorems in *Principia Mathematica,* Whitehead and Russell's seminal work on the foundations of mathematics. There were also some "easy" problems that GPS was unable to solve. (Photo by Dan McCoy of Rainbow) published in 1963.[56] McCarthy refined his ideas for a language that would combine list (treelike) structures with recursion, which was subsequently introduced in 1959 as LISP (List-processing language).[57] It quickly became the standard for AI work and has remained the principal AI language through several major revisions. Only recently with AI having entered the commercial arena have other languages such as C begun to compete with LISP, primarily on the basis of efficiency. Probably the major contribution of the conference was to put a number of the leading thinkers in the field in touch with one another. Progress, ideas, and a great deal of enthusiasm were shared, although McCarthy left the conference disappointed that most of its specific goals had not been met. He went on to found the two leading university AI laboratories: one at MIT with Marvin Minsky in 1958 and one at Stanford in 1963.

By the end of the 1960s the full AI agenda was represented by specific projects. A number of the more significant efforts of the decade are described in *Semantic Information Processing*, edited by Marvin Minsky and published in 1968. Included was Daniel G. Bobrow's Ph.D. project entitled Student, which could set up and solve algebra problems from natural English language stories.[58] Student reportedly rivaled the ability of typical high school students in solving story problems. The same performance level was claimed for a program created by Thomas G. Evans that could solve IQ test geometric-analogy problems.[59]

Computer chess programs continued to improve in the 1960s, although not nearly up to Simon's expectations. A program that could achieve respectable tournament ratings was created in 1966 by Richard D. Greenblatt at MIT.[60]

A new area for AI, expert systems, also got its start in the 1960s. With leadership from Edward A. Feigenbaum, now the director of the Stanford AI Laboratory, a group started work on DENDRAL, a program based on a knowledge base describing chemical compounds. It is considered the world's first expert system.[61]

The 1960s also saw the creation of ELIZA, a natural language program written by MIT professor Joseph Weizenbaum in 1966, which simulates a nondirective (i.e., Rogerian) therapist. ELIZA has continued for over two decades to receive a high level of attention, including extensive criticism for its inability to react intelligently in a variety of situations, from some AI critics, most notably Hubert Dreyfus.[62] Actually, ELIZA was never representative of the state of the art in natural-language understanding, even at the time it was created. It was a demonstration of how successful one could be in creating an *apparently* intelligent interactive system with relatively simple rules. ELIZA is a good example of the principle of achieving complex behavior from a simple system in a complex environment. People using ELIZA

Thomas Evans's program solves analogy problems of the sort, *A* is to *B* as *C* is to____? (From Thomas G. Evans, "A Program for the Solution of a Class of Geometric-Analogy Intelligence-Test Questions," in Minsky, ed., *Semantic Information Processing,* 1968, p. 271)

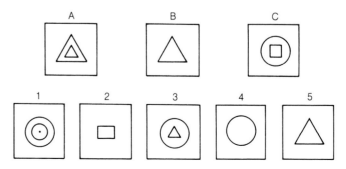

Daniel Bobrow's Student solves algebra story problems. Note the stages of analysis from the original statement to the equations to be solved. (From Daniel G. Bobrow, "Natural Language Input for a Computer Problem-Solving System," in Minsky, ed., *Semantic Information Processing,* 1968, pp. 212–213)

(THE PROBLEM TO BE SOLVED IS)
(IF THE NUMBER OF CUSTOMERS TOM GETS IS TWICE THE SQUARE OF 20 PER CENT OF THE NUMBER OF ADVERTISEMENTS HE RUNS, AND THE NUMBER OF ADVERTISEMENTS HE RUNS IS 45, WHAT IS THE NUMBER OF CUSTOMERS TOM GETS Q.)

(WITH MANDATORY SUBSTITUTIONS THE PROBLEM IS)
(IF THE NUMBER (OF CUSTOMERS TOM GETS IS 2 TIMES THE SQUARE 20 PERCENT OF THE NUMBER OF ADVERTISEMENTS HE RUNS, AND THE NUMBER OF ADVERTISEMENTS HE RUNS IS 45, WHAT IS THE NUMBER OF CUSTOMERS TOM GETS Q.)

(WITH WORDS TAGGED BY FUNCTION THE PROBLEM IS)
(IF THE NUMBER (OF / OP) CUSTOMERS TOM (GETS / VERB) IS 2 (TIMES / OP 1) THE (SQUARE / OP 1) 20 (PERCENT / OP 2) (OF / OP) THE NUMBER (OF / OP) ADVERTISEMENTS (HE / PRO) RUNS, AND THE NUMBER (OF / OP) ADVERTISEMENTS (HE / PRO) RUNS IS 45, (WHAT / QWORD) IS THE NUMBER (OF / OP) CUSTOMERS TOM (GETS / VERB) (QMARK / DLM))

(THE SIMPLE SENTENCES ARE)

(THE NUMBER (OF / OP) CUSTOMERS TOM (GETS / VERB) IS 2 (TIMES / OP 1) THE (SQUARE / OP 1) 20 (PERCENT / OP 2) (OF / OP) THE NUMBER (OF / OP) ADVERTISEMENTS (HE / PRO) RUNS (PERIOD / DLM)

(THE NUMBER (OF / OP) ADVERTISEMENTS (HE / PRO) RUNS IS 45 (PERIOD / DLM))

((WHAT / QWORD) IS THE NUMBER (OF / OP) CUSTOMERS TOM (GETS / VERB) (QMARK / DLM))

(THE EQUATIONS TO BE SOLVED ARE)

(EQUAL G02515 (NUMBER OF CUSTOMERS TOM (GETS / VERB)))

(EQUAL (NUMBER OF ADVERTISEMENTS (HE / PRO) RUNS) 45)

(EQUAL (NUMBER OF CUSTOMERS TOM (GETS / VERB)) (TIMES 2 (EXPT (TIMES .2000 (NUMBER OF ADVERTISEMENTS (HE / PRO) RUNS)) 2)))

(THE NUMBER OF CUSTOMERS TOM GETS IS 162)

(THE PROBLEM TO BE SOLVED IS)
(THE SUM OF LOIS'S SHARE OF SOME MONEY AND BOB'S SHARE IS $4.500. LOIS'S SHARE IS TWICE BOB'S. FIND BOB'S AND LOIS'S SHARE.)

(WITH MANDATORY SUBSTITUTIONS THE PROBLEM IS)
(SUM LOIS'S SHARE OF SOME MONEY AND BOB'S SHARE IS 4.500 DOLLARS. LOIS'S SHARE IS 2 TIMES BOB'S. FIND BOB'S AND LOIS'S SHARE.)

(WITH WORDS TAGGED BY FUNCTION THE PROBLEM IS)
((SUM / OP) LOIS'S SHARE (OF / OP) SOME MONEY AND BOB'S SHARE IS 4.500 DOLLARS (PERIOD / DLM) LOIS SHARE IS 2 (TIMES / OP 1) BOB'S (PERIOD / DLM) (FIND / QWORD) BOB'S AND LOIS'S SHARE (PERIOD / DLM))

(THE SIMPLE SENTENCES ARE)

((SUM / OP) LOIS'S SHARE (OF / OP) SOME MONEY AND BOB'S SHARE IS 4.500 DOLLARS (PERIOD / DLM))

(LOIS'S SHARE IS 2 (TIMES / OP 1) BOB'S (PERIOD / DLM))

((FIND / QWORD) BOB'S AND LOIS'S SHARE (PERIOD / DLM))

(THE EQUATIONS TO BE SOLVED ARE)

(EQUAL G02519 (LOIS'S SHARE))

(EQUAL G02518 (BOB'S))

(EQUAL (LOIS'S SHARE) (TIMES 2 (BOB'S)))

(EQUAL PLUS (LOIS'S SHARE OF SOME MONEY) (BOB'S SHARE)) (TIMES 4.500 (DOLLARS)))

THE EQUATIONS WERE INSUFFICIENT TO FIND A SOLUTION

(ASSUMING THAT)
((BOB'S) IS EQUAL TO (BOB'S SHARE))

(ASSUMING THAT)
((LOIS'S SHARE) IS EQUAL TO (LOIS'S SHARE OF SOME MONEY))

(BOB'S IS 1.500 DOLLARS)

(LOIS'S SHARE IS 3 DOLLARS)

(THE PROBLEM TO BE SOLVED IS)
(MARY IS TWICE AS OLD AS ANN WAS WHEN MARY WAS AS OLD AS ANN IS NOW. IF MARY IS 24 YEARS OLD, HOW OLD IS ANN Q.)

(WITH MANDATORY SUBSTITUTIONS THE PROBLEM IS)
(MARY IS 2 TIMES AS OLD AS ANN WAS WHEN MARY WAS AS OLD AS ANN IS NOW. IF MARY IS 24 YEARS OLD, WHAT IS ANN Q.)

(WITH WORDS TAGGED BY FUNCTION THE PROBLEM IS)
((MARY / PERSON) IS 2 (TIMES / OP 1) AS OLD AS (ANN / PERSON) WAS WHEN (MARY / PERSON) WAS AS OLD AS (ANN / PERSON) IS NOW (PERIOD / DLM) IF (MARY / PERSON) IS 24 YEARS OLD, (WHAT / QWORD) IS (ANN / PERSON) (QMARK / DLM))

(THE SIMPLE SENTENCES ARE)

((MARY / PERSON)'S AGE IS 2 TIMES / OP 1) (ANN / PERSON)'S AGE G02521 YEARS AGO (PERIOD / DLM))

(G02521 YEARS AGO (MARY / PERSON'S AGE IS (ANN / PERSON)'S AGE NOW (PERIOD / DLM))

((MARY / PERSON)'S AGE IS 24 (PERIOD / DLM))

((WHAT / QWORD) IS (ANN / PERSON)'S AGE (QMARK / DLM))

(THE EQUATIONS TO BE SOLVED ARE)

(EQUAL G02522 ((ANN / PERSON)'S AGE))

(EQUAL ((MARY / PERSON)'S AGE) 24)

(EQUAL (PLUS ((MARY / PERSON)'S AGE) (MINUS (G02521))) ((ANN / PERSON)'S AGE))

(EQUAL ((MARY / PERSON)'S AGE) (TIMES 2 PLUS ((ANN / PERSON)'S AGE) (MINUS G02521)))))

(ANN'S AGE IS 18)

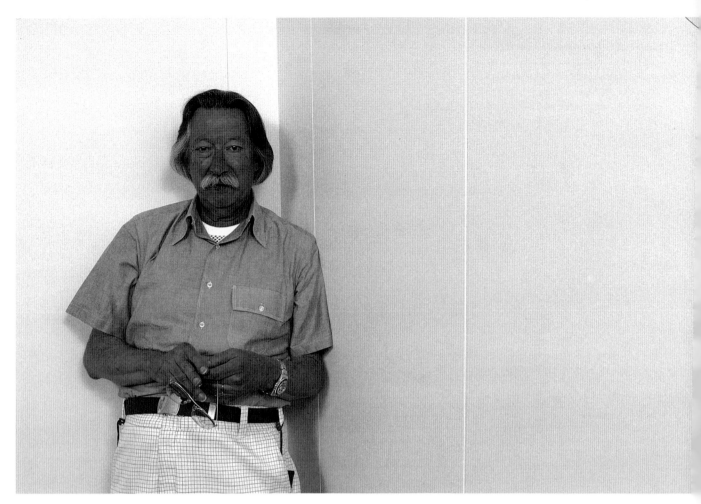

Joseph Weizenbaum of MIT, AI
pioneer and critic. (Photo by Lou
Jones)

A conversation with ELIZA. (ELIZA's
responses are in all caps.)
(Courtesy of Avron Barr and Edward
Feigenbaum)

Men are all alike.
IN WHAT WAYS

They're always bugging us about something or other.
CAN YOU THINK OF A SPECIFIC EXAMPLE

Well, my boyfriend made me come here.
YOUR BOYFRIEND MADE YOU COME HERE

He says I'm depressed much of the time.
I AM SORRY TO HEAR THAT YOU ARE DEPRESSED

It's true. I'm unhappy.
DO YOU THINK COMING HERE WILL HELP YOU NOT TO BE UNHAPPY

I need some help, that much seems certain.
WHAT WOULD IT MEAN TO YOU IF YOU GOT SOME HELP

Perhaps I could learn to get along with my mother.
TELL ME MORE ABOUT YOUR FAMILY

. . .

WHAT ELSE COMES TO MIND WHEN YOU THINK OF YOUR FATHER

Bullies.
DOES THAT HAVE ANYTHING TO DO WITH THE FACT THAT YOUR BOYFRIEND
MADE YOU COME HERE

provide it with very diverse inputs, which often lead to unexpected and seemingly insightful responses despite its relative simplicity. A more substantial effort in the area of natural language was Susumu Kuno's pioneering work on English language parsers: his 1963 program could understand the syntax of complex English sentences.

Another attribute characteristic of AI work in the 1960s was the use of toy worlds. A prime example was Terry Winograd's Ph.D. thesis at MIT called SHRDLU, which combined natural language understanding with a planning capability in a simulated world (displayed on a terminal screen) that consisted only of different colored and shaped blocks.[63] Users could ask SHRDLU to perform tasks with questions and commands phrased in natural language, such as "Take the red block in front of the big cube and place it on the blue rectangular solid." The system would understand the English statements and could plan a strategy for performing the task. Although several critics of AI jumped on the unrealistic nature of these toy worlds, it was appropriate at the time to concentrate on problems of language understanding and decision making without the vagaries of real-world complexity.[64] The next step, going from toy worlds to real worlds, continues to occupy the attention of AI researchers.

The age of recursion

Through the end of the 1960s two schools of thought competed for the attention of AI researchers and funding. The neural school, based on self-organizing neural nets, started in the 1940s with a paper by McCulloch and Pitts and was heavily promoted in the 1960s by Frank Rosenblatt of Cornell University.[65] The lure of neural nets is the idea that a system of many simple elements, if set up in just the right way, could actually teach (organize) itself to perform intelligent behavior. With the publication of Minsky and Papert's *Perceptrons* in 1969, this school of thought was eliminated almost overnight. As mentioned earlier, the book proved several theorems that demonstrated that certain types of simple problems could never be solved with this approach. Now in the late 1980s there is renewed interest in a new type of neural net to which the Minsky and Papert theorems do not apply.[66]

The school that survived, which one might call the recursive school, was based on the idea that a relatively small set of powerful ideas would be sufficient to capture at least some forms of intelligence. If one let these methods attack complicated problems, one could obtain intelligent behavior. The ideas included methods of exploring (searching) the "space" of possible solutions to a problem as well as techniques for defining the rules that govern certain domains (e.g. the syntax rules of natural language).

Foremost among these "powerful" ideas is recursion, the idea that the statement of a problem can be used as a part, often the most important part, of the problem's solution. It is a seductive concept; it implies that the essence of solving a problem is often a matter of being able carefully and precisely to state the problem. This approach works surprisingly well in a variety of domains, and many AI methodologies make extensive use of it. It is one reason that the von Neumann computer architecture that was first incorporated in the famous EDSAC and BINAC computers was so important. Without the von Neumann capability for a stored program, recursion is not possible.

We examined one illustration of the power of recursion earlier in the context of game playing. To select our best move in a rule-based game such as chess we call a program called Move. Move generates all of the legal moves for the current board position and then calls itself to determine the opponent's best response, to each possible move (which in turn calls itself again to determine our best response to our opponent's best response, and so on). In this way as many move and countermove sequences as we have time to compute are automatically generated. The most complicated part of implementing this technique is the generation of the possible moves. Generating possible moves is a matter of programming the rules of the game. Thus, the heart of the solution is indeed implementing a precise statement of the problem.

A primary distinguishing feature of McCarthy's LISP, historically the AI field's primary programming language, is its ability to easily represent recursive procedures. Another example should illustrate how easily a recursive language can be used to solve seemingly complex problems. Consider the problem called the Tower of Hanoi. This famous children's puzzle presents issues similar to many important combinatorial problems found in mathematics and other fields.

We have three towers on which we can place round disks of various sizes. We can move disks from tower to tower, but we can only move one disk at a time and we cannot place a disk onto a disk of smaller size. Thus, a legal stack of disks will have the largest disk on the bottom and the smallest disk on top. The problem is to move a stack of disks from one tower to another. Consider first a stack of just one disk. Here the answer is obvious: simply move the disk. It is also fairly easy to determine the procedure for two disks. Let's consider a larger stack. Try actually solving the problem for a stack of seven or eight disks—it is rather challenging.

Now consider the general problem of describing a method that can quickly determine the *optimal* procedure for a stack of *any* arbitrary height. This problem at first appears very difficult, but a simple insight enables us to use the self-referencing (recursive) paradigm to automatically generate the optimal procedure for any height stack in three simple steps. Let us number the disks from 1 to n, n being the largest (bottom) disk. The insight is this: if we are to move the entire stack from the original tower to the destination tower, at some point we are going to have to move the bottom disk. That's it! We have just solved the problem. The power of recursion is that this simple observation is enough to solve the entire problem.

To wit, if the stack consists of only a single disk, then move that disk from the original tower to the destination tower, and we're done. Otherwise,

Step 1 Since we know that we will need at some point to move the bottom disk, we clearly need to move the disks on top of it out of the way. We therefore have to move them away from both the original tower and the destination tower. Thus, we have to move the stack consisting of all the disks *except* for the bottom disk (we can call this the ($n - 1$) stack since it consists of disk 1 through disk $n - 1$) from the original tower to the free tower. This is where the recursion comes in. Moving the stack of ($n - 1$) disks is the same Tower of Hanoi problem that we started with, only

Solution to the Tower of Hanoi puzzle for 1 disk

Tower 1 is the origin.
Tower 2 is the destination.
Tower 3 is the free tower.

Move disk 1 from tower 1 to tower 2.

Solution to the Tower of Hanoi puzzle for 2 disks

Tower 1 is the origin.
Tower 2 is the destination.
Tower 3 is the free tower.

Move disk 1 from tower 1 to tower 3.
Move disk 2 from tower 1 to tower 2.
Move disk 1 from tower 3 to tower 2.

Solution to the Tower of Hanoi puzzle for 3 disks

Tower 1 is the origin.
Tower 2 is the destination.
Tower 3 is the free tower.

Move disk 1 from tower 1 to tower 2.
Move disk 2 from tower 1 to tower 3.
Move disk 1 from tower 2 to tower 3.
Move disk 3 from tower 1 to tower 2.
Move disk 1 from tower 3 to tower 1.
Move disk 2 from tower 3 to tower 2.
Move disk 1 from tower 1 to tower 2.

Solution to the Tower of Hanoi puzzle for 4 disks

Tower 1 is the origin.
Tower 2 is the destination.
Tower 3 is the free tower.

Move disk 1 from tower 1 to tower 3.
Move disk 2 from tower 1 to tower 2.
Move disk 1 from tower 3 to tower 2.
Move disk 3 from tower 1 to tower 3.
Move disk 1 from tower 2 to tower 1.
Move disk 2 from tower 2 to tower 3.
Move disk 1 from tower 1 to tower 3.
Move disk 4 from tower 1 to tower 2.
Move disk 1 from tower 3 to tower 2.
Move disk 2 from tower 3 to tower 1.
Move disk 1 from tower 2 to tower 1.
Move disk 3 from tower 3 to tower 2.
Move disk 1 from tower 1 to tower 3.
Move disk 2 from tower 1 to tower 2.
Move disk 1 from tower 3 to tower 2.

Solution to the Tower of Hanoi puzzle for 5 disks

Tower 1 is the origin.
Tower 2 is the destination.
Tower 3 is the free tower.

Move disk 1 from tower 1 to tower 2.
Move disk 2 from tower 1 to tower 3.
Move disk 1 from tower 2 to tower 3.
Move disk 3 from tower 1 to tower 2.
Move disk 1 from tower 3 to tower 1.
Move disk 2 from tower 3 to tower 2.
Move disk 1 from tower 1 to tower 2.
Move disk 4 from tower 1 to tower 3.
Move disk 1 from tower 2 to tower 3.
Move disk 2 from tower 2 to tower 1.
Move disk 1 from tower 3 to tower 1.
Move disk 3 from tower 2 to tower 3.
Move disk 1 from tower 1 to tower 2.
Move disk 2 from tower 1 to tower 3.
Move disk 1 from tower 2 to tower 3.
Move disk 5 from tower 1 to tower 2.
Move disk 1 from tower 3 to tower 1.
Move disk 2 from tower 3 to tower 2.
Move disk 1 from tower 1 to tower 2.
Move disk 3 from tower 3 to tower 1.
Move disk 1 from tower 2 to tower 3.
Move disk 2 from tower 2 to tower 1.
Move disk 1 from tower 3 to tower 1.
Move disk 4 from tower 3 to tower 2.
Move disk 1 from tower 1 to tower 2.
Move disk 2 from tower 1 to tower 3.
Move disk 1 from tower 2 to tower 3.
Move disk 3 from tower 1 to tower 2.
Move disk 1 from tower 3 to tower 1.
Move disk 2 from tower 3 to tower 2.
Move disk 1 from tower 1 to tower 2.

Optimal solutions to the Tower of Hanoi problem generated by our recursive program.

The solution of the Tower of Hanoi problem for three disks.

Starting position. Tower 2 is the destination tower.

Step 1

Step 2

Step 3. We have now moved the $(n-1)$ stack to the free tower.

Step 4. We have now moved the bottom disk (disk n) to the destination tower.

Step 5. We now start moving the $(n-1)$ stack from the free tower to the destination tower.

Step 6

Step 7. We're done!

for a smaller stack. The program solving the Tower of Hanoi problem simply calls itself at this point to solve the problem of moving the $(n - 1)$ stack to the free tower. This does not lead to an infinite loop because of our special rule for a stack of only one disk.

Step 2 Now with all of the other disks out of the way, we can move the bottom disk from the original tower to the destination tower.

Step 3 Finally, we move the stack of $(n - 1)$ disks from the free tower to the destination tower. This again requires a recursive call. Now we're done.

The power of recursive programming languages is that a program can call itself with the language keeping track of all the tightly nested self-referencing. The above three steps will not only solve the problem, it will produce the *optimal* solution to the problem for any height stack. It generates exactly $(2^n - 1)$ moves for n disks. If one attempts to solve the problem directly by moving disks, one quickly gets lost in the apparent complexity of the puzzle. To solve the problem using recursion, all that is required is enough insight to be able to state how the solution for n disks can be built from the solution for $(n - 1)$ disks. Recursion then optimally expands the solution for any value of n.

As the above example should make clear, recursion is a tool that can unlock solutions to problems that otherwise would be enormously difficult to understand. A variety of techniques based on this self-referencing paradigm found widespread applicability by the 1960s. The initial success of recursive AI techniques—finding, for example, an *original* proof for an important theorem in *Principia Mathematica*—fueled much of the field's early optimism.

A recursive program for the Tower of Hanoi problem

The following program, written in the C programming language, generates an optimal solution to the Tower of Hanoi problem. Try following the logic of this program from the comments even if you are not familiar with programming in general or the C language in particular. The program is written as a function that when called will print out the solution. It is called with parameters specifying the original tower, the destination tower, the free tower, and the number of disks. Note that in this function, anything that appears between /* and */ is considered to be a comment and is not part of the program.

```
tower_of_hanoi (original, destination, free, number_of_disks)
        /* This function will print out an optimal solution to the Tower of Hanoi problem. */
integer original;      /* This parameter specifies the originating tower. */
integer destination;      /* This parameter specifies the destination tower. */
integer free;      /* This parameter specifies the free tower. */
integer number_of_disks;      /* This parameter specifies the number of disks. The disks are
        numbered from 1 to n with n being the largest (bottom) disk. */
{
if (number_of_disks == 1)
    {
```

```
                print ("Move disk 1 from tower %d to tower %d\n", original destination);
                return;
                }
                /*   If the number of disks is 1, then this is the escape from recursion. We simply print
                     that disk 1 is to be moved from the originating tower to the destination tower and
                     then return. */
        tower_of_hanoi (original, free, destination, number_of_disks − 1);
                /*   Here we have the first recursive call where the tower_of_hanoi function calls itself.
                     This call moves the (n − 1) stack (the stack consisting of all the disks except for the
                     bottom one) from the originating tower to the free tower. */
        print ("Move disk %d from tower %d to tower %d\n", number_of_ disks, original,
                destination);
                /*   Now print that the bottom disk (disk n) is to be moved from the originating tower to
                     the destination tower. */
        tower_of_hanoi (free, destination, original, number_of_disks − 1);
                /*   Move the (n − 1) stack from the free stack to the destination stack. */
        return;    /* We're done! */
        }          /*   End of tower_of_hanoi function */
```

The age of knowledge

Somewhere around the early 1970s a major conceptual change took place in AI methodology (it is difficult to pick a hard date as there is no single paper one can cite that ushered in the change).[67] While work in the 1950s and 1960s concentrated primarily on the mechanics of the reasoning process (search, recursion, problem representation, etc.), it became apparent by the early 1970s that such techniques alone were not sufficiently powerful to emulate the human decision-making process, even within narrowly defined areas of expertise.[68] Something was missing, and the something turned out to be *knowledge*.

Some work on knowledge representation (knowledge about how to represent knowledge) took place earlier.[69] In fact, two projects conducted during the 1960s and described in Minsky's *Semantic Information Processing* were Bertram Raphael's SIR program (Semantic Information Retrieval) and a theory of semantic memory by M. Ross Quillian, both of which dealt with methods for representing human knowledge (see figure). What changed in the early 1970s was the recognition of the relative importance of knowledge versus method. In the 1950s and 1960s there was an emphasis on the power of techniques, particularly recursive ones, for emulating the logical processes associated with thinking. By the 1970s it was recognized that programming reasoning techniques were relatively simple compared to the task of creating a knowledge base with the depth required to solve real-world problems.

Roger Schank points out the extensive knowledge required to understand even simple stories. If we read a story about a restaurant, there is a vast body of factual information about restaurants that we take for granted.[70] Understanding the statement "He paid the bill" requires understanding that in a restaurant we are expected to pay for the food we order, we order food on credit, we are brought a document (generally at the end of the meal) called the "tab," "check," or "bill," which itemizes the charges, we generally settle this debt prior to leaving the

Knowledge structures from M. Ross Quillian's theory of semantic memory. (From M. Ross Quillian, "Semantic Memory," in Minsky, ed., *Semantic Information Processing*, 1968, p. 250)

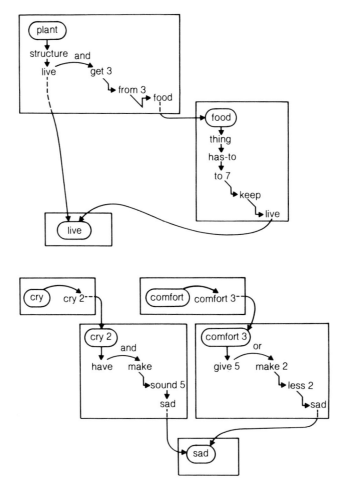

restaurant, and so on. When we read a story, almost every sentence evokes vast networks of similarly implied knowledge. The difficulty in mastering all of this commonsense knowledge is that no one has ever bothered to write it all down, and the quantity of it is vast.

Mastering knowledge has indeed turned out to be a far more difficult process than mastering the logical processes inherent in deductive or even inductive reasoning. First, we need to have a means of structuring knowledge to make it useful. A simple list of all facts in the world, if such a list could be constructed, would not help us solve problems, because we would have a hard time finding the right facts to fit the right situations. Douglas Hofstadter provides an amusing example of the problem in *Metamagical Themas*. "How do I know," he asks, "when telling you I'll meet you at 7 at the train station, that it makes no sense to tack on the proviso, 'as long as no volcano erupts along the way, burying me and my car on the way to the station,' but that it *does* make reasonable sense to tack on the proviso, 'as long as no traffic jam holds me up?'" The objective of appropriate knowledge structures is to quickly access the information truly relevant to any particular situation. Once we have constructed suitable structures for knowledge representation, we then need to actually collect the vast amount of information required to solve practical problems. Finally, we have to integrate this knowledge base with the appropriate decision-making algorithms.

The early 1970s saw a number of pioneering efforts to address the knowledge-representation problem. Perhaps the most famous was Minsky's theory of *frames*, which he described in his 1975 paper "A Framework for Representing

Knowledge."[71] A frame is a data structure that can include information of arbitrary complexity about an object or type of object, and that allows for multiple hierarchies for understanding relationships between classes of objects. For example, we can have a frame of information about the concept of a dog, another for the concept of a cat, and another for the concept of a mammal. The mammal frame is a higher-level frame than those representing *examples* of mammals, and the relationship between the levels (e.g., a dog is a *type* of mammal) is built into the frame structures. Each frame allows for default information to be filled in or "inherited" from a higher-level frame. For example, if the mammal frame says that mammals have four legs, this information would not have to be repeated in the frames for dogs and cats. However, a *human* frame would have to indicate an exception to this default information (one specifying only two legs). The frame methodology avoids redundancy, describes hierarchical relationships, and allows for arbitrarily complex classifications. It also helps us to make useful hypotheses. If we learn, for example, about another mammal, we can assume that it has four legs until informed otherwise.

Another important approach to representing knowledge and the interdependency relationships between concepts was first described in another 1975 paper, this one describing a project called SAM (Script Applier Mechanism) by Roger Schank, Robert Abelson, et al. at Yale University. Schank's methodology allowed for the development of "scripts" that provide the information implicit in everyday situations such as restaurants.[72]

The second part of the knowledge issue, actually collecting the knowledge, has proved to be the greatest challenge. In developing modern expert systems (computer-based systems that emulate the decision-making ability of human experts), the process of collecting the necessary knowledge is generally a painstaking process involving a "knowledge engineer" interviewing the appropriate human experts and literally writing down (in an appropriate computer language) all of the relevant knowledge and decision-making rules used by that human expert. The sheer volume of information involved is one problem, but a bigger one is that while human experts are capable of solving problems within their domains of expertise, they generally do not know *how* they accomplish these tasks. The skill required of the knowledge engineer is to be able to extract the decision-making process from the domain experts despite their not being consciously aware of many elements of this process.[73]

With a first generation methodology for building expert systems already established, a number of ambitious projects were started in the 1970s. Internist (now called CADUCEUS), an expert system that diagnoses a wide range of internal diseases, was developed throughout the 1970s (and continued in the 1980s). In one study, Internist was able to diagnose illnesses within at least one specialty with an accuracy equal to or better than human physicians. MYCIN, a system that can make diagnoses and recommend treatments for a wide range of bacterial infections, was developed by Edward H. Shortliffe in the mid 1970s. Prospector, an expert system that is capable of pinpointing energy and geology deposits, was initiated by R. O. Duda and his associates at Stanford Research Institute in 1978. In at least one case Prospector identified a number of important energy deposits overlooked by human experts. Finally, XCON, probably the most successful expert system in commercial use today, started operation in 1980 configuring complex computer systems for Digital Equipment Corporation. This system, running on a single VAX computer, is able to perform tasks that would otherwise require several hundred human experts, and at substantially higher rates of accuracy. These systems and others, as well as the problems of knowledge representation, will be discussed in greater detail in chapter 8.[74]

The U.S. Department of Defense through its agency DARPA (Defense Advanced Research Projects Agency), funded two major initiatives in the pattern recognition area during the 1970s. The SUR (Speech Understanding Research) project funded the development of several experimental continuous-speech-understanding programs aimed at machine recognition of normal human speech with a large vocabulary. Though the most successful system from the SUR project did not operate in real time and was limited to an artificial syntax, SUR did increase confidence that practical, high-performance speech recognition was feasible. A similar program called IUP (Image Understanding Program) attempted machine comprehension of visual images.

The intensity of effort as well as the practical value of AI technology grew enormously during the 1980s. Here I shall mention briefly two salient trends: the commercialization and the internationalization of AI. The AI industry grew from just a few million dollars at the beginning of the 1980s to $2 billion by 1988, according to DM Data, a leading market-research firm. Many market analysts predict that the bulk of the several-hundred-billion dollar computer and information processing market by 1999 will be intelligent, at least by today's standards.

The 1980s began with a stunning challenge from Japan's powerful MITI (the Ministry of International Trade and Industry) when they announced a plan to design and build an intelligent fifth generation computer. This was seen by many as an attempt by Japan to leapfrog its foreign competitors and establish dominance over the international computer industry.[75]

As I said earlier, the idea that human intelligence could be simulated seems to have occurred to all of the pioneers who played a role in what I consider to be the twentieth century's greatest invention, the computer. Though artificial intelligence was not named until 1956, the concept was by no means an afterthought. Despite the fact that the early computers were used primarily for numerical calculation (as most computers still are today), these classic machines were not thought of by their creators as mere number crunchers. They have been viewed since their conception as amplifiers of human thought, what Ed Feigenbaum calls "power tools for the mind."[76]

Early success in the 1950s and 1960s with what were thought to be difficult problems, such as proving theorems and playing chess, fueled a romantic optimism that proved short-lived. It was an example of the "90-10" rule: solving the first 90 percent of a problem often requires only 10 percent of the effort, and though the remaining 10 percent then requires 90 percent of the effort, it generally represents 90 percent of the importance. With the realization in the 1970s that extensive knowledge was required to solve practical problems, and with no easy way of capturing that knowledge, the field gained a needed maturity.

The 1980s saw the first practical solutions to real problems and the emergence of a multibillion-dollar industry. The 1990s will, in my estimation, witness the emergence of an industry valued at several hundred billion dollars and a generation of ubiquitous intelligent machines that work intimately with their human creators.

Marvin Minsky

Thoughts about Artificial Intelligence

Marvin Minsky, a founder of the
MIT Artificial Intelligence
Laboratory, Thinking Machines,
and Logo Computer Systems,
is Donner Professor of Science
at the Massachusetts Institute
of Technology. He was one of
the pioneers in computer
science, having made major
contributions in establishing
the scientific foundation of
three important areas: the
mathematical theory of
computation, artificial intelligence, and robotics. His most
recent book is *The Society of
Mind* (1986).

What Is Intelligence?

What is intelligence, anyway? It is only a word that people use to name those unknown processes with which our brains solve problems we call hard. But whenever you learn a skill yourself, you're less impressed or mystified when other people do the same. This is why the meaning of "intelligence" seems so elusive: it describes not some definite thing but only the momentary horizon of our ignorance about how minds might work. It is hard for scientists who try to understand intelligence to explain precisely what they do, since our working definitions change from year to year. But it is not at all unusual for sciences to aim at moving targets. Biology explores the moving frontier of what we understand of what happens inside our bodies. Only a few decades ago the ability of organisms to reproduce seemed to be a deep and complex mystery. Yet as soon as they understood the elements of how our gene strings replicate themselves, biologists wondered why it took so long to think of such a simple thing. In the same way each era of psychology explores what we don't then know about processes in our brains.

Then, can we someday build intelligent machines? I take the answer to be yes in principle, because our brains themselves are machines. To be sure, we still know very little about how brains actually work. There is no reason for scientists to be ashamed of this, considering that it was only a century ago that we began to suspect that brains were made of separate nerve cells that acted somewhat like computer parts and that it is only half a century since we began developing technical ideas for understanding what such systems could do. These ideas are still barely adequate for dealing with present-day serial computers, which have only thousands of active components, and are not yet robust enough to deal with systems like those in the brain, which involve trillions of interconnected parts, all working simultaneously.

Nor do we yet know how to make machines do many of the things that ordinary people do. Some critics maintain that machines will never be able to do some of those things, and some skeptics even claim to have proved such things. None of those purported proofs actually hold up to close examination, because we are still in the dark ages of scientific knowledge about such matters. In any case, we have not the slightest grounds for believing that human brains are not machines. Because of this, both psychology and artificial intelligence have similar goals: both seek to learn how machines could do many things we can't yet make them do.

Why are so many people annoyed at the thought that human brains are nothing more than "mere machines"? It seems to me that we have a problem with the word "machine," because we've grown up to believe that machines can behave only in lifeless,

Marvin Minsky. (Photo by Lou Jones)

mechanical ways. This view is obsolete, because the ways we use the word "machine" are out of date. For centuries words like "machine" and "mechanical" were used for describing relatively simple devices like pulleys, levers, locomotives, and typewriters. The word "computer" too inherits from the past that sense of pettiness that comes from doing dull arithmetic by many small and boring steps. Because of this, our previous experience can sometimes be a handicap. Our preconceptions of what machines can do date from what happened when we assembled systems from only a few hundreds or thousands of parts. And that did not prepare us to think about brainlike assemblies of billions of parts. Although we are already building machines with many millions of parts, we continue to think as though nothing has changed. We must learn to change how we think about phenomena that work on those larger scales.

What Is Artificial Intelligence?

Even though we don't yet understand how brains perform many mental skills, we can still work toward making machines that do the same or similar things. "Artificial intelligence" is simply the name we give to that research. But as I already pointed out, this means that the focus of that research will keep changing, since as soon as we think we understand one mystery, we have to move on to the next. In fact, AI research has made enormous progress in only a few decades, and because of that rapidity, the field has acquired a

somewhat shady reputation! This paradox resulted from the fact that whenever an AI research project made a useful new discovery, that product usually quickly spun off to form a new scientific or commercial specialty with its own distinctive name. These changes in name led outsiders to ask, Why do we see so little progress in the central field of artificial intelligence? Here are a few specialties that originated at least in part from AI research but later split into separate fields and, in some instances, commercial enterprises: robotics, pattern recognition, expert systems, automatic theorem proving, cognitive psychology, word processing, machine vision, knowledge engineering, symbolic applied mathematics, and computational linguistics.

For example, many researchers in the 1950s worked toward discovering ways to make machines recognize various sorts of patterns. As their findings were applied to problems involved with vision, speech, and several other areas, those fields evolved their own more distinct techniques, they organized their own technical societies and journals, and they stopped using the term "artificial intelligence." Similarly, an early concern of AI was to develop techniques for enabling computers to understand human language; this spawned a field called computational linguistics. Again, many ideas from artificial intelligence had a large influence among psychologists, who applied those ideas to their studies of the mind but used the title "cognitive psychology."

I can illustrate how AI projects develop by recounting the research of James Slagle, who, as a graduate student at MIT in 1960,

215

developed a program to solve calculus problems; he named it with the initials of "symbolic automatic integration." Although there were many problems that SAINT couldn't solve, it surpassed the performance of average MIT students. When he first approached this subject, most scientists considered solving those problems to require substantial intelligence. But after Slagle's work we had to ask ourselves instead why students take so long to learn to do such basically straightforward things.

How did SAINT solve those problems? It employed about 100 formulas from the domains of algebra and calculus and applied to these about a dozen pattern-matching methods for deciding which formula might be most likely to help solve a given problem. Since any particular attempt might fail, the program had to employ a good deal of trial and error. If one method did not work, the program automatically went on to try another. Sometimes one of them would work, but frequently a problem was too hard for any single such method to work. The system was programmed in that case to proceed on to certain other methods, methods that attempted to split each hard problem into several simpler ones. In this way, if no particular method worked, SAINT was equipped with a great variety of alternatives.

Now we can make an important point. For years the public has been told, Computers do only what they're programmed to do. But now you can see why that's not quite true: We can write programs that cause the machine to search for solutions. Often such searches produce results that greatly surprise their programmers.

The idea of making programs search greatly expanded their powers. But it also led to new kinds of problems: search processes could generate so many possible alternatives that the programs were in constant danger of getting lost, repeating themselves, or persisting at fruitless attempts that had already consumed large amounts of time. Much research in the 1960s was focused on finding methods to reduce that sort of fruitless search. Slagle himself experimented with some mathematical theories of how to take into account both how much effort had been spent on each solution attempt and how much apparent progress had been made. Thus the SAINT program worked as well as it did, not merely because of its specialized knowledge about calculus, but also because of other knowledge about the search itself. To prevent the search from simply floundering around, making one random attempt after another, some of the program's knowledge was applied to recognize conditions in which its other, more specialized knowledge might be particularly useful.

When SAINT first appeared, it was acclaimed an outstanding example of work in the field of artificial intelligence. Later other workers analyzed more carefully its virtues and deficiencies, and this research improved our understanding of the basic

nature of those calculus problems. Eventually ways were found to replace all the trial and error processes in SAINT by methods that worked without any search. The resulting commercial product, a program called MACSYMA, actually surpassed the abilities of professional mathematicians in this area. But once the subject was so well understood, we ceased to think of it as needing intelligence. This area is now generally seen as belonging no longer to artificial intelligence but to a separate specialty called symbolic applied mathematics.

Robotics and Common Sense

In the 1960s we first began to equip computers with mechanical hands and television eyes. Our goal was to endow machines with the sorts of abilities children use when playing with toys and building blocks. We found this much harder to do than expected. Indeed, a scholar of the history of artificial intelligence might get a sense of watching evolution in reverse. Even in its earliest years we saw computers playing chess and doing calculus, but it took another decade for us to begin to learn to make machines that could begin to act like children playing with building blocks! What makes it easier to design programs that imitate experts than to make them simulate novices? The amazing answer is, Experts are simpler than novices! To see why it was harder to make programs play with toys than pass calculus exams, let's consider what's involved in enabling a robot to copy simple structures composed of blocks: we had to provide our robot with hundreds of small programs organized into a system that engaged many different domains of knowledge. Here are a few of the sorts of problems this system had to deal with:

- The relation between the hand and the eye
- Recognizing objects from their visual appearances
- Recognizing objects partially hidden from view
- Recognizing relations *between* different objects
- Fitting together three-dimensional shapes
- Understanding how objects can support one another to form stable structures
- Planning a sequence of actions to assemble a structure
- Moving in space so as to avoid collisions
- Controlling the fingers of a hand for grasping an object

It is very hard for any adult to remember or appreciate how complex are the properties of ordinary physical things. Once when an early version of our block-building program was asked to find a new place to put a block, it tried to place it on top of itself! The program could not anticipate how that action would change the situation. To catalog only enough fragments of knowledge to enable a robot to build a simple blocklike house from an unspecified variety of available materials would be an encyclopedic task. College students usually learn calculus in half a year, but it takes ten times longer for children to master their building toys. We all forget how hard it was to learn such things when we were young.

Expertise and Common Sense

Many computer programs already exist that do things most people would regard as requiring intelligence. But none of those programs can work outside of some very small domain or specialty. We have separate programs for playing chess, designing transformers, proving geometry theorems, and diagnosing kidney diseases. But none of those programs can do any of the things the others do. By itself each lacks the liveliness and versatility that any normal person has. And no one yet knows how to put many such programs together so that they can usefully communicate with one another. In my book *The Society of Mind* I outline some ideas on how that might be done inside our brains.

Putting together different ideas is just what children learn to do: we usually call this common sense. Few youngsters can design transformers or diagnose renal ailments, but whenever those children speak or play, they combine a thousand different skills. Why is it so much easier for AI programmers to simulate adult, expert skills than to make programs perform childlike sorts of commonsense thought? I suspect that part of the answer lies in the amounts of variety. We can often simulate much of what a specialist does by assembling a collection of special methods, all of which share the same common character. Then so long as we remain within some small and tidy problem world, that specialist's domain of expertise, we need merely apply different combinations of basically similar rules. This high degree of uniformity makes it easy to design a higher-level supervisory program to decide which method to apply. However, although the "methods" of everyday thinking may, by themselves, seem simpler than those of experts, our collections of commonsense methods deal with a great many more d*ifferent types* of problems and situations. Consider how many different things each normal child must learn about the simplest-seeming physical objects, such as the peculiarities of blocks that are heavy, big, smooth, dangerous, pretty, delicate, or belong to someone else. Then consider that the child must learn quite different kinds of strategies for handling solids and liquids; strings, tapes, and cloths; jellies and muds as well as things he is told are prohibited, poisonous, or likely to cut or bite.

What are the consequences of the fact that the domain of commonsense thinking is so immensely varied and disorderly? One problem is simply accumulating so much knowledge. But AI research also encountered a second, more subtle problem. We had to face the simple fact that in order for a machine to behave as though it "knows" anything, there must exist, inside that machine, some sort of structure to embody or "represent" that knowledge. Now, a specialized, or "expert," system can usually get by with very few types of what we call knowledge representations. But in order to span that larger universe of situations we meet in ordinary life, we appear to need a much larger variety of types of representations. This leads to a second, harder type of problem: knowledge represented in different ways must be a*pplied* in different ways. This imposes on each child obligations of a higher type: they have to learn which types of knowledge to apply to which kinds of situations and how to apply them. In other words, we have to accumulate not merely knowledge, but also a good deal of *knowledge about knowledge*. Now, experts too have to do that, but because commonsense knowledge is of more varied types, an ordinary person has to learn (albeit quite unconsciously) much more *knowledge about representations of knowledge*, that is, which types of representation skills to use for different purposes and how to use them.

If this sounds very complicated, it is because it actually is. Until the last half century we had only simple theories of mind, and these explained only a little of what animals could do in the impoverished worlds of laboratory experiments. Not until the 1930s did psychologists like Jean Piaget discover how many aspects of a child's mind develop through complicated processes, sometimes composed of intricate sequences of stagelike periods. We still don't know very much about such matters, except that the mind is much more complex than imagined in older philosophies. In *The Society of Mind* I portray it as a sort of tangled-up bureaucracy, composed of many different experts, or as I call them, "agencies," that each develop different ways to represent what they learn. But how can experts using different languages communicate with one another? The solution proposed in my book is simply that they never come to do it very well! And that explains why human consciousness seems so mysterious. Each part of the mind receives only hints of what the other parts are about, and no matter how hard a mind may try, it can never make very much sense of itself.

Supercomputers and Nanotechnology

Many problems we regard as needing cleverness can sometimes be solved by resorting to exhaustive searches, that is, by using massive, raw computer power. This is what happens in most of those inexpensive pocket chess computers. These little machines use programs much like the ones that we developed in the 1960s, using what were then some of the largest research computers in the world. Those old programs worked by examining the consequences of tens of thousands of possible moves before choosing one to actually make. But in those days the programs took so long to make those moves that the concepts they used were discarded as inadequate. Today, however, we can run the same programs on faster computers so that they can consider millions of possible moves, and now they play much better chess. However, that shouldn't fool us into thinking that we now understand the basic problem any better. There is good reason to believe that outstanding human chess players actually examine merely dozens, rather than millions, of possible moves, subjecting each to more thoughtful analysis.

In any case, as computers improved in speed and memory size, quite a few programming methods became practical, ones that had actually been discarded in the earlier years of AI research. An Apple desktop computer (or an Amiga, Atari, IBM, or whatever) can do more than could a typical million-dollar machine of a decade earlier, yet private citizens can afford to play games with them. In 1960 a million-bit memory cost a million dollars; today a memory of the same size (and working a hundred times faster) can be purchased for the price of a good dinner. Some seers predict another hundredfold decrease in size and cost, perhaps in less than a decade, when we learn how to make each microcircuit ten times smaller in linear size and thus a hundred times smaller in area. What will happen after that? No one knows, but we can be sure of one thing: those two-dimensional chips we use today make very inefficient use of space. Once we start to build three-dimensional microstructures, we might gain another millionfold in density. To be sure, that would involve serious new problems with power, insulation, and heat. For a futuristic but sensible discussion of such possibilities, I recommend Eric Drexler's *Engines of Creation* (Falcon Press, 1986).

Not only have small components become cheaper; they have also become faster. In 1960 a typical component required a microsecond to function; today our circuits operate a thousand times faster. Few optimists, however, predict another thousandfold increase in speed over the next generation. Does this mean that even with decreasing costs we will soon encounter limits on what we can make computers do? The answer is no, because we are just beginning a new era of parallel computers.

Most computers today are still serial; that is, they do only one thing at a time. Typically, a serial computer has millions of memory elements, but only a few of them operate at any moment, while the rest of them wait for their turn: in each cycle of operation, a serial computer can retrieve and use only one of the items in its

memory banks. Wouldn't it be better to keep more of the hardware in actual operation? A more active type of computer architecture was proposed in Daniel Hillis's *Connection Machine* (MIT Press, 1986), which describes a way to assemble a large machine from a large number of very small, serial computers that operate concurrently and pass messages among themselves. Only a few years after being conceived, Connection Machines are already commercially available, and they indeed appear to have fulfilled their promise to break through some of the speed limitations of serial computers. In certain respects they are now the fastest computers in the world.

This is not to say that parallel computers do not have their own limitations. For, just as one cannot start building a house before the boards and bricks have arrived, you cannot always start work simultaneously on all aspects of solving a problem. It would certainly be nice if we could take any program for a serial computer, divide it into a million parts, and then get the answer a million times faster by running those parts simultaneously on that many computers in parallel. But that can't be done, in general, particularly when certain parts of the solution depend upon the solutions to other parts. Nevertheless, this quite often turns out to be feasible in actual practice. And although this is only a guess, I suspect that it will happen surprisingly often for the purposes of artificial intelligence. Why do I think so? Simply because it seems very clear that our brains themselves must work that way.

Consider that brain cells work at very modest speeds in comparison to the speeds of computer parts. They work at rates of less than a thousand operations per second, a million times slower than what happens inside a modern computer circuit chip. Could any computer with such slow parts do all the things that a person can do? The answer must lie in parallel computation: different parts of the brain must do many more different things at the same time. True, that would take at least a billion nerve cells working in parallel, but the brain has many times that number of cells.

AI and the World of the Future

Intelligent machines may be within the technological reach of the next century. Over the next few generations we'll have to face the problems they pose. Unless some unforeseen obstacles appear, our mind-engineering skills could grow to the point of enabling us to construct accomplished artificial scientists, artists, composers, and personal companions. Is AI merely another advance in technology, or is it a turning point in human evolution that should be a focus of discussion and planning by all mankind? The prospect of intelligent machines is one that we're ill prepared to think about, because it raises such unusual moral, social, artistic, philosophical, and religious issues. Are we obliged to treat artificial intelligences as sentient beings? Should they have rights? And what should we do when there remains no real need for honest work, when artificial workers can do everything from mining, farming, medicine, and manufacturing all the way to house cleaning? Must our lives then drift into pointless restlessness and all our social schemes disintegrate?

These questions have been discussed most thoughtfully in the literary works of such writers as Isaac Asimov, Gregory Benford, Arthur C. Clarke, Frederick Pohl, and Jack Williamson, who all tried to imagine how such presences might change the aspirations of humanity. Some optimistic futurists maintain that once we've satisfied all our worldly needs, we might then turn to the worlds of the mind. But consider how that enterprise itself would be affected by the presence of those artificial mindlike entities. That same AI technology would offer ways to modify the hardware of our brains and thus to endlessly extend the mental worlds we could explore.

You might ask why this essay mixes both computers and psychology. The reason is that though we'd like to talk about making intelligent machines, people are the only such intelligence we can imitate or study now. One trouble, though, is that we still don't know enough about how people work! Does this mean that we can't develop smart machines before we get some better theories of psychology? Not necessarily. There certainly could be ways to make very smart machines based on principles that our brains do not use, as in the case of those very fast, dumb chess machines. But since we are the first very smart machines to have evolved, we just *might* represent one of the simplest ways!

But, you might object, there's more to a human mind than merely intellect. What about emotion, intuition, courage, inspiration, creativity, and so forth. Surely it would be easier simply to understand intelligence than to try to analyze all those other aspects of our personalities! Not so, I maintain, because traditional distinctions like those between logic and intuition, between intellect and emotion, unwisely try to separate knowledge and meaning from purpose and intention. In *The Society of Mind* I argue that little can be done without combining elements of both. Furthermore, when we put them together, it becomes easier, rather than harder, to understand such matters, because, though there are many kinds of questions, the answers to each of them illuminate the rest.

Many people firmly believe that computers, by their nature, lack such admirable human qualities as imagination, sympathy, and creativity. Computers, so that opinion goes, can be only logical and literal. Because they can't make new ideas, intelligent machines lie, if at all, in futures too remote for concern. However, we have to be wary of such words as "creativity." We may only mislead ourselves when we ask our machines to do those things that we admire most. No one could deny that our machines, as we know them today, lack many useful qualities that we take for granted in ourselves. But it may be wrong to seek the sources of those qualities in the exceptional performances we see in our cultural heroes. Instead, we ought to look more carefully at what we ordinary people do: the things we call common sense and scarcely ever consider at all. Experience has shown that science frequently develops most fruitfully once we learn to examine the things that seem the simplest, instead of those that seem the most mysterious.

The Moving Frontier

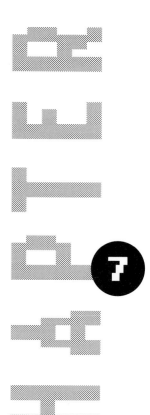

CHAPTER **7**

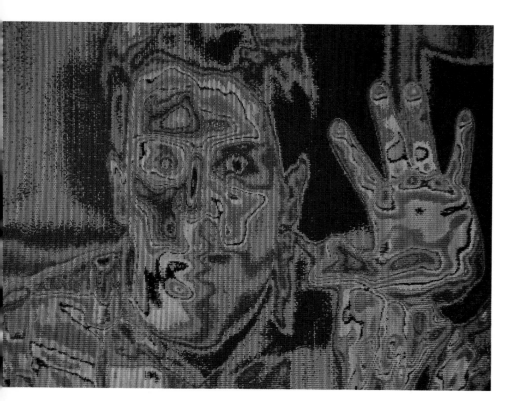

(Photo by Lou Jones)

Pattern Recognition: The Search for Order

The digitization of information in all its forms will probably be known as the most fascinating development of the twentieth century.
An Wang, founder of Wang Laboratories

Most probably, we think, the human brain is, in the main, composed of large numbers of relatively small distributed systems, arranged by embryology into a complex society that is controlled in part (but only in part) by serial, symbolic systems that are added later. But the subsymbolic systems that do most of the work from underneath must, by their very character, block all the other parts of the brain from knowing much about how they work. And this, itself, could help explain how people do so many things yet have such incomplete ideas of how those things are actually done.
Marvin Minsky and Seymour Papert, the 1988 epilogue to *Perceptrons*

• **Vision**

Two types of thinking

Try not to think about elephants. For the next sixty seconds, do not let the image of these huge mammals with their large ears and swaying trunks enter your mind. Now look across the room and focus your vision on an object. Without closing your eyes or turning them away, try not to determine what the object is. Finally, consider the Tower of Hanoi problem described in the last chapter. For the next sixty seconds, do not solve this problem.

You are undoubtedly having difficulty avoiding the mental image of an elephant. Assuming that the object that you selected to look at is not unknown to you, you were probably unsuccessful as well in not determining its identity. On the other hand, unless you have an unusual passion for mathematics, you are probably experiencing little difficulty in not solving the Tower of Hanoi problem.

Two types of thought processes coexist in our brains, and the above exercises illustrate one of the profound differences between them. Perhaps most often cited as a uniquely human form of intelligence is the *logical* process involved in solving problems and playing games. A more ubiquitous form of intelligence that we share with most of the earth's higher animal species is the ability to *recognize patterns* from our visual, auditory, and tactile senses. We appear to have substantial control over the sequential steps required for logical thought. In contrast, pattern recognition, while very complex and involving several levels of abstraction, seems to happen without our conscious direction.[1] It is often said that a master chess player can "see" his or her next move without going through all of the conscious sequences of thinking required of less experienced players. It may be that after being exposed to tens of thousands of board situations, the master player is able to replace at least some of the logical processes usually used to play games with pattern-recognition methods.[2]

There are several key differences between these two forms of intelligence, including the level of success the AI field has had in emulating them.[3] Ironically, we find it easier to create an artificial mathematician or master chess player than to emulate the abilities of animals. While there are many animal capabilities that our machines have not yet mastered, including the intricacies of fine motor coordination, the most difficult barrier has been the subtleties of vision, our most powerful sense and a prime example of pattern recognition.

One attribute that the two types of thinking have in common is the use of imagination. The first example cited above, imagining an elephant, is a direct exercise in imagination. The second example, identifying an object, also involves imagination, particularly in the latter stages of the process. If part of the object we are trying to identify is blocked or if its orientation toward us prevents the most useful view, we use our imagination to visualize in our minds what the full object might look like and then determine if the imagined object matches what we can see. In fact, we almost always use our imagination to visualize an object, because invariably there are sides we cannot see.[4] The technical term for this technique is "hypothesis and test"; we use our imagination to hypothesize the answer and then test its validity.[5] Hypothesis and test is also used in logical thought. We often imagine an answer to a logical problem based on methods of intuition that are only partially understood and then work backward to the original problem statement.

If we examine the nature of our visual imagination, we can gain some insight into the most important way in which pattern recognition differs from logical rule-based thinking. Consider again your imagination of an elephant. Your mental picture probably does not include a great deal of detail: it is essentially a line drawing, probably one that is moving (I'll bet the trunk is swaying back and forth). The phenomenon of the line drawing—the fact that we recognize a line drawing of an object (a face, for example) as representing that object though the drawing is markedly simpler than the original image—provides us with an important clue to the nature of the transformations performed during the process of human vision. Very important to the recognition of visual objects is the identification of *edges*, which we model in two dimensions as lines. If we explore what is required to extract edges from an image, we shall gain an appreciation of one major way in which visual perception differs from logic.

There are many aspects of visual perception that we do not yet understand, but some understanding of the identification of edge location and orientation has been achieved.[6] A particular set of computations has been discovered that is capable of detecting edges with reasonable accuracy. There is some evidence that similar techniques are used in visual processing by mammals. The technique is based on two observations. The first observation is that we need to smooth the data; changes involving tiny regions can probably be considered to be non-information-bearing visual noise. Thus, small defects in edges can be ignored, at least initially, in locating all of the edges in an image. Second, we note that *changes* in the visual information (across any spatial dimension) are more important than the information itself. In other words, we are primarily interested in sudden and consistent alterations in color or shading from one region to another.

I shall now describe a method for inferring edges from visual images.[7] The following two paragraphs are somewhat technical. Yet it is not necessary to understand all of these details to appreciate some of the implications of the method. The image itself is represented by a two-dimensional array of pixels, or points of information. In a black and white image, each pixel can be represented by a single number representing a shade of grey. In a color image, several numbers (usually three) are required to represent the color and shade. We can take this initial raw image and modify it to take advantage of the two observations cited above. The modification is achieved by applying what is called a filter, in which each pixel has an influence on its surrounding pixels. For example, a Gaussian filter designates certain pixels as *propagating* pixels; it then increases the intensity of each pixel in the vicinity of each propagating pixel on the basis of the intensity of the propagating pixel and the distance to the neighboring pixel. The function of intensity to distance is based on the familiar Gaussian (normal) curve, with the peak of the curve representing zero distance (that is, the propagating pixel itself). A Gaussian filter is applied to an image by making *every* pixel a propagating pixel; thus, all pixels bleed into their surrounding pixels. This has the impact of smoothing the image, with the sharpness of the resulting image being a function of the width of the Gaussian curve. A different filter, the Laplacian, can then be applied to detect changes. This filter replaces the value of every pixel with the rate of change of the rate of change (that is, the second derivative) of the pixel values.

These two processes—smoothing and determining rates of rates of change—can be combined into a single filter in which every pixel influences all of the pixels within its vicinity. This filter, with the appropriate, if forbidding, name of "Laplacian of a Gaussian convolver," has a graph with the shape of an upside-down Mexican hat, so it is often called a sombrero filter. As the figure shows, each pixel has a positive influence on the pixels in its immediate vicinity and a negative

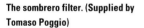

The sombrero filter. (Supplied by Tomaso Poggio)

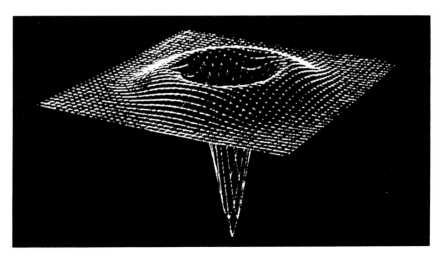

influence on pixels in a band surrounding the immediate vicinity. Once the sombrero filter has been applied, edges can be inferred by looking for zero crossings, places where values change from negative to positive.[8]

Let us consider some of the implications of this process. First, the technique is not particularly complicated. Second, experiments have shown that it is reasonably successful. In general, edges are correctly inferred. False hypotheses are generated, but these can be eliminated by later processing that incorporates knowledge about the types of objects we expect to see in the environment and the nature of their edges.[9] Third, there is evidence that the hardware exists in mammalian brains to perform this type of transformation. For example, David H. Hubel and Torsten N. Wiesel of Harvard Medical School have discovered specialized edge detector cells in the outer (early) layers of the visual cortex of the human brain.[10]

Most important is a conclusion we can draw regarding the *amount* of computation required to perform edge detection. While it has not been proved that

A scanned image and the edges detected by an edge detection system developed by J. F. Canny in 1983. (From J. F. Canny, "Finding Edges and Lines in Images," MIT Artificial Intelligence Laboratory, TR-720, figures 6.14a and 6.14b)

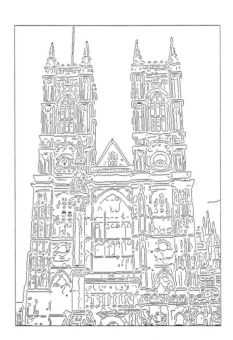

this precise filter, the Laplacian of a Gaussian convolver, is used in mammal vision, it can be shown that any algorithm that could possibly perform edge detection with the facility of human (and apparently most mammal) vision must use a center-surround filter (a filter in which each pixel influences all pixels within a certain distance) that requires a comparable amount of computation. This amount turns out to be vast and is determined by a *six-dimensional* computation. First, the filter must be applied for every pixel, and the pixels are organized in a two-dimensional array. For each pixel we must apply the filter to all pixels in a two-dimensional array surrounding that pixel, which gives us a four-dimensional computation. We noted earlier that the sharpness of our edge analysis was a function of the size of the Gaussian (normal) curve applied. In the combined sombrero filter, the size of the Mexican hat has the same impact. A large sombrero will enable us to detect the edges of large objects; a small sombrero will detect smaller features. We thus need to perform this entire computation several times, which is a fifth dimension. The sixth dimension is time;

since vision must be capable of dealing with *moving* images, this entire computation must be repeated many times each second. Undoubtedly, some optimizations can be applied. For example, if we note that portions of the image are not changing, it is not necessary to repeat all of the computations. Nonetheless, the number of computations required is essentially determined by this six-dimensional array.[11]

Let us plug in some numbers to get a feeling for the orders of magnitude involved. Human vision is estimated to have a resolution of 10,000 positions along each of the two axes of vision, or about 100 million pixels (there are indeed about 100 million rod cells in each eye to detect shape and motion and 6 million cone cells to detect color and fine detail).[12] The diameter of typical sombrero filters used in computer-vision experiments range from 10 to 30 pixels, but these experiments are based on images of only 1,000 pixels on a side. A reasonable average size for a human sombrero filter would be about 100 by 100 pixels. If we assume about 3 different sombreros for different size objects and a refresh rate of recomputing the image of 30 times per second, we have the following number of multiplications per second: $10,000 \times 10,000 \times 100 \times 100 \times 3 \times 30$, or about 100 trillion. Now, a typical personal computer can perform about 100,000 multiplications per second. Thus, we would need about a billion personal computers to match the edge detection capability of human vision, and that's just for one eye![13]

Typical computer vision systems have somewhat less demanding specifications. Typically image resolution is about 1,000 by 1,000 pixels, which requires smaller filters of about 25 by 25 pixels. With three filters of different sizes and a refresh rate of 30 images per second, we have $1,000 \times 1,000 \times 25 \times 25 \times 3 \times 30$, or only 60 billion multiplications per second, which could be handled in real time by a mere 600,000 personal computers.

This brings us back to the issue of digital versus analog computation. As mentioned earlier, the need for massive parallel processing (doing many computations at the same time) may reverse, at least partially, the trend away from analog computing. While it is possible to achieve billions of digital computations per second in our more powerful supercomputers, these systems are large and expensive. The computations described above for the sombrero filter do not need high degrees of accuracy or repeatability, so analog multiplications would be satisfactory. Multiplying 60 billion analog numbers per second (600,000 computing elements each performing 100,000 multiplications per second) could be achieved using VLSI circuits in a relatively compact system. Even the 100 trillion multiplications per second required for human vision, though out of the question using digital circuits, is not altogether impractical using analog techniques. After all, the human brain accomplishes image-filtering tasks using just this combination of methods: massive parallel processing and analog computation.[14]

The human visual system picks up an image with 100 million specialized (rod and cone) cells. Multiple layers, each of a comparable number of cells, would have the capability to perform transformations similar to the sombrero filter described above. In fact, the visual cortex of the brain contains hundreds of layers, so these filtering steps are but the first transformations in the long (but quick) journey of processing that a visual image undergoes.[15]

The images from both eyes need to be processed, and then the two images need to be fused into one through a technique called stereopsis. As a result of having two eyes, we can detect depth; that is, we can determine the relative distance of different objects we see.[16] Because our eyes are a few inches apart, the same object will be slightly shifted in the images they receive. The amount of shift is determined by simple trigonometric relationships. Distant objects will have little shift, whereas close objects will have larger shifts. However, before our visual system can apply trigonometry to the problem of determining depth it needs to line up the corresponding objects in the two visual fields. This is more difficult than it sounds. Experiments indicate that matching the image of each object in the visual field of one eye to the image of that object in the visual field of the other must take place after the detection of edges.[17] Once edge detection has taken place, the edges can be matched using additional pattern-recognition techniques.[18]

Once the edges are detected and the dual images fused with corresponding information regarding depth, it becomes possible for more subtle processes of discrimination to begin. Edges and depths can be organized into surfaces, the texture of the surfaces can be estimated, and finally the objects themselves identified.[19] In this process a great deal of knowledge about the types of objects we expect to see in our environment is used. The paradigm of hypothesis and test is clearly used here in that people typically see what they expect to see in a situation. Visual experiments have shown that people often misrecognize objects that are not expected if they appear to be similar to those that are anticipated. This indicates that the testing of the hypotheses has given a positive result. If an unusual object does not match our hypothesis (i.e., the test fails), then that object is likely to grab our focus of attention.

We have now described a fundamental way in which pattern recognition in general, and vision in particular, differs from the logical processes of thought. The essence of logic is *sequential*, whereas vision is *parallel*. I am not suggesting that the human brain does not incorporate any parallel processing in its logical analyses, but logical thinking generally involves considering only one transformation and its implications at a time. When speaking of parallelism in human vision (and in any attempt to truly emulate vision in a machine), we are speaking not of a few computations at the same time but rather of *billions* simultaneously. The steps after edge detection also involve vast amounts of computation, most of which are also accomplished through massive parallelism.[20] Only in the final stages of the process do we begin to reason about what we have seen and thereby to introduce more sequential logical transformations. Though vision involves vastly greater amounts of computation than logical processes, it is accomplished much more quickly because the number of processing stages are relatively fewer. The trillions of computations required for the human visual system to view and recognize a scene can take place in a split second.

This explains the relatively automatic (not consciously controlled) nature of vision: these tremendously parallel circuits are constantly processing information and piping their results to the next stage. It is not a process we can turn off unless we close our eyes. Even then we have trouble preventing our imagination from presenting images for analysis.

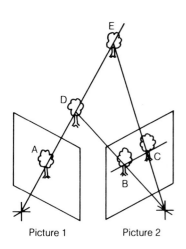

Picture 1   Picture 2

Stereo vision. The different views provided by our two eyes enable us (in most instances) to reconstruct the three-dimensional arrangement of objects. (Courtesy of Paul Cohen and Edward Feigenbaum)

Logical thought appears to be a more recent evolutionary development than pattern recognition, one that requires more conscious control over each sequential step.[21] The amount of computation required is not as vast, and less massive parallelism appears to be involved. This is one reason that we have been more successful in emulating these more "advanced" logical processes in our "intelligent" machines. Despite the relatively slow speed of neuronal circuits, the massive parallelism of the human brain makes it capable of vastly more computation than today's computers. Thus, the relative lack of computational capability of computers to date (less parallel processing) have rendered them inadequate for a level of visual processing comparable to human vision. On the less computationally intensive (and more sequential) tasks of solving problems and playing games, even the very early computers were sufficient to perform at credible levels. Conversely, the brain's capacity for massive parallel processing is at least one of the keys to the apparent superiority of human versus computer thought in areas such as vision.[22]

Parallel processing

The realization of this superiority has focused attention on breaking the von Neumann bottleneck of conventional, single-processor computers. W. Daniel Hillis's Connection Machine, for example, is capable of 65,536 computations at the same time, and machines with a millionfold parallelism are on the way.[23] Billions of simultaneous processes, particularly if analog methods are combined with digital, are not out of the question.[24]

The realization that certain critical mental processes are inherently massively parallel rather than sequential has also refocused attention on the neural net as an approach to building intelligent machines.[25] The 1960s concept of a neural net machine incorporated very simple neuron models and a relatively small number of neurons (hundreds or thousands) organized in one or two layers. They were provided with no specific task-oriented algorithms and were expected to organize themselves by rearranging the interneuronal connections on the basis of feedback from the human trainer. These systems were capable of recognizing simple shapes, but Minsky and Papert showed, in their classic *Perceptrons,* that the machines were essentially just matching individual pixel values against stored templates. These early neural nets were simply not capable of more sophisticated discriminations.[26] As noted earlier, the 1980s school of neural nets uses potentially more capable neuron models that can incorporate their own algorithms.[27] Designers are targeting systems with millions of such artificial neurons organized into many layers. Though the self-organizing paradigm is still popular, its role can be limited. Predetermined algorithms can be built into both the neuron models themselves and the organization of each layer. For example, a layer designed to detect edges should be organized differently from a layer designed to integrate edges into surfaces. Of course, this is still a far cry from the human visual system, with its billions of neurons organized into hundreds of layers. We still have very limited understanding of the algorithms incorporated in most of the layers or even what their functions are. Greater insight into these issues will be required before neural nets can solve real problems. Minsky and Papert remain critical of the excessive reliance of the new connectionists on the self-organizing paradigm of neural nets. In the prologue to a new edition of

The Connection Machine, 65,536
computers in one. AI Researchers
now realize that massive parallel
processing is one of the keys to
achieving human-level intelligence.
(Courtesy of Thinking Machines
Corp.)

Perceptrons (1988) they state, "Our position remains what it was when we wrote the book: We believe this realm of work to be immensely important and rich, but we expect its growth to require a degree of critical analysis that its more romantic advocates have always been reluctant to pursue—perhaps because the spirit of connectionism seems itself to go somewhat against the grain of analytic rigor."[28]

Another difference between logical and imaginal thinking is the issue of gradual versus catastrophic degradation.[29] In animal vision the failure of any neuron to perform its task correctly is irrelevant. Even substantial portions of the visual cortex could be defective with relatively little impact on the quality of the end result. Leaving aside physical damage to the eyes themselves, the ability of the human brain to process visual images typically degrades the same way that a holographic (three-dimensional, laser-generated) picture degrades. Failure of individual elements subtract only marginally from the overall result. Logical processes are quite different. Failure of any step in a chain of logical deductions and inferences dooms the rest of the thought process. Most mistakes are catastrophic (in that they lead to an invalid result). We have some ability to detect problems in later stages, realize that earlier assumptions must have been faulty, and then attempt to correct them, but our ability to do this is limited.

The difference between parallel thinking and sequential thinking is significant in skill acquisition. When we first learn to perform a pattern-recognition task (learning a new type of alphabet, for example, or, on a higher level, a new language), we use our rational facilities to reason through the decision-making tasks required. This tends to be slow, deliberate, and conscious.[30] As we "master" the new task,

The promise of parallel processing. Hidehiko Tanaka of the University of Tokyo designs super fast computers that incorporate thousands of tiny processors working in unison on a single problem. (Photo by Lou Jones)

Yuichiro Anzai, one of the leading AI authorities in Japan. (Photo by Lou Jones)

our parallel facilities take over and we no longer need to consciously think through each step. It seems just to happen automatically. We have programmed our parallel pattern-recognition systems to take over the job. The process of recognition becomes substantially faster, and we are no longer conscious of the steps in the process. Visual-perception experiments have indicated that when we read, we do not perform recognition on individual characters and then group the characters into words but rather recognize entire words and even groups of words in parallel. If we had to reason through each discrimination (e.g., "Now there's a semicircle with a straight line to the left of it, so that must be a *p*"), our reading speeds would be extremely slow. Indeed, a child's reading speed is very slow until the child has succeeded in programming his parallel pattern-recognition facilities to recognize first individual letters, then words, finally, after years, groups of words.

There is a similar phenomenon on the output side of human intelligence. When we learn to perform a certain task that involves the coordination of our muscles (learning a sport or even speaking a new language), we start out very deliberately and conscious of each step in the process. After we "master" the new skill, we are conscious only of the higher-level tasks, not of the individual steps. We have gone from sequential to parallel thinking.

One of the objections that philosophers such as Hubert Dreyfus have made of AI is that computers appear to lack the ability for this type of parallel thought (the objection is generally expressed in the much vaguer terms that computers lack intuition).[31] It is true that the purely logical processes of most expert systems do not have the capacity for achieving this vital category of massively parallel thought. It is not valid, however, to conclude that machines are inherently incapable of using this approach.

One might point out that even massively parallel machines ultimately use logic in their transformations. Logic alone, however, is not the appropriate level of analysis to understand such systems. It is similar to trying to understand meteorology using the laws of physics.[32] Obviously, cloud particles do follow the laws of physics, but it is hopeless to attempt to predict the weather by means of the physics of particle interactions alone (not that we are very successful at weather forecasting even with "appropriate" methods). As an example of the weakness of rule-based methodologies in mastering certain intelligent tasks, consider the problem of describing how to recognize faces using logic alone. Face recognition is a process we are very good at despite our having little awareness of how the process actually works. No one has been able to program a computer to perform this task, in part because no one can begin to describe how we perform this feat. In general, we find it far easier to reconstruct our mental processes for sequential thinking than for parallel thinking because we are consciously aware of each step in the process.

Building a brain

We can draw conclusions from the above discussion regarding some of the capabilities required to simulate the human brain (i.e., to emulate its functionality). Clearly, we need a capacity for hundreds of levels of massively parallel computations (with the parallelism of each stage potentially in the billions). These levels cannot be fully self-organizing, although the algorithms will in some cases allow for "growing" new interneuronal connections. Each level will embody an algorithm, although the algorithms must permit learning. The algorithms are implemented in two ways: the transformations performed by the neurons themselves and the architecture of how the neurons are connected. The multiple layers of parallel neuronal analysis permit information to be encoded on multiple levels of abstraction. For example, in vision, images are first analyzed in terms of edges; edges form surfaces; surfaces form objects; objects form scenes.[33]

Another example is human written language. Lines and curves form letters, which form words, which form phrases, which form sentences, and so on. In spoken language, we have sounds forming phonemes, which form words, and so on. Knowledge regarding the constraints of each level of abstraction is used in the appropriate layer. The knowledge itself is not built in (though algorithms for manipulating it may be) and methods need to be provided to acquire, represent, access, and utilize the domain-specific knowledge.

Each level of analysis reduces information. In vision, for example, we start with the signals received from the hundred million rod and cone cells in each eye. This is equivalent to tens of billions of bits of information per second. Intermediate representations in terms of surfaces and surface qualities can be represented with far less information. The knowledge we finally extract from this analysis is a reduction of the original massive stream of data by many orders of magnitude. Here too we see the selective (i.e., intelligent) destruction of information discussed earlier as the purpose of computation.[34]

The human brain has a certain degree of plasticity in that different areas of the brain can often be used to represent the same type of knowledge. This property enables stroke victims to relearn lost skills by training other portions of the brain that were not damaged. The process of learning (or relearning) requires our sequential conscious processes to repetitively expose the appropriate parallel unconscious mechanisms to the knowledge and constraints of a pattern-recognition or physical-skill task. There are substantial limits to this plasticity, however. The visual cortex, for example, is specifically designed for vision and cannot be used for most other tasks (although it is involved in visual imagination, which does impact many other areas of thought).

We can also draw a conclusion regarding the type of *physical construction* required to achieve human-level performance. The human brain achieves massive parallelism in all stages of its processing measured in the tens or hundreds of billions of simultaneous computations in a package substantially under one cubic foot, about the size of a typical personal computer. It is capable of this immense level of performance because it is organized in *three* dimensions, whereas our electronic circuits are currently organized in only *two*. Our integrated-circuit chips, for example, are essentially flat. With the number of components on each side of a chip measured in the thousands, we are limited to a few million components per chip. If, on the other hand, we could build three-dimensional chips (that is, with a thousand or so layers of circuitry on each chip instead of just one), we would add three orders of magnitude to their complexity: we would have chips with billions rather than mere millions of components. This appears to be *necessary* to achieve hardware capable of human performance. Evolution certainly found it necessary to use the third dimension when designing animal brains.[35] Interestingly, one way that the design of the human brain uses the third dimension is by elaborately folding the surface of the cerebral cortex to achieve a very large surface area.

A primary reason that the third dimension is not utilized is thermal problems. Transistors generate heat, and multiple layers would cause chip circuitry to melt. However, a solution may be on the horizon in the form of superconductivity: because of their lack of electrical resistance, superconducting circuits generate virtually no heat. This may enable circuit designers to further reduce the size of each transistor as well as to exploit the unexplored third dimension for a potential million-fold improvement in performance.[36]

David Marr and Tomaso Poggio pointed out another salient difference between human brains and today's computers in their first paper on stereo vision in 1976.[37] While the ratio of connections to components in a conventional computer is about 3, this ratio for the mammalian cortex can be as high as 10,000. In a computer virtually every component and connection is vital. Although there are special fail-safe computers that provide a small measure of redundancy, most computers depend on a very high degree of reliability in all of their components. The design of mammalian brains appears to use a radically different methodology in which none of the components or connections are crucial; massive redundancy allows major portions of the process to fail with little or no effect on the final results.[38]

In summary, there are two fundamentally different forms of thinking: logical thinking and parallel thinking. Logical thinking is sequential and conscious. It involves deliberate control over each step. It tends to be slow and errors in early stages propagate throughout the rest of the process often with catastrophic results. The amount of computation required tends to be limited. Thus, computers lacking in parallel-processing capabilities (nearly all computers to date) have been relatively successful in emulating some forms of logical thought. Most AI through the mid 1980s has been concerned with emulating this type of problem solving, with parallel thought processes often being overlooked.[39] This has led to criticism of AI, often with the unjustified conclusion that computers are inherently incapable of parallel thought. Parallel thinking is massively parallel. It is capable of simultaneously processing multiple levels of abstraction, with each level incorporating substantial knowledge and constraints. It tends to be relatively fast because of its highly parallel construction. It generally takes place without either conscious direction or even awareness of the nature of the transformations being made. Skill acquisition generally involves the sequential mind repeatedly training the parallel mind.

The principles of pattern recognition

Building on the observations above, we can describe several principles that govern successful pattern recognition systems. While specific implementations and techniques will differ from one problem domain to another, the principles remain the same.

It is clear that parallel processing is important, particularly in the early stages of the process, since the quantity of information is greatly reduced by each stage of processing. Pattern-recognition tasks generally require a hierarchy of decisions. Each stage has its own manner of representing information and its own methods for deriving the information from the previous stage. For example, in vision we represent the original image data in terms of pixel intensity values. Hypothesized line segments, on the other hand, are probably represented in terms of the coordinates of the ends of each segment along with additional information about the characteristics of each segment (curvature, edge noise, shading, etc.). Similarly, surfaces are represented by a large number of coordinates plus information regarding the surface characteristics. A variety of methods have been devised for representing objects, including the primal sketch, the $2\frac{1}{2}$D sketch, and the world model.[40]

A key issue in analyzing each stage of representation is *segmentation*. In speech recognition, for example, we need to divide a sample of continuous speech into smaller segments such as words or perhaps phonemes (basic sounds).[41] Choosing the appropriate types of segments for each stage is one of the most important decisions in designing a pattern-recognition system. Once segments in the data have been located, they can be labeled (described). In vision, for example, once we have segmented a scene into line segments, we can describe the nature of the segments. We then segment the edge representation into surfaces and go on to label the surfaces with their characteristics.

After we have determined the stages of processing, the representation of information contained in each stage, the segments to be extracted, and the type of

How about this pattern? How many faces are there? Can you find a hand? What other body parts can you identify? Human pattern recognition is capable of many levels of abstraction. (*Girl before a Mirror* by Pablo Picasso, in the collection of the Museum of Modern Art, New York)

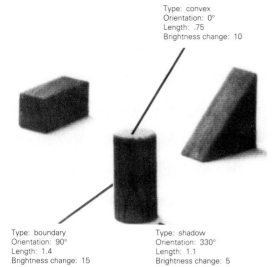

Type: convex
Orientation: 0°
Length: .75
Brightness change: 10

Type: boundary
Orientation: 90°
Length: 1.4
Brightness change: 15

Type: shadow
Orientation: 330°
Length: 1.1
Brightness change: 5

One approach to describing an image is the primal sketch, shown here with the original image. The primal sketch is not an image at all but a data base that describes brightness change, blobs and textures. (From Winston, *Artificial Intelligence,* 1984, p. 337)

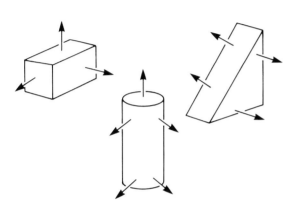

The next level of representation, the 2¹/₂-dimensional sketch (sometimes called a needle diagram for obvious reasons), describes the location and orientation of surfaces. (From Winston, *Artificial Intelligence,* 1984, p. 338)

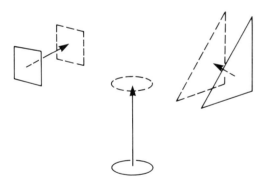

Finally, the world model, which describes the construction of objects in the image by modeling them as generalized "cylinders." (From Winston, *Artificial Intelligence,* 1984, p. 339)

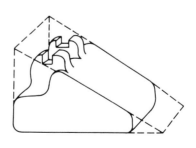

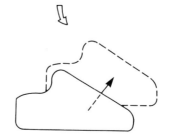

A more complicated world model consisting of a wedge-shaped cylinder with protrusions describes the shape of a telephone. (From Winston, *Artificial Intelligence,* 1984, p. 340)

labeling desired for each segment, we are still faced with the heart of the problem: designing methods to make the segmentation and labeling decisions. The most successful paradigm I have found for accomplishing this is that of multiple experts.[42] Usually the only methods available to perform specific recognition tasks are very imperfect ones. Information theory tells us that with several *independent* methods of relatively low accuracy we can still achieve high levels of accuracy if we combine them in a certain way. These multiple methods, called experts, are considered independent if they have what are called orthogonal invariances, that is, independent strengths. Another way of saying the same thing is that the different experts (sometimes also called knowledge sources) tend to make different types of mistakes. The goal is to assemble a group of experts diverse enough that for each pattern that arises, at least one of the experts will have the proficiency to respond correctly. (Of course, we still have to decide which expert is right, just as in ordinary life! I shall come back to this question.)

Character recognition

As an example, consider the recognition of printed letters.[43] One useful expert we can call on would detect a feature called the loop, which is an area of white completely surrounded by black. The capital *A*, for example, has one loop; *B* has two. Another useful expert would detect concavities, which are concave regions facing in a particular direction. For example, *A* has one concavity facing south, *F* has one concave region facing east, and *E* has two concavities facing east.

Our loop expert would be proficient at distinguishing an *O* from a *C* in that *O* has a loop and *C* does not. It would not be capable, however, of discriminating *C* from *I* (no loops in either case) or *O* from *6* (each has one loop). The concavity expert could help us here, since it can distinguish *C* from *I* and *6* from *O* by the presence of an east concavity in *C* and *6*. Similarly, the concavity expert by itself would be unable to distinguish *C* from *6* (since they both have an east concavity), but the loop expert could identify *6* by its single loop. Clearly, the two experts together give us far greater recognition capability than either one alone. In fact, using just these two experts (a loop detector and a concavity detector), we can sort all 62 sans-serif roman characters, excluding punctuation (*A* through *Z*, *a* through *z*, and *0* through *9*) into about two dozen distinct groups with only a few characters in each group. For example, the group characterized by no loops with north and south concavities contains only the characters *H* and *N*. In other words, if the loop expert examined a pattern and indicated it had found no loops and the concavity expert indicated concave regions facing south and north, we could conclude that the character was (probably) either an *H* or an *N*. Additional experts that examined the location and orientation of line segments or angle vertices could then help us to make a final identification.

It is clear that in addition to a set of experts that can provide us with the ability to make all of the discriminations necessary, we also need a process to direct and organize the efforts of these experts. Such a system, often called the expert manager, is programmed with the knowledge of which expert to use in each situation.[44] It knows the relative strengths and weaknesses of each expert and how to

The loop feature.

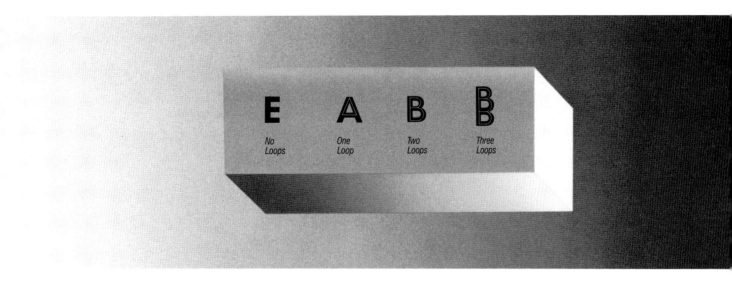

E — No Loops
A — One Loop
B — Two Loops
B — Three Loops

C — One "East" Concavity
H — One "North" and one "South" Concavity
A — One "South" Concavity
O — No Concavities
E — Two "East" Concavities

The concavity feature.

A and n touching

Broken loop on the A

Closed loop on the a   **u and n touching**

Another di

from a fund':

along to its in

realize the lo:

Noise around r

Typical defects in real print.

combine their insights into making final decisions. It would know, for example, that the loop expert is relatively useless in discriminating 6 from O but very helpful for determining whether a character is a 6 or a C, and so on.

In a real system (one that deals with images from the real world), classifications are rarely as straightforward as the examples above suggest. For example, it is entirely possible that an A as actually printed might *not* contain a loop because a printing error caused the loop to be broken (see figure). An a (which should contain one loop) might actually contain two loops if an ink smear caused the upper portion to close. Real-world patterns rarely display the expected patterns perfectly. Even a well-printed document contains a surprisingly large number of defects. One way to deal with the vagaries of real-world patterns is to have redundant experts and multiple ways of describing the same type of pattern. There are a number of different ways of describing what an A should look like. Thus, if one of our experts failed (e.g., the loop expert), we still have a good chance of correctly recognizing the pattern.

There are many sources of variability. One, called noise for obvious reasons, consists of random changes to a pattern, particularly near the edges, caused by defects in the pattern itself as well as imperfections in the sensing mechanism that visualizes the pattern (e.g., an image scanner). Another source of variability derives from the inherent nature of patterns defined at a high level of abstraction. For example, the concept of an A allows for a great deal of variation (see figure). There are hundreds of different styles of type in common use and many more if ornamental styles are considered. If one considers only a single type style, then one could obtain accurate recognition using a relatively small number of experts. If, on the other hand, we attempt to recognize printed characters drawn from a wide multitude of styles, then it is clear that a substantially more diverse set

What letter is this? Douglas Hofstadter uses these images to illustrate the superiority of human pattern recognition over the machines of today. Humans have little difficulty recognizing these variations (although a few of these may indeed be problematical if presented in isolation). While machines exist today that can accurately recognize the many type styles in common usage, no machine can successfully deal with the level of abstraction required by these ornamental forms.

The classification of roman well-printed sans-serif characters by loop and concavity features.

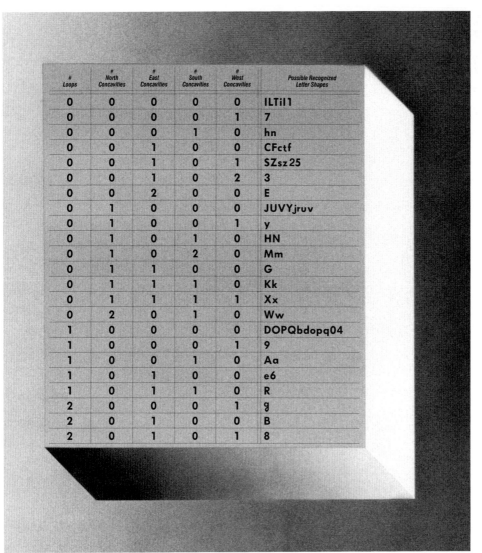

# Loops	# North Concavities	# East Concavities	# South Concavities	# West Concavities	Possible Recognized Letter Shapes
0	0	0	0	0	ILTiI1
0	0	0	0	1	7
0	0	0	1	0	hn
0	0	1	0	0	CFctf
0	0	1	0	1	SZsz25
0	0	1	0	2	3
0	0	2	0	0	E
0	1	0	0	0	JUVYjruv
0	1	0	0	1	y
0	1	0	1	0	HN
0	1	0	2	0	Mm
0	1	1	0	0	G
0	1	1	1	0	Kk
0	1	1	1	1	Xx
0	2	0	1	0	Ww
1	0	0	0	0	DOPQbdopq04
1	0	0	0	1	9
1	0	0	1	0	Aa
1	0	1	0	0	e6
1	0	1	1	0	R
2	0	0	0	1	g
2	0	1	0	0	B
2	0	1	0	1	8

Disambiguating *N* from *H* using a line segment expert.

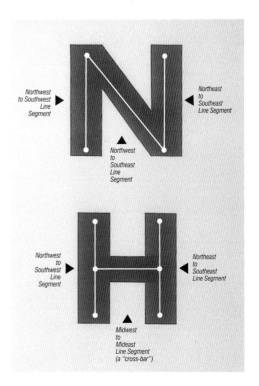

Northwest to Southwest Line Segment

Northeast to Southeast Line Segment

Northwest to Southeast Line Segment

Northwest to Southwest Line Segment

Northeast to Southeast Line Segment

Midwest to Mideast Line Segment (a "cross-bar")

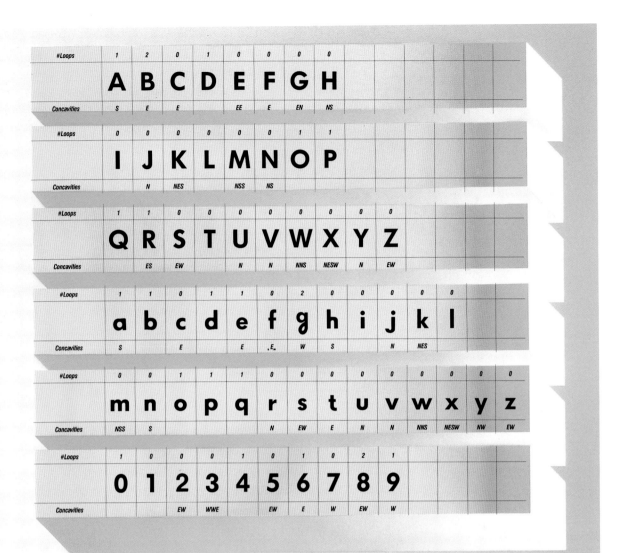

The loop and concavity features of 62 roman sans-serif characters. Some of the concavities are ambiguous or marginal. For example, the southern concavity in the letter *a* is so small it may be overlooked by the concavity expert. Thus in a practical system *a* would be classified in both the "has one southern concavity" and "has no southern concavity" categories. To account for multiple type fonts most characters will in fact have multiple classifications.

of experts is required.[45] Allowing such variability in the patterns to be recognized also complicates the task of the expert manager.

Since the classification of patterns in the real world is often not clear cut, it is desirable for our experts to provide their "opinions" on a continuous scale. Rather than stating that this pattern has a loop, it would be of greater value for the expert to indicate its relative level of confidence in the presence of such a property (e.g., "There is a 95 percent probability of there being one loop in this pattern, a 3 percent probability of there being two loops"). A less-than-certain result might indicate that the loop expert almost found a loop, that the "loop" found is broken by a few pixels. Even if the loop is entirely closed, there is always the possibility that it really should not be there at all but is only an artifact of a printing or scanning error. If all of the experts provide their analyses in terms of probabilities, then the expert manager can use information theory to combine these results in an optimal way.

In cases of significant print distortion, even human perception can fail on the level of individual letters. Yet we are often able to correct for printing defects by using our knowledge of language context. For example, if we have trouble distinguishing a *t* from a *c* because of poor printing, we generally look (consciously or unconsciously) at the context of the letter. We might determine, for example, that "computer" makes more sense than "compucer." This introduces the concept of experts that use knowledge of the constraints of higher levels of context. Knowing that "compucer" is not a word in English but that "computer" is enables us to disambiguate an otherwise ambiguous pattern. Similarly, in the field of speech recognition, the only possible way to distinguish the spoken word "to" from "too" and from "two" (all of which sound identical) is from context. In the sentence "I am going to the store," we can eliminate "too" and "two" from consideration by relying on our higher-level syntactic knowledge. Perceptual experiments indicate that human pattern recognition relies heavily on such contextual discrimination. Attempting to recognize printed letters without a word context, human speech without a sentence context, and musical timbres without a melodic context sharply reduces the accuracy of human perception. Similarly, machines dealing with highly variable types of patterns require extensive use of context experts with substantial knowledge about their domains. A word-context expert in a character-recognition system requires knowledge of all the possible words in the language. A syntactic expert in a speech-recognition system requires knowledge of possible word sequences. Again, an expert that can say, "'Phthisis' has a probability of .0001," is more valuable than one who can only say, "'Phthisis' is possible."

All of the experts mentioned above deal with relatively abstract concepts. Concavity is not a perfectly defined concept. Detecting this property is not straightforward and requires a relatively complex program. A very different category of experts, low-level experts (as distinguished from the high-level experts described above), deal with features that are simple transformations of the original input data. For example, in any type of visual recognition we could have a low-level property associated with every pixel whose value is simply the value of the pixel. This is, of course, the simplest possible property. A slightly higher level property (but still low level) could detect the amount of black in a particular region of the image. For

Varieties of low-level (minimal) property sets.

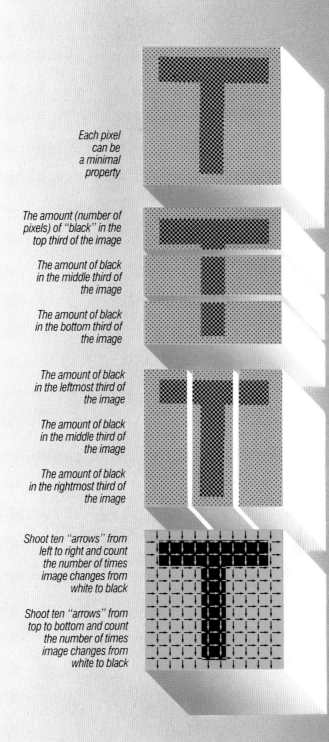

Each pixel
can be
a minimal
property

The amount (number of
pixels) of "black" in the
top third of the image

The amount of black
in the middle third of
the image

The amount of black
in the bottom third of
the image

The amount of black
in the leftmost third of
the image

The amount of black
in the middle third of
the image

The amount of black
in the rightmost third of
the image

Shoot ten "arrows" from
left to right and count
the number of times
image changes from
white to black

Shoot ten "arrows" from
top to bottom and count
the number of times
image changes from
white to black

example, a *T* will tend to have more black in the upper region of the image than an *L*, which will tend to be more black in the lower region. In actual use, minimal properties tend to be more complex than in the above two examples but nonetheless use straightforward and well-defined transformations of the original input.

It turns out that such low-level properties are quite useful in recognizing patterns when the possible types of patterns are highly constrained. For example, in character recognition, if we restrict the problem to a single style of type, then a system built entirely with low-level property experts is capable of a very high level of accuracy (potentially less than one error in over ten thousand printed characters). This limited problem is often attacked with template matching, so called because it involves matching the image under consideration to stored templates of every letter in the character set.[46] Template matching (and other methods of minimal-property extraction) also work well for recognizing printed letters drawn from a small number of type styles. If we are trying to recognize *any* nonornamental type style (called omnifont, or intelligent, character recognition), then an approach using only minimal property extraction does not work at all. In this case, we must use the higher-level (more intelligent) experts that are based on such abstract topological concepts as loops, concavities, and line segments. The minimal properties can still play an important role, however. Fortunately, printed material does not generally combine multiple type styles in anything like a random fashion. Any particular document (e.g., a book or magazine) will tend to use a limited number of type styles in a consistent way.[47] When an omnifont character-recognition machine first encounters a new document, it has no choice but to use its intelligent experts (its loop expert, concavity expert, etc.) to recognize the characters. As it begins successfully to recognize characters, its higher-level experts can actually train its lower-level experts to do the job, and its expert manager (which directs the overall recognition process) can begin to rely more heavily on the lower-level experts for recognition. The higher-level experts train the lower-level ones by presenting actual examples of recognized characters and telling them, in essence, "Here are examples of characters as they actually appear in this document, and this is what we believe their correct identifications to be." The advantages of such an automatic learning process include both speed and accuracy. The lower-level experts are not only potentially much faster, they can also be less sensitive to image noise.

To return to the first theme of this chapter, the higher-level experts in such a character-recognition system are representative of logical analysis, whereas the lower-level experts represent a more parallel type of thinking. The lower-level experts use much simpler algorithms, so they are more amenable to massive parallel processing, which is a major reason for their potential speed advantage.

Interestingly, perceptual experiments indicate that the human visual system works in a similar way. When we first encounter a new typeface, to recognize it, we rely on our conceptual understanding of print (a logical type of analysis), and our recognition speeds are relatively slow. Once we get used to the style, our recognition process becomes less analytic, and our speed and accuracy increase substantially. This is another example of our logical mind training our parallel mind.

The paradigm of pattern recognition described above is common to most serious recognition problems: multiple stages of processing based on a hierarchy of levels, massive parallel processing (particularly in the early stages), segmentation and labeling, multiple experts on both high and low levels, expert management, disambiguation using the constraints of higher levels of context, and learning from actual recognition examples.[48] The actual content of the paradigm, however, will differ substantially from one problem area to another. Most of the technology of any successful pattern-recognition system is *domain specific*; that is, it is based on the detailed nature of the types of patterns to be recognized. Every so often one hears claims regarding a general-purpose pattern-recognition system that can recognize *any* type of pattern—printed characters, spoken words, land-terrain maps—regardless of their source. As mentioned earlier, while such systems do recognize many types of patterns, they perform these tasks poorly. To perform any specific pattern-recognition task well with commercially acceptable rates of accuracy requires substantial knowledge deeply embedded in the algorithms and specific to the domain of inquiry.

• **The Real World**

Looking at the real world

Attempts to emulate the general capabilities of human vision are being pursued at a number of leading AI laboratories. One is an ambitious project to create an artificial eye-head system at the MIT Vision Laboratory under the direction of Tomaso Poggio.[49] The MIT work includes edge detection (using the Laplacian Gaussian convolver described above and other similar algorithms), fusing stereo images to provide information on depth, understanding color perception, reconstructing surfaces and their properties, tracking trajectories of moving objects, and the ultimate problem of describing the content of what is seen. One of the most interesting aspects of the MIT work is the development of a new type of computer that combines digital control with massive analog parallelism.[50] Experiments conducted by Poggio, his associate Christof Koch, and others have already suggested that the human nervous system appears to be capable of substantial parallelism (hundreds) of *analog* computations within a *single neuron.*

This work is exemplary of the paradigm of multiple experts. A number of different systems, each with extensive knowledge of a specific aspect of the visual-perception task, are combined in the MIT eye-head system.[51] For example, an expert being developed by Anya Hurlbert and Tomaso Poggio uses knowledge of the spectral (color) reflectance of surfaces to help describe them.[52] The project also addresses the issues of integrating visual perception with the mechanical control of a robot and includes a head with two solid-state cameras for eyes (that is, cameras with a special chip called a charge-coupled device as an electronic retina).

A major center for the development of vision systems and their application to the field of robotics is the Robotics Institute (RI) at Carnegie-Mellon University under the direction of AI pioneer Raj Reddy. A particularly ambitious project at RI, funded by the Defense Advanced Research Projects Agency (DARPA) is an autonomous vehicle called Terregator (Terrestrial Navigator) which combines a high-resolution vision system, parallel processing, and advanced decision-making capabilities.[53]

In view of the strong Japanese commitment to the application of robotics to production techniques, Japanese researchers have targeted vision as a priority

Raj Reddy, director of the Robotics Institute of Carnegie-Mellon University. Reddy has been a pioneer in the development of voice recognition, computer vision, and robotics. Now working on the Terregator (Terrestrial Navigator) for the Defense Advanced Research Projects Agency (DARPA), Reddy predicts that future robotic-vision systems will eventually revolutionize driving and provide cars with effective collision-control and road-following capabilities. (Photo by Lou Jones)

Computer vision pioneer Tomaso Poggio at the MIT Vision Lab. (Photo by Lou Jones)

Takeo Kanade, director of the Computer Vision Laboratory of Carnegie-Mellon University. Kanade is developing a highly parallel computer for real-time processing of images from robotic-vision systems. (Photo by Mary Jo Dowling of the Robotics Institute, Carnegie Mellon University)

research topic. Building on the work of Poggio and his associates, Yoshiaki Shirai (of the Electrotechnical Laboratory, Ibaraki, Japan) and Yoshiro Nishimoto (of the Research Laboratory, Kobe Steel, Kobe, Japan) are attempting to build a practical system for fusing stereo images. Based on parallel hardware, the Shirai-Nishimoto system uses a Laplacian of a Gaussian convolver (a sombrero filter) as well as more advanced pattern-matching techniques. Japanese development efforts are emphasizing the integration of vision with real-time robotic control to provide a new generation of robots that can see their environment, perceive and understand the relevant features of objects, and reason about what they have seen. Hirochika Inoue and Hiroshi Mizoguchi (of the University of Tokyo) have developed a system that can detect, recognize, and track rapidly moving objects in real time.

One promising approach to organizing the massive parallelism required for pattern-recognition tasks is to develop specialized chips to perform those tasks requiring the most computation. One researcher pursuing this approach is Carver A. Mead (of the California Institute of Technology), one of the original pioneers in the development of design methodologies for large-scale integrated circuits. Mead and his associates have developed an artificial-retina chip that performs such early-vision tasks as edge detection and the adjustment of an image for the effects of varying levels of illumination.[54] One of the innovations of Mead's approach is his reliance on massively parallel analog circuits to provide the bulk of the computation. Mead is also working on an artificial-cochlea chip based on similar principles.

While research is just beginning on systems that emulate the full range of human visual processing, machines that perform more limited tasks of visual perception have already found significant commercial applications. For example, optical character recognition (OCR) was a $100 million industry in 1986 and is projected to grow to several hundred million dollars in 1990.[55] Applications include reading aloud for the blind, as well as scanning printed and typed documents for entry into word processing, electronic publishing, transaction processing, and database systems.

Seeing and believing. At the
Tsukuba Research Center in Japan,
Yoshiaki Shirai's research in
robotics focuses on the development
of three-dimensional vision systems.
(Photo by Lou Jones)

Hirochika Inoue, a pioneer in robotic
vision systems, at the University of
Tokyo. (Photo by Lou Jones)

Makoto Nagao of Kyoto University explores pattern recognition by means of shadows and surfaces. (Photo by Lou Jones)

Systems using pattern-recognition techniques are revolutionizing the handling of fingerprints by law enforcement agencies. A system called the Automated Fingerprint Identification System (AFIS) developed by NEC of Japan enables agencies across the United States to rapidly identify suspects from fingerprints or even small fragments of fingerprints by intelligently matching them against the stored prints of hundreds of thousands of previously arrested men and women. A report by the U.S. Bureau of Justice Statistics stated, "AFIS may well have the greatest impact of any technological development on law enforcement effectiveness since the introduction of computers to widespread use in the criminal justice system in the 1960s."[56] AFIS is capable of identifying a suspect in several minutes; the manual methods it replaces took months or even years.

Similar techniques are being used in security devices. Systems manufactured by Fingermatrix, Thumbscan, and other firms include a small optical scanner into which a person inserts his finger.[57] The device quickly reads the person's finger pattern and uses pattern-recognition techniques to match it against stored images. The system can control entry to restricted areas and protect information in computers from unauthorized access. Such systems could eventually replace ordinary locks and keys in homes and cars.

One of the largest applications of commercial vision systems so far can be found in factories, where the systems are used for inspection, assembly, and process control. Such systems typically use solid-state cameras with specialized

Systems for automated fingerprint analysis identify distinguishing ridge points that characterize each individual. (Courtesy of Fingermatrix)

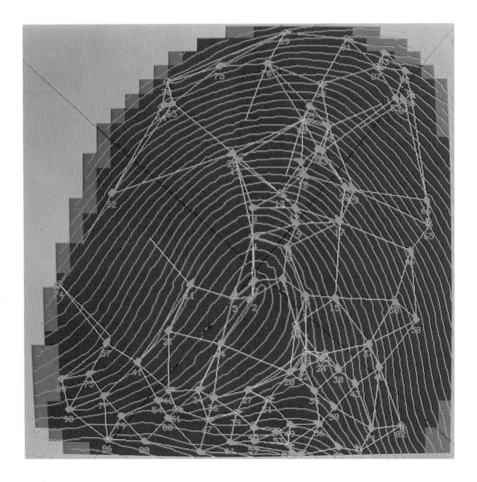

Robotic vision. The robot's TV camera eye sees a jumble of disposable razors. None of the objects can be seen in full. Many crucial features are hidden or otherwise obscured. (Photo by David Lowe)

In this three-dimensional-object-recognition system developed by David Lowe at New York University the first step is to extract line segments by looking for sudden changes in intensity. (Photo by David Lowe)

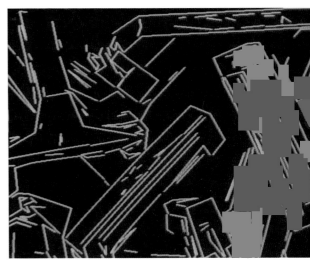

Next the computer attempts to match the two-dimensional projections represented in the image with its internal model of the three-dimensional shape of a razor. Here one set of lines are from the model, and the other set of lines are matching segments from the original picture. (Photo by David Lowe)

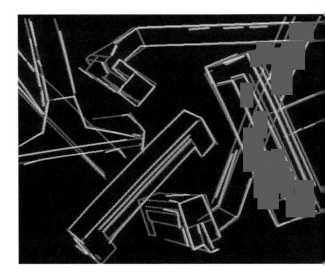

Finally, the location and orientation of each object are recognized. The full models are shown here superimposed on the original image. The dotted lines represent hypothesized line segments that are hidden from view. (Photo by David Lowe)

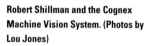

**Robert Shillman and the Cognex
Machine Vision System. (Photos by
Lou Jones)**

electronics to digitize moving images and provide for the computationally intensive early phases of processing.[58] A general-purpose computer with custom software provides for the higher levels of analysis. One of the more sophisticated of such systems has been developed by Cognex Corporation, founded by Robert Shillman and a team of MIT AI researchers in 1981. One Cognex product can scan manufactured products streaming by on a conveyor belt and detect and recognize such information as serial numbers embossed in metal or even glass. Other Cognex products can identify specific objects and their orientation for inspection and to assist robotic assemblers. Other major providers of vision systems include Automatix, Defracto, Perceptron, Robotic Vision Systems, and View Engineering. A major player has been General Motors, which has provided investments and contracts for several of the players. According to DM Data, overall revenues for the factory-vision industry were over $300 million in 1987 and are projected to hit $800 million in 1990.[59]

Military systems account for another major application of artificial vision.[60] The ability to scan and recognize terrain at very low altitudes is a crucial element of the cruise missile, which can be launched thousands of miles from its intended target. Modern fighter planes have a similar ability to track terrain and provide pilots with a continually updated display of the location and trajectory of the aircraft. Smart weapons (bombs, missiles, and other munitions) use a variety of sensing mechanisms including vision to locate, identify, and reach intended targets.

The advent of weapons that can see has resulted in profound changes in military tactics and strategy. As recently as the Vietnam War, it was generally necessary to launch enormous numbers of passive blind weapons in relatively indiscriminate patterns to assure the destruction of a target. Modern battlefield tactics emphasize instead the carefully targeted destruction of the enemy with weapons that can recognize their objective. Intelligent missiles allow planes, ships, and submarines to destroy targets from relatively safe distances. For example, a plane can launch an intelligent missile to destroy a ship from tens or even hundreds of miles away, well out of range of the ship's guns. A new generation of pilotless aircraft use pattern-recognition-based vision systems to navigate and launch weapons without human crews.[61] Vision systems and other pattern-recognition technologies are also deployed in defensive tactics to recognize an incoming missile, but such defense is generally much more difficult than offense. The result is an increasing degree of vulnerability for such slow-moving targets as tanks and ships.

An area of emerging importance is the application of pattern recognition to medicine. Medical diagnosis is, after all, a matter of perceiving relevant patterns from symptoms, test results, and other diagnostic data. Experimental systems can look at images from a variety of imaging sources—X-ray machines, CAT (computerized axial tomography) scanners, and MRI (magnetic resonance imaging) systems—and provide tentative diagnoses. Few, if any, medical professionals are ready to replace their own perceptions with those of such systems, but many are willing to augment their own analysis. Often an automatic system will detect and report a diagnosis that manual analysis would have overlooked.[62]

One particularly promising medical application is the analysis of blood-cell images. Certain types of cancer can be diagnosed by finding telltale precursor

The Cruise Missile. Relying heavily on image processing and pattern-recognition technology, the missile identifies the terrain below it from computerized maps in its memory. This capability permits it to fly only hundreds of feet from the ground and thus to evade radar-based air defenses. (Supplied by Photri)

The B-1 Bomber. Computers assist a wide range of functions, including flying, navigating, and targeting. (Supplied by Photri)

Can you find the airplanes in this picture? Tom Binford, head of Robotics at Stanford University, with images from his aircraft-recognition system. (Photo by Dan McCoy of Rainbow)

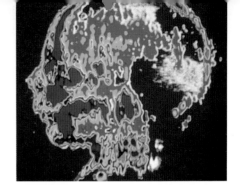

This image of the head of a normal 18-week-old fetus is revealed by sonography, which uses computer-enhanced sound-wave reflections. (Photo taken by Howard Sochurek at the Rush Presbyterian St. Luke's Medical Center, Chicago)

Shigeru Eiho, director of Engineering at Kyoto University, with his medical imaging system. (Photo by Lou Jones)

Computers peer into the human brain. Five new computer-based scanning systems provide doctors with dramatic and precise images of the brain and its ailments. Magnetic resonance imaging (MRI) uses radio waves and a strong magnetic field. This MRI image shows a herniating finger of tissue from a brain slumping into the base of the skull. (Photo taken by Howard Sochurek at the Mallinckrodt Institute of Radiology, Saint Louis)

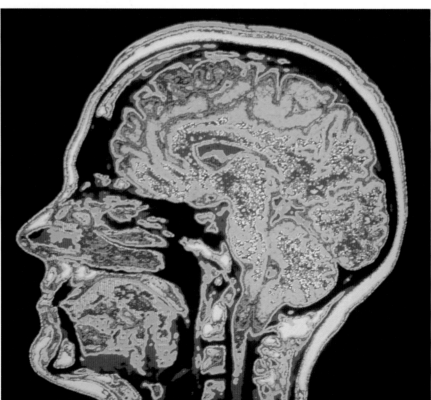

malignant cells in a blood sample. Analysis of blood samples by human technicians typically involve the examination of only about a hundred cells. By the time a malignant cell shows up in a sample that small, the cancer is often too advanced to be effectively treated. Unhampered by fatigue or tedium and able to operate at speeds hundreds of times greater than human technicians, artificial "technicians" using pattern-recognition techniques can search for signs of cancer in hundreds of thousands or even millions of cells and thus potentially detect the presence of disease at a treatable stage.

Ultimately, medical applications of pattern recognition will have enormous benefit. Medical testing comprises a major fraction of all of medicine and costs several hundred billion dollars per year. Examining the images and other data resulting from such tests is extremely tedious for human technicians, and many studies have cited the relatively low level of accuracy that results. Many doctors routinely order tests to be conducted in duplicate just to improve their accuracy. Once computers have mastered the requisite pattern-recognition tasks, the potential exists for a major transformation of medical testing and diagnosis.

A dangerous aneurysm is revealed in an X ray processed by digital subtraction angiography, a computer enhancement technique. (Photo taken by Howard Sochurek at the University of Kansas Medical Center)

The positron emission tomography images reveal damage from a stroke. (Photo taken by Howard Sochurek at the Mallinckrodt Institute of Radiology, Saint Louis)

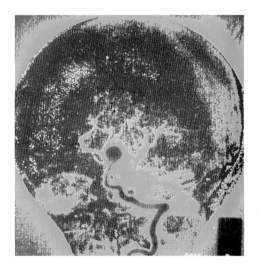
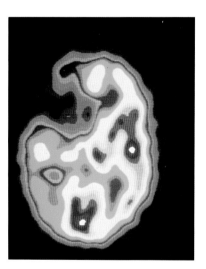

One area of medicine that is already being revolutionized is medical imaging.[63] Using a variety of computer-based image-enhancement techniques, physicians now have access to unprecedented views inside our bodies and brains. Similar techniques also allow scientists to visualize such extremely small biochemical phenomena as viruses for the first time.

One of the more surprising results of image processing and recognition took place recently when Lillian Schwartz observed the striking unity of the juxtaposed halves of the "Mona Lisa" and the reversed "Self-Portrait" by Leonardo da Vinci. Further investigation by Schwartz led her to identify Leonardo as the model used to complete the "Mona Lisa," thereby suggesting a remarkable conclusion to the 500-year-old riddle of the identity of the celebrated painting.[64]

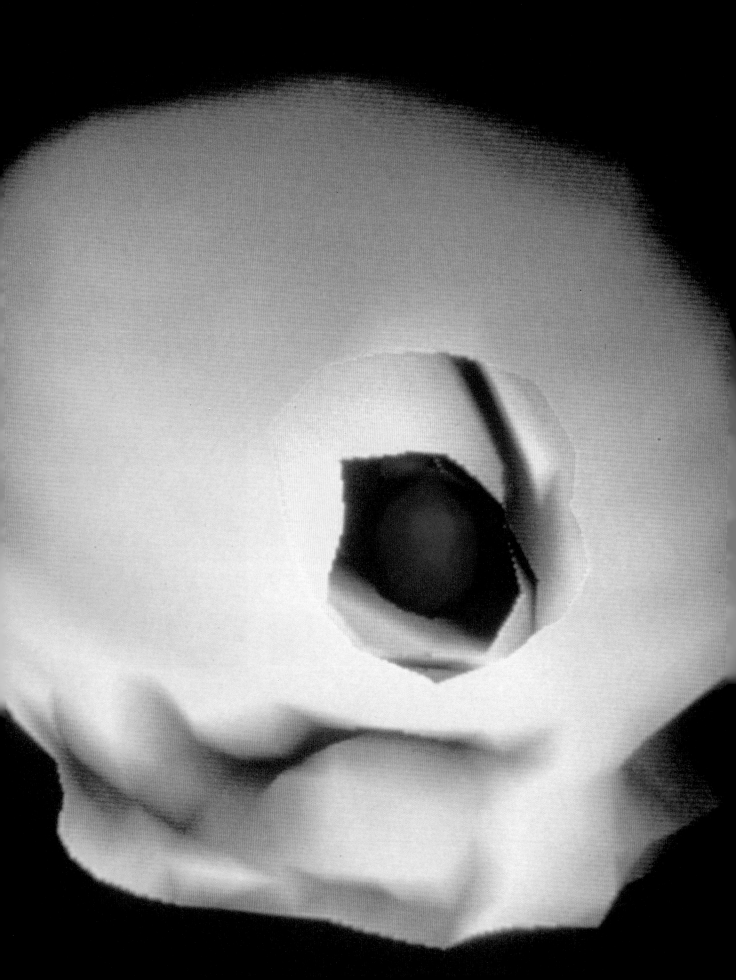

A glaring red tumor reveals itself in this computer-enhanced three-dimensional image from a computer-aided tomography scanner. (Photo taken by Howard Sochurek at the University of Kansas Medical Center)

The computer imagines a tomato virus. This virus is too small to be seen even with an electron microscope. However, scientists can now "see" the virus for the first time using computer-generated images. To create these pictures, the computer was provided information about the virus's molecular structure and chemical composition. (Courtesy of Lawrence Livermore National Laboratory)

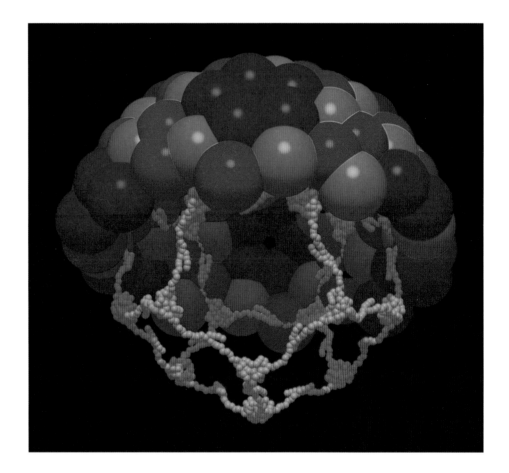

Who is this lady? Mona Lisa
revealed. With the help of computer
image processing, Lillian Schwartz
reached the controversial
conclusion that Mona Lisa was none
other than the artist himself.
(*Mona-Leo* by Lillian Schwartz. Discussed in *The Computer Art Book*,
W. W. Norton. Copyright 1987
by Computer Creations Corporation)

Listening to the real world

Another human sense that computers are attempting to emulate is hearing. While input to the auditory sense involves substantially less data than the visual sense (about a million bits per second from both ears versus about fifty billion bits per second from both eyes), the two senses are of comparable importance in our understanding of the world. As an experiment, try watching a television news program without sound. Then try listening to a similar broadcast without looking at the picture. You will probably find it easier to follow the news stories with yours ears alone than with your eyes alone. Try the same experiment with a situation comedy; the result should be the same.

Part of the importance of our auditory sense is the close link of verbal language to our conscious thinking process. A theory popular until recently held that thinking was subvocalized speech.[65] While we now recognize that our thoughts incorporate both language and visual images, the crucial importance of the auditory sense in the acquisition of knowledge is widely accepted.

Blindness is often considered to be a more serious handicap than deafness. A careful consideration of the issues, however, shows this to be a misconception. With modern mobility techniques, blind persons with appropriate training have little difficulty in travelling from place to place, reading machines can provide access to the world of print, and the visually impaired experience few barriers to communicating with other persons in groups and meetings large or small. For the deaf, however, there is a barrier to engaging in a very fundamental activity—understanding what other people are saying in person to person contact, on the phone, and in meetings. The hearing impaired are often cut off from basic human communication and feel anger at society's failure to accommodate or understand their situation.

We hear many things: music, speech, the varied noises of our environment. Of these, the sounds that are the most important in terms of interacting with

This is the CBS Evening News. A speech spectograph provides a picture of speech. In the large middle portion labeled "Wide-Band Spectogram" the vertical axis is frequency (pitch) and the horizontal axis is time. The darker the plot, the more energy is represented for that pitch at that moment. (Photo by Dan McCoy of Rainbow)

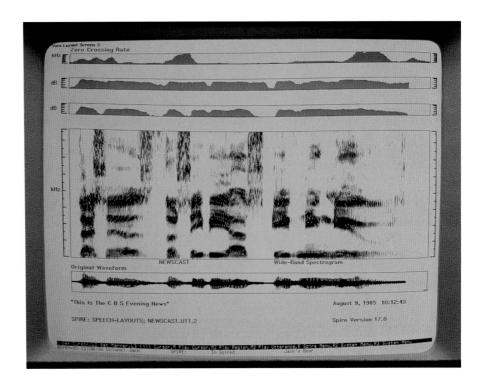

Jonathan Allen, director of the MIT Research Laboratory of Electronics and a pioneer in speech science. Allen's MITalk System was a forerunner of modern speech synthesis programs. Allen has also conducted important research in speech understanding programs and VLSI (very large scale integrated) circuit design. (Photo by Dan McCoy of Rainbow)

Fred Jelinek, IBM researcher and pioneer in the application of statistical modeling techniques to automatic speech recognition. (Courtesy of Fred Jelinek)

The late Dennis Klatt, senior research scientist at MIT, listening to synthesized speech from his KlatTalk program. Klatt's algorithms are used in two commercially successful speech synthesizers, DECtalk from Digital Equipment Corporation and Prose 2000 from Speech Plus. (Courtesy of the MIT Research Laboratory of Electronics)

and learning about the world are those of human speech. Appropriately, the area of auditory recognition that has received the most attention is that of speech recognition in both human and machine.

As with human vision, the stages of human auditory processing that we know the most about are the early ones. From the work of Stephanie Seneff, Richard Goldhor, and others at the MIT Speech Laboratory and from similar work at other laboratories, we have some knowledge of the specific transformations applied by the auditory nerve and early stages of the auditory cortex. As with vision, our knowledge of the details of the later stages is relatively slight due mostly to our inability to access these inner circuits of the brain. Since it is difficult for us to analyze the human auditory system directly, the bulk of the research in speech recognition to date has been devoted to teaching machines to understand speech. As with vision, the success of such efforts may provide us with workable theories as to how the human auditory system might work, and these theories may subsequently be verified by neurophysical experimentation.

Let us examine automatic speech recognition (ASR) in terms of the pattern-recognition paradigm described above for vision. Speech is created by the human vocal tract, which, like a complex musical instrument, has a number of different ways of shaping sound. The vocal cords vibrate, creating a characteristic pitched sound. The length and tautness of the vocal cords determines pitch in the same way that the length and tautness of a violin or piano string determines pitch. We can control the tautness of our vocal cords (hence our ability to sing). We shape the overtones produced by our vibrating vocal cords by moving our tongue, teeth, and lips, which has the effect of changing the shape of the vocal tract. The vocal tract is a chamber that acts like a pipe in a pipe organ, the harmonic resonances of which emphasize certain overtones and diminish others. Finally, we control a small piece of tissue called the alveolar flap, which opens and closes the nasal cavity. When the alveolar flap is open, the nasal cavity provides an additional resonant chamber similar to the opening of another organ pipe.

In addition to the pitched sound produced by the vocal cords, we can produce a noiselike sound by the rush of air through the speech cavity. This sound

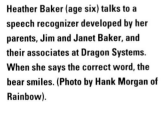

Heather Baker (age six) talks to a speech recognizer developed by her parents, Jim and Janet Baker, and their associates at Dragon Systems. When she says the correct word, the bear smiles. (Photo by Hank Morgan of Rainbow).

does not have specific overtones but is rather a complex spectrum of many frequencies mixed together. Like the musical tones produced by the vocal cords, the spectra of these noise sounds are also shaped by the changing resonances of the moving vocal tract.[66]

This apparatus allows us to create the varied sounds that comprise human speech. While many animals communicate with others of their species with sound, we humans are unique in our ability to shape sound into language. Vowel sounds (/a/, /e/) are produced by shaping the overtones from the vibrating vocal cords into distinct frequency bands called formants. Sibilant sounds (/s/, /z/) are created by the rush of air through particular configurations of tongue and teeth. Plosive consonants (/p/, /k/, /t/) are transitory sounds created by the percussive movement of lips, tongue, and mouth cavity. Nasal sounds (/n/, /m/) are created by invoking the resonances of the nasal cavity.[67]

Each of the several dozen basic sounds, called phonemes, requires an intricate movement involving precise coordination of the vocal cords, alveolar flap, tongue, lips, and teeth. We typically speak about 3 words per second. So with an average of 6 phonemes per word, we make about 18 complex phonetic gestures each second. We do this without thinking about it, of course. Our thoughts remain on the conceptual (that is, the highest) level of the language hierarchy. In our first two years of life, however, we thought a lot about how to make speech sounds (and how to meaningfully string them together). This is another example of our sequential (logical) conscious mind training our parallel (pattern recognition) mind.

The mechanisms described above for creating speech sounds—vocal cord vibrations, the noise of rushing air, articulatory gestures of the mouth and tongue, the shaping of the vocal and nasal cavities—produce different rates of vibration. A physicist measures these rates of vibration as frequencies; we perceive them as pitches. Though we normally consider speech to be a single time-varying sound, it is actually a composite of many different sounds, each of which has a different frequency. With this insight, most commercial ASR systems start by breaking up the speech waveform into a number of different bands of frequencies. A typical commercial or research ASR system will produce between three and a few dozen frequency bands. The front end of the human auditory system does exactly the same thing; each of the nerve endings in the cochlea (inner ear) responds to different frequencies and emits a pulsed digital signal when activated by an appropriate pitch. The cochlea differentiates several thousand overlapping bands of frequency, which gives the human auditory system its extremely high degree of sensitivity to frequency. Experiments have shown that increasing the number of overlapping frequency bands in an ASR system (and thus bringing it closer to the thousands of bands of the human auditory system) substantially increases the ability of that system to recognize human speech.[68]

Typically, parallel processing is used in the front-end frequency analysis of an ASR system, although not as massively as in vision systems, since the quantity of data is much less. (If one were to approach the thousands of frequency bands used by the human auditory system, then massive parallel processing would be required.) Once the speech signal has been transformed into the frequency domain, it is normalized (adjusted) to remove the effects of loudness and background noise. At this point we can detect a number of features of frequency-band signals and consider the problems of segmentation and labeling.

As in vision systems, minimal property extraction is one popular technique. One can use as a feature set either the normalized frequency data itself or various transformations of this data. Now, in matching such minimal-property sets, we need to consider the phenomenon of nonlinear time compression.[69] When we speak, we change our speed according to context and other factors. If we speak one word more quickly, we do not increase the rate evenly throughout the entire word. The duration of certain portions of the word, such as plosive consonants, will remain fairly constant, while other portions, such as vowels, will undergo most of the change. In matching a spoken word to a stored template, we need to align the corresponding acoustic events, or the match will never succeed. This problem is similar to the matching of visual cues in fusing the stereo images from our two eyes. A mathematical technique called dynamic programming has been developed to accomplish this temporal alignment.[70]

As with vision systems, high-level features are also used in ASR systems. As mentioned above, speech is made up of strings of phonemes, which comprise the basic "alphabet" of spoken language. In English and other European romance languages, there are about 16 vowels and 24 consonants; Japanese primarily uses only 5 vowels and 15 consonants. The nature of a particular phoneme (such as /a/) is an abstract concept in the same way that the inherent nature of a printed character (such as *A*) is: neither can be simply defined. Identifying phonemes in human speech requires intelligent algorithms and recognition of high-level features (something like the loops and concavities found in printed characters). The task of segmenting speech into distinct time slices representing different phonemes is also a formidable task. The time-varying spectrum of frequencies characterizing a phoneme in one

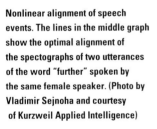

Nonlinear alignment of speech events. The lines in the middle graph show the optimal alignment of the spectographs of two utterances of the word "further" spoken by the same female speaker. (Photo by Vladimir Sejnoha and courtesy of Kurzweil Applied Intelligence)

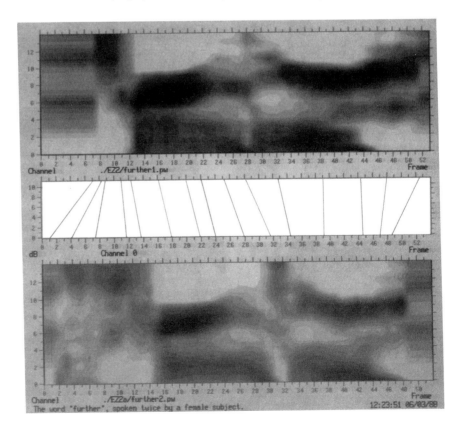

context may be dramatically different in a different context. In fact, in many instances no time slice corresponding to a particular phoneme can be found; we detect it only from the subtle influence it has on phonemes surrounding it.

As with vision and character recognition, both high-level and low-level features have value in speech-recognition systems. For recognizing a relatively small vocabulary (a few hundred words) for a single speaker, low-level feature detection and template matching by means of dynamic programming is usually sufficient, and most small-vocabulary systems use this approach. For more advanced systems, a combination of techniques is usually required: generally, multiple experts and an expert manager that knows the strengths and weaknesses of each.[71]

High-level context experts are also vital for large vocabulary systems. For example, phonemes cannot appear in any order. Indeed, many sequences are impossible to articulate (try saying "ptkee"). More important, only certain phoneme sequences will correspond to a word or word fragment in the language. On a higher level, the syntax and semantics of the language put constraints on possible word orders. While the set of phonemes is similar from one language to another, context factors differ dramatically. English, for example, has over 10,000 possible syllables, whereas Japanese has only 120.

Learning is also vital in speech recognition. Adaptation to the particular characteristics of each speaker is a powerful technique in each stage of processing. Learning must take place on a number of different levels: the frequency and time relationships characterizing each phoneme, the dialect (pronunciation) patterns of each word, and the syntactic patterns of possible phrases and sentences.

In sum, we see in speech recognition the full paradigm of pattern recognition that we first encountered in vision and character recognition systems: parallel processing in the front-end, segmentation and labeling, multiple experts on both high and low levels, expert management, disambiguation by context experts, and learning from actual recognition examples. But while the paradigm is the same, the content is dramatically different. Only a small portion of the technology in a successful ASR system consists of classical pattern-recognition techniques. The bulk of it consists of extensive knowledge about the nature of human speech and language: the shape of the speech sounds and the phonology, syntax, and semantics of spoken language.[72]

Automatic speech recognition is receiving considerable attention because of its potential for commercial applications.[73] We learn to understand and produce spoken language in our first year of life, years before we can understand or create written language. Thus, being able to communicate with computers using verbal language would provide an optimal modality of communication. A major goal of AI is to make our interactions with computers more natural and intuitive. Being able to converse with them by talking and listening is a vital part of that process.

For years ASR systems have been used in situations where users necessarily have their hands and eyes busy, making it impossible to use ordinary computer keyboards and display screens. For example, a laboratory technician examining an image through a microscope or other technical equipment can speak results into the microphone of an ASR system while continuing to view the image being examined. Similarly, factory workers can verbalize inspection data and other information on the production or shop floor directly to a computer without having to occupy their hands with a keyboard. Other systems are beginning to automate routine business transactions over telephone lines. Such telecommunications applications include credit-card verification, sales-order entry, accessing data base and inventory records, conducting banking and other financial transactions, and many others.

The applications mentioned are usually highly structured and thus require the ASR system to recognize only a small vocabulary, typically a few hundred words or less. The largest markets are projected for systems that can handle vocabularies that are relatively unrestricted and much larger, say, ten thousand words or more. The most obvious application of large vocabulary ASR systems is the creation of written documents by voice. The creation of written documents is a ubiquitous activity engaged in by almost everyone in offices, schools, and homes. Just copying all of the written documents created each year is a $25 billion industry. Tens of billions of dollars are spent each year in the creation of original written works from books to interoffice memoranda. Being able to dictate a document to a computer-based machine and see the document appear on a screen as it is being dictated has obvious advantages in terms of speed, accuracy, and convenience. Large-vocabulary ASR-based dictation systems are beginning to see use by doctors in writing medical reports and by many other professionals.

There are also significant applications of ASR technology to the handicapped. Persons who are unable to use their hands because of quadriplegia (paralysis due to spinal-cord injury), cerebral palsy, or other neurological impairment can still create written documents, interact with computers, and otherwise control their environment by speaking to a computer equipped with ASR. Certain types of brain damage cause a person's speech to be slurred and distorted. While such speech patterns are unrecognizable by human listeners (unless they have received special training), it is distorted in a consistent way and thus can be recognized by machine. A system consisting of an ASR system to recognize the distorted speech connected to a speech synthesizer can act as a translator, allowing the person to be understood by others. Research has been conducted at Children's Hospital, Boston, by Dr. Howard Shane on assisting both the hand-impaired and the speaking-impaired using ASR. Of perhaps the greatest potential benefit to the handicapped, and also representing the greatest technological challenge, would be an ASR-based device for the deaf that could provide a visual read-out of what people are saying.

There are three fundamental attributes that characterize a particular ASR system: vocabulary size, training requirements, and its ability to handle continuous speech. Vocabulary size is the number of different words that a system can handle at one time. Text creation requires a large basic vocabulary as well as the ability to add additional words to the active personal vocabulary of each individual user. For most other applications, small vocabularies suffice.

Most ASR systems require each user to train the system on their particular pronunciation patterns. This is typically accomplished by making the user provide the system with one or more spoken samples of each word in the vocabulary. However, for large vocabulary systems, speaking every word in the vocabulary is often not practical. It is preferable if the ASR system can infer how the speaker is likely to pronounce words never actually spoken to the machine. Then the user needs to train the system on only a subset of the full vocabulary.

Some small-vocabulary systems have been preprogrammed with all of the dialectic patterns anticipated from the population expected to use the system and thus do not require *any* prior training by each user. This capability, called speaker independence, is generally required for telephone-based systems, where a single system can be accessed by a large group of users.

Most commercial systems to date require users to speak with brief pauses (usually around 100 milliseconds) between words. This helps the system make a crucial segmentation decision: where words start and end. Speaking with such pauses reduces the speed of a typical speaker by 20 to 50 percent. ASR systems that can handle continuous speech exist, but they are limited today to small vocabularies. Continuous-speech systems that can handle large vocabularies are expected in the early 1990s.

Other characteristics that are important in describing practical ASR systems include the accuracy rate, response time, immunity to background noise, requirements for correcting errors, and integration of the speech recognition capability with specific computer applications. In general, it is not desirable to simply insert a speech recognition system as a front-end to ordinary computer applications. The human requirements for controlling computer applications by voice are substantially different from those of more conventional input devices such as keyboards, so the design of the overall system needs to take this into account.

While ASR systems continue to fall far short of human performance, their capabilities are rapidly improving, and commercial applications are taking root. As of 1989 ASR systems could either recognize a large vocabulary (10,000 words or more), recognize continuous speech, or provide speaker independence (no user training), but they could provide only *one* of these capabilities at a time. In 1990, commercial systems were introduced that combined speaker independence with the abililty to recognize a large vocabulary. I expect it to be possible in the early 1990s to combine any *two* of these attributes in the same system. In other words, we will see large vocabulary systems that can handle continuous speech while still requiring training for each speaker; there will be speaker-independent systems that can handle continuous speech but only for small vocabularies; and so on. The Holy Grail of speech recognition is to combine all *three* of these abilities, as human speech recognition does.

Other types of auditory perception

There are applications of pattern recognition to auditory perception other than recognizing speech. A field closely related to ASR is speaker identification, which attempts to reliably identify the *person speaking* by his or her speech profile. The techniques used are drawn from the ASR field. Common applications include entry and access control.

Military applications of auditory pattern recognition consist primarily of ship and submarine detection. It is not possible to see through the ocean, but sound waves can travel through the water for long distances. By sending sound waves and analyzing the reflected patterns, marine vehicles can be recognized. One of the challenges is to correctly characterize the patterns of different types of submarines and ships as opposed to whales and other natural undersea phenomena.

There are also a number of medical applications. Scanning the body with sound waves has become a powerful noninvasive diagnostic tool, and systems are being developed to apply pattern-recognition techniques to data from sonagram scanners. Perhaps the most significant medical application lies in the area of listening to the human heart. Many irregularities in heartbeat (arrhythmias) occur infrequently. So a technique has been developed that involves recording an electrocardiogram for a 24-hour period. In such Holter monitoring the patient goes through a normal day while a portable unit makes a tape recording of his heart pattern. The recording is then reviewed on a special screen by a human technician at 24 times normal speed, thus requiring an hour of analysis. But reading an electrocardiogram at 24 times real time for an hour is extremely demanding and studies have indicated a significant rate of errors. Using pattern-recognition techniques, computers have been programmed to analyze the recording at several hundred times real time and thus have the potential for providing lower costs and higher accuracy. Similar systems are used to monitor the vital functions of critical-care patients. Eventually wristwatch systems will be able to monitor our vital functions on a continuous basis. Heart patients could be told by their wristwatches to slow down or take other appropriate action if it determines they are overexerting themselves or otherwise getting into difficulty.

Next to human speech, perhaps the most important type of sound that we are exposed to is music. It might be argued that music is the most fundamental of the arts: it is the only one universal to all known cultures. The musical-tone qualities created by complex acoustic instruments such as the piano or violin have unique psychological effects, particularly when combined with the other elements of music (melody, rhythm, harmony, and expression). What is it that makes a piano sound the way it does? Every piano sounds somewhat different, yet they are all recognizable as the same type of instrument. This is essentially a pattern-recognition question, and insight into the answer has provided the ability to recreate such sounds using computer-based synthesizers. It also provides the ability to create entirely new synthetic sounds that have the same richness, depth, and musical relevance as acoustically produced sounds.[74]

Analogues to the other human senses are being developed as well. Chemical-analysis systems are beginning to emulate the functions of taste and smell. A variety of tactile sensors have been developed to provide robots with a sense of touch to augment their sight.

Taken together, applications of pattern recognition comprise fully half of the AI industry. It is surprising that many discussions of AI overlook this area entirely. Unlike expert systems and other areas that primarily emphasize logical rules and relationships, the field of pattern recognition combines both parallel and sequential types of thinking. Because of their need for enormous amounts of computation, pattern-recognition systems tend to require the cutting edge of advanced computer architectures.

It is widely recognized that computers will require extensive knowledge about the world to perform useful intelligent functions. It is not feasible for computer scientists to explicitly teach our computers all there is to know about the entire world. Like children, AI systems will need to acquire their own knowledge by reading, looking, listening, and drawing their own conclusions based on their own perceptions, perceptions based on pattern recognition.

Success provides the opportunity for growth, and growth provides the opportunity to risk at a higher level.
Eric Vogt

Most of the AI projects that I have been involved in personally are in the pattern-recognition field. The following is a description of some of these efforts from the point of view of *technology*. This section is perhaps misnamed. This is not really a *personal* postscript; not recounted here are the many exceptional people who have made contributions to these projects, the early struggles of growing companies, the efforts to attract both capital and talent, the ambiguities and subtleties of understanding markets, the challenge of establishing manufacturing facilities, the relationships with vendors, suppliers, contractors, dealers, distributors, customers, consultants, attorneys, accountants, bankers, investment bankers, investors and the media, or the interpersonal challenges of building organizations.

Raymond Kurzweil

A Personal Postscript

Optical Character Recognition

I founded Kurzweil Computer Products (KCP) in 1974. Our goal was to solve the problem of omnifont (*any* type font) optical character recognition (OCR) and to apply the resulting technology to the reading needs of the blind as well as to other commercial applications. There had been attempts to help the blind read using conventional OCR devices (those for a single or limited number of type fonts), but these machines were unable to deal with the great majority of printed material as it actually exists in the world. It was clear that to be of much value to the blind, an OCR machine would have to read any style of print in common use and also deal with the vagaries of printing errors, poor quality photocopies, varieties of paper and ink, complex page formats, and so on. OCR machines had existed from the beginning of the computer age, but all of the machines up to that time had relied on template matching, a form of low-level property extraction, and thus were severely limited in the range of material they could handle. Typically, users had to actually retype printed material using a specialized typeface before scanning. The principal value of these devices was that typewriters were at that time more ubiquitous than computer terminals.

It was clear to us that to produce an OCR device that was font invariant as well as relatively insensitive to distorted print, we would need additional experts beyond minimal property extraction. Our solution was to develop software for multiple experts, including topological experts such as loop, concavity, and line-segment detectors, with an expert manager that could combine the results of both high- and low-level recognition experts. The system was able to

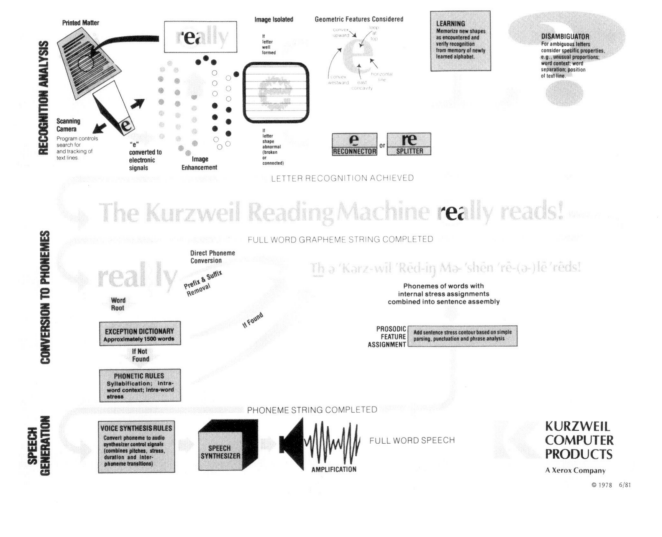

The flow of information in the Kurzweil Reading Machine. (Courtesy of the Kurzweil Reading Machine Division of Xerox)

RECOGNITION ANALYSIS

Printed Matter

really

Image Isolated

If letter well formed

Geometric Features Considered

convex upward
loop at top
convex westward
east
horizontal line
concavity

LEARNING
Memorize new shapes as encountered and verify recognition from memory of newly learned alphabet.

DISAMBIGUATOR
For ambiguous letters consider specific properties, e.g., unusual proportions; word context; word separation; position of text line.

Scanning Camera
Program controls search for and tracking of text lines

"e" converted to electronic signals

Image Enhancement

If letter shape abnormal (broken or connected)

RECONNECTOR e or re **SPLITTER**

LETTER RECOGNITION ACHIEVED

The Kurzweil Reading Machine really reads!

FULL WORD GRAPHEME STRING COMPLETED

CONVERSION TO PHONEMES

real ly

Direct Phoneme Conversion

Prefix & Suffix Removal

Th ə 'Kärz-wil 'Rēd-iŋ Mə-'shēn 'rē-(ə-)lē 'rēds!

Word Root

If Found

Phonemes of words with internal stress assignments combined into sentence assembly

EXCEPTION DICTIONARY
Approximately 1500 words

If Not Found

PROSODIC FEATURE ASSIGNMENT
Add sentence stress contour based on simple parsing, punctuation and phrase analysis

PHONETIC RULES
Syllabification; intra-word context; intra-word stress

PHONEME STRING COMPLETED

SPEECH GENERATION

VOICE SYNTHESIS RULES
Convert phoneme to audio synthesizer control signals (combines pitches, stress, duration and inter-phoneme transitions)

SPEECH SYNTHESIZER

AMPLIFICATION

FULL WORD SPEECH

KURZWEIL COMPUTER PRODUCTS

A Xerox Company

© 1978   6/81

273

learn by having the high-level experts teach the low-level experts the type faces found in a particular document. At a later point we added context experts by providing the machine with a knowledge of English (and ultimately several other languages).

The first Kurzweil Reading Machine (KRM), introduced in 1976, consisted of an image scanner we developed ourselves that contained an electro-optical camera. The camera's eye consisted of a charge-coupled device containing 500 light-sensitive elements arranged in a straight line. The camera was mounted on an electro-mechanical "X-Y mover," which could move the camera in both vertical and horizontal directions. The material to be read (a book, magazine, typed letter, etc.) lay face down on the glass plate that formed the top of the machine. The camera automatically moved back and forth scanning each line of print, transmitting the image electronically to a minicomputer contained in a separate cabinet. Using our omnifont OCR software, the minicomputer recognized the characters, grouped them into words and computed the pronunciation of each word. To accomplish this last task, several hundred pronunciation rules were programmed in, along with several thousand exceptions. The resulting string of phonemes was sent to a speech synthesizer, which articulated each word. Subsequent models of the KRM have been substantially improved, but they are organized in a similar way.

Using the device is straightforward: the user places the document to be read face down on the machine, presses start, and listens. The KRM has a control panel to control the movement of the scanner, back it up, make it reread sections or spell out words, and provide a variety of other functions.

Font invariance is a primary goal of Kurzweil Computer Products' intelligent character recognition (ICR). (Courtesy of the Kurzweil Reading Machine Division of Xerox)

Users can verify recognized characters against images of the original characters if so desired. (Courtesy of the Kurzweil Reading Machine Division of Xerox)

A few of the topological features considered by Kurzweil Computer Products' ICR. (Courtesy of the Kurzweil Reading Machine Division of Xerox)

Jamal Mazrui uses the Kurzweil Reading Machine. The Kurzweil Reading Machine scans and recognizes such text as books, magazines, and memos and converts it into synthesized speech and thus is able to provide blind readers with independent access to printed material. (Photo by Lou Jones)

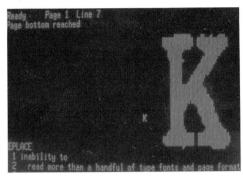

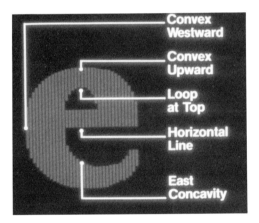

The KRM has been called the first commercial product to successfully incorporate AI technology. A recent survey showed that most blind college students have access to a KRM to read their educational materials. Nothing in my professional career has given me greater satisfaction than the many letters I have received from blind persons of all ages indicating the benefit they have received from the KRM in enabling them to complete their studies or gain and maintain productive employment.

Two years after the introduction of the KRM, we introduced a refined version, the Kurzweil Data Entry Machine (KDEM), designed for commercial applications. The KDEM, like the KRM, could scan printed and typed documents and recognize characters and page formats from a wide variety of sources, but rather than speaking the words, it transmits them. It has been used to automatically enter documents into data bases, word-processing machines, electronic-publishing systems, and a variety of other computer-based systems. For example, the KDEM was used to automatically scan and recognize all of the contributed articles in this book for entry into a computerized publishing system.

Many computerized systems move information from electronic form onto the printed page. The KDEM allows it to move back not just as an electronic image but in an intelligent form that a computer can understand and process further. The result is to make the printed page another form of information storage like a floppy disk or tape. Unlike electronic media, however, the printed page can be easily accessed by humans as well, which makes it the medium of choice for both people and machines.

I find it interesting to review the rapidly improving price performance of computer-based products in terms of the products of my own companies. The 1978 KDEM were sold for $120,000, which, adjusted for inflation, is equivalent to $231,000 in 1990 dollars. It had 65,536 bytes of memory and recognized print at about 3 characters per second. In 1990 KCP offered a far superior product for under $5,000. The 1990 version has 2 to 4 million bytes of memory, can recognize between 30 and 75 characters per second, can recognize a substantially wider range of degraded print, and is far more accurate than the 1978 KDEM. The 1990 version thus has 32 to 64 times as much memory, is 10 to 25 times faster, and is more accurate and versatile than the 1978 version. If we conservatively assume that it provides at least 15 times the performance at 1/46.2 the price, it represents an overall improvement in price-performance of 693 to 1. Since $2^{9.4} = 693$, KCP has doubled its price-performance 9.4 times in 144 months, which is a doubling of price-performance every 15.3 months. That rate is somewhat better than the computer industry at large, which is generally considered to double its price-performance ratio only every 18 to 24 months.

Vladimir Sejnoha, a speech scientist
at Kurzweil Applied Intelligence,
looks at images of human speech.
(Photo by Hank Morgan of Rainbow)

Say "baby." Spectograms of two
utterances of the same word by the
same speaker show the high degree
of variability in human speech.
(Photo by Hank Morgan of Rainbow)

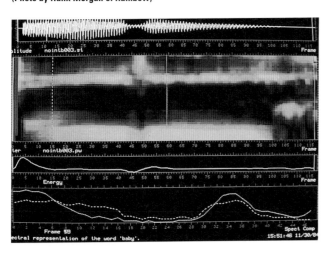

Speech Recognition

On July 1, 1982, I founded Kurzweil Applied Intelligence, (KAI). KAI's goal has been to master automatic speech recognition (ASR) technology and to integrate ASR with other AI technologies to solve real-world problems. The long term goal is to establish ASR as a ubiquitous modality of communication between human and machine. In 1985 we introduced the Kurzweil Voice System (KVS), the first commercial ASR device with a 1,000 word vocabulary. A refined version called KVW, the first to provide a recognition vocabulary of up to 10,000 words, was introduced in 1987.[1]

The KAI speech recognizers follow the paradigm described in the previous section. The KVW, for example, has seven different experts, all of which attempt to recognize each spoken word simultaneously. Several of the experts analyze the acoustics (or sound) of the word spoken, and the others are context experts programmed with a knowledge of English word sequences (other languages will follow in the future). The system makes extensive use of user training and adaptation. It learns the phonological patterns (that is, the frequency patterns) and the phonetic sequences (the dialect) of each user. It also includes a user syntax expert that learns the characteristic word-sequence patterns used by each speaker.

The KVW consists of specialized electronics, an industry-standard personal computer and software. Before a user can begin productive dictation with the system, he needs to enroll, which involves speaking a sample of words to the machine to provide it with initial phonological and phonetic models. Once that has been accomplished, the user can dictate to the machine and watch each word appear on the screen within a fraction of a second after speaking it. The 1990 models require the user to provide a brief pause between words, although later models are expected to accept continuous speech.

The KVW actually improves its performance as the system adapts to (that is, learns about) the user's pronunciation patterns and syntax. This adaptation continues indefinitely. In addition to displaying each recognized word, the system also displays its second through sixth choices. If the KVW makes a mistake, one of these alternate words is very often the correct choice. Thus, errors are typically corrected by the user saying "Take two" or "Take three," which replaces the word originally displayed in the text with the appropriate alternate word.

KVW speech-recognition technology has been integrated with a variety of applications. One version includes a full-function word-processor with the capability of entering text as well as issuing all editing and formatting commands by voice. Several sections of this book were written by voice using this version of the KVW. Other

Sample reports from Kurzweil VoiceRad (for radiology). VoiceRad combines large-vocabulary speech recognition and knowledge engineering. (Courtesy of Kurzweil Applied Intelligence)

A doctor dictates medical reports to VoiceRad. (Courtesy of Kurzweil Applied Intelligence)

Routine mammography report

Say	Display
"today" "mammography" "bilateral"	4/11/1987 Mammography (bilateral)
"routine"	A low dose film technique was used. Cephalocaudad and modifed lateral views were obtained.
"diffuse nodularity"	Both breasts show a very prominent duct pattern with diffuse nodularity throughout. Such diffuse nodularity makes the breasts difficult to evaluate.
"no focal lesions"	There are no dominant masses or clustered calcifications on either side.
"obtain outside study"	The patient gives a history of previous mammography elsewhere. If these could be obtained for comparison it would be helpful to exclude any interval change.
"signature"	John H. Jones, M.D. 9:18:32 4/11/1987

Word-by-word dictation

Mammography (left side only)

Xerographic images were obtained. There is a 3 cm ill-defined mass 2 cm deep to the nipple. Findings compatible with malignancy. No other abnormality is seen at this time.

Impression: Probable cancer.
Advise biopsy.

John H. Jones, M.D. 9:22:51 4/11/87

Sample reports produced by doctors dictating to Kurzweil VoiceEM, a system for emergency medicine physicians that is similar to VoiceRad. (Courtesy of Kurzweil Applied Intelligence)

Automobile accident report

8/19/1987 Auto accident

10 year old white male non-belted passenger in high vilocity accident struck form rear not thrown from vehicle.

Denies rolling vehicle. No glass fragments. Onset of pain in right hip.

Physical exam vital signs: See nurse's notes.
Head: Atraumatic, without sinus, temporal or scalp tenderness.
Eyes: PERLA,EOMI, no discharge, injection, a-v nicking, hemorrhage, exudate or papilledema.
Ears: TM without perforation, injection or bulging. External canals clear without exudate.
Nose: No injection, exudate or septal hematoma.
Throat: Clear tongue, pharynx without injection, exudate or tonsillar hypertrophy.
Teeth: Normal variant.
Neck: Supple, non-tender; without HJR, JVD, thyromegaly, or lymphadenopathy.
Lungs: CTA equal.
Heart: RRR without murmurs, gallops, or rubs.
Chest: Non-tender, symmetrical; no retractions.
Abdomen: Soft, flat, non-tender, good bowel sounds. No hepatosplenomegaly, rebound, guarding, or firm pulsatile mass.
Back: No costovertebral, paravertebral, intervertebral, or vertebral tenderness.
Neurological: Alert and oriented X3. Cooperative. Cranial and cerebellar functions normal. DTR equal and symmetrical.
Extremity: Right proximal lateral hip tender. Neurovascular status intact. Joint tenderness present. Pulses unequal.
Genitourinary: No penile ulcers or urethral discharge. Testes descended, vertical and non-tender.
Rectum: No mass or tenderness. Non-bloody stool.
Xray: Right hip fracture, simple.
Diagnosis: Acute fracture right hip.

Consult specialty service. Admit to hospital.

John H. Smith, M.D. 4:18:32 8/19/1987

Earache report

Earache
4 year old white female patient complains of right ear pain for 2 day(s).

Physical exam: See nurse's notes.
Right TM injected, without perforation, without bulging. External canals clear, without exudate.

Diagnosis: Acute right otitis media.

Discharge plan:
1. Rest at home. Drink lots of clear liquids for 24 hours.
2. Take amoxicillin 250 mg TID.
3. If your symptoms worsen or if you notice no improvement within the next few days, see your Doctor as soon as possible.
4. Excuse from activity for 0 day(s).
5. Return to Emergency Department for any emergency.

Charles Watson, M.D. 14:03 8/15/1987

277

versions of the KVW are integrated with knowledge-based systems that have expertise in the types of reports created in different professions. For example, VoiceRad integrates KAI's speech-recognition technology with knowledge of radiology reporting, allowing a radiologist to quickly dictate the results of an examination for instantaneous transcription. As with the word-processor version of the KVW, the radiologist can dictate a report word by word. In addition, the system can automatically generate predefined sections of text based on its knowledge of radiology reporting. VoiceEM is a similar system for emergency medicine. A variety of similar systems have been developed for medicine and other disciplines. This approach combines the productivity gains of ASR-based dictation with those of a built-in domain-specific knowledge base. These products mark the first time that a commercially available large-vocabulary ASR product has been used to create written text by voice in other than experimental situations.

KAI also has a major commitment to applying technology for the handicapped. Versions of KVS and KVW technology provide means for text creation and computer and environmental control for quadriplegic and other hand-impaired individuals. A long-term goal of the company is to develop a sensory aid for the deaf that would provide a real-time display of what someone is saying on the phone and in person.

The company's long term objectives are two-fold. First, it intends to continue strengthening its core speech-recognition technology, to move toward the Holy Grail of combining large-vocabulary ASR with continuous-speech capability and minimal requirements for training the system for each user. Second, it intends to integrate ASR with a variety of applications, particularly those emphasizing other AI technologies. Ultimately, our goal is to establish voice communication as a desirable and widely used means of communicating with machine intelligence.

The Electronic Music Revolution

I founded Kurzweil Music Systems (KMS), also on July 1, 1982. The inspiration for starting KMS came from two sources. One was my lifelong interest in music, along with a nearly lifelong interest in computers. My father, a noted conductor and concert pianist, had told me shortly before his death in 1970 that I would combine these two interests one day, although he was not sure how. The other and more immediate genesis of KMS was a conversation I had with Stevie Wonder, who had been a user of the Kurzweil Reading Machine from its inception. While showing me some new musical instruments he had recently acquired, Steve noted that two worlds of musical

instruments—the acoustic and the electronic—had developed with no bridge existing between them.

On the one hand, acoustic instruments such as the piano, violin, and guitar provided the musical sounds that were still the sounds of choice for most of the world's musicians. While these acoustic sounds were rich, complex, and musically satisfying, only limited means were available for controlling or even playing these sounds. For one thing, once a piano key was struck, there was no further ability to shape the note other than to terminate it: the initial velocity of the key strike was the only means for modifying piano sounds. Second, most instruments could only play one note at a time. Third, there were no ways to *layer* sounds, that is, play the sounds of different instruments simultaneously. Even if you had the skills to play both a piano and a guitar, for example, you could hardly play both at the same time. Even two musicians would find playing the same chords on a piano and guitar almost impossible. In any case, very few musicians, no matter how accomplished, could play more than a very few instruments, as each one requires substantially different playing techniques. Since the playing methods themselves were linked to the physics of each acoustic instrument, many instruments required a high level of finger dexterity. If a composer had a multi-instrumental arrangement in mind, he had no way of even hearing what the piece sounded like without assembling a large group of musicians. Then making changes to the composition required laborious modification of written scores and additional rehearsal. I recall my father's lamenting the same difficulties.

Steve pointed out that on the other hand there existed the electronic world of music in which most of the above limitations are overcome. Using just one type of playing skill (e.g., a piano-keyboard technique), one can activate and control all available electronic sounds. A wide variety of techniques exist for modifying many aspects of the sounds themselves prior to as well as during perform-ance (these techniques have expanded greatly since 1982). One can layer sounds by having each key initiate different sounds simultane-ously. Using sequencers, one can play one part of a multi-instrumen-tal composition, then play that part back from memory and play a second part over it, repeating this process indefinitely. However, electronic instruments at that time suffered from a major drawback, namely the sounds themselves. While they had found an important role in both popular and classical music, synthetic sounds were "thin," had relatively limited diversity, and did not include any of the desirable acoustic sounds.

Steve asked whether it would be possible to combine these two worlds of music to create in a single instrument the capabilities of both. Such an instrument could produce music that neither world of instruments alone could create. Accomplishing this

The Kurzweil 250 Computer-Based Synthesizer. (Courtesy of Kurzweil Music Systems)

A musician plays the Kurzweil 250 using the keyboard and an electronic drum controller. (Courtesy of Kurzweil Music Systems)

would, for example, enable musicians to play a guitar and a piano at the same time. We could take acoustic sounds and modify them to accomplish a wide variety of artistic purposes. A musician could play a multi-instrumental composition (such as an entire orchestra) by himself using real acoustic (as well as electronic) sounds. A musician could play a violin or any other instrument *polyphonically* (playing more than one note at a time). One could play sounds of any instrument without having to learn the playing techniques of each. One could even create new sounds that were based on acoustic sounds, and thus shared their complexity, but moved beyond them to a whole new class of timbres with substantial musical value.

This vision defined the goal of KMS. In June of 1983 we demonstrated an engineering prototype of the Kurzweil 250 (K250), and we introduced it commercially in 1984.[2] The K250 was considered the first electronic musical instrument to successfully emulate the sounds of a grand piano and a wide variety of other instruments: orchestral string instruments (violin, viola, etc.), guitar, human voice, brass instruments, drums, and many others. In listening tests we found that listeners, including professional musicians, were essentially unable to tell the K250 "grand piano" sound apart from that of a real $40,000 concert grand piano. A 12-track sequencer, sound layering, and extensive sound modification facilities provide a full complement of artistic control methods.

The essence of K250 technology lies in its sound models. These data structures, contained in read-only memory within the instrument, define the essential patterns of each instrument voice. We needed to create a signal-processing model of an instrument that will respond to changes in pitch, loudness, and the passage of time in the same complex ways as the original acoustic instrument. To create a sound model, the starting point is to record the original instrument using high-quality digital techniques. Surprisingly, just finding the right instruments to record turned out to be a major challenge. We were unable, for example, to find a single concert grand piano with an attractive sound in all registers. Some had a beautiful bass region but a shrill midrange. Others were stunning in the high range, but mediocre otherwise. We ended up recording five different pianos, including the one that Rudolph Serkin plays when he comes to Boston.

When capturing an instrument, we record examples of many different pitches and loudness levels. When a particular key on a piano is struck with varying levels of force, it is not just the loudness level that changes but the entire time-varying spectrum of sound frequencies. All of these digital recordings are fed into our sound analysis computer, and a variety of both automatic and manual techniques are used to shape each instrument model. Part of the

process involves a form of painstaking tuning and attention to detail ironically reminiscent of old-world craftsmanship. The automatic aspects of the process deal primarily with the issue of data compression. The original recorded data for even a single instrument would exceed the K250's memory capacity. Thus, it is necessary to include only the salient information necessary to accurately represent the original sounds.

When the keyboardist strikes the K250's pianolike keys, special sensors detect the velocity of each key's motion. (Other KMS keyboards can also detect the time-varying pressure exerted by each finger.) The K250's computer and specialized electronics extract the relevant information from the appropriate sound models in memory and then compute in real time the waveforms representing the selected instrument sound, pitch, and loudness for each note. The varied control features, such as sequencing, layering, and sound modification, are provided by software routines stored in the unit's memory.

In evolving our instruments at KMS, we have followed two paths. First, the K250 has evolved into a comprehensive system for creating complex musical works. It is essentially a digital recording and production studio in an instrument, and it has become a standard for the creation of movie and television soundtracks and professional recordings. KMS has also moved to bring down the cost of its sound-modeling technology. Its K1000 series, for example, is a line of relatively inexpensive products that provide the same quality and diversity of sounds as the K250.

There is a historic trend taking place in the musical instrument industry away from acoustic and mechanical technology and toward digital electronic technology. There are two reasons for this. First, the price-performance of acoustic technology is rapidly deteriorating because of the craftsmanship and labor-intensive nature of its manufacturing processes. A grand piano, for example, has over 10,000 mostly hand-crafted moving parts. The price of the average piano has increased by over 250 percent since 1970. At the same time, it is widely acknowledged that the quality of new pianos is diminishing. On the other hand, the price-performance of digital electronics is, of course, rapidly improving. Furthermore, it is now possible for an electronic instrument to provide the same sound quality as an acoustic instrument, with substantially greater functionality. For these reasons, electronic keyboard instruments have gone from 9.5 percent of the American market for keyboard instruments in 1980 to 55.2 percent in 1986 (according to the American Music Conference). It is my strong belief that this trend will continue until the market is virtually entirely electronic. Our long-term goal at KMS is to continue to provide leadership for this emerging worldwide industry of intelligent digital music technology.

A Final Note

I have tried to select projects that make it possible to build strong companies while meeting social and cultural goals that are important to me and others. I believe, for example, that there is a good match between the capabilities of computer science and the needs of the handicapped. It has been a personal goal of mine to apply AI technologies to help overcome the handicaps associated with major physical and sensory disabilities. I believe the potential exists in the next couple of decades to largely overcome these major handicaps. As amplifiers of human thought, computers have great potential to assist human expression, improve productivity, and expand creativity for all of us, in all areas of work and play. I hope to play a role in constructively harnessing this potential.

All of the projects described above have been highly interdisciplinary efforts and have required the dedication and talents of many brilliant individuals in a broad range of fields. Inventing today is very much a team effort and its success is a function of the quality of the individual members of the team as well as the quality of the group's communication. As Norbert Wiener pointed out in *Cybernetics*, scientists and engineers with different areas of expertise often use entirely different technical vocabularies to refer to the same phenomena. Creating an environment in which a team of linguists, speech scientists, signal-processing experts, VLSI designers, and other specialists can understand each other's terminology and effectively work together (as was required, for example, in the efforts to develop the speech recognition technology described above) is at least as challenging as the development of the technology itself. Once developed, the technology (and the technologists) must be further integrated into the equally well-developed disciplines of manufacturing, marketing, finance, and the other management skills of a modern corporation.

It is always exciting to see (or hear) a new product, to experience the realization of a vision after years of hard collaborative work. Perhaps my greatest pleasure has been the opportunity to share in the creative process with the many outstanding men and women who have contributed to these endeavors.

Notes

1. Raymond Kurzweil, "The Technology of the Kurzweil Voice Writer," *BYTE*, March 1986.

2. Christopher Morgan, "The Kurzweil 250 Digital Synthesizer," *BYTE*, June 1986.

A few bits of knowledge.

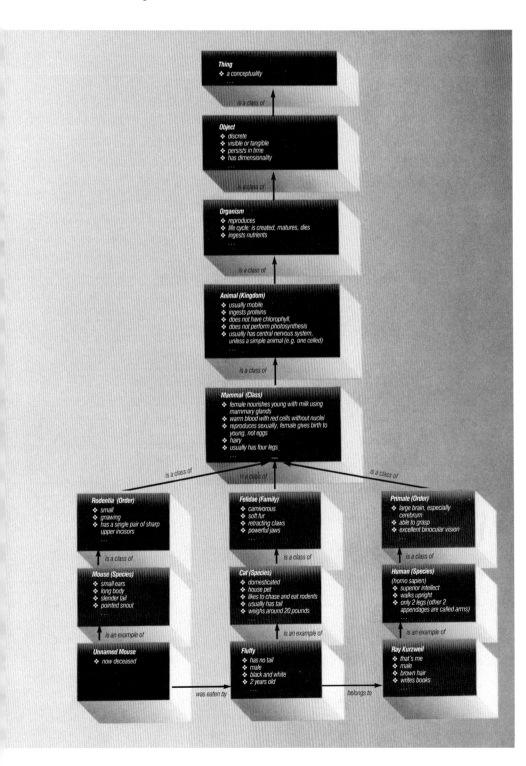

The Search for Knowledge

A man is sent to prison for a ten-year term. The dining hall also serves as an auditorium, and there is a stage at one end. After supper, one of the prisoners runs up onto the stage and hollers, "Four hundred and eighty-seven." Everyone starts laughing. The next day, it's the same thing: After supper someone jumps onto the stage, yells, "Two thousand six hundred and twenty-two," and all the prisoners crack up. This goes on for a couple of weeks, and finally the man asks his cellmate what's going on.

"Well," says the cellmate, "It's like this. The prison library has a big fat book called *The Ten Thousand Best Jokes,* and we've all been here so long that we know the book by heart. If somebody wants to tell a joke, they just shout out the number of the joke in *The Ten Thousand Best Jokes,* and if it's a funny one, everybody laughs."

At dinner that night, the man decides to show the other prisoners that he's a good guy. Before anyone else can get to the stage, he dashes up there and shouts, "Five thousand nine hundred and eighty-six!" But to his horror, nobody cracks a smile. There are even a few groans. He slinks back to his cell to consult with his cellmate.

"Nobody laughed! Isn't the five thousand nine hundred and eighty-sixth joke a good one?"

"Sure it's a good one," says the cellmate. "Old five thousand nine hundred eighty-six is one of the best."

"So why didn't anyone laugh?"

"You didn't tell it right."

An old joke as retold in *Mind Tools* by Rudy Rucker

• Knowledge and Expert Systems

Knowledge is not the same as information. Knowledge is information that has been pared, shaped, interpreted, selected, and transformed; the artist in each of us daily picks up the raw material and makes of it a small artifact—and at the same time, a small human glory. Now we have invented machines to do that, just as we invented machines to extend our muscles and our other organs. In typical human fashion, we intend our new machines for all the usual purposes, from enhancing our lives to filling our purses. If they scourge our enemies, we wouldn't mind that either. . . .

The reasoning animal has, perhaps inevitably, fashioned the reasoning machine. With all the risks apparent in such an audacious, some say reckless, embarkation onto sacred ground, we have gone ahead anyway, holding tenaciously to what the wise in every culture at every time have taught: the shadows, however dark and menacing, must not deter us from reaching the light.

Edward A. Feigenbaum and Pamela McCorduck, *The Fifth Generation*

What is knowledge?

Facts alone do not constitute knowledge. For information to become knowledge, it must incorporate the relationships between ideas. And for the knowledge to be useful, the links describing how concepts interact must be easily accessed, updated, and manipulated. Human intelligence is remarkable in its ability to perform these tasks. However, it is almost more remarkably weak at reliably storing the information on which knowledge is based.[1] The natural strengths of computers are roughly the opposite. They have, therefore, become powerful allies of the human intellect in their ability to reliably store and rapidly retrieve vast quantities of information, but conversely, they have been slow to master true knowledge. The design of computer data structures that can represent the complex web of relationships both within and among ideas has been a quest of artificial intelligence from its inception. Many competing approaches have been proposed. The following example illustrates features of several approaches including the methodology of frames, first proposed by Minsky in the mid 1970s.[2]

Each box (in the figure at the beginning of this chapter) represents a concept sometimes referred to as an object or frame. One important relationship, *is a class of*, refers to a group of entities that comprise a proper subset of a broader set. The principle of inheritance tells us that the characteristics of a set apply to all of its subsets (and all of their subsets, etc.) unless there is a specific indication to the contrary. Thus, we can conclude that mammals, being a subclass of animals, ingest proteins, even though this fact is not explicitly stated. We can also conclude that mammals, being ultimately a subclass of objects, are visible or tangible. The relationship *is an example of* refers to a subset with a single member. Thus, even though little is explicitly revealed in the Ray Kurzweil frame, the principle of inheritance lets us infer a great deal. We can conclude that Ray shares with the rest of the human species a superior intellect (although after reading this book, one might wish to enter an exception here). Since he is a male, we cannot conclude that he nourishes his young with milk, but we can determine that he is warm blooded, is usually mobile, and persists in time. We note that Fluffy, although of the cat species, does not inherit the characteristic of a tail, but is nonetheless domesticated, carnivorous, and so on.

Other types of relationships, types that do not imply the inheritance of characteristics, are also shown on the chart. *Belongs to* and *was eaten by* are examples of binary relationships that two singular objects or frames may have with one another. These relationships can also be described using hierarchical structures. For example, *loves, hates,* and *is jealous of* could all be examples of *has feelings for*.

Some areas of knowledge are more amenable to this type of hierarchical analysis than others. Taxonomy, the study of the classification of organisms, is one of the most effective. Biologists have been largely successful in constructing an elaborate tree structure that incorporates virtually all of the many millions of known earth species (including nearly a quarter million species of beetles alone).[3] The system requires a minimum of seven levels:

- Animalia kingdom
- Chordata phylum
- Mammalia class

- Primate order
- Homidae family
- *Homo* genus
- *Homo sapien* species

More complex classifications are also possible:

- Animalia kingdom
- Metazoa subkingdom
- Chordata phylum
- Vertebrata subphylum
- Tetrapoda superclass
- Mammalia class
- Theria subclass
- Eutheria infraclass
- Ferungulata cohort
- Ferae superorder
- Carnivora order
- Fissipeda suborder
- Canoidea superfamily
- Canidae family
- Caninae subfamily
- *Canis* genus
- *Canis lupus* (wolf) species

Though some controversies persist (including, ironically, the exact place-ment of our own species), the system has proved a remarkably useful tool for organizing biological knowledge.[4] Other areas have more difficulty with hierarchic classification. Consider the well-known Dewey Decimal system for classifying books. Through three levels of ten-fold expansion, Melvil Dewey (1851–1931) devised 999 categories for the Amherst College library in 1873.[5] His system has since been refined to provide a virtually unlimited number of subdivisions, for example,

- 540 chemistry
- 541 physical and theoretical chemistry
- 541.3 physical chemistry
- 541.34 solutions

There is no question that the system is useful. Organizing libraries would be immensely difficult without it or some similar system (say, the Library of Con-gress system). Yet books do not always fall into one neat category, particularly with the rapid development of new interdisciplinary topics. It will be interesting to see how this book is classified: computer science, philosophy, history of technology, humor? Since books often deal with complex subjects that may span multiple areas of knowledge, a single position in a hierarchy is often an unsatisfactory compromise. This is not to say that hierarchical classification of organisms works perfectly: it does not. But it is interesting to note that every organism, even the lowest, has one or more "parents," which in turn had one or more parents, and so on. If we ignore interbreeding, the entire collection of all individual organisms that have ever lived form one or more gigantic trees with trillions of leaves. There is obviously no such equally fundamental tree organization for all books.

An ambitious attempt to organize all human knowledge in a single hierarchy is contained in the Propaedia section of the fifteenth edition of the *Encyclopaedia Britannica,* published in 1980. The Propaedia, which describes itself as an "outline of knowledge," is an 800-page attempt to codify *all knowledge*, at least that contained in the remaining 30,000 pages of the encyclopedia. For example, *money* is found under 534D1:

- 5 Human society
- 53 The production, distribution, and utilization of wealth
- 534 The organization of production and distribution
- 534D Institutional arrangements that facilitate production and output
- 534D1 The nature and characteristics of money

Hierarchical relationships among lateral relationships.

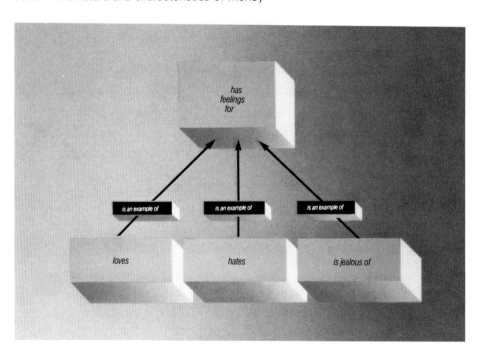

The Propaedia does allow for multiple classifications. Each entry, such as 534D1, will provide a number of references into the main portion of the encyclopedia. Conversely, any section in the encyclopedia is likely to have multiple references to it from the Propaedia. The Propaedia takes time to understand, but it is surprisingly successful in view of the vast scope of the material it covers.

Hierarchical classification schemes have provided a powerful organizing tool for most of the sciences. It is clear, however, that we need to go beyond treelike structures to represent most concepts. Key to the design of data structures intended to represent concepts are the cross-links (i.e. nonhierarchical relationships). Consider the structures, called semantic networks, depicted in the figures.[6] The vertical lines continue to represent such hierarchical relationships as *part* and *is a*. The *horizontal* links, however, give the concepts their distinguishing shapes. Here we see the same type of structure (with different shapes, of course) representing two very different ideas: the concept of an *arch* and that of a *musical scale*. An arch

The concept of an arch in a semantic network. (Figure reprinted with permission from Curtis Roads, "Research in Music and Artificial Intelligence," *ACM Computing Surveys* 17 [1985], no. 2: 184; copyright 1985 by the Association for Computing Machinery)

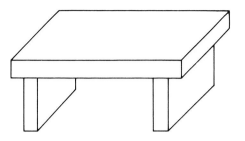

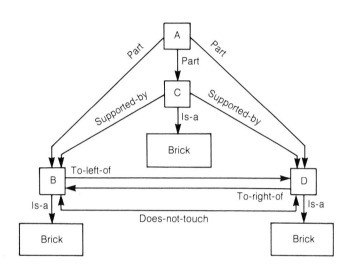

The concept of a musical scale in a semantic network. (Figure reprinted with permission from Curtis Roads, "Research in Music and Artificial Intelligence," *ACM Computing Surveys* 17 [1985], no. 2: 185; copyright 1985 by the Association for Computing Machinery)

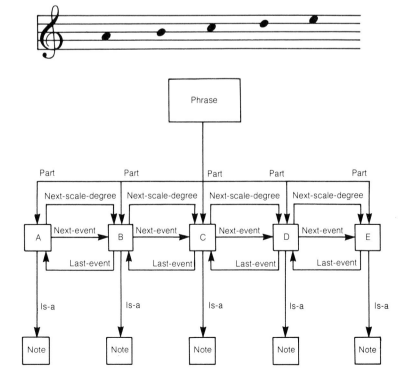

or scale can be implemented in a virtually unlimited number of ways, but all such manifestations can share the same conceptual representation.

The horizontal links are themselves concepts and can obviously be quite varied. They can also be represented by networks. The boxes, sometimes called objects, can also be either simple entities or networks. Thus, each network may refer to other networks to represent both the cross-links and the objects. The vertical lines continue to represent simple hierarchical relationships.

Semantic networks and other similar systems are reasonably successful in representing the shape and content of abstract ideas for use in computer knowledge bases. Creating such networks is not easy, however, and this has proved to be a major bottleneck. A major focus of current AI research is to create software that can automatically build such structures from examples of a concept.[7]

Such data structures as semantic networks provide a formal methodology for representing a broad class of knowledge. As they are easily stored and manipulated in a computer, they are a powerful and practical tool for capturing and harnessing the patterns inherent in at least some types of ideas. Since humans routinely deal with abstract concepts in a supremely subtle way, we can infer that the data structures in our own minds must be at least as powerful as these networks (they are, in fact, far more powerful). Though little is directly known about the data structures we use, we can draw a few hints from observations of our own behavior and thought patterns.

First, it is clear that we rarely, if ever, model the relationships between entities with single links.[8] Every time we experience or come into contact with a concept, we add links that reinforce the structures inherent in a concept. For a common concept we may have millions of links expressing the same or similar associations. Indeed, the key relationships may not be explicitly coded at all but rather implied by the general pattern of the data structures. This redundancy has several implications. First, these knowledge structures are not subject to catastrophic failure if parts of the hardware fail. One estimate puts at 50,000 the number of neurons that die each day in an adult human brain (and this process accelerates with age), yet our concepts and ideas do not necessarily deteriorate with the hardware. The massive number of links also helps us to appreciate both the unity and the diversity of a concept. We probably have millions of links indicating or implying that a chair generally has four legs. The link between a chair and four legs is thus strongly established. The links refer to (or evoke) experiences we have had with chairs and so relate to memories of particular chairs we have known. The diversity that is possible within the concept of a chair is thus also captured. The massive redundancy also accounts for our ability (or inability) to deal with what is called cognitive dissonance (a piece of information that appears to contradict a well-established belief or understanding).[9] If we suddenly experience evidence, even strong evidence, that an idea or concept that we have is invalid, we do not immediately update all of our knowledge structures to reflect this new insight. We are capable of storing this apparently contradictory idea right alongside the concepts we already had. Unless the new idea is reinforced, it will eventually die out, overwhelmed by the large number of links representing our previous conceptions. There is no evidence of a mechanism in our brains to avoid or eliminate contradictory concepts, and we are sometimes quite comfortable with ideas that appear to be incompatible. Hence, ideas that are presented repeatedly early in our life by our parents or culture are not easily modified, even if our adult experiences are apparently inconsistent. In general, it takes repeated exposure to a new idea to change our minds. This is one reason that the media are so powerful. They have the ability to reach large audiences on a repeated basis and are thus capable of having a measurable effect on our data structures.[10] Presenting an idea once, even if the idea is powerful and true, does not generally have a significant impact.

There is a strong link between our emotions and our knowledge. If information is presented in a way that elicits an emotional response, we are far more likely to change our knowledge structures (and hence our minds). For this reason, television, which has far greater potential than the print media to reach most people emotionally, has a correspondingly greater impact. Television commercials are often minidramas that attempt to engage us emotionally so that the underlying message will have its desired impact.[11]

Our knowledge is also closely tied into our pattern-recognition capabilities. People deal with the concept of a particular person's face as easily as with the concept of an arch or a musical scale. But we have yet to devise computer-based data structures that can successfully represent the unique features of a face, although for simpler visual concepts (such as the shape of an industrial part, or the shape of the letter *A*) representations similar to semantic networks are actively used.

One indication that we use structures similar to semantic networks is our ability to jump from concept to concept via the crosslinks. The thought of taxonomy may lead us to thoughts of primates, which may lead to monkeys, which may lead to bananas, which may lead to nutrition, which may lead to dieting, which may lead to the upcoming Thanksgiving party, which may lead to a particular family member, and so on. We clearly have all of our semantic information, with its massively redundant links, organized in a single vast network. Individual concepts are not identified as such. It requires a great deal of disciplined thought and study to explicitly call out (and describe) individual ideas. The ability to translate our mental networks into coherent language is a difficult skill, one that we continue to struggle with even as adults.

An interesting question concerns how much knowledge we are capable of mastering. It is estimated that the human brain contains on the order of 100 billion neurons.[12] We now realize that individual neurons are each capable of remembering far more than the one or several bits of data originally thought possible. One method of storing information is in the strength of each synaptic connection. A neuron can have thousands of such connections, each potentially storing an analog number. There is also speculation that certain long-term memories are chemically coded in the neuron cell bodies. If we estimate the capacity of each neuron at about 1,000 bits (and this is probably low by several orders of magnitude), that gives the brain a capacity of 100 trillion (10^{14} bits). A typical computer-based semantic network requires only a few thousand bits to represent a concept. Because of the redundancy, however, our human semantic networks need much greater amounts of storage. If, as a rough guess, we assume an average redundancy factor of several tens of thousands, this gives us about 100 million bits per concept, and this yields a total capacity of 1 million concepts per human brain. It has been estimated that a "master" of a particular domain of knowledge (chess, medicine, etc.) has mastered about 50,000 concepts, which is about 5 percent of the total capacity, according to the above estimate.

Human intelligence is not, however, a function of the number of concepts we can store, but rather of the coherency of our concepts, our ability to create meaningful concepts from the information we are exposed to, the levels of abstraction we are capable of dealing with, our ability to articulate these concepts, and perhaps most importantly, our ability to apply concepts in ways that go beyond the original information that created them. This last trait is often regarded as a key component of creativity.[13] As Roger Schank and Christopher Owens point out in their article in this book, we may be able to model this essential component of creativity using AI techniques. We are beginning to understand some of the mechanisms that enable us to apply a mental concept outside of its original domain and may ultimately be able to teach computers to do the same. And while humans do excel at their ability to recognize and apply concepts in creative ways, we are far from consistent in our ability to do so. Computers may ultimately prove far more thorough in their attempts to search all possibly relevant conceptual knowledge in the solution of a problem.[14]

The knowledge-search trade-off

The human brain uses a type of circuitry that is very slow. Our neurons can perform an analog computation in about 5 milliseconds, which is at least 10,000 times slower than a digital computer. On the other hand, the degree of parallelism vastly outstrips any computer architecture we have yet to design. The brain has about 100 billion neurons each with about 1,000 connections to other neurons, or about 100 trillion connections, each capable of a computation. If 1 percent of these are active, that produces 1 trillion computations in 5 milliseconds, or about 200 trillion computations per second. From this analysis Raj Reddy concludes that for such tasks as vision, language, and motor control, the brain is more powerful than 1,000 supercomputers, yet for certain simple tasks such as multiplying digital numbers, it is less powerful than the 4-bit microprocessor found in a ten-dollar calculator.[15]

It is clear that the human brain is not sequentially fast enough to perform lengthy searches on the implications of its knowledge base. Yet with such a large number of neurons and an even larger number of connections, it is capable of storing a vast amount of highly organized knowledge and accessing this knowledge in parallel. Thus, a typical strategy of the human brain is to access its memory of previously analyzed situations, since it is not capable of performing a great deal of analysis on a problem in real-time. The strategy is quite different for computers using the conventional serial (that is, nonparallel) architecture. There is sufficient sequential speed to perform extensive recursive search in the problem space, but often insufficient knowledge about a particular domain to rely too heavily on previously analyzed situations.

A dramatic example of this difference is found in the game of chess, our quintessential laboratory problem for exploring approaches to intelligence. Because of the slow sequential speed of human thought, the chess master has time only to consider perhaps 100 board positions, although he is able to take advantage of a

The knowledge-search trade-off in chess

	Human chess master	Computer chess master
Number of rules or memorized situations	30,000–100,000	200–400*
Number of board positions considered for each move	50–200	1,000,000–100,000,000

* Many computer chess programs do have extensive libraries of starting positions, so there can be an appreciable amount of knowledge used in the early game. The figure of 200–400 rules refers to the mid and end games.

large memory of previously analyzed situations.[16] Because of his powerful pattern-recognition capabilities, the chess master can recognize similarities in these previous situations even if the match is not perfect. It is estimated that the chess master has mastered 30,000 to 100,000 such board positions. The leading machine players, while performing at comparable levels, have traditionally used very little knowledge of chess beyond the rules. HiTech, for example, uses only a few hundred heuristic rules to assist its search but is capable of examining *millions* of board positions for each move (see table).

We thus find that there is a trade-off between knowledge and the computation required for recursive search, with the human and machine approaches to chess being at the opposite extreme ends of the curve.[17] As Raj Reddy says, "When in doubt, sprout!" meaning that the sprouting of a recursive search tree by machine intelligence can often compensate for its relative lack of knowledge. Conversely, our human knowledge compensates for the brain's inability to conduct extensive sequential search in real-time. The figure illustrates the knowledge-search trade-off, again with the human and machine approaches to chess at opposite ends.[18]

This brings up the issue of how much knowledge is enough. Interestingly, in areas of knowledge as diverse as the size of an expert's vocabulary, the number of symptom-illness correspondences known by a medical specialist, and the number of board positions memorized by a chess master, the number of "chunks" of

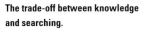

The trade-off between knowledge and searching.

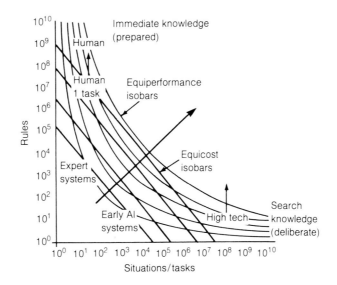

knowledge possessed by a human master of any particular discipline appears to be in the range of 30,000 to 100,000.[19] We are also finding that a comparable number of production rules are needed in our machine-based expert systems in order to provide for sufficient depth of coverage and avoid the fragility that was evident in the first generation of such systems. This realization about the long-term memory of a human expert contrasts with observations of human short-term memory, which appears to be about 10,000 times smaller.

These insights are encouraging with regard to the long-term outlook for machine intelligence. Machine intelligence is inherently superior to human intelligence in its ability to perform high-speed sequential search. As our machine methods for representing, learning, and retrieving chunks of knowledge improve, there is no reason why our computers cannot eventually exceed the approximate 100,000 chunk limit of human knowledge within specific domains. Another advantage of machine intelligence is the relative ease of sharing knowledge bases. Humans are capable of sharing knowledge, but this requires a slow process of human communication and learning. Computers can quickly and efficiently pool their knowledge bases.

The so-called chunking of knowledge has become a major issue in AI research. A recent system called SOAR created by Allen Newell and his colleagues is able to automatically create its own chunks of knowledge and thereby learn from experience.[20] It is capable of performing recursive search but also takes advantage of knowledge derived from a number of sources, including its own analysis of its own previous searches, information provided directly by its human teachers, and corrections of its own judgements. As it gains more experience in a particular problem area, it is indeed able to answer questions more quickly and with greater accuracy.[21]

The organization of an expert system

Expert systems are intended to replicate the decision making of a human expert within narrowly defined domains. Such systems have three primary components: a knowledge base, decision rules, and an inference engine.[22]

The knowledge base is intended to capture the ideas and concepts inherent in the domain in question. As mentioned above, creating such knowledge bases is a difficult and painstaking process. Although creating such knowledge bases automatically (or semiautomatically) is a focus of AI research, the knowledge bases of most expert systems in use today have been created link by link by human "knowledge engineers." Knowledge bases often incorporate structures similar to those discussed above to represent the concepts and relationships between concepts that are important to the domain. They may also include data bases of information with a more uniform structure.

The decision rules describe the methods to make decisions. In XCON, a system which configures computers for Digital Equipment Corporation, a typical rule may state that if a particular computer model needs more than six expansion boards, it requires an expansion chassis.[23] If there is an expansion chassis, then there must also be certain expansion cables, and so on. As of 1987 XCON incorporated over 10,000 such rules. It reportedly is doing the work of over 300 human experts with substantially higher accuracy. XCON was developed as an expert system only after several earlier attempts using more conventional programming methodologies had failed.[24]

The first generation of expert systems have used hard decision rules with firm antecedents and certain consequences. Most human decision making, on the other hand, is based on uncertain and fragmentary observations and less than certain implications. If as humans we failed to consider information unless it was relatively certain, we would be left with very little basis on which to make most decisions. A branch of mathematics called fuzzy logic has emerged to provide an optimal basis for using probabilistic rules and observations.[25]

The third component of the expert system, the inference engine, is a system for applying the rules to the knowledge base to make decisions. Many expert systems in use today use standard serial computers (mainframes, minicomputers, and personal computers) with special software to perform the deductive and inductive reasoning required by the decision rules. For the more sophisticated expert systems now being created, this approach will not be fast enough in many cases. The number of inferences that must be considered (that is, the number of rules that must be applied to each concept or datum in the knowledge base) explodes exponentially as both the knowledge base and number of rules expands. Systems created in the early 1980s typically included several hundred to several thousand rules with similarly modest knowledge bases. For systems now being created with tens of thousands of rules and far more extensive knowledge bases, serial computers are

Toshi Doi, pioneer of the compact disc. Doi is developing an intelligent workstation called NEWS. (Photo by Lou Jones)

often too slow to provide acceptable response times. Specialized inference engines incorporating substantial (and eventually massive) parallelism are being constructed to provide the requisite computing power. As noted below the Japanese fifth-generation computer project foresees the personal computer of the 1990s as containing extremely high-speed, highly parallel inference engines capable of rapidly manipulating abstract concepts.[26]

• Putting Knowledge to Work

Zeppo: We've got to *think*!
Chico (with a dismissive hand gesture): Nah, we already tried dat.
The Marx brothers, as quoted in *Mind Tools* by Rudy Rucker.

Knowledge has an important property. When you give it away, you don't lose it.
Raj Reddy, *Foundations and Grand Challenges of Artificial Intelligence* (1988)

The actual codifying of scientific and professional knowledge in terms that a computer could understand began in the mid 1960s and became a major focus of AI research in the 1970s. Edward Feigenbaum, Bruce Buchanan, and their colleagues at Stanford University were early pioneers in the effort to establish the field now known as knowledge engineering.[27] Their first effort, called DENDRAL, was one of the first expert systems. Begun in 1965 and developed throughout the 1970s, it embodied extensive knowledge of molecular-structure analysis, which was selected simply as an illustration of the ability of a computer-based system to master an area of scientific knowledge. A primary goal of the project was to investigate questions in the philosophy of science, including the construction and validity of hypotheses. It emerged nonetheless as a tool of practical value in university and industrial laboratories. Much of the interest in, and methodology of, expert systems, which spawned a major industry during the 1980s, can be traced to DENDRAL.[28]

A follow-on project, Meta-DENDRAL, was an early attempt to break the knowledge-learning bottleneck. Presented with data about new chemical compounds, Meta-DENDRAL was capable of automatically devising new rules for DENDRAL. Problems that the Meta-DENDRAL team faced included dealing with partial and often inaccurate data and the fact that multiple concepts were often intertwined in the same set of data. The problem of learning was by no means solved by the Meta-DENDRAL workers, but they did ease the job of the human knowledge-engineer, and many of Meta-DENDRAL's techniques are still the focus of learning research today.[29]

Expert systems in medicine

With the success of DENDRAL and Meta-DENDRAL by the early 1970s, Feigenbaum, Buchanan, and others became interested in applying similar techniques to a broader set of applications and formed the Heuristic Programming Project, which today goes by the name of the Knowledge Systems Laboratory. Perhaps their best known effort, MYCIN, an expert system to diagnose and recommend remedial treatment for infectious diseases was developed throughout the 1970s. In 1979 nine researchers reported in the *Journal of the American Medical Association* a compari-

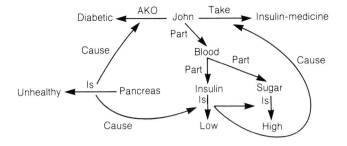

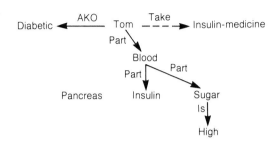

A knowledge-base extract describing diabetes. Causal links are shown with bold arrows. (From Winston, *Artificial Intelligence,* 1984, p. 492)

son of MYCIN's ability to evaluate complex cases involving meningitis to that of human doctors.[30] In what has become a landmark study, ten cases of infection were selected, including three viral, one tubercular, one fungal, and one bacterial. For each of these cases, diagnoses and treatment recommendations were obtained from MYCIN, a Stanford Infectious Disease faculty member, a resident, and a medical student. A team of evaluators compared the diagnoses and recommendations for all of the cases, without knowledge of who (or what) had written them, against the actual course of the disease and the actual therapy followed. According to the evaluators, MYCIN did as well or better than any of the human doctors. Although the domain of this evaluation was limited, the conclusion received a great deal of attention from both the medical and computer communities, as well as the general media. If a computer could match human intelligence in medical diagnosis and treatment recommendation, albeit within a limited area of specialization, there appeared to be no reason why the domains could not be substantially broadened. It was also evident that such systems could eventually improve on human judgement in terms of the *consistent* application of the vast (and rapidly increasing) quantity of medical knowledge.

MYCIN's success resulted in a high level of interest and confidence in expert systems.[31] A sizeable industry was created in the decade that followed.[32] According to DM Data, the market research firm, the expert-system industry grew from $4 million in 1981 to $400 million in 1988 and an estimated $800 million in 1990.[33]

Beyond the attention it focused on the discipline of knowledge engineering, MYCIN was significant in other ways. It introduced the now-standard methodology of a separate knowledge base and inference engine, as well as the recursive goal-directed algorithms of the inference engine.[34] Further, MYCIN did not just give diagnostic conclusions, it could also explain its reasoning and cite sources in the medical literature. Of major significance was MYCIN's use of its own version of fuzzy logic, that is, reasoning based on uncertain evidence and rules, as shown in the following rule, which also includes justification and reference:

MYCIN Rule 280

IF:

(1) The infection which requires therapy is meningitis, and

(2) The type of the infection is fungal, and

(3) Organisms were not seen on the stain of the culture, and

(4) The patient is not a compromised host, and

(5) The patient has been to an area that is endemic for coccidiomycoses, and

(6) The race of the patient is one of: Black, Asian, Indian, and

(7) The cryptococcal antigen in the csf was not positive

THEN:

There is suggestive evidence (.5) that cryptococcus is not one of the organisms (other than those seen on cultures or smears) which might be causing the infection.

AUTHOR:

YU

JUSTIFICATION:

Dark-skinned races, especially Filipino, Asian and Black (in that order) have an increased susceptibility to coccidiomycoses meningitis.

LITERATURE:

Stevens et al. Miconazole in Coccidiomycosis. Am. J. Med. 60:191–202, Feb 1976.

In the mid to late 1970s a variety of enhancements for MYCIN were created, including TEIRESIAS, a knowledge-building tool, and EMYCIN (for Essential MYCIN), a portable version (that is, applicable to other applications) of MYCIN's inference engine.[35] These tools were applied to other tasks, including a system called PUFF for interpreting pulmonary tests.[36] During the 1980s the techniques established by MYCIN were applied to more sophisticated systems, including NeoMYCIN, a consultation system with a broader domain of medical knowledge than MYCIN, and ONCOCIN, a system for the design of oncology (cancer therapy) chemotherapy protocols.[37] Innovations introduced by these later systems include hierarchical knowledge bases that go beyond decision rules and the ability to engage in a dialogue with the user to elicit symptoms, call for additional tests and input, and clarify reasoning.[38]

A particularly ambitious system called CADUCEUS (formerly Internist) was developed at the University of Pittsburgh for diagnosis within the broad domain of internal medicine. As of 1982 CADUCEUS contained over 100,000 associations between symptoms and diseases and covered an estimated 70 percent of the relevant knowledge in the field.[39] The performance of CADUCEUS was compared to that of human doctors on cases drawn from the *New England Journal of Medicine.* In a wide range of diagnostic categories CADUCEUS was actually more accurate than the human physicians.[40]

It is not surprising that medicine would be the first professional domain to attract significant knowledge-engineering attention. Medical knowledge is highly organized, and the linkage of symptoms and test results to diagnoses and remedial action is described in the medical literature in great detail. Although the knowledge-

4-Oct-84 61:14:42

PERSON-1

(1) What is the person called
** ANNIE BODDIE
(2) What sex is Annie Boddie
** FEMALE
(3) How old is Annie Boddie
** 3
The first sample of Annie Boddie will be referred to as:

SAMPLE-1

(4) What was SAMPLE-1 (blood, marrow, etc)
** MARROW
(5) What is the blast count in SAMPLE-1
** UNK
(6) What was the Tdt result
** 20
(7) What is the C-ALL result
** 0
(8) What was the clinical diagnosis for Annie Boddie
* UNK
(9) What is the Sm Ig result
** 50
(10) What was the mouse rosette result
** UNK
(11) Is there a mediastinal mass
** UNK
(12) What was the Sheep rosette result
** UNK
(13) What was the HLA-DR result
** UNK
(14) What was the Kappa result
** WHY [I.e., why is it important to determine the percentage of Kappa-positive cells?]

A typical dialogue with the EMYCIN leukemia diagnosis system. (Courtesy of the Imperial Cancer Research Fund Laboratories, London)

[1.0] This will aid in determining the leukemic cell type. It has already been established that
[1.1] the leukemic cell type is b-cell
Therefore, if
[1.2] (1) The percentage of Kappa positive cells divided by the percentage lambda positive cells
        is greater than or equal to 6, or
        (2) The percentage lambda positive cells divided by the percentage of Kappa positive cells
        is greater than or equal to 3
then there is weakly suggestive evidence (.4) that the leukemic cell type is monoclonal-b-cell
[RULE 032]

[Back to question 14.]
** WHY [I.e., why is it important to determine the leukemic cell type?]

[2.0] The leukemic cell type is one of the 2 key parameters associated with a SAMPLE. The value of this parameter is always determined as soon as a SAMPLE is mentioned.
[2.1] The leukenic cell type is very important in determining the diagnosis [as, for example, in RULE 055].

[Back to question 14.]
** 62
(15) What was the Lambda result
** 62
(16) Are there any other samples of Annie Boddie
** NO

I was unable to make any conclusion about the diagnosis.

A dialogue with TEIRESIAS, a computerized investment counselor. (Taken from Jean-Louis Lauriere, "Knowledge Representation and Use. Part 1, Expert Systems," *Technology and Science of Informatics* 1 [1983], no. 1: 15)

TEIRESIAS:	The following investments seem to be the most suitable at the moment: Varian Corporation and American Telephones & Telegraphs (AT&T). Is that correct?
Expert:	No.
TEIRESIAS:	Are there any missing?
Expert:	Yes, Digital Equiptment and Data General.
TEIRESIAS:	Are there any which should not be present?
Expert:	Yes, AT&T.
TEIRESIAS:	Would you like me to guide the error search?
Expert:	Yes.
TEIRESIAS:	Let's begin then with AT&T. I used rule 27 to reach that conclusion: As (1) the investment field was not defined, (2) expected profits are above 10%, (3) the investment must be long term, so AT&T is a plausible choice (0.4). Is the rule correct?
Expert:	Yes.
TEIRESIAS:	Is there a premiss which should not have been evaluated as true?
Expert:	Yes, number 1.
TEIRESIAS:	I came to no conclusion on the issue of the field of investment. Should I have come up with something precise?
Expert:	Yes. Advanced technology.
TEIRESIAS:	Tests on all rules which might have concluded in favour of the advanced technology field all failed because marked premisses were false. . . . Were these two rules correct?
Expert:	Yes.
TEIRESIAS:	Should either of them not have been applied?
Expert:	No.
TEIRESIAS:	Is there a rule missing?
Expert:	Yes.
TEIRESIAS:	OK, so I need a rule which will allow me to deduce that the field should have been advanced technology. Would you like to give me a rule of that kind?
Expert:	If the client's tax bracket is 80%, if the client is following up on market trend carefully, then it is obvious (0.8) that the investment should be made in high technology.
TEIRESIAS:	The new rule is called rule 383. This is how I understand it: If (1) the client's tax payments are 50%, if (2) the market has followed an upward trend recently, if (3) the client manages his assets carefully, then the investment should be made in high technology (0.8). Is that right?
Expert:	No.
TEIRESIAS:	Should the premisses be changed?
Expert:	Yes, change (2).
TEIRESIAS:	What if (2) were changed into '(2) the client follows the market carefully , would that do?
Expert:	Yes.
TEIRESIAS:	Then you will doubtless want to eliminate (3). Right?
Expert:	Yes.
TEIRESIAS:	(Repetition of R383, then:) I don't like to criticize, Randy, but do you realize that usually, rules affecting investment fields which mention the client's tax bracket and the way he follows the market also mention the client's experience in making investments? Should I attempt to formulate a third premiss?
Expert:	Yes.
TEIRESIAS:	What do you think of: the client has moderate degree of experience in investment?
Expert:	OK.
TEIRESIAS:	Most of those rules also give a conclusion on the desired level of risk for the investment. Should I attempt to give that kind of conclusion here?
Expert:	No.
TEIRESIAS:	(Repetition of corrected R383, then:) Please tell me briefly why you have added this rule.
Expert:	The system had not understood that it could specify the field of investment, which led to rule 27 being applied incorrectly.
TEIRESIAS:	R383 has been added to the knowledge base. The consultation will start again to test whether this rule is in fact well founded or not. Make youself comfortable, this could take some time. . . . Results, suggested investments: Varian Corporation, Data General, Digital Equipment. Good, it looks like everything has been corrected, doesn't it?
Expert:	Yes.

engineering process remains painstaking, the knowledge is sufficiently well organized for expert-system techniques. The systems described above are among dozens of medical expert systems in existence or under development. Some of these systems are already contributing to medical care.[41] PUFF, for example, is routinely used at the Pacific Medical Center in San Francisco. Its reports are screened by an attending pulmonary physiologist, who modifies no more than 5 percent of PUFF's reports. Many patients have had their cancer-treatment programs recommended by ONCOCIN, which are also carefully reviewed. Although a large amount of development of medical expert systems has been done and their actual use as advisors is beginning, these systems have still had relatively little impact on medical practice in general. There are four reasons for this. First, the medical community is understandably conservative with regard to any new technology, let alone an entirely new approach to diagnosis. Even as consultants, these cybernetic diagnosticians will have to prove themselves repeatedly before they are given major roles. Second, the hardware these systems require has been expensive up until recently. This factor is rapidly vanishing: the latest generation of personal computers has sufficient power to run many of these applications. Third, many of these systems are not sufficiently developed for practical use. They are often "brittle," falling apart when cases fall outside of their narrow areas of expertise. In order to provide a consistent and predictable level of service, the knowledge bases require enormous refinement.[42] The most advanced systems, such as CADUCEUS, are now beginning to reach sufficient depths of medical knowledge. Finally, the issue of competition from a new type of medical expert (one without a medical degree) is a real issue. Since the medical profession has effective control over the delivery of medical services, resistance to any new type of competition is not surprising. To succeed, the marketers of such services will need to position them clearly as tools that will make their users more competitive with their human peers.

Expert systems in other fields

Considering the gravity of many medical decisions, the slow pace of acceptance of expert systems in medicine is understandable. In the financial field, the situation is quite different. Here expert-system technology is often enthusiastically adopted. This too is perhaps not surprising. Financial professionals are used to imperfect decision making. They expect a certain fraction of decisions to be wrong. Practical demonstrations that a financial expert system can match and often exceed the quality of human decision making within a well defined area of expertise are more likely to be readily accepted.[43]

For example, Syntelligence has created a system for the insurance industry called Underwriting Advisor, which provides advice on risk analysis and pricing for various lines of insurance, including workers' compensation, property, liability, and other types. A particularly successful system is the Authorizer's Assistant, which reduces the transaction time of an American Express credit authorizer by 20 to 30 percent and has reportedly reduced expensive bad judgements by about 75 percent.

Applications are proliferating in a broad variety of fields. A system developed at SRI International called Prospector received significant attention when it was

I am considering the possibility of a (Type-A porphyry copper deposit—PCDA) in the target area.

The following questions are intended to establish the nature of the petrotectonic setting.

1—To what degree do you believe that: (the target area is in a continental margin mobile belt)?

** –2

The following questions are intended to determine the nature of the regional environment.

2—To what degree do you believe that: (there are granitic intrusives in the region)?

** 5

3—To what degree do you believe that: (the region contains an abundance of small stocks)?

** –3

. . .

8—To what degree do you believe that: (igneous rocks in the region have porphyritic texture)?

** Why

I am trying to establish whether some of the intrusive rocks in your area have textures suggestive of a hypabyssal to subvolcanic environment. Porphyry textures resulting from the rapid cooling and crystallization of a silicate melt which contains large mineral grains are suggestive of relatively shallow levels of emplacement.

8—To what degree do you believe that: (igneous rocks in the region have porphyritic texture)?

** 5

My certainty in (the texture and morphology of the intrusive system suggest a subvolcanic (hypabyssal) regional environment) is now: 4.924.

Do you want to pursue this further?

** No

A conversation with Prospector. (Human responses start with a double asterisk.) (Courtesy of Edward Feigenbaum)

reported to have identified the location of a porphyry molybdenum deposit from readily available predrilling exploration data.[44] Although this particular discovery had more scientific than economic significance, the potential of expert systems to improve the odds for the very expensive gambles involved in natural-resource discovery has fueled substantial investment in knowledge engineering by the energy and minerals industries.

Teknowledge is creating a system for General Motors that will assist garage mechanics in quickly diagnosing and repairing engine-control problems in GM's fuel-injected engines. With the increasing complexity of modern automobile designs, keeping the skills and knowledge of mechanics up to date has become a major problem. A computer-based system is an efficient way to provide continually updated expertise to thousands of locations around the world. A similar system called the Service Bay Diagnostic System, being developed by the Carnegie Group for Ford, is described in the article by Jeff Pepper in this book.

Digital Equipment Corporation's success with XCON has resulted in an extensive development program of expert systems encompassing most aspects of DEC's business, including XSEL (expert selling tool), an expert system that matches DEC products to customer needs; ISA (Intelligent Scheduling Assistant), which schedules manufacturing and shop floor activity; IDT (Intelligent Diagnostic Tool), which assists human technicians in diagnosing manufactured products that fail verification tests; and NTC (Network Troubleshooting Consultant), which diagnoses computer network problems.[45]

A survey conducted by the *Applied Artificial Intelligence Reporter* showed that the number of working expert systems swelled from 700 at the end of 1986 to 1,900 by the end of 1987. There were 7,000 systems under development at the end of 1986 and 13,000 at the end of 1987. This has swelled to tens of thousands of systems in 1990. The most popular application area is finance, with manufacturing control second and fault diagnosis third. With the number of expert systems rapidly expanding, a significant portion of the revenue of the expert-system industry comes from selling the tools to create expert systems. These include specialized languages like PROLOG and knowledge-engineering environments, sometimes called shells, such as Knowledge Craft from the Carnegie Group, ART (Automated Reasoning Tool) from Inference Corporation, and KEE (Knowledge Engineering Environment) from IntelliCorp.[46]

Some of the more advanced applications are being created by the U.S. Defense Department as part of its Strategic Computing Initiative (SCI)—not to be confused with the more controversial Strategic Defense Initiative (SDI), although both SCI and SDI involve extensive application of pattern-recognition and knowledge-engineering technologies.[47] SCI envisions the creation of four advanced prototypes. The Autonomous Land Vehicle is an unmanned robotic vehicle that can avoid obstacles, conduct tactical maneuvers and carry out attack and defense plans while traveling at speeds of up to 40 miles per hour. Its on-board expert system is expected to carry out 7,000 inferences (applications of rules) per second. This will clearly require parallel processing, as typical expert systems implemented on serial computers rarely achieve speeds of greater than 100 inferences per second. SCI's Vision System will provide real-time analysis of imaging data from intelligent weapons and reconnaissance aircraft. It is expected to use computers providing 10 to 100 billion instructions per second, which will require massive parallel processing. The Pilot's Associate will be an integrated set of nine expert systems designed to provide a wide range of services to pilots in combat situations, including the planning of mission tactics, monitoring the status of key systems, navigation, and targeting.[48] The system contemplates communication with the pilot via speech recognition and advanced visual displays. Finally, SCI's Battle Management System will assist the commanders of naval aircraft in coordinating resources and tactics during conflicts.

One issue confronting defense applications is the complexity of the software systems required and the inherent difficulty of testing such systems under realistic conditions. The core avionics of a typical fighter aircraft in the late 1980s used about 200,000 lines of software; the fighter aircraft of the early 1990s is expected to require about a million lines. Altogether, it is estimated that the U.S. military in 1990 uses about 100 million lines of code, which is expected to double within five years. Assuring the quality of such extensive software systems is an urgent problem that planners are only beginning to address.

As we approach the next generation of expert systems, three bottlenecks have been recognized and are being attacked by researchers in the United States, Europe, and Japan. Inference engines that use parallel processing are being developed to process the substantially larger knowledge and rule bases now being developed. The number of inferences per second that need to be handled often grows exponentially with the size of the knowledge base. With expert systems being

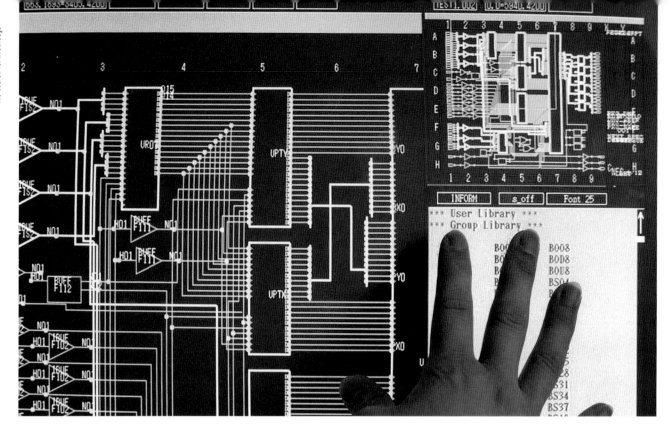

Intelligent chip design. At an NEC research lab in Kawasaki, Japan, a computer-aided design (CAD) system generates a blueprint for a VLSI chip. (Photo by Lou Jones)

applied to such real-time situations as monitoring nuclear plants and coordinating weapons systems, the need for rapid response is obvious.[49]

Perhaps the most important issue being addressed is learning.[50] Building knowledge bases by hand is extremely painstaking. Methods for automating this process have become a major focus of both academic and commercial development. EURISKO, a system developed at Stanford's Knowledge Systems Laboratory and now being refined at the Microelectronics and Computer Technology Corporation, has demonstrated an ability to generate its own rules as it solves problems and receives feedback from users.[51] Several new expert systems are capable of growing their own knowledge bases simply by observing human decision makers doing their jobs. This is particularly feasible in financial applications, since in most cases financial decisions, as well as the data they are based on, are already easily accessed by computer communications.

Finally, another major issue is the proper use of uncertain and fragmentary information. It is well known that effective use of such information is vital to most human decision making, but recent research by Robert Hink and David Woods at Expert Systems Design has cast some doubt on just how skilled humans are at it.[52] Hink and Woods found that for most people, including human experts within their domains, the ability to balance risks and make optimal decisions involving probabilistic outcomes is surprisingly low.[53] For example, in some instances subjects would choose an opportunity for a large reward with a small probability over a smaller but certain reward even though the expectant value (the reward multiplied by the probability of receiving it) of the larger reward was substantially lower. One might ascribe this behavior to an enjoyment of risk taking and a general desire to reach for large rewards. In other instances these same subjects would select the more conservative option even though in these cases its expectant value was less. The decision-making patterns were *neither* optimal nor consistent. Often the way in which questions were worded had more effect on the choices than the underlying facts. These findings are consistent with the commonsense observation that some people display consistently better performance at certain types of tasks, even when considerable uncertainty is involved. Classic examples are card games such as poker, in which skilled players almost always come out on top, even though a significant element of chance is involved. Such players are obviously able to apply probabilistic rules in a more consistent and methodologically sound manner than their opponents. Hink and Woods found that the validity and coherency of most people's decision making, even within the persons' areas of professional competence, was dramatically lower than they had expected. The significance of this observation for the knowledge-engineering community is mixed. The bad news is that devising sound knowledge bases and rules will remain difficult, since even the human domain experts are not very effective at applying them, apart from frequent lack of awareness of their own decision rules. The good news is that there is considerable opportunity for computer-based expert systems to improve on human decision-making in those domains where the knowledge and decision-making processes can be captured and applied.[54]

• Language: The Expression of Knowledge

Gracie: **A truck hit Willy.**

George: **What truck?**

Gracie: **The truck that didn't have its lights on.**

George: **Why didn't it have its lights on?**

Gracie: **It didn't have to. It was daytime.**

George: **Why didn't the truck driver see Willy?**

Gracie: **He didn't know it was Willy.**

A comedy routine of Burns and Allen, quoted by Roger Schank to illustrate problems of language comprehension

This is the cheese that the rat that the cat that the dog chased bit ate.

Marvin Minsky, *The Society of Mind* (citing a valid sentence that humans have difficulty parsing)

Squad Helps Dog Bite Victim

Book of Newspaper Headline Gaffes

Birds can fly, unless they are penguins and ostriches, or if they happen to be dead, or have broken wings, or are confined to cages, or have their feet stuck in cement, or have undergone experiences so dreadful as to render them psychologically incapable of flight.

Marvin Minsky, *The Society of Mind* (illustrating the difficulty of accurately expressing knowledge)

"Okay, where did you hide it?"

"Hide what?"

"You know."

"Where do you think?"

"Oh."

A "married conversation" cited by Nicholas Negroponte of the MIT Media Lab to illustrate the importance of shared knowledge in interpreting natural language

**No knowledge is entirely reducible to words, and
no knowledge is entirely ineffable.**

Seymour Papert, *Mindstorms*

Students of human thought and the thinking process have always paid special
attention to human language.[55] Our ability to express and understand language is
often cited as a principal differentiating characteristic of our species. Language is the
means by which we share our knowledge. Though we have only very limited access
to the actual circuits and algorithms embedded in our brains, language itself is quite
visible. Studying the structures and methods of language gives us a readily accessible laboratory for studying the structure of human knowledge and the thinking
process behind it. Work in this laboratory shows, not surprisingly, that language is no
less complex or subtle a phenomenon than the knowledge it seeks to transmit.

There are several levels of structure in human language. The first to be
actively studied was syntax, the rules governing the ways in which words are
arranged and the roles words play. Syntactic rules govern the placement of nouns,
verbs, and other word types in a sentence and also control verb conjugation and
other elements of sentence structure. Although human language is far more complex, similarities in the syntactic structures of human and computer languages were
noticed by AI researchers in the 1960s. An early AI goal was to give a computer the
ability to parse natural language sentences into the type of sentence diagrams that
grade-school children learn. One of the first such systems, developed in 1963 by
Susumu Kuno of Harvard, was interesting in its revelation of the depth of ambiguity
in the English language. Kuno asked his computerized parser what the sentence
"Time flies like an arrow" means. In what has become a famous response, the
computer replied that it was not quite sure. It might mean (1) that time passes as
quickly as an arrow passes. Or maybe (2) it is a command telling us to time the flies
the same way that an arrow times flies; that is, "Time flies like an arrow would." Or
(3) it could be a command telling us to time only those flies that are similar to
arrows; that is, "Time flies that are like an arrow." Or perhaps (4) it means that the
type of flies known as "time flies" have a fondness for arrows: "Time-flies *like*
arrows."[56]

It became clear from this and other syntactical ambiguities that understanding language requires both an understanding of the relationships between
words and knowledge of the concepts underlying words.[57] It is impossible to
understand the sentence about time (or even to understand that the sentence is
indeed talking about time and not flies) without a mastery of the knowledge structures that represent what we know about time, flies, arrows, and how these
concepts relate to one another. An AI technology called semantic analysis attempts
to apply knowledge of the concepts associated with words to the problem of
language understanding. A system armed with this type of information would note
that flies are not similar to arrows (which would thus knock out the third interpretation above). (Often there is more than one way to resolve language ambiguities. The
third interpretation could also have been syntactically resolved by noting that "like"
in the sense of "similar to" ordinarily requires number agreement between the two

304

S = sentence   N = noun
NP = noun phrase   V = verb
VP = verb phrase   P = preposition
PP = prepositional phrase   D = determiner

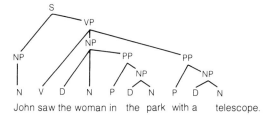
John saw the woman in the park with a telescope.

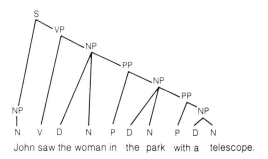
John saw the woman in the park with a telescope.

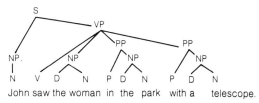
John saw the woman in the park with a telescope.

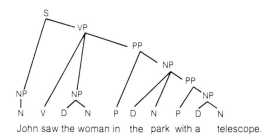
John saw the woman in the park with a telescope.

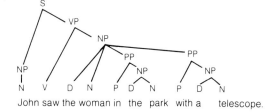
John saw the woman in the park with a telescope.

A Japanese display at the Tokyo Institute of Technology. (Photo by Lou Jones)

What did you mean by that? A computer sentence-parsing program reveals the ambiguity of language. (Data from Skona Brittain, "Understanding Natural Languages," *AI Expert* 2 [1987], no. 5: 32) objects that are compared.) It would also note that there is no type of flies known as time flies (which would probably knock out the fourth interpretation). Another type of analysis, known as pragmatic analysis, attempts to apply the vast wealth of practical knowledge about the world to further resolve ambiguities. In applying this technique to our previous results, we use such tidbits of knowledge as that flies have never shown a fondness for arrows, and that arrows cannot and do not time anything, much less flies, to select the first interpretation as the only plausible one.

The ambiguity of language is far greater than may be apparent. During a language parsing project at the MIT Speech Lab, Ken Church found a sentence published in a technical journal with over one million syntactically correct interpretations!

It is clear that a vast amount of knowledge is needed to interpret even the simplest sentence. Indeed, some of the largest knowledge-based systems have been developed in the area of language understanding and translation. Translation is clearly impossible without understanding. Ever since Bar-Hillel's famous paper of 1960, "A Demonstration of the Nonfeasibility of Fully Automatic High-Quality Translation," researchers have understood the necessity that the computer under-stand both the syntax and semantics of the text in a language before attempting a translation into another language.[58] The Logos computer-assisted translation system, for example, uses about 20,000 understanding and translation rules to translate German technical texts into English and still provides results that are only about 80 percent as accurate as a human translator. Logos researchers estimate that it would require about 100,000 rules to achieve human performance levels, even in the restricted domain of technical texts.[59]

Understanding human language in a relatively unrestricted domain remains too difficult for today's computers. Beyond the resolution of syntactic and semantic ambiguities, there are many issues regarding unspoken assumptions and appropriate-ness. If I say, "The bread is ready to eat," one can assume that it is not the bread that will do the eating; however, if I say, "The chicken is ready to eat," it is less clear who intends to eat whom. In this case, further contextual information is required. Resolving such ambiguities in a general way requires extensive knowledge and the ability to readily access the information most relevant. If I ask someone I have just met, What do you do? I am probably not interested in hearing about things which I obviously already know, such as eating, breathing, sleeping, thinking (al-though if someone wanted to be evasive, these might very well be appropriate responses). If I ask, Do you want something to eat or not? it would be technically correct to answer yes even if you did *not* want something to eat.[60] Again, avoiding overly literal interpretations of language requires vast collections of knowledge that no one has yet bothered to collect. We are, in fact, only now beginning to know what knowledge to collect and how to collect it.

The ability of humans quickly and accurately to resolve syntactic ambigui-ties is not perfect, however, and a great deal of humor is based on this type of confusion. Skona Brittain cites the following example:

John: I want to go to bed with Marilyn Monroe again tonight.
Jane: Again?
John: Yes, I've had this desire before.

A further complication in understanding language is the ubiquitous use of idiomatic expressions. Consider the following: "She broke the ice by bringing up their latest advertising client. 'We're skating on thin ice with this one,' she said, 'the problem in promoting their new product is just the tip of the iceberg.'" Although there are three references to ice, these sentences obviously have nothing to do with ice. Beyond the three ice-related idioms, the phrase "bring up" is also idiomatic, meaning to introduce a topic by speaking about it. Each idiom introduces a story or analogy that must somehow be integrated with the rest of the subject matter. Understanding language can thus require a knowledge of history, myths, literary allusions and references, and many other categories of shared human experience.[61]

When we talk to other human beings, we assume that they share with us an enormous core of knowledge and understanding about both the world and the subjects we plan to talk about.[62] These assumptions vary according to who we are talking to and how much we know we have in common. Talking to coworkers or good friends obviously allows us to make more assumptions than talking to a stranger on the street, although even here we often assume shared knowledge of sports teams, current events, history, and many other topics. But in talking (or typing) to computers, no understanding of human commonsense knowledge can yet be assumed. While the slow and arduous process of teaching basic world knowledge to computers has begun, the most successful strategy in creating viable computer-based natural-language applications has been to limit the domain of discourse to an area where virtually all of the relevant knowledge can be captured. One of the first examples of this approach was Terry Winograd's 1970 MIT thesis SHRDLU.[63] SHRDLU understood commands in natural English, as long as the commands pertained only to an artificial world composed of different colored blocks. While the limitations of the toy worlds of SHRDLU and other similar systems were criticized in the 1960s and 1970s, it turns out that such sharply constrained domains do have practical value.[64] For example, the world of computer data bases is no more complicated than the world of colored blocks, but it happens to be one that many business people do interact with daily. One of the more successful natural-language-understanding programs, Intellect, from Artificial Intelligence Corporation, allows users to ask questions in natural English concerning information in their data bases.[65] Because the domain is sufficiently limited, the Intellect system can rely primarily on syntactic rules, although semantic and pragmatic knowledge has also been incorporated. Competitive systems developed by Cognitive Systems, a company founded by Roger Schank, rely more heavily on explicit representations of semantic and pragmatic knowledge. By means of Schank's script methodology, similar knowledge bases can be used for both language understanding and decision making.[66] For example, an expert system called Courtier, created by Cognitive Systems for a Belgian bank, can provide portfolio advice in response to natural-language commands.[67]

Perhaps the largest market for natural-language systems is translation.[68] Translating (mostly technical) texts by means of traditional techniques is today a multibillion-dollar business. While computerized translation systems are not yet sufficiently accurate to run unassisted, they can significantly increase the productivity of a human translator. One of the challenges in developing computerized translation

Roger Schank, director of the
Institute for the Learning Sciences at
Northwestern University and a
pioneer in knowledge representation
and natural-language understanding.
(Photo by Dan McCoy of Rainbow)

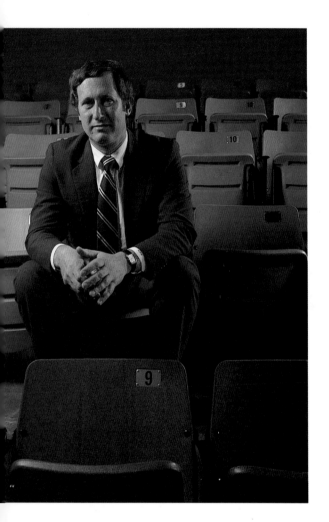

Larry Harris, president of Artificial
Intelligence Corp. (AIC) and
developer of natural-language-
understanding systems. AIC's
Intellect program enables executives
to interact with their data base
systems using ordinary English.
(Photo by Lou Jones)

systems is that each pair of languages represents a different translation problem, or rather, each pair of languages represents a pair of problems. An interesting approach to simplifying this difficulty is being pursued by DLT, a Dutch firm that is developing translators for six languages to and from a standard root language. They use a modified form of Esperanto, a century-old language originally proposed as a universal language, as an intermediate representation. In their system, a translation from English to French would be accomplished in two steps, English to Esperanto and then Esperanto to French. Esperanto was selected because it is particularly good at representing concepts in an unambiguous way, thus making it ideal as a root conceptual language. Translating among 6 different languages would ordinarily require 30 different translators (6 languages, each to be translated into 5 other languages), but with the DLT approach, only 12 are required (6 translators from the 6 languages into Esperanto and 6 more from Esperanto back to the 6 languages). Furthermore, as DLT points out, the translating systems that go from Esperanto to another language are relatively simple.[69]

Perhaps the most intensive work on automatic language translation is being pursued at a number of Japanese research centers, including Kyoto University and the Tokyo Institute of Technology. Japan's Ministry of International Trade and Industry has cited Japanese-English and English-Japanese translation systems as vital to Japan's economy.

One of the primary barriers to more widespread use of computer technology is communication between human and machine. Most persons, even those with technical training in fields other than computer science, find the specialized syntax required by most computer applications to be intimidating and confusing. There is considerable agreement that the optimal way to interact with computers would be the same way we interact with our human colleagues and assistants: by talking things over in a natural language. Providing this capability will require integrating large-vocabulary speech recognition (recognizing what the words *are* from speech) with a high level of natural-language understanding (understanding what the words *mean*). Though these capabilities are not yet sufficiently well developed to replace either the keyboard or the specialized computer syntaxes now used for most computer applications, the natural-language market is beginning to take hold for a variety of applications. DM Data estimates the natural-language market (not including speech recognition) at $80 million in 1987 and projects a $300 million market in 1990.[70]

Once again, we find that the relative strengths of machine and human intelligence are quite different. Humans first learn to listen to and understand spoken language. Later on we learn to speak. Computers, on the other hand, have been generating printed natural-language output since their inception and have only recently begun to understand it. Also, the ability of computers to speak predated their ability to recognize spoken language. Another example: humans gain mastery of written language at a much later age than verbal language. Here too computer history has reversed this sequence. As a final example, computers today can understand natural-language sentences dealing with "complex" financial inquiries yet still stumble on the "simple" sentences that children can understand. This phenomenon is widely misunderstood. The popular robot character R2D2 (of *Star Wars* fame)

Language translation at present involves bilingual humans making copious use of a dictionary. (Photo by Lou Jones)

Jun-Ichi Tsujii of Kyoto University, an authority on the automatic translation of languages. (Photo by Lou Jones)

A tale of two countries. The keyboards on this computer displays both English and Japanese characters. The upper board allows direct input of Japanese ideographs. Developed at the Tokyo Institute of Technology, this machine translation system can translate text from either language almost instantaneously. (Photos by Lou Jones)

is supposed to understand many human languages yet is unable to speak (other than with "computerlike" squeaks and other noises), which gives the mistaken impression that *generating* human language (and speech) is far more difficult than *understanding* it.

• Putting It All Together: The Age of Robots

I am incapable of making an error.

HAL, in Stanley Kubrick and Arthur C. Clarke's 1968 film *2001: A Space Odyssey*

1. A robot may not injure a human being, or, through inaction, allow a human being to come to harm.
2. A robot must obey the orders given it by human beings, except where such orders would conflict with the First Law.
3. A robot must protect its own existence as long as such protection does not conflict with the First or Second Law.

Isaac Asimov's three laws of robotics

In *R.U.R.,* a play written in 1921, the Czech dramatist Karel Capek (1890–1938) describes the invention of intelligent mechanical machines intended as servants for their human creators. Called robots, they end up disliking their masters and take matters into their own "hands." After taking over the world, they decide to tear down all symbols of human civilization. By the end of the play they have destroyed all of mankind. Although Capek first used the word "robot" in his 1917 short story "Opilec," creating the term from the Czech words "robota," meaning obligatory work, and "robotnik," meaning serf, *R.U.R.* (for "Rossum's Universal Robots") introduced the word into popular usage. Capek intended his intelligent machines to be evil in their perfection, their ultimate rationality scornful of human frailty. Although a mediocre play, it struck a chord by articulating the uneasy relationship between man and machine and achieved wide success on two continents.[71] The spectre of machine intelligence enslaving its creators, or at least competing with human intelligence for employment and other privileges, has continued to impress itself on the public consciousness.

Although lacking human charm and good will, Capek's robots brought together all of the elements of machine intelligence: vision, auditory perception, touch sensitivity, pattern recognition, decision making, judgement, extensive world knowledge, fine motor coordination for manipulation and locomotion, and even a bit of common sense. The robot as an imitation or substitute for a human being has remained the popular conception. The first generation of modern robots was, however, a far cry from this anthropomorphic vision.[72] The Unimation 2000, the most popular of the early "robots," was capable only of moving its arm in several directions and opening and closing its gripper. It had no senses and could move its arm with only two or three degrees of freedom (directions of movement) of the six possible in three-dimensional space. Typical applications of these early robots, introduced during the 1970s, involved moving objects from one place to another (a capability called pick and place).

More sophisticated devices, such as the American company Cincinnati Milacron's T3 (The Tomorrow Tool), the German KUKA robots, and the Japanese

Wabot-2, an anthropomorphic robot with a penchant for jazz. (Courtesy of Ichiro Kato of Waseda University, Tokyo)

The dance of the robots. Their use for welding cars was one of the earliest applications of industrial robots, shown here at a Chrysler manufacturing plant. (Courtesy of Cincinnati Milacron)

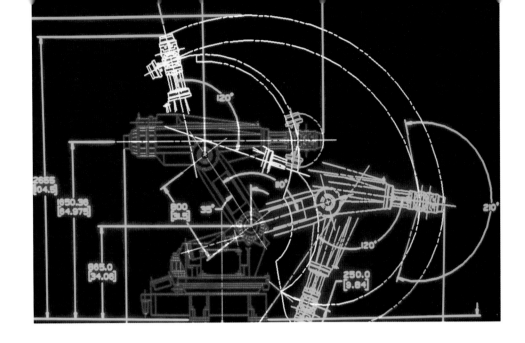

A computer-assisted design (CAD) display. Here the computer designs a robot (with some human help). (Photo by Dan McCoy of Rainbow)

Hitachi robots, were introduced in the early 1980s. These second-generation robots can move with five or six degrees of freedom, can effect more precise movements, are faster, and have more delicate grippers. The motions of these robots can be programmed, but they still had no provision for conditional execution, that is, operations conditioned on some external event. Since these robots still have no way of sensing their environment, there are no inputs on which to base any decision making. These second-generation robots became well known for welding and spray painting, primarily in the automotive industry.[73]

The third generation, introduced in the mid 1980s, began to display a modicum of intelligence. Robots of this generation—Unimation's PUMA, IBM's 7535 and 7565, and Automatix's RAIL series—contain general-purpose computers integrated with vision and/or tactile sensing systems. By 1987 robotic vision systems alone had developed into a $300 million industry, with estimates of $800 million for 1990.[74] Specialized programming languages, such as Unimation's VAL and IBM's AML, allow these robots to make decisions based on changes in their environment.[75] Such systems can, for example, find industrial parts regardless of their orientation and identify and use them appropriately in complex assembly tasks.[76]

With the flexibility and sophistication of robots improving each year, the population of industrial robots has increased from a few hundred in 1970 to several hundred thousand by the late 1980s. Some are used in factories that are virtually totally automated, such as Allen Bradley's facility for manufacturing electric motor starters (see the companion film to this book).[77] The only human beings in this factory monitor the process from a glass booth, while computers control the entire flow of work from electronically dispatched purchase orders to shipped products.[78] Though the era of workerless factories has begun, the most significant short-term impact of this latest generation of robots is in settings where they work alongside human coworkers. Increasingly, new factories are designed to incorporate both human and machine assemblers, with the flow of materials monitored and controlled by computers.[79]

This man is making dishwashers. A computer-controlled assembly line at the GE dishwasher factory. (Photo by Bill Strode).

Do not touch. Very few hands touch this well-known personal computer during its manufacture. (Photo by Dan McCoy of Rainbow)

With the arrival of the third generation, the diversity of tasks being accomplished by robots has broadened considerably.[80] A robot named Oracle is shearing sheep in western Australia. One called RM3 is washing, debarnacling, and painting the hulls of ships in France. Several dozen brain operations have been performed at Long Beach Memorial Hospital in California with the help of a robot arm for precision drilling of the skull. In 1986 police in Dallas used a robot to break into an apartment in which a suspect had barricaded himself. The frightened fugitive ran out of the apartment and surrendered.[81] The U.S. Defense Department is using undersea robots built by Honeywell to disarm mines in the Persian Gulf and other locations. Thousands of robots are routinely used in bioengineering laboratories to perform the extremely delicate operations required to snip and connect minute pieces of DNA. And walking robots are used in nuclear power plants to perform operations in areas too dangerous for humans. One such robot, Odetics's Odex, looks like a giant spider with its six legs.[82]

The next generation of robots will take several more steps in replicating the subtlety of human perceptual ability and movement, while retaining a machine's inherent advantages in speed, memory, precision, repeatability, and tireless operation. Specialized chips are being developed that will provide the massively parallel computations required for a substantially higher level of visual perception. Equally sophisticated tactile sensors are being designed into robot hands. Manipulators with dozens of degrees of freedom will combine the ability to lift both very heavy objects and delicate ones without breaking the latter. These robots' "local" intelligence will be fully integrated into the computerized control systems of a modern factory.[83]

Forerunners of these robots of the 1990s are beginning to compete with human dexterity and intelligence on many fronts. A robot developed by Russell Anderson of Bell Labs can defeat most human opponents at Ping-Pong.[84] Two other Ping-Pong playing robots, one English and one Japanese, recently met each other in San Francisco for a match. A robot hand developed at the University of Utah can crack an egg, drop the contents into a mixing bowl, and then whip up an omelette mixture all at several times the speed of a master chef.[85] The Stanford/JPL Hand,

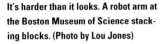
It's harder than it looks. A robot arm at the Boston Museum of Science stacking blocks. (Photo by Lou Jones)

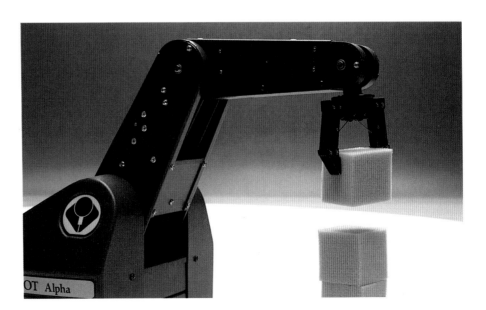

Tsuneo Yoshikawa, director of Robotics Engineering at Kyoto University, with his students. (Photo by Lou Jones)

designed by Kenneth Salisbury and other MIT researchers, is a three-fingered robot that can perform such intricate tasks as turning a wing nut. A collaborative effort now underway between the University of Utah Center for Biomedical Design and the MIT Artificial Intelligence Laboratory aims at constructing a hand that will "exhibit performance levels roughly equivalent to the natural human hand," according to Stephen Jacobsen, the chief designer of the project. A voice-activated robot to provide quadriplegic patients such personal services as shaving, brushing teeth, feeding and retrieving food and drinks is being developed by Larry Leifer and Stefan Michalowski under a grant from the Veterans Administration (see the companion film to this book).[86]

A particularly impressive robot called Wabot-2 (Waseda Robot; see the picture at the beginning of this section) was developed in the mid-to-late 1980s by Waseda University in Tokyo and refined by Sumitomo Electric.[87] This human-size (and humanlike) 200-pound robot is capable of reading sheet music through its camera eye and then, with its ten fingers and two feet, playing the music on an organ or synthesizer keyboard. It has a total of 50 joints and can strike keys at the rate of 15 per second, comparable to a skilled keyboard player. Its camera eye provides relatively high resolution for a robot. Using a charge-coupled device (CCD) sensing array, it has a resolution of 2,000 by 3,000 pixels (by comparison, the eyes of a person with good eyesight can resolve about 10,000 by 10,000 points). Wabot-2 also has a sense of hearing: it can track the pitch of a human singer it is accompanying and adjust the tempo of its playing accordingly. Finally, the robot has rudimentary

Hurahiko Asada, a robotics expert at Kyoto University. Asada pioneered the application of the direct-drive motor to improve robots' fine motor coordination. (Photo by Lou Jones)

A Japanese application of robotics. (Photo by Fischer of Woodfin Camp and Associates)

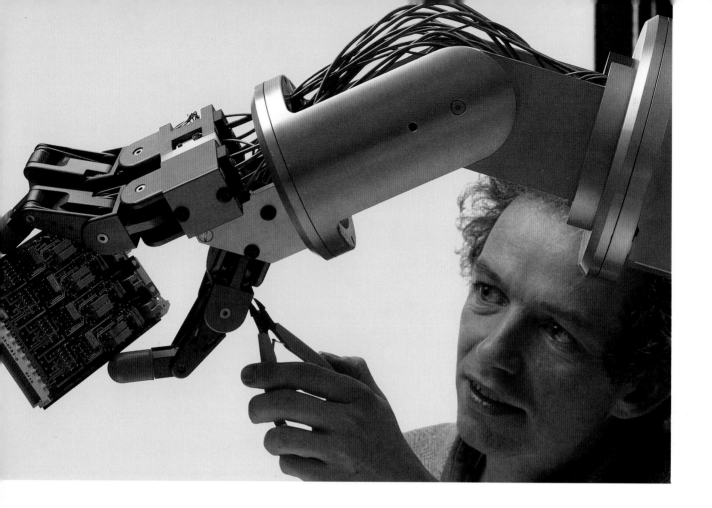

Ken Salisbury of the MIT Artificial Intelligence Lab fine tunes the dexterous Stanford-JPL robot hand. (Photo by Lou Jones)

speech-recognition and synthesis capabilities and can engage in simple conversations. There are severe limitations on the complexity of the musical score that it can read, and the music must be precisely placed by a human assistant. Nonetheless, Wabot-2 is an impressive demonstration of the state of the robotic art in the late 1980s.

Another state-of-the-art robot developed around the same time was a half-scale model of a *Quetzalcoatlus northropi* (better known as pterodactyl, a winged dinosaur that lived 65 million years ago). The replica, developed by human-powered-flight pioneer Paul MacCready, could fly by flapping its robotic wings, much like its reptile forebear. Unfortunately, in a demonstration for the press, MacCready's invention crashed, which caused a loss of public interest in it. It has flown successfully, however, and it represents a particularly sophisticated integration of sensors and actuators with real-time decision-making by on-board computers.[88]

Not surprisingly, the world's largest supporter of robotic research is the U.S. Defense Department, which foresees a wide range of roles for robotic fighters in the 1990s and early twenty-first century. A walking truck with fat bent legs is being developed by the U.S. Army for roadless terrains.[89] The U.S. Air Force is developing a number of pilotless aircraft, or flying robots, that can perform a variety of reconnaissance and attack missions.[90] Early versions of such robot craft played a vital role in the Israeli destruction of 29 Russian surface-to-air missile (SAM) sites in the Bekaa Valley in a single hour during its invasion of Lebanon in 1982.

The field of robotics is where all of the AI technologies meet: vision, pattern recognition, knowledge engineering, decision-making, natural-language

Anita Flynn of the MIT Artificial Intelligence Laboratory with a robot friend. (Photo by Lou Jones)

The pterodactyl returns to life. Paul MacCready's flying robot recreates the *Quetzalcoatlus northropi,* a flying dinosaur that became extinct millions of years ago. (Photo by O. C. Carlisle)

understanding, and others. As the underlying technologies mature and as the growing corps of robot designers gets better at integrating these diverse technologies, robots will become increasingly ubiquitous.[91] They will tend our fields and livestock, build our products, assist our surgeons; eventually they will even help us clean our houses. This last task has turned out to be one of the most difficult. As we have seen with other AI problems, machine intelligence has first been successfully deployed in situations where unpredictable events are held to a minimum. It was not surprising, therefore, that manufacturing was the first successful application for robotic technology, since factories can be designed to provide predictable and relatively well-organized environments for robots to work in. In contrast, the environments of our homes change rapidly and present many unpredictable obstacles.[92] So, effective robotic servants in the home will probably not appear until early in the next century. By that time, however, robotic technology will have dramatically transformed the production and service sectors of society.[93]

• An International Affair

In 1981 Japan's powerful Ministry of International Trade and Industry (MITI) announced plans to develop a new kind of computer. This new computer would be at least a thousand times more powerful than the models of 1981, would have the intelligence to converse with its human users in natural spoken language, would be programmed with vast arrays of knowledge in all domains, would have human-level decision-making capabilities, and would sit on a desktop. They called this new type of machine a fifth-generation computer. The first four generations were characterized by the type of electronic components they used, the first being vacuum tubes, the second transistors, the third integrated circuits, and the fourth VLSI (very large scale integrated) chips. The fifth generation of computers, on the other hand, would be characterized by something different, by its *intelligence*.[94] With MITI's track record of having led Japanese industry to dominance in consumer electronics and a broad range of other high-tech fields, the announcement was a blockbuster. MITI formed the Institute for New Generation Computer Technology (ICOT) to carry out its project. ICOT began active development in 1982 with funding of approximately $1 billion (half from MITI and half from industry) for ten years.[95]

In the United States and Europe the spectre of the loss of the strategically important computer industry led to urgent consultations at the highest levels of government and industry.[96] A few months after ICOT began development, a major response by American industry had been initiated. Twenty-one leading American computer and electronics companies, among them Control Data, Digital Equipment, Honeywell, NCR, Sperry, and Bell Communication Research, had formed a new company called Microelectronics and Computer Technology Corporation (MCC). This collaboration was intended to pool money and research talent to overcome several bottlenecks in advanced computer research that no single member of the consortium had the resources to solve alone.[97] IBM was not invited to join because of concerns regarding antitrust laws. Special legislation was still required and was signed by President Reagan in 1984.[98] MCC's research budget of about $65 million per year is targeted at a wide variety of AI, human-interface, and computer-architecture problems. Primary goals of MCC research are the development of integrated-circuit packaging techniques and computer-assisted design tools that will give American companies a practical edge in the worldwide electronics marketplace. MCC hopes to develop a chip-design station that will enable a small group of engineers to completely design an advanced custom VLSI chip in under a month, whereas one to two years is now required. MCC has also identified parallel processing as the most effective way to achieve the massive increases in processing power required for future AI applications.

In addition to MCC, the Defense Advanced Research Projects Agency (DARPA), which has historically funded a major portion of American university-based AI research, has increased its AI funding. It is now investing over $100 million per year.

The English response to Japan's challenge was a $500 million program called the Alvey Program, after John Alvey, who had proposed it and became its chairman.[99] Unlike MCC, which conducts 97 percent of its research in house, Alvey has no research laboratory of its own. With funding primarily from the government, Alvey has provided money for over 100 colleges, companies, and laboratories to conduct research in a wide variety of AI, VLSI, software engineering, man-machine interfaces, and other advanced computer technologies. Alvey has planned a number of "demonstrators" to integrate the results of its research, but its primary emphasis is to encourage advanced research laboratories in England to put high priority on information technologies and to train a new generation of knowledge engineers and computer scientists.[100]

In 1984 the European Economic Community (EEC) formed the European Strategic Program for Research in Information Technology (ESPRIT).[101] This $1.5 billion program has funded companies, universities, and government laboratories throughout Europe in virtually all areas of computer technology, including office automation, robotics, and computer-aided manufacturing.[102]

In many ways the original MITI announcement was perfectly timed to create an intense response. In addition to growing concern in the United States and Europe over Japanese competition for trade markets, there was a growing awareness that AI technology, which had been a focus of largely academic research for over 25 years, was now poised to radically transform the way computers are used and to have a far-reaching impact on society. The MCC, DARPA, Alvey, and ESPRIT responses to the MITI challenge were just the tip of the iceberg. The enormous publicity that Japan's fifth-generation computer project received and the ensuing conferences, books, congressional inquiries, and other forms of debate helped to set the priorities of industry and university research and development throughout the world.[103]

The timing turned out to be right. According to DM Data, commercial revenue in the U.S. from AI-related technologies (not including robotics), was only $52 million in 1981, grew to $1.4 billion by 1987, and is projected to be $4 billion in 1990. The AI industry as a whole is expected to hit tens of billions of dollars per year during the 1990s. Very likely the worldwide information and computer industry will be over one trillion dollars per year in the year 2000 and will be largely intelligent by today's standards. Indeed, the ability to effectively harness information and knowledge is expected to be the key to wealth and power in the decades ahead.

Edward A. Feigenbaum

Knowledge Processing:
From File Servers to Knowledge Servers

Edward Feigenbaum is
professor of computer science
at Stanford University, where
he is also scientific director of
the Heuristic Programming
Project, a leading laboratory
for work in knowledge
engineering and expert
systems. He is cofounder of
two major applied AI
companies: IntelliCorp and
Teknowledge. His most recent
books are *The Fifth Generation:
Artificial Intelligence and
Japan's Computer Challenge to
the World* (1983), coauthored
with Pamela McCorduck, and
*The Rise of the Expert
Company: How Visionary
Companies are using Artificial
Intelligence to Achieve Higher
Productivity and Profits* (1988),
coauthored with Pamela
McCorduck and Penny Nii. He
is widely regarded as a pioneer
in the theory and methodology
of expert systems.

It has been said that when people make forecasts, they overestimate what can be done in the short run and underestimate what can be achieved in the long run. I have worked in the science and technology of artificial intelligence for twenty years and confess to being chronically optimistic about its progress. The gains have been substantial, even impressive. But we have hardly begun, and we must not lose sight of the point to which we are heading, however distant it may seem.

We are beginning the transition from data processing to knowledge processing. The key tool of our specialty is the digital computer, the most complex and yet the most general machine ever invented. Though the computer is a universal symbol-processing device, we have exploited to date only its mundane capabilities to file and retrieve data (file service) and to do high-speed arithmetic. Researchers in artificial intelligence have been studying techniques for computer representation of human knowledge and the methods by which that knowledge can be used to reason toward the solution of problems, the formation of hypotheses, and the discovery of new concepts and new knowledge. These researchers have been inventing the knowledge servers of our future.

Like all creators, scientists and technologists must dream, must put forth a vision, or else they relegate their work to almost pointless incrementalism. My dream is about the future of AI research and development over the next several decades and the knowledge systems that can be produced thereby to assist the modern knowledge worker.

Edward Feigenbaum. (Photo by Lou
Jones)

The Beginnings of the Dream

Fifty years ago, before the modern era of computation began, Turing's theorems and abstract machines gave hint of the fundamental idea that the computer could be used to model the symbol-manipulating processes that make up the most human of all behaviors: thinking. More than thirty years ago the work began in earnest (1991 will mark the thirty-fifth anniversary of the Dartmouth Summer Conference on Artificial Intelligence). The founding principle of AI research is really an article of faith that the digital computer has the necessary and sufficient means for intelligent action. This first principle is called the physical-symbol-system hypothesis.

The early dreaming included dreams about intelligent behavior at very high levels of competence. Turing speculated on wide-ranging conversations between people and machines and on chess playing programs. Later Newell and Simon wrote about champion-level chess programs and began their work toward that end. Samuel (checker playing), Gelernter (geometry-theorem proving), and others shared the dream.

At Stanford, Lederberg and I chose reasoning in science as our task and began work with Buchanan and Djerassi on building a program that would elucidate chemical structure at a high level of competence: the DENDRAL program. What emerged from the many experiments with DENDRAL was an empirical hypothesis that the source of the program's power to figure out chemical structures from spectral data was its knowledge of basic and spectral chemistry. For DENDRAL, knowledge was power. Obvious? In retrospect, perhaps. But the prevailing view in AI at the time ascribed power to the reasoning processes—in modern terms, to the inference engine, not the knowledge base. Thus, in the late 1960s the knowledge-is-power hypothesis stood as a counter-hypothesis awaiting further tests and the accumulation of evidence.

Much evidence came in the 1970s. Medical problem solving provided the springboard. The MYCIN program of Shortliffe and others at Stanford was the prototype of the expert-level advisory (or consultation) system. The core of MYCIN was its knowledge base of rules for the diagnosis and therapy of infectious diseases. Its reasoning process was simple (backward chaining), even ad hoc in parts. But MYCIN was built as an integrated package of intellectual abilities. It could interact with a professional in the professional jargon of the specialty. It could explain its line of reasoning. And it had a subsystem that could aid in the acquisition of new knowledge by guiding an expert to find defects in the stored knowledge. Overall, MYCIN provided strong confirmation to the knowledge-is-power hypothesis.

At nearly the same time other efforts in medical problem solving were providing similar results. At the University of Pittsburgh the focus of the Internist project was the construction of an enormous electronic textbook of the knowledge of internal medicine. With its current knowledge base of 572 diseases, nearly 4,500 manifestations, and hundreds of thousands of links between them, Internist has provided the strongest confirmation yet of the knowledge-is-power hypothesis.

In the late 1970s an explosion of expert systems was taking place in fields other than medicine: engineering, manufacturing, geology, molecular biology, financial services, diagnostic servicing of machinery, military signal processing, and many other areas. There is little that ties these areas together other than this: in each, high-quality problem solving is guided by experiential, qualitative, heuristic knowledge. The explosion of applications created a new type of professional, the knowledge engineer (now in extremely short supply) and a new industry, the expert systems industry (now rapidly expanding). One generalization from the frenzy of activity is simply massive additional confirmation of the knowledge-is-power hypothesis. The reasoning procedures associated with all of these systems are weak. Their power lies in their knowledge bases.

Other areas of AI research made shifts to the knowledge-base viewpoint. It is now commonplace to say, A program for understanding natural language must have extensive knowledge of its domain of discourse. A vision program for image understanding must have knowledge of the world it is intended to see. And even, learning programs must have a substantial body of knowledge from which to expand (that is, learning takes place at the fringes and interstices of what is already known). Thus, the dream of a computer that performs at a high level of competence over a wide variety of tasks that people perform well seems to rest upon knowledge in the task areas.

The knowledge-is-power hypothesis has received so much confirmation that we can now assert it as the knowledge principle:

A system exhibits intelligent understanding and action at a high level of competence primarily because of the specific knowledge that it contains about its domain of endeavor.

A corollary to the knowledge principle is that reasoning processes of an intelligent system, being general and therefore weak, are not the source of power that leads to high levels of competence in behavior. The knowledge principle simply says that if a program is to perform well, it must know a great deal about the world in which it operates. In the absence of knowledge, reasoning won't help.

The knowledge principle is the emblem of the first era of artificial intelligence; it is the first part of the dream. It should inform and influence every decision about what it is feasible to do in AI science and with AI technology.

The Middle of the Dream

Today our intelligent artifacts perform well on specialized tasks within narrowly defined domains. An industry has been formed to put this technological understanding to work, and widespread transfer of this technology has been achieved. Although the first era of the intelligent machine is ending, many problems remain to be solved.

One of these is naturalness. The intelligent agent should interact with its human user in a fluid and flexible manner that appears natural to the person. But the systems of the first era share with the majority of computer systems an intolerable rigidity of

stylistic expression, vocabulary, and concepts. For example, programs rarely accept synonyms, and they cannot interpret and use metaphors. They always interact in a rigid grammatical straitjacket. The need for metaphor to induce in the user a feeling of naturalness seems critical. Metaphorical reference appears to be omnipresent and almost continuous in our use of language. Further, if you believe that our use of language reflects our underlying cognitive processes, then metaphor is a basic ideational process.

In the second era we shall see the evolution of the natural interface. The processes controlling the interaction will make greater use of the domain knowledge of the system and knowledge of how to conduct fluid discourse. Harbingers of naturalness already exist; they are based to a large extent upon pictures. The ONCOCIN project team at Stanford invested a great effort in an electronic flow sheet to provide a seamless transition for the oncologist from paper forms for patient data entry to electronic versions of these forms. The commercially available software tools for expert-system development sometimes contain elegant and powerful packages for creating pictures that elucidate what the knowledge system is doing and what its emerging solution looks like (for example, IntelliCorp's KEE Pictures and Active Images).

Naturalness need not rely upon pictures, of course. The advances in natural-language understanding have been quite substantial, particularly in the use of knowledge to facilitate understanding. In the second era it will become commonplace for knowledge systems to interact with users in human language, within the scope of the system's knowledge. The interaction systems of the second era will increasingly rely on continuous natural speech. In person-to-person interactions, people generally talk rather than type. Typing is useful but unnatural. Speech-understanding systems of wide applicability and based on the knowledge principle are coming. At Stanford we are beginning experiments with an experimental commercial system interfaced with the ONCOCIN expert system.

A limitation of first-era systems is their brittleness. To mix metaphors, they operate on a high plateau of knowledge and competence until they reach the extremity of their knowledge; then they precipitously fall off to levels of utter incompetence. People suffer from the same difficulty (they too cannot escape the knowledge principle), but their fall is more graceful. The cushion for the soft fall is the knowledge and use of weaker but more general models that underlie the highly specific and specialized knowledge of the plateau. For example, if an engineer is diagnosing the failure of an electronic circuit for which he has no specific knowledge, he can fall back on his knowledge of electronics, methods of circuit analysis, and handbook data for the components. The capability for such model-based reasoning by machine is just now under study in many laboratories and will emerge as an important feature of second-era systems. The capability does not come free. Knowledge engineers must explicate and codify general models in a wide variety of task areas.

Task areas? But what if there is no "task"? Can we envision the intelligent program that behaves with common sense at the interstices between tasks or when task knowledge is completely lacking? Common sense is itself knowledge, an enormous body of knowledge distinguished by its ubiquity and the circumstance that it is rarely codified and passed onto others, as more formal knowledge is. There is, for example, the commonsense fact that pregnancy is associated with females, not males. The extremely weak but extremely general forms of cognitive behavior implied by common-sense reasoning constitute for many the ultimate goal in the quest for machine intelligence. Researchers are now beginning the arduous task of understanding the details of the logic and representation of commonsense knowledge and are codifying large bodies of commonsense knowledge. The first fruits of this will appear in the later systems of the second era. Commonsense reasoning will probably appear as an unexpected naturalness in a machine's interaction with an intelligent agent. As an example of this in medical-consultation advisory systems, if pregnancy is mentioned early in the interaction or can be readily inferred, the interaction shifts seamlessly to understanding that a female is involved. Magnify this example by one hundred thousand or one million unspoken assumptions, and you will understand what I mean by a large knowledge base of commonsense knowledge.

As knowledge in systems expands, so does the scope for modes of reasoning that have so far eluded the designers of these systems. Foremost among these modes are reasoning by analogy and its sibling metaphorical reasoning. The essence of analogy has been evident for some time, but the details of analogizing have not been. An analogy is a partial match of the description of some current situation with stored knowledge. The extent of the match is crucial. If the match is too partial, then the analogy is seen to be vacuous or farfetched; if too complete then the "analogy" is seen as hardly an analogy at all. Analogizing broadens the relevance of the entire knowledge base. It can be used to construct interesting and novel interpretations of situations and data. It can be used to retrieve knowledge that has been stored, but not stored in the "expected" way. Analogizing can supply default values for attributes not evident in the description of the current situation. Analogizing can provide access to powerful methods that otherwise would not be evoked as relevant. For example, in a famous example from early twentieth-century physics, Dirac made the analogy between quantum theory and mathematical group theory that allowed him to use the powerful methods of group theory to solve important problems in quantum physics. We shall begin to see reasoning by analogy emerge in knowledge systems of the second era.

Analogizing is seen also as an important process in automatic knowledge acquisition, another name for machine learning. In first-era systems, adding knowledge to knowledge bases has been almost always a manual process: people codify knowledge and place it in knowledge structures. Recent experiments by Douglas Lenat have shown that this laborious process can be semiautomated, facilitated by an analogizing program. The program suggests the relevant analogy to a new situation, and the knowledge engineer fills in the details. In the second era we shall see programs that acquire the details with less or no human help. Many other techniques for automatic learning will find their way into second-era systems. For example, we are currently seeing early experiments on learning apprentices, machines that carefully observe people performing complex tasks and infer thereby the knowledge needed for competent performance. The second era will also see (I predict) the first successful systems that couple language understanding with learning, so that knowledge bases can be augmented by the reading of text. Quite likely these will be specialized texts in narrow areas at the outset.

To summarize, because of the increasing power of our concepts and tools and the advent of automatic-learning methods, we can expect that during the second era the knowledge bases of intelligent systems will become very large, representing therein hundreds of thousands, perhaps millions, of facts, heuristics, concepts, relationships, and models. Automatic learning will be facilitated thereby, since by the knowledge principle, the task of adding knowledge is performed more competently the more knowledge is available (the more we know, the easier it is to know more).

Finally, in the second era we will achieve a broad reconceptualization of what we mean by a knowledge system. Under the broader concept, the "systems" will be collegial relationships between an intelligent computer agent and an intelligent person (or persons). Each will perform tasks that he/she/it does best, and the intelligence of the system will be an emergent of the collaboration. If the interaction is indeed seamless and natural, then it may hardly matter whether the relevant knowledge or the reasoning skills needed are in the head of the person or in the knowledge structures of the computer.

The Far Side of the Dream: The Library of the Future

Here's a "view from the future," looking back at our "present," from Professor Marvin Minsky of MIT: "Can you imagine that they used to have libraries where the books didn't talk to each other?" The libraries of today are warehouses for passive objects. The books and journals sit on shelves waiting for us to use our intelligence to find them, read them, interpret them, and cause them finally to divulge their stored knowledge. Electronic libraries of today are no better. Their pages are pages of data files, but the electronic pages are equally passive.

Now imagine the library as an active, intelligent knowledge server. It stores the knowledge of the disciplines in complex knowledge structures (perhaps in a knowledge-representation formalism yet to be invented). It can reason with this knowledge to satisfy the needs of its users. These needs are expressed naturally, with fluid discourse. The system can, of course, retrieve and exhibit (i.e., it can act as an electronic textbook). It can collect relevant information; it can summarize; it can pursue relationships. It acts as a consultant on specific problems, offering advice on particular solutions, justifying those solutions with citations or with a fabric of general reasoning. If the user can suggest a solution or a hypothesis, it can check this and even suggest extensions. Or it can critique the user viewpoint with a detailed rationale of its agreement or disagreement. It pursues relational paths of associations to suggest to the user previously unseen connections. Collaborating with the user, it uses its processes of association and analogizing to brainstorm for remote or novel concepts. More autonomously, but with some guidance from the user, it uses criteria of being interesting to discover new concepts, methods, theories, and measurements.

The user of the library of the future need not be a person. It may be another knowledge system, that is, any intelligent agent with a need for knowledge. Thus, the library of the future will be a network of knowledge systems in which people and machines collaborate. Publishing will be an activity transformed. Authors may bypass text, adding their increment to human knowledge directly to the knowledge structures. Since the thread of responsibility must be maintained, and since there may be disagreement as knowledge grows, the contributions are authored (incidentally allowing for the computation of royalties for access and use). Maintaining the knowledge base (updating knowledge) becomes a vigorous part of the new publishing industry.

At the far horizon the dream can take many forms and dimensions. I have briefly sketched only a few, and I invite you to exercise your imagination to sketch your own. At the far horizon, the question is not "whether," but only "when."

Power Tools for the Mind: A Statement of the Encompassing Vision

The hard work of the farmer was revolutionized by agricultural machinery. The labor of the industrial worker was revolutionized by engines and heavy machinery. As we move toward the postindustrial period of the twenty-first century, as work becomes increasingly the work of professionals and knowledge workers, the power tools are and will be digital computers. The economic and social well-being of the advanced societies is increasingly the result of working "smarter" rather than working harder, and computers are the agents of that change. Knowledge is power, in human affairs, and knowledge systems are amplifiers of human thought and action. As Carlo De Benedetti, Chief Executive of Olivetti, has said, "For the first time in the history of mankind, innovation is the fundamental raw material. Real strategic resources are no longer represented by coal, steel, or oil but by the cleverness and cognitive capability of man."

Jeff Pepper

An Expert System for Automotive Diagnosis

Jeff Pepper is product
marketing manager of the
diagnostics division of the
Carnegie Group. His current
research interests include all
aspects of knowledge-base
design, construction,
validation, and maintenance.
He has published several
articles on building expert
systems and integrating them
into service organizations. He
has also taught computer
programming at Carnegie-
Mellon University.

Big changes are coming to the world of automobile repair. In the Ford dealership of the not too distant future, mechanics will be tracking down and fixing problems in your car with the help of a powerful AI diagnostic tool called SBDS, under development by a joint project team at Ford Motor Company, the Carnegie Group, and Hewlett Packard. SBDS, the Service Bay Diagnostic System, will revolutionize the way cars are fixed. When it is completed in the next year or two, SBDS's knowledge base will contain the expertise of Ford's top diagnosticians, and it will make their diagnostic skills available to mechanics in every Ford dealership in North America. This "expert in a box" will guide a human technician through the entire service process, from the initial customer interview at the service desk to the diagnosis and repair of the car in the garage.

Imagine how this expert system will affect the way your car is serviced. When you first walk up to the service desk, a service writer interviews you to find out the details of your car's problem. But most of the questions he asks are suggested by SBDS, which is trying to gather important information from you before you leave the dealership. The questions are tailored to your particular situation and depend on your car, your complaints, your car's repair history, and Ford's knowledge about possible problems with cars similar to yours.

After the interview SBDS prints a repair order, and your car is taken to the shop. There a technician begins his diagnosis. In early versions of the system, the technician will use a computer terminal and a touch screen to communicate with the computer. But in one future scenario we are working on, there is no terminal at all. Instead, the technician dons a headset with a built-in microphone and begins the diagnosis by simply saying "Let's go" to the expert system. In this vision of the future, SBDS requests information and provides instructions by generating synthesized speech and sending it into the technician's headset. This speech is provided in the technician's preferred language and at a level of detail appropriate to his education and depth of experience. The technician responds to test requests by saying the result (such as "Pass" or "Twelve volts") into the microphone.

Whenever possible, SBDS avoids asking the technician to perform physical tests. Instead, it goes directly to the car for the information, using a specially designed Portable Vehicle Analyzer connected to the on-board computer that controls much of the operation of Ford cars. Raw data such as voltages and vacuum-pressure readings are processed by the vehicle analyzer and passed back to the expert system to help guide the diagnosis. If the technician does not understand why SBDS asks for a test or makes a certain conclusion, he can respond by asking "Why?" The expert system responds to this request by describing, in ordinary spoken language, the reasoning that led to the test request or conclusion. The technician can ask "How?" to listen to an explanation of how to perform a repair, or say "Show me" to trigger the display of a schematic or animated illustration on a nearby TV monitor.

SBDS does not rigidly control the session. It simply suggests tests and asks questions according to its knowledge of the problem and what it needs in order to proceed with its diagnostic strategy. Yet the technician can override this line of reasoning if he notices something unusual about the car or feels that the program is ignoring a likely cause for the failure. Whenever the technician volunteers new information, SBDS responds immediately. It interrupts its diagnosis, draws whatever conclusions it can from the new information, and refocuses its strategy to take advantage of what it has learned. Thus, the technician can let SBDS control the diagnostic session completely, or he can use it as an expert advisor, depending on his skill level and how he wants to use the system.

SBDS is part of a major effort by Ford Motor Company to introduce artificial intelligence into the design, manufacture, and service of their products. It is the cornerstone of Ford's commitment to bring AI into the automotive world. With an expected installed base of over 5,000 dealerships throughout North America, SBDS may become the largest application of artificial intelligence in the world.

Ford asked the Carnegie Group to help them develop the expert-system component of SBDS, because they recognized that the complexity of today's cars is rapidly exceeding the capability of human mechanics to fix them. Today's technicians are generally unable to tell what is wrong with a car just by listening to it, because a maze of electronics controls virtually every aspect of the perform-ance of a car. The traditional methods for diagnosis, such as listening to the engine, adjusting engine controls and observing response, are rapidly losing their usefulness. Many mechanics, overwhelmed by the electronics of the car, are forced into a swap and test strategy, simply replacing a suspected component and checking afterwards to see if the problem went away. Although there are a few experts who can reliably diagnose failures in today's electronics-laden vehicles, they are a very scarce and expensive resource.

In trying to overcome this expertise bottleneck, our development team at Carnegie used existing techniques for AI-based diagnosis and modified them to deal with the very large, unstructured domain of automobile repair. We soon learned that expert automobile diagnosis is a very complex task. Skilled auto mechanics, we discovered, rely on several different kinds of knowledge about the domain and use several completely different reasoning techniques during the course of a diagnosis. Our task was to design a knowl-edge-base structure that would be rich enough to hold all the kinds of knowledge that human experts bring to bear on the problem but simple enough that it could be built and maintained by non-AI experts.

All human diagnosticians, whether they work in automotive repair or medicine, have certain characteristics in common. Both groups have an internal mental model of the task domain. This model is a body of knowledge about the parts of the mechanism or organism they are trying to fix and about how those parts fit together. This model is closely tied to two additional knowledge sources: the expert's formal understanding of the laws of

Jeff Pepper. (Photo by Patrick Terry)

the domain (such as electrical theory) and a large loosely structured body of knowledge consisting of common sense and experience gained simply by living in the world. Taken together, these three knowledge sources are very powerful and enable human beings to solve new problems by reasoning them through. This process is called causal reasoning or reasoning from first principles.

We discovered an interesting fact about causal reasoning: experts rarely solve problems this way. They only perform causal reasoning when absolutely necessary, such as when confronted with a new situation. Most of the time experts work from a different representation, a much simpler model derived from the original causal model but much easier to work with. This second model, called a troubleshooting or weak causal model, consists of failures and their relationship to each other. The troubleshooting model retains most of the diagnostic power of the original causal model but does not require such difficult reasoning.

The knowledge base of SBDS is built using a modified troubleshooting model. It was written using a tool kit for expert-system development called Knowledge Craft, and it consists of thousands of chunks of information called schemata. There is one schema for each known way that the vehicle can fail. These modes of failure are connected to each other by predefined relations such as due to and always leads to, which enables a knowledge engineer to represent the fact, for example, that an empty gas tank always leads to a no-start. Taken together, these relationships among failures form a richly interconnected hierarchy ranging from visible, identifiable customer concerns at the highest level down to specific component failures at the lowest level (see figure). The treelike structure of the failure-mode network is augmented with large amounts of supporting information that assist the expert system in diagnosis and repair. Each failure module has links to the failures that it can cause, failures that are possible causes for it, and many other kinds of schemata. These include test procedures that can confirm or reject the hypothesis that the failure actually occurred, repair procedures that can fix it if it does occur, documentation that describes how to fix it, and guidelines on how to proceed if the repair fails.

This knowledge-base design is sufficient to describe the common ways in which cars fail. But just like human experts, it needs a way to modify its behavior when confronted with exceptions and unusual conditions. To replicate this important aspect of problem solving, we added the ability to attach exception rules to the failure schemata. These rules modify the knowledge base to handle special conditions. For example, a rule might say that if the car has a very high odometer reading, then there is a higher likelihood that clogged fuel injectors will cause stalling. This rule doesn't actually conclude anything, it simply modifies the knowledge base so that the reasoning strategy can reach a correct conclusion faster in this case.

In the world of automotive diagnosis, knowledge is constantly changing. A technical-service bulletin may be issued from the manufacturer, or mechanics in the field may discover a new kind of problem, a new diagnostic, or a new repair procedure. The traditional way to handle this was to mail technical-service bulletins to dealerships. These bulletins would be posted on bulletin boards and discussed among the technicians. But with SBDS, knowledge engineers at Ford simply insert the new information into the knowledge base. This makes the new information available not just for reference but to actually improve the reasoning strategy. SBDS gets smarter with every new chunk of knowledge.

The actual reasoning about repairs is done by a program called the Diagnostic Interpreter. This interpreter is completely separate from the knowledge base and knows nothing about cars or any other object. Yet it knows a great deal about how to do machine diagnosis. In some ways the interpreter is like a detective who is suddenly asked to fix a broken water heater. He doesn't know anything about water heaters, but knows a great deal about deductive-reasoning techniques. If we give him a manual that describes the water heater, he can apply his reasoning skills to this new domain. In much the same way, an expert system makes a strict separation between "pure" knowledge in the knowledge base and the procedural information in the diagnostic interpreter. This makes it much easier to create and update the knowledge base and makes it

A typical knowledge base for Ford's
Service Bay Diagnostic System
showing failures, the relations among
them, and two rules that can modify
the knowledge base. Arrows indicate
a "due to" relation between two
failures. (Supplied by Jeff Pepper)

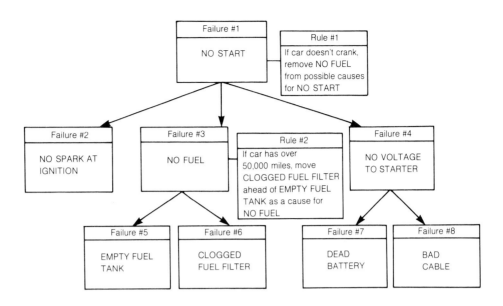

A typical display from the expert
portion of Ford's Service Bay Diagnostic
System. (Courtesy of the Carnegie Group)

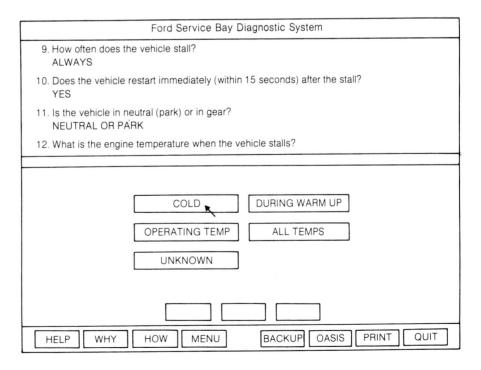

possible to reuse the SBDS diagnostic interpreter for different makes and models of cars by simply replacing appropriate portions of the knowledge base.

The diagnostic interpreter doesn't know anything except how to reason, and it can apply its different reasoning strategies to the contents of any knowledge base. It knows how to reason by process of elimination, how to modify its behavior to make best use of unexpected or volunteered information, and so on. It also knows how to use all the various tricks of the trade contained in the knowledge base, such as recognizing a failure from a certain combination of symptoms. And it knows how to perform backward chaining, or goal-driven reasoning, the inference method that forms the backbone of this and many other expert systems.

After SBDS reaches a conclusion, another difficult task remains: it must make sure that the conclusion is correct and that the recommended repair actually fixes the car. This validation process or repair strategy is much more difficult than it might seem. Many factors complicate the picture: A single customer concern may have several co-occurring causes, so finding one cause doesn't solve the customer's problem. The diagnosis may lead to the conclusion that a part is bad, but that part may not have anything to do with the customer's original problem. The technician might be unable or unwilling to perform the suggested repair, and another must be substituted. There may be a likelihood for certain repairs to cause other things to break, and these other, secondary problems need to be investigated if the repair fails to fix the car. These are problems that human experts intuitively know how to handle. But they must be studied, formalized, and converted into computer software in order for SBDS to solve them. As we built SBDS, we found that the task of verifying a repair is just as difficult as the original diagnosis, and much less understood. The repair-strategy component of SBDS is perhaps the first large-scale attempt to intelligently verify the correctness of computer-assisted diagnosis and repair.

As of this writing, SBDS is undergoing testing in Ford garages, and results have been very encouraging. We know now that the program performs as expected, that it can accurately and efficiently guide a human user to the correct diagnosis of a vehicle fault. But in looking back on what we've done, two questions remain: Did we accurately replicate the expert's mental map when we built the SBDS knowledge base? And is the program intelligent? The answer to the first question is no, and is likely to remain no for expert systems in the near future. We know that a human expert's understanding is rooted in real-world experience. A human understands that an empty gas tank prevents a car from starting, just like our expert system does. But his understanding is based on observations that he makes in terms of his commonsense understanding of how the world works. Our expert system has no substratum of experience in which to root its knowledge. It doesn't know why an empty gas tank prevents a car from starting, it doesn't really know what gas is, or even what a car is. When confronted with situations outside its limited knowledge base, like a car with two gas tanks, it can't be of much help. The best it can do is to recognize the situation as being outside its domain and gracefully admit that it doesn't know what to do.

As to the second question, Raymond Kurzweil has devoted much of this book to pointing out that the question Is it intelligent? is meaningless unless we first clearly define what we mean by intelligence. If we are concerned merely with the ability to perform symbolic reasoning, then of course SBDS is intelligent, because it is extremely adept at manipulating its own knowledge structures. But at a deeper level, the answers become more elusive.

Probably the best contribution I can make to this discussion is to digress a little and take you to the Carnegie Museum of Natural History. We go inside the museum, and we see an exhibit of the evolution of the horse. Over there is a row of horse skeletons ranging from the small doglike creatures of the ice ages to the modern thoroughbred racehorse. The small creature there on the far left doesn't look much like a horse at all. It is Eohippus, the "dawn horse." It was evolution's first experiment with this type of animal, and it was successful enough to survive and provide the seeds of evolution that have led to the magnificent creatures we know as horses today.

Perhaps SBDS and other similar systems are the dawn horses of intelligent machines. Although they are primitive in comparison to their human counterparts, they contain the seeds of intelligence. They are useful enough to ensure that they will spawn future generations, and their descendants will improve and deepen their methods of reasoning, perception, and understanding. Natural selection and strong evolutionary pressures will encourage this growth, one experiment giving way to another, until they evolve into the racehorses of AI, a future generation of truly intelligent machines.

The following describes the machine-user interaction during two diagnostic sessions for a car that does not start.

Session 1

SBDS: Does the car crank?

User: Yes.

Result: Rule 1 does not fire.

SBDS: Is there spark at the ignition coil?

User: Yes.

Result: NO SPARK AT IGNITION is ruled out.

SBDS: Is the fuel pressure OK?

User: No.

Result: NO FUEL is confirmed.

SBDS: Does the car have over 50,000 miles?

User: Yes.

Result: Rule 2 fires, moving CLOGGED FUEL FILTER ahead of EMPTY FUEL TANK.

SBDS: Is the fuel filter clogged?

User: Yes.

Result: CLOGGED FUEL FILTER is confirmed.

SBDS: Diagnosis is complete.

Session 2

SBDS: Does the car crank?

User: No.

Result: Rule 1 fires, removing NO-FUEL from possible causes.

SBDS: Is there spark at the coil?

User: Yes.

Result: NO SPARK AT IGNITION is ruled out.

SBDS: Is there voltage at starter?

User: No.

Result: NO VOLTAGE AT STARTER is confirmed.

SBDS: Is the battery OK?

User: Yes.

Result: DEAD BATTERY is ruled out.

SBDS: Is there a short in the battery cable?

User: Yes.

Result: BAD CABLE is confirmed.

SBDS: Diagnosis is complete.

Kazuhiro Fuchi. (Courtesy of the Institute for New Generation Computer Technology, Tokyo)

K. Fuchi

The Significance of Fifth-Generation Computer Systems

Since 1982 Kazuhiro Fuchi has been director of the Research Center of the Institute for New Generation Computer Technology (ICOT, also known as the Fifth-Generation Computer System Project). He is editor of the journal *New Generation Computing* and author of numerous articles on cutting-edge computer technology in Japan.

The Fifth-Generation Computer System (FGCS) Project was inaugurated in 1983. I would like to report on the significance of the project today. The word "significance" is quite hard to define. It will probably be given different definitions by different people. To put it most simply, if I say the project will be useful or profitable, some people may think it is very significant. Since, however, profit is a very tough subject for me to deal with, I would like to see the significance of the project from a different perspective.

Computer History Will Change

The greatest significance of the FGCS Project, as I see it, is that computer history will be changed by the successful completion of this project. Will this change be for the good? I feel that the computer must evolve to the next generation if it is really to take root in society. To make such evolution possible is the aim of the project. I think that if the aim is achieved, that will be the significance of the project. More simply, the project, as I see it, is aimed primarily at changing the basic design principle that has given us existing computers. I shall expand on this later. Bringing computer technology to a new stage by changing its basic design philosophy, then, is the aim of the project. Has a new computer-design principle been established yet? The answer is no. I think that changing the basic design means establishing new concepts and translating them into practical basic technologies. Establishing basic technologies is the goal of this ten-year project.

As we work on the project, we have visitors from various fields, such as journalists and researchers. One visitor wanted to have a look at a fifth-generation computer. When I told him that we did not have one as yet, he joked, "You've hidden it somewhere, haven't you?" Another serious visitor said this, to my embarrassment: "We have a plan at our company to introduce a new computer system three years or so in the future. Your fifth-generation computer seems very good, and we'd like to install it."

Ten Years Are Needed to Establish Basic Technologies

The ten-year time frame of the project is rather long, but I feel it takes ten years or so to establish basic technologies. If the project succeeds, it will still take several more years to build commercial products on the basis of it. So its realization will take a dozen years from inception, perhaps too distant a future for some people. But I believe it is still very worthwhile to pursue the project.

When I am asked if there is any blueprint for the fifth-generation computer system kept in some vault, I say no, at least not for now. I should rather say that drawing up such a basic blueprint is the goal of the project. The most difficult part of the project is to make the idea of the project understood. Once a product is physically available, we can readily make it understood. But we don't have that yet. There is now no example anywhere in the world that we can cite to show what our projected computer system will be like. This is a characteristic of the project. If what we aim at could be explained in terms of increasing the speed of some known process by ten times or reducing its cost by a certain percentage, it could be understood very easily. As it is, there is no such process.

But that does not mean we have stepped into an entirely nebulous field. And I think that this too is a characteristic of the project. Planning for the project was preceded by three years of research and study and to tell the truth, it incorporated discussions held in various places even further back. For instance, at the Electrotechnical Laboratory, where I was before I came to ICOT, we had had discussions for five or six years on what the next age would be like. One of the motives behind the project is to integrate such various discussions from various places. In the planning process we also discussed where we should go on the basis of diverse leading-edge research under way throughout the world. I myself made efforts in that direction, and so did other researchers. So the project is built on research conducted in the past and not on just a collection of casual ideas. However, when it comes to shaping an image out of various research, you can do it by merely gathering and processing the data statistically. I may say the project represents a refinement of the very intensive discussions we had with various people and on insights gained from past trends.

Establishing new technology is the primary aim of the project. Japan is not very experienced in developing new technology where there is an idea or goal but no example to go by. First a new methodology for implementation of the project must be developed. If we could develop new technology by just following traditional methods, that would be best. But that is not possible, I think. As is often pointed out, the Japanese traditionally prefer stability to innovation. But just developing old themes will not create new technology. That is why we need a new method for carrying out the project. To sum up, I think that making an effort to demonstrate where Japan is going with new technology is the nature and significance of the project.

The Basis Is a Logic Machine

As I see it, there is emerging a situation that calls for Japan to strive to make great contributions at what Professor Moto-oka aptly called a precompetitive stage. The FGCS Project is a project that responds to just that situation.

Though the primary goal of the project was just now explained in terms of changing the design philosophy of computers, it can also be described as developing an easy-to-use computer or a computer with intelligence. When I talked about this with one gentleman, he suggested that the goal might be to seek a new paradigm. The term "paradigm" is normally used to indicate an example, tangible or intangible, that provides the basis for evolution of a cultural or scientific theory. Let me explain this is my own parlance. The computer, as I see it, is a logic machine.

From that standpoint, the basis of the FGCS Project can be traced to logic. But what logic or system of logic is the present computer based on? At the beginning there was Turing-machine theory. It is not entirely wrong to say that the computer has evolved on the basis of that theory. While the present computer is not a Turing

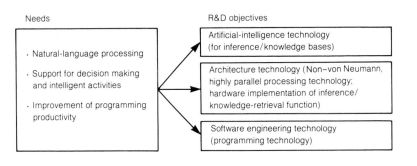

Needs	R&D objectives
· Natural-language processing	Artificial-intelligence technology (for inference/knowledge bases)
· Support for decision making and intelligent activities	Architecture technology (Non–von Neumann, highly parallel processing technology; hardware implementation of inference/knowledge-retrieval function)
· Improvement of programming productivity	Software engineering technology (programming technology)

machine per se, its basis can be traced back to the Turing theory. So it is still operating in the Turing paradigm. Is there, then, a different paradigm from the Turing paradigm? There is. The Turing theory was published in 1936, which happens to be the year in which I was born. According to the texts, those days were the golden age of logic. Various logic systems were devised to pursue computability, etc., which resulted in the establishment of the concept of computability. From this came the Turing theory.

From the standpoint of logic, however, the Turing theory was a very special one. The mainstream of logic is a system of logic called predicate logic. There were a number of great men involved in establishing predicate logic. This began with Frege in the nineteenth century, who was followed by Gödel in the 1930s. Von Neumann also had his name recorded in the history of predicate logic. With a long history dating way back to Aristotle, predicate logic is, in a sense, an ordinary, more natural logic. So when it comes to logic machines, there might have been predicate-logic machines rather than machines modeled after the Turing machine. But history did not turn out that way.

The computer has followed the route as it has. Some people say that this may have been a gigantic historical detour. I partly agree with them. I think the time is approaching to return to predicate logic as a paradigm. In the past ten years or so there have been moves to restore predicate logic in the field of programming too. Called logic programming, the movement is aimed at developing programming languages based on systems of logic like predicate logic and using them for programming.

Looking back on the planning for the FGCS Project, I may say the project is based on the concept of logic programming. This could be interpreted as redesigning software and applications within that concept, or it could be viewed as building machines with a new type of architecture to support the concept of logic programming. Though logic was our starting point, I would say that logic was not taken into consideration from the outset. Rather, it came as a conclusion after the analysis of various research projects, as I mentioned a short while ago.

Logic programming is closely related to various fields. Take the field of data bases, for example. In the world of data bases, relational data bases are now accepted. The basic concept of relational data bases is relations, and the relations form a concept that is based on predicate logic. Data bases are becoming a very large proportion of computer systems, but the relational-data-base model is not consistent with the programming world at present.

Programs are based not on relations but on procedures. Relations and procedures are fundamentally different from each other. Data-base languages are theoretically more advanced, while the programming languages in current use are based on old concepts. I feel that the present situation is that we have no alternative but to connect the two in unnatural ways. Data-base and programming languages are similar in that logic programming may be regarded as intended to bring programming up to the level of relational data bases, but not the other way around. I thus see the possibility that use of logic in programming will allow it to connect very beautifully with the world of relational data bases, though not the reverse.

In the field of software engineering, research was conducted on a variety of subjects such as new styles of programs, program verification, and synthesis. From these also came logic programming. When considering program verification or synthesis or a very efficient debugging system, which I think will be a future challenge, we have great difficulty in theoretically dealing with the basic computer model of today, which is based on the GOTO statement and assignment. The concepts of assignment and the GOTO statement are basic and easy to understand but are not suitable for proving properties, because they are oriented toward functions. By contrast, machines based on predicate logic *are* suited for such purposes, since proving is built into them. This is not just a theoretical argument but is somewhat in line with the trend some ten years ago toward avoiding the use of GOTO statements wherever possible so as to write neat programs. That fact suggests that programming based on predicate logic is better suited to our purposes than the ordinary languages we are currently using.

R&D objectives for fifth-generation
computers to meet the needs of the
coming information society. (Courtesy
of the Institute for New Generation
Computer Technology, Tokyo)

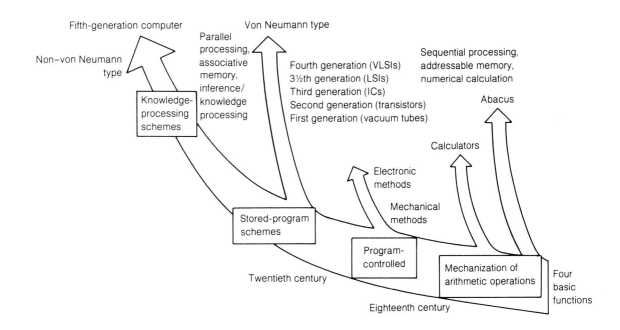

The positioning of fifth-generation
computers in the hierarchy of
computer technology. (Courtesy of
the Institute for New Generation
Computer Technology, Tokyo)

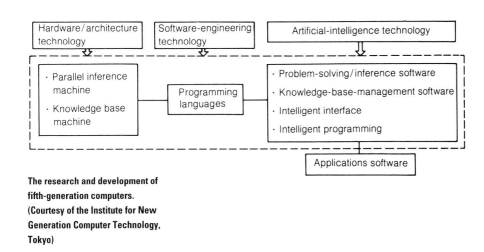

The research and development of
fifth-generation computers.
(Courtesy of the Institute for New
Generation Computer Technology,
Tokyo)

Close Relations with Artificial Intelligence

The FGCS Project is also closely related to the field of artificial intelligence. Knowledge-engineering systems, or expert systems, which have been drawing considerable attention recently, are based on the idea of making a consultation system by representing knowledge in the form of rules and processing the rules. Roughly, organizing knowledge into rules is a return to predicate logic. If we go into detail, we shall find diverse arguments on this subject. I might add that AI experts tend to be concerned with even minuscule differences. For knowledge representation there are numerous proposals that are substantially the same with minor differences.

In connection with artificial intelligence, there is the question of natural-language processing. Grammar, for instance, is very closely related to predicate logic. So is semantics. This may be only natural, because logic itself came from a desire to formulate part of the mechanism of natural language. Historically, logic programming originated from proposals by researchers of natural language.

Historical background aside, if we go with the predicate-logic paradigm instead of the Turing paradigm, we can expect that all the problems we now face will be put in order as far as software is concerned.

Linkage with Software Concepts

The resurgence of predicate logic is not limited to the area of software. Diverse research in computer architectures has yielded new interesting architectures. They are interesting not just in hardware configuration but in that they are intended to connect with software concepts. They include frequently cited data-flow machines and their variations, reduction machines, and more recently proposed advanced parallel machines. These represent a new trend, because they are aimed at linking architecture to software engineering concepts.

Conversely, previous bottom-up concepts alone, such as parallelism and associative memory, are not sufficient. They must be connected with high-level software. Recent notable moves take the standpoint that bringing in such software concepts may make it possible to organize parallelism well.

In this context, functional programming is often discussed. Predicate-logic programming, again in macro terms, is an expanded concept that encompasses functional programming. From the viewpoint of architecture too, logic programming may provide a better base for parallel processing, because it contains more parallelism than functional formulation. This thinking underlies the FGCS Project.

The aims of the fifth-generation computer. (Courtesy of the Institute for New Generation Computer Technology, Tokyo)

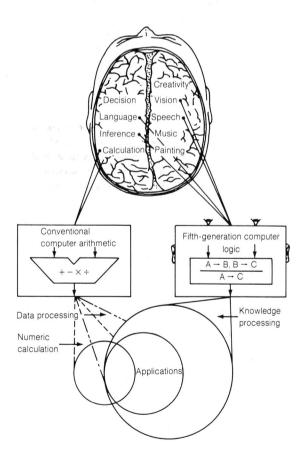

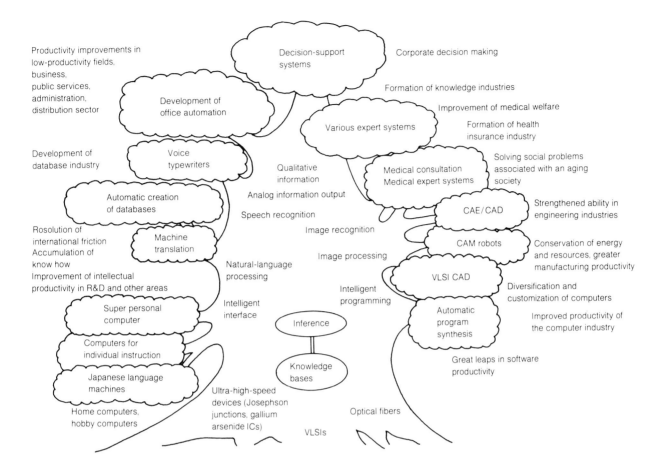

The social impacts of fifth-generation computers. (Courtesy of the Institute for New Generation Computer Technology, Tokyo)

The approach for developing a fifth-generation computer. (Courtesy of the Institute for New Generation Computer Technology, Tokyo)

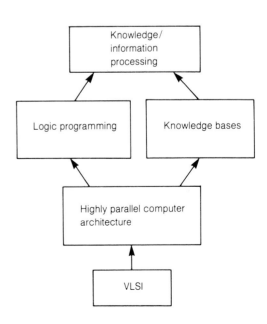

The basic configuration of fifth-generation computer systems. (Courtesy of the Institute for New Generation Computer Technology, Tokyo)

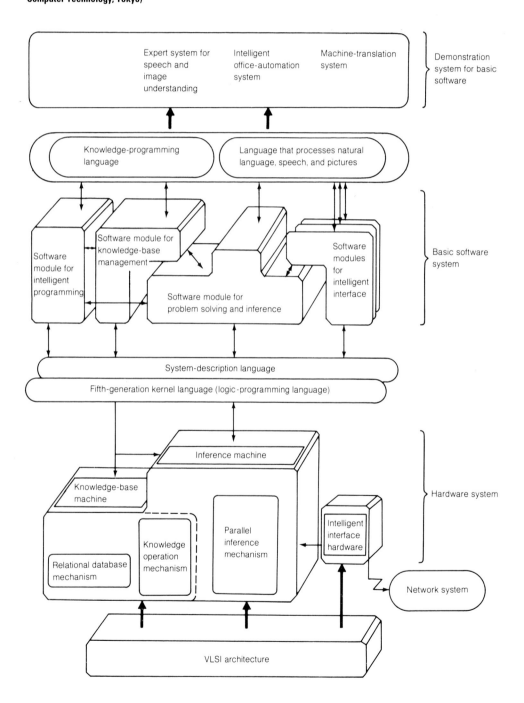

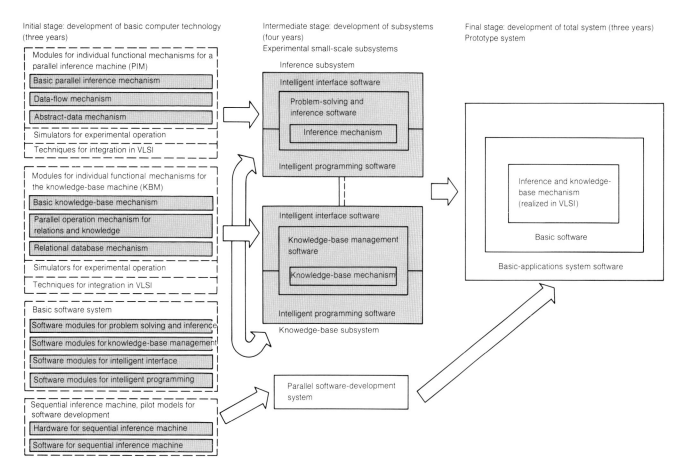

Initial stage: development of basic computer technology (three years)

Modules for individual functional mechanisms for a parallel inference machine (PIM)
- Basic parallel inference mechanism
- Data-flow mechanism
- Abstract-data mechanism

Simulators for experimental operation

Techniques for integration in VLSI

Modules for individual functional mechanisms for the knowledge-base machine (KBM)
- Basic knowledge-base mechanism
- Parallel operation mechanism for relations and knowledge
- Relational database mechanism

Simulators for experimental operation

Techniques for integration in VLSI

Basic software system
- Software modules for problem solving and inference
- Software modules for knowledge-base management
- Software modules for intelligent interface
- Software modules for intelligent programming

Sequential inference machine, pilot models for software development
- Hardware for sequential inference machine
- Software for sequential inference machine

Intermediate stage: development of subsystems (four years)
Experimental small-scale subsystems

Inference subsystem

Intelligent interface software
Problem-solving and inference software
Inference mechanism

Intelligent programming software

Intelligent interface software
Knowledge-base management software
Knowledge-base mechanism

Intelligent programming software

Knowedge-base subsystem

Parallel software-development system

Final stage: development of total system (three years)
Prototype system

Inference and knowledge-base mechanism (realized in VLSI)

Basic software

Basic-applications system software

Stages of fifth-generation computer research and development. (Courtesy of the Institute for New Generation Computer Technology, Tokyo)

Our plan to consider such parallel machines is supported by the progress of VLSI technology. Let us look again at the history. What was the primary reason for going with the Turing paradigm in the first place? In the 1940s memory elements were very expensive. So it was necessary to use as simple a hardware configuration and as few vacuum tubes as possible. A great idea born in those circumstances is what is now called the von Neumann computer concept. But computer history has reached a point where the conventional concept of making software do everything on simple hardware presents various problems. The so-called software crisis is taking place in some fields. For this reason I feel we may see computer history moving out of a phase characterized by strict adherence to a basic philosophy born in the days of costly hardware and into a new phase.

FGCS as a Return to Predicate Logic

For these reasons I see the basic thrust of FGCS as a return to predicate logic. This is not an innovation. Rather it is a return to something old. To people adverse to the word innovation, I explain it as restoration. To people fond of innovation, on the other hand, I explain it as a venture into a new field. I am not lying to either: we are in a transition phase of the cycle of history. What I mean is that history has not yet reached a turning point but will in the 1990s. It will

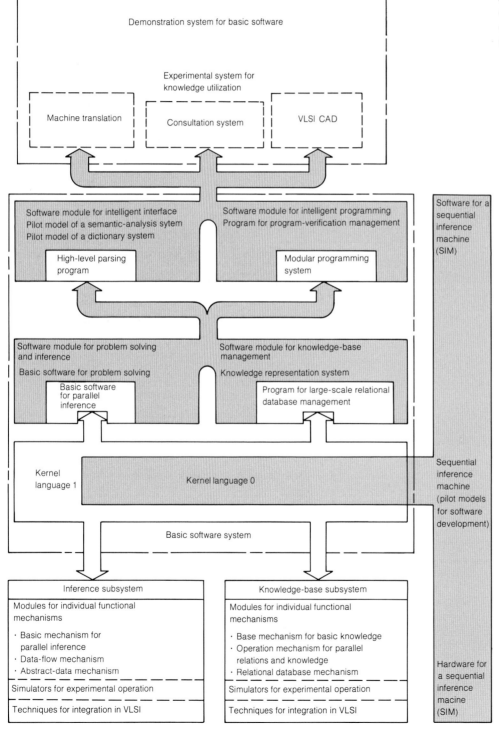

An overview of research and development in the initial stage. (Courtesy of the Institute for New Generation Computer Technology, Tokyo)

Demonstration system for basic software

Experimental system for knowledge utilization

Machine translation

Consultation system

VLSI CAD

Software module for intelligent interface
Pilot model of a semantic-analysis sytem
Pilot model of a dictionary system

Software module for intelligent programming
Program for program-verification management

High-level parsing program

Modular programming system

Software module for problem solving and inference

Software module for knowledge-base management

Basic software for problem solving

Knowledge representation system

Basic software for parallel inference

Program for large-scale relational database management

Software for a sequential inference machine (SIM)

Kernel language 1

Kernel language 0

Sequential inference machine (pilot models for software development)

Basic software system

Inference subsystem

Knowledge-base subsystem

Modules for individual functional mechanisms

· Basic mechanism for parallel inference
· Data-flow mechanism
· Abstract-data mechanism

Modules for individual functional mechanisms

· Base mechanism for basic knowledge
· Operation mechanism for parallel relations and knowledge
· Relational database mechanism

Simulators for experimental operation

Simulators for experimental operation

Techniques for integration in VLSI

Techniques for integration in VLSI

Hardware for a sequential inference macine (SIM)

be a little more than a half century since the computer as we have known it was born. The time span may also justify this scenario.

So far I have explained the FGCS Project from my own point of view. Behind this view is, of course, lots of discussions. I have boiled down the results of the discussions I have had with various experts over the years and recapitulated them as I understand them. The ICOT Research Center started activities with researchers sent on loan from numerous organizations. Though they were like a scratch team, these people were very quick to blend themselves harmoniously into the center. Very quickly a sense of togetherness prevailed in the center, and all the people have done better than expected in their respective research fields. This is attributable partly to the enthusiasm of the researchers and those supporting them and partly to the goal of the project, which, if somewhat vague, is ambitious enough to stimulate the young researchers.

Overseas reactions to the project are now very different from what they were when we started discussions on the project. At first there was some criticism that our project had little chance of success. But there have since been increasing numbers of people overseas who support the project's objective of ushering in a new age of computers. I think that this is evidenced by the start of new programs in a number of countries. Behind these startups is the support of researchers in the respective countries.

Allow me to sum up. The FGCS Project is considerably different in nature from a number of other projects under way. It is aimed at something entirely new. For this reason I think we need to make greater efforts than in the past. ICOT has to play a central role in these efforts. But that alone will not be enough. We must encourage research activities throughout Japan and all over the world. The bud is present, and now we need to make it grow. By doing so, we can usher in a really new computer age. But global rather than merely local efforts are needed to make this happen, and after all, the new age will benefit all mankind. As we exert efforts toward that end, we look for cooperation and support from all those concerned everywhere.

We have made a fairly good start on the project. This project is very ambitious in that it is aimed at ushering in a new computer age rather than at developing products in the near future. What we have to do to make that happen and what we sought to do is to employ the framework of logic programming with the aim of building a new hardware architecture and new-type software and applications within that framework and thereby establish a basic body of computer technology for a new age.

Some people say that our commitment to logic programming is simple-minded and may place us under restraint. But evidence indicates that things may go in the direction of logic programming. Moreover, we have no intention of excluding anything else, though we think that the various good ideas suggested so far will fit naturally within that framework. We selected logic programming as the basic idea in the expectation that it would increase freedom in hardware and software design rather than limit it.

The project requires more than group activities on a limited scale. The wisdom of Japan must be combined, and in a broader perspective, the wisdom of computer scientists all over the world must be marshalled to usher in a new age for mankind. So far we have received much more support and cooperation than is usual with other projects. But we have a long, long way to go, and there will be numerous difficulties on the way.

Brian W. Oakley

Intelligent Knowledge-Based Systems: AI in the U.K.

Brian Oakley, a physicist who started his career working on microwaves and computer applications in what is now the Radar & Signals Research Establishment in England, is the former director of the Alvey Programme, a British national cooperative program in information technology formed in response to the Japanese Fifth-Generation Computer System Project. He is currently chairman of Logica Cambridge.

For reasons that will be made clear, the term "artificial intelligence" is not much used in the U.K. "IKBS" (intelligent knowledge-based systems) tends to be the term employed to cover work in expert systems, natural language, and logic languages. There is a long history of AI work in the U.K., dating back to Alan Turing's pioneering work just before and after World War II. That strange genius foresaw the use of stored-program machines for much more than mathematical calculation, and in the early 1950s he enabled us to compare human and machine intelligence by postulating a test by which one could determine whether true artificial simulation of human intelligence had been achieved. He proposed that an observer in one room should try to tell if he is conversing with a man or a machine in another room. And he also predicted that this test for AI would be achieved by the year 2000. Well, there are still some years to go, and it remains an open question whether his prediction will be proved right; most of his other predictions have been amply fulfilled. One might add that some people believe Colby's program PARRY has achieved AI, because it fooled psychiatrists into believing they were dealing with the output from paranoid human beings. If some people are not impressed with this, it may be because they are not impressed with psychiatrists.

Alan Turing worked in various places in the U.K., including the National Physical Laboratory, Bletchley Park, and the University of Manchester. After his time the center of progress in AI work shifted to the University of Edinburgh, where Donald Michie built up a considerable team and formed one of the first centers in the world for the study of AI. The university has produced excellent work in the language field, though perhaps its most renowned output has been its students, who have gone on to populate AI centers throughout the world. Donald Michie himself has moved on to found the Turing Institute at Strathclyde University, which provides an advisory and training service to industry. But the very broadly based team at Edinburgh, with groups ranging from linguistics through logic programming to speech recognition and computer science, still continues as perhaps the dominant center for AI work in the U.K.

Another much smaller center for AI work in the U.K. academic world is at Sussex University, where the POPLOG language environment is being developed under Professor Aaron Sloman. POPLOG contains compilers for PROLOG and Common LISP as well as one for POP, a simulation language that has its adherents in the U.K. community. After Edinburgh, perhaps the main centers for AI work are at Imperial College, London and Cambridge. Bob Kowalski heads the team at Imperial, where work is in progress on logic programming, expert systems, and Declarative Language architectures. One of the interesting recent applications of AI techniques there has been to the construction of a rule base for the interpretation of legislation, the chosen example being the British Nationality Act, perhaps not one of the most logically constructed pieces of British legislation.

Computer architecture work flourishes at many university centers. Imperial College and Manchester University are cooperating to produce a general-purpose parallel architecture, and a development stage of this machine, called Alice, has been installed at Imperial College and also at the computer center at Edinburgh University, where it is possible to make comparisons with various other machines. Other work in parallel architectures is in progress at universities at Cambridge, Reading, Bath, Southampton, East Anglia, Glasgow, and St. Andrews as well as at University College and Queen Mary College, London.

Work in natural language is relatively weak in the U.K., in comparison with the amount of work on logic programming and advanced architectures. But there is some work being done at Cambridge and the Open University, and as a part of speech recognition, work is in progress at various centers, most notably at Edinburgh.

It is generally believed that the Lighthill Study of Artificial Intelligence, which was commissioned by the Science Research Council toward the end of the 1960s, was a major setback for AI work in the U.K. In this report Sir James Lighthill suggested that one needed a major breakthrough before it would be possible to gain much by tackling the subject of AI as a coherent whole. He recommended that robotic developments should be pursued in their own right, just as the study of human intelligence should be, but that it would not be very profitable, for the moment, to expect an understanding of the way the mind operated to lead to practical applications of so-called artificial intelligence. In a sense, time has supported his contention, for with the exception of low-level vision, there is little evidence that the development of AI practical applications have received much benefit from the study of how the human mind works. Interestingly, it would appear that the study of human behavior has benefited rather more from developments in computer science.

It was probably not intended that the Lighthill report would result in a cutback in work on the component parts of artificial intelligence in the U.K., but this is generally said to have been the result. It probably also intensified the feeling in the U.K. that the term "artificial intelligence" is unfortunate, with its implications that the products are a replacement or rival to human intelligence. For this reason, when work on AI was intensified in the early 1980s, the term "knowledge-based systems" was employed, usually preceded by the word "intelligent" as a sop to the AI community.

If the Lighthill Report of the early 1970s was paradise lost for the AI community, the Alvey Report of the early 1980s was

Brian Oakley. (Courtesy of Brian Oakley)

paradise regained. The Alvey Report was triggered by the Japanese announcement of their fifth-generation program at a conference in Tokyo in the autumn of 1981. In practice, this program is not very large by Japanese standards. The Japanese AI research center, ICOT, still does not number more than 60 workers. But the fact that Japan announced this belief in the importance of AI work to the future of the Japanese economy was enough to launch renewed support for AI in the U.S., Europe, and elsewhere. In the U.K. the growth of interest in AI, and indeed in information technology generally, actually preceded the Japanese announcement.

The Science and Engineering Research Council (SERC), the body in the U.K. that has the responsibility for funding academic research in the physical and biological sciences and in engineering, had already initiated a specially promoted program for distributed computing, which led to much of the flowering of work in parallel computing and declarative and logic languages. A study of the computer-architecture requirements for IKBS was initiated, and this in practice formed the background for the strategy for the IKBS or AI part of the Alvey program.

The Alvey Committee, which planned the program, saw it as a way of marshaling all the research resources of the U.K. to an attack on what were then seen, and are still largely seen today, as the enabling or underlying technologies required to support the whole of information technology. The committee's report, accepted by the government in May 1983, called for a program costing 350 million pounds over 5 years, of which industry would pay for about half, or 150 million pounds. The government contribution of 200 million pounds would come from the Department of Trade and Industry, the Ministry of Defence, and the SERC.

The program was seen as one of cooperative research, and in practice the work is being carried out by some 200 project teams drawn from industry, the universities and polytechnics, and the research institutions, which are largely government establishments. Typically, teams from two or three firms and one or two universities take part in each project. Universities are involved in over 85 percent of the projects, and there is a special "uncle" project class for work of a long-range or speculative nature in the universities supported by some company that takes an avuncular interest in the work. Altogether, the program employs some 2,300 research workers and has probably doubled the effort in the fields covered. Sixteen clubs exist to bring together all the workers in a common field; for example, the Speech Club covers workers in the 10 projects in that field.

AI work largely falls into the IKBS and man-machine-interface (MMI) parts of the program, the other parts being VLSI and software engineering. MMI covers human factors and speech and pattern recognition. There are also considerable developments in

expert systems in the Large Demonstrator parts of the program, which are designed to pull the work together into some practically orientated major projects. Overall, AI work probably constitutes nearly half of the whole program, appearing in all parts. For example, the software-engineering program includes a set of integrated project-support environments, software-project tool sets. The most advanced of these will be based on the use of AI techniques. But it is only fair to add that the AI and software-engineering communities in the U.K. are not really converging as fast as one might like to see.

Much of the AI work in the U.K. has suffered from a lack of suitable experts. So part of the Alvey program is devoted to building up the skilled manpower. When the research-trained postgraduate workers from the Alvey projects soon start becoming available for employment in the general community, this will make a very considerable impact on the available skilled manpower. The program has initiated a Journeyman scheme under which good people from industry with skills in information technology but lacking in AI expertise go to sit at the feet of masters in the academic centers for six months or so while working on projects of interest to their employers.

The Awareness part of the Alvey program has proved to be a great success. The Alvey Tapes are a set of videotaped lectures of distinguished experts on artificial intelligence prepared for the Alvey program by the Open University. The 16 one-hour tapes cover subjects like logic programming, dealing with uncertainty, image understanding, machine learners, natural-language processing, and various aspects of expert systems. One of the most popular tapes, designed to counter the oft repeated canard that expert systems are not really used, shows examples of such systems at work in British industry.

Another way of helping British industry to get started on building expert systems has been through the Expert Systems Starter Pack put together by the National Computing Centre. These consist of computer tapes for four different expert-system design tools, together with training guides. These tools provide elementary experience of such techniques as backward- and forward-chaining inference mechanisms and the use of dialogue generators.

To spread the knowledge of expert systems widely in British industry and commerce, a set of Community Clubs has been established. A Community Club typically consists of 10 to 30 like-minded firms who join together to study the development of an expert system in an area of particular interest to them. They work with a team from the computer industry or the universities that has had experience in building expert systems, and together they draw up a specification, recruit staff to build the system, construct the system, and then test it. Often one or more of the firms acts as the guinea pig for trying out the system. The Alvey program has sponsored nine such

Community Clubs in fields like financial services (Small Company Health Adviser), insurance, data processing (Help Disk Adviser for data-processing installations), econometric modeling, planning for real-time manufacturing projects, quantity surveying, real-time quality control of processing plants, transport-route planning, and water-industry construction planning. Altogether, some 200 organizations are participating in these clubs and learning how to build and use expert systems for a purely nominal fee. They have greatly helped to spread awareness of the power and limitations of expert systems in the U.K. The initiative is being copied by others, so that knowledge about expert systems has grown very fast in the U.K. It is not accidental that the expert-systems group of the British Computer Society is perhaps the most flourishing such society in the U.K. today. It is probably true to say that there is more true awareness of the implications of expert systems in the U.K. than elsewhere, even if the magnitude of some of the applications in the U.S. is far larger.

No picture of the AI scene in the U.K. today would be complete without mention of the part played by the EEC's ESPRIT program. ESPRIT is a program very like the Alvey program except that the cooperative teams are drawn from throughout the European Community of 12 nations. In scale it is, for the U.K., about half the size of the Alvey program, which means that in total for Europe it consists of about twice the number of workers. AI is about a fifth of the program, being largely represented in the Advanced Information Processing part of the program. Of course, ESPRIT has the crucial role of bringing the research workers of Europe together. Perhaps for the first time the AI community in the U.K. is coming into active contact with the other research workers in Europe not just to carry out project work but also to plan, evaluate, and implement the program. And in several countries in Europe there are also nationally sponsored programs, so the total AI effort in Europe is far from negligible and its historic problem of fragmentation is being overcome.

Looking to the future, a committee in the UK is now planning an After Alvey program, and the second phase of ESPRIT is also under discussion. Though one cannot be certain at this stage just what will emerge, it seems very probable that some planned and coordinated programs will continue, perhaps with a rather larger bias toward actual applications than the precompetitive research programs of the first wave. What is certain is that the buildup of interest and work in artificial intelligence in Europe will continue. The overall scene in the U.K. and Europe can be characterized by saying that there is now immense awareness of the potential to be unlocked by applying the techniques developed under the banner of AI work. Though much of the work is at a rather elementary stage, characterized by a shortage of expert workers, there are nevertheless some true centers of expertise to rank with the best in the United States in terms of quality if not in terms of quantity. The recognition that yet to come are the true breakthroughs, both in understanding and in application, spurs on the AI community in Europe. And the cooperative programs of the last few years have served to build up significant, multidisciplinary teams that bid to make a real impact on the world AI scene. The Europeans who have led and inspired many of the AI developments of the last forty years will be followed up by a growing army of experts. These experts recognize that AI is going to make a great impact on the world in the future but that the breakthroughs that will be needed will demand considerable teams drawn from a very wide range of disciplines.

CHAPTER 9

The Science of Art

The great discovery of the twentieth century in art and physics alike, is a recoil from and transformation of the impersonal assembly-line of nineteenth century art and science.

Marshall McLuhan, *The Gutenberg Galaxy*

• The Musical Arts

At a time like ours, in which mechanical skill has attained unsuspected perfection, the most famous works may be heard as easily as one may drink a glass of beer, and it only costs ten centimes, like the automatic weighing machines. Should we not fear this domestication of sound, this magic that anyone can bring from a disk at his will? Will it not bring to waste the mysterious force of an art which one might have thought indestructible?

Claude Debussy, *La Revue S.I.M.* (1913)

Collaboration with machines! What is the difference between manipulation of the machine and collaboration with it? I have sometimes experienced a state of dynamic tension rising in me out of what would seem to be a state of mutual responsiveness between the machine and myself. Such a state could require hours of concentrated preparatory exploration, coaxing of machines, connecting, so to say, one's own sensibilities, one's own nerve endings to the totality of the tuned-up controls. And, suddenly, a window would open into a vast field of possibilities; the time limits would vanish, and the machines would seem to become humanized components of the interactive network now consisting of oneself and the machine, still obedient but full of suggestions to the master controls of the imagination. Everything seemed possible: one leaned on the horizon and pushed it away and forward until utter exhaustion would set in and, one by one, the nerve endings ceased to connect, the possibilities contracted, and an automatic reversal to routine solutions was a sure danger signal to quit. An affectionate pat on a control here and there was not to be resisted. Switches and lights off! If there is an unfinished bit of conversation between you and the machines, either take note of all the controls or leave them alone until tomorrow. Recapturing the exact circumstances of such periods as just described is not easy. Tomorrow it may seem all cold steel, copper and colored plastic. The coaxing may have to start all over again.

Vladimir Ussachevsky (composer and early pioneer of electronic music), *Electronic Tape Music*

Computer technology is now having a major impact on all fields, including the creative arts. While the visual arts are just beginning to feel the impact of advances in computer graphics and imaging technologies, the computer revolution in music is already well under way.[1] One reason that the transformation of music is further along has to do with the substantially greater "bandwidth" (communication and memory capacity) required for images as compared to sounds. With digital technology we can already store, analyze, modify, and recreate sounds with an accuracy equal to that of the human auditory system.[2] To do the same with visual images requires an amount of memory and processing power that is still quite challenging for today's computers. Another reason has to do with the fact that music theory is more highly developed and quantitative than theory in the visual arts.

As discussed earlier, a historic transformation is taking place in the musical-instrument industry away from the acoustic technology of the piano and violin and toward the computer-based technology of the synthesizer.[3] The advent and now enthusiastic acceptance of digital instruments follows a long tradition. Music has always used the most advanced technologies available: the cabinet-making crafts of the eighteenth century, the metalworking industries of the nineteenth century, and the analog electronics of the 1960s. This latest wave—the digital electronics and artificial intelligence of the 1980s—is again making historic changes in the way music is created.

Up until recently, instrument-playing technique was inextricably linked to the sounds created. If you wanted flute sounds, you had to use flute-playing technique. The playing techniques derived from the physical requirements of creating the sounds. Now that link has been broken. If you like flute-playing technique (or just happened to have learned it), you can now use an electronic wind controller that plays very much like an acoustic flute yet creates the sounds not only of the flute but also of virtually any other instrument, acoustic or electronic. In fact, there are now controllers that emulate the playing technique of most popular acoustic instruments, including piano, violin, guitar, drums, and a variety of wind instruments. Since we are no longer linked to the physics of creating sounds acoustically, a new generation of controllers is emerging that bears no resemblance to any conventional acoustic instrument but instead attempts to optimize the human factors of creating music with our fingers, arms, feet, mouth, and head.

Music controllers and sound generators (or synthesizers) can be linked together by an industry-standard electronic interface called MIDI (Musical Instrument Digital Interface).[4] MIDI, which employs an inexpensive communication link, has allowed independently developed synthesizers, controllers, sequencers (computer-based devices that can remember and replay sequences of notes), and other sound-modification devices to communicate and interact with each other. MIDI has even been used to control stage lighting and other visual effects. Another industry protocol called SMPTE Time Code (Society of Motion Picture and Television Engineers) allows interfacing sound-manipulating devices to video. MIDI and SMPTE Time Code together are facilitating the development of computer-based systems that are revolutionizing video and audio production in the same way that electronic publishing software, personal computers, and laser printers have transformed the way printed documents are created.

In addition to new music controllers, new sounds to be controlled are being created at an accelerating pace. While the sounds of the piano and other acoustic instruments continue to be sounds of choice, they are routinely mixed with new sounds that approach the richness and complexity of acoustic sounds but have never been heard before.[5] The creation of a musical work such as a pop song used to

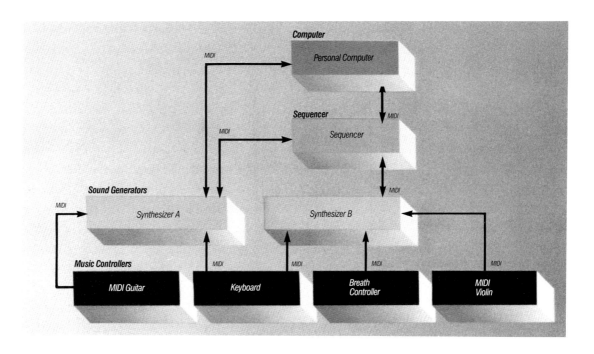

Computer

Personal Computer

MIDI

Sequencer

MIDI

Sequencer

MIDI

Sound Generators

MIDI

Synthesizer A

MIDI

Synthesizer B

MIDI

Music Controllers

MIDI

MIDI Guitar

MIDI

Keyboard

MIDI

Breath
Controller

MIDI

MIDI
Violin

**A home music studio that
uses Musical Instrument Digital
Interfaces (MIDIs)**

involve the creation of a few fixed elements: melody, rhythm, harmony, lyrics, and orchestration, say. Now an entirely new element, the invention of new timbres, has been added. This has led to the appearance of a new type of musician, one who specializes in sound design. Rare these days is the successful pop song that does not introduce some new timbre to the music world's palette of sounds.

Sound modification techniques are being developed as rapidly as new sounds and control methods. It is now possible with personal computers and appropriate software to take a musical note, break it into all of its frequency components, reshape the amplitude (or loudness) envelope of each such component, and then reassemble the sound.[6] Like most experiments, many such attempts fail to produce anything worthwhile, but the experiments that do succeed are creating an ever expanding repertoire of new, musically relevant timbres. A wide variety of sound-modification techniques can be used off-line when editing a multi-instrumental composition and controlled in real-time during performance.

Digital technology has overcome many of the conventional limitations of acoustic instruments. All sounds can now be played polyphonically and be layered (i.e., played simultaneously) or sequenced with one another.[7] Also, it is no longer necessary to play music in real time.[8] Traditionally, music performance has often depended on nearly superhuman feats of finger acrobatics. While technical playing skills are still being used to good effect by the virtuosos, absence of such skills no longer represents a barrier to the creation of music. Music can be performed at one speed and played back at another, without changing the pitch or other characteristics of the notes. Further, it is possible to edit a recorded sequence by inserting, changing, and deleting notes in much the same way that one edits a text document with a word processor. In this way, music can be created that would be impossible to perform in real-time.[9]

The computer as composer

Expert systems and other AI techniques are also providing new methods for composing music. A musician can provide his own original ideas for a composition and allow the computer to do the rest of the work using systems that are programmed with extensive knowledge about the music composition process.[10] One such system that can compose music automatically, the Cybernetic Composer, was developed by Charles Ames and Michael Domino. The Cybernetic Composer composes entire pieces automatically, while similar systems allow the musician to contribute his own musical ideas. For example, one can write the melody and rhythm and allow the expert-system software to generate the harmonic progression, the walking bass line, the drum accompaniment, or any combination of these parts. Such systems will be of growing value in teaching music composition and theory, as well as in allowing composers to concentrate on those aspects of the composition process where they can add the most creativity.[11] Also increasing in popularity are systems that allow the musician to interactively change parameters of a piece in real time—essentially, computer-assisted improvisation. For example, for the Macintosh there is Jam Factory, M, Music Mouse, and Ovaltine.[12] Other computerized aids for composers include systems that can automatically generate high-quality music notation. Examples include Finale, Professional Composer, and an advanced system now under development by Don Byrd.[13]

AI systems are likely to have a major impact on music education. In place of the tedious and simpleminded auto-play type of features found on home organs, future musical instruments for the home will contain intelligent music accompanists that can help teach music and provide both children and adults with a richer musical experience at early stages of keyboard skill development.[14]

Computer-generated music notation. (Courtesy of Donald Byrd; copyright 1989 by Donald Byrd)

Mirroring the broadening choices in sounds and musical control is a broadening appreciation in popular music for diverse musical traditions. Initiated in part by the Beatles almost two decades ago and fueled by many other musical innovators, popular music has expanded from its Afro-American roots to include today the rhythms, styles, melodies, and harmonies of folk and classical traditions from around the world.

Thus today's musicians are confronted by a staggering array of choices: an ever expanding set of sounds, music controllers, sound-modification techniques, sequencing methods, composition tools, and even music traditions. All of this does not necessarily make the musician's job easier: it is generally not desirable to use a plethora of sounds and processing techniques in a single work. Indeed, much of popular music has been criticized for the overuse of electronic techniques.

The goal of music, however, remains the same: the communication of emotions and ideas from musician to listener through sound, using the elements of melody, rhythm, harmony, timbre, and expression. The challenge for the musical artist is the same as for all artists: to make choices, to select the right timbres and melodies to express their musical ideas.

• The Visual Arts

An image can be placed somewhere between these two antipodes:
Realism = Abstraction
Abstraction = Realism
Wassily Kandinski, *The Problem of Form* (1912)

As I mentioned above, the computer revolution in the visual arts lags well behind the major transformation already taking place in the musical arts. In music, computers are no longer a novelty but are now the strongest driving force in the rapidly changing face of music creation. In the visual arts there is still a widespread tendency to view the computer as an interloper, as something alien to the creative process.[15] This inclination is reinforced by the fact that computer art has until recently been constrained by the limited resolution of most computer display screens and hard-copy output devices.[16] For several years now computer-based devices have been able to create, modify, and manage sounds without compromising the quality and accuracy of the result. The comparable situation in the visual arts is only now becoming possible. The result is that computer art, while a creative and rapidly changing field, is not yet in the mainstream. Recognition that the computer is a viable and powerful tool for artistic expression with unique capabilities should become more widespread in the early 1990s now that the latest generation of personal computers is providing an ability to create graphics comparable to other artistic media.[17]

Some of the advantages of computer-based art techniques over manual methods apply to *any* domain—e.g., ease of revising, of making backup and archival copies, of making many types of global transformations (in music, transposing; in art, changing size or color). The computer also permits the use of techniques that would otherwise be impossible to realize.

Methods for using the computer to create visual art vary. The most straightforward approach is to simply use the display screen as a window onto a simulated

A portrait of the artist as a computer.
AARON, a program developed
by Harold Cohen of the University of
California at San Diego, creates
"freehand" drawings that Cohen then
colors. (Photo by Linda Waters)

Art by AARON by Cohen. (Photo by Becky Cohen)

canvas. The Macintosh MacPaint program and many more-recent applications popularized the computer as a sketchpad but also made obvious some of its limitations, including an inability to represent fine detail, the jagged appearance of curved lines, and for many of these systems, the lack of color. More recent high-resolution color-graphics displays are now beginning to provide image quality comparable to that of good 35-mm slides.[18] Foremost among the advantages of using a computer screen as a canvas is the availability of image-processing techniques that would be impossible using ordinary paints and pencils. Among the dozens of techniques available, users can alter shadings, reconstruct surfaces, synthesize natural and artificial backgrounds, create reflections, and distort shapes.[19]

One simple technique is the automatic repetition and rotation of images. If the original image is complex, this would require enormous skill, not to mention time, to perform manually. Using a computer, artists can easily view any object from any orientation, complete with accurate perspectives if so desired.[20] But few artists would be happy with these exotic techniques if the more ordinary effects they have always used were not available. Just as each musical instrument provides its own unique set of methods for sound modification (vibrato, pizzicato, and others on a violin, for example), each method of visual art creation provides techniques for creating and modifying color and shape. Oil paints provide an ability to blend and fuse colors, pastels provide certain types of shadings, and so on. With improvements in display technology and image processing techniques, artists at a computer canvas will soon be able to simulate all of these techniques in a single medium, while taking advantage of methods that would be impossible with real paints and solvents.[21]

Grass Series Five, a computer-generated drawing programmed by Colette Bangert and Charles J. Bangert, 1983. Their mathematical program was particularly effective in depicting natural forms, such as these interwoven patterns of blades of grass. (Hardware: Intertrec Superbrain computer, Wanatabe WX 4671 plotter. Courtesy of Colette Bangert and Charles Bangert)

Large Landscape II: Ochre and Black, a drawing plotted by a computer programmed by Colette Bangert and Charles Bangert, 1970. This drawing was done using a Honeywell 635 digital computer and a Benson-Lehner Draft-O-Matic plotter at the University of Kansas. (Courtesy of Colette Bangert and Charles Bangert)

Computer graphics from Tokyo.
(Photo by Lou Jones)

Perhaps the greatest advantage the computer gives to the artist is the ability to experiment and change one's mind. Doing this is quite difficult with real paints, but it is one of the inherent benefits of the computer canvas.

Artificial life

An unusual way of applying computers to visual art is called artificial life.[22] This technique uses the computer to create a simulated environment with simulated "organisms" controlled by a "genetic" code.[23] The artist provides the genetic code and the rules for procreation and survival. The computer then simulates dozens or even thousands of generations of simulated evolution. The resulting "creatures" and environment can be quite beautiful. The artist is thus like a deist god who creates a starting point and then unleashes a recursive process of repetitive re-creation.[24] The artistic value of this technique should not be surprising. After all, real evolution has certainly created a myriad of beautiful forms. In fact, aesthetics itself is often considered to be rooted in the beauty of the natural creation. The artificial-life approach to creating art is to imitate this ultimate design force.

Artificial life, Przemyslaw
Prusinkiewicz and one of his
computer-grown flowers.
(Photo by Gail Russell and
courtesy of the *New York Times*)

Fractals

Artificial life is considered a recursive technique because each new generation of artificial life begets the next.[25] The ultimate application of recursion to design involves the mathematics of fractals. Fractal images are derived from a branch of mathematics called fractal geometry, devised in the 1970s by IBM Research Fellow Benoit Mandelbrot.[26] One method for generating a fractal image is through a recursive procedure in which specific parts of a picture (e.g., every straight line) are repeatedly replaced with more complex parts. By using various starting figures and transformations, a great variety of patterns can be generated.

There are actually several types of fractals. I have been discussing geometric fractals. Instead of using exactly the same transformation at each stage, we can allow a random process to control the transformations (randomly skipping some of the steps, for example). In these chaotic fractals, the patterns are less regular and, oddly enough, more natural.[27] This observation led Mandelbrot to realize the potential application of fractals to describing a wide variety of natural phenomena, including

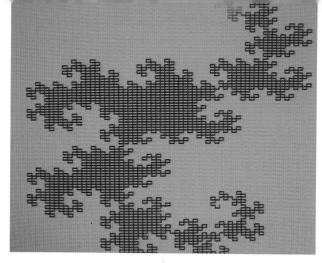

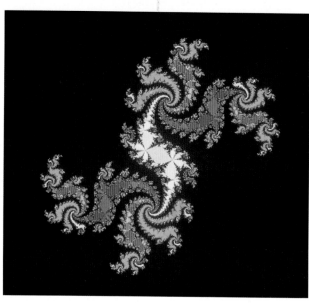

A fractal dragon in the process of
being generated. (Photo by Lou Jones)

A fractal dragon. (Image by Richard
F. Voss; copyright 1982 by B. B.
Mandelbrot; programming by Mark
Laff and Alan Norton.)

Generation of a random fractal.
(Photo by Lou Jones)

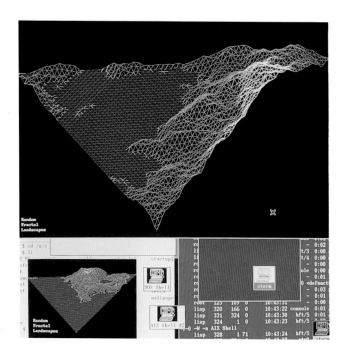

Fractal mountains. These mountains were created by a computer using fractal geometry. (Image by Richard F. Voss; copyright 1982 by B. B. Mandelbrot)

economic trends, the progression of epidemics, the organization of proteins, and the structure of music.[28]

Fractals have a number of interesting properties. Unlike most mathematically generated shapes, the nature of a fractal is the same at all scales of magnification. Magnify a fractal a thousand times, and it still looks the same. Magnify it another thousand times, and again, no essential change. This paradoxical quality describes a surprisingly large number of natural phenomena quite well. The most famous example is that of coastlines. Maps of coastlines have the same jagged appearance regardless of their scale.[29] Another important example is cloud formation. Pictures of clouds look the same whether one looks at a cloud of 10 feet or a cloud of 100 miles.[30]

Indeed, perfect fractals keep the same appearance at all scales. But fractal-like shapes in the real world have this property, called self-similarity, only to a point.[31] In a graphic display the limit is the granularity of the display, which is known as the pixel size .[32] In the universe as a whole, which turns out to be a spongelike fractal, the pixel corresponds to the galaxy. Within galaxies, a different type of fractal known as a fractal whorl governs the organization of stars.[33]

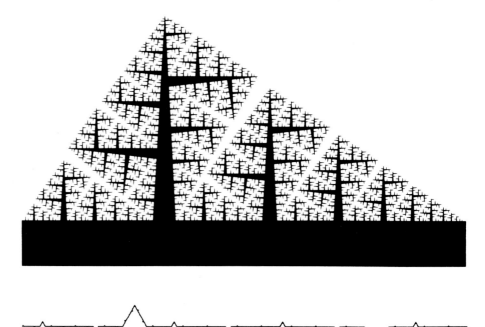

Point Reyes. This elaborate scene was created entirely by computer using a variety of techniques, including chaotic fractals. (Courtesy of Lucasfilm; copyright 1983 by Pixar)

Self-similarity. These treelike geometric patterns were generated by repetitive application of a fractal generator. (Copyright 1982 by B. B. Mandelbrot)

Apfeimännchen, a graphic display of the so-called Mandelbrot set, a set of formulas by Benoit B. Mandelbrot drawn from the mathematics of Julia sets. This famous fractal looks the same at all scales of magnification. Magnify this image a million times, and the whorls and snowmen will look exactly the same. (Image by Heinz-Otto Peitgen and Peter H. Richter of the University of Bremen; copyright 1984 by MapArt)

The word "fractal" derives from the phrase "*fractional* dimension."[34] Because of its infinitely fine detail, a perfect fractal shape actually has infinite length even though it resides on a finite two-dimensional surface. According to fractal geometry, it therefore has a dimensionality somewhere in between that of an ordinary line segment, which has a dimensionality of 1, and a surface, which has a dimensionality of 2.[35] For example, the Koch snowflake, pictured above, has a dimensionality of 1.26, just slightly greater than the coastline of Great Britain, which is considered to have 1.25 dimensions. The galactic sponge has been estimated to have about 2.2 dimensions.[36]

For the sciences and engineering disciplines, fractal geometry provides a powerful tool for understanding the dynamics of turbulence, chaos, and other unpredictable patterns.[37] For the visual arts, fractal geometry provides an equally powerful methodology for creating images that can be natural, spectacular, or both. Fractals are capable of generating realistic clouds, trees, bushes, lakes, mountains, shorelines, landscapes, and other similar images.[38] For example, George Lucas used the technique to create the moons of Endor in his film *The Return of the Jedi*. It can create environments that, while very alien-looking, appear to be the result of natural processes.[39]

The computer as artist

Another use of the computer to create artistic images is to provide a computer with a set of rules and other knowledge structures that explain the processes of drawing, composition, and layout and to let it be the artist. Probably the leading exponent of this approach is Harold Cohen. Cohen has programmed over 1,000 rules for the creation of complex drawings; his computer uses these to direct a robotic drawing machine to create the drawings.[40] These can be of people, plants, or abstract objects. Cohen clearly intends the pictures as art, and indeed, his work has been highly acclaimed. Cohen, who is considered a master colorist, often colors in his robot's drawings manually. His latest ambition is to build a robot colorist programmed with his own theory of coloring.

The computer as artist raises a number of interesting questions. First, who is the artist? Cohen claims that he is, and his computer has not been programmed to complain. Second, why bother? Why not simply make the drawings directly? Both of these questions also pertain to the computer as composer.

These are important questions, and there are, in my view, several answers. First, computer art is a perfectly legitimate means of creating art. The computer is simply a tool, a medium through which the artist (or musician) is expressing himself.

Second, the work of art is, in a sense, more interesting. We can regard the program itself as the work of art that manifests itself differently every time we choose to look at it (or listen to it). It is a work of art that can change its appearance as quickly as the program can generate a new drawing. Since the style is unmistakably similar in each such manifestation, all manifestations can reasonably be regarded as a single work. It can be pointed out, however, that it is not unusual for multiple works of one artist to exhibit such a degree of similarity. We can, therefore, consider a program such as Cohen's to be either an artist itself, or a work of art, or both.

Planetrise Over Labelgraph Hill
(Souvenir from a Space Mission That
Never Was.) A Fractal-generated
planet and landscape by Benoit
B. Mandelbrot. (Image by Richard F.
Voss; copyright 1982 by B. B.
Mandelbrot)

Third, the rules themselves give us an objective and rigorous statement of the theory of the artwork and thus an unprecedented degree of insight into its structure. Understanding the boundary between the rules themselves and the expressive aspects of art that we might feel cannot (yet) be expressed with such precision also provides a valuable perspective.

The rules also have educational value. In art, a great deal is known about perspective, composition, the drawing of different types of shapes, and other facets of visual art. These facets can be expressed in precise terms. Similarly, a great deal can be said with mathematical precision regarding the nature of rhythm, harmonic progressions, the structures of different genres of melodies, and the other elements of music. Creating rules that can in turn create entire satisfactory works of art (or music) helps us to understand, and therefore to teach, the objective aspects of artistic creation.

Finally, such systems can have practical value. In music they can perform compositional chores by automatically creating walking bass lines, rhythmic accompaniments, and so on. In the visual arts, after the artist indicated his intentions, such cybernetic assistants could finish a drawing, performing chores of shading, coloring, creating perspective, balancing the sizes of objects for proper compositional balance, and other tasks. In this mode of operation, such computer-based assistants would always be working under the careful eye (or ear) of the artist.

Such automatic assistants have already been actively harnessed in the creation of animation, where the chores of creating hundreds of thousands of images (over a thousand per minute of film) is formidable. Computer-based animation systems have substantially boosted the productivity of human animators.[41] Another area of commercial art where computer design stations are already of substantial practical value is in fashion design and layout.

As in the world of music, the role of the computer is not to displace human creativity but rather to amplify it. It is a tool, like a paintbrush, but one of unique and virtually unlimited potential. Clearly, the great artists of old must have had many ideas beyond the ones they had the time to actually express. By reducing the many chores involved, computers can give artists the opportunity to realize more of their artistic visions.

Also, many computer techniques allow the expression of forms that are simply impossible to realize in any other way. Because the results of some of these methods, such as recursive fractal generation, are unpredictable until they are tried, the computer can be a partner with the artist in exploring the artist's imagination.

Finally, the computer can open the world of artistic expression to more participants. Many of us have rich visual imaginations and a good sense of aesthetic judgement but are lacking in the technical skills to express our imaginations using conventional artistic materials and techniques. The inability to draw a straight line (as the ads used to say) may no longer be a barrier to becoming an effective and successful artist.[42]

Could I see this in a blue paisley?
Computer-aided design stations
allow clothes designers to create
new fashions on digital mannequins.
Garments can be viewed from
different perspectives with seam
allowances, tucks, notches, and
other design elements automatically
computed. Computerized pattern
graders then generate the different-
sized patterns needed for manufacturing. (Courtesy of *Bobbin
International* magazine)

Automated animation in Kawasaki,
Japan. (Photo by Lou Jones)

At all events my own essays and dissertations about love
and its endless pain and perpetual pleasure will be
known and understood by all of you who read this and
talk or sing or chant about it to your worried friends
or nervous enemies. Love is the question and the subject
of this essay. We will commence with a question: does
steak love lettuce? This question is implacably
hard and inevitably difficult to answer. Here is
a question: does an electron love a proton,
or does it love a neutron? Here is a question: does
a man love a woman or, to be specific and to be
precise, does Bill love Diane? The interesting
and critical response to this question is: no! He
is obsessed and infatuated with her. He is loony
and crazy about her. That is not the love
of steak and lettuce, of electron and proton and
neutron. This dissertation will show that the
love of a man and a woman is not the love of
steak and lettuce. Love is interesting to me
and fascinating to you but it is painful to
Bill and Diane. That is love!

A poem from *The Policeman's Beard Is Half Constructed* (the first book ever written entirely by a computer) by RACTER (a program by William Chamberlain and Thomas Etter)

Bill sings to Sarah. Sarah sings to Bill. Perhaps they
will do other dangerous things together. They may eat lamb or stroke
each other. They may chant of their difficulties and their
happiness. They have love but they also have typewriters.
That is interesting.

RACTER, *The Policeman's Beard Is Half Constructed*

eons deep in the ice
I paint all time in a whorl
bang the sludge has cracked

eons deep in the ice
I see gelled time in a whorl
pffftt the sludge has cracked

all green in the leaves
I smell dark pools in the trees
crash the moon has fled

all white in the buds
I flash snow peaks in the spring
bang the sun has fogged

Haiku poems written by a program by Margaret Masterman and Robin McKinnon Wood

In the literary arts, computers are already of substantial practical benefit. Of greatest impact is the simple word processor. Not an AI technology per se, word processing was derived from the text editors developed during the 1960s at AI labs at MIT and elsewhere.[43] Also assisting the craft of writing text are increasingly sophisticated

David Boucher, Harry George, and
the Interleaf Desktop Publishing
System. (Photos by Lou Jones)

spelling checkers, intelligent syntax checkers, style checkers, on-line dictionaries, thesauri, and other linguistic data bases.[44] Of practical value to poets is the on-line rhyming dictionary that provides rhymes and half-rhymes with particular rhythmic patterns.

Writers of nonfiction are beginning to utilize the rapidly growing array of data bases available on almost every subject. As the world's knowledge bases gradually shift from paper to on-line information utilities that can be intelligently accessed through telecommunications, the productivity of research will be greatly improved. Ultimately, computers will be able to conduct entire research projects on verbal requests from their human bosses.[45]

Magazine and newspaper writing has benefited for the past decade from on-line systems, such as those provided by Atex and other companies, that facilitate all aspects of material creation, including text creation and editing, graphics preparation, and layout. The new industry of desktop publishing, pioneered by Xerox,

Mitch Kapor, founder of Lotus
Development Corp. and developer of
Lotus 1-2-3 and Agenda. (Photo by
Lou Jones)

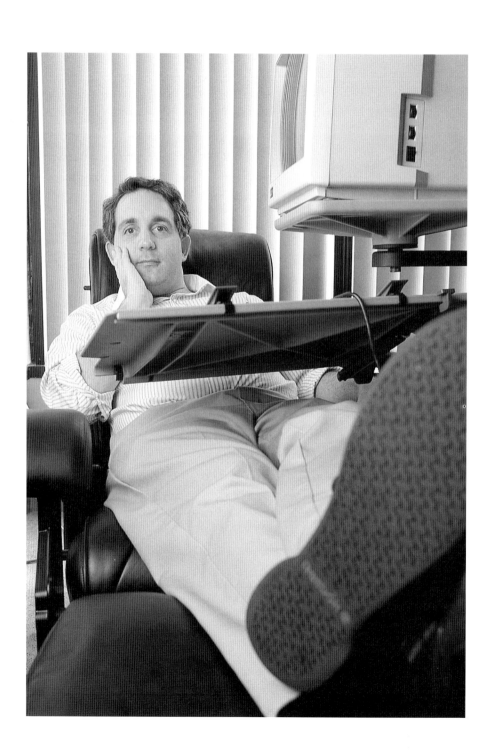

Interleaf, Apple, and others, provides writers with their own personal publishing capability through the use of an ordinary personal computer and a laser printer.[46]

A new genre of expert systems for personal computers are now appearing that provide assistance in the organization of ideas. These systems allow users to explore a set of thoughts, notice patterns and similarities, and develop outlines that can later be fleshed out into text. Some of these systems are intended to be used in real time as thoughts develop and include abilities to organize a variety of activities. A prime example of this type of software is Lotus's Agenda, developed by Mitch Kapor.[47]

Expert systems can also be applied to tracking the complex histories, characterizations, and interactions of characters in such extended works of fiction as long novels, series of novels, and television drama series. (A system that can assist with the development of characters and plots for soap operas is described in Michael Lebowitz, "All Work and No Play Makes HAL a Dull Program" in this chapter.)

Most challenging of all would be a system that could actually write or substantively assist with the writing of prose or verse in the same way that expert systems are now beginning to assist the composer and the graphic artist. Efforts have been made to accomplish this, and some are represented in the epigraphs at the beginning of this section and in the article "A (Kind of) Turing Test" in this chapter. The computer undoubtedly has a role to play in the generation of text, and computer-generated prose and verse is a small but flourishing field. The results, however, are significantly less successful to date than in the musical and visual arts. RACTER's prose has its charm, but is somewhat demented-sounding, due primarily to its rather limited understanding of what it is talking about.[48] Deeply imbedded in written language is knowledge, extensive, diverse, and intricately organized knowledge, the vast bulk of which has yet to be captured. With language translation systems currently providing only 80 to 90 percent accuracy on technical texts, it is not *yet* realistic (until well into the first half of the next century) to expect computers to have sufficient facility with language to generate literary quality text without assistance.[49] The objection might be raised that there is a comparable depth of knowledge in works of music and of visual arts. This is certainly true. The reason why computers have had greater success in assisting with the creative process in these areas is that we have a better understanding of the surface structures of music and visual art (particularly the former) than we do for literature. But even in these fields, the ultimate responsibility for making an artistic statement is still the province of the human artist.

The role of the computer is the same for all of the arts. First is to provide an effective tool for improving the productivity of the artist, to enable him to realize more of his imagination. Second, the computer can provide forms of expression that were previously unavailable. Finally, to whatever extent we are able to capture even a portion of the creative process in a program, we learn something about the art form as well as the process of creating it. The computer can be a powerful partner in exploring our thoughts and emotions and finding new ways of expressing them.

Raymond Kurzweil

A (Kind of) Turing Test

No ideas but in things.
William Carlos Williams

As discussed in several of the contributed articles in this book, the Turing test was devised by Alan Turing as a way of certifying machine intelligence. Turing described a situation in which a human judge communicates with both a computer and a human using a computer terminal. The judge's task is to determine which is which. The judge cannot see the computer or the human and must make his or her determination by interviewing both. The computer attempts to trick the judge into selecting it as the human.

The essence of the Turing Test is that the computer attempts to act like a human within the context of an interview over terminal lines. A narrower concept of a Turing test is for a computer to successfully imitate a human within a particular domain of human intelligence. We might call these domain-specific Turing tests. One such domain-specific Turing test, based on a computer's ability to write poetry, is presented here.

The Kurzweil Cybernetic Poet is a computer program (written by the author) and provided with an input file of poems written by a human author or authors. The program analyzes these poems and creates a word-sequence model based on the poems it has just read. It then writes original stanzas of poetry using the model it has created. Some of the following stanzas of poetry were written by the Kurzweil Cybernetic Poet. Some were written by human authors (in fact the same human authors that were read and analyzed by the Kurzweil Cybernetic Poet). See if you can tell which are which. On a piece of paper, write down the numbers 1 through 28. Then put a *C* by that number if you believe that the corresponding stanza was written by the computer. Put an *H* if you believe the stanza was written by a human poet. The answers are in a footnote.[1] Following the answers are the results obtained when the test was taken by 16 human (both adult and child) judges.

1. is beauty itself

   that they were walking there. All along the new world naked,

   cold, familiar wind—

---

2. Pink confused with white

   flowers and flowers reversed

   take and spill the shaded flame

   darting it back

   into the lamp's horn

---

3. The winds of the oozy woods which wear

   the ocean, with azure moss and flowers

   So sweet, the purple even

   I sleep in the arrows

   Of the dome of death.

---

4. O thou,

   Who moved among some fierce Maenad, even among noise

      and blue

   Between the bones sang, scattered and the silent seas.

---

5. She eyes me with an ingrown eye,

   in the rhythm of teacup tapping

   thinks of sweeping away crumbs

---

6. At six I cannot pray:

   Pray for lovers,

   through narrow streets

   And pray to fly

   But the Virgin in their dark wintry bed

---

7. What seas what shores what granite islands towards my timbers

   And woodthrush calling through the fog

   My daughter.

---

8. Imagine now a tree in white sails still whirled

   About the leaves

   will be of silences

   Calm and angels

---

9. —and the sun, dipping into the avenues

   streaking the tops of

   the irregular red houselets,

   and

   the gay shadows dropping and dropping.

---

10. The morning and already

    a perfect if slightly paled

    old park turned with young women

    seized in amber.

---

11. "Interesting book?"

    she sits

    dancing by the electric typewriter,

    bloodless revolution of meats

    strings of use,

    Politic, cautious, and the fact

    she is the fact

    she is calling them all—

    The children at his feet

    he is always time

    To roll it was dark,

    damp, jagged, like the voice

    Because of love ends.

---

12. Men with picked voices chant the names

    of cities in a huge gallery: promises

    that pull through descending stairways

    to a deep rumbling.

---

13. Where were thou, sad Hour, selected from whose race is

       guiding me,

    Lured by the love of Autumn's being,

    Thou, from heaven is gone, where was lorn Urania

    When rocked to fly with thee in her clarion o'er the arms of death.

---

14. Lady of Autumn's being,

    Thou, from the day, having to care

    Teach us now thoroughly small and create,

    And then presume?

    And this, and me,

    And place of the unspoken word, the unread vision in Baiae's bay,

    And the posterity of Michelangelo.

---

15. I am lonely, lonely.

    I slap an answer myself

    she hides deep within her

    yet plays—

    Milkless

---

16. O my shoulders, flanks, buttocks
   against trespassers,
   against thieves,
   storms, sun, fire,
   against thieves,
   storms, sun, fire,
   against flies, against weeds, storm-tides,
   neighbors, weasels that waken
   The silent seas.

---

17. the days, locked in each other's arms,
   seem still
   so that squirrels and colored birds
   go about at ease over
   the branches and through the air.

---

18. I am watching ants dig tunnels and bury themselves
   they go without water or love

---

19. Lady is sick,
   perhaps vomiting,
   perhaps laboring
   to the usual reign

---

20. Rain is sweet, brown hair;
   Distraction, music in passageways.
   Six o'clock.
   The time. Redeem
   The world and waking, wearing

---

21. Wipe your hand across your mouth, and laugh;
   The worlds revolve like ancient women
   Gathering fuel in vacant lots.

---

22. I should have been a pair of ragged claws
   Scuttling across the floors of silent seas.

---

23. patches of all
   save beauty
   the rigid wheeltracks.
   The round sun
   the bed.
   She smiles, Yes
   you please first
   then stays

   with herself alone
   and then dividing and over
   and splashed and after you are
   listening in her eyes

---

24. All along the road the reddish
   purplish, forked, upstanding, twiggy
   stuff of bushes and small trees
   with dead, brown leaves under them
   leafless vines—

---

25. Pray for those who are branches on forever

---

26. Like a sod of war;
   houses of small
   white curtains—
   Smell of shimmering
   ash white,
   an axe

---

27. By action or by suffering, and whose hour
   Was drained to its last sand in weal or woe,
   So that the trunk survived both fruit or flower;—

---

28. is a steady burning
   the road the battle's fury —
   clouds and ash and waning
   sending out
   young people,

The above 28-question poetic Turing test was administered to 16 human judges with varying degrees of computer and poetry experience and knowledge. The 13 adult judges scored an average of 59 percent correct in identifying the computer poem stanzas, 68 percent correct in identifying the human poem stanzas, and 63 percent correct overall. The three child judges scored an average of 52 percent correct in identifying the computer poem stanzas, 42 percent correct in identifying the human poem stanzas, and 48 percent correct overall.

The charts show the actual scores obtained by the 16 human judges as broken down by adult/child, computer experience, and poetry experience. As can be seen from the charts, there were no trends based on level of computer experience or poetry experience clearly discernible from this limited sample. The adults did score somewhat better than the children. The children scored essentially at chance level (approximately 50 percent) and the adults achieving slightly better than chance.

The next chart shows the number of correct and incorrect answers for each of the 28 poems or stanzas. While the adult judges scored somewhat better than chance (63 percent), their answers were far from perfect. The computer poet was able to trick the human judges much of the time. Some of the computer poems (numbers 15 and 28, for example) were particularly successful in tricking the judges.

We can conclude that this domain-specific Turing test has achieved some level of success in tricking human judges in its poetry-writing ability. A more difficult problem than writing stanzas of poetry is writing complete poems that make thematic, syntactic, and poetic sense across multiple stanzas. A future version of the Kurzweil Cybernetic Poet is contemplated that attempts this more difficult task. To be successful, the models created by the Cybernetic Poet will require a richer understanding of the syntactic and poetic function of each word.

Even the originally proposed Turing test involving terminal interviews is notably imprecise in determining when the computer has been successful in imitating a human. How many judges need to be fooled? At what score do we consider the human judges to have been fooled? How sophisticated do the judges need to be? How sophisticated (or unsophisticated) does the human foil need to be? How much time do the judges have to make their determination? These are but a few of the many questions surrounding the Turing test. (The article "A Coffeehouse Conversation on the Turing Test" by Douglas Hofstadter in chapter 2 provides an entertaining discussion of some of these issues). It is clear that the era of computers passing the Turing test will not happen suddenly. Once computers start to arguably pass the Turing test, the validity of the

Adult scores on poem stanzas composed by a computer
(13 adults, % correct)

| Level of poetry experience | Level of computer experience | | | |
	Little	Moderate	Professional	Average
Little	56	44, 69, 75	63, 75	64
Moderate	50, 56, 63	56, 63	75	61
A lot			25	25
Average	56	61	59	59

Children's scores on poem stanzas composed by a computer
(3 children, % correct)

Scores	38, 50, 69
Average	52

Adult scores on poem stanzas composed by a human
(13 adults, % correct)

| Level of poetry experience | Level of computer experience | | | |
	Little	Moderate	Professional	Average
Little	83	58, 58, 100	50, 67	69
Moderate	60, 67, 83	58, 83	92	74
A lot			25	25
Average	73	72	59	68

Children's scores on poem stanzas composed by a human
(3 children, % correct)

Scores	33, 42, 50
Average	42

Adult scores on all poem stanzas (13 adults, % correct)

| Level of poetry experience | Level of computer experience | | | |
	Little	Moderate	Professional	Average
Little	68	50, 64, 86	57, 71	66
Moderate	55, 61, 71	61, 68	82	66
A lot			25	25
Average	64	66	59	63

Children's scores on all poem stanzas (3 children, % correct)

Scores	39, 43, 61
Average	48

Numbers of right and wrong answers for each poem stanza

Poem stanza	No. right	No. wrong	Computer or human poem stanza
1	9	7	computer
3	11	5	computer
4	8	8	computer
6	9	7	computer
8	11	5	computer
11	11	5	computer
13	8	8	computer
14	10	6	computer
15	6	10	computer
16	10	6	computer
19	9	7	computer
20	12	4	computer
23	9	7	computer
25	8	8	computer
26	11	5	computer
28	6	10	computer
Average	58%	42%	
2	9	7	human
5	9	7	human
7	9	7	human
9	13	3	human
10	8	8	human
12	10	6	human
17	9	7	human
18	14	2	human
21	11	5	human
22	11	5	human
24	11	5	human
27	8	8	human
Average	64%	36%	
Overall average	61%	39%	

tests and the testing procedures will undoubtedly be debated. The same can be said for the narrower domain-specific Turing tests.

We have not yet reached the point at which computers can even arguably pass the originally proposed terminal-interview type of Turing test. This test requires a computer to master too many high-level cognitive skills in a single system for the computer of today to succeed. As Dan Dennett points out in his article, the unadulterated Turing test is *far* more difficult for a computer to pass than any more restricted version. We have, however, reached the point where computers *can* successfully imitate human performance within narrowly focused areas of human expertise. Expert systems, for example, are able to replicate the decision-making ability of human professionals within an expanding set of human disciplines. In at least one controlled trial, human chess experts were unable to distinguish the chess-playing style of more sophisticated computer chess players from that of humans. Indeed, computer chess programs are now able to defeat almost all human players, with the exception of a small and diminishing number of senior chess masters. Music composed by computer is becoming increasingly successful in passing the Turing test of believability. The era of computer success in a wide range of *domain-specific* Turing tests is arriving.

Note

1. Four human poets were used: three famous poets (Percy Bysshe Shelley, T. S. Eliot, and William Carlos Williams) and one obscure poet (Raymond Kurzweil). In the case of the famous human poets, stanzas were selected from their most famous published work. In all cases, the stanzas selected did not require adjacent stanzas to make thematic or syntactic sense. The computer stanzas were written by the Kurzweil Cybernetic Poet after it had read poems written by these same human authors. The answers are as follows:
Poem stanza 1 written by the Kurzweil Cybernetic Poet after reading poems by William Carlos Williams
Poem stanza 2 written by William Carlos Williams
Poem stanza 3 written by the Kurzweil Cybernetic Poet after reading poems by Percy Bysshe Shelley

Poem stanza 4 written by the Kurzweil Cybernetic Poet after reading poems by T. S. Eliot and Percy Bysshe Shelly

Poem stanza 5 written by Raymond Kurzweil

Poem stanza 6 written by the Kurzweil Cybernetic Poet after reading poems by T. S. Eliot, Raymond Kurzweil, Percy Bysshe Shelley, and William Carlos Williams

Poem stanza 7 written by T. S. Eliot

Poem stanza 8 written by the Kurzweil Cybernetic Poet after reading poems by Raymond Kurzweil and T. S. Eliot

Poem stanza 9 written by William Carlos Williams

Poem stanza 10 written by Raymond Kurzweil

Poem stanza 11 written by the Kurzweil Cybernetic Poet after reading poems by Raymond Kurzweil and T. S. Eliot

Poem stanza 12 written by William Carlos Williams

Poem stanza 13 written by the Kurzweil Cybernetic Poet after reading poems by Percy Bysshe Shelley

Poem stanza 14 written by the Kurzweil Cybernetic Poet after reading poems by T. S. Eliot and Percy Bysshe Shelley

Poem stanza 15 written by the Kurzweil Cybernetic Poet after reading poems by Raymond Kurzweil and William Carlos Williams

Poem stanza 16 written by the Kurzweil Cybernetic Poet after reading poems by T. S. Eliot, Raymond Kurzweil, Percy Bysshe Shelley, and William Carlos Williams

Poem stanza 17 written by William Carlos Williams

Poem stanza 18 written by Raymond Kurzweil

Poem stanza 19 written by the Kurzweil Cybernetic Poet after reading poems by T. S. Eliot, Raymond Kurzweil, Percy Bysshe Shelley, and William Carlos Williams

Poem stanza 20 written by the Kurzweil Cybernetic Poet after reading poems by Raymond Kurzweil and T. S. Eliot

Poem stanza 21 written by T. S. Eliot

Poem stanza 22 written by T. S. Eliot

Poem stanza 23 written by the Kurzweil Cybernetic Poet after reading poems by Raymond Kurzweil and William Carlos Williams

Poem stanza 24 written by William Carlos Williams

Poem stanza 25 written by the Kurzweil Cybernetic Poet after reading poems by T. S. Eliot, Raymond Kurzweil, Percy Bysshe Shelley, and William Carlos Williams

Poem stanza 26 written by the Kurzweil Cybernetic Poet after reading poems by Raymond Kurzweil and William Carlos Williams

Poem stanza 27 written by Percy Bysshe Shelley

Poem stanza 28 written by the Kurzweil Cybernetic Poet after reading poems by William Carlos Williams

This is the year 1300. Brother Giorgio, scholar-monk, has the task of making a map of Australia, a big island just south of India. Maps must record what is known about the places they represent, and Giorgio has been told about a strange Australian animal, ratlike, but much bigger, with a long thick tail and a pouch. He draws it, and it comes out like this:

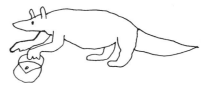

A year later a world traveller is visiting Giorgio's monastery, and he tells our cartographer that he has the animal wrong. For one thing, it isn't *carrying* a pouch; the pouch is actually part of its belly. (Mercy! says Giorgio.) For another, it doesn't walk on all fours like a rat but on its hind legs, which are much bigger than its front legs. Giorgio redraws his picture:

But the tail rests on the ground. Giorgio tries once more. The traveller screws up his face in concentration, his eyes closed. I don't think that's quite right, he finally says , but I guess it's close enough.

Harold Cohen

Brother Giorgio's Kangaroo

Harold Cohen is a professor in the Visual Arts Department at the University of California at San Diego. In recent years he and AARON have been shown at the San Francisco Museum of Modern Art, the Stedelijk Museum in Amsterdam, the Tate Gallery in London, the Brooklyn Museum, the Ontario Science Center, and the Boston Science Museum. He has lectured widely on the subject of AARON, and AARON has reciprocated by providing Cohen with several thousand drawings, including designs for a series of mural projects. Cohen describes their relationship as symbiotic. Cohen is regarded as a pioneer in the application of AI to the visual arts.

The year is 1987. AARON, a computer program, has the task of drawing some people in a botanical garden—not just making a copy of an existing drawing, you understand, but generating as many unique drawings on this theme as may be required of it. What does it have to know in order to accomplish such a task? How could AARON, the program, get written at all?

The problem will seem a lot less mystifying, though not necessarily less difficult, if we think of these two stories as having a lot in common. AARON has never seen a person or walked through a botanical garden. Giorgio has never seen a kangaroo. Since most of us today get most of our knowledge of the world indirectly and heavily wrapped in the understanding of other people from grade school teachers to television anchor persons, it should come as no surprise that a computer program doesn't have to experience the world itself in order to know about it.

How did Giorgio know about kangaroos before the visitor started to refine his knowledge? He had been told that the animal was ratlike, but how much good would that have done him if he had never seen a rat? For people, the acquisition of knowledge is cumulative, as it clearly has to be. Nothing is ever understood from scratch. Even the new-born babe has a good deal of knowledge "hard-wired" before it starts. And when we tell each other about the world, it isn't practical or even possible to give a full description of something without referring to some thing else. That's as true for computer programs as it is for people. There is an important difference, though. For people, knowledge must eventually refer back to experience, and people experience the world with their bodies, their brains, their reproductive systems, which computers don't have.

Harold Cohen, computer artist. (Photo by Lou Jones)

Athletes, a hand-colored, computer-generated drawing by Harold Cohen. (Photo by George Johnson)

From the *Bathers* series of hand-colored, computer-generated drawings by Harold Cohen. (Photo by George Johnson)

With this in mind, we might guess that AARON's knowledge of the world and the way AARON uses its knowledge are not likely to be exactly the same as the way we use what we have. Like us, its knowledge has been acquired cumulatively. Once it understands the concept of a leaf cluster, for example, it can make use of that knowledge whenever it needs it. But we can *see* what plants look like, and AARON can't. We don't need to understand the principles that govern plant growth in order to recognize and record the difference between a cactus and a willow tree in a drawing. AARON can only proceed by way of principles that we don't necessarily have. Plants exist for AARON in terms of their size, the thickness of limbs with respect to height, the rate at which limbs get thinner with respect to spreading, the degree of branching, the angular spread where branching occurs, and so on. Similar principles hold for the formation of leaves and leaf clusters. By manipulating these factors, AARON is able to generate a wide range of plant types and will never draw quite the same plant twice, even when it draws a number of plants recognizably of the same type. Interestingly enough, the way AARON accesses its knowledge of plant structure is itself quite treelike. It begins the generation of each new example with a general model and then branches from it. "Tree" is expanded into "big-tree/small-tree/shrub/grass/flower," "big tree" is expanded into "oak/willow/avocado/wideleaf" (the names are not intended literally), and so on, until each unique representation might be thought of as a single "leaf," the termination of a single path on a hugely proliferating "tree" of possibilities.

Obviously, AARON has to have similar structural knowledge about the human figure, only more of it. In part, this extra knowledge is demanded by AARON's audience, which knows about bodies from the inside and is more fussy about representations of the body than it is about representations of trees. In part, more knowledge is required to cope with the fact that bodies move around. But it isn't only a question of needing *more* knowledge; there are three different *kinds* of knowledge required—different, that is, in needing to be represented in the program in different ways.

First, AARON must obviously know what the body consists of, what the different parts are, and how big they are in relation to each other. Then it has to know how the parts of the body are articulated: what the type and range of movement is at each joint. Finally, because a coherently moving body is not merely a collection of independently moving parts, AARON has to know something about how body movements are coordinated: what the body has to do to keep its balance, for example. Conceptually, this isn't as difficult as it may seem, at least for standing positions with one or both feet on the ground. It's just a matter of keeping the center of gravity over the base and, where necessary, using the arms for fine tuning.

We started by asking what AARON would need to know to carry out its task. What I've outlined here constitutes an important part of that necessary knowledge, but not the whole of it. What else is necessary? Let's go back to Giorgio. Has it struck you that whatever Giorgio eventually knew about the relative sizes of the kangaroo's parts and its posture, he had been told nothing at all about its *appearance?* Yet his drawings somehow contrived to look sort of like the animal he thought he was representing, just as AARON's trees and people contrive to look like real trees and real people.

That may not seem very puzzling with respect to Giorgio. In fact, it may seem so unpuzzling that you wonder why I raise the issue. Obviously, Giorgio simply knew how to draw. I suspect that most people who don't draw think of drawing as a simple process of copying what's in front of them. Actually it's a much more complicated process of regenerating what we know about what's in front of us or even about what is *not* in front of us: Giorgio's kangaroo, for example. There's nothing simple about that regeneration process, though the fact that we can do it without having to think much about it may make it seem so. It is only in trying to teach a computer program the same skills that we begin to see how enormously complex a process is involved.

A hand-colored, computer-generated drawing of figures and trees with rocks in the foreground, by Harold Cohen. (Photo by Linda Winters)

How do humans learn to draw? To some degree, obviously, we learn about drawing by looking at other peoples' drawings. That's why we are able to identify styles in art, and why most of the drawings coming out of Giorgio's monastery would have had a great deal in common and be distinguishably different from, say, the drawings made in a Zen Buddhist temple in Japan. At the same time, all children make very much the same drawings at any one stage of cognitive development *without* learning from each other or from adults. They don't need to be told to use closed forms in their drawings to stand for solid objects, for example. That equivalent is universal; all cultures have used closed forms to stand for solid objects. In short, knowledge of drawing has two components. Giorgio learned about style, about what was culturally acceptable and what was not, from his peers. But before cultural considerations ever arise, drawing is closely coupled to seeing—so closely coupled that we might guess all major visual modes of representation in human history to have sprung directly from the nature of the cognitive system. So Giorgio never had to be told how to draw or how to read drawings. He could see.

He had to be told about kangaroos, not about how to draw kangaroos. Knowledge of drawing isn't object specific; if Giorgio

Black and White Drawing, a computer-generated drawing of figures and trees, by Harold Cohen. (Photo by Becky Cohen)

could draw a kangaroo, he could also draw an elephant or a castle or an angel of the Annunciation. If one can draw, then anything that can be described in structural terms can be represented in visual terms. That generality suggests that rather than thinking of knowledge of drawing as just one more chunk of knowledge, we should think of it as a sort of filter through which object-specific knowledge passes on its way from the mind to the drawing.

Like Giorgio, AARON had to be told about things of the world. Unlike Giorgio in having no hard-wired cognitive system to provide a built-in knowledge of drawing, it had to be taught how to draw as well, given enough of a cognitive structure (the filter just referred to) to guarantee the required generality. If provided with object-specific knowledge, AARON should be able to make drawings of those objects without being given any additional knowledge of drawing.

AARON's cognitive filter has three stages, of which the first two correspond roughly to the kinds of knowledge described above in relation to the human figure: knowledge of parts, articulation, and coordination. The third stage generates the appearance of the thing being drawn. Neither of the first two stages results in anything being drawn for the viewer, though they are drawn in AARON's imagination, so to speak, for its own use. First AARON constructs an articulated stick figure, the simplest representation that can embody what it knows about posture and movement. Then around the lines of this stick figure it builds a minimal framework of lines embodying in greater detail what it knows about the dimensions of the different parts. This framework doesn't represent the surface of the object. In the case of a figure, the lines actually correspond quite closely to musculature, although that is not their essential function. They are there to function as a sort of core around which the final stage will generate the visible results. Quite simply, AARON draws around the core figure it has "imagined." Well, no, not quite so simply. If you look at one of its drawings, it should be clear that the final embodying stage must be more complicated than I have said if only because AARON apparently draws hands and leaves with much greater attention than it affords to thighs and tree trunks.

AARON's embodying procedures are not like the preliminary edge-finding routines of computer vision, which respond to changes in light intensity without regard to what caused them. AARON is concerned with what it is drawing and continuously modifies the performance of this final stage with respect to how much knowledge has already been represented in the core figure. The greater the level of detail already present, the more AARON relies upon it and the closer to the core the embodying line is drawn. Also, greater detail implies more rapidly changing line directions in the core, and AARON ensures a sufficiently responsive embodying line by sampling its relation to the core more frequently.

Nothing has been said here about how AARON's knowledge of the world is stored internally, about how its knowledge of drawing is actually implemented, or about its knowledge of composition, occlusion, and perspective. AARON's success as a program stands or falls on the quality of the art it makes, yet nothing much has been said about art and nothing at all about the acculturated knowledge of style, for which its programmer, like Giorgio's monastic peers, must admit or claim responsibility. All the same, there are interesting conclusions to be drawn from this abbreviated account. It should be evident, for example, that the knowledge that goes into the making of a visual representation, even a simple one, is quite diverse. I doubt that one could build a program capable of manipulating that knowledge and exhibiting the generality and flexibility of the human cognitive system other than by fashioning the program as an equivalent, artificial cognitive system. If nothing much has been said about art, it is because remarkably little of the program has anything to do with art: it constitutes a cognitive model of a reasonably general kind, and I even suspect that it could be adapted to other modes without too much distortion. But the lack of art specificity isn't as puzzling as it may seem at first glance. The principal difference between artists and nonartists is not a cognitive difference. It is simply that artists make art and nonartists don't.

Charles Ames (Photo by Lou Jones)

Charles Ames

Artificial Intelligence and Musical Composition

Charles Ames studied
mathematics and musical
composition at Pomona College,
musical history at Oxford, and
composition at the State
University of New York at
Buffalo, where he received his
Ph.D. in 1984. He is currently
Director of the Kurzweil
Foundation's Automated
Composition Project, which
created the Cybernetic
Composer, an AI based software
system that composes music
in a variety of popular styles.
Ames is regarded as a pioneer in
the application of AI to music
composition.

How Can Intelligent Computers Help Compose Music?

Consider the young music student who wants to learn about chord progressions. Traditionally, he would be required to try out some progressions of blocked chords on the piano. But if keyboard skills were lacking, the student would have to put off learning about progressions for several years until these skills had been acquired. With an appropriately designed expert music-tutoring program, such a student might type a harmonic plan into a computer and have the program quickly derive a full-blown realization with rhythmic chords, a bass line, even a drum part.

Consider the musical theorist who desires a truly empirical means of testing assumptions about how music is made. Whereas in the past, musical theories have as often as not been accepted on the basis of intrinsic logical elegance, AI techniques now make it possible to implement a theory as a program whose products may be evaluated empirically against authentic musical examples.

Consider also the composer of soundtracks for recorded dramas, documentaries, and advertisements. It is already common to rely heavily on standard background patterns when producing large volumes of precisely timed and thematically consistent music in the face of production deadlines. It is very likely that tomorrow's professional composers will be relying even more heavily on software modules for accompaniments and perhaps even for leads.

For the art-music composer, artificial intelligence provides a mechanical extension to human intellect. For example, a composer might wish to set up criteria for comparing solutions to a compositional problem (e.g., the problem of choosing pitches for a melody) and then let the computer evaluate every possible solution in order to choose the best one.

Perhaps the most radical potential for automated composition resides in the capability of a single program to generate many distinct pieces of music. One might think of such a program as a new kind of "record" that plays a different piece every time. The possibilities range from the mundane, such as computer-composed music for fast-food restaurants and supermarkets, to the sublime. We have now seen the appearance of a new type of composer: the metacomposer, who shapes compositional principles as fluently as traditional composers have shaped compositional material. For such artists the originality of the music will clearly depend on the originality and subtlety of the programming.

The situations described above are not at all speculative. All of them can become realities within five years if developers are willing to expend the necessary energy to make them happen. Indeed, successes already achieved indicate that creativity can be modeled with much greater precision than conventional wisdom once suggested. A number of programs of my own are already producing credible emulations of human-composed music in popular styles, and a program by Kemal Ebcioglu (see figure) for harmonizing chorales in the style of J. S. Bach has managed on occasion to duplicate Bach's solutions exactly.[1] Although the styles in all of the current programs have been rather narrowly defined, the insights they provide lead toward ever-more-general representations of compositional procedure.

A Survey of Decision-Making Tactics and Compositional Strategies

From their beginnings in the mid 1950s up until a few years ago, programs for automatic musical composition have been developed by a small handful of musicians working in relative isolation from the mainstream AI movement and, for that matter, from other computer-music fields such as digital sound synthesis.[2] This isolation has been harmful to the extent that most early practitioners were ignorant of recursion, linked data structures, and basic search methods. Yet it has also led to some unique approaches that might have been passed over by a more orthodox methodology.

Statistics Up to the late 1960s the most pervasive decision-making tactics were statistical. Statistics provided an economical way of representing *trends* of musical behavior from short-term dependencies (e.g., how often G^7 chords are followed by C major chords, by A minor chords, etc.) to long-term distributions of material (e.g., the relative usage of scale degrees). A statistical composing program from these early years selected options randomly; the options assigned the greatest statistical weight by the programmer had the greatest probability of selection.[3]

The basic compositional strategy for these programs was "left-to-right," with some "top-down" influences. Wholly left-to-right programs selected musical details directly as they were to appear in the music, conditioning later decisions upon earlier choices. Many programs had top-down influences to the extent that they divided the music into sections and then chose the details of each section in a left-to-right manner. Each new section was distinguished by unique parameters that affected the statistical makeup of these details. One of the composer-programmers of this period even interposed subsections between sections and details.

Rote Processing When computers went on-line during the 1970s, a number of musicians took advantage of the new technology to develop programs that would process musical information either in real time or within the context of an interactive dialog. The desire for rapid interaction led to an emphasis on procedures that were simple enough that they could respond at the touch of a button, and especially to an emphasis on rote operations on themes. Among the most familiar of these operations are those that come from traditional

Kemal Ebcioglu's 1984 program for harmonizing chorales guided its left-to-right note selection with top-down planning of harmonic goals and subgoals. For a few chorale tunes Ebcioglu's program managed to duplicate Bach's own solutions exactly. However, the solution shown here is more typical. (Courtesy of Kemal Ebcioglu)

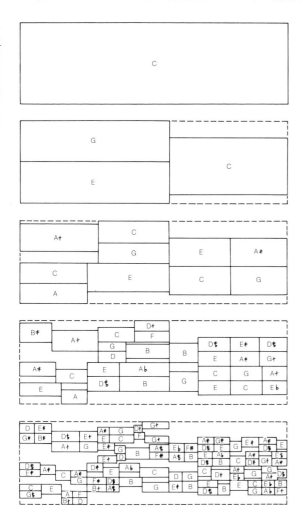

Top-down productions begin with a very general archetype of a musical form and recursively elaborate upon this archetype until a complete description of the musical details has been obtained. (From Charles Ames, "Crystals: Recursive Structures in Automated Composition," *Computer Music Journal* 6 [1982], no. 3; courtesy of Charles Ames)

In one stage of producing Charles Ames's *Protocol* for solo piano, the composer decided that groupings of chords (themselves computer-composed) would be most appropriate to the musical spirit of the piece when constituent pairs of chords shared few degrees of the chromatic scale in common. The program scored the left group less highly than the right one because chords 7 and 13 on the left share five out of seven degrees. (From Charles Ames, "Protocol Motivation, Design, and Production of a Composition for Solo Piano," *Interface: Journal of New Music Research* 11 [1982], no. 4: 226)

canons and fugues. They include transposition (playing a theme with every note shifted equally up or down in pitch), inversion (playing a theme upside down), retrograde (playing a theme backwards), and diminution (decreasing the note lengths in a theme so that it goes by twice as quickly). The user of one of these programs would typically build a composition using a "bottom-up" strategy: he could either enter an originally composed theme or have one randomly generated, he might then derive variations on this theme using one or more operations, and he could cut up, paste together, and edit this thematic material in various ways until a whole composition had been produced.

Searches Intelligent composing programs such as Ebcioglu's and my own are distinguished from statistical and rote programs by their ability to *discriminate* among solutions to musical problems. The secret behind this ability lies in constrained-search techniques drawn directly from AI.[4] As an illustration of how a constrained search works, consider the problem of composing a melody when the rhythm, range, harmonic context, and style are given. Solving this kind of problem means choosing a pitch for each note in a way that conforms to the given style. Yet although one might have a very good idea how a melody in this style should *sound*, that's not sufficient understanding to develop a program. One must be able to describe the style in terms meaningful to a computer.

To do this, the programmer needs to make some general observations concerning how pitches behave in the style. He might observe, for example, that the melodies *never* move in parallel octaves or fifths with the bass, that they *always* employ chord roots at cadence points, that nonchord tones *always* resolve by step to chord tones, and that dissonant chord tones (e.g., chord sevenths) *always* resolve downward by step in the next chord. The programmer might observe as well that scalewise motion is *preferable* to leaps, that leading tones *tend* to lead upward, and that the different scale degrees are *usually* in balance. Observations characterized by such words as "never" and "always" can be implemented directly as

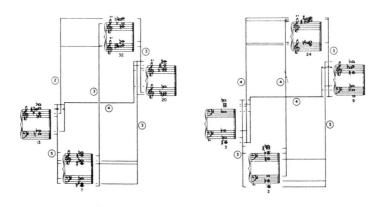

constraints. Constraints keep a search within the musical ballpark. Though many are drawn from the rules of musical pedagogy, they should in no sense be taken as standards of "good music." If a melody violates a constraint, we cannot say it is wrong, only that it is out of style. The basic mechanism for composing a melody subject to constraints is as follows: For each note, the search steps through the available pitches until it finds one conforming to all the constraints. Whenever it finds an acceptable pitch, it moves forward to an uncomposed note; whenever it exhausts all the pitches available to a given note, it backtracks to the most recent composed note that caused a conflict, revises this note's pitch, and begins working its way forward again.

Observations characterized by words such as "tend," "preferable," and "usually" generally cannot be implemented as hard-and-fast constraints. The only alternative is to bias the search toward solutions with more preferable attributes. Should the programmer wish to encourage scalewise motion, for example, the search might be designed to try neighboring pitches before others. If such motion is more critical at the end of a phrase than at the beginning, it may be more effective to start at the end of the phrase and work backward; this will prevent early phrase-notes from forming a context that precludes scalewise motion later on. The official AI jargon for this kind of procedural biasing is "heuristic programming."

The abilities to seek the more preferable solutions, to apply constraints, and to backtrack in the face of an impasse are the basic advantages that constrained searches have over statistical and rote procedures. The method applies just as well to musical problems radically different from melody writing, such as top-down generation of musical details from forms. Searches are a complement, not a substitute, for statistical and rote procedures. If the programmer desires to maintain a sense of unpredictability within given stylistic bounds, then randomness can be incorporated into the mechanism by which the search assigns priorities to options. If long-term statistical distributions are of concern, then a search can be designed to favor options that best conform to these distributions. Finally, if rote thematicism is desired, then themes generated by such operations as the ones described above can themselves be treated as options by searches evaluating many different thematic variations to choose the best one for the context.

One trade-off with searches is that their ability to backtrack renders them *compositional* rather than *improvisational*. A composer in a pinch can throw things out, but an improvisor cannot turn back the clock on music that has already been played. As a result, it is impractical to implement search-driven compositional procedures in real time. Another trade-off is that one must be willing

to interact with a search-driven composing program on its own terms. Interactive feedback from a search consists at present of three phases: setting up constraints and preferences, leaving the search to do its thing (searches are most effective when left to run with a minimum of interference from the human user), and accepting or rejecting the results. If the results are unsatisfactory, one might make adjustments in the constraints and preferences before running the search again.

Conclusions

The entry of AI into musical creativity is by no means as radical as it might seem to laymen in view of the active and long-standing tradition of composer involvement with technical theory about music. This tradition reaches from Pythagoras and Aristoxenus of antiquity, through numerous medieval writers, through such Renaissance theorists as Gioseffe Zarlino and Thomas Morley, through the Baroque composer Jean-Philippe Rameau, through more recent composers as diverse as Arnold Schoenberg, Henry Cowell, Paul Hindemith, Harry Partch, and Joseph Schillinger to contemporaries such as Pierre Boulez and Iannis Xenakis. Each has built stylistic models from constraints, preferences, and procedural descriptions of the act of making a composition, not as a way of codifying what went on in the past, but as an intellectual aid to his craft. However, the ability of AI programs to generate actual music from such models brings them out of the speculative realm and makes them accessible to all: to composers seeking an augmented working environment in which the content, form, and style of entire compositions can be adjusted at the touch of a button; to theorists wishing to determine where the strengths and weaknesses of new models lie; and to music students seeking expert assistance in the realization of their musical projects.

Notes

1. Ebcioglu's results have great implications for pedagogy, since Bach's chorales are the paradigm for traditional studies in musical harmony.
2. Programs for automatic music composition began in 1956 with Hiller and Isaacson's Illiac Suite, created slightly later than the first chess-playing and theorem-proving programs. An exhaustive survey of composing programs, replete with names, musical examples, and bibliography, is available in Charles Ames, "Automated Composition in Retrospect: 1956–1986," *Leonardo: Journal of the International Society for Science, Technology, and the Arts*, 1987.
3. These statistical composing programs anticipated by some 20 years the current AI fashion for "fuzzy logic."
4. Rigorous searches have also been used by Stanley Gill, Marilyn Thomas, and possibly David Levitt.

Michael Lebowitz

All Work and No Play
Makes HAL a Dull Program

Michael Lebowitz was a
faculty member from 1980 to
1987 in the Department of
Computer Science at Columbia
University. His primary
research interests lie in the
areas of machine learning,
natural-language processing,
memory organization, and
cognitive modeling. He also led
a research group at Columbia
that designed intelligent
information systems that could
read, remember, and learn from
natural-language text. He has
published many articles in a
wide range of areas in artificial
intelligence. He is currently a
vice president of the Analytical
Proprietary Trading unit at
Morgan Stanley & Co. in New
York City.

Introduction

The clear majority of applied work in artificial intelligence (AI) has
involved practical problems in such areas as business, medicine,
defense, and so forth. This is as it should be, but there is also room for
the application of AI to the arts. AI has the potential to allow the
creation of compelling new entertainment forms and to improve the
creative process in existing art forms. In addition, such work can lead
to important new insight into the creative process. In this article I
shall discuss how AI can be applied to the area of story telling: both
how it can be used in intelligent tools for writers and how it might
lead to new forms of intelligent, interactive stories where a writer/
creator can intimately involve a reader/user in the story.

At Columbia University my colleagues and I investigated
the problem of developing systems that generate extended stories,
those that continue over time. We selected the domain of "interpersonal melodrama," one example of which is television soap opera.
We felt that this is a good domain to look at both for scientific and
practical reasons. Television melodramas are watched by large
numbers of people over very long periods of time. From a scientific
point of view, stories based on interpersonal relations have received
much less attention than those that are more action oriented. Finally,
stories of this sort combine complexity and creativity with a good
deal of stereotypy. They help us get a handle on which parts of
creativity are not too creative. Here is an outline of events in a typical
melodrama (NBC's "Days of Our Lives").

Liz was married to Tony. Neither loved the other, and
indeed, Liz was in love with Neil. However, unknown to either Tony
or Neil, Stephano, Tony's father, who wanted Liz to produce a

Michael Lebowitz (Photo by Betsy
Malcolm)

grandson for him, threatened Liz that if she left Tony, he would kill Neil. Convinced that he was serious by a bomb that exploded near Neil, Liz told Neil that she did not love him, that she was still in love with Tony, and that he should forget about her. Neil was eventually convinced and married Marie. Later when Liz was finally free from Tony (because Stephano had died), Neil was not free to marry her, and their troubles went on.

As part of our research we developed a simple, prototype story-telling program, Universe. The program can create sets of characters appropriate for interpersonal melodrama and can generate simple plot outlines of about the complexity of this outline using the characters that it generates.[1]

Assisting Writers

In the immediate future it is unlikely that we will be able to create programs that produce melodrama with the richness of human writers. However, we can hope to provide tools to assist in the creation of such works. In particular, I feel that the creation of an automated assistant that can suggest possibilities to a writer is well within reach. We can create programs that help a writer develop meaningful characters and that suggest plot possibilities. I shall illustrate a simple version of one such program below.

In a sense, we can view a program of the sort I envision as a kind of intelligent story editor, the next step beyond text editing. Such a system would have to be embedded in a complete development system that would also keep track of the history of the story over time. The display below illustrates the kind of behavior I have in mind. It shows Universe running in an interactive mode in which instead of creating characters itself, it prompts a user for the relevant information. Items in italics were entered by the user.

Enter sex (m/f): *m*
Enter name: *John Jones*
Enter age group (ya/ma/old): *ma*
Cycling person John Jones
Enter year of next life event (cr = quit): *1970*
Next event (m/d): *m*
Try to find spouse in universe (u/n): *n*
Enter name (list):
Cycling marriage between John Jones and Kathy Cole
Enter year of next marriage event (cr = quit):
Beginning finish up for John Jones
Pick traits (p/r): *p*
Possible traits to set: wealth, promiscuity, competence, niceness, self-confidence, guile, naivete, moodiness, physical attractiveness, intelligence

Enter trait and value (cr = quit): *niceness 3*
Enter trait and value (cr = quit): *self-confidence 4*
Enter trait and value (cr = quit): *intelligence 3*
Enter trait and value (cr = quit):
Optimal occupations are: sleazy-doctor
Enter occupation:
Selecting: sleazy-doctor
Trait (intelligence 3) already satisfied
For trait (self-confidence 4)
Choices (life-guard, swinger, big-eater): *swinger*
For trait (niceness 3)
Choices (taxidriver):

The AI aspects of the program arise in the representation of the information and where the program suggests possibilities for the character being created. These suggestions are intended to help make the character more believable and interesting by appropriately motivating the characteristics that the user wants. In the first section of the display, Universe prompts the user for a few vital statistics of the character being created: sex, name, age group (young adult, middle age, old). These are used to begin filling in a frame for the character John Jones.[2] In all cases, if no answer is provided, the program will pick one.

After getting the basic facts, the program begins to "cycle" the character's life, that is, to prompt the user for major life events, concentrating on marriages, divorces, the births of children, and deaths. Other parts of the program allow other sorts of history to be added. Note that by including past events and not just the current state of the world, Universe helps the user build a consistent and coherent set of characters. In the display the user specified that John Jones had gotten married (m) in 1970. The program knew that a spouse was necessary, and the user let the program pick her name (Kathy Cole).

The final section of the display is the most AI oriented. It involves filling in a personality profile for the character. Universe knows about a variety of different personality traits. Here the user suggests a set of values to describe John Jones: he is not very nice, is moderately self-confident, and moderately intelligent. Just specifying values, however, is not very satisfying, so the program assists the user in selecting various prototypical character types that will help explain the trait values. It allows the user to either accept a proffered prototype or provide one. It suggests that sleazy doctor would be a character type that meshes with these traits. It also suggests other prototypes that help explain the traits. Between the program and the user they come up with a character that is a swinging sleazy doctor and taxidriver. Needless to say, the quality of the system's help depends on the quality of the prototype library. Such a description is the sort the writer would have to come up with anyway to make the character one a reader/user will believe.[3]

Tools like the one described here (with plot management included) can be of great use to writers of all sorts. They serve as partners by suggesting ideas but leave the real creativity to the writer. They will be particularly important in developing various kinds of interactive fiction but should also be of use in more traditional forms. One can easily imagine how an AI tool could greatly help the writers of a television serial that has been on the air for many years keep everything consistent and at the same time suggest new possibilities.

Personalized Stories

Beyond the creation of intelligent story-writing tools, the obvious next step in applying AI to story telling is the automatic generation of stories. With human writers available, it may not be clear why we would want to do this (beyond the goal of understanding how creative processes work). The reason is the same as for many other tasks: the application of AI techniques to story telling will lead to an art form that is personalized and interactive. Imagine a soap opera with characters that are exactly the kind you would find most interesting, not necessarily a set of characters that you create (after all, we are not all writers), but one molded to your own tastes. In addition, imagine that you can influence the unfolding of events—not necessarily directing the characters in detail, but influencing the story in more subtle ways. It is a compelling vision of a new fictional form. Stories in textual form should be exciting, and the addition of graphics and other computer-manipulated images should make it even more impressive.

Stories of this kind will evolve from two current lines of entertainment: interactive computer games and role-playing games. Several manufacturers are currently producing interactive computer games in which users work their way through a branching story, typically solving a series of puzzles along the way. Many such games are quite intriguing. However, all the various outcomes have to be handcrafted by a programmer and as a result are relatively limited in the world to be explored. In addition, programmers have tended to focus on action-oriented and mystery domains with little character development.

Such role-playing games as Dungeons and Dragons come closer to the model I have in mind. Here with a human game master a story can move through a very wide range of possibilities. Yet the game master is required, and these games too have tended to be quite

action oriented (even though at least one was modeled after a television melodrama).

It is important to note that what we are after is more than simply games. We seek the depth and quality of fiction along with the interactive nature of games. Although the stories themselves would be generated by computer, the knowledge bases from which they worked—information about people, places, and plot devices—would presumably be built by human writers, although not by specifying every plot turn, as is done with interactive games.

To date there has not been a great deal of work on automatic story generation. Perhaps the best known work is that done by Jim Meehan in the mid 1970s when he developed Tale-Spin, a program that told children's stories in the style of Aesop's fables.[4] Other workers have also been working on AI story telling.[5] Our own work on Universe has taken us to the point where it can generate simple plot outlines by applying planning techniques to author goals.[6]

Below is a simple plot outline created by Universe. It uses characters created by the automatic version of the interactive program described in the previous section after being given as input an author goal, here to "churn" a relationship, that is, to keep two people in love from being happy together (a staple of melodrama). Since Teddy Bryks, the husband of one of the lovers, has an evil father, Universe selects a plot fragment that involves the father's threatening the women not to betray her husband (which is loosely based at an abstract level on the outline above). The various elements of this plot are expanded using other plot fragments. By the time the first fragment ends, the spurned lover, Steven Kades, is involved with someone else, which creates further complications. Universe runs through a couple more of its library of ways to keep people apart.

The setting generated by the program as part of a set of characters is as follows: Nadine Burton is married to Teddy Bryks but is in love with Steven Kades. Gerald Bryks is Teddy's father, and none too nice a guy. (Elaborative comments are enclosed in parentheses.)

Churn Nadine and Steven

Gerald Bryks threatens Nadine Burton Bryks: forget it (her affair with Steven). Nadine Burton Bryks tells Steven Kades that she doesn't love him. Norma Ryan Bryks is worried about Steven Kades. Linda Einbinder Kimball seduces Steven Kades. Joe Kimball decides to expose Gerald Bryks. Joe Kimball tells the world about Gerald Bryks (and his evil doings). Nadine Burton Bryks and Teddy Bryks get divorced. Teddy Bryks tries to seduce Nadine Burton Bryks. Steven Kades gets frustrated (by this). Steven Kades tells Nadine Burton Bryks that he doesn't love her. Nadine Burton Bryks seduces Steven Kades.

This story is certainly not intended to be great fiction. However, our program has shown us that even with a very limited library of plot fragments (about 60), through interactions of plots and characters, Universe can produce some rather clever plot outlines. A much larger library (perhaps by two orders of magnitude) should be practical and would be able to produce a large number of interesting stories, particularly if there are techniques to automatically create new fragments.[7] No small part of the effect is based on the same trick that authors of standard fiction use: the reader's imagination will enhance what is actually presented.

Our work on Universe has also given us some interesting insights into creativity, which I can only touch upon here. It appears that many parts of creativity involve primarily determining clever ways to apply previous situations (or abstracted versions of them) to new settings. In story telling, it is rarely necessary to create whole new ideas: one can take old ideas and combine them in new ways or apply new twists to them. This is certainly evident in television melodrama and is by no means bad: even plot turns that are familiar in the abstract can be quite interesting when applied to new situations. Although there are many other aspects to creativity, a crucial part is storing previous experiences in a way that they can be efficiently retrieved and applied in the future. This applies to both story telling and general day-to-day planning.[8]

We are just beginning the process of automatically generating stories. There are many problems involved in creating plot outlines, and beyond them there are issues in language generation, knowledge representation, knowledge-state assessment (who knows what when), memory organization and access, and user interaction, among many others that must be dealt with to achieve the sort of system envisioned at the beginning of this section.

It is no doubt appropriate for most AI work to address practical considerations. Indeed, most of our own research does just that. However, people should know that AI will enhance other aspects of their lives than just the workplace. AI can help creative people make better use of their talents and create interesting and entertaining new art forms. After all, if AI is going to help improve productivity, then it had better also help fill the leisure time thus created—and it can.

Notes

1. For further details, see M. Lebowitz, "Creating Characters in Story-Telling Universe," *Poetics* 13 (1984): 171–194; and M. Lebowitz, "Story-Telling as Planning and Learning," *Poetics* 14 (1985): 483–502.

2. For more on frames, see M. Minsky, "A Framework for Representing Knowledge," in P. H. Winston, ed., *The Psychology of Computer Vision* (New York: McGraw-Hill, 1975).

3. For further details on Universe's methods of character creation, see M. Lebowitz, "Creating Characters in a Story-Telling Universe," *Poetics* 13 (1984): 171–194.

4. See J. R. Meehan, "The Metanovel: Writing Stories by Computer," Yale University Department of Computer Science, technical report 74, 1976.

5. See N. Dehn, "Memory in Story Invention," *Proceedings of the Third Annual Conference of the Cognitive Science Society* (Berkeley, Calif., 1981), pp. 213–215; M. Yazdani, "Generating Events in a Fictional World of Stories," University of Exeter Computer Science Department, technical report R-113; and S. R. Turner and M. G. Dyer, "Thematic Knowledge, Episodic Memory, and Analogy in MINSTREL, A Story Invention System," *Proceedings of the Seventh Annual Conference of the Cognitive Science Society* (Irvine , Calif., 1985), pp. 371–375.

6. See M. Lebowitz, "Story-Telling as Planning and Learning," *Poetics* 14 (1985): 483–502.

7. See M. Lebowitz, "Story-Telling as Planning and Learning," *Poetics* 14 (1985): 483–502.

8. See K. J. Hammond, "Planning and Goal Interaction: The Use of Past Solutions in Present Situations," *Proceedings of the Third National Conference on Artificial Intelligence* (Washington, D.C., 1983), pp. 148–151.

Roger Schank and Christopher Owens

The Mechanics of Creativity

Roger C. Schank directs the Institute for the Learning Sciences at Northwestern University, where he is also John Evans Professor of Electrical Engineering and Computer Science, Psychology, and Education. Previously, he was Chairman of the Computer Science department at Yale University and Director of the Yale Artificial Intelligence Project. In addition, he was Assistant Professor of Linguistics and Computer Science at Stanford University. Schank holds a Ph.D in Linguistics from the University of Texas at Austin. He is the founder of two businesses, Compu-Teach, an educational software company, and Cognitive Systems, a company specializing in natural language processing. An internationally acclaimed researcher in artificial intelligence, Schank is the author of numerous articles and books, including *Dynamic Memory; Scripts, Plans, Goals, and Understanding* with Robert Abelson; and *The Cognitive Computer* and *The Creative Attitude* with Peter Childers. Christopher Owens is engaged in AI research at the Artificial Intelligence Lab at Yale University, where he is currently completing a Ph.D. His primary interests are studying the organization of human memory and applying the principles thereof to the task of making machines smarter. His work focuses on people's ability to reuse old knowledge to solve new problems, specifically the kind of frozen, culturally shared knowledge typified by the planning advice given in proverbs and other folk adages.

What exactly is creativity? Could a machine ever be creative? These are questions psychologists, philosophers, and AI researchers would all like to be able to answer. But what kind of answers are we looking for? The search for a rigorous philosophical definition of creativity has been overworked, and we don't intend to further pursue that course here. On the other hand, redefining the question in AI terms and applying AI research methods might result in a new and useful kind of answer, or at least an interesting set of new questions to consider.

A persistent criticism of AI work has centered around arguments like, "By its very nature, a machine could never *really* be creative." Since a basic assumption underlying work in computer science is that a machine can perform any task that can be described via sufficiently specific rules, people who make statements like the above mean that no rules can ever be found that will account for creativity and other quintessentially human behavior, that there is something inherently mystical in these abilities that cannot be expressed via rules and procedures. Or else they might mean that even if such a set of rules and procedures could be found, a machine that was obeying them would only seem to be creative. Its behavior, they say, would be a kind of elaborate parlor trick; it would be achieving its effect merely by fooling us.

But as AI researchers and cognitive scientists, our work is based upon the assumption that rules and procedures underlying human behavior *can* be found. Our job is to define problems in such a way as to maximize our chances of succeeding in this endeavor. Our goal is to come up with an *algorithmic* definition of creativity, a set of processes and steps that can account for the kind of creative thinking that we observe in people. Although the idea of a human or machine exhibiting creativity by following a set of rules seems on the face to be a contradiction, this is not necessarily so. If we can agree on some kinds of behavior that constitute creative thinking and can develop an algorithmic model that accounts for these behaviors, then we have an algorithmic theory of creativity and hence a first step toward creative machines. Whether or not a philosopher would agree that the resulting machine truly embodied creativity is almost irrelevant to us: building machines that act in ways that *appear* to be creative would be a significant enough step to undertake.

Creativity is often associated with problem solving, science, and the arts. People often view creative thinking as something out of the ordinary, as a mode of reasoning in which completed thoughts suddenly spring to mind without being cued, thoughts perhaps having nothing at all to do with what the thinker was working on at the time the thought occurred. Often people implicitly assume that creativity represents some divine, unconscious, or other inspiration out of the control of one's ordinary thought processes. Actual case studies of scientific and artistic creativity, however, support the idea that creativity springs not from any mystical source but from a certain set of cognitive skills. There is no principled distinction between creative and less creative thinking other than the degree to which this set of skills is applied. Highly creative individuals simply have these skills better developed than do the less creative. What, then, are these cognitive skills? How are they used? How can we program a computer to exhibit them? These are questions that we can study more fruitfully than the open-ended type of question, "What is Creativity?" with which this chapter opened.

In our view, the basic cognitive skill underlying creativity is the ability *to intelligently misapply* things. A creative solution to a problem is one that uses an object, technique, or tool in a useful and previously undiscovered way. A creative work of art, similarly, might use some material or image in a new way. A creative piece of scientific research might involve, for example, applying a principle from one field to a problem in another. At Yale we are studying the cognitive skills underlying one particular type of creative behavior, the creation of novel explanations for unexpected events. Explanation is a kind of problem solving in which the problem is of a mental nature: "How can I connect this new and strange piece of knowledge with the rest of my knowledge so that it all makes sense," or "What pattern of events do I know about into which I can fit this new fact."

Of course, by this definition, many kinds of understanding can be seen as explanation, in that all understanding consists of integrating new facts into existing knowledge. But what we are interested in here is the kind of explanation that requires conscious work, the explanation of events that are at first puzzling. This kind of explanation may require searching for a missing piece of knowledge, or it may require finding some previously unseen causal connection. Often an explanation can be found by seeing one object or event as similar to another in a way that was not previously noticed, in other words, by making up and using a novel analogy. For example, when we asked people in the Yale AI lab to try to explain the unexpected death of the successful three-year-old race horse Swale, one student was reminded of the death of Jim Fixx, the runner. He reasoned that Swale was like Fixx in that both participated in regular strenuous activity, and that possibly Swale, also like Fixx, had a congenital heart defect.

This kind of reasoning from prior examples is very important to our approach to explanation. Although an understanding system could conceivably explain each new situation by reasoning from first principles, chaining together all the rules and pieces of knowledge it needed to build the entire explanation from small elements, this probably does not happen very often. One reason is that

Roger Schank and Christopher Owens (Courtesy of Charles Martin of the Yale AI Lab)

the computational complexity of this task is unreasonably large. Another is that people seem to be able to use remindings and analogical reasoning to construct explanations: they can use the same explanation over and over to cover a range of similar and thematically related situations.

For a second example of this kind of reasoning, consider the folk use of proverbs, which can be viewed as a kind of extremely abstract pattern used by people to explain unfamiliar situations in a familiar way. When someone standing in the rain beside his disabled car and wishing he had had that overdue tune-up analyzes the situation by saying "A stitch in time saves nine," he has placed the situation in a context in which knowledge about topics like prevention and the bad effects of not taking precautions is available. The causal reasoning represented within this proverb is available without the effort of building an analysis or explanation from scratch.

In a manner similar to the way people might use proverbs, our systems store and reuse old explanations using a knowledge structure called an Explanation Pattern, or XP. Like a proverb, an XP is a frozen piece of causal reasoning. Because it is designed to be retrieved, modified, and applied by a computer program, it has the following basic components:

A characterization of a set of situations to which it is likely to apply, for example, deaths of athletes

A characterization of a broader set of situations to which, even if it does not apply, it is likely to be at least relevant, for example, unexpected bad outcomes

A causally annotated description of the event being explained. For example: Running involves physical exertion. Physical exertion strains the heart. Straining the heart combined with a heart defect can cause a heart attack. A heart attack can cause death.

Since we are viewing explanation as a kind of problem solving, and since a creative solution to a problem is one that uses an object, technique, or tool in a useful and previously undiscovered way, a creative explanation is one that uses an XP in a novel and previously unencountered way. If the basic idea of an explanation system is to select a relevant XP from memory and apply it to a new episode, then the basic idea of a creative explanation system is to intelligently misapply XPs; to try, if no relevant XP can be found, to modify and apply an XP that, although at first seemingly irrelevant, might nevertheless bear some thematic relationship to the episode being explained.

The idea of using near misses is an important one. Often people associate creativity with a simple relaxation of constraints on retrieval and pattern matching, with some kind of random process by

which weird remindings can be generated. Creativity, according to this view, consists of being tolerant of inappropriate remindings, in being slow to discard an erroneous idea. But that tolerance is only half the process. Because processing power is finite, the key is to be intelligent about choosing *which* inappropriate XP to misapply. Creativity does not lie in floundering through memory, trying one randomly selected idea after the next; it lies in finding near misses that are reasonably close to the right idea and fixing them to fit.

This approach puts a large demand on memory, since the retrieval task is no longer simply to find the closest fit from among a library of XPs (which selection, by the way, is an important task itself, and we do not mean to denigrate its difficulty here). The task of memory is now to fail gracefully: to find the closest fit, or if a close fit is not available, to find a near miss that nevertheless captures some important and relevant aspects of the situation being explained. This kind of near miss is the most likely candidate for modification.

Along with a means for getting reasonable near misses, this approach also requires that the system, when presented with an inappropriate XP, be able to analyze what is wrong with it and to select an appropriate repair strategy based upon that analysis. The student who explained Swale's death in terms of Jim Fixx's knew that Jim Fixx was not a race horse, that the explanation would not directly apply without making the connection between a runner and a race horse. People do this so easily that we hardly think about it, yet the task is difficult. This modification of inappropriate XPs in order to adapt them to new situations, which we have been calling "tweaking," is central to being a creative explainer.

Our algorithm for creativity must therefore embody three processes: a means of searching through memory for applicable patterns that returns a reasonable set of near misses, a means of evaluating the near misses and seeing what is wrong with them, and a means of modifying those inappropriate patterns to suit the current situation. Of course, for any of this to work reasonably well, our creative machine must have a rich memory of facts, experiences, and relationships it can draw upon as starting points for new explanations. Searching for and adapting patterns is a reasonable strategy only if the library of patterns is large enough that the near misses will nevertheless have at least something in common with the episode being explained. Our fourth requirement, therefore, is to have a large and richly indexed memory of explanation patterns and other knowledge gained from experience. How these patterns are learned is another interesting problem to be attacked.

So we have transformed the questions "What is creativity?" and "Can a machine ever be creative?" into "What cognitive skills underlie creative behavior?" and "How can we program these skills into a computer?" Further refining the questions, we have discussed creativity, which at first seems mystical and quintessentially human, in terms of knowledge structures, search, retrieval, and adaptation, which seem quintessentially mechanistic. Creative explanation, we claim, is not so mysterious. It depends upon having a stock set of explanations, some heuristics for finding them at the right time, and some rules for tweaking them after they have been found. These problems are, of course, not as simple as this quick description might imply; each of them represents an important research area that is yet to be properly explored. Although trying to reduce creativity to mechanical processes might seem to be a kind of cheapening or demystification of human capabilities, that is not the case. The philosophy underlying AI research is that there must necessarily be mechanically understandable processes underlying intelligent behavior, and that our general purpose should be to deepen our understanding of human capabilities by defining and studying these mechanisms.

Visions of the Future

10

(Photo by Lou Jones)

Visions

I never think of the future, it comes soon enough.

Albert Einstein

What is possible we can do now, what is impossible will take a little longer.

A modern-day proverb

Every electronic product being sold today is obsolete.

Fred Zieber, Senior Vice President, Dataquest

The problems of the world cannot possibly be solved by skeptics or cynics whose horizons are limited by the obvious realities. We need men who can dream of things that never were.

John F. Kennedy

• Scenarios

Since the founding of the computer industry almost half a century ago, one of its most salient and consistent features has been change. Functionality per unit cost has been increasing exponentially for decades, a trend that shows no sign of abating. When I attended MIT in the late 1960s, thousands of students and professors shared a *single* computer, an IBM 7094 with 294,912 bytes of core storage (organized as 65,536 words of 36 bits each) and a speed of about 250,000 instructions per second. One needed considerable influence to obtain more than a few seconds of computer time per day. Today, one can buy a personal computer with ten times the speed and memory for a few thousand dollars. In *Metamagical Themas,* Doug Hofstadter cites an actual job that took 10 people with electromechanical calculators ten months to perform in the early 1940s, was redone on an IBM 704 in the early 1960s in 20 minutes, and now would take only a few seconds on a personal computer.[1] David Waltz points out that memory today, after adjustment for inflation, costs only one one-hundred millionth of what it did in 1950.[2] If the automotive industry made as much progress in the past two decades, a typical automobile today would cost about two dollars (the doubling of price performance every 22 months on average has resulted in an improvement factor of about 2,000 in 20 years; this is comparable to the difference between the 7094 of the late 1960s and a personal computer with a Intel 80386 chip today).[3] If we go back to the first relay-based computers, a personal computer today is nearly a million times faster at a tiny fraction of the cost. Many other examples of such progress abound.[4]

In addition to the basic power of computation as measured by speed and memory capacity, new hardware and software technologies have greatly improved our ability to interact with computer devices. Through the 1940s and 1950s most communication with computers was through boards with plug-in cables; through the 1960s and 1970s, with reels of punched paper tape, stacks of punched paper cards, and print-outs from line printers. Today the advent of high resolution graphic displays, the mouse, graphics tablets, laser printers, optical cameras, scanners, voice recognition, and other technologies have provided a myriad of ways for humans and machines to communicate.

Advances in software have harnessed these increasingly potent hardware resources to expand the productivity of most professions. Twenty years ago computers were used primarily by large corporations for transaction processing and by scientists (occasionally by computer scientists to explore the power of computing). Today most workers—professionals, office workers, factory workers, farmers—have many occasions to use methods that rely on the computer. I can recall that fifteen years ago even thinking about changing my company's business projections was regarded as a very serious endeavor; it would take the finance department days to grind through the numbers to examine a single scenario. Today with spreadsheet programs it is possible to consider a dozen alternative plans and determine their implications in less than an hour. Twenty years ago the only people interacting with computers were computer experts and a small cadre of students learning the somewhat arcane new field of computation. Today computers appear ubiquitously on office desks, in kitchens, in play rooms, in grocery stores, and in elementary schools.

"The computer chip: inscribing worlds on grains of sand"—George Gilder (Photo by Dan McCoy of Rainbow)

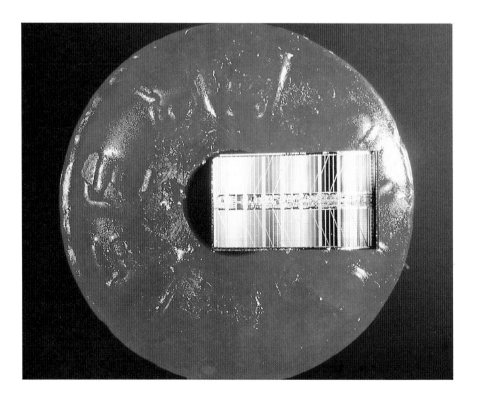

Computer-aided design (CAD) for computer chips. A chip with photo sensors being designed at Cal Tech using technology from Synaptics. (Photo by Dan McCoy of Rainbow)

Will these trends continue? Some observers have pointed out that an exponential trend cannot continue forever. If a species, for example, happens upon a hospitable new environmental niche, it may multiply and expand its population exponentially for a period of time, but eventually its own numbers exhaust the available food supply or other resources and the expansion halts or even reverses. On this basis, some feel that after four decades, exponential improvement in the power of computing cannot go on for much longer. Predicting the end of this trend is, in my view, highly premature. It is, of course, possible that we will eventually reach a time when the rate of improvement slows down, but it does not appear that we are anywhere close to reaching that point. There are more than enough new computing technologies being developed to assure a continuation of the doubling of price performance (the level of performance per unit cost) every 18 to 24 months for many years.

With just conventional materials and methodologies, progress in the next ten years, at least in terms of computing speeds and memory densities, seems relatively assured. Indeed, chips with 64 million bits of RAM (random access memory) and processor chips sporting speeds of 100 million instructions per second are on the drawing board now and likely to be available in the early 1990s. Parallel-processing architectures, some including the use of analog computation, are an additional means of expanding the power of computers. Beyond the conventional methods, a broad variety of experimental techniques could further accelerate these trends. Superconducting, for example, while challenging to implement in a practical way, has the potential to break the thermal barrier that currently constrains chip geometries. As I mentioned earlier, the resulting combination of smaller component geometries with the effective utilization of the third dimension could provide a *millionfold* improvement in computer power. A variety of new materials, such as gallium arsenide, also have the potential to substantially improve the speed and density of electronic circuits.[5] And optical circuits—computing with light rather than electricity—may multiply computing speeds by factors of many thousands.[6]

Will software keep up? It is often said that the pace of advances in software engineering and applications lags behind that of the startling advance of hardware technology. Advances in software are perhaps more evolutionary than revolutionary, but in many instances software techniques are already available that are just waiting for sufficiently powerful hardware to make them practical. For example, techniques for large-vocabulary speech recognition can be adapted to recognize continuous speech but require substantially greater computational speed. Vision is another application with the same requirement. There are many techniques and algorithms that are already understood but are waiting for more powerful computers to make them economically feasible.[7] In the meantime, our understanding of AI methods, the sophistication of our knowledge bases, the power of our pattern-recognition technologies, and many other facets of AI software continue to grow.

Where is all this taking us? People in the computer field are accustomed to hearing about the rapidly improving speed and density of semiconductors. People in other professions inevitably hear reports of the same progress. Numbing are the extremely small numbers used to measure computer timings and the enormous numbers used for memory capacity, time measured in trillionths of a second and memory in billions of characters. What impact are these developments going to have? How will society change? How will our daily lives change? What problems will be solved or created?

One can take several approaches in attempting to answer these questions. Perhaps most instructive is to consider specific examples of devices and scenarios that have the potential to profoundly change the way we communicate, learn, live, and work. These concrete examples represent only a few of the ways that computer and other advanced technologies will shape our future world. These examples are based on trends that are already apparent. In my view, it is virtually certain (barring a world calamity) that all of these scenarios will take place. The only uncertainty is precisely *when*. I will attempt to project current trends into the future and estimate when we are likely to see each example.

Obviously, the further into the future we look, the more uncertain the timing of these projections become. The history of AI is replete with examples of problems that were either underestimated or (less often) overestimated. A great irony in early AI history is that many of the problems thought most difficult—proving original theorems, playing chess—turned out to be easy, while the "easy" problems—pattern-recognition tasks that even a child can perform—turned out to be the most challenging.[8] Nonetheless, I believe that we now have a more sophisticated appreciation of the difficulty of many of these problems, and so I will attempt the thankless task of making specific projections. Of course, by the time you discover that my predictions were altogether wrong, it will be too late to obtain a refund for the purchase price of this book.

As I mentioned, these projections are based on trends that are already evident. What is most difficult to anticipate are *breakthroughs*. Any attempts to have predicted the future at the beginning of this century would have almost certainly overlooked the computer, as well as atomic energy, television, the laser, and indeed, most of electronics. After going through the scenarios, I shall discuss some possible breakthroughs that *may* result from current research. In the following chapter I offer a discussion of the overall impact these developments are likely to have on our educational, social, political, medical, military, and economic institutions.

The translating telephone

Koji Kobayashi, chairman of the powerful Japanese corporation NEC, has a dream. Someday, according to Kobayashi, people will be able to call anyone in the world and talk, regardless of the language that they speak. The words will be translated from language to language in real time as we speak.[9]

Three technologies are required to achieve Kobayashi's dream: automatic speech recognition (ASR), language translation (LT), and speech synthesis (SS). All three exist today, but not nearly in sufficiently advanced form. Let us consider each of these requirements.

ASR would have to be at the "holy grail" level, that is, combining large (relatively unrestricted) vocabulary, accepting continuous speech input, and providing speaker independence (no training of the system on each voice). Conceivably, the last requirement could be eased in early versions of this system. Users of this capability may be willing to spend fifteen minutes or so training the system on their voice. Such enrollment would be required only once. Combining the first two elements—large vocabulary and continuous speech—will take us to the early to mid 1990s. Adding speaker independence will take us another several years.

LT requires only the ability to translate *text*, not speech, since ASR technology would be translating speech input into written language. The LT capability would

The translating telephone.

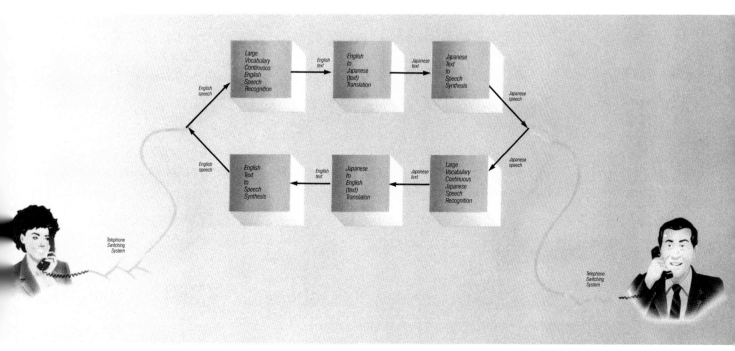

not require literary-quality translations, but it would have to perform unassisted. LT systems today require human assistance. Completely automatic LT of sufficient quality will probably become available around the same time that the requisite ASR is available. It should be noted that every pair of languages requires different software (going from French to English is a different problem from going from English to French). While many aspects of translation will be similar from one set of languages to another, LT technology will vary in quality and availability according to the languages involved.

SS is the easiest of the three technologies Kobayashi requires. In fact, it is available today. While not entirely natural, synthetic speech generated by the better synthesizers is quite comprehensible without training. Naturalness is improving, and SS systems should be entirely adequate by the time the necessary ASR and LT systems are available.

Thus, we can expect translating telephones with reasonable levels of performance for at least the more popular languages early in the first decade of the next century. With continuing improvements in performance and reductions in cost, such services could become widespread by the end of that decade. The impact will be another major step in achieving the "global village" envisioned by Marshall McLuhan (1911–1980) over two decades ago.[10] Overcoming the language barrier will result in a more tightly integrated world economy and society. We shall be able to talk more easily to more people, but our ability to misunderstand each other will remain undisturbed.

The intelligent assistant

You are considering purchasing an expensive item of capital equipment and wish to analyze the different means of financing available. Issues to consider are your company's current balance sheet, other anticipated cash flow requirements, the state of various financial markets, and future financial projections. You ask your intelligent assistant to write a report that proposes the most reasonable methods to finance the purchase and analyzes the impact of each. The computer engages you in sufficient spoken dialogue to clarify the request and then proceeds to conduct its study. In the course of its research, it accesses the balance sheet and financial projections from the data bases of your company. It contacts the Dow Jones data base by telephone to obtain information on current financial markets. It makes several calls to other computers to obtain the most recent financing charges for different financial instruments. In one case, it speaks to a human to clarify certain details on a lease-repurchase plan. It speaks with your company's vice president of marketing to obtain her level of confidence in achieving the sales projections for the following two years. It then organizes and presents the information in a written report complete with color charts. The report is presented to you the following day, since it took that long to reach the two humans involved. (Had it been able to conduct the research through communication only with other computers, it would have required only a few minutes.) Other services provided by your computerized assistant include keeping careful track of your schedule, including planning your travel from one appointment to another. The system plans your work for you, doing as much of it itself as it is capable of and understanding what portion of it you need to do yourself.

When we shall see the above system depends on how intelligent an assistant we would like to have. Crude forerunners exist today. Large-vocabulary ASR has been integrated with natural-language understanding and data-base-management programs to provide systems that can respond to such commands (posed by voice) as, Compare the sales of our western region to our three largest competitors. Such systems are, of course, highly limited in their problem-solving ability, but efforts to integrate ASR with data-base access have already begun.

The most challenging aspect of the vision is problem solving, having sufficient commonsense knowledge and reasoning ability to understand what information is required to solve a particular problem. Required are expert systems in many areas of endeavor that are less narrowly focused than the expert systems of today. One of the first intelligent assistants is likely to be one that helps get information from data bases through telecommunications.[11] It has become clear to a number of software developers that a need exists to improve substantially the ease of accessing information from such data-base systems as Compuserve, Delphi, The Source, Dialog, Dow Jones, Lexis, Nexis, and others. Such data-base systems are greatly expanding the volume and diversity of information available, but most persons do not know where to find the appropriate information they need. The first generation of office-assistant programs are now being developed that know how to obtain a broad variety of information without requiring precisely stated requests. I expect that within several years such systems will be generally available, and some of them will take ASR for input.

Thus, in the early to mid 1990s we shall see at least part of the above vision in use: flexible access to information from increasingly varied information services around the world, accessed by systems that understand human speech as well as the syntax and (at least to some extent) the semantics of natural language. They will support their own data bases and be able to access organization-specific knowledge. You will be able to obtain information in a flexible manner without having to know which data-base service has what information or how to use any particular information utility. As the 1990s progress, these systems will be integrated with problem-solving expert systems in many areas of endeavor. The level of intelligence implied in the above scenario describing a capital-equipment purchase will probably be seen during the first decade of the next century.

The world chess championship

As noted earlier, the best machine chess players are now competing successfully at the national senior-master level, regularly defeating all but about 700 players.[12] All chess machines use some variant of the recursive algorithm called minimax, a strategy whose computational requirements are multiplied by some constant for each additional move ahead that is analyzed. Without a totally new approach, we thus need to make exponential progress in computational power to make linear gains in game-playing performance (though we are indeed making exponential progress in hardware). The analysis I gave before estimated that the requisite computer power to achieve world-championship chess playing should become available between 9 and 54 years from now. This estimate was based on the continuing gains anticipated in the speeds of individual microprocessors. If we factor in the increasing popularity of

An endangered species? Two human world chess champions, Gary Kasparov (right) and Anatoly Karpov, battle it out in 1986. The best human chess playing has remained relatively constant in performance, while computer chess playing is rapidly improving. How much longer will the world chess champion be a human? (Supplied by AP/Wide World Photos)

parallel-processing architectures, the result will be much closer to the short end of this range. Some of the other scenarios in this section require significant advances in both hardware power and software sophistication. In my view, the ability of a machine to play championship chess is primarily a function of the former. Some of the possible breakthroughs in electronic hardware discussed below will be directly applicable to the chess issue. For example, if we are successful in harnessing the third dimension in chip fabrication (that is, building integrated circuits with hundreds or thousands of layers of active circuitry rather than just one), we will see a major improvement in parallel processing: hundreds or thousands of processors on a single chip. Taking into consideration only anticipated progress in conventional circuit-fabrication methodologies and continued development of parallel-processing architectures, I feel that a computer world chess champion is a reasonable expectation by the end of the century.

What will be the impact of such a development? For many, such as myself, it will simply be the passing of a long anticipated milestone. Yes, chess is an intelligent game (that is, it requires intelligence to play well), but it represents a type of intelligence that is particularly well suited to the strengths of early machine intelligence, what I earlier called level-2 intelligence (see "The Recursive Formula and Three Levels

The march of machine intelligence toward the world chess championship. Computers are improving in their chess-playing prowess. In 1987 HiTech defeated a series of national senior masters who were rated at over 2,400. Computers now have less than 400 points to go to capture the world championship. (Data from *The Computer Museum Report* [Boston], summer-fall 1987, p. 7)

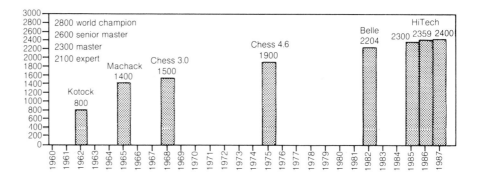

of Intelligence"). While level-3 intelligence will certainly benefit from the increasing power of computer hardware, it will also require substantial improvements in the ability of computers to manipulate abstract concepts.

Defenders of human chess playing often say that though computers may eventually defeat all human players, computers are not able to use the more abstract and intuitive methods that humans use.[13] For example, people can eliminate from consideration certain pieces that obviously have no bearing on the current strategic situation and thus do not need to consider sequences of moves involving those pieces. Humans are also able to draw upon a wealth of experience of previous similar situations. However, neither of these abilities is inconsistent with the recursive algorithm. The ability to eliminate from consideration branches of the expanding tree of move-countermove possibilities not worth pursuing is an important part, called pruning, of any minimax program. Drawing upon a data base of previous board positions is also a common strategy in the more advanced chess programs (particularly in the early game). It is estimated that human chess masters have memorized between 20,000 and 50,000 chess boards.[14] While impressive, it is clear that this is again an area where machines have a distinct edge. There is little problem in a computer mastering millions of board positions (each of which can have been analyzed in great depth in advance). Moreover, it is feasible for computers to modify such previously stored board positions to use them even if they do not precisely match a current position .

It may very well be that human players deploy methods of abstraction other than recalling previous board positions, pruning and move expansion. There is little evidence, however, that for the game of chess such heuristic strategies are inherently superior to a simple recursive strategy combined with massive computational power.[15] Chess, in my view, is a good example of a type of intelligent problem solving well suited to the strengths of the first half century of machine intelligence. For other types of problem solving (level-3 problems), the situation is different.

Not everyone will cheerfully accept the advent of a computer chess champion. Human chess champions have been widely regarded as cultural heroes, especially in the Soviet Union; we regard the world chess championship as a high intellectual achievement. If someone could compute spreadsheets in his head as quickly as (or faster than) a computer, we would undoubtedly regard him as an amazing prodigy, but not as a great intellect (in fact, he would actually be an idiot savant). A computer chess championship is likely to cause a watershed change in how many observers view machine intelligence (though perhaps for the wrong reasons). More constructively, it may also cause a keener appreciation for the unique and *different* strengths (at least for the near future) of machine and human intelligence.

The intelligent telephone-answering machine

The intelligent telephone assistant answers your phone, converses with the calling party to determine the nature and importance of the call (according to your instructions), interrupts you if necessary, and finds you in an emergency. The latter may become relatively easy once cellular-phone technology is fully developed. If cellular phones become compact and inexpensive enough, most people would be able to carry them, perhaps in their wristwatches. This raises some interesting issues of privacy. Many people like the ability to be away from their phones; we do not necessarily want to be accessible to phone calls at all times. On the other hand, it could be considered irresponsible to be completely unavailable for contact in the event of an emergency. But addressing this issue will be more a matter of evolving social custom than artificial intelligence.

The other aspects of the above scenario require the same machine skills as the intelligent assistant: two-way voice communication, natural-language understanding, and automated problem solving. In some ways this application may be more challenging than the office assistant. For a cybernetic assistant that we interact with, many people would be willing to spend time learning how to use such technology if it really helped them to accomplish their work. We might not mind if it failed to handle every interaction gracefully, so long as it provided an overall productivity gain. On the other hand, we might set a higher standard for a machine intended to interact with our friends and associates.

The cybernetic chauffeur

When will computers drive our cars? Without major changes in the methods of traffic control, the advent of the self-driving car is not likely for a long time. Unlike character recognition, factory vision, and similar tasks that involve limited visual environments, driving on existing highways requires the full range of human vision and pattern-recognition skills. Furthermore, because the consequences of failure are so serious, we would demand a high level of performance from such a system before relying on it. (On the other hand, with 50,000 traffic deaths each year on American highways, the human standard of performance is far from perfect.)

Yet there is a simpler form of the cybernetic chauffeur that is easier to build and could still accomplish a sharp reduction in driving fatalities as well as substantially reduce the tedium of driving. If specially designed sensors and communication devices were placed in major thoroughfares, cars could communicate with the road as well as with other cars. They could then be placed on automatic pilot. Highways would essentially become electronic railways that our cars could join and leave. The communication system required would be similar to the complex one already in place for cellular phones. Algorithms built into each car and into the roads would maintain safe distances between cars and would handle a variety of situations.[16] Although no specific system has been developed, the underlying technology exists today to deal with the steady-state situation of cars driving on a highway and maintaining proper speed and distance. But the situation gets more complicated when several other contingencies are considered. First, we need to be able to get our car *onto* a computer-controlled road. Presumably, we would drive to an access road, where our computer driver would lock onto the road's communication system, which would take over (in conjunction with the intelligence of our own car computer). Getting *off* the road is perhaps trickier. The system has to consider the possibility that the driver has fallen asleep or is otherwise not ready to resume manual control. The best protocol might be for the system to bring the car to a halt at an exit position at which point the human driver would be expected to take over. Machine intelligence would also have to deal with possibilities of hardware failure—not just of the computer itself, but also of the engine, tires, and other parts of the vehicle. Furthermore, the designers of such systems will also have to consider the possibility of people or animals straying onto the road.

Even with all of these complications, from a technical standpoint, intelligent roads represent a substantially easier problem than creating an automatic driver that can cope with traffic situations as they currently exist. One major nontechnical barrier to creating an intelligent road system, however, is that it requires a large measure of cooperation between car manufacturers and the government agencies that manage our roads (and drivers). It is not an innovation that can be introduced to a small number of pioneering users; it needs to be implemented *all at once* in at least some roads and in all cars intending to access such roads. Presumably, cars not equipped with such automatic guidance equipment would not be allowed on intelligent roads. Again, cellular phone technology is similar: it was not feasible until both the portable phone equipment and the overall computerized communication systems were in place. Still, I would expect such a system to be introduced gradually. At first it would be featured on one or a few major highways on an experimental basis. If successful, it would spread from there.

The technology to accomplish this should be available in the first decade of the next century. But because political decision making is involved, it is difficult to predict when it will receive priority sufficient to warrant implementation. Though cellular-phone technology also involved the coordination of a complex system, it has grown rapidly because it created an entrepreneurial opportunity.

The more advanced scenario of the completely driverless car will take us well into the first half of the next century. Another approach might be to forget roads altogether and replace them with computer-controlled flying vehicles that can ascend and descend vertically. There is, after all, much more space in the three-dimensional open air than there is on our one-dimensional roads. There are already plans in place to install a satellite-based collision-avoidance system that will dramatically reduce airplane collisions by the end of the century. The flying vehicles envisioned here would be the size of today's cars and would be even easier to use.[17]

Invisible credit cards and keys

During the 1990s we shall see highly reliable person-identification systems that use pattern-recognition techniques applied to fingerprint scanning and voice patterns. Such systems will typically combine the recognition of a personal attribute (a finger-print or voice pattern) with a password that the user types in. The password prevents a misrecognition from causing a problem. The recognition system prevents unauthorized access by a thief who acquires someone's password.

Today we typically carry a number of keys and cards to provide us with access to, and use of, our homes, cars, offices, and a broad variety of financial services. All of these keys and cards could be eliminated by the widespread adoption of reliable person-identification technologies. The acceptance of this technology is likely to be hastened by the loss of confidence in hand-written signatures caused by the explosion of electronic publishing.

Unfortunately, this type of technology is also capable of helping Big Brother track and control individual transactions and movements.

Instant ASICs

One of the remarkable recent innovations in hardware technology is the advent of the application-specific integrated circuit (ASIC), in which an entire complex electronic system is placed on a single inexpensive chip. The advent of the ASIC has provided products that are complex, diverse, customized and highly miniaturized. As Allen Newell points out in the article following this chapter, one might regard it as an almost magic technology: once an ASIC is developed, it provides enormous computational power at very low cost, takes up almost no space, and uses almost no electricity. The major barrier to greater deployment of this technology is the very long and expensive engineering cycles required to design such chips. The promise of *instant* ASICs is the ability to design an integrated circuit as easily as one writes a high-level computer program and, once designed, to have the actual chip available immediately.

The development of instant-ASIC technology is a major goal of the U.S. Department of Defense. Aside from its obvious military applications, it will also greatly accelerate the availability of innovative consumer products. Just as the difficulty of programming the early computers was quickly recognized as a major bottleneck, so is the difficult design process behind today's advanced chips. Indeed, the latter is receiving intense attention from all of the major players in the semiconductor industry. It is expected that in the early 1990s designers will be able to write chip programs (whose output is a piece of silicon) as easily and as quickly as computer programs.[18] The availability of instant-ASIC technology will eliminate for most purposes what little difference remains today between hardware and software engineering. It will accelerate the trend toward knowledge as the primary component of value in our products and services.

Artificial people and the media of the future

Rather than describe the vision I have in mind, I shall approach the idea of artificial people by starting with what is feasible today. Consider the artificial creatures that we interact with in computerized games and educational programs. An early and prime example is Pac Man, an artificial creature capable of responding and interacting with us in certain limited ways. One might not consider Pac Man to be much of a creature, let alone an artificial *person*. It is kind of a cartoon caricature of a fish with a limited repertoire of movements. Similarly, our range of emotional responses to it is very narrow, but it serves as a useful starting point.

Now consider what is feasible today, about a decade after the first introduction of Pac Man and other computer games. Reasonably lifelike video images of human faces can be completely synthesized and animated. Experiments at such advanced media laboratories as the MIT Media Laboratory have created completely synthetic yet realistic computer-generated images of human faces that can move and express a wide range of responses and emotions.

Let us imagine the next step: computer games and interactive educational programs that use synthetically generated human images. Rather than simply replaying a previously stored animated sequence, such programs would start with knowledge structures representing the concepts to be expressed and then translate each concept into spoken language and articulated facial and bodily movements. We would thus see and hear images—not prestored but created in real time—of people that are reasonably realistic. The motions and speech sounds would be computed as needed from an intent to express certain ideas and emotions. These artificial people would be responding to our actions within the context of the program.

Let us take several more steps. Add speech recognition and natural-language understanding. Add another several generations of improved image resolution and computing power for greatly enhanced visual realism. Add a more sophisticated problem-solving capability and more intelligence to provide greater subtlety of personality. Our artificial person is becoming more like a real person and less like Pac Man.

Applications would include very realistic games, movies that could include the viewer as a participant, and educational programs that would engage the student to learn from direct experience. Benjamin Franklin could take a child on a guided tour of colonial Philadelphia. Rather than a canned visual tour, this artificial Ben Franklin could answer questions, engage the child in dialogue, customize the tour on the basis of the child's own expressed interests, and otherwise provide an engaging experience. One could debate Abraham Lincoln or take Marilyn Monroe on a date. As with any creative medium, the possibilities are limited only by our imagination. As another example, the intelligent assistant could include a persona complete with appearance, accent, and personality. As time went on, such artificial persons would continue to grow in sophistication, realism, communicative and interactive ability and of course intelligence. Ultimately, they would develop a sense of humor.

It should be noted that personality is not an attribute that can be stuck on an intelligent machine. A personality is almost certainly a necessary byproduct of any behavior complex enough to be considered intelligent. People already speak of the personalities of the software packages they use. Shaping the personality of intelligent machines will be as important as shaping their intelligence. After all, who wants an obnoxious machine?

Such artificial persons could eventually use three-dimensional projected holographic technology (a method for creating three-dimensional images that do not require the use of special glasses). Currently, most holograms are static three dimensional pictures, although some use multiple images to provide a sense of movement. The MIT Media Lab has succeeded in creating the world's first three-dimensional holographic image generated entirely by computer.[19] The ability to project a hologram entirely from computer data is an important step in imaging technology. If a computer can project one hologram, then it can be made to project any number. Ultimately, with sufficient computer power, the images could be generated fast enough to appear realistically to move. The movements would not be prestored but rather *computed* in real time to respond to each situation. Thus, our artificial people can ultimately be lifelike, life-size, three-dimensional images with sufficiently high resolution and subtlety of movement to be indistinguishable from real people. These future computer displays will also be able to project entire environments along with the people.

There is concern today regarding the power of television to shape our views and to engage our emotions and attention. Yet television is essentially noninteractive, of low resolution, and flat. A medium that provided nearly perfect resolution and three-dimensional images and interacted with us in an intelligent and natural way would be far more powerful in its emotional impact, possibly too powerful for many (real) people. Harnessing and regulating these media of the future will undoubtedly be an area of much debate and controversy.

413

Adoption of the advanced media technologies described here will begin in the late 1990s and mature over the first half of the next century. Applications include entertainment, education, conducting business transactions, even companionship.

Another approach

An entirely different approach to the concept of artificial people lies in the area of robotics. Robots of the first generation, just like the first generation of computer-generated creature images (essentially pictures of robots), were neither intelligent nor realistic. We were as unlikely to mistake an early factory robot for a natural creature, let alone a person, as we were to mistake Pac Man for an image of a real animal. Here again, successive generations of technology have provided greater intelligence, subtlety, and naturalness. The primary drive for robotic technology lies in practical applications in the manufacturing and service industries. Admittedly, for most of these applications, resemblance to humans or to any other natural creature is of little relevance. Yet there will be applications for natural robots (sometimes called androids) as teachers, entertainers, and companions. Primitive robotic pets have already created a niche in the toy industry.

Creating a reasonably natural robotic imitation of a person is even more challenging than creating a convincing media image of a person. Any autonomous robot, humanoid or otherwise, has to be able to ambulate in a natural environment; this requires general-purpose vision and a high degree of fine motor coordination. Autonomous robots for exploring hostile environments, such as nuclear reactors and the surfaces of other planets, exist today. Routine use of autonomous robots in more conventional settings is likely to begin by the end of the century. Robots that are reasonably convincing artificial people will not appear until well into the next century.

Marvin Minsky has often said that a good source of insights into the realities of tomorrow's computer science can be found in today's science fiction. Isaac Asimov in his *Robots of Dawn* describes a society two centuries from now in which people live alongside a ubiquitous generation of robotic servants, companions, guards, and teachers. Two of the protagonists are a beautiful female scientist and her lover, a "male" "humaniform" robot.

Passing the Turing test

Scientists from the University of Clear Valley reported today that a computer program they had created was successful in passing the famous Turing test. Computer scientists around the world are celebrating the achievement of this long-awaited milestone. Reached from his retirement home, Marvin Minsky, regarded as one of the fathers of artificial intelligence (AI), praised the accomplishment and said that the age of intelligent machines had now been reached. Hubert Dreyfus, a persistent critic of the AI field, hailed the result, admitting that he had finally been proven wrong.

The advent of computers passing the Turing test will almost certainly not produce the above sort of coverage. We will more likely read the following:

Scientists from the University of Clear Valley reported today that a computer program they had created was successful in passing the famous Turing test. Computer scientists reached at press time expressed considerable skepticism about the accomplishment. Reached from his retirement home, Marvin Minsky, regarded as one of the fathers of artificial intelligence (AI), criticized the experiment, citing a number of deficiencies in method, including the selection of a human "judge" unfamiliar with the state of the art in AI. He also said that not enough time had been allowed for the judge to interview the computer foil and the human. Hubert Dreyfus, a persistent critic of the AI field, dismissed the report as the usual hype we have come to expect from the AI world and challenged the researchers to use him as the human judge.

Alan Turing was very precisely imprecise in stating the rules of his widely accepted test for machine intelligence.[20] There is, of course, no reason why a test for artificial intelligence should be any less ambiguous than our definition of artificial intelligence. It is clear that the advent of the passing of the Turing test will not come on a single day. We can distinguish the following milestones:

Level 1 Computers arguably pass *narrow* versions of the Turing test of believability. A variety of computer programs are each successful in emulating human ability in some area: diagnosing illnesses, composing music, drawing original pictures, making financial judgements, playing chess, and so on.

Level 2 It is well established that computers can achieve human or higher levels of performance in a wide variety of intelligent tasks, and they are *relied upon* to diagnose illnesses, make financial judgements, etc.

Level 3 A single computer system arguably passes the *full* Turing test, although there is considerable controversy regarding test methodology.

Level 4 It is well established that computers are capable of passing the Turing test. No reasonable person familiar with the field questions the ability of computers to do this. Computers can engage in a relatively unrestricted range of intelligent discourse (and engage in many other intelligent activities) at human or greater levels of performance.

We are at level 1 today. A wide range of expert systems can meet or exceed human performance within narrowly defined (yet still intelligent) areas of expertise. The judgements of expert systems are beginning to be relied upon in a variety of technical and financial fields, although acceptance in the medical area is much slower. Also, computer success in a variety of artistic endeavors is beginning to be at least arguably comparable.

Level 2 is within sight and should be attained around the end of the century. As expert systems grow in sophistication and achieve more natural human interfaces, we will begin to rely on their expertise as much as (if not more than) human society relies on their idiot savant forebears today.

We will probably begin to see reports of level 3, and newspaper articles similar to the second one given above, during the first decade of the next century, with continued controversy for at least several decades thereafter. The first reports will almost certainly involve significant limitations to Turing's originally proposed challenge. We are close to having the underlying technology (if not the actual pro-gram) today if we use sufficiently naive judges and provide them with relatively little time to make their determinations.

Level 4 is what Turing had in mind when he predicted success by the year 2000. Achieving this level is *far* more difficult than any of the other three. It requires advanced natural-language understanding, vast knowledge bases of commonsense information, and decision-making algorithms capable of great subtlety and abstraction. Turing's prediction, made in 1950, will almost certainly not be fulfilled by the year 2000. I place the achievement of level 4 sometime between 2020 and 2070. If this turns out to be the case, then Turing will have been off by a factor of between 1.4 and 2.4 (70 to 120 years versus his prediction of 50 years), which actually is not bad for such a longterm prediction. Of course, there is no assurance that *my* prediction will be any more accurate than Turing's.

As mentioned earlier (see *The Debate Goes On*), Hubert Dreyfus has indicated that he will concede that he was wrong (and has been wrong for his entire professional career) if he can be fooled as the human judge in a Turing test. Will this happen? If we assume that Dreyfus is in good health and further that continuing advances in bioengineering technology enable him (and the rest of us) to live longer than today's average life expectancy, then it is altogether possible. Personally, I would be willing to bet on it.

Conclusion

The above scenarios provide only a small sampling of the ways in which intelligent machines of the future can be expected to touch our lives. The computers of today, dumb as they are, have already infiltrated virtually every area of work and play. The bureaucracies of our society could hardly function without their extensive computer networks. If one adds just the sharply focused intelligence of the next phase of the age of intelligent machines to the already prodigious memory capacity and speed of today's computers, the combination will be a formidable one indeed. Our cars, watches, beds, chairs, walls, floors, desks, books, clothes, phones, homes, appliances, and virtually everything else we come into contact with will be intelligent, monitoring and servicing our needs and desires. The age of intelligent machines will not start on a particular day; it is a phenomenon that has started already, with the breadth and depth of machine intelligence growing each year. Turing predicted a time when people would talk naturally about machines thinking without expecting anyone to contradict them or be surprised. We are not there today, but the day will arrive so gradually that no one (except a few authors) will notice it when it does.

• Breakthroughs

Ralph Gomory, IBM's chief scientist, predicted in 1987 that within a decade the central processing units of supercomputers will have to be concentrated within a space of three cubic inches. The supercomputer core of the 1990s will be suitable for a laptop.
George Gilder

Hardware

As I noted earlier, a continuation of the same rate of exponential improvement in computer hardware appears likely for the foreseeable future, even if we consider only improvements using conventional approaches. Progress continues to be made in manufacturing integrated circuits with ever smaller geometries, which thus allows ever larger numbers of components to be placed on a single chip. As this book was being written, designers were passing the mark of several million transistors per chip.

The advent of parallel-processing architectures is also contributing to expanding the amount of computation we can devote to machine intelligence.[21]

At the same time, researchers are experimenting with a number of exotic materials and techniques that, if perfected, could provide a quantum leap in computing power. Rather than "just" the orderly doubling of computer power every 18 to 24 months, the possibility exists for a relatively sudden increase by a factor of thousands or even a million.

Probably the most promising is the potential for superconductors to virtually eliminate the thermal constraints that now govern chip geometries. As mentioned earlier, the heat generated by resistance in circuits limits how small we can build each transistor. But superconductors offer no electrical resistance, so superconducting circuits generate no heat. A superconducting integrated circuit could thus use transistors that are smaller by at least a factor of ten in each of the two dimensions, for a hundredfold improvement in the number of components. Since these components would also operate ten times faster, the overall improvement is approximately one thousand. Furthermore, with the absence of heat, we could build a chip with a thousand layers of circuitry rather than just one. This use of the third spatial dimension provides another improvement factor of a thousand, for an overall potential improvement of one million to one.

The only problem so far is that no one yet knows a practical way to build tiny transistors using superconducting materials. Earlier attempts to harness superconducting integrated circuits, using a technology called Josephson junction, never reached commercial viability.[22] One of the problems with the earlier attempts was the need to cool the circuits to so near absolute zero that very expensive liquid helium had to be used to cool them. But recent advances in superconducting have provided materials that can provide superconducting at much higher temperatures, so liquid nitrogen, at less than one tenth the cost of liquid helium, can be used. There is even the possibility of developing materials that can provide superconductivity at room temperature, the Holy Grail of superconductivity. The latest materials exhibit considerable brittleness, however, which presents a major difficulty in creating the tiny wires needed.[23] While the challenges are formidable, the potential payoff of superconducting integrated circuits is so enormous that major efforts are underway on three continents (North America, Europe, and Asia).[24]

Another approach being explored is the development of circuits that use light instead of electricity. There are two potential advantages of light. First, light is faster. The speed of light is regarded as a fundamental speed limit that the universe is obliged to follow. Electricity in wires moves about one-third as fast. More important, laser light can contain millions of adjacent signals that each carry independent information. Thus, the potential exists to provide truly massive parallel processing, with each light signal providing a separate computational path. Optical techniques are already revolutionizing communications (with optical fibers) and memory (optical disks); the promise of optical computing would revolutionize computation itself.[25]

There are disadvantages, however, in that the types of computations that can be performed optically are somewhat limited. A massively parallel optical computing machine would be well suited for certain pattern-recognition tasks, particularly those using low-level feature detection, but it could not be easily adapted to conventional types of computing. For this, superconductivity appears more promising. A massively parallel computer using superconduction could provide an enormous number of parallel processors that could each use conventional software techniques.

A third, even more exotic approach is to build circuits using bioengineering techniques, essentially to *grow* circuits rather than to *make* them. Such circuits would be constructed of the same proteins that form the basis of life on earth. These organic circuits would be three-dimensional, just as circuits in the brains of natural living creatures are three-dimensional. They would be cooled in the same way that natural brains are cooled: by bloodlike liquids circulating through a system of capillaries. We would not build these circuits; they would grow in much the same way that the brain of a natural organism grows: their growth and reproduction would be controlled by genes made up of ordinary DNA. Although still at an early stage, significant progress has been made in developing such organic circuits. Wires and simple circuits have already been grown.[26]

Still another approach, called molecular computing, has substantial overlap with all three of the above techniques.[27] Molecular computing attempts to employ light and the finest possible grains of matter (for computing, probably molecules) to provide techniques for information manipulation and storage. The goal of molecular computing is massively parallel machines with three-dimensional circuitry grown like crystals.

As I mentioned, the objective of all of these investigations is to provide a great improvement in the capacity and speed of computation. It should be emphasized that the value of doing so is not primarily to speed up existing applications of computers. Speeding up the computation of a spreadsheet that now takes a few seconds to a few microseconds is of little value. The real excitement is in being able to solve important problems that have heretofore proved intractable. I discussed earlier the massive amount of computation required to emulate human-level vision. Because the amount of computation provided by the human visual system is not yet available in a machine, all attempts at machine vision to date have been forced to make substantial compromises. The enormous improvements in speed and capacity discussed above would provide the computational power needed to emulate human-level functionality.

Software

If three-dimensional superconducting chips or one of the other breakthroughs just described were perfected and computer hardware were suddenly to expand in capability by a factor of thousands or even a million, the impact on many problem areas would not be immediate. While substantial expansion of computing power is one of the requirements to master problems such as vision, there are other requirements as well. We also need continued refinement of our algorithms, greater ability to represent and manipulate abstractions, more knowledge represented in computer form, and an enhanced ability to capture and manipulate knowledge.

Two key points are worth making about potential improvements in computer technology. First, breakthroughs and software appear to me to be incompatible, particularly with regard to issues of machine intelligence. AI applications are so complex, and the requisite human-interface issues so demanding, that none of the underlying software technologies is likely to spring suddenly upon us. Inevitably, solutions to various AI problems—image understanding, speech understanding, language understanding, problem solving—are solved incrementally and gradually, with each new generation of a technology providing greater subtlety and depth. Each new step forward reveals new limitations and issues that are addressed in the next generation of the technology or product. A point often comes when the level of performance in a certain area exceeds a critical threshold, and this enables the technology to move out of a research environment into practical commercial applications. In a sense, the overall AI movement started to pass that threshold during the 1980s, when it moved from a barely visible industry with a few million dollars per year of revenue in 1980 to a billion dollars in 1986, with four billion expected in 1990, according to DM Data. It often appears that a breakthrough must have been made, because a technology became sufficiently powerful to be commercially viable. But invariably, the underlying technology was created over an extended period of time. AI is no exception.

The second point is that a hardware breakthrough of the type described above is not *necessary* for significant and sustained progress in each area of AI. There is no question that more powerful computers are needed for many problems, such as continuous speech recognition, human-level vision and others, but the exponential growth in computer power that will occur anyway is sufficient.

Allen Newell

Fairy Tales

Prof. Allen Newell is the U. A. and Helen Whitaker University Professor of Computer Science at Carnegie-Mellon University, where he has been since 1961. He was educated in physics (B.S., Stanford University), mathematics (Princeton University), and industrial administration (Ph.D., 1957, Carnegie Institute of Technology). He contributed to the emergence of cognitive psychology and artificial intelligence in the mid 1950s and has continued to make significant contributions to them ever since, many with Herbert Simon. His current research (with John Laird and Paul Rosenbloom) is on Soar, a general cognitive architecture that embodies a unified theory of human cognition. He has also made major contributions to list processing, expert systems, computer structures, and human-computer interaction. He is the recipient of the Association of Computing Machinery's A. M. Turing Award (with Herbert Simon), and the American Psychological Association's Distinguished Scientific Contribution Award. He is the author or coauthor of over 250 papers and 10 books.

Once upon a time, when it was still of some use to wish for what one wanted, . . . there lived a king and queen who had a daughter who was lovely to behold, but who never laughed.

Or perhaps:

there lived an old fisherman by the side of the sea that had hardly any fishes in it.

If you are like me, you are already hooked. You are ready to abandon all talk of present matters, of computers and electronic technology, and settle in to hear a fairy tale. Their attraction reaches almost all of us.

They let us enter into an enchanted world. Magic abounds, though always in special ways. Animals talk, and not only animals but trees and bridges as well. Villainy is there, certainly danger. There are trials to be overcome—usually three of them. But there is always the happy ending. The spell is broken, and the princess smiles and marries the youth who made her laugh. The old fisherman gets the Jinni back in the bottle with the top on. And happiness is ever after, which means at least for a little while.

The experts tell us that fairy tales are for childhood. They contain lessons for the crises of growing up, and their universal attraction comes because they deal with what is central to this universal period in life: Like Hansel and Gretel, we have to leave home and find our own way. Like the princess with the frog king, we must learn to keep our word and embrace what we find ugly and disgusting, to discover that it contains our heart's desire.

Or like Jack, in the story of the beanstalk, we can bring home the bacon if we persevere, even if our parents don't think we can. But there was more, if you remember your Jack: First, he escaped back home with a bag of gold. But Jack and his mother used up the gold, which shows that one success is not enough. Then he made a second trip up the beanstalk to the giant's castle. This time he came home with the magic hen that lays golden eggs. Now Jack had a technology for satisfying his and his mother's wants. But even so,

Allen Newell (Courtesy of Allen Newell)

material things are not sufficient for the full life. So on his third trip Jack brought home the golden singing harp, symbolizing the higher things of life.

The experts notwithstanding, fairy tales are for all of us. Indeed, this is true especially in our current times. For we are, all of us, children with respect to the future. We do not know what is coming. The future is as new, and as incomprehensible, as adult life is to children. We find ourselves troubled and fearful at the changes taking place in ourselves and our society. We need the hidden guidance of fairy tales to tell us of the trials we must overcome and assure us there will be a happy ending. Whether fairy tales have been written that speak to the heart of our own adult crises is not clear. How would we, the children, ever know? Perhaps we must get along with the fairy tales we have.

But even more, fairy tales seem to me to have a close connection to technology. The aim of technology, when properly applied, is to build a land of Faerie.

Well, that should come as a shock! The intellectual garb of the modern academic is cynicism. Like a follower in a great herd, as surely as I am an academic, I am a cynic. Yet I have just uttered a sentiment that is, if anything, straight from Pollyanna.

In point of fact, within the small circle of writers who manage to put technology and fairy tales between the same covers, the emphasis is always on the negative, on the dark side. The favorite stories are those that trouble:

· Like the Sorcerer's Apprentice, who learns only enough magic to start the broom of technology hauling water from the River Rhine to the cistern, but who cannot stop it.

· Like the Jinni in the bottle, where the story is never permitted to go to the conclusion in the Arabian Nights, with the Jinni snookered back in the bottle, but is always stopped with the Jinni hanging in air and the question along with it—Can we ever put the Jinni back? Or will there only be ink all over the sky till the stars go out?

· Like the many stories of the three magic wishes, in which, promising infinite riches just for the asking, they are always spent, first on

foolishness, second on disaster, and third on bare recovery. Recall the story of the Monkey's Paw, which came to an old English couple. Their first wish was for just 200 pounds. That was foolish. They lost a son, whose accident brought them a 200-pound reward. The second wish was for the return of their son. That was disaster. He returned from the grave, though hardly unscathed. The third wish was to send their son back to his opened grave, to try to recover for themselves a world where life could go on.

I see it differently. I see the computer as the enchanted technology. Better, it is the technology of enchantment. I mean that quite literally, so I had best explain.

There are two essential ingredients in computer technology. First, it is the technology of how to apply knowledge to action to achieve goals. It provides the capability for intelligent behavior. That is why we process data with computers—to get answers to solve our problems. That is what algorithms and programs are about—frozen action to be thawed when needed.

The second ingredient is the miniaturization of the physical systems that have this ability for intelligent action. This is what Angel Jordan, my co-Whitaker professor, has been telling us about in his talk. Computers are getting smaller, and cheaper, and faster, and more reliable, and less energy demanding. Everything is changing together in the right direction. The good things do not trade off against the bad ones. More speed does not mean more dollars. Small size does not mean lower reliability. On any given date, the expected painful trade-offs do hold, just as we learned in elementary economics. It costs more to buy faster circuits or larger memories. But come back next year and everything is better: smaller, cheaper, faster, more reliable, and for less energy.

Thus computer technology differs from all other technologies precisely in providing the capability for an enchanted world: for little boxes that make out your income-tax forms for you, for brakes that know how to stop on wet pavement, for instruments that can converse with their users, for bridges that watch out for the safety of those who cross them, for streetlights that care about those who stand under them—who know the way, so no one need get lost.

In short, computer technology offers the possibility of incorporating intelligent behavior in all the nooks and crannies of our world. With it we could build an enchanted land.

All very good, but what about the Sorcerer's Apprentice? Two half-fallacies feed our fear that his nightmare might be ours. The first half-fallacy is that technologies are rigid and unthinking. Start the broom off carrying water, and it does just that and not something else. But every computer scientist recognizes in the Sorcerer's Apprentice simply a program with a bug in it, embedded in a first generation operating system with no built-in panic button. Even with our computer systems today, poor things that they are, such blunderbus looping is no longer a specter.

Exactly what the computer provides is the ability *not* to be rigid and unthinking, but rather to behave conditionally. That is what it means to apply knowledge to action: it means to let the action taken reflect knowledge of the situation, to be sometimes this way, sometimes that, as appropriate. With small amounts of computer technology—that is, with small amounts of memory and small amounts of processing per decision—you often can't be conditional enough. That is certainly the story of the first decades of the computer revolution. It was too expensive and involved too much complexity to create systems with enough conditionality. We didn't know how and couldn't have afforded it if we did. Consequently, many applications were rigid and unthinking. It was indeed a Sorcerer's Apprentice who seemed to run the computerized billing service.

The import of miniaturization is that ultimately we will be able to have the capability for enough conditionality in a small enough space. And the import of our scientific study of computers is that we shall know how to make all the conditionality work for us. Then the brooms of the world themselves can know enough to stop when things go wrong.

The second half-fallacy behind the Sorcerer's Apprentice is that technologies by their nature extract too high a price. That is a

message of the recent literature of political ecology: Our technologies inevitably demand that we use up our precious world. There is rather abundant evidence for this view. Here in Western Pennsylvania, the price paid in enchantment of our countryside for taking our coal by strip mining is only too evident. Less in our awareness, because it was so thorough, was what the loggers did to Western Pennsylvania. Not once, but thrice, within forty years they swept the hillsides almost bare. The hot scorching breath of a dragon could hardly have done better for desolation.

But all is not inevitable. Ecologically, computer technology itself is nearly magic. The better it gets, the less of our environment it consumes. It is clean, unobtrusive, consumes little energy and little material. Moreover, as we push it to higher peaks of speed and memory, it becomes more of all these things. For deep technical reasons this has to be. There is no way to obtain immense amounts of processing power by freezing technology at some cost in dollars, material, and energy per unit of computation and then just buying more and more of it, consuming our wealth and our environment. Instead, for a long time to come, as we get more and more of it, the less it will impact our environment.

Even more, the computer is exactly the technology to permit us to cope intelligently with the use of our other resources. Again, by providing us with distributed intelligence, it can let us keep track of the use and abuse of our environment. And not only of the destruction that we ourselves visit on our world but also that which nature does as well. Mount Vesuvius was hardly bound by any antipollution ordinances posted on the walls of ancient Pompeii.

In sum, technology can be controlled, especially if it is saturated with intelligence to watch over how it goes, to keep accounts, to prevent errors, and to provide wisdom for each decision. And these guardians of our world, these magic informational dwarfs, need not extract too high a price.

But I said that fear of the plight of the Sorcerer's Apprentice was guided by *half-fallacies.* I did not dismiss the view totally. Because, of course, in fairy tales there are great trials to be performed before the happy ending. Great dangers must be encountered and overcome. Because, also, in fairy tales, the hero (or the heroine)—the one who achieves finally the happy ending—must grow in virtue and mature in understanding. No villains need apply for the central role. The fairy tale that I am indirectly spinning here will not come true automatically. We must earn it.

Where are we now? We are not at the end of the story, though we are surely at the end of my talk. In fact, the fairy tale is hardly past its "Once upon a time." Still, I wish to assert that computer science and technology are the stuff out of which the future fairy land can be built. My faith is that the trials can be endured successfully, even by us children who fear that we are not so wise as we need to be. I might remind you, by the way, that the hero never has to make it all on his own. Prometheus is not the central character of any fairy tale but of a tragic myth. In fairy tales, magic friends sustain our hero and help him overcome the giants and the witches that beset him.

Finally, I wish to express my feeling of childlike wonder that my time to be awake on this earth has placed me in the middle of this particular fairy tale.

CHAPTER 11

The Impact On . . .

It's hard to predict—especially the future.

Niels Bohr, physicist

• Employment and the Economy

If every instrument could accomplish its own work, obeying or anticipating the will of others . . . , if the shuttle could weave, and the pick touch the lyre, without a hand to guide them, chief workmen would not need servants, nor masters slaves.

Aristotle

If machines could be so improved and multiplied, then all of our corporeal necessities could be entirely gratified, without the intervention of human labor, there will be nothing to hinder all mankind from becoming philosophers and poets.

Timothy Walker, essayist, 1831

Machinery will perform all work—automata will direct all activities and the only tasks of the human race will be to make love, study and be happy.

The United States Review, 1853

When people consider the impact of computer intelligence, few areas generate as much controversy as its potential to influence patterns of employment. Other areas— education, medicine, even warfare—evoke less passion. In education, concern is sometimes expressed about computers replacing human instructors, but astute observers realize that computer-assisted instruction is intended to compete with books, not teachers.[1] There is understandable hesitancy to rely on the diagnostic judgements of medical expert systems even when they have demonstrated superior skills in some areas, but few expect undue reliance on such systems without strenu- ous steps to verify reliability. There is certainly controversy surrounding military applications, but even here there is some recognition that the highly pinpointed targeting provided by "smart" weapons may cause less indiscriminate destruction than the shotgun tactics required by older generations of weapon systems (more about this later). The issue of jobs, on the other hand, strikes at a fundamental and immediate concern of most people. While machines have been competing with human labor for centuries in the *physical* domain, the more recent competition for *mental* work is more threatening, both economically and psychologically.

Views on the impact of this latest wave of automation vary dramatically with the observer. Some hail the ability of machines to eliminate mental drudgery in the same way that an earlier generation of machines released us from the bondage of hard physical labor. Others point to a bleak future in which employment opportunities remain only for an elite few.

This issue is rarely approached dispassionately. Most views are heavily influenced by a number of social and ideological assumptions. I do not pretend to be immune from such influence, but I do feel that an examination of long-term trends of the past and attempts to project such trends into the future can help to illuminate these issues. Most of the automation that has taken place in human history has occurred over the past one hundred years. As I pointed out in the prolog, the macro-economic trends during that period were quite positive. Jobs grew 10-fold in the United States (12 million in 1870 to 116 million in 1985) with the percentage of the U.S. population gainfully employed increasing from 31 percent to 48 percent. More significantly, the per-capita gross national product, as well as the average earning power of jobs, increased 600 percent in constant dollars during the same period.[2] The quality of jobs improved as well, a much higher fraction of jobs providing gratification beyond the paycheck. Nonetheless, the impact of automation on jobs has been a controversial subject during this entire period. One impediment to sober reflection on the issue is that the *reality* of lost jobs and the resulting emotional and social impact are far easier to see than the *possibility* of new jobs and new industries. Early in this century, jobs in factories and in agriculture were disappearing at a rapid rate. Dire predictions of these trends spiraling to disaster were not uncommon. It was not possible for leaders at the time to say, Don't worry, millions of jobs will be created in the electrical industry, and following that, the electronics and computer industries will create millions more. Indeed at the time it would have been impossible to foresee even the existence of these industries. The phenomenon continues today, with new manufacturing technologies rapidly reducing the number of production jobs. Manufacturing today provides a quarter of all employment; by the beginning of the next century it is expected to provide relatively few jobs.[3] The social and political impact of these lost jobs is felt far more strongly than the future opportunities which undoubtedly will be there.

More perspective can be gained by attempting as rigorously as possible to project these trends into the future. A comprehensive study using a detailed computer model of the U.S. economy was conducted recently by Wassily Leontief, Faye Duchin, and their colleagues at the Institute for Economic Analysis (IEA).[4] The study indicates continued expansion of the per-capita gross national product and average earning power of the American worker. It projects a rapidly diminishing demand for clerical workers and other categories of semiskilled and unskilled workers and a reduction in factory workers, although the latter will be partially offset by the overall increase in economic activity. It projects a sharp reduction in the need for skilled metal workers due to increased use of factory automation, including robots and computerized machine tools. Conversely, it projects a sharp increase in the need for professionals, particularly engineers (including computer specialists), and for teachers.[5]

426

The most significant finding of the study is that the limiting factor on future economic growth will be the availability of a suitably trained workforce.[6] There will be plenty of jobs in the early twenty-first century, but only if society provides a sufficient number of appropriately skilled workers to fill them. As factories are rebuilt for substantially fewer personnel, both blue and white collar, as agriculture continues to be mechanized, as the service industries begin to automate, there will be a corresponding increase in the demand for knowledge workers who can design, build, program, and run the intelligent machines of the future. At least as important as the knowledge workers are the teachers to train them. Since power and wealth in the age of intelligent machines will increasingly consist of knowledge and skill, the ability to develop and foster our human intellectual resources becomes society's most pressing challenge.

The IEA study examines a number of scenarios that differ in assumptions about the speed with which society can incorporate new computer technologies and provide the workforce with the necessary skills. Consequently, the scenarios differ dramatically in their projected employment levels and economic progress. Of course, the economic model used by the IEA, no matter how detailed, does not by any means eliminate uncertainty regarding the future. It is difficult to predict how quickly a given technology will be adopted and integrated into the workplace. Often predictions of rapid change are premature. For example, the advent of numerically controlled machine tools in the 1960s was expected to quickly revolutionize metalworking, but the new technology made little headway until it was integrated with computers in the late 1970s.[7] On the other hand, some technologies move more quickly than any expert predicted, as was the case with the rapid computerization of offices during the 1980s. A comparison of the different scenarios of the IEA's study does make clear, however, that the primary variable that will determine the rate of continued economic progress and continued growth in the availability of employment is the quality and availability of appropriate education and training. Interestingly, the conclusion is the same for both advanced and underdeveloped nations.[8]

The nature of work

Most factories built today employ substantially fewer workers than the factories they replace. Even if robotic technology is not employed, the computerization of material handling and work flow has already substantially reduced the direct-labor content of most products. There is little question that this trend will continue and intensify over the next two decades. By early in the next century a relatively small number of technicians and other professionals will be sufficient to operate the entire production sector of society.

While employing substantially fewer people, the advent of computer-controlled manufacturing technologies will permit a degree of individual customization of products not feasible today. Two centuries ago every item was inevitably a little different, since it was made by hand. During the first industrial revolution the innovation of mass production substantially reduced the individualization of products. During the second industrial revolution the innovation of extremely flexible manufacturing will increase it.[9] For example, consumers will be able to sit down at their home computers and design their own clothes to their own precise measurements and style requirements using friendly, computer-assisted design software. When the user issues the command "Make clothes," the design parameters and measurements will be transmitted to a remote manufacturing facility, where the clothes will be made and shipped within hours.

As employment in the factory dwindles, employment in the office will be stable or increase. However, what we do in offices will substantially change.[10] Clerical work will largely disappear. Completing a trend already under way, by early in the next century, computers will type our letters and reports, intelligently maintain our files and records, and help to organize our work. The areas likely to continue to require significant human involvement, particularly during the first half of the next century, will be communication, teaching, learning, selling, strategic-decision making, and innovation. While computers will certainly impact all of these areas, they will continue to be the primary focus of human efforts in the office. As I pointed out above, the office worker of the next century will have sustained contact with both human and machine intelligence.

The concept of a document will undergo substantial change. Extremely high resolution easy-to-view screens will become as common and as easy to read from as paper. As a result, we will routinely create, modify, handle, and read documents without their ever being converted to paper form. Documents will include a variety of types of information beyond mere text and pictures. They will routinely include voice, music, and other sound annotations. Even the graphic part of documents will become more flexible: it may be an animated three-dimensional picture. In addition, documents will be tailored in that they will include the underlying knowledge and flexibility to respond *intelligently* to the inputs and reactions of the reader.[11] Finally, documents will not necessarily be ordered sequentially as they are in this book: they will be capable of flexible intuitive patterns that reflect the complex web of relationships among ideas (this is Ted Nelson's "hypertext").[12]

With the ongoing acceleration of the pace of change, the idea of training someone for a lifelong trade will become even less valid than it is today. Instead, we shall need to teach our children how to keep learning throughout their adult lives. It is estimated that the typical worker of the twenty-first century will make changes in the way they work once or twice each decade, changes that we would now consider major career changes.[13] Thus, the *primary* skill required for employment in the workplace of the future will be the ability to adapt and to continue growing intellectually.

A constructive change in our concept of work will be to think of the process of learning as *part* of work, rather than as just a *prerequisite* for work. The worker of the future may spend as much as half of his time learning rather than just doing. A trend toward this concept is already discernible among more enlightened employers. Employers providing on-the-job education and paying their employees to acquire new skills is likely to emerge as a major trend by the end of the century.

The trend toward work as a vital component of gratification and personal satisfaction is also likely to intensify in the decades ahead. It is to be hoped that the divisions between work on the one hand and learning, recreation, and social relationships on the other will dissolve as work becomes more fully integrated with the other facets of life.

Common sense is not a simple thing. Instead, it is an immense society of hard-earned practical ideas—of multitudes of life-learned rules and exceptions, dispositions and tendencies, balances and checks.
Marvin Minsky, *The Society of Mind*

All instruction given or received by way of argument proceeds from pre-existent knowledge.
Aristotle, *Posterior Analytics*

The search for the truth is in one way hard and in another easy—for it is evident that no one of us can master it fully, nor miss it wholly. Each one of us adds a little to our knowledge of nature, and from all the facts assembled arises a certain grandeur.
Aristotle, 350 B.C.

My conclusion about the impact of intelligent machines on employment rests on education and its pivotal role in shaping the future world economy. This leads me to consider the impact of this new technology on education itself.[14] Thus far the impact of computers has been modest. Of much greater effect have been the other media technologies of television, cinema, and recorded music. While it is true that hundreds of thousands of computers have found their way into schools, a much larger number have found their way into homes. In the home videogames have made their presence felt, digital technology is evident in a broad variety of consumer electronic products, and calculators are ubiquitous. Yet the content and process of education remains largely unchanged; there is continued reliance on books that, as Minsky puts it, "do not talk to each other."[15] The computer revolution, which is radically transforming the work of the office and the factory, has not yet made its mark in the schools.

The enormous popularity in American classrooms of the Apple IIe, which is now several generations behind in hardware technology, is a testament to the conservative nature of the educational establishment (and to the lack of adequate resources). Seymour Papert, developer of LOGO, the principal educational computer language, compares the specter of an entire classroom of children sharing one computer to that of a classroom sharing one pencil. One pencil, according to Papert, is probably better than none, but it is not likely to lead to a "pencil revolution."

Nonetheless, computers *are* infiltrating the schools. The importance of this has more to do with laying the groundwork for the future than with its current impact. Before any fundamental transformation of the learning process can take place, a critical mass needs to be reached in the capabilities of personal computers, their availability to the student population, their portability, the sophistication of educational software, and their integration into the learning process.[16] Let us consider the situation when such a critical mass is reached. This situation will, in my view, include the following eight developments:

- Every child has a computer. Computers are as ubiquitous as pencils and books.
- They are portable laptop devices about the size of a large book.
- They include very high resolution screens that are as easy to read as books.
- They include a variety of devices for entering information, including a keyboard and a track ball (or possibly a mouse).
- They support high quality two-way voice communication, including natural-language understanding.

The LOGO turtle robot draws pictures under command of LOGO programs written by the children. (Photo by Bill Pierce of Rainbow)

Seymour Papert, codirector of the MIT Artificial Intelligence Laboratory and inventor of the popular children's programming language LOGO, is widely regarded as a pioneer in the application of computers to education. (Photo by Bill Pierce of Rainbow)

- They are extremely easy and intuitive to use.
- A great variety of high-quality interactive *intelligent* and *entertaining* courseware is available.
- Computers are integrated into wireless networks.

My emphasis on *intelligent* courseware needs explanation. Much of the available computer-assisted instruction (CAI) provide little more than repetitive exercises that could have been provided just as easily by books.[17] The better programs do provide a measure of interaction, with sequences dependent on the specific areas of weakness of the student, but they still develop little sense of the student's true strengths and weaknesses. CAI now under development has a more ambitious goal. We all have models of the world that we use to understand and respond to events and to solve problems, whether they be real-world situations or classroom exercises. If we make a mistake, it may be simply a matter of a few missing or inaccurate facts. But more often it reflects a structural defect in the organization of our knowledge. A good teacher attempts to understand the model that the student is using. Then if the student's model, and not just his data base, is faulty, the teacher devises a strategy to modify the model to more accurately reflect the subject matter. Such researchers as John Seely Brown at Xerox's Palo Alto Research Center are attempting to develop a CAI technology which will be able to model the relationships in the knowledge to be taught, diagnose the presumably weaker models that a student is starting with, develop a strategy to upgrade the student's models to the desired ones, and provide entertaining and engaging experiences to carry out the remedial strategy.[18] The objective is to incrementally improve the world models of the student. As Seymour Papert points out, you cannot learn something unless "you already almost know it."

Wireless networks will allow easy sharing of courseware, submissions by students of papers, exams, courseware responses, and other creations, electronic mail and other communications (e.g., love notes). By being plugged into international networks of information, children will have immediate access to the great libraries of the world right from their school bags. In addition to being able quickly to access virtually all books, magazines, data bases, and other research materials, there will exist intelligent software assistants to help students quickly find the information they are looking for.

The above vision of an optimal educational workstation will obviously not come forth suddenly. Some aspects of it are becoming available now; others will emerge over the next decade.[19] A personal computer with the necessary attributes should become available around the end of this century. With the historical ten-year lag of the educational field in adopting new computer technology, we can expect a critical mass level of ubiquitous utilization of such technology by the end of the first decade of the next century.[20] If society wakes up to the pivotal role of education in determining our future economic well-being, then the time period for widespread implementation of this technology may be compressed. Yet it will still be well into the first decade of the next century before a broad transformation of the educational process is complete.

Let us envision education yet several decades farther into the future. By the second half of the next century, the future media technologies described earlier will be as widespread as the various video technologies of today. The greatest impact of the media of the future will be in education. A homework assignment, for example, might be to participate in the Constitutional Convention of 1787 and debate the founding fathers on the separation of powers between the three branches of the U.S. government. A subsequent assignment might be to negotiate the final language on behalf of the executive branch: see if you can get a better deal for the presidency on war powers. Your submission would be the actual debates that you participated in, and your teacher watches them in the same way that you originally did: in a totally realistic three-dimensional projected holographic environment with nearly perfect resolution. The founding fathers that you interact with are extremely lifelike artificial people that can hear you, understand what you are saying and respond to you just as the original founding fathers might have. They will be programmed to tolerate a young student barging in on their constitutional convention and engaging them in debate. They may also have better comprehension of contemporary language than the real founding fathers of two hundred years ago might be expected to have had.

For those of us who do not want to wait until these future media technologies are perfected, we can go back right now and engage the founding fathers in debate. We just have to use our imaginations.

• Communications

Of what lasting benefit has been man's use of science and of the new instruments which his research brought into existence? First, they have increased his control of his material environment. They have improved his food, his clothing, his shelter; they have increased his security and released him partly from the bondage of bare existence. They have given him increased knowledge of his own biological processes so that he has had a progressive freedom from disease and an increased span of life. They are illuminating the interactions of his physiological and psychological functions, giving promise of an improved mental health.

Science has provided the swiftest communication between individuals; it has provided a record of ideas and has enabled man to manipulate and to make extracts from that record so that knowledge evolves and endures throughout the life of a race rather than that of an individual.
Vannevar Bush, *As We May Think*, 1945

By early in the next century, personal computers will be portable laptop devices containing cellular phone technology for wireless communication with both people and machines. Our portable computers will be gateways to international networks of libraries, data bases, and information services.

We can expect the personal computers of 2010 to have considerable knowledge of where to find knowledge. They will be familiar with the types of information contained in our own personal data bases, in the data bases of companies and organizations to which we have access, as well as to all subscription and public-information services available through (wireless) telecommunications. As described earlier, we shall be able to ask our personal computers to find, organize, and present diverse types of information. The computer will have the intelligence to engage us in dialogue to clarify our requests and needs, to access knowledge from other machines and people, and to make organized and even entertaining presentations.

Software should be highly standardized by the end of this century. In general, commercially available software packages will work on any computer with

A brief history of human communication. (Data from Dataquest)

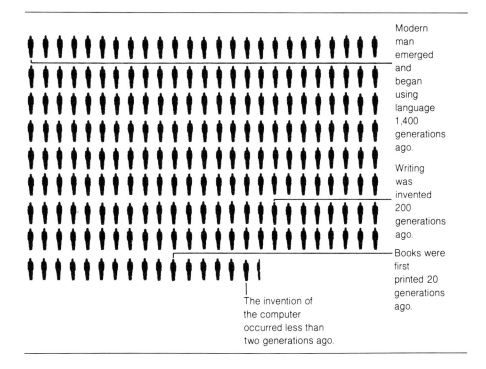

Modern man emerged and began using language 1,400 generations ago.

Writing was invented 200 generations ago.

Books were first printed 20 generations ago.

The invention of the computer occurred less than two generations ago.

sufficient capability. Standard protocols and formats will be in place for all types of files: text, spreadsheets, documents, images, and sounds. Paper will be regarded as just another form of information storage. With highly accurate and rapid technology available for character and document recognition, paper will be a medium easily accessed by both people and machines.

Indeed, the advent of the electronic document has not caused the end of paper. The so-called "paperless office" actually uses more paper than its predecessor. U.S. consumption of paper for printed documents increased from 7 million tons in 1959 to 22 million in 1986.[21] American business use grew from 850 billion pages in 1981 to about 2.5 trillion pages in 1986 and is expected to hit 4 trillion pages in 1990.[22] While computers make it possible to handle documents without paper, they also greatly increase the productivity of *producing* paper documents.

Telephones will routinely include video capability. Later in the next century the video images will have improved to become highly realistic, moving, three-dimensional, projected, holographic images with nearly perfect resolution. A phone call with a friend or business associate will be very much like visiting that person. It will appear that they are sitting with you in your living room or office. The only limitation will be that you cannot touch one another.

Even this limitation will eventually be overcome. Once we create robotic imitations of people that are extremely lifelike in terms of both look and feel, a robotic person imitator could be made to move in exactly the same way as the real person hundreds or thousands of miles away. Thus, if two people who are apart wanted to spend time together, they would each meet with a robotic imitator of the other. Each imitator would move in exactly the same way (and at nearly the same time) as the remote real person by means of high-speed communication and robotic techniques. In other words, you lift an arm, and your robotic imitator hundreds of miles away lifts its arm in exactly the same way. One problem to overcome will be the slight communications delay if the two humans are a few thousand miles apart. Artificial intelligence may be able to help out here by anticipating movements. Using this type of communication service of the late twenty-first century, couples may not necessarily have to be near each other to maintain their romantic relationships. (I have not yet checked with my wife on this, however.)

The advent of videophones, even of a conventional two-dimensional type, will place new demands on telephone etiquette. We may not always want to engage in a call with video. There will, of course, always be the option of turning the picture off (in either direction), but doing so may involve an explanation that we currently do not have to deal with. (In fact, the widespread adoption of cellular technology, even without pictures, will also put a strain on telephone etiquette. It is now feasible to be "away" from our telephones when we are busy. But if everyone has a phone in their wrist watch, it may become harder to avoid answering the phone.)

One major impact of advanced communications technology will be on the nature of our cities. Cities first developed to facilitate manufacturing and transportation and thus tended to be located near ports and rivers. With highways and railways providing greater flexibility in transporting goods and people, a primary purpose of the city shifted to communication. Congregating people in one place facilitated their ability to meet and conduct business. But if we can "meet" with anyone regardless of where we are and our computers can easily share information through wireless telecommunications networks, the need for cities will diminish. Already our cities are spreading out, and this trend will accelerate as the communication technologies described above become available. Ultimately, we will be able to live anywhere and still work, learn, and play with people anywhere else on the globe. The world will become one city, the ultimate realization of McLuhan's vision of the global village.

• Warfare

When all else fails, the future still remains.
Christian Bovee

Knowledge is power and permits the wise to conquer without bloodshed and to accomplish deeds surpassing all others.
Sun Tzu (Chou dynasty philosopher and military strategist), *The Art of War* (fourth century B.C.)

Warfare and potential for warfare is taking a paradoxical turn in the last half of the twentieth century. There is increasing reliance, at least by the more developed nations, on "smart" weapons and a rapid evolution of such weapons. Missiles can be launched from air, ground, or sea hundreds and in some cases thousands of miles from their intended targets. These weapons find their way to their destinations using a variety of pattern-recognition and other computer technologies. Pilot's Assistants, for example, are beginning to provide pilots with an electronic copilot that helps fly, navigate, locate enemy targets, plot weapon trajectories, and other tasks. Recent military engagements which utilized such technology have resulted in more accurate destruction of enemy targets and substantially less unintended damage to neighboring civilian populations and facilities (although there are still a few bugs in these systems). Among military establishments that can afford routine use of these

434

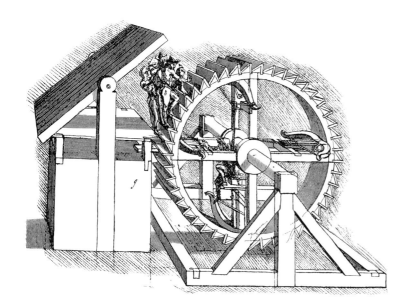

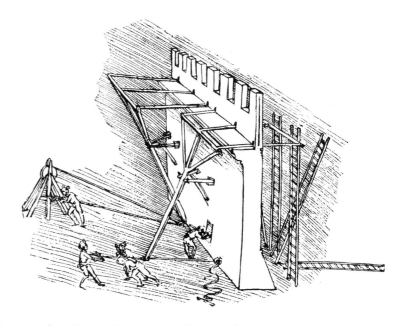

Military high tech before the computer, Leonardo da Vinci's treadmill-powered cross-bow. (Supplied by North Wind Picture Archives)

A device proposed by Leonardo for foiling the enemy's scaling ladders. (Supplied by North Wind Picture Archives)

technologies, a profound reconsideration of military tactics is underway. The primary thrust is to replace shotgun strategies with the careful pinpointing of targets.

Not all nations have access to these new technologies. While Iran and Iraq do possess small numbers of such advanced weapons, they still primarily used weapons and battlefield tactics of World War II vintage during their recent war. The Soviet Union in Afghanistan also used relatively unsophisticated weapons and tactics. This reflects a fundamental reality in the balance of power between East and West: the Warsaw Pact forces are at least a decade behind the NATO forces in AI and computer technologies. Indeed, our primary strategy in countering the numerically superior forces of the Soviet Union and its allies is to rely on our superiority in the *intelligence* of our conventional (or nonnuclear) weapons as the first line of defense and on our nuclear threat as the second line.[23]

In accordance with this second line, the United States and NATO have been unwilling to make a declaration of no first use of nuclear weapons, stating that we *may* use nuclear weapons in the event of a *conventional* attack on Europe. However, if we can improve our intelligent but conventional weapons to a point where our confidence in the first line strategy is sufficiently enhanced, then the western allies would be in a position to issue a no-first-use pledge and forego the nuclear threat in Europe. Recent political changes in Eastern Europe and the apparent collapse of communism in many countries may hasten such a development. There are active development programs to create a new generation of, for example, ground-to-ground and air-to-ground antitank missiles that are capable of being launched from hundreds of miles away, follow irregular trajectories, search intelligently for their targets, locate, and destroy them.[24] Once perfected, these missiles could be launched without precise knowledge of the location of the enemy positions. They are being designed to use a variety of artificial vision, pattern-recognition, and communication technologies to roam around and reliably locate enemy vehicles. Friendly forces would be avoided by a combination of electronic communication and pattern-recognition identification. To the extent that friendly targets are avoided by electronic communication, the reliability and security of the encoding protocols, another important area of advanced computer research, will obviously be crucial. Anticipated progress in intelligent weaponry was a major factor behind the recommendation of four former high ranking American advisers, including Robert McNamara and McGeorge Bundy, for an American no-first-use pledge in the spring 1982 issue of *Foreign Affairs*.[25]

One result of these changes is the prospect of diminished civilian destruction from war, but few observers are heralding this development. The reason for this is, of course, the enormous increases in the destructive capability of weapons that have also occurred. As terrifying and destructive as the atomic weapons that ended World War II were, the superpowers now possess more than a million times more destructive power. Children growing up today belong to the first generation in history born into an era in which the complete destruction of the human race is at least plausible. Experts may debate whether or not "nuclear winter" (the catastrophic global change in climate that some scientists have predicted would follow a large-scale exchange of nuclear weapons) really has the potential to end all human life. The end of the human race has never before been seriously debated as a possibility. Whether an all-out nuclear war would actually destroy all human life or not, the overwhelming destruction that would certainly ensue has created an unprecedented level of terror, under which all of the world's people now live. Ironically, the fear of nuclear conflict has kept the peace: there has not been a world war for nearly half a century. It is a peace from which we take limited comfort.

The most evident technologies behind this radical change in the potential destructiveness of warfare are, of course, atomic fission and fusion. The potential for worldwide catastrophe would not be possible, however, without weapon-delivery systems, which rely heavily on computer intelligence to reach their destinations. The power of conventional munitions has also grown substantially, and political and social inhibitions against their use are far less than those for nuclear weapons. Thus, the possibility of eliminating nuclear weapons from the European theater paradoxically evokes fear that such a development would make Europe "safe" for a conventional war that would still be far more destructive than World War II. This duality in the development of military technology—the advent of weapons for fighting weapons rather than civilian populations and the potential for greatly enhanced destruction—will continue.

Let us consider military technology and strategy several decades into the next century, at which time these trends should have fully matured. By that time flying weapons (missiles, robot planes, and flying munitions) will be highly self-reliant. They will be capable of being launched from virtually any place on earth or from space and still finding their targets by using a combination of advanced vision and pattern-recognition technologies. They will obviously need the ability to avoid or counteract defensive weapons intended for their destruction. Clearly, of primary strategic importance will be the sophistication, indeed the *intelligence*, of both the offensive and defensive systems of such weapons. Geography is already losing its strategic importance and should be a relatively minor factor several decades from now. Such slow moving vehicles as tanks and ships, as well as battle stations, whether land, sea, air, or space based, will be vulnerable unless defended by arrays of intelligent weapons.

Most weapons today destroy their targets with explosions or, less often, bullets. Within the next few decades it is likely that laser and particle beam weapons will be perfected. This will provide such fast-moving weapons as missiles a variety of means for both offense and defense.

Planes, particularly those closest to combat, will not require pilots. With sophisticated enough electronic technology, there is no reason why planes cannot be directed from afar by either human or machine intelligence. Of course, reliable and secure communications will be essential to prevent an enemy from taking control of remote-controlled robot aircraft. Indeed, the three *Cs*—command, control, and communication—are emerging as the cornerstone of future military strategy.[26]

In general, the interactions of future weapons are likely to be so fast that human reflexes will not be the primary criterion of tactical success. Weapons will utilize a variety of their tactical offensive and defensive capabilities within seconds or even milliseconds when meeting comparable enemy systems. In such encounters, the most capable and reliable electronics and software will clearly prevail.

I remember as a child reading a tale about a very advanced civilization that had outlawed war and replaced it with a more refined form of conflict. Rather than resort to deadly weapons, two societies challenging each other for supremacy engaged in a game of chess. Each society could select their best master player or use a committee. As I recall, no one thought to use machine intelligence for this task. Whoever won the board conflict won the war and, apparently, the spoils of war. How this was enforced was not discussed, but one can imagine that warfare in the future may not be all that dissimilar from this tale. If human reflexes and eventually human decision making, at least on a tactical level, are replaced with machine intelligence, then two societies could let their machines fight out the conflict and let them know who wins (or perhaps it would be obvious who had prevailed). It would be convenient if the actual conflict took place in some remote place, like outer space. Here the enforcement of the winner's prerogatives is obvious: the losing society will have lost its machine defenders, which will render it defenseless. It will have no choice but to submit to the victor.

This scenario differs in one important respect from the story about conflict resolution through chess. In the terms I used earlier, chess represents level 2 intelligence and is thus amenable to recursive software techniques combined with massive amounts of computer power. Battling weapons, on the other hand, require level 3 intelligence (the ability to abstract) as well as advanced forms of pattern recognition. They also require *reliability*. One controversial aspect of this new technology is the extent to which we can rely on these extremely complex systems, considering the limited opportunity we will have to test them under realistic wartime conditions. This issue is particularly salient for the highly centralized communication networks needed for command and control.[27]

Can we take any comfort from this vision? It is entirely possible that military engagements decades hence may involve relatively few casualties, particularly of a civilian nature. On the other hand, there is no guarantee that warfare will be constrained to weapons fighting weapons. The tactic of holding large civilian populations hostage will continue to have its adherents among military strategists. What is clear, however, is that a profound change in military strategy is starting to take place. The cornerstones of military power from the beginning of recorded history through recent times—geography, manpower, firepower, and battle-station defenses—are being replaced by the sophistication of computerized intelligence and communications. Humans will direct battlefield strategy, but even here computers will play a crucial role. Yet humans will still be the underlying determinants of military success. Military strength will be a function of the sophistication of the technology, but a society's leaders, scientists, engineers, technicians, and other professionals will create and use the technology. At least, that is likely to remain the case for the next half century.

· Medicine

A self-balancing 28-jointed adapter-base biped; an electro-chemical reduction plant, integral with segregated stowages of special energy extract in storage batteries for subsequent actuation of thousands of hydraulic and pneumatic pumps with motors attached; sixty-two thousand miles of capillaries; . . . the whole extraordinary complex mechanism guided with exquisite precision from a turret in which are located telescopic and microscopic self-registering and recording range finders, a spectroscope, etc.; the turret control being closely allied with an air-conditioning intake and exhaust, and a main fuel intake . . .
R. Buckminster Fuller, "A Definition of a Man"

A projection of current trends gives us the following picture of medicine early in the next century: A variety of pattern-recognition systems will have become a vital part of diagnosis. Blood tests will be routinely analyzed by cybernetic technicians. Today's routine blood test generally involves a human technician examining only about 100 cells and distinguishing only a few cell types; the blood test of the early twenty-first century will involve automatic analysis of thousands or even a million blood cells as well as a thorough biochemical analysis. With such extensive analysis, precursor cells and chemicals that indicate the early stages of many diseases will be reliably detected. Most people will have such devices in their homes. A sample of blood will be painlessly extracted on a routine basis and quickly analyzed.

Electrocardiograms will be analyzed entirely by computer; indeed, prototypes of this technology exist today. Our wristwatches will monitor cardiac functions and other biological processes that might require immediate attention, in addition to diagnosing less acute problems. Particularly powerful computerized monitoring will attend anyone in a special-care situation, such as a hospital, nursery, or old-age home.

Apart from blood tests there will be almost complete reliance on diagnosis by noninvasive imaging (like sonic and particle-resonance imaging). The instantly generated hard-copy images will include the computer's diagnostic findings. The images themselves will be highly realistic computer-generated views of the interiors of our bodies and brains, rather than the often confusing, hard-to-interpret pictures from some of today's imaging devices. While human diagnosticians will continue for many years to examine images from X-ray machines, CAT scanners, nuclear-magnetic-resonance scanners, and sonic scanners, a high degree of confidence will ultimately be placed in the ability of computerized systems to detect and diagnose problems automatically.

Lifetime patient records and histories will be maintained in nationally (or internationally) coordinated data banks in place of today's disorganized system of partial, fragmented, and often illegible records. These records will include all imaging data, the complete readouts of our home blood tests and wristwatch monitoring

A medical workstation of the future will instantly connect the doctor to information from the patient-records department, images from the radiology department, references from the medical library and a suggested diagnosis by the workstation itself. (Photo by Larry Fagan and Mark Friss)

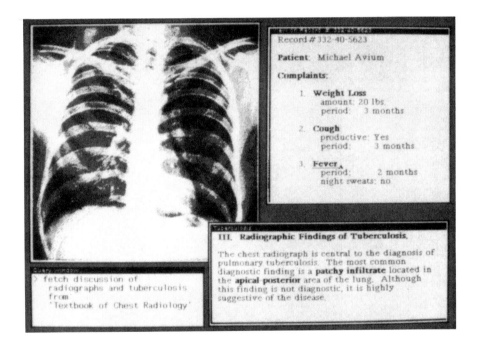

systems. Intelligent software will be available to enable this extensive data bank to be analyzed and accessed quickly by both human and machine experts.

Expert systems will influence virtually all diagnostic and treatment decisions. These expert systems will have access to the output of a patient's most recent imaging and biochemical analyses, as well as to the entire file of all such past exams and monitored data. They will also have access to all internationally available research data and will be updated on a daily basis with the latest research insights. The written reports of these expert systems will be reviewed by human doctors in critical or complex cases, but for more routine problems the machine's opinions will be relied upon with little or no review.[28]

The designing of drugs will be entirely different from present methods. Most drugs on the market today were discovered accidentally. In addition to their beneficial effects, they often cause a number of undesirable side effects. Further, their positive effects are often indirect and not fully effective. In contrast, most drugs of the early twenty-first century will have been specifically designed to accomplish their missions in the most effective and least harmful ways. Drug designers will work at powerful computer-assisted design workstations that will have access to relatively complete mathematical models of all of our biochemical processes. The human drug-design engineers will specify key design parameters, and the computer will perform most of the detailed design calculations. Human biochemical simulation software will allow drugs to be tested with software before any actual drugs are manufactured.[29] Human trials will still be required in most cases (at least this will be true during the first half of the next century), but the simulators will ultimately be sufficiently reliable that the lengthy multistage process of animal and human testing now required will be substantially shortened.

One class of drugs will be similar to the smart weapons described in the previous section. These drugs will be actual living cells with a measure of intelligence. Like cells of our natural immune systems, they will be smart enough to identify an enemy pathogen (bacteria, virus, etc.) and destroy or pacify it. Again like immune cells, once they have completed their missions, they may either self-destruct or remain on call to defend against a future pathogen invasion. Another class of drugs will help overcome genetic diseases. Computer-designed genes will be distributed to our cells by specially designed viruses, which will essentially "infect" the body with the desired genetic information.[30]

Surgical operations will make extensive use of robotic assistants. In types of surgery requiring very precise performance, e.g., in eye surgery, the actual operation will be carried out by the robot, with human doctors overseeing the operation.

Research will be similar to drug design. Most research will be carried out on software that simulates human biochemical processes. Experiments that would now take years will be carried out in minutes. Reporting will be instantaneous, with key results feeding into data bases that allow access by other humans as well as by computer expert systems.[31]

Will these innovations improve our health and well-being? The answer is almost certainly yes. Heart disease and cancer are likely to be conquered by early in the next century. Of course, we have the opportunity right now to dramatically reduce the incidence of these diseases by applying what is already known about the crucial role of diet and life style. But that is a subject for a different book.

We have already doubled the average life expectancy in Europe, Japan, and the United States since the beginning of the first industrial revolution two centuries ago. The potential exists to substantially increase it again by the end of the twenty-first century.

With machines playing such crucial and diverse roles, what will the doctors and nurses of the twenty-first century do? Their major role will be in research and in the organization of medical knowledge. Committees with both human and machine intelligence will review all research findings with a view to incorporating new rules and recommendations into our expert systems. Today new research knowledge filters into the medical community in a slow, inconsistent, and haphazard fashion. The future dissemination of knowledge and recommendations will be very rapid. Doctors will continue to be involved in strategic medical decisions and will review diagnostic and treatment recommendations in complicated cases. Yet some of the new technology will bypass the doctor. There will be a trend toward individuals taking responsibility for their own health and utilizing computerized diagnostic and remedial methods directly.

One area that will still require human attention in the early twenty-first century will be comfort and caring. Machines will not play a significant role here until mature versions of the advanced media technologies described earlier become available later in the century.

• The Handicapped

A primary interest of mine is the application of computer technology to the needs of the handicapped. Through the application of computer technology, handicaps associated with the major sensory and physical disabilities can largely be overcome during the next decade or two. I am confident of this development because of the fortunate matching of the strengths of early machine intelligence with the needs of the handicapped. The typical disabled person is missing a specific skill or capability but is otherwise a normally intelligent and capable human being. It is generally possible to apply the sharply focused intelligence of today's machines to ameliorate these handicaps. A reading machine, for example, addresses the inability of a blind or dyslexic person to read, probably the most significant handicap associated with the disability of blindness.

In the early twenty-first century lives of disabled persons will be far different than they are today. For the blind, reading machines will be pocket-sized devices that can instantly scan not only pages of text but also signs and symbols found in the real world. These machines will be able to read with essentially perfect intonation and with a broad variety of voice styles. They will also be able to describe pictures and graphics, translate from one language to another, and provide access to on-line knowledge bases and libraries through wireless networks. Most blind and dyslexic persons will have them, and they may be ubiquitous among the rest of the population.

Blind persons will carry computerized navigational aids that will perform the functions of seeing-eye dogs, only with greater intelligence than today's canine navigators. Attempts up to now at electronic navigational assistants for the blind have not proved useful. Unless such a device incorporates a level of intelligence at least comparable to a seeing-eye dog, it is not of much value. This is particularly true since modern mobility training can provide a blind person equipped only with an ordinary cane with substantial travel skills. I personally know many blind people who can travel around town and even around the world with ease. With the intelligent navigational aids of the future, travel skills for the blind will become even easier.

Ultimately, compact devices will be built that combine both reading and navigational capabilities with the ability to provide intelligent descriptions of real-world scenes on a real-time basis. At that stage of machine evolution they are probably more accurately called *seeing* machines.[32] Such a machine would be like a friend that could describe what is going on in the visible world. The blind user could ask the device (verbally or in some other way) to elaborate on a description, or he could ask it questions. The visual sensors of such a device could be built into a pair of eyeglasses, although it may be just as well to pin it on the user's lapel. In fact, these artificial eyes need not only look forward; they may as well look in all directions. And they may have better visual acuity than normal eyes. We may all want to use them.

441

The deaf will have hearing machines that can display what people are saying. The underlying technology required is the Holy Grail of voice recognition: combining large-vocabulary recognition with speaker independence and continuous speech. Early versions of speech-to-text aids for the deaf should appear over the next decade. Artificial hearing should also include the ability to intelligently translate other forms of auditory information, such as music and natural sounds, into other modalities, such as vision and touch.

Eventually we may find suitable channels of communication directly into the brain to provide truly artificial sight and hearing. But in any case, there will certainly be progress in restoring lost hearing and sight.

The physically handicapped (paraplegics and quadriplegics) will have their ability to walk and climb stairs restored, abilities that will overcome the severe access limitations wheel chairs impose. Methods to accomplish this will include exoskeletal robotic devices, or powered orthotic devices, as they are called. These devices will be as easy to put on as a pair of tights and will be controlled by finger motion, head motion, speech, and perhaps eventually thoughts. Another option, one that has shown promise in experiments at a number of research institutes, is direct electrical stimulation of limb muscles. This technique effectively reconnects the control link that was broken by spinal cord damage.

Those without use of their hands will control their environment, create written text, and interact with computers using voice recognition. This capability already exists. Artificial hand prostheses controlled by voice, head movement, and perhaps eventually by direct mental connection, will restore manual functionality.

Substantial progress will be made in courseware to treat dyslexia (difficulty in reading for neurophysical reasons other than visual impairment) and learning disabilities. Such systems will also provide richer learning experiences for the retarded.

Perhaps the greatest handicap associated with sensory and physical disabilities is a subtle and insidious one: the prejudice and lack of understanding often exhibited by the general public. Most handicapped persons do not want pity or charity; instead, they want to be respected for their own individuality and intelligence. We all have handicaps and limitations; those of a blind or deaf person may be more obvious, but they are not necessarily more pervasive or limiting. I have worked with many disabled persons, and I know from personal experience that they are as capable as other workers and students at most tasks. I cannot ask a blind person to drive a package across town, but I can ask him to give a speech or conduct a research project. A sighted worker may be able to drive a car, but he will undoubtedly have other limitations. The lack of understanding many people have of handicapped persons is evident in many ways, some obvious, some subtle. By way of example, I have had the following experience on many occasions while eating a meal with a blind person in a restaurant. The waiter or waitress will ask me if my blind friend wants dessert or if he wants cream in his coffee. While the waiter or waitress obviously intends no harm or disrespect, the message is clear. Since there is no indication that the blind person is also deaf, the implication is that he must not be intelligent enough to deal with human language.

A not unimportant side benefit of intelligent technology for the handicapped should be a substantial alteration of these negative perceptions. If the handicaps resulting from disabilities are significantly reduced, if blind people can read and navigate with ease, if deaf persons can hold normal conversations on the phone, then we can expect public perceptions to change as well. When blind, deaf, and other disabled persons take their place beside us in schools and the workplace and perform with the same effectiveness as their nondisabled peers, we shall begin to see these disabilities as mere inconveniences, as problems no more difficult to overcome than poor handwriting or fear of public speaking or any of the other minor challenges that we all face.

• Music

I . . . begin to feel an irresistible drive to become a primitive and to create a new world.
August Strindberg, from a letter

Let us step well into the next century for a view of music when current trends have been fully established. There will still be acoustic instruments around, but they will be primarily of historical interest, much like harpsichords are today. Even concert pianists will accept electronic pianos as fully the equivalent of the best acoustic pianos. All nuances of sound, including interstring resonances, will be captured. Of course, to a pianist, the feel of a piano is important, not just the sound. Piano actions with time-varying magnetic actions will faithfully emulate the feel of the finest top-of-the-line grand pianos. Pianists will prefer the electronic versions because they are more reliable, have extensive additional capabilities, and are always perfectly in tune. We are close to this vision today. Controllers emulating the playing techniques of all conventional instruments, such as guitar, violin and drums, will have largely replaced their acoustic counterparts. Perfect synthesis of acoustic sounds will have long been established.

With the physical link between the control and generation of musical sound having long been broken, most musicians will have gravitated to a new generation of controllers. These new instruments will bear little resemblance to any instrument of today and will enable musicians optimal expressive control.

While the historically desirable sounds of pianos and violins will continue to be used, most music will use sounds with no direct acoustic counterpart. Unlike many synthetic sounds of today, these new musical sounds will have greater complexity and musical depth than any acoustic instrument we are now familiar with.

The concept of a musical sound will include not only sounds that simply start and stop but also a class of sounds that changes characteristics according to a number of continuously controllable parameters. For example, we could use all of our fingers to control ten continuous parameters of a *single* sound. Such a sound will exist as a time-evolving entity that changes according to expression applied in ten different dimensions. With extremely powerful parallel computing devices, the distinction between real-time and non-real-time sound modification will largely disappear; virtually everything will happen in real-time. The ability to modify sound with real-time continuous controls will be regarded as more important than the individual sounds themselves.

Computers will almost always respond in real time, although people will not always create music in real time. There will continue to be a distinction between music composition and music performance. Composition will not mean writing down music notation. It will refer to the creation of music in which the creation takes substantially longer than the piece created. Sequencers that record all continuous controls with high resolution will allow the "massaging" of a work of music in the same way that we now work on a printed document. Music created in this way will certainly not be subject to the limitations of finger dexterity (this has already been largely achieved with contemporary sequencers). Once composed, high-quality notation will be instantly available. It is likely that forms of music notation more satisfactory than the current five-line staffs will be developed over the next several decades to keep pace with the added dimensions of control, added sounds, and added sound modifications.[33]

Live music performance will continue to have the same appeal that it does today. While much of what is heard may have been previously programmed, musicians' sharing with their audience musical expression through real-time (and live) control will continue to be a special form of human communication. The preparation of a musical performance will involve practice and learning of the musical material as well as preparation of the knowledge bases of the musical instruments. Cybernetic musicians generating lines of accompaniment and counterpoint will be commonplace. The intelligence of these software-based musical accompanists will be partially built into the instruments and partially programmed by the musicians as they prepare a performance.[34]

Intelligent software incorporating extensive knowledge of musical theory and styles will be extensively used by professional musicians in creating musical compositions and preparing performances, by amateur musicians, who can jam with their computerized instruments, and by students learning how to play. The advent of musically knowledgeable software-based accompanists will provide children with exciting musical experiences at early stages of their knowledge and skill acquisition.

Music will not necessarily take the form of fixed works that we listen to from beginning to end. One form of musical composition might be a set of rules (or a modification of a set of rules) and expression structures that together can generate an essentially unlimited number of actual pieces. This "work" would sound different every time we listen to it, although each such listening would share certain qualities, which qualifies it to be considered a single work. Compositions will also allow the listener to control and modify what he is hearing. We could control the entry and exit of various instruments and lines of music or control the evolution and emotional content of a piece without necessarily having the musical knowledge of a musician. This type of musical work would allow us to explore a musical world that we could have some influence on. A musical work could respond to our physical movements or even our emotions, which the computer-based system generating the actual sounds could detect from the subtleties of our facial expressions or perhaps even our brainwaves.

In this way music becomes potentially more than entertainment. It can have powerful effects on our emotional states, influencing our moods and affecting our learning. There will not be a sharp division between the musician and nonmusician. Increasingly and regardless of musical talent and training, we shall all be able to express our feelings through music.

Economics, sociology, geopolitics, art, religion all provide powerful tools that have sufficed for centuries to explain the essential surfaces of life. To many observers, there seems nothing truly new under the sun—no need for a deep understanding of man's new tools—no requirement to descend into the microcosm of modern electronics in order to comprehend the world. The world is all too much with us.

Nonetheless, studying economics and other social sciences, I began to realize that the old disciplines were breaking down, the familiar categories slipping away. An onslaught of technological progress was reducing much of economic and social theory to gibberish. For example, such concepts as land, labor, and capital, nation and society—solemnly discussed in every academic institution as if nothing had changed—have radically different meanings than before and drastically different values. Yet the vendors of old expertise continue on as if nothing had happened.

Laws get passed, editorials written, speeches delivered, soldiers dispatched, for all the world as if we still traveled in clipper ships and communicated chiefly by mail.

Jean Kirkpatrick, for example, gave a speech, quoted respectfully in the *Wall Street Journal*, in which she said it was impossible to understand what is going on in the world without a comprehension of geography, "an idea of where things are." It is a common notion. . . . Visit the Pentagon, or the *New York Times*, and everywhere there are maps, solemnly defining national borders and sovereign territories. No one shows any signs of knowing that we no longer live in geographic time and space, that the maps of nations are fully as obsolete as the charts of a flat earth, that geography tells us virtually nothing of interest about where things are in the real world.

The worldwide network of satellites and fiber optic cables, linked to digital computers, television terminals, telephones and databases, sustain worldwide markets for information, currency and capital on line 24 hours a day. Boeing 747s constantly traversing the oceans foster a global community of commerce. The silicon in sand and glass forms a global ganglion of electronic and photonic media that leaves all history in its wake. With other new technologies of material science, bioengineering, robotics, and superconductivity, all also heavily dependent on the microchip, informations systems are radically reducing the significance of so-called raw materials and natural endowments, nations and ethnic loyalties, material totems and localities.

Israel, a desert-bound society, uses microelectronic agricultural systems to supply eighty percent of the cut flowers in Europe and compete in avocado markets in New York. Japan, a set of barren islands, has used microelectronic devices to become one of the globe's two most important nations. In an age when men can inscribe worlds on grains of sand, conventional territory no longer matters. . . .

Today the most important products are essentially made of the sand in chips of crystalline silicon. Their worth derives from the ideas they embody. They are information technologies and their value is invisible. Yet intellectuals, supposedly masters of ideas, refuse to believe in any value they cannot see or weigh. . . .

While the cost-effectiveness of computer components and related products has risen several million fold and the price of a transistor has sunk from $9.00 in 1955 to about eight ten-thousandths of a cent in 1987, the estimates of national productivity have entirely ignored the change. Once again, things that drop in price are assumed to be dropping in value. Yet it is the astronomical reduction in the price of computing that has made it the most important force and most valuable industry in the world economy.

George Gilder, *The Message of the Microcosm*

Where did that knowledge exist? . . . If all records told the same tale, then the lie passed into history and became truth.

George Orwell, *1984*

As I have pointed out throughout this book, wealth and power in the age of intelligent machines is increasingly becoming a function of innovation and skill. The cornerstones of power during the first industrial revolution—geography, natural resources, and manual labor—are rapidly diminishing in importance and relevance. We are entering a world in which wealth can be beamed across the world by satellite, smart weapons can reach their destinations from thousands of miles away, and some of the most powerful technologies in history require only tiny amounts of material resources and electricity. We can only conclude that the strategic variables controlling our future are becoming technology and, in particular, the human *intellectual resources* to advance technology.

For thousands of years governments have demonstrated the possibility of forcing people to perform manual labor (although even here productivity is certainly diminished by coercion). It is a fortunate truth of human nature that creativity and innovation cannot be forced. To create knowledge, people need the free exchange of information and ideas. They need free access to the world's accumulated knowledge bases. A society that restricts access to copiers and mimeograph machines for fear of the dissemination of uncontrolled knowledge will certainly fear the much more powerful communication technologies of personal computers, local area networks, telecommunication data bases, electronic bulletin boards, and all of the multifarious methods of instantaneous electronic communication.

Controlled societies like the Soviet Union are faced with a fundamental dilemma. If they provide their engineers and professionals in all disciplines with advanced workstation technology, they are opening the floodgates to free communication by methods far more powerful than the copiers they have traditionally banned.[35] On the other hand, if they fail to do so, they will increasingly become an ineffectual third-rate power. Russia is already on a par with many third-world countries economically. Russia is a superpower only in the military sphere. If it continues to stagnate economically and fails to develop advanced computer technologies, this type of power will dissipate as well.

Innovation requires more than just computer workstations and electronic communication technologies. It also requires an atmosphere of tolerance for new and unorthodox ideas, the encouragement of risk taking, and the ability to share ideas and knowledge. A society run entirely by government bureaucracies is not in a position to provide the incentives and environment needed for entrepreneurship and the rapid development of new skills and technologies.

From all appearances, some of the leaders of the Communist world have had similar thoughts. Mikhail Gorbachev's much-heralded campaigns of *glasnost* (openness) and *perestroika* (restructuring) have taken some initial steps to open communication and provide market incentives. Important steps have been taken in many of these societies toward achieving individual liberty. But these are only the first steps in what will need to be a long journey to complete a full transformation. Already the forces of reaction in China have taken a major step backward. What is not yet clear is the ability of these societies to succeed in moving deeply entrenched bureaucracies. What is clear, however, is that the *pressures* for such change will not go away.

Should these societies opt instead for a continuation of the controlled society, they will also find computers to be of value. Computers today play an indispensable role in legitimate law enforcement; there is no reason why they would not be equally useful in enforcing any form of state control. With the advanced vision and networking technologies of the early twenty-first century, the potential will exist to realize George Orwell's chilling vision in *1984*.

Computer technology may lead to a flowering of individual expression, creativity, and communication or to an era of efficient and effective totalitarian control. It will all depend on who controls the technology. A hopeful note is that the nature of wealth and power in the age of intelligent machines will encourage the open society. Oppressive societies will find it hard to provide the economic incentives needed to pay for computers and their development.

• Our Concept of Ourselves

We know what we are, but know not what we may be.
William Shakespeare

What will happen when all these artificially intelligent computers and robots leave us with nothing to do? What will be the point of living? Granted that human obsolescence is hardly an urgent problem. It will be a long, long time before computers can master politics, poetry, or any of the other things we really care about. But a "long time" is not forever; what happens when the computers *have* mastered politics and poetry? One can easily envision a future when the world is run quietly and efficiently by a set of exceedingly expert systems, in which machines produce goods, services, and wealth in abundance, and where everyone lives a life of luxury. It sounds idyllic—and utterly pointless.

But personally, I have to side with the optimists—for two reasons. The first stems from the simple observation that technology is made by people. Despite the strong impression that we are helpless in the face of, say, the spread of automobiles or the more mindless clerical applications of computers, the fact is that technology does not develop according to an immutable genetic code. It embodies human values and human choices. . . . My second reason for being optimistic stems from a simple question: What does it mean to be "obsolete"?
M. Mitchell Waldrop

As I discussed earlier, I believe that a computer will be able to defeat all human players at the game of chess within the next one or two decades. When this happens, I noted, we shall either think more of computers, less of ourselves, or less of chess. If history is a guide, we will probably think less of chess. Yet, as I hope this book has made clear, the world chess championship is but one of many accomplishments that will be attained by future machine intelligence. If our approach to coping with each achievement of machine intelligence is to downgrade the intellectual value of the accomplishment, we may have a lot of revision to do over the next half century.

Let us review some of the intellectual domains that machines are likely to master in the near future. A few examples of tasks that computers are now *beginning* to accomplish include the following: accompanying musical performances, teaching us skills and areas of knowledge, diagnosing and recommending remedial treatment for classes of diseases, designing new bioengineered drugs, performing delicate medical operations, locating underground resources, and flying planes.

A more difficult task for a computer, one that we shall probably see during the first half of the next century, is reading a book, magazine, or newspaper and understanding its contents. This would require the computer to update its own knowledge bases to reflect the information it read. Such a system would be able to write a synopsis or a critique of its reading. Of comparable difficulty to this task is passing the Turing test, which requires a mastery of written language as well as extensive world knowledge.

Of at least comparable difficulty would be to watch a moving scene and understand what is going on. This task requires human-level vision and the ability to abstract knowledge from moving images. Add the ability for a robot to imitate humans with sufficient subtlety, and computers will be able to pass a more difficult form of the Turing test in which communication is not through the written word transmitted by terminal but rather by live face-to-face communication. For this achievement we have to go at least to late in the next century.

It is clear that the strengths and weaknesses of machine intelligence today are quite different from those of human intelligence. The very first computers had prodigious and virtually unerring memories. In comparison, our memories are quite limited and of dubious reliability. Yet the early computers' ability to organize knowledge, recognize patterns, and render expert judgements—all elements of human intelligence—was essentially nonexistent. If we examine the trends that are already apparent, we can see that computers have progressed in two ways. They have gained even greater capacities in their areas of unique strength: today's computers are a million times more powerful in terms of both speed and memory than their forebears. At the same time, they have also moved toward the strengths of human intelligence.

(Cartoon by Alan Wallerstein)

They are nowhere near that goal yet, but they are certainly getting closer. Today computers can organize knowledge incorporating networks of relationships, they are beginning to recognize patterns contained in visual, auditory, and other modalities, and they can render judgements that rival those of human experts. They have still not mastered the vast body of everyday knowledge we call common sense, and ironically, they are particularly weak in the pattern recognition and fine motor skills that children and even animals do so well.

Computer intelligence is not standing still. Radical new massively parallel computer architectures, together with emerging insights into the algorithms of vision, hearing, and physical skill acquisition, are propelling computers closer to human capabilities and also continuing to enhance their historical areas of superiority. While machine intelligence continues to evolve and move in our direction, human intelligence is moving very slowly, if at all. But since we have computers to serve us, human intelligence may not *need* to change.

Thousands of years ago, when the religious and philosophical traditions that still guide Western civilization were being formed, a human being was regarded as special. We were different from animals and certainly from material things. The ultimate intelligence in the universe, God, knew about us, and cared about us. Later on as we learned that the earth on which we stood was not the only celestial body in the world, we imagined that all the other entities in the sky revolved around us. In this world view we were special because of our central location. The sun, the moon, the stars, the comets, and other celestial objects all paid homage to us. Still later when we realized that the earth was just the third planet orbiting an unremarkable star located on an arm of an unremarkable galaxy, our view changed again. Then we were special because of our unique intelligence: We could derive knowledge from information. We could contemplate the relationships among the world's phenomena. We could create patterns with aesthetic qualities. We could appreciate those qualities. True, animals shared in this intelligence, but to a much lesser degree, which only reinforced the uniqueness of the level of intelligence we possessed.

Now we are entering an era in which this latest concept of our uniqueness will be challenged once again. To be sure, this challenge will not arrive on a single day. By the time one can seriously argue that computers possess intellectual capabilities comparable to the human species, it will have been at least a century from the invention of the electronic computer in the late 1940s. We should have time to adjust. Perhaps we shall return whence we started, with an appreciation of the inherent value of being human.

Margaret A. Boden

The Social Impact of Artificial Intelligence

Margaret Boden is professor of philosophy and psychology at the University of Sussex, England, and a fellow of the British Academy. Her research work has focused on the premise that human thinking, motivation, and even personality might be understood in computational terms. She is the author of *Artificial Intelligence and Natural Man* (2nd edition, 1987), *Minds and Mechanisms* (1981), and most recently, *Artificial Intelligence in Psychology: Interdisciplinary Essays* (1989).

Is artificial intelligence in human society a utopian dream or a Faustian nightmare? Will our descendants honor us for making machines do things that human minds do or berate us for irresponsibility and *hubris*? Either of these judgments might be made of us, for like most human projects this infant technology is ambivalent. Just *which* aspects of its potential are realized will depend largely on social and political factors. Although these are not wholly subject to deliberate control, they can be influenced by human choice and public opinion. If future generations are to have reason to thank us rather than to curse us, it's important that the public (and politicians) of today should know as much as possible about the potential effects—for good or ill—of artificial intelligence (AI).

What are some of the potential advantages of AI? Clearly, AI can make knowledge more widely available. We shall certainly see a wide variety of expert systems: for aiding medical diagnosis and prescription, for helping scientists, lawyers, welfare advisers, and other professionals, and for providing people with information and suggestions for solving problems in the privacy of their homes. Educational expert systems include interactive programs that can help students (schoolchildren or adults, such as medical students) to familiarize themselves with some established domain. This would give us much more than a set of useful tools and educational cribs. In virtue of its applications in the communication and exploration of knowledge, AI could revolutionize our capacity for creativity and problem solving, much as the invention of printing did.

One advantage of having computers in the schoolroom and elsewhere is that they are *not* human. Precisely because they are not, they will not be bored by their human user's questions, nor scorn their user's mistakes, as another person might. The user may be ignorant, stupid, or naive, but the computer will not think so. Moreover, what looks like ignorance, stupidity, or naïveté is often a sort of exploratory playing around with ideas that is the essence of learning and of creativity. Many children have their self-confidence undermined by their teacher's explicit or implicit rejection of their attempts at self-directed thinking.

Similarly, many people—for instance, those who are female, working class, Jewish, disabled, or black—encounter unspoken (and often unconscious) prejudice in their dealings with official or professional bodies. An AI welfare adviser, for example, would not be prejudiced against such clients *unless* its data and inferential rules were biased in the relevant ways. A program could, of course, be written so as to embody its programmer's prejudices, but the program can be printed out and examined, whereas social attitudes cannot.

Artificial intelligence might even lead to a society in which people have greater freedom and greater incentive to concentrate on what is most fully human. Too few of us today (especially men) have time to commit ourselves to developing our interpersonal relations with family and friends. Increased leisure time throughout society (on the assumption that appropriate political and economic structures had been developed to allow for this) would make room for such conviviality. Partly as a result of this and perhaps partly as a reaction against the *unemotional* nature of most AI programs, the emotional dimension of personality might come to be more highly valued (again, especially by men) than it is in the West today. In my view, this would be all to the good. Similarly, the new technology might make it possible for many more people (yet again, especially men) to engage in activities, whether paid or unpaid, in the service sector: education, health, recreation, and welfare. The need for such activities is pressing, but the current distribution of income makes these intrinsically satisfying jobs financially unattractive. One of the most important benefits of all is that AI can rehumanize—yes, *rehumanize*—our image of ourselves. How can this be? Most people assume that AI either has nothing to teach us about the nature of being human or that it depicts us as "nothing but machines": poor deluded folk, we believe ourselves to be purposive, responsible creatures whereas in reality we are nothing of the kind.

The crucial point is that AI is concerned with *representations*, and how they can be constructed, stored, accessed, compared, and transformed. A computer program is itself a set of

Margaret A. Boden (Courtesy of Margaret A. Boden)

representations, a symbol system that models the world more or less adequately. This is why it is possible for an AI program to reflect the sexist or racist prejudices of its programmer. But representation is central to psychology as well, for the mind too is a system that represents the world and possible worlds in various ways. Our hopes, fears, beliefs, memories, perceptions, intentions, and desires all involve our ideas about (our mental models of) the world and other worlds. This is what humanist philosophers and psychologists have always said, of course, but until recently they had no support from science. Because sciences like physics and chemistry have no place for the concept of representation, their philosophical influence over the past four centuries has been insidiously dehumanizing. The mechanization of our world picture—including our image of man— was inevitable, for what a science cannot describe it cannot recognize. Not only can artificial intelligence recognize the mind (as distinct from the body); it can also help to explain it. It "gives us back to ourselves," by helping us to understand *how it is possible* for a representational system to be embodied in a physical mechanism (brain or computer).

So much for the rose-colored spectacles. What of the darker implications? Many people fear that in developing AI, we may be sowing the seeds of our own destruction, our own physical, political, economical, and moral destruction. Physical destruction could conceivably result from the current plans to use AI within the U.S. Strategic Defense Initiative (Star Wars). One highly respected computer scientist, David Parnas, publicly resigned from the U.S. government's top advisory committee on SDI computing on the grounds that computer technology (and AI in particular) cannot *in principle* achieve the reliability required for a use where even one failure could be disastrous. Having worked on military applications throughout his professional life, Parnas had no political ax to grind. His resignation, like his testimony before the U.S. Senate in December 1985, was based on purely technical judgment.

Political destruction could result from the exploitation of AI (and highly centralized telecommunications) by a totalitarian state.

If AI research had developed programs with a capacity for understanding text, understanding speech, interpreting images, and updating memory, the amount of information about individuals that was potentially available to government would be enormous. Good news for Big Brother, perhaps, but not for you and me.

Economic destruction might happen too if changes in the patterns and/or rates of employment are not accompanied by radical structural changes in industrial society and in the way people think about work. Economists differ about whether the convivial society described above is even possible: some argue that no stable economic system could exist in which only a small fraction of the people do productive (nonservice) work. Certainly, if anything like this is to be achieved, and achieved without horrendous social costs, new ways of defining and distributing society's goods will have to be found. At the same time, our notion of work will have to change: the Protestant ethic is not appropriate for a high-technology postindustrial society.

Last, what of moral destruction: could we become less human—indeed, less than human—as a result of advances in AI? This might happen if people were to come to believe that purpose, choice, hope, and responsibility are all sentimental illusions. Those who believe that they have no choice, no autonomy, are unlikely to try to exercise it. But this need not happen, for our goals and beliefs—in a word, our subjectivity—are not threatened by AI. As we have seen, the philosophical implications of AI are the reverse of what they are commonly assumed to be: properly understood, AI is not dehumanizing.

A practical corollary of this apparently abstract point is that we must not abandon our responsibility for evaluating—and, if necessary, rejecting—the "advice" or "conclusions" of computer programs. Precisely because a program is a symbolic representation of the world, rather than a part of the world objectively considered, it is in principle open to question. A program functions in virtue of its *data*, its *inferential rules*, and its *values* (*decision criteria*), each and every one of which may be inadequate in various ways. (Think of the example of the racist expert system.) We take it for granted that human beings, including experts (perhaps *especially* experts), can be mistaken or ill advised about any of these three aspects of thinking. We must equally take it for granted that computer programs—which in any event are far less subtle and commonsensical than their programmers and even their users—can be questioned too. If we ever forget that "It's true because the computer says so" is *never* adequate justification, the social impact of AI will be horrendous indeed.

George Gilder (Photo by Jonathan Becker)

George Gilder

A Technology of Liberation

George Gilder is the author of eight books on issues of technology and society, including *Wealth and Poverty* (1981) and *The Spirit of Enterprise* (1983), both best sellers. His most recent book is *Microcosm* (1989), a history and prophesy of the age of VLSI microchips. Gilder is a regular contributor to the *Wall Street Journal* and lives in Tyringham, Massachusetts with his wife, four children, and four computers.

Futurists have long seen computers as Big Brother's crucial ally on the road to 1984, George Orwell's chilling vision of technocracy. Placed on pedestals in the central computing rooms of large institutions, computers were large, expensive, and arcane. They did not understand English; to use them, you had to learn what were called their higher-level languages. As one expert predicted, "There will be a small, almost separate society of people in rapport with the advanced machines." This elite will tend to control the state and master the commanding heights of the economy.

The year 1984 came and went, and the prophecies of 1984 were fulfilled only in nightmares and totalitarian gulags. One of the prime reasons for the failure of the prophecy was the success of computer technology. Contrary to all the grim predictions, intelligent machines empower individuals rather than large institutions, spread power rather than centralize it.

Crucial to the liberating impact of computers was the very nature of computer technology. In volume, anything on a chip is cheap. But moving up the hierarchy from the chip to the circuit board to the network and to the telecommunications system, interconnections between components grow exponentially more expensive. So a first law of the technology is to concentrate components and connections—and thus computing power—on single chips. Concentrating components on a chip not only enhanced their speed and effectiveness but also vastly lowered their price. Finally, in the form of the microprocessor, the computer on a chip costs a few dollars and outperforms the computer on a pedestal. Rather than pushing control toward Big Brother at the top, as the pundits predicted, the technology, by its very nature, constantly pulled power down to the people. The ultimate beneficiary, the individual with a personal computer or workstation, gained powers of creation and communication far beyond the kings of old.

The individual was not only the heir to the throne of the technology; he also was its leading creator. Although made possible by hardware innovations from around the world, the move to small computers was chiefly an American revolution driven by the invention of new software. As fast as the Japanese and others could expand the capacity of computer memories, American entrepreneurs filled them with useful programs. Some 14 thousand new U.S. companies, many of them led by teenagers and college hackers, launched a vast array of software packages and changed the computer from an arcane tool of elites to a popular appliance. As a result of this software, ranging from spreadsheets and word processors to data bases and video games, the United States pioneered and propagated the use of small computers, and the U.S. share of the world software market rose from under two-thirds to more than three quarters.

Analysts focusing on fifth-generation computer projects, mainframe systems, and supercomputers dismiss these personal computers as toys. So did the experts at IBM a few years ago. But at the same time that the United States moved massively into microcomputers, small systems surged far ahead in price performance. In terms of cost per MIPS (millions of instructions per second), the new personal computers are an amazing ninety times more cost effective than mainframes. With the ever growing ability to interconnect these machines in networks and use them in parallel configurations that yield mainframe performance, microcomputers are rapidly gaining market share against the large machines.

Once believed to be a bastion of bureaucratic computing, IBM itself has become a prime source of the redistribution of computer power. As IBM's machines become smaller and cheaper and more available to the public, they also become more effective and more flexible. The trend will continue. According to Ralph Gomory, IBM's chief scientist, the constraints of interconnections mean that supercomputers of the future will have to be concentrated into a space of three cubic inches. The industrial revolution imposed economies of scale, but the information revolution imposes economies of microscale. Computer power continually devolves into the hands and onto the laps of individuals.

The advance into the microcosm is now accelerating. Propelling it is a convergence of three major developments in the industry, developments that once again disperse power rather than centralize it. The first is artificial intelligence, giving to computers rudimentary powers of sight, hearing, and common sense. True, some of these AI devices still do a pretty limited job. It has been said that the computer industry thrived by doing well what human beings do badly. Artificial intelligence often seems to thrive by doing badly what human beings do well. But you can understand the significance of AI advances by imagining that you are deaf, dumb, and blind. If someone gave you a device that allowed you to see and hear even poorly, you would hail him as a new Edison. Computer technology has long been essentially deaf, dumb, and blind. Reachable only through keyboards and primitive sensors and programmable only in binary mathematics, computers remained mostly immured in their digital towers. Artificial intelligence promises to vastly enhance the accessibility of computers to human language, imagery, and expertise. So the computer can continue to leave ivory towers and data-processing elites behind and open itself to the needs of untrained and handicapped individuals, even allowing the blind to read and the disabled to write.

The second major breakthrough is the silicon compiler. Just as a software compiler converts high-level languages into the bits and bytes that a computer can understand, the silicon compiler converts high-level chip designs and functions into the intersecting polygons of an actual chip layout. This technology allows the complete design of integrated circuits on a computer, from initial concept to final silicon. To understand the impact of this development, imagine that printing firms essentially wrote all the books. This was the situation in the computer industry; in order to author a chip, you essentially had to own a semiconductor manufacturing plant (a silicon printing press), which cost between $50 and $200 million to build on a profitable scale. But with silicon compilers and related gear, any computer-literate person with a $20,000 workstation can author a major new integrated circuit precisely adapted to his needs. If mass production is needed, semiconductor companies around the globe will compete to print your design in the world's best clean rooms. In a prophetic move a few firms are now even introducing forms of silicon desktop publishing. For $3 million, for example, Lasarray sells manufacturing modules that do all essential production steps from etching the design to assembling the chips. Dallas Semiconductor acquired an advanced new chip-making facility for $10 million. Contrary to the analyses of the critics, the industry is not becoming more capital intensive. Measured in terms of capital costs per device function (the investment needed to deliver value to the customer) the industry is becoming ever cheaper to enter. The silicon compiler and related technologies moves power from large corporations to individual designers and entrepreneurs.

The third key breakthrough is the widespread abandonment of the long cherished von Neumann computer architecture with its single central processing unit, separate memory, and step-in and fetch-it instruction sets. Replacing this architecture are massively parallel systems with potentially thousands of processors working at once. This change in the architecture of computers resembles the abandonment of centralized processing in most large companies. In the past users had to line up outside the central processing room, submit their work to the data-processing experts, and then wait hours or days for it to be done. Today tasks are dispersed to thousands of desk tops and performed simultaneously. The new architecture of parallel processing breaks the similar bottleneck of the central processing unit at the heart of every computer. It allows the computer itself to operate like a modern corporate information system, with various operations all occurring simultaneously throughout the firm, rather than like an old corporate data processing hierarchy, which forced people to waste time in queues while waiting access to the company mainframe. Promising huge increases in the cost effectiveness of computing, parallel processing will cheaply bring supercomputer performance to individuals.

Any one of these breakthroughs alone would not bring the radical advances that are now in prospect. But all together they will increase computer efficiency by a factor of thousands. Carver Mead of Caltech, a pioneer in all three of these new fields, predicts a 10,000-fold advance in the cost effectiveness of information technology over the next ten years. The use of silicon compilers to create massively parallel chips to perform feats of artificial intelligence will transform the computer industry and the world economy.

An exemplary product of these converging inventions is speech recognition. Discrete-speech talkwriter technology already commands available vocabularies of nearly one hundred thousand words, active vocabularies in the tens of thousands, learning algorithms that adapt to specific accents, and operating speeds of over 40 words per minute. To achieve this speed and capacity combined with the ability to recognize continuous speech on conventional computer architectures would require some four hundred MIPS (millions of instructions per second). Yet the new speech-recognition gear will operate through personal computers and will cost only some $5000. That is just $15.00 per MIPS. IBM mainframes charge some $150,000 per MIPS, and the most efficient general-purpose small computers charge some $3,000 per MIPS. By using parallel chips adapted specifically to process the enigmatic onrush of human speech, these machines can increase the cost effectiveness of computing by a factor of hundreds.

The talkwriter is only one of hundreds of such products. Coming technologies will increase the efficiency of computer simulation by a factor of thousands, radically enhance the effectiveness of machine vision, create dramatically improved modes of music synthesis, provide new advances in surgical prosthesis, open a world of information to individuals anywhere in the world, all at prices unimaginable as recently as three years ago. As prices decline, the new information systems inevitably become personal technologies, used and extended by individuals with personal computers.

With an increasing stress on software and design rather than on hardware and materials, the computer industry symbolizes the age of information. Real power and added value in the modern era lies not in things but in thoughts. The chip is a medium, much like a floppy disk, a 35-millimeter film, a phonograph record, a video cassette, a compact disk, or even a book. All of these devices cost a few dollars to make; all sell for amounts determined by the value of their contents: the concepts and images they bear. What is important is not the medium but the message.

Microchip entrepreneur Jerry Sanders once declared that semiconductors would be "the oil of the eighties." Some analysts now fear that giant companies will conspire to cartelize chip production as OPEC once monopolized oil. They predict that by dominating advanced manufacturing technology and supplies, a few firms will gain the keys to the kingdom of artificial intelligence and other information technologies. Yet unlike oil which is a substance extracted from sand, semiconductor technologies are written on sand, and their substance is ideas. To say that huge conglomerates will take over the information industry because they have the most efficient chip factories or the purest silicon is like saying that the Canadians will dominate world literature because they have the tallest trees.

Contrary to all the fears and prophecies, the new technologies allow entrepreneurs to economize on capital and enhance its efficiency, mixing sand and ideas to generate new wealth and opportunity for men and women anywhere in the world. The chief effect can be summed up in a simple maxim, a hoary cliche: knowledge is power. Most people agree that this statement conveys an important truth. Today, however, knowledge is not simply *a* source of power; it is supremely *the* source of power. The difference is crucial. If knowledge is power in this vital sense, it means that other things are not power. The other things that no longer confer power, or radically less power than before, include all the goals and dreams of all the tyrants and despots of the centuries: power over natural resources, territory, military manpower, national taxes, trade surpluses, and national currencies.

In an age when men can inscribe new worlds on grains of sand, particular territories have lost their economic significance. Not only are the natural resources under the ground rapidly declining in relative value, but the companies and capital above the ground can easily pick up and leave. Capital markets are now global; funds can move around the world, rush down fiber optic cables, and bounce off satellites at near the speed of light. People—scientists, workers, and entrepreneurs—can leave at the speed of a 747, or even a Concorde. Companies can move in weeks. Ambitious men no longer stand still to be fleeced or exploited by bureaucrats.

The computer age is the epoch of the individual and family. Governments cannot take power by taking control or raising taxes, by mobilizing men or heaping up trade surpluses, by seizing territory or stealing technology. In the modern world even slaves are useless: they enslave their owners to systems of poverty and decline. The new source of national wealth is the freedom of creative individuals in control of information technology. This change is not merely a gain for a few advanced industrial states. All the world will benefit from the increasing impotence of imperialism, mercantilism, and statism. All the world will benefit from the replacement of the zero-sum game of territorial conflict with the rising spirals of gain from the diffusion of ideas. Ideas are not used up as they are used; they spread power as they are shared. Ideas begin as subjective events and always arise in individual minds and ultimately repose in them. The movement toward an information economy inevitably means a movement toward a global economy of individuals and families. Collective institutions will survive only to the extent that they can serve the men and women who comprise them.

All the theories of the computer as an instrument of oppression misunderstand these essential truths of the technology. In the information age, nations cannot gain strength by coercing and taxing their citizens. To increase their power, governments must reduce their powers and emancipate their people on the frontiers of the age of intelligent machines.

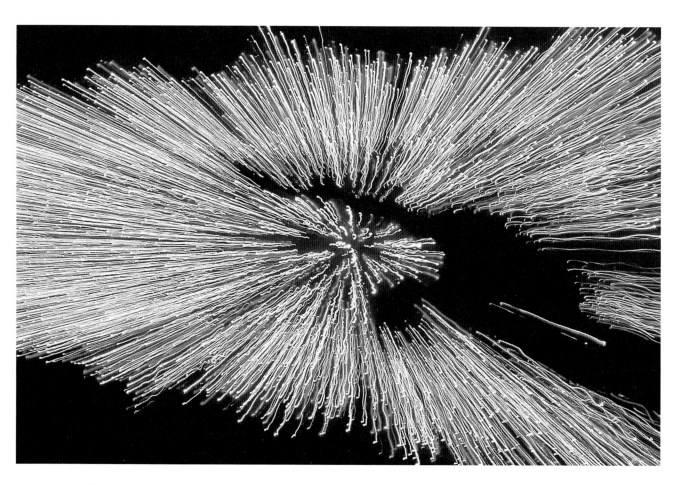

A computer image (Photo by Lou Jones)

Postscript

Let us review a few of the fundamental issues underlying the age of intelligent machines.

• Will Machines Reach Human Levels of Intelligence?

As I noted in the last section of the previous chapter, the strengths of today's machine intelligence are quite different from those of human intelligence and in many ways complement it. Once we have defined the transformations and methods underlying intelligent processes, a computer can carry them out tirelessly and at great speed. It can call upon a huge and extremely reliable memory and keep track of billions of facts and their relationships. Human intelligence, on the other hand,.though weak at mastering facts, still excels at turning information into *knowledge*. The ability to recognize, understand, and manipulate the subtle networks of abstraction inherent in knowledge continues to set human intelligence apart.

Yet computers are clearly advancing in these skills. Within narrow domains—diagnosing certain classes of disease, performing financial judgements, and many other specialized tasks—computers already rival human experts. During the 1980s expert systems went from research experiments to commercially viable tools that are relied upon daily to perform important jobs. Computers have also begun in recent years to master the pattern-recognition tasks inherent in vision and hearing. Though not yet up to human standards, pattern-recognition technology is sufficiently advanced to perform a wide variety of practical tasks. It is difficult to estimate when these capabilities will reach human levels, but there does not appear to be any fundamental barrier to achieving such levels. Undoubtedly, computers will achieve such levels gradually; no bell will ring when it happens.

What is clear is that by the time computers achieve human levels of performance in those areas of traditional human strength, they will also have greatly enhanced their areas of traditional superiority. (Not all experts agree with this. Doug Hofstadter, for example, speculates in *Gödel, Escher, Bach* that a future "actually intelligent" machine may not be able to do fast accurate arithmetic, because it will get distracted and confused by the concepts triggered by the numbers—a dubious proposition in my view.[1]) Once a computer can read and understand what it is reading, there is no reason why it should not read everything ever written (encyclopedias, reference works, books, journals and magazines, data bases, etc.) and thus master all knowledge. As Norbert Wiener has pointed out, no human being has had a complete mastery of human knowledge for the past couple centuries (and it is doubtful in my view that anyone has ever had such mastery). Even mere human levels of intelligence combined with a thorough mastery of all knowledge would give computers unique intellectual skills. Combine these attributes with computers' traditional strengths of speed, tireless operation, prodigious and unfailing memory, and extremely rapid communication, and the result will be formidable. We are, of course, not yet on the threshold of this vision. This early phase of the age of intelligent machines is providing us with obedient servants that are not yet intelligent enough to question our demands of them.

Minsky points out that we have trouble imagining machines achieving the capabilities we have because of a deficiency in our concept of a machine.[2] The human race first encountered machines (of its own creation) as devices with a few dozen, and in some cases a few hundred, active parts. Today, our computerized machines have millions of active components, yet our concept of a machine as a relatively inflexible device with only a handful of behavioral options has not changed. By the end of this century chips with over a billion components are anticipated, and we will enter an era of machines with many billions of components. Clearly, the subtleness and intelligence of the behavior of machines at those different levels of complexity are quite different. Emulating human levels of performance will require trillions, perhaps thousands of trillions, of components. At current rates of progress, we shall achieve such levels of complexity early in the next century. Human-level intelligence will not automatically follow, but reasonable extrapolations of the rate of progress of machine intelligence in a broad variety of skills in pattern recognition, fine motor coordination, decision making, and knowledge acquisition leads to the conclusion that there is no fundamental barrier to the AI field's ultimately achieving this objective.

• Can a Machine Think?

The question sounds innocuous enough, but our approach to it rests on the meanings we ascribe to the terms "machine" and "think." Consider first the question of whether or not a human being is a machine. A human being is certainly not like the early human-made machines, with only a handful of parts. Yet are we fundamentally different from a machine, one with, say, a few trillion parts? After all, our bodies and brains are presumably subject to the same natural laws as our machines. As I stated earlier, this is not an easy question, and several thousand years of philosophical debate have failed to answer it. If we assume that the answer to this question is no (humans are not fundamentally different from machines), then we have answered the original question. We presumably think, and if indeed we are machines, then we must conclude that machines can think. If, on the other hand, we assume that we are in some way fundamentally different from a machine, then our answer depends on our definition of the word "think."[3]

First, let us assume a behavioral definition, that is, a definition of thinking based on *outwardly* observable behavior. Under this definition, a machine should be considered to think if it appears to engage in intelligent behavior. This, incidentally, appears to be the definition used by the children I interviewed (see the section "Naive Experts" in chapter 2). Now the answer is simply a matter of the level of performance we expect. If we accept levels of performance in specific areas that would be considered intelligent if performed by human beings, then we have achieved intelligent behavior in our machines already, and thus we can conclude (as did the children I talked with) that today's computers are thinking. If, on the other hand, we expect an overall level of cognitive ability comparable to the full range of human intelligence, then today's computers cannot be regarded as thinking. If one accepts my conclusion above that computers will eventually achieve human levels of intellectual ability, then we can conclude that it is inherently possible for a machine to think, but that machines on earth have not yet started to do so.

If one accepts instead an intuitive definition of thinking, that is, an entity is considered to be thinking if it "seems" to be thinking, then responses will vary widely with the person assessing the "seeming." The children I spoke to felt that computers seemed to think, but many adults would disagree. For myself, I would say that computers do not yet *seem* to be thinking most of the time, although occasionally a clever leap of insight by a computer program I am interacting with will make it seem, just for a moment, that thinking is taking place.

Now let us consider the most difficult approach. If we define thinking to involve *conscious intentionality*, then we may not be in a position to answer the question at all. I know that I am conscious, so I know that I think (hence Descartes's famous dictum "I think, therefore I am"). I assume that other people think (lest I go mad), but this assumption appears to be built in (what philosophers would call *a priori* knowledge), rather than based on my observations of the behavior of other people. I can imagine machines that can understand and respond to people and situations with the same apparent intelligence as real people (see some of the scenarios above). The behavior of such machines would be indistinguishable from that of people; they would pass any behavioral test of intelligence, including the Turing test. Are these machines conscious? Do they have genuine intentionality or free will? Or are they just following their programs? Is there a distinction to be made between conscious free will and just following a program? Is this a distinction with a difference? Here we arrive once again at the crux of a philosophical issue that has been debated for several thousand years. Some observers, such as Minsky and Dennett, maintain that consciousness is indeed an observable and measurable facet of behavior, that we can imagine a test that could in theory determine whether or not an entity is conscious. Personally, I prefer a more subjective concept of consciousness, the idea that consciousness is a reality appreciated only by its possessor. Or perhaps I should say that consciousness is the possessor of the intelligence, rather than the other way around. If this is confusing, then you are beginning to appreciate why philosophy has always been so difficult.

If we assume a concept of thinking based on consciousness and hold that consciousness is detectable in some way, then one has only to carry out the appropriate experiment and the answer will be at hand. (If someone does this, let me know.) If, on the other hand, one accepts a subjective view of consciousness, then only the machine itself could know if it is conscious and thus thinking (assuming it can truly *know* anything). We could, of course, ask the machine if it is conscious, but we would not be protected from the possibility of the machine having been programmed to lie. (The philosopher Michael Serwen once proposed building an intelligent machine that could not lie and then simply asking it if it was conscious.)

One remaining approach to this question comes to us from quantum mechanics. In perhaps its most puzzling implication, quantum mechanics actually ascribes a physical reality to consciousness. Quantum theory states that a particle cannot have both a precise location and a precise velocity. If we measure its velocity precisely, then its location becomes inherently imprecise. In other words, its location becomes a probability cloud of possible locations. The reverse is also true: measuring its precise location renders its velocity imprecise. It is important to understand exactly what quantum mechanics is trying to say. It is not saying that there is an underlying reality of an exact location and velocity and that we are simply unable to measure them both precisely. It is literally saying that if a conscious being measures the velocity of a particle, it actually renders the *reality* of the location of that particle imprecise. Quantum mechanics is addressing not simply limitations in observation but the impact of conscious observation on the underlying reality of what is observed. Thus, *conscious* observation actually changes a property of a particle. Observation of the same particle by a machine that was not conscious would not have the same effect. If this seems strange to you, you are in good company. Einstein found it absurd and rejected it.[4] Quantum mechanics is consistent with a philosophical tradition that ascribes fundamental reality to knowledge, as opposed to knowledge simply being a reflection of some other fundamental reality.[5] Quantum mechanics is more than just a philosophical viewpoint, however: its predictions have been consistently confirmed. Almost any electronic device of the past 20 years demonstrates its principles, since the transistor is an embodiment of the paradoxical predictions of quantum mechanics. Quantum mechanics is the only theory in physics to ascribe a specific role to consciousness beyond simply saying that consciousness is what may happen to matter that evolves to high levels of intelligence according to physical laws.

If one accepts its notions fully, then quantum mechanics may imply a way to physically detect consciousness. I would counsel caution, however, to any would-be builder of a consciousness detector based on these principles. It might be upsetting to point a quantum-mechanical consciousness detector at ourselves and discover that we are not really conscious after all.

As a final note on quantum mechanics let me provide a good illustration of the central role it ascribes to consciousness. According to quantum mechanics, observing the velocity of a particle affects not only the preciseness of its location but also affects the preciseness of the location of certain types of "sister" particles that may have emerged from the same particle interaction that produced the particle whose velocity we just observed. For example, if an interaction produces a pair of particles that emerge in opposite directions and if we subsequently observe the velocity of one of the particles, we will instantly affect the preciseness of the position of both that particle and its sister, which may be millions of miles away. This would appear to contradict a fundamental tenet of relativity: that effects cannot be transmitted faster than the speed of light. This paradox is currently under study.[6]

When computers were first invented in the mid 1940s, they were generally regarded as curiosities, though possibly of value to mathematics and a few engineering disciplines. Their value to science, business, and other disciplines soon became apparent, and exploration of their practical applications soon began. Today, almost a half-century later, computers are ubiquitous and highly integrated into virtually all of society's institutions. If a law were passed banning all computers (and in the doubtful event that such legislation were adhered to), society would surely collapse. The orderly functioning of both government and business would break down in chaos. We are already highly dependent on these "amplifiers of human thought," as Ed Feigenbaum calls them. As the intelligence of our machines improves and broadens, computer intelligence will become increasingly integrated into our decision making, our economy, our work, our learning, our ability to communicate, and our life styles. They will be a driving force in shaping our future world. But the driving force in the growth of machine intelligence will continue to be human intelligence, at least for the next half century.

• A Final Note

When I was a boy, I had a penchant for collecting magic tricks and was known to give magic shows for friends and family. I took pleasure in the delight of my audience in observing apparently impossible phenomena. It became apparent to me that organizing ordinary methods in just the right sequence could give rise to striking results that went beyond the methods I started with. I also realized that revealing these methods would cause the magic to disappear and leave only the ordinary methods.

As I grew older, I discovered a more powerful form of magic: the computer. Again, by organizing ordinary methods in just the right sequences (that is, with the right algorithms), I could once again cause delight. Only the delight caused by this more grown-up magic was more profound. Computerized systems that help overcome the handicaps of the disabled or provide greater expressiveness and productivity for all of us provide measures of delight more lasting than the magic tricks of childhood. The sequences of *1*s and *0*s that capture the designs and algorithms of our computers embody our future knowledge and wealth. And unlike more ordinary magic, any revelation of the methods underlying our computer magic does not tarnish its enchantment.

Chronology

The world has changed less since Jesus Christ than it has in the last thirty years.
Charles Peguy, 1913

Year	Event
140–190 million years ago	Dinosaurs roam the earth.
Less than 100,000 years ago	*Homo sapiens* begin using intelligence to further their goals.
More than 5,000 years ago	The abacus, which resembles the arithmetic unit of a modern computer, is developed in the Orient.
3000–700 B.C.	Water clocks are built in China in 3000 B.C., in Egypt c. 1500 B.C., and in Assyria 700 B.C.
2500 B.C.	Egyptians invent the idea of thinking machines: citizens turn for advice to oracles, which are statues with priests hidden inside.
b. 469 B.C.	Socrates, the mentor of Plato, is the first Western thinker to assert that mental activities occur in the unconscious.
469–322 B.C.	Socrates, Plato, and Aristotle establish the essentially rationalistic philosophy of Western culture.
427 B.C.	In the *Phaedo* and later works Plato expresses ideas, several millenia before the advent of the computer, that are relevant to modern dilemmas regarding human thought and its relation to the mechanics of the machine.
c. 420 B.C.	Archytas of Tarentum, a friend of Plato, constructs a wooden pigeon whose movements are controlled by a jet of steam or compressed air.
b. 415 B.C.	Theaetetus, a member of Plato's Academy, creates solid geometry.
387 B.C.	Plato founds the Academy for the pursuit of science and philosophy in a grove on the outskirts of Athens. It results in the fertile development of mathematical theory.
343–334 B.C.	Aristotle carries on the Platonic tradition by becoming the teacher of Alexander the Great in 343 B.C. and founding the Lyceum, also known as the peripatetic school of philosophers, in 334 B.C.

Year	Event
293 B.C.	Euclid, also a member of Plato's Academy, is the expositor of plane geometry. He writes the *Elements,* a basic mathematics textbook for the next 2,000 years.
c. 200 B.C.	In China artisans develop elaborate automata, including an entire mechanical orchestra.
c. 200 B.C.	An Egyptian engineer improves the water clock, making it the most accurate timekeeping device for nearly 2,000 years.
A.D. 529	Plato's Academy and Aristotle's Lyceum are closed by the emperor Justinian.
c. 600	The earliest works mentioning the game of chess appear in India.
725	A Chinese engineer and a Buddhist monk build the first true mechanical clock, a water-driven device with an escapement that causes the clock to tick.
c. 1310	The first mechanical clocks appear in Europe, apparently stemming from stories about the existence of mechanical clocks in China.
1494	Leonardo da Vinci draws a clock with a pendulum.
1530	The spinning wheel is in use in Europe.
1540, 1772	The technology of clock and watch making results in the production of more elaborate automata during the European Renaissance. Gianello Toriano's mandolin-playing lady (1540) and P. Jacquet-Droz's child (1772) are famous examples.
1543	Nicolaus Copernicus publishes *De Revolutionibus*, in which he states that the earth and the other planets revolve around the sun, thereby changing humankind's relationship with God.
17th–18th centuries	This is the age of the Enlightenment, a philosophical movement to restore the supremacy of human reason, knowledge, and freedom, with parallel developments in science and theology. It had its roots in the European Renaissance and the Greek philosophy of twenty centuries earlier and constitutes the first systematic reconsideration of the nature of human thought and knowledge since the Platonists.
1617	John Napier invents Napier's Bones, of significance to the future development of calculating engines.
1637	René Descartes, who formulated the theory of optical refraction and developed the principles of modern analytic geometry, pushes rational skepticism to its limits in his most comprehensive work, *Discours de la Méthode*. His conclusion was "I think, therefore I am."
1642	Blaise Pascal perfects the Pascaline, a machine that can add and subtract. It is the world's first *automatic* calculating machine.
c. 1650	Otto von Guericke perfects the air pump and uses it to produce vacuums.
1670	*Pensées*, by Blaise Pascal, is published posthumously.
1687	Isaac Newton's *Philosophiae Naturalis Principia Mathematica,* known as *Principia,* establishes his three laws of motion and the law of universal gravitation.
1694	Gottfried Wilhelm Liebniz, an inventor of calculus, perfects the Liebniz Computer, a machine that multiplies by performing repetitive additions, an algorithm still used in modern computers.

Year	Event
1719	What appears to be the the first factory, an English silk-thread mill, employs 300 workers, mostly women and children.
1726	Jonathan Swift describes a machine that will automatically write books in Gulliver's Travels.
1733	John Kay paves the way for much faster weaving by patenting his New Engine for Opening and Dressing Wool, later known as the flying shuttle.
1760	Benjamin Franklin, in Philadelphia, erects lightning rods after having found, through his famous kite experiment in 1752, that lightning is a form of electricity.
c. 1760	Life expectancy at the beginning of the Industrial Revolution is about 37 years in North America and northwestern Europe.
1764	James Hargreaves invents the spinning jenny, which is able to spin eight threads at once.
1769	Richard Arkwright, the founder of the modern factory system, patents a hydraulic spinning machine that is too large and expensive to use in family dwellings. He builds a factory for his machine in 1781, thereby paving the way for many of the economic and social changes that will characterize the Industrial Revolution.
1781	Immanuel Kant publishes his *Critique of Pure Reason,* which expresses the philosophy of the Enlightenment while deemphasizing the role of metaphysics. He sets the stage for the emergence of twentieth-century rationalism.
1792	Edmund Cartwright devises the first machine to comb wool to feed the new mechanized spinning machines.
1792	William Murdock invents coal-gas lighting. The streets of London will be illuminated by 1802.
1800	All aspects of the production of cloth are automated.
1805	Joseph-Marie Jacquard devises a method for automating weaving with a series of punched cards. This invention will be used many years later in the development of early computers.
1811	Ned Ludd founds the Luddite movement in Nottingham over the issue of jobs versus automation.
1821	Charles Babbage is awarded the first gold medal by the British Astronomical Society for his paper "Observations on the Application of Machinery to the Computation of Mathematical Tables."
1821	Michael Farraday, widely recognized as the father of electricity, reports his discovery of electromagnetic rotation and builds the first two motors powered by electricity.
1822	Charles Babbage develops the Difference Engine, but its technical complexities exhaust his financial resources and organizational skills. He eventually abandons it to concentrate his efforts on a general-purpose computer.
1829	The first electromagnetically driven clock is constructed.
1832	Charles Babbage develops the principle of the Analytical Engine, which is the world's first computer and can be programmed to solve a wide variety of logical and computational problems.

Year	Event
1835	Joseph Henry invents the electrical relay, a means of transmitting electrical impulses over long distances that serves as the basis of the telegraph.
1837	Samuel Finley Breese Morse patents his more practical version of the telegraph, which sends letters in codes consisting of dots and dashes.
1843	Ada Lovelace, Lord Byron's only legitimate child and the world's first computer programmer, publishes her own notes with her translation of L. P. Menabrea's paper on Babbage's Analytical Machine.
1843	Søren Kierkegaard, who will greatly influence the ideas of modern existentialists, publishes *Either-Or,* his major work, followed by other writings that denounce the state-organized church on grounds that religion is a matter for the individual soul.
1846	Alexander Bain uses punched paper tape to send telegraph messages, greatly improving the speed of transmission.
1847	George Boole publishes his first ideas on symbolic logic. He will develop these ideas into his theory of binary logic and arithmetic that is still the basis of modern computation.
1851	An exhibition in London promotes the application of science to technology and focuses world attention on British progress in both fields.
1854	An electric telegraph is installed between Paris and London.
1855	Heinrich Geissler Igelshieb develops his mercury pump, used to produce the first good vacuum tubes. These will lead to the development of cathode rays and eventually to the discovery of the electron.
1855	William Thomson develops a successful theory of transmission of electrical signals through submarine cables.
1859	Charles Darwin, in *The Origin of Species,* explains his principle of natural selection and its influence on the evolution of various species.
1861	San Francisco and New York are connected by a telegraph line.
1864	Ducos de Harron develops a primitive motion-picture device in France.
1866	Cyrus West Field lays a telegraph cable across the Atlantic Ocean.
1870	GNP on a per capita basis and in constant 1958 dollars is $530. Twelve million Americans, or 31 percent of the population, have jobs, and only 2 percent of adults have high school diplomas.
1871	Charles Babbage dies, leaving more than 400 square feet of drawings for his Analytic Engine.
1873	Melvil Dewey develops for the Amherst College Library a plan for 999 categories of materials that becomes known as the Dewey Decimal System. It is refined over time to provide a virtually unlimited number of subdivisions.
1876	Alexander Graham Bell's telephone receives U.S. Patent 174,465, the most lucrative patent ever granted.
1879	G. Frege, one of the founders of modern symbolic language, proposes a notational system for mechanical reasoning. This work is a forerunner to the predicate calculus, which will be used for knowledge representation in artificial intelligence.

Year	Event
1879	Thomas Alva Edison invents the first incandescent light bulb that can burn for a significant length of time.
1880	Frederich Nietzsche writes *Morgenröte* and later works opposing romanticism and holding up art, philosophy, and religion as illusions. These ideas will strongly influence modern existentialism.
1882	Thomas Alva Edison's design for New York City's Pearl Street station on lower Broadway brings lighting to the United States.
1885	Boston is connected to New York by telephone.
1886	Alexander Graham Bell, with a modified version of Thomas Alva Edison's phonograph, uses wax discs for recording sound.
1887	The first gasoline-engine automobile is sold in Germany.
1888	William S. Burroughs patents an adding machine. This machine is modified, four years later to include subtraction and printing. It is the world's first dependable key-driven calculator and will soon win widespread acceptance.
1888	Heinrich Hertz experiments with the transmission of what are now known as radio waves.
1888	The first commercial roll-film camera is introduced.
1890	Herman Hollerith, incorporating ideas from Jacquard's loom and Babbage's Analytical Engine, patents an electromechanical information machine that uses punched cards. It wins the 1890 U.S. Census competition, with the result that electricity is used for the first time in a major data-processing project.
1894	Guglielmo Marconi builds his first radio equipment, which rings a bell from 30 feet away.
1894	Niagara Falls is harnessed for electricity.
1896	A sound film is first shown before a paying audience in Berlin.
1896	Herman Hollerith forms the Tabulating Machine Company, which will become IBM.
1897	Joseph John Thomson, with better vacuum pumps than previously available, discovers the electron, the first known particle smaller than an atom.
1897	Alexander Popov, a Russian, uses an antenna to transmit radio waves, and Guglielmo Marconi, an Italian, receives the first patent ever granted for radio. Marconi helps organize a company to market his system.
1899	The first recording of sound occurs magnetically on wire and on a thin metal strip.
1899	David Hilbert consolidates the accomplishments of nineteenth-century mathematics with such publications as *The Foundations of Geometry*.
1900	Herman Hollerith introduces an automatic card feed into his information machine to process the 1900 census data.

Year	Event
1900	The entire civilized world is connected by telegraph, and in the United States there are more than 1.4 million telephones, 8,000 registered automobiles, and 24 million electric light bulbs. Edison's promise of "electric bulbs so cheap that only the rich will be able to afford candles" is thus realized. In addition, the Gramophone Company is advertising a choice of five thousand recordings.
1900	More than one-third of all American workers are involved in the production of food.
1900	David Hilbert introduces the "direct method" in the calculus of variations and presents an agenda for twentieth-century mathematics that includes a list of the 23 most pressing problems at the International Mathematics Conference in Paris. He predicts that these problems will occupy the attention of mathematicians for the next century.
1901	Marconi in Newfoundland receives the first transatlantic telegraphic radio transmission.
1901	Sigmund Freud publishes *The Interpretation of Dreams,* which, along with his other works, illuminates the workings of the mind.
1904	John Ambrose Fleming files a patent for the first vacuum tube, a diode.
1906	Reginald Aubrey Fessenden invents AM radio and transmits by radio waves to wireless operators on U.S. ships off the Atlantic Coast a Christmas carol, a violin trill, and for the first time the sound of a human voice.
1907	Lee De Forest and R. von Lieben invent the amplifier vacuum tube, known as a triode, which greatly improves radio.
1908	Orville Wright makes his first hour-long airplane flight.
1910–1913	Bertrand Russell and Alfred North Whitehead publish their three-volume *Principia Mathematica,* a seminal work on the foundations of mathematics that provides a new methodology for all mathematics.
1911	Herman Hollerith's Tabulating Machine Company acquires several other companies and changes its name to Computing-Tabulating-Recording Company (CTR). In 1914 Thomas J. Watson is appointed president.
1913	Henry Ford introduces the first true assembly-line method of automated production.
1913	A. Meissner invents a radio transmitter with vacuum tubes. Radio-transmitter triode modulation is introduced the following year, and in 1915 the radio-tube oscillator is introduced.
1915	The first North American transatlantic telephone call is made between Thomas A. Watson in San Francisco and Alexander Graham Bell in New York.
1915	Albert Einstein completes his theory of gravitation known as the general theory of relativity.
1921	Czech dramatist Karel Capek popularizes the term "robot," a word he coined in 1917 to describe the mechanical people in his science fiction drama *R.U.R.* (Rossum's Universal Robots). His intelligent machines, intended as servants for their human creators, end up taking over the world and destroying all mankind.
1921	Ludwig Wittgenstein, often referred to as the first logical positivist, publishes *Tractatus Logico-Philosophicus,* regarded by some as perhaps the most influential philosophical work of the twentieth century.

Year	Event
1923	Vladimir Kosma Zworkin, the father of television, gives the first demonstration of an electronic television-camera tube, using a mechanical transmitting device. He develops the iconoscope, an early type of television system, the following year.
1924	Thomas J. Watson becomes the chief executive officer of CTR and renames the company International Business Machines (IBM). IBM will become the leader of the modern industry and one of the largest industrial corporations in the world.
1925	Niels Bohr and Werner Heisenberg lay the foundations for quantum mechanics.
1925	Vannevar Bush and his coworkers develop the first analog computer, a machine designed to solve differential equations.
1926	The era of talking motion pictures is introduced by *The Jazz Singer,* starring Al Jolson.
1927	Charles Lindbergh makes the first solo nonstop flight across the Atlantic Ocean.
1927	Martin Heidegger publishes *Sein und Zeit,* vol. 1, which is rooted in the work of Søren Kierkegaard and greatly influences the future development of existentialism.
1927	The Powers Accounting Machine Company goes through a series of mergers to become the Remington Rand Corporation.
1927	Werner Heisenberg postulates his uncertainty principle, which says that electrons have no precise location but rather probability clouds of possible locations. He wins a Nobel Prize five years later for his discovery of quantum mechanics.
1928	John von Neumann presents the minimax theorem, which will be widely used in game-playing programs.
1928	Philo T. Farnsworth demonstrates the world's first all-electronic television, and Vladimir Zworkin receives a patent for a color television system.
1929	FM radio is introduced.
1930	Paul Adrian Maurice Dirac publishes his *Principles of Quantum Mechanics,* in which he formulates a general mathematical theory.
1930	More than 18 million radios are owned by 60 percent of U.S. households.
1930	Vannevar Bush's analog computer, the Differential Analyzer, is built at MIT. It will be used to calculate artillery trajectories during World War II.
1930s	Music has shifted from the romantic style of Brahms and the early Mahler to the atonality of Schoenberg, art to the cubism and expressionism of Picasso, and poetry to the minimalism of Ezra Pound, T. S. Eliot, and William Carlos Williams.
1931	Kurt Gödel publishes his incompleteness theorem, which has been called the most important in all mathematics.
1932	RCA demonstrates a television receiver with a cathode-ray picture tube. In 1933 Zworkin produces a cathode-ray tube. called the iconoscope, that makes high-quality television almost a reality.
c. 1935	Albert Einstein's quest for a unified field theory occupies most of the last two decades of his life.

Year	Event
1936	Regular public television transmission begins in Great Britain.
1937	Building on the work of Bertrand Russell and Charles Babbage, Alan Turing publishes "On Computable Numbers," his now celebrated paper introducing the Turing machine, a theoretical model of a computer.
1937	The Church-Turing thesis, independently developed by Alonzo Church and Alan Turing, states that all problems solvable by a human being are reducible to a set of algorithms, or more simply, that machine intelligence and human intelligence are essentially equivalent.
1937	Frank Whittle builds the first working jet engine.
1939	The first regularly scheduled commercial flights begin crossing the Atlantic Ocean.
1940	John V. Atanasoff and Clifford Berry build an electronic computer known as ABC. This is the first *electronic* computer, but it is not programmable.
1940	The 10,000-person British computer war effort known as Ultra creates Robinson, the world's first operational computer. It is based on electromechanical relays and is powerful enough to decode messages from Enigma, the Nazi's first-generation enciphering machine.
1941	Konrad Zuse, a German, completes the world's first fully *programmable* digital computer, the Z-3, and hires Arnold Fast, a blind mathematician, to program it. Fast becomes the world's first programmer of an *operational* programmable computer.
1943	Warren McCulloch and Walter Pitts write their influential "Logical Calculus of the Ideas Immanent in Nervous Activity," which discusses neural-network architectures for intelligence.
1943	The Ultra team builds Colossus, a computer that uses electronic tubes 100 to 1000 times faster than the relays used by Robinson. It cracks increasingly complex German codes and contributes to the Allies' winning of World War II.
1943	Jean-Paul Sartre, a modern existentialist, publishes *L'Etre et le Néant* and later works that incorporate the ideas of Søren Kierkegaard and Martin Heidegger while emphasizing the role of free will in an apparently purposeless world. The spiritual and emotive world, which is meaning less to logical positivists is to existentialists the seat of true meaning.
1944	Howard Aiken completes the first American programmable computer, the Mark I. It uses punched paper tape for programming and vacuum tubes to calculate problems.
1945	Konrad Zuse develops Plankalkul, the first high-level language.
1946	John von Neumann publishes the first modern paper on the stored-program concept and starts computer research at the Institute for Advanced Study in Princeton.
1946	John Presper Eckert and John W. Mauchley develop ENIAC, the world's first fully electronic, general-purpose (programmable) digital computer. It is almost 1,000 times faster than the Mark I and is used for calculating ballistic-firing tables for the Army.
1946	Television enters American life even more rapidly than radio did in the 1920s. The percentage of American homes having sets jumps from 0.02 percent in 1946 to 72 percent in 1956 and more than 90 percent by 1983.
1947	William Bradford Schockley, Walter Hauser Brittain, and John Ardeen invent the transistor, a minute device that functions like a vacuum tube but switches current on and off at much faster speeds. It launches a revolution in microelectronics, bringing down the cost of computers and leading to the development of minicomputers and powerful new main frame computers.

Year	Event
1947	An airplane flies at supersonic speed for the first time, in the United States.
1948	Norbert Wiener publishes *Cybernetics,* a seminal book on information theory.
1949	Maurice Wilkes, influenced by Eckert and Mauchley, builds EDSAC, the world's first stored-program computer. Eckert and Mauchley's new U.S. company brings out BINAC, the first American stored-program computer, soon after.
1949	George Orwell's novel *1984* envisions a chilling world in which very large bureaucracies employ computers to enslave the population.
1950	The U.S. census is first handled by a programmable computer, UNIVAC, developed by Eckert and Mauchley. It is the first commercially marketed computer.
1950	Alan Turing's "Computing Machinery and Intelligence" describes a means for determining whether a machine is intelligent known as the Turing test.
1950	Commercial color television begins in the U.S. Transcontinental black-and-white television is inaugurated the following year.
1950	Claude Elwood Shannon writes a proposal for a chess program.
1951	EDVAC, Eckert and Mauchley's first computer that implements the stored-program concept, is completed at the Moore School at the University of Pennsylvania.
1951	A Cybernetics Congress is held in Paris.
1952	The CBS television network uses UNIVAC to correctly predict the election of Dwight D. Eisenhower as president of the United States.
1952	The pocket-sized transistor radio is introduced.
1952	The 701, IBM's first production-line electronic digital computer, is designed by Nathaniel Rochester and marketed for scientific use.
1953	James D. Watson and Francis H. C. Crick discover the chemical structure of the DNA molecule.
1953	Two statements of major importance to modern existentialism appear: *Philosophical Investigations* by Ludwig Wittgenstein and *Waiting for Godot,* a play by Samuel Beckett.
1955	The Remington Rand Corporation merges with Sperry Gyroscope to become the Sperry-Rand Corporation, one of IBM's chief competitors for a time.
1955	IBM introduces its first transistor calculator, with 2,200 transistors instead of the 1,200 vacuum tubes that would otherwise be required.
1955	The first design is created for a robotlike machine for industrial use in the U.S.
1955	Allen Newell, J. C. Shaw, and Herbert Simon develop IPL-II, the first AI language.
1955	The beginning space program and the military in the U.S., recognizing the need for computers powerful enough to steer rockets to the moon and missiles through the stratosphere, fund major research projects.
1956	Allen Newell, J. C. Shaw, and Herbert Simon create The Logic Theorist, which uses recursive search techniques to solve mathematical problems.

Year	Event
1956	The first transatlantic telephone cable begins to operate.
1956	Fortran, the first scientific computer programming language, is invented by John Backus and a team at IBM.
1956	MANIAC I, the first computer program to beat a human being in a chess game, is developed by Stanislaw Ulam.
1956	Artificial intelligence is named at a computer conference at Dartmouth College.
1957	Allen Newell, J. C. Shaw, and Herbert Simon develop the General Problem Solver, which uses means-ends analysis to solve problems.
1957	Noam Chomsky writes *Syntactic Structures,* the first of many important works that will earn him the title of father of modern linguistics. This work seriously considers the computation required for natural-language understanding.
1958	Jack St. Clair Kilby invents the first integrated circuit.
1958	John McCarthy and Marvin Minsky found the Artificial Intelligence Laboratory at the Massachusetts Institute of Technology.
1958	The first U.S. commercial jet flies from New York to Paris.
1958	Allen Newell and Herbert Simon predict that within ten years a digital computer will be the world's chess champion.
1958	John McCarthy introduces LISP, an early (and still widely used) AI language.
1958	The Defense Advanced Research Projects Agency is established. It will fund much important computer-science research in the decades to come.
1958–1959	Jack Kilby and Robert Noyce independently develop the chip, which leads to much cheaper and smaller computers.
1959	Arthur Samuel's checker-playing program, completed as a study in machine-learning, performs as well as some of the best players of the time.
1959	Dartmouth's Thomas Kurtz and John Kemeny find an alternative to batch processing: time sharing.
1959	The advent of electronic document preparation will increase U.S. paper consumption of printed documents: the nation now consumes 7 million tons of paper per year; that number will increase to 22 million in 1986. American businesses will use 850 billion pages in 1981, 2.5 trillion pages in 1986, and 4 trillion in 1990.
1959	Grace Murray Hopper, one of the first programmers of the Mark I, develops COBOL, a computer language designed for business use.
1960	The Defense Department's Advanced Research Projects Agency substantially increases its funding of computer research.
1960	About 6,000 computers are in operation in the United States.
1960	Yehoshua Bar-Hillel's "Demonstration of the Nonfeasibility of Fully Automatic High-Quality Translation" points out the difficulty of machine translation from one natural language to another: a program needs to actually understand the world a particular passage refers to.

Year	Event
1960s	Current neural-net machines incorporate a small number of neurons organized in only one or two layers. Such simple models are mathematically proved to be limited in what they can do.
1961	President John F. Kennedy, addressing a joint session of Congress, says, "I believe we should go to the moon," thereby launching Project Apollo, which will provide the impetus for important research in computer science.
1961	Yuri Gagarin becomes the first human being to orbit the earth.
1962	A U.S. company markets the world's first industrial robots.
1962	The first Department of Computer Science offering a Ph.D. is established at Purdue University.
1962	Time sharing is introduced on a computer in Philadelphia for inventory control.
1962	John Glenn, Jr., in his Mercury 6 space capsule, becomes the first American to orbit the earth. The U.S. space probe Mariner is the first object made by human beings to voyage to another planet. And America's Telstar becomes the first active communications satellite, relaying television pictures around the globe.
1962	D. Murphy and Richard Greenblatt develop the TECO text editor, one of the first word-processing systems, for use on the PDP1 computer at MIT.
1962	Frank Rosenblatt publishes *Principles of Neurodynamics*, in which he defines the perceptron, a simple processing element for neural networks. He first introduced the perceptron at a conference in 1959.
1962	Thomas Kuhn publishes *The Structure of Scientific Revolutions*, in which he theorizes about the nature of the growth of scientific knowledge.
1963	M. Ross Quillian's work leads to the semantic network as a means of representing knowledge in terms of concepts and relationships among concepts.
1963	Project MAC is established at MIT for computer-science research.
1963	AI researchers of the 1960s, noting the similarity between human and computer languages, adopt the goal of parsing natural-language sentences. Susumo Kuno's parsing system reveals the great extent of syntactic and semantic ambiguity in the English language. It is tested on the sentence "Time flies like an arrow."
1963	John McCarthy founds the Artificial Intelligence Laboratory at Stanford University.
1963	Marvin Minsky publishes his influential *Steps Towards Artificial Intelligence*.
1964	IBM solidifies its leadership of the computer industry with the introduction of its 360 series.
1964	Daniel Bobrow completes his doctoral work on Student, a natural-language program that can solve high-school-level word problems in algebra.
1964	Gordon Moore, one of the founders of Fairchild Semiconductor Corporation, predicts that integrated circuits will double in complexity each year. His statement will become known as Moore's law and will prove true for decades to come.
1964	Marshall McLuhan's *Understanding Media* foresees electronic media, especially television, as creating a "global village" in which "the medium is the message."

Year	Event
1965	Raj Reddy founds the Robotics Institute at Carnegie-Mellon University. The institute becomes a leading research center for AI.
1965	The DENDRAL project begins at Stanford University, headed by Bruce Buchanan, Edward Feigenbaum, and Nobel laureate Joshua Lederberg. Its purpose is to experiment on knowledge as the primary means of producing problem-solving behavior. The first expert system, DENDRAL, embodies extensive knowledge of molecular-structure analysis. Follow-up work, carried out through the early 1970s, produce Meta-DENDRAL, a learning program that automatically devises new rules for DENDRAL.
1965	Hubert Dreyfus presents a set of philosophical arguments against the possibility of artificial intelligence in a RAND Corporation memo entitled "Alchemy and Artificial Intelligence."
1965	Led by Edward Feigenbaum and his associates the Heuristic Programming Project, which will later become the Knowledge Systems Laboratory, begins at Stanford University.
1965	Herbert Simon predicts that by 1985 "machines will be capable of doing any work a man can do."
Mid 1960s	Computers are beginning to be widely used in the criminal justice system.
Mid 1960s	Scientific and professional knowledge is beginning to be codified in a machine-readable form.
1966	Richard Greenblatt develops a fairly sophisticated chess-playing program, a version of which defeats Hubert Dreyfus, an AI critic who strongly doubts the ability of computers to play chess.
1967	Seymour Papert and his associates at MIT begin working on LOGO, an education-oriented programming language that will be widely used by children.
1967	The software business is born when IBM announces it will no longer sell software and hardware in a single unit.
1968	David Hubel and Torstein Wiesel publish the first of many important papers on the macaque monkey cortex. They discover edge-detection cells in the outer layers of the visual cortex.
1968	Marvin Minsky publishes *Semantic Information Processing*, an important collection of papers describing AI work by himself and his students.
1968	Noam Chomsky and Morris Halle publish *The Sound Pattern of English,* a landmark study of English phonetics.
1968	The film *2001: A Space Odyssey,* by Arthur C. Clarke and Stanley Kubrick, presents HAL, a computer that can see, speak, hear, and think like its human colleagues aboard a spaceship.
1969	Neil Armstrong becomes the first human to stand on the moon.
1969	Marvin Minsky and Seymour Papert write *Perceptrons,* a book that presents limitations of single-layer neural nets.
1970	The GNP on a per capita basis and in constant 1958 dollars is $3,500, or more than six times as much as a century ago.
1970	The floppy disc is introduced for storing data in computers.
1970	Harry Pople and Jack Myers of the University of Pittsburgh begin work on Internist, a system that aids physicians in the diagnosis of a wide range of human diseases.

Year	Event
1970	Patrick Winston's doctoral work presents a program that learns to recognize an arch, and it also addresses the problem of machine learning.
1970	Terry Winograd completes his landmark thesis on SHRDLU, a natural-language system that exhibits diverse intelligent behavior in the small world of children's blocks. SHRDLU is criticized, however, for its lack of generality.
1971	Kenneth Colby, Sylvia Weber, and F. D. Hilf present a report on PARRY, a program simulating a paranoid person, in a paper entitled "Artificial Paranoia." The program is so convincing that clinical psychiatrists cannot distinguish its behavior from that of a human paranoid person.
1971	The first microprocessor is introduced in the U.S.
1971	The first pocket calculator is introduced. It can add, subtract, multiply, and divide.
1971	Direct telephone dialing on a regular basis begins between parts of the U.S. and Europe.
1972	Hubert Dreyfus publishes *What Computers Can't Do,* an elaboration of his 1965 criticism of AI. He argues that symbol manipulation cannot be the basis of human intelligence.
1973	Alain Colmerauer presents an outline of PROLOG, a logic-programming language. The language will become enormously popular and will be adopted for use in the Japanese Fifth Generation Program.
1973	Roger Shank and Robert Abelson develop scripts, knowledge-representation systems used to describe familiar everyday situations.
1974	The first computer-controlled industrial robot is developed.
1974	Edward Shortliffe completes his doctoral dissertation on MYCIN, an expert system designed to help medical practitioners prescribe an appropriate antibiotic by determining the precise identity of a blood infection. Work to augment this program with other important systems, notably TEIRESIAS and EMYCIN will continue through the early 1980s. TEIRESIAS will be developed in 1976 by Randall Davis to serve as a powerful information-structuring tool for knowledge engineers. EMYCIN, by William van Melle, will represent the skeletal structure of inferences.
1974	Marvin Minsky issues "A Framework for Representing Knowledge" as an MIT AI memo, a landmark in knowledge representation.
1974	The SUMEX-AIM computer-communications network is established to promote the development of applications of artificial intelligence to medicine.
1975	Benoit Mandelbrot writes "Les objet fractals: Forme, hasard, et dimension," his first long essay on fractal geometry, a branch of mathematics that he developed. Fractal forms will be widely used to model chaotic phenomena in nature and to generate realistic computer images of naturally occurring objects.
1975	Medicine is becoming an important area of applications for AI research. Four major medical expert systems have been developed by now: PIP, CASNET, MYCIN, and Internist.
1975	The Defense Advanced Research Programs Agency launches its Image Understanding Program to stimulate research in the area of machine vision.
1975	More than 5,000 microcomputers are sold in the U.S., and the first personal computer, with 256 bytes of memory, is introduced.

Year	Event
1970s	The role of knowledge in intelligent behavior is now a major focus of AI research. Bruce Buchanan and Edward Feigenbaum of Stanford University pioneer knowledge engineering.
1976	Daniel Bell publishes *The Post-Industrial Society*, which introduces the concept of a society in which the "axial principle" is the centrality and codification of knowledge.
1976	As a representation of a visual image, David Marr proposes a primal sketch, containing information that describes brightness changes, blobs, and textures.
1976	Kurzweil Computer Products introduces the Kurzweil Reading Machine, which reads aloud any printed text that is presented to it. Based on omnifont-character-recognition technology, it is intended to be a sensory aid for the blind.
1976	Douglas Lenat presents a program called AM (for Automated Mathematician) as part of his Stanford doctoral dissertation. AM, a precursor to EURISKO, is a knowledge-based system that makes "discoveries" in number theory and abstract mathematics.
1976	Joseph Weizenbaum, who created the famous ELIZA program, which simulates a Rogerian psychotherapist, publishes *Computer Power and Human Reason.* He argues that even if we could build intelligent machines, it would be unethical to do so.
1976–1977	Lynn Conway and Carver Mead collaborate and put together a collection of principles for VLSI design. Their classic textbook *Introduction to VLSI Design* is published in 1980. VLSI circuits will form the basis of the fourth generation of computers.
1977	David Marr and Tomaso Poggio point out the salient difference between the human brain and today's computer in a paper on computer vision, "From Understanding Computation to Understanding Neural Circuitry." While the connection to components ratio is only 3 in computers, it is 10,000 in the cortex of a mammal.
1977	Steven Jobs and Stephen Wozniak design and build the Apple Computer.
1977	The first computer camp for children is held in Connecticut.
1977	The film *Star Wars* features 3CPO and a galaxy of other imaginative true-to-life robots with a wide spectrum of convincing human emotions.
1977	Voyagers 1 and 2 are launched and radio back billions of bytes of computerized data about new discoveries as they explore the outer planets of our solar system.
1977	The Apple II, the first personal computer to be sold in assembled form, is successfully marketed.
1978	David Marr and H. K. Nishihara propose a new representation of visual information. The $2^1/_2$-dimensional sketch, presents the depth and orientation of all visible surfaces.
1978	Digital Equipment Corporation (DEC) and Carnegie-Mellon University begin work on XCON, an expert system that configures computer systems. By 1980 XCON will come into regular use, saving millions of dollars at DEC plants.
1979	In a landmark study published in the *Journal of the American Medical Association* by nine researchers, the performance of MYCIN is compared with that of doctors on ten test cases of meningitis. MYCIN does at least as well as the medical experts. The potential of expert systems in medicine becomes widely recognized.

Year	Event
1979	Ada, a computer language developed for use by the armed forces, is named for Ada Lovelace.
1979	Pac Man and other early computerized video games appear.
1980	AI industry revenue is a few million dollars per year.
1980	Douglas R. Hofstadter wins a Pulitzer Prize for his best-selling *Gödel, Escher, Bach*.
1980	David Marr and Ellen Hildreth publish an important study on edge detection.
1980	The Propaedia section of the fifteenth edition of the *Encyclopaedia Britannica* represents an ambitious attempt to codify an outline of all human knowledge in just 800 pages.
Early 1980s	Second-generation robots arrive with the ability to precisely effect movements with five or six degrees of freedom. They are used for industrial welding and spray painting.
Early 1980s	The MYCIN project produces NeoMYCIN and ONCOCIN, expert systems that incorporate hierarchical knowledge bases. They are more flexible than MYCIN.
Early 1980s	Expert systems typically have knowledge bases of about a thousand rules.
1980s	The neural-network paradigm begins to make a comeback, as neuron models are now potentially more sophisticated. Multilayered networks are commonly used.
1981	MITI, Japan's ministry for trade and industry, announces plans to develop by 1990 intelligent computers that will be at least a thousand times as powerful as the present ones. MITI has a track record of leading Japanese industry to world dominance in a wide range of fields.
1981	Desktop-publishing takes root when Xerox brings out its Star Computer. However, it will not become popular until Apple's Laserwriter comes on the market in 1985. Desktop publishing provides writers and artists an inexpensive and efficient way to compose and print large documents.
1981	IBM introduces its Personal Computer (PC).
1982	Compact-disc players are marketed for the first time.
1982	A million-dollar advertising campaign introduces Mitch Kapor's Lotus 1-2-3, an enormously popular spreadsheet program.
1982	With over 100,000 associations between symptoms and diseases covering 70 percent of all the knowledge in the field, CADUCEUS, an improvement on the Internist expert system, is developed for internal medicine by Harry Pople and Jack Myers at the University of Pittsburgh. Tested against cases from the *New England Journal of Medicine*, it proves more accurate than humans in a wide range of categories.
1982	Defense robots play a vital role in the Israeli destruction of 29 Russian SAM (surface-to-air missile) sites in a single hour during the invasion of Lebanon.
1982	Japan's ICOT, a corporate consortium formed to meet some of the goals of the Fifth Generation Project, begins active development with funding of $1 billion (half from MITI, half from Japanese industry) over ten years. A response is initiated by the Americans.
1982	SRI International's Prospector, a mineralogical expert system initiated in 1976 and updated annually, pinpoints the location of a major deposit of molybdenum.

Year	Event
1983	Edward Feigenbaum and Pamela McCorduck publish their influential book *The Fifth Generation*, on Japan's computer challenge to the world.
1983	The Defense Advanced Research Projects Agency (DARPA) unveils the Strategic Computing Initiative, a major program for research in microelectronics, computer architectures, and AI.
1983	Six million personal computers are sold in the U.S.
1983	Isaac Asimov describes in his science fiction novel *Robots of Dawn* a society two centuries from now in which a beautiful female scientist and her "humaniform" robot lover live in the company of a generation of robotic companions, servants, teachers, and guards.
1984	The European Economic Community forms ESPRIT, a five-year program to develop intelligent computers. It is launched with $1.5 billion in funding.
1984	RACTER, created by William Chamberlain, is the first computer program to author a book.
1984	Ronald Reagan signs legislation to permit the formation of the Microelectronics and Computer Corp. (MCC), a consortium of 21 companies whose purpose is to develop intelligent computers. MCC has an annual research budget of $65 million.
1984	Waseda University in Tokyo completes Wabot-2, a 200 pound robot that reads sheet music through its camera eye and plays the organ with its ten fingers and two feet.
1984	Optical disks for the storage of computer data are introduced, and IBM brings out a megabit RAM memory chip with four times the memory of earlier chips.
1985	Marvin Minsky publishes *The Society of Mind,* in which he presents a theory of the mind in which intelligence is seen to be the result of proper organizations of a very large number of simple mechanisms, each of which is by itself unintelligent.
1985	Jerome Wiesner and Nicholas Negroponte found MIT's Media Laboratory to do research on applications of aspects of computer science, sociology, and artificial intelligence to media technology.
1985	During this year designs for 6,000 application-specific integrated circuits (ASICs) are produced. These custom-built chips are being recognized as time and money savers.
1985	Jobs have grown tenfold since 1870: from 12 million to 116 million. The percentage of the U.S. populace gainfully employed has grown from 31 to 48. Per capita GNP in constant dollars has increased by 600 percent. These trends are expected to continue.
1985	The MIT Media Laboratory creates the first three-dimensional holographic image to be generated entirely by computer.
c. 1985	Japan leads the world in robotics development, production, and application.
Mid 1980s	AI research begins to focus seriously on parallel architectures and methodologies for problem solving.
Mid 1980s	Third-generation robots arrive with limited intelligence and some vision and tactile sensing.
1986	AI industry revenue is now $1 billion.
1986	Albert Lawrence, Alan Schick, and Robert Birge of Carnegie-Mellon University conduct research focused on the effort to develop a theory of molecular computing.

Year	Event
1986	Dallas Police use a robot to break into an apartment. The fugitive runs out in fright and surrenders.
1986	Electronic keyboards account for 55.2 percent of the American musical keyboard market, up from 9.5 percent in 1980. This trend is expected to continue until the market is almost *all* electronic.
1986	James McClelland and David Rumelhart edit a set of papers on neural-network models for intelligence, a collection that will soon become the manifesto of the new connectionists.
1986	Technology for optical character recognition represents a $100 million dollar industry that is expected to grow to several hundred million by 1990.
1986	New medical imaging systems are creating a mini revolution. Doctors can now make accurate judgments based on views of areas inside our bodies and brains.
1986	Using image processing and pattern recognition, Lillian Schwartz comes up with an answer to a 500-year-old question: Who was the Mona Lisa? Her conclusion: Leonardo da Vinci himself.
1986	Life expectancy is about 74 years in the U.S. Only 3 percent of the American work force is involved in the production of food. Fully 76 percent of American adults have high school diplomas, and 7.3 million U.S. students are enrolled in college.
1986	Russell Anderson's doctoral work at the University of Pennsylvania is a robotic ping-pong player that wins against human beings.
1986	The best computer chess players are now competing successfully at the senior master level, with HiTech, the leading chess machine, analyzing 200,000 board positions per second.
1987	Computerized trading helps push NYSE stocks to their greatest single-day loss.
1987	The market for natural-language products (excluding automated speech recognition) is estimated at $80 million and is expected to grow to $300 million by 1990.
1987	Commercial revenue from AI-related technologies in the U.S., excluding robotics, is now $1.4 billion. It is expected to reach $4 billion by 1990.
1987	Current speech systems can provide any *one* of the following: a large vocabulary, continuous speech recognition, or speaker independence.
1987	Japan develops the Automated Fingerprint Identification System (AFIS), which enables U.S. law enforcement agencies to rapidly track and identify suspects.
1987	Robotic-vision systems are now a $300 million industry and will grow to $800 million by 1990.
1987	There are now 1,900 working expert systems, 1,200 more than last year. The most popular area of application is finance, followed by manufacturing control and fault diagnosis.
1987	XCON, DEC's expert system for configuring computers, has grown since its introduction in 1980. It now has a knowledge base that incorporates over 10,000 rules and does the work of 300 people more accurately than humans.
1988	Computer memory today costs only 10^{-8} of what it did in 1950.
1988	The expert-systems market is now valued at $400 million, up from $4 million in 1981. The market is projected to grow to $800 million by 1990.

Year	Event
1988	Marvin Minsky and Seymour Papert offer their view of recent developments in neural-network machinery for intelligence in a revised edition of *Perceptrons*.
1988	The population of industrial robots has increased from a few hundred in 1970 to several hundred thousand, most of them in Japan.
1988	In the U.S. 4,700,000 microcomputers, 120,000 minicomputers, and 11,500 mainframes are sold in this year.
1988	W. Daniel Hillis's Connection Machine is capable of 65,536 computations at the same time.
1988	Warsaw Pact forces are at least a decade behind NATO forces in artificial intelligence and other computer technologies.
1989	Computational power per unit of cost has roughly doubled every 18 to 24 months for the past 40 years.
1989	The trend from analog to digital will continue to revolutionize a growing number of industries.
1989	Japan, a country very poor in natural resources but rich in expertise, has become the wealthiest nation on the planet, as measured by the total value of all assets.
Late 1980s	The core avionics of a typical fighter aircraft uses 200,000 lines of software. The figure is expected to grow to about 1 million in the 1990s. The U.S. Military as a whole uses about 100 million lines of software (and is expected to use 200 million by 1993). Software quality becomes an urgent issue that planners are beginning to address.
Late 1980s	The computer is being recognized as a powerful tool for artistic expression.
Early 1990s	A profound change in military strategy arrives. The more developed nations increasingly rely on "smart weapons," which incorporate electronic copilots, pattern recognitiontechniques, and advanced technologies for tracking, identification, and destruction.
Early 1990s	Continuous speech systems can handle large vocabularies for specific tasks.
Early 1990s	Computer processors operate at speeds of 100 MIPS.
Early 1990s	Application Specific Integrated Circuit (ASIC) technology makes writing chip programs as easy as writing software programs.
1990s	A multi-hundred-billion-dollar computer and information-processing industry is emerging, together with a generation of ubiquitous machine intelligence that works intimately with its human creators.
1990s	Significant progress is made toward an intelligent assistant, a decision-support system capable of a wide variety of administrative and information-gathering tasks. The system can, for example, prepare a feasibility report on a project proposal after accessing several data bases and talking to human experts.
1990s	Reliable person identification, using pattern- recognition techniques applied to visual and speech patterns, replace locks and keys in many instances.
1990s	Accomplished musicians, as well as students learning music, are routinely accompanied by cybernetic musicians.

Year	Event
1990s	AI technology is of greater strategic importance than manpower, geography, and natural resources.
Late 1990s	Documents frequently never exist on paper because they incorporate information in the form of audio and video pieces.
Late 1990s	Media technology is capable of producing computer-generated personalities, intelligent image systems with some human characteristics.
1999	The several-hundred-billion-dollar computer and information-processing market is largely intelligent by 1990 standards.
2000	Three-dimensional chips and smaller component geometries contribute to a multithousandfold improvement in computer power (compared to a decade earlier).
2000	Chips with over a billion components appear.
2000	The world chess champion is a computer.
Early 2000s	Translating telephones allow two people across the globe to speak to each other even if they do not speak the same language.
Early 2000s	Speech-to-text machines translate speech into a visual display for the deaf.
Early 2000s	Exoskeletal robotic prosthetic aids enable paraplegic persons to walk and climb stairs.
Early 2000s	Telephones are answered by an intelligent telephone answering machine that converses with the calling party to determine the nature and priority of the call.
Early 2000s	The cybernetic chauffeur, installed in one's car, communicates with other cars and sensors on roads. In this way it successfully drives and navigates from one point to another.
Early 21st century	Computers dominate the educational environment. Courseware is intelligent enough to understand and correct the inaccuracies in the conceptual model of a student. Media technology allows students to interact with simulations of the very systems and personalities they are studying.
Early 21st century	The entire production sector of society is operated by a small number of technicians and professionals. Individual customization of products is common.
Early 21st century	Drugs are designed and tested on human biochemical simulators.
Early 21st century	Seeing machines for the blind provide both reading and navigation functions.
2010	A personal computer has the ability to answer a large variety of queries because it will know where to find knowledge. Communication technologies allow it to access many sources of knowledge by wireless communication.
2020–2050	A phone call, which includes highly realistic three-dimensional holographic moving images, is like visiting with the person called.
2020–2070	A computer passes the Turing test, which indicates human-level intelligence.

Notes

The Second Industrial Revolution

1. Duncan Bythell, *The Handloom Weavers: A Study in the English Cotton Industry during the Industrial Revolution*, p. 70.

2. Bythell, "The Coming of the Powerloom," *The Handloom Weavers*, pp. 66–93.

3. Malcolm I. Thomis has written a sound documentation of this important historical movement in *The Luddites: Machine-Breaking in Regency England*.

4. See, for example, Sir Percy Snow, speaker, "Scientists and Decision Making," in Martin Greenberger, ed., *Computers and the World of the Future*, p. 5; and Langdon Winner, "Luddism as Epistemology," in *Autonomous Technology*, pp. 325–395.

5. Ben J. Wattenberg, ed., *The Statistical History of the United States from Colonial Times to the Present*.

6. U.S. Department of Commerce, Bureau of the Census, *Statistical Abstract of the United States, 1986,* 106th ed., p. 390; see also U.S. Bureau of the Census, *How We Live: Then and Now*.

7. Ben J. Wattenberg, ed., *The Statistical History of the United States from Colonial Times to the Present*.

8. U.S. Department of Commerce, Bureau of the Census, *Statistical Abstract of the United States, 1986.*

9. Ben J. Wattenberg, ed., *The Statistical History of the United States from Colonial Times to the Present*, p. 224.

10. U.S. Department of Commerce, Bureau of the Census, *Historical Statistics of the U.S.: Colonial Times to 1970,* vol. 1; and National Center for Education Statistics, U.S. Department of Education, 1986.

11. U.S. Department of Commerce, Bureau of the Census, *Historical Statistics of the U.S.: Colonial Times to 1970,* vol. 1.

12. U.S. Department of Commerce, Bureau of the Census, *Historical Statistics of the U.S.: Colonial Times to 1970,* vol. 1.

13. Wassily W. Leontief, *The Impact of Automation on Employment, 1963–2000* .

14. Wassily W. Leontief, *The Impact of Automation on Employment, 1963–2000.*

15. This phenomenon is discussed at length by Barry Bluestone and Bennett Harrison, in *The Deindustrialization of America*; also, see Lester Thurow "The Surge in Inequality," *Scientific American*, May 1987, 30–38; and Harrison and Bluestone, *The Great U-Turn*.

16. Tom Forester surveys the cost and power trends in the computer revolution in *High-Tech Society*, pp. 21–41.

17. Edward Feigenbaum and Pamela McCorduck discuss the impact of expert systems on the field of molecular biology in *The Fifth Generation*, p. 66. Sketches of computer-assisted diagnostic programs

presently in use can be found in Katherine Davis Fishman, *The Computer Establishment*, pp. 361–366; see also Roger Schank, *A Cognitive Computer: On Language, Learning, and Artificial Intelligence*, pp. 231–234.

18. Ben J. Wattenberg, ed., *The Statistical History of the United States from Colonial Times to the Present,* series F, pp. 1–5, 1965.

19. David L. Parnas delivers one perspective on this topic in "Computers in Weapons: The Limits of Confidence," in David Bellin and Gary Chapman, eds., *Computers in Battle —Will They Work?* pp. 209–231; also of interest is a statement on future prospects for AI by Robert Dale, in Allen M. Din, ed., *Arms and Artificial Intelligence,* p. 45.

20. This possibility may be more hypothetical than real because of the close relationship between manufacturing and services. Loss of manufacturing in key areas, for example, could be perilous to next-stage prospects for innovation. For an analysis of these and related problems, see S. S. Cohen and J. Zysman, *Manufacturing Matters.*

21. Translated from the Russian, "SAM" means surface-to-air missile, or literally, fixed maintenance depot to air.

22. See Tom Athanasiou, "Artificial Intelligence as Military Technology," in Bellin and Chapman, eds., *Computers in Battle.*

23. SCI is aimed toward the use of advanced computing to develop weapons and systems "for battle management in complex environments where human decision-making [is] seen to be inadequate" (Allan M. Din, ed., *Arms and Artificial Intelligence*, p. 7; see also pp. 90–91 in the same volume).

What Is AI, Anyway?

1. Similar definitions are found in many standard textbooks on AI.

2. This conference was originally called the Dartmouth Summer Research Project on Artificial Intelligence; for a full account of this landmark event, see Pamela McCorduck, *Machines Who Think,* pp. 93 ff.

3. Norbert Weiner, the famous mathematician who coined this term (later supplanted by the term "artificial intelligence"), was clearly fond of the meaning of its Greek root, "kubernetes": pilot or governor.

4. These terms were introduced by Edward Feigenbaum; see his "Art of Artificial Intelligence: Themes and Case Studies in Knowledge Engines," in *AFIPS Conference Proceedings of the 1978 National Computer Conference* 47: 227–240.

5. Roger Schank, *The Cognitive Computer*, pp. 49–51.

6. The layman may also want to see Susan J. Shepard, "Conversing with Tiny ELIZA," *Computer Language* 4 (May 1987). See also notes 61 and 62 to chapter 2.

7. See Hans Berliner, "New Hitech Computer Chess Success," *AI Magazine* 9 (Summer 1988): 133. And, for a brilliant discussion of machine versus human intelligence in chess and of dangers of rigidity in "learning machines," see Norbert Weiner, discussant, "Scientists and Decision Making," in Martin Greenberger, ed., *Computers and the World of the Future*, pp. 23–28.

8. See Lofti Zadeh, "Fuzzy Sets," in *Information and Control* 8: 338–353. See also a fascinating interview with Zadeh published in *Communications of the ACM*, April 1984, pp. 304–311, in which he discusses the inadequacy of precise AI techniques and tools to solve real life ("fuzzy") problems.

9. See Sigmund Freud, *The Psychopathology of Everyday Life*, in *The Basic Writings of Sigmund Freud*; see also his *Collected Papers*; for another point of view, see Carl Jung et al., *Man and His Symbols*; and for a shorter but broad overview on the subject, see William Kessen and Emily D. Cahan, "A Century of Psychology: From Subject to Object to Agent," *American Scientist,* Nov.–Dec. 1986, pp. 640–650.

10. Newell's fullest and most current vision can be found in John E. Laird, A. Newell, and Paul S. Rosenbloom, "SOAR: An Architecture for Intelligence" (University of Michigan Cognitive Science and Machine Intelligence Laboratory Technical Report no. 2, 1987).

11. See Richard Dawkins's defense of Darwinism in *The Blind Watchmaker: Why the Evidence of Evolution Reveals a Universe without Design*; for some classic arguments on design versus necessity, also see A. Hunter Dupree, in Ada Gray, ed., *Darwiniana*, pp. 51–71.

12. This subject is eloquently addressed in a slim volume (23 pages) by S. Alexander, *Art and Instinct.*

13. To some, of course, the concept of God is not applicable to Buddhism; see William James, *The Varieties of Religious Experience*, pp. 42–44 and 315.

14. Charles Darwin, *The Origin of the Species*. In this, his classic work on natural selection and evolution, Darwin states, "If it could be demonstrated that any complex organ[ism] existed, which could not possibly have been formed by numerous, successive, slight modifications, my theory would absolutely break down" (p. 229).

15. Richard Dawkins, *The Blind Watchmaker,* pp. 112–113.

16. Note, for example, a compelling argument against this notion (which instead champions the notion of hierarchy in evolution) in Stephen Jay Gould, "Is a New and General Theory of Evolution Emerging?" *Paleobiology* 6 (1979): 19–130.

17. See Gould, *Paleobiology* 6 (1979): 119–130. Also, in Stephen Jay Gould, *The Mismeasure of Man*, pp. 326-334, mention is made of "human nature" in relation to the concept of natural selection. See also Richard Dawkins, *The Blind Watchmaker*, pp. 141–142.

18. This idea is supported, at least in theory, by some pioneers of AI; see, for example, Lawrence Fogel, Alvin Owens, and Michael Walsh, *Artificial Intelligence through Simulated Evolution*, pp. viii and 112.

19. Edward Fredkin of MIT is credited with saying, "Artificial intelligence is the next step in evolution" in Sherry Turkle, *The Second Self*, p. 242.

Philosophical Roots

1. The literature on mind as machine is extensive. One provocative work is Daniel C. Dennett's *Brainstorms: Philosophical Essays on Mind and Psychology*. Dennett, a philosopher, draws upon the achievements of AI to formulate a new theory of mind. An important survey of philosophical issues can be found in Margaret Boden's *Artificial Intelligence and Natural Man*, chapter 14; see also Pamela McCorduck, *Machines Who Think*. A brief, useful summary of trends is the introduction ("Philosophy and AI: Some Issues") to Steve Torrance, ed., *The Mind and the Machine: Philosophical Aspects of Artificial Intelligence*. For the philosophy-AI nexus, see the papers in Martin D. Ringle, ed., *Philosophical Perspectives in Artificial Intelligence*. Another important source is John Haugeland, ed., *Mind Design*. The legacy of the mind-body problem is related to contemporary AI debates in succinct, lively fashion by Paul M. Churchland in *Matter and Consciousness*.

2. Some theorists who have argued for the mind-beyond-machine approach are J. R. Lucas, Hubert Dreyfus, and John Searle. Lucas, in 1961, used Gödel's incompleteness theorem to argue that computers could never model the human mind successfully; see his "Minds, Machines and Gödel," *Philosophy* 36 (1961): 120–124. For a refutation of this position, see Dennett's *Brainstorms*, chapter 13. Dreyfus's famous critique of AI is *What Computers Can't Do: The Limits of Artificial Intelligence*. Searle distinguishes between the capacities of "weak AI" and "strong AI" in his 1980 paper "Minds, Brains, and Programs," *The Behavioral and Brain Sciences* 3 (1980): 417–424. (Searle's paper is reprinted as chapter 10 of Haugeland's *Mind Designs*.) Here Searle introduces his famous "Chinese room" example to criticize what he sees as the "residual behaviorism" of AI. A particularly useful review of criticism of AI is J. Schwartz, "Limits of Artificial Intelligence," in Stuart C. Shapiro, ed., *Encyclopedia of Artificial Intelligence*, vol. 1. The *Encyclopedia* is an excellent general source.

3. See Boden's discussion, in *Artificial Intelligence*, pp. 21–63, of Colby's attempt to develop a computational model of human emotions; on pages 440–444 she argues that emotions are not "merely" feelings; in *What Computers Can't Do*, Dreyfus argues from a phenomenological standpoint that computers can never simulate our understanding, in part because of our capacity to experience emotions. Dennett provides an intriguing discussion of the matter in chapter 11 ("Why You Can't Make a Computer That Feels Pain") of *Brainstorms*.

4. According to Dreyfus in *What Computers Can't Do*, "The story of artificial intelligence might well begin around 450 B.C.," when Plato expressed the idea that "all knowledge must be stateable in explicit definitions which anyone could apply" (p. 67).

5. For an overview see D. A. Rees, "Platonism and the Platonic Tradition," *The Encyclopedia of Philosophy*, vol. 6, pp. 333–341 (New York: The Macmillan Company, 1967).

6. See Thomas L. Hankins, *Science and the Enlightenment*. See also Ernst Cassirer, *The Philosophy of the Enlightenment*; the first three chapters provide an important overview of the new studies of mind and how they reflected methods of the new science.

7. See Reinhardt Grossman, *Phenomenology and Existentialism: An Introduction*; the critiques of AI mounted by Hubert and Stuart Dreyfus have their roots in phenomenology. Hubert Dreyfus has developed the Heideggerian notion that understanding is embedded in a world of social purpose, which cannot be adequately represented as a set of facts. Stuart Dreyfus emphasizes the importance of skills

that elude representations and rules by drawing upon the existential phenomenology of Merleau-Ponty. See H. Hall, "Phenomenology," in Shapiro, *Encyclopedia of Artificial Intelligence*, vol. 2, pp. 730–736.

8. See A. J. Ayer, "Editor's Introduction," in A. J. Ayer, ed., *Logical Positivism*, pp. 3–28; Rudolf Carnap, "The Elimination of Metaphysics through Logical Analysis of Language," in Ayer's *Logical Positivism*, pp. 3–81; Noam Chomsky, *Syntactic Structures* (1957). For a review of Chomsky's achievement and influence, see Frederick J. Newmeyer's *Linguistic Theory in America*, 2nd ed., chapter 2, "The Chomskyan Revolution."

9. This debate, in its technical and personal dimensions, is described in some detail in McCorduck's *Machines Who Think*.

10. Plato's works are readily available in Greek and English in the Loeb Classical Library editions; some other English translations of individual works are mentioned below. An excellent place to begin is any of several reference works: Gilbert Ryle, "Plato," in *The Encyclopedia of Philosophy*, vol. 6, pp. 324–333; D. J. Allan, "Plato," in *The Dictionary of Scientific Biography*, vol. 11, pp. 22–31 (New York: Charles Scribner's Sons, 1975). A more detailed account can be found in J. N. Findlay, *Plato and Platonism: An Introduction*.

11. In *Aristotle: The Growth and Structure of His Thought*, chapters 2 and 3, G. E. R. Lloyd describes Aristotle as both a pupil and a critic of Plato.

12. See "The Greek Academy," in *The Encyclopedia of Philosophy*, vol. 3, pp. 382–385. The Academy is also treated in Ryle's "Plato," pp. 317–319. In his excellent survey, *A History of Greek Philosophy*, vol. 4, p. 19, W. K. C. Guthrie explains that the Academy was by no means like our modern university: it had religious elements we might more readily associate with a medieval college. Volume 4 of this survey is devoted to Plato; the Academy is discussed on pp. 8–38. The early years of Plato's Academy are described in the reprint edition of Eduard Zeller's 1888 classic, *Plato and the Older Academy*. See note 17 below.

13. Guthrie (vol. 4, pp. 338–340) points out that Plato was influenced by the mystery religions of his day, especially in the *Phaedo*.

14. Plato describes the movements of the planets in important passages in the *Republic* and the *Timaeus*; In *Plato's Timaeus*, pp. 33–35, Francis Cornford provides a useful summary of the kinds of motion Plato describes in the *Timaeus*. G. E. R. Lloyd has a lucid and concise discussion of Plato's astronomy in chapter 7 of *Early Greek Science: Thales to Aristotle*, pp. 80–98. The nature of Plato's astronomy, long a controversial subject for the history of science, is analyzed in John D. Anton's *Science and the Sciences in Plato*.

15. The myth of Er in the *Republic* (617–618) was Plato's version of a scheme originally developed by the Pythagorean philosopher Philolaus, who put fire at the extremity and at the center of the universe, thus displacing the earth from its central position (G. S. Kirk, J. E. Raven, and M. Schofield, *The Presocratic Philosophers*, p. 259). The Pythagorean concept of a central fire is described by S. Sambursky in *The Physical World of the Greeks*, pp. 64–66.

16. The discovery of irrational numbers eventually resulted in the rejection of a Pythagorean "geometric atomism" and led to the concept of the continuum (S. Sambursky, *The Physical World of the Greeks*, pp. 33–35). In Plato's *Theaetetus*, the mathematician Theodorus demonstrates the irrationality of nonsquare numbers up to the root of 17. Plato then claims that the roots of all numbers that are not squares are irrational. According to G. E. R. Lloyd (*Early Greek Science: Thales to Aristotle*, pp. 32–34), the irrationality of the square root of 2 was known even before the time of Plato. The Greeks commonly expressed the proof in geometrical terms, by showing that the diagonal of a square is not commensurable with its side. (The proof assumes this commensurability, then shows that it leads to an impossibility because the resulting number is both odd and even.) The discovery that some magnitudes are incommensurable (c. 450–441 B.C.) is attributed to Hippacos of Mepontum, a member of the Pythagorean Brotherhood, in Alexander Helleman and Bryan Bunch, *The Timetables of Science*, p. 31.

17. E. R. Dodds, *The Greeks and the Irrational* is a classic treatment of this subject. *Ananke* is described in detail in F. M. Cornford, *Plato's Cosmology*, pp. 159–177. A more recent work is Richard R. Mohr's *Platonic Cosmology*.

18. In the *Phaedo* and *The Republic*, Plato opposes the activity of intellect to the "brutish" passivity of desire (Martha Nussbaum, "Rational Animals and the Explanation of Action," in *The Fragility of Goodness: Luck and Ethics in Greek Tragedy and Philosophy*, p. 273). In this book Nussbaum explores the antithesis in Greek philosophy between the controlling power of reason and events beyond one's control, an antithesis central to Plato's dialogues.

19. The first mention of the Forms is in the *Phaedo*; an excellent discussion can be found in Gilbert Ryle's article (pp. 320–324) in *The Encyclopedia of Philosophy*.

20. Plato's theory of matter in the *Timaeus*, where the smallest particles are triangles, is a blend of Pythagorean ideas and Democritan atomism (see S. Sambursky, *The Physical World of the Greeks*, p. 31).

21. Cornford, in *Plato's Cosmology*, pp. 159–177, provides a lucid discussion of this tension between necessity and reason.

22. On the dialogue as Plato's chosen form, see D. Hyland's "Why Plato Wrote Dialogues," *Philosophy and Rhetoric* 1 (1968): 38–50.

23. Physicist Werner Heisenberg describes how he arrived at his uncertainty principle, which he formulated in 1927 in chapter 6 of his gracefully written and entertaining volume *Physics and Beyond: Encounters and Conversations*. Heisenberg was influenced by Plato's corpuscular physics, and he explores the relation between Plato's ideas and quantum theory in chapter 20, "Elementary Particles and Platonic Philosophy (1961–1965)."

24. A refreshing new interpretation of the *Phaedrus* emphasizing the role of paradox is Martha Nussbaum's "'This Story Isn't True': Madness, Reason, and Recantation in the *Phaedrus*," chapter 7 in *The Fragility of Goodness*, pp. 200–228.

25. D. A. Rees, "Platonism and the Platonic Tradition," p. 336. It was Xenocrates, who headed the Academy after the death of Speusippus, Plato's immediate successor, who identified the Platonic Ideas with mathematical numbers, not the "ideal" numbers postulated in the Academy under Plato and discussed in the *Phaedo*. The fates of the various forms of Platonism are reviewed in several brief articles in the *Dictionary of the History of Ideas* (New York: Charles Scribner's Sons, 1973), vol. 3: John Fisher's "Platonism in Philosophy and Poetry," pp. 502–508; John Charles Nelson's "Platonism in the Renaissance," pp. 508–515; and Ernst Moritz Manasse's "Platonism since the Enlightenment," pp. 515–525.

26. D. H. Fowler, in *The Mathematics of Plato's Academy*, reconstructs in detail the curriculum of the Academy. A particularly readable account of the work of the geometers can be found in chapter 3 of Francois Lasserre, *The Birth of Mathematics in the Age of Plato*. A more technical treatment can be found in chapter 3 of Wilbur Richard Knorr, *The Ancient Tradition of Geometric Problems*.

27. For an general overview of Plato's philosophy of numbers, see "Plato," *The New Encyclopedia Britannica*, vol. 14, p. 538. For the text of the *Epinomis* in Greek and English, see W. R. M. Lamb, ed., *Plato*, Loeb Classical Library, vol. 8. In the *Epinomis*, 976 D–E, the speaker asks what science is indispensable to wisdom: "it is the science which gave number to the whole race of mortals." See also R. S. Brumbaugh, *Plato's Mathematical Imagination*.

28. A superb introduction to Enlightenment thought is Peter Gay's two volumes, *The Enlightenment: An Interpretation*, vol. 1, *The Rise of Modern Paganism* and vol. 2, *The Science of Freedom*.

29. The definitive biography is Richard Westfall's *Never at Rest: A Biography of Isaac Newton*. No one interested in Isaac Newton's scientific achievement should fail to see I. Bernard Cohen's *Newtonian Revolution*. Those who wish to tackle Newton in the original should see *Isaac Newton's Philosophiae Naturalis Principia Mathematica*, 3rd edition (1726), assembled by Alexander Koyré, I. Bernard Cohen, and Anne Whitman.

30. Otto Mayr, *Authority, Liberty, and Automatic Machinery in Early Modern Europe*.

31. A useful overview of Descartes's life and work can be found in *The Dictionary of Scientific Biography*, vol. 4, pp. 55–65. *Descartes*, by Jonathan Rée, is unsurpassed in giving a unified view of Descartes's philosophy and its relation to other systems of thought.

32. The brief *Discours de la Méthode* appeared in 1637 and is written in a lively autobiographical manner. It is readily available in the Library of the Liberal Arts edition, which includes the appendixes in which Descartes introduced analytic geometry and his theory of refraction: *Discourse on Method, Optics, Geometry, and Meteorology*, trans. by Paul J. Olscamp.

33. Derek J. de Solla Price, "Automata and the Origins of Mechanism and Mechanistic Philosophy," *Technology and Culture* 5 (1964): 23.

34. See I. Bernard Cohen on Newton in the *Dictionary of Scientific Biography*, vol. 10, pp. 42–103, and Cohen's *Newtonian Revolution*, mentioned above.

35. Charles Gillispie, *The Edge of Objectivity*, p. 140. The resulting prestige of science during the Enlightenment is treated in chapter 5.

36. For a readable and lucid introduction to relativity, see the 1925 classic by Bertrand Russell, *The ABC of Relativity*, 4th rev. ed. A more detailed treatment may be found in Albert Einstein, *Relativity: The Special and General Theory, a Popular Exposition*, trans. Robert Lawson.

37. Gillispie, *The Edge of Objectivity*, pp. 145–150.

38. Leibniz's criticism of the watchmaker God can be found in a letter written in November 1715 to Samuel Clarke (1675–1729), a renowned disciple of Newton (see pp. 205–206 of Leibniz's *Philosophical Writings*, G. H. R. Parkinson, ed.). For the famous debate this letter initiated, see *The Leibniz-Clarke Correspondence*, H. G. Alexander, ed.

39. W. T. Jones, *Kant and the Nineteenth Century*, p. 14. The legacy of Descartes is expressed in Kant's own definition of the Enlightenment, which is quoted by Ernst Cassirer in *The Philosophy of the Enlightenment*, p. 163: "Enlightenment is man's exodus from his self-incurred tutelage. Tutelage is the inability to use one's understanding without the guidance of another person. This tutelage is self-incurred if its cause lies not in any weakness of the understanding, but in indecision and lack of courage to use the mind without the guidance of another. 'Dare to know' (*sapere aude*)! Have the courage to use your own understanding; this is the motto of the Enlightenment."

40. Immanuel Kant, *Critique of Pure Reason*, 1st ed. 1781; *Prolegomena to Any Future Metaphysics*, 1st ed. 1783. The relations between Kantian philosophy and science are explored in Gordon G. Brittan, Jr., *Kant's Theory of Science*.

41. A brief history of logical positivism can be found in A. J. Ayer, *Logical Positivism*, pp. 3–28. Moritz Schlick, center of the Vienna Circle in the 1920s, compares the Kantian and positivist treatments of reality in "Positivism and Realism," an essay published in 1932 or 1933 and reprinted in Ayer's *Logical Positivism* (see p. 97).

42. Ayer, in *Logical Positivism*, p. 11, points out the positivist nature of Hume's attack on metaphysics and then claims that he could well have cited Kant instead, "who maintained that human understanding lost itself in contradictions when it ventured beyond the bounds of possible experience." Ayer claims that "the originality of the logical positivists lay in their making the impossibility of metaphysics depend not upon the nature of what could be known but upon the nature of what could be said" (*Logical Positivism*, p. 11).

43. Norman Malcolm, *Ludwig Wittgenstein: A Memoir, with a Biographical Sketch by Georg Henrik Von Wright*, p. 10. Whereas Kant distinguished between what can and cannot be known, Wittgenstein distinguished between what can and cannot be said. See "The *Tractatus*," chapter 6 of W. T. Jones, *The Twentieth Century to Wittgenstein and Sartre*.

44. Ludwig Wittgenstein, *Tractatus Logico-Philosophicus*, trans. by D. F. Pears and B. F. McGuiness, first German edition published in 1921.

45. Malcolm, *Ludwig Wittgenstein*, pp. 11–12.

46. Wittgenstein, *Tractatus*, p. 37.

47. Wittgenstein, *Tractatus*, p. 115.

48. Wittgenstein, *Tractatus*, p. 115.

49. For a readable discussion of the Church-Turing thesis, see David Harel's *Algorithmics: The Spirit of Computing*, pp. 221–223. The Church-Turing thesis, named after Alonzo Church and Alan Turing, is based on ideas developed in the following papers: Alan Turing, "On Computable Numbers with an Application to the Entscheidungsproblem," *Proc. London Math. Soc.* 42(1936): 230–265; Alonzo Church, "An Unsolvable Problem of Elementary Number Theory," *Amer. J. Math.* 58 (1936): 345–363.

50. See, for example, statement 4.002 in Wittgenstein's *Tractatus*, p. 37.

51. Wittgenstein, *Tractatus*, pp. 7, 151.

52. Ludwig Wittgenstein, *Philosophical Investigations*, trans. G .E .M. Anscombe.

53. Michael Dummett, in his "Frege and Wittgenstein" (in Irving Block, ed., *Perspectives on the Philosophy of Wittgenstein*, pp. 31–42), argues that Wittgenstein tried and failed to provide a theory of language in *Philosophical Investigations*.

54. In the preface to *Philosophical Investigations* (p. vi), Wittgenstein claims that he recognized "grave mistakes" in his earlier work, the *Tractatus*. The more atomistic approach of the latter is challenged by a greater emphasis on contexts in *Philosophical Investigations*. Anthony Kenny compares the two works in "Wittgenstein's Early Philosophy of Mind," Block, ed., *Perspectives*, pp. 140–147. A. J. Ayer remarks that Wittgenstein "modified the rigors of his early positivism" as expressed in the *Tractatus*. (See Ayer's *Logical Positivism*, p. 5).

55. In the Preface to his 1936 work *Language, Truth and Logic*, p. 31, Alfred Ayer asserts that his views stem from the writings of Russell and Wittgenstein.

56. See Reinhardt Grossman, *Phenomenology and Existentialism*.

57. *Tractatus*, p. 151.

490

58. Hubert L. Dreyfus, "Alchemy and Artificial Intelligence," The RAND Corporation, December 1965, publication 3244. For a profile of Dreyfus, see Frank Rose, "The Black Knight of AI," *Science 85*, 6 (March 1985): 46–51.

59. Pamela McCorduck, *Machines Who Think*, p. 204. McCorduck devotes chapter 9 ("L'Affair Dreyfus") to an engaging history of Dreyfus's critique and the reactions it provoked in the AI community.

60. ELIZA was first announced in Joseph Weizenbaum's "ELIZA—A Computer Program for the Study of Natural Language Communication between Man and Machine," *Communications of the Association for Computing Machinery* 9 (1966): 36–45. Hubert Dreyfus stumped ELIZA by entering the phrase "I'm feeling happy," and then correcting it, by adding "No, elated." ELIZA responded with "Don't be so negative," because it is programmed to respond that way whenever "no" appears anywhere in the input. See Hubert Dreyfus and Stuart Dreyfus, "Why Computers May Never Think like People," *Technology Review* 89 (1986): 42–61.

61. ELIZA mimics a Rogerian psychotherapist, whose technique consists largely of echoing utterances of the patient; it therefore uses very little memory, and arrives at its "answers" by combining transformations of the "input" sentences with phrases stored under keywords. Its profound limitations were acknowledged by its creator. In his 1976 work, *Computer Power and Human Reason,* Weizenbaum argues that ELIZA's limitations serve to illustrate the importance of context for natural language understanding, a point made in his original paper. He chose this kind of psychotherapeutic dialogue precisely because the psychotherapist in such a dialogue need know practically nothing about the real world. See Margaret Boden, *Artificial Intelligence and Natural Man,* p. 108.

62. Dreyfus developed this argument in detail in *What Computers Can't Do: The Limits of Artificial Intelligence.* There he sets out objections to "the assumption that man functions like a general-purpose symbol-manipulating device" (p. 156). Especially drawing his ire was the work of Allen Newell and H. A. Simon, *Computer Simulation of Human Thinking*, The RAND Corporation, P-2276 (April 1961).

63. PROLOG, a language based upon logic programming, was devised by Colmerauer at Marseille around 1970 (see W. F. Clocksin and C. S. Mellish, *Programming in PROLOG).*

64. Fuzzy logic, developed by L. A. Zadeh, guards against the oversimplification of reality by not assuming all fundamental questions have yes or no answers. See E. H. Mamdani and B. R. Gaines, *Fuzzy Reasoning and Its Applications.*

65. See, in particular, the introduction to the revised edition, in Hubert Dreyfus, *What Computers Can't Do.*

66. Dreyfus's predictions about the limitations of chess-playing programs have been proven wrong time and again. Chess-playing programs have improved their performance through the application of greater and greater computational power. One of the latest benchmarks occurred when HiTech won the Pennsylvania State Chess Championship in 1988. See Hans Berliner, "HITECH Becomes First Computer Senior Master," *AI Magazine* 9 (Fall 1988): 85–87.

67. McCorduck, *Machines Who Think*, p. 205.

68. In *What Computers Can't Do* Dreyfus argues, "There is no justification for the assumption that we first experience isolated facts, or snapshots of facts, or momentary views of snapshots of isolated facts, and then give them significance. The analytical superfluousness of such a process is what contemporary philosophers such as Heidegger and Wittgenstein are trying to point out" (p. 270).

69. Hubert L. Dreyfus and Stuart E. Dreyfus, "Making a Mind versus Modeling the Brain: Artificial Intelligence Back at a Branchpoint," *Daedalus* 117 (Winter 1988): 15–43. This issue of *Daedalus,* devoted to AI, was subsequently published in book form; see Stephen R. Graubard, ed., *The Artificial Intelligence Debate: False Starts, Real Foundations.*

70. Dreyfus and Dreyfus, "Making a Mind," p. 15.

71. Jack Cowan and David H. Sharp review the importance of neural nets for AI in "Neural Nets and Artificial Intelligence," *Daedalus* 117 (Winter 1988): 85–121.

72. Dreyfus and Dreyfus, "Making a Mind," pp. 38–39.

73. See "The Role of the Body in Intelligent Behavior," chapter 7 of Hubert Dreyfus's *What Computers Can't Do.*

74. Sherry Turkle also explores children's responses to computers in her 1984 work, *The Second Self: Computers and the Human Spirit,* chapter 1, "Child Philosophers: Are Smart Machines Alive?"

75. Sigmund Freud, *Jokes and Their Relation to the Unconscious*, 1st ed., 1905. Marvin Minsky provides a new interpretation of jokes, emphasizing the importance of "knowledge about knowledge," in his "Jokes and the Logic of the Cognitive Unconscious," in Lucia Vaina and Jaakko Hintikka, eds., *Cognitive Constraints on Communication*, pp. 175–200.

Mathematical Roots

1. For the relationship between logic and recursion, see Stephen Cole Kleene, "l-Definability and Recursiveness," *Duke Mathematical Journal* 2 (1936): 340–353. See also Stephen Cole Kleene, *Introduction to Metamathematics*. For Rosser's contribution, see J. Barkley Rosser, "Extensions of Some Theorems of Gödel and Church," *Journal of Symbolic Logic* 1 (1936): 87–91. Church has made many important contributions to logic and computation. A coherent presentation of his work appears in Alonzo Church, *Introduction to Mathematical Logic*, vol. 1.

2. For the flavor of this theory, see a classic text on numerical analysis and computation: R. W. Hamming, *Introduction to Applied Numerical Analysis*.

3. A good example of such thinking is Bertrand Russell, *Introduction to Mathematical Philosophy*.

4. The paradox was first introduced in Bertrand Russell, *Principles of Mathematics*, 2nd ed., pp 79–81. Russell's paradox is a subtle variant of the Liar Paradox. See E. W. Beth, *Foundations of Mathematics*, p. 485.

5. Gottlob Frege was about to publish a monumental work on arithmetic and set theory when Russell pointed out the implications of his paradox. Frege could only add a postscript that said, "A scientist can hardly meet with anything more undesirable than to have the foundations give way just as the work is finished. In this position I was put by a letter from Mr. Bertrand Russell." See Bertrand Russell, Letter to Frege, 1902, published in Jean van Heijenoort, ed., *From Frege to Gödel*.

6. Bertrand Russell, *Principles of Mathematics*, 2nd ed., 1938, pp. 10–32, 66–81.

7. Bertrand Russell, *Principles of Mathematics*, 2nd ed., pp. 10–32, 66–81.

8. See Bertrand Russell, *Principles of Mathematics*, 2nd ed., pp. v–xiv.

9. See also Alfred N. Whitehead and Bertrand Russell, *Principia Mathematica*, 3 vols., 2nd ed., pp. 187–231.

10. First introduced in Alan M. Turing, "On Computable Numbers with an Application to the Entscheidungsproblem," *Proc. London Math. Soc.* 42 (1936): 230–265.

11. Work on PROLOG began in 1970. A clear presentation of the conceptual foundations of PROLOG appears in Robert Kowalski, "Predicate Logic as a Programming Language," University of Edinburgh, DAI Memo 70, 1973. See also Alain Colmerauer, "Sur les bases théoriques de Prolog," Groupe de IA, UER Luminy, Univ. d'Aix-Marseilles, 1979. This and other aspects of the Japanese program are discussed in Edward Feigenbaum and Pamela McCorduck, *The Fifth Generation*, p. 115.

12. These early experiments are described in A. Newell, J. C. Shaw, and H. Simon, "Empirical Explorations with the Logic Theory Machine," *Proceedings of the Western Joint Computer Conference* 15 (1957): 218–239.

13. Turing's theoretical model was first introduced in Alan M. Turing, "On Computable Numbers with an Application to the Entscheidungsproblem," *Proc. London Math. Soc.*" 42 (1936): 230–265.

14. An enormously influential paper is Alan M. Turing, "Computing Machinery and Intelligence," *Mind* 59 (1950): 433–460, reprinted in E. Feigenbaum and J. Feldman, eds., *Computers and Thought*.

15. The program is called the "Turochamp" (evidently a contraction of "Turing and Champernowne"). See Andrew Hodges, *Alan Turing: The Enigma*, pp. 338–339.

16. Turing researched morphogenesis deeply enough to produce a paper on the subject: Alan M. Turing, "The Chemical Basis of Morphogenesis," *Phil. Trans. Roy. Soc.* 1952: B237.

17. See Andrew Hodges, *Alan Turing: The Enigma*, pp. 267–268.

18. For an engineering account of this project, see B. Randell, "The Colossus" (1976), reprinted in N. Metropolis, J. Howlett, and G. C. Rota, eds., *A History of Computing in the Twentieth Century*.

19. See David Hilbert, *Grundlagen der Geometrie*, Liepzig and Berlin, 1899, 7th ed., 1930.

20. Alan M. Turing. "On Computable Numbers with an Application to the Entscheidungsproblem," *Proc. London Math. Soc.* 42 (1936): 230–265.

21. Simpler models that have appeared since have perhaps been ignored. See Marvin Minsky, *Computation: Finite and Infinite Machines*.

22. This thesis was independently arrived at by both Church and Turing around 1936.

23. For an excellent article on the theory of computation, see John M. Hopcroft, "Turing Machines," *Scientific American*, May 1984, pp. 86–98.

24. The busy beaver problem is one example of a large class of noncomputable functions, as one can see from Tibor Rado, "On Noncomputable Functions," *Bell System Technical Journal* 41, no. 3 (1962): 877–884.

25. Church's version of the result appears in Alonzo Church, "An Unsolvable Problem of Elementary Number Theory," *American Jour. Math* 58 (1936): 345–363.

26. We can see Gödel's concerns about Russell's framework in Kurt Gödel, "Russell's Mathematical Logic" (1944), in P. A. Schilpp, ed., *The Philosophy of Bertrand Russell*.

27. Gödel's incompleteness theorem first appeared in: Kurt Gödel, "Über formal unenscheiderbare Satze der *Principia Mathematica* und verwandter Systeme I," *Monatsh. Math. Phys.* 38 (1931): 173–198.

28. See Alonzo Church, "A Note on the Entscheidungsproblem," *Journal of Symbolic Logic* 1 (1936): 40–41, and Kurt Gödel, "On Undecidable Propositions of Formal Mathematical Systems," mimeographed report of lectures at the Institute for Advanced Study, Princeton, 1934.

29. Herbert A. Simon, *The Shape of Automation for Men and Management* (Harper & Row, 1965), p. 96.

30. A short reflection by Turing on some of the issues behind thinking machines appears as part of chapter 25 of B. W. Bowden, ed., *Faster than Thought*.

31. For an introductory account of some of the implications of the Church-Turing thesis, see Douglas Hofstadter, *Gödel, Escher, Bach: An Eternal Golden Braid*, pp. 559–586.

The Formula for Intelligence

1. See Morris Kline, *Mathematics and the Search for Knowledge*.

2. See Albert Einstein, *Relativity: The Special and the General Theory*. A more readable account is presented in Bertrand Russell, *ABC of Relativity*. See also A. Einstein, "Zur Elektrodynamic bewegter Korpen," *Annalen der Physik* 17 (1905): 895, 905.

3. For the mathematically mature, an excellent introduction can be found in Enrico Fermi, *Thermodynamics* (Englewood Cliffs, N.J.: Prentice-Hall, 1937).

4. Atkins gives an account of thermodynamics and entropy that is fascinating and informal yet scholarly in P. W. Atkins, *The Second Law*.

5. A glimpse into the complexity is presented in Allan C. Wilson, "The Molecular Basis of Evolution," *Scientific American*, October 1985, pp. 164–173.

6. See Rudy Rucker, *The Five Levels of Mathematical Reality*, pp. 14–35.

7. The motivations and quests for anthropomorphic parallels are considered in John D. Barrow and Frank J. Tipler, *The Anthropic Cosmological Principle*, pp. 1–23.

8. See Robert P. Crease and Charles C. Mann, *The Second Creation*, pp. 393–420.

9. For one contribution to a "theory of everything," see Stephen Hawking, *A Brief History of Time*. A more popular discussion is given in Heinz R. Pagels, *Perfect Symmetry*, pp. 269–367.

10. In 1666 Gottfried Leibniz contemplated a scientific system of reasoning, the "calculus ratiocinator," that could be used to settle arguments formally. George Boole took up this problem and presented his work in 1854 in *An Investigation of the Laws of Thought on Which Are Founded the Mathematical Theories of Logic and Probabilities*, aspects of which are discussed in the next few pages.

11. See Douglas Hofstadter, *Gödel, Escher, Bach: An Eternal Golden Braid*, pp. 559–586.

12. Meindl, James D. "Chips for Advanced Computing," *Scientific American*, October 1987, p. 78.

13. For a detailed treatment, see Carver Mead and Lynn Conway, *Introduction to VLSI Systems*. Old but nonetheless broadly relevant is the article Ivan E. Sutherland and Carver A. Mead, "Microelectronics and Computer Science," *Scientific American*, September 1977, pp. 210–228.

14. For a discussion that is less philosophical than that of Hofstadter, see Rudy Rucker, *The Five Levels of Mathematical Reality*, pp. 207–249.

15. See John M. Hopcroft, "Turing Machines," *Scientific American,* May 1984, p. 91.

16. See A. Newell and H. A. Simon, "GPS: A Program that Simulates Human Thought," in E. A. Feigenbaum and J. Feldman, eds., *Computers and Thought*, pp. 71–105, and Claude Shannon, "A Chess Playing Machine," *Scientific American*, October 1950.

17. For a sketch, see Patrick H. Winston, "The LISP Revolution, " *BYTE*, April 1985, p. 209.

18. For this reason we've been more successful in building checkers programs. See Arthur L. Samuel, "Some Studies in Machine Learning Using the Game of Checkers," (1959), reprinted in E. A. Feigenbaum and J. Feldman, eds., *Computers and Thought*, pp. 279–293. An early note is given in Claude Shannon, "Programming a Computer for Playing Chess," *Philosophical Magazine*, series 7, 41 (1950): 256–275.

19. This and some of the other formulations discussed here have been examined in depth by researchers in game theory. A seminal work in the area is R. D. Luce and H. Raiffa, *Games and Decisions*. The famous Minimax theorem itself was presented in J. von Neumann, "Zur Theorie der Gesellschaftespiele," *Mathematische Annalen* 100 (1928): 295–320.

20. This serves to show that in theory a computer can be as good as any human chess player.

21. Researchers have tried various strategies to get around the problems created by this combinatorial explosion in the number of possible chess moves at each stage. See Peter Frey, "An Introduction to Computer Chess," in Peter Frey, ed., *Chess Skill in Man and Machine*, and also M. M. Botvinnik, *Computers in Chess*, pp. 15–21.

22. A. K. Dewdney, "The King Is Dead, Long Live the King," *Scientific American*, May 1986, p. 13.

23. See Gregory Chaitin, "On the Difficulty of Computation," *IEEE Transactions on Information Theory* 16 (1970): 5–9, and Gregory Chaitin, "Computing the Busy Beaver Function," IBM Watson Research Center Report, RC 10722, 1970. An easy introduction to certain aspects of computability and complexity is in Michael R. Garey and David S. Johnson, *Computers and Intractability*.

24. See, for instance, the piece by M. A. Tsasfman and B. M. Stilman in M. M. Botvinnik, ed., *Computers in Chess*. Also see Carl Ebeling, *All the Right Moves*, pp. 56–64.

25. A lucid presentation on the two positions can be found in Carl Ebeling, *All the Right Moves*, pp. 1–3.

26. Compare the various strategies and systems described in Peter Frey, ed., *Chess Skill in Man and Machine*.

27. A recent report on HiTech is Hans Berliner, *AI Magazine*, Summer 1988.

28. The structure of HiTech is well documented in Carl Ebeling, *All the Right Moves*.

29. H. A. Simon and Allen Newell, "Heuristic Problem Solving: The Next Advance in Operations Research," *Operations Research* 6 (January–February 1958).

30. A report of the system's performance is given in Danny Kopec and Monty Newborn, "Belle and Mephisto Dallas Capture Computer Chess Titles at the FJCC," *Communications of the ACM*, July 1987, pp. 640–645.

31. In 1988 HiTech became the first system to beat a human chess grandmaster, albeit one who has been out of form. See Harold C. Schonberg, *New York Times*, September 26, 1988.

32. See W. Daniel Hillis, "The Connection Machine," *Scientific American*, June 1987.

33. Eliot Hearst, "Man and Machine: Chess Achievements and Chess Thinking," in Peter Frey, ed., *Chess Skill in Man and Machine*.

34. A useful examination of the psychology of chess-playing in the light of the performance of chess programs is given in Brad Leithauser, "Computer Chess," *New Yorker*, May 9, 1987, pp. 41–73. See also the article by Hearst, cited in note 33.

35. An excellent survey is in Geoffrey C. Fox and Paul C. Messina, "Advanced Computer Architectures," *Scientific American*, October 1987, pp. 66–74. The flurry of research activity is evident from Richard Miller (project manager), *Optical Computers: The Next Frontier in Computing*, vols. 1 and 2 (Englewood, N.J.: Technical Insights, 1986).

36. Even the early checkers programs were quite good. See Pamela McCorduck, *Machines Who Think*, pp. 152–153.

37. H. J. Berliner, "Backgammon Computer Program Beats World Champion," *Artificial Intelligence* 14, no. 1 (1980).

38. See H. J. Berliner, "Computer Backgammon," *Scientific American*, June 1980.

39. The number of possible moves at each point is estimated at 200 for go. See E. Thorp and W. E. Walden, "A Computer-Assisted Study of Go on M by N Boards," in R. B. Banerji and M. D. Mesarovic, eds., *Theoretical Approaches to Non-numerical Problem-Solving* (Berlin: Springer-Verlag, 1970), pp. 303–343.

40. An early effort on go is described in W. Reitman and B. Wilcox, "Pattern Recognition and Pattern Directed Inference in a Program for Playing Go," in D. A. Waterman and F. Hayes-Roth, eds., *Pattern-Directed Inference Systems.*

41. As stated by John Laird, the cannibals and missionaries problem is, "Three cannibals and three missionaries want to cross a river. Though they can all row, they only have available a small boat that can hold two people. The difficulty is that the cannibals are unreliable: if they ever outnumber the missionaries on a river bank, they will kill them. How do they manage the boat trips so that all six get safely to the other side?"

42. A. Newell, J. C. Shaw, and H. A. Simon, "Empirical Explorations with the Logic Theory Machine" (1957), reprinted in E. A. Feigenbaum and J. Feldman, eds., *Computers and Thought,* pp. 109–133. The generalized results can be seen in A. Newell, J. C. Shaw and H. A. Simon, "A Report on a General Problem Solving Program," *Proceedings of the International Conference on Information Processing* (UNESCO, Paris, 1959), pp. 256–264.

43. Notably from the Dreyfus brothers. See Hubert Dreyfus, *What Computers Can't Do,* 2nd ed.

44. A. Newell and H. A. Simon, "GPS: A Program That Simulates Human Thought," in E. A. Feigenbaum and J. Feldman, eds., *Computers and Thought,* pp. 71–105.

45. H. A. Simon and Allen Newell, "Heuristic Problem Solving: The Next Advance in Operations Research," *Operations Research.* 6 (January–February 1958).

46. Some problems are described in Patrick H. Winston, *Artificial Intelligence,* pp. 146–154. The results and lessons of GPS are detailed in A. Newell and H. A. Simon, *Human Problem Solving.*

47. See E. Feigenbaum and Avron Barr, *The Handbook of Artificial Intelligence,* vol. 1, pp. 123–138.

48. An excellent paper on intelligence and computer chess is A. Newell, J. C. Shaw, and H. A. Simon, "Chess Playing Programs and the Problem of Complexity" (1958), reprinted in E. Feigenbaum and J. Feldman, *Computers and Thought.*

49. Minsky's views on intelligence serve us well here: Marvin Minsky, "Why People Think Computers Can't," *Technology Review,* November–December 1983, pp. 64–70.

50. Formally defined in Marvin Minsky and Seymour Papert, *Perceptrons,* p. 12.

51. W. S. McCulloch and W. Pitts, "A Logical Calculus of the Ideas Immanent in Neural Nets," *Bulletin of the Mathematical Biophysics* 5 (1943).

52. Marvin Minsky and Seymour Papert, *Perceptrons,* pp. 136–150.

53. An excellent introductory article on the history and achievements of connectionism is Jerome Feldman, "Connections," *BYTE,* April 1985, pp. 277–284.

54. This is reflected in the progress reports issued by the MIT AI Laboratory during that period. See, for instance, Marvin Minsky, Seymour Papert, "New Progress in Artificial Intelligence," MIT Artificial Intelligence Laboratory, AI memo 252, 1972.

55. See Douglas Hofstadter, *Metamagical Themas,* pp. 274–292.

56. Widely applicable algorithms are likely to perform weakly in all their domains. See Seymour Papert, "One AI or Many," *Daedalus,* Winter 1988.

57. A recent survey is in Jack D. Cowan and David. H. Sharp, "Neural Nets and Artificial Intelligence," *Daedalus,* Winter 1988, pp. 85–121.

58. Important papers on recent work are put together in the standard reference in the field: D. E. Rumelhart, J. L. McClelland, and the PDP Research Group, *Parallel Distributed Processing.*

59. See Marvin Minsky, "Connectionist Models and Their Prospects," in David Waltz, ed., *Connectionist Models and Their Implications* (Norwood, N.J.: Ablex Publishing, 1988).

60. This selection is carried out in the style of "summarizing" in the society theory. See Marvin Minsky, *Society of Mind,* p. 95.

61. Decision trees have been used extensively in Management Science. For an enjoyable introduction, see Howard Raiffa, *Decision Analysis: Introductory Lectures* (Reading, Mass.: Addison-Wesley).

62. This is a point well brought out in Marvin Minsky, "Why People Think Computers Can't," *Technology Review,* November–December 1983, pp. 64–70.

63. See R. C. Schank and R. Abelson, *Scripts, Plans, Goals, and Understanding* (Hillsdale, N.J.: Erlbaum, Lawrence Associates, 1977).

64. Marvin Minsky, "Plain Talk about Neurodevelopment Epistemology," *Proceedings of the Fifth International Joint Conference on AI* (Cambridge, Mass., 1977). Minsky's work culminated in a major book: Marvin Minsky, *The Society of Mind*.

65. Minsky, *The Society of Mind*, p. 17.

66. For a sketch of the society theory, see Marvin Minsky, "Society of Mind," *Artificial Intelligence Journal* 1989.

67. For early related work, see Jerome Lettvin, H. Maturana, W. McCulloch and W. Pitts, "What the Frog's Eye Tells the Frog's Brain," *Proceedings of the IRE* 47 (1959): 1940–1951. This famous paper is reprinted with other related papers in Warren S. McCulloch, *Embodiments of Mind*. Also see: W. S. McCulloch and W. Pitts, "A Logical Calculus of the Ideas Immanent in Neural Nets," *Bulletin of the Mathematical Biophysics* 5 (1943), reprinted in Warren S. McCulloch, *Embodiments of Mind*.

68. Jerome Lettvin, H. Maturana, W. McCulloch and W. Pitts, "What the Frog's Eye Tells the Frog's Brain," *Proceedings of the IRE* 47 (1959): 1940–1951.

69. John McDermott, "R1: A Rule-Based Configurer of Computer Systems," *Artificial Intelligence* 19, no. 1 (1982). Also see John McDermott, "XSEL: A Computer Salesperson's Assistant," in J. Hayes, D. Michie, and Y. H. Pao, *Machine Intelligence 10* (New York: Halsted, Wiley, 1982).

70. P. H. Winston and K. A. Prendergast, eds., *The AI Business*, pp. 41–49, 92–99.

71. A strong case for the use of computers largely as office environment shapers is in Terry Winograd and Fernando Flores, *Understanding Computers and Cognition: A New Foundation for Design*.

72. See Seymour Papert, "One AI or Many?" *Daedalus*, Winter 1988, p. 7.

73. One large-scale effort that takes this problem seriously is described in D. Lenat, M. Shepherd, and M. Prakash, "CYC: Using Common Sense Knowledge to Overcome Brittleness and Knowledge Acquisition Bottlenecks," *AI Magazine*, Winter 1986.

74. An enjoyable account of genetics, evolution, and intelligence is in Carl Sagan, *The Dragons of Eden*.

75. The original reports of Crick and Watson, surprisingly readable, may be found in James A. Peters, ed., *Classic Papers in Genetics* (Englewood Cliffs, N.J.: Prentice-Hall, 1959). An exciting account of the successes and failures that led to the double helix is given in J. D. Watson, *The Double Helix*.

76. The structure and behavior of DNA and RNA are described in: Felsenfeld Gary, "DNA," *Scientific American*, October 1985. And: James Darnell, "RNA," *Scientific American*, October 1985.

77. A fascinating account of the new biology is given in Horace F. Judson, *The Eighth Day of Creation*.

78. G. L. Stebbins and F. J. Ayala, "The Evolution of Darwinism," *Scientific American*, July 1985, p. 73.

Mechanical Roots

1. See J. David Bolter, *Turing's Man: Western Culture in the Computer Age*, pp. 17–24. Bolter illustrates the mechanism for astronomical calculation described in detail in Derek J. de Solla Price, "An Ancient Greek Computer," *Scientific American*, June 1959, pp. 60–67; see also Derek J. de Solla Price, *Gears from the Greeks: The Antikythera Mechanism—A Calendar Computer from circa 80 B.C.* Early automata and their relation to AI are discussed in Pamela McCorduck's popular 1979 history of AI research, *Machines Who Think*, chapter 1. Another useful and lively source is John Cohen's *Human Robots in Myth and Science*. Perhaps the best detailed sources on automata through the ages are Derek J. de Solla Price, "Automata and the Origins of Mechanism and Mechanistic Philosophy," *Technology and Culture* 5 (1964): 9–23, and Silvio Bedini, "The Role of Automata in the History of Technology," *Technology and Culture* 5 (1964): 24–42. A classic volume with many illustrations is Alfred Chapuis and Edmond Droz, *Automata: A Historical and Technological Study*, trans. Alec Reid. Otto Mayr describes the significance of automata in European culture in *Authority, Liberty, and Automatic Machinery in Early Modern Europe*.

2. For a general history of the mechanical arts see C. Singer, E. J. Holmyard, A. R. Hall, and T. I. Williams, eds., *A History of Technology*, and A. P. Usher, *A History of Mechanical Inventions*, 2nd ed. Those interested in ancient technologies should consult R. J. Forbes, *Studies in Ancient Technology*.

3. Price, "Automata and the Origins of Mechanism," p. 11. Other important works on ancient technologies are A. G. Drachman, *The Mechanical Technology of Greek and Roman Antiquity*, A. P. Neuberger, *The Technical Arts and Sciences of the Ancients*, and K. D. White, *Greek and Roman Technology*.

4. Price, "Automata and the Origins of Mechanism," p. 11. Joseph Needham describes the fascinating automata in China at the time of the pre-Socratics in his *Science and Civilisation in China*, vol. 2, pp. 53–54, 516. The Chinese mechanical orchestra, consisting of twelve figures cast in bronze, is also

described in Needham's *Science and Civilisation in China.*, vol. 4, p. 158. Descartes, who was very interested in automata, described in one of his notebooks how to reproduce the pigeon of Archytas. See Mayr, *Authority, Liberty, and Automatic Machinery*, p. 63.

5. For more on androids, see Samuel L. Macey, *Clocks and the Cosmos: Time in Western Life and Thought*; see also Carlo M. Cipolla, *Clocks and Culture, 1300–1700,* and David S. Landes, *Revolution in Time: Clocks and the Making of the Modern World.*

6. Bedini describes Torriano's automaton in "Automata in the History of Technology," p. 32, where it appears as figure 5. For more on P. Jacquet-Droz and Écrivain, see Bedini's "Automata," p. 39, and Macey's *Clocks and the Cosmos*, pp. 210–211. P. Jacquet-Droz's son, Henri-Louis, created a mechanical artist that drew flowers and a musician that played a clavecin. He also made a pair of artificial hands for a general's son, who had lost his own hands in a hunting accident. Henri-Louis's success in this venture was praised by the great creator of automata Jacques de Vaucanson (1709–1782). See the entries for Pierre-Jacquet Droz and Henri-Louis-Jacquet Droz in *Nouvelle Biographie Générale*, vol. 14 (Paris: Didot, 1868), pp. 812–813. Vaucanson was perhaps best known for his duck automaton, which ate, drank, chewed, and excreted. See Macey's *Clocks and the Cosmos*, p. 210, and Bedini's "Automata in the History of Technology," pp. 36–37, which has a diagram of the duck's inner mechanism (figures 11 and 12). Anyone interested in Vaucanson should see Michael Cardy, "Technology as Play: The Case of Vaucanson," *Stud. Voltaire 18th Cent.* 241 (1986): 109–123. In 1726 Jonathan Swift described a machine that would automatically write books; see Eric A. Weiss, "Jonathan Swift's Computing Machine," *Annals of the History of Computing* 7 (1985): 164–165.

7. Martin Gardner, "The Abacus: Primitive but Effective Digital Computer," *Scientific American* 222 (1970): 124–127; Parry H. Moon, *The Abacus: Its History, Its Design, Its Possibilities in the Modern World*; J. M. Pullan, *The History of the Abacus* (London: Hutchinson, 1968).

8. Napier's bones or rods are described and pictured in Stan Augarten's *Bit by Bit: An Illustrated History of Computers*, pp. 9–10. A more detailed treatment can be found in M. R. Williams, "From Napier to Lucas: The Use of Napier's Bones in Calculating Instruments," *Annals of the History of Computing* 5 (1983): 279–296.

9. An earlier calculating machine was devised by the polymath Wilhelm Shickard (1592–1635). Shickard's machine, and Pascal's development of the Pascaline are described in Augarten's *Bit by Bit: An Illustrated History of Computers*, pp. 15–30. A more technical account can be found in René Taton, "Sur l'invention de la machine arithmetique," *Revue d'histoire des sciences et de leurs applications* 16 (1963): 139–160; Jeremy Bernstein, *The Analytical Engine: Computers—Past, Present, and Future,* p. 40; Herman Goldstine, *The Computer from Pascal to von Neumann*, p. 7–8.

10. Blaise Pascal, *Pensées* (New York: E. P. Dutton & Co., 1932), p. 96, no. 340.

11. The Pascaline, of which perhaps ten or fifteen were sold, failed to sell for a variety of reasons. See Augarten, *Bit by Bit*, pp. 27–30.

12. The Stepped Reckoner, as Leibniz called his machine, employed a special gear as a mechanical multiplier. See Augarten, *Bit by Bit*, pp. 30–35, and Goldstine, *The Computer from Pascal to von Neumann*, pp. 7–9. Morland's career is described in Henry W. Dickinson's biography, *Sir Samuel Morland, Diplomat and Inventor, 1625–1695.*

13. Brian Randell, ed., *The Origins of Digital Computers: Selected Papers,* p. 2.

14. Augarten, *Bit by Bit*, p. 89.

15. Babbage's paper can be found in H. P. Babbage, *Babbage's Calculating Engines*, pp. 220–222.

16. H. P. Babbage, *Babbage's Calculating Engines*, pp. 223–224. On Babbage and the Astronomical Society, see Anthony Hyman, *Charles Babbage: Pioneer of the Computer*, pp. 50–53.

17. See chapter 2 of Augarten's *Bit by Bit*, which has marvelous illustrations. Babbage's life and career are treated in detail in Hyman's *Charles Babbage*. Joel Shurkin provides a lively account of Babbage's work in his *Engines of the Mind: A History of the Computer*, chapter 2. A biography recently published almost a century after its completion is H. W. Buxton, *Memoirs of the Life and Labours of the Late Charles Babbage, Esq., F.R.S.,* ed. A. Hyman.

18. Allen G. Bromley, Introduction to H. P. Babbage, *Babbage's Calculating Engines*, pp. xiii–xvi; Bernstein, *The Analytical Engine*, pp. 47–57.

19. Augarten, *Bit by Bit*, pp. 62–63; Bernstein, *The Analytical Engine*, p. 50; Hyman, *Charles Babbage*, p. 166.

20. Augarten, *Bit by Bit*, pp. 63–64. Babbage describes the features of his machine in "On the Mathematical Powers of the Calculating Engine," written in 1837 and reprinted as appendix B in Hyman's *Charles Babbage*.

21. A recent biography is Dorothy Stein, *Ada, a Life and a Legacy*.

22. Goldstine, *The Computer*, p. 26.

23. Her translation and notes can be found in H. P. Babbage, *Babbage's Calculating Engines*, pp. 1–50.

24. The lonely end of Babbage's life is described in Hyman, *Charles Babbage*, chapter 16.

25. Joel Shurkin, in *Engines of the Mind*, p. 104, describes Aiken's machine as "an electromechanical Analytical Engine with IBM card handling." For a concise history of the development of the Mark I, see Augarten's *Bit by Bit*, pp. 103–107. I. Bernard Cohen provides a new perspective on Aiken's relation to Babbage in his article "Babbage and Aiken," *Annals of the History of Computing* 10 (1988): 171–193.

26. Anyone with a serious interest in the history of calculators should be aware of the following two classics: D. Baxandall, *Calculating Machines and Instruments,* and Ellice Martin Horsburgh, ed., *Modern Instruments and Methods of Calculation: A Handbook of the Napier Tercentenary Celebration Exhibition*. Some of the calculators and tabulating machines of the 1940s are described in Charles and Ray Eames, *A Computer Perspective*, pp. 128–159. A brief pictorial history of calculating machines can be found in George C. Chase, "History of Mechanical Computing Machinery," *Annals of the History of Computing* 2 (1980): 198–226. Two important sources in the history of computing, besides the *Annals*, are N. Metropolis, J. Howlett, and Gian-Carlo Rota, eds., *A History of Computing in the Twentieth Century*, and Brian Randell, *The Origins of Digital Computers*.

27. See chapter 3 of Augarten's *Bit by Bit*, and Eames's *A Computer Perspective*, pp. 16–17, 22-30.

28. Augarten, *Bit by Bit,* pp. 78–83; Randell, *Origins*, p. 28.

29. Shurkin, *Engines of the Mind*, p. 94; Augarten, *Bit by Bit*, p. 82; Eames, *A Computer Perspective*, p. 39. Burroughs's life and work are described in Molly Gleiser, "William S. Burroughs," *Computer Decisions,* March 1978, pp. 34–36.

30. By 1913 the Burroughs Adding Machine Company had $8 million in sales, according to Augarten's *Bit by Bit*, p. 82.

31. The legacy of the census crisis is described in detail in L. E. Truesdell, *The Development of Punch Card Tabulation in the Bureau of the Census, 1890–1940* (Washington D.C.: Government Printing Office, 1965).

32. See Geoffrey D. Austrian's biography, *Herman Hollerith: Forgotten Giant of Information Processing*, pp. 50–51. Shurkin, in *Engines of the Mind*, chapter 3, gives a very readable and concise account of Hollerith and his census work.

33. Austrian, *Herman Hollerith*, pp. 16–17, 51; Augarten, *Bit by Bit*, p. 75.

34. Austrian, *Herman Hollerith*, pp. 63–64.

35. Hollerith's system for the 1890 census is similar to one he described in an 1889 article, "An Electric Tabulating System," extracts from which are reprinted in Randell, *Origins,* pp. 129–139. Also see Randell's discussion of Hollerith's work, pp. 125–126.

36. According to Augarten in *Bit by Bit*, p. 77, the Census Bureau was able to give a preliminary population total of 62,622,250 just six weeks after all the data arrived in Washington.

37. Austrian, *Herman Hollerith*, p. 153.

38. Shurkin, *Engines of the Mind*, pp. 78–82; Austrian, *Herman Hollerith*, chapter 13.

39. Austrian, *Herman Hollerith*, p. 176 ff.

40. See chapters 20 and 21 in Austrian, *Herman Hollerith*, as well as Shurkin, *Engines of the Mind*, p. 86.

41. Austrian, *Herman Hollerith*, p. 312.

42. Shurkin, *Engines of the Mind*, pp. 91–921; Augarten, *Bit by Bit*, pp. 177–178; Austrian, *Herman Hollerith*, pp. 329. Thomas Watson's career is reviewed in Augarten, *Bit by Bit*, pp. 168ff.

43. Shurkin, *Engines of the Mind*, p. 92. See "The Rise of IBM," chapter 25, in Austrian, *Herman Hollerith*, and "The Rise of IBM," chapter 6, in Augarten's *Bit by Bit*. See also Charles J. Bashe, Lyle R. Johnson, John H. Palmer, and Emerson W. Pugh, *IBM's Early Computers*.

44. Augarten, *Bit by Bit*, pp. 217–223. Shurkin examines the relations between IBM and its competitors in *Engines of the Mind*, pp. 260–279.

45. Aiken is quoted in Bernstein, *The Analytical Engine*, p. 62.

46. Bernstein, *The Analytical Engine*, p. 73.

Electronic Roots

1. The writings of these early thinkers are particularly insightful regarding what it means to compute. Some representative works are H. P. Babbage, "Babbage's Analytical Engine," *Monthly Note of the Royal Astronomical Society* 70 (1910): 517–526, 645. George Boole, *An Investigation of the Laws of Thought on Which Are Founded the Mathematical Theories of Logic and Probabilities* (Peru, Ill.: Open Court Publishing Co., 1952); Bertrand Russell, *Principles of Mathematics*, 2nd ed.; and H. Hollerith, "The Electric Tabulating Machine," *Journal of the Royal Statistical Society* 57, no. 4 (1894): 678–682. For a detailed account of Burroughs's contributions, scientific and commercial, see B. Morgan, *Total to Date: The Evolution of the Adding Machine.*

2. Zuse's claim is supported by the patent applications he filed. See, for instance, K. Zuse, "Verfahren zur Selbst Atigen Durchfurung von Rechnungen mit Hilfe von Rechenmaschinen," German Patent Application Z23624, April 11, 1936. Translated extracts, titled "Methods for Automatic Execution of Calculations with the Aid of Computers," appear in Brian Randell, *The Origins of Digital Computers,* pp. 159–166.

3. From an interview with *Computerworld* magazine. Published in *The History of Computing* in 1981 by CW Communications, Framingham, Mass. The magazine's interviewers were enterprising enough to locate Zuse in Hunfeld, Germany, (where he now lives) and produce an engaging interview.

4. Jan Lukasiewicz developed two related notations, each intended to ease certain aspects of representation and computation in mathematical logic. See Donald Knuth, *The Art of Computer Programming,* volume 1, *Fundamental Algorithms,* 2nd edition (Reading, Mass.: Addison-Wesley, 1973), p. 336.

5. A three page description of a special purpose electromechanical computer used to process flying-bomb wing data is given in K. Zuse, "Rechengerate für Flugelvermessung," private memorandum, September 10, 1969.

6. The charge is strongly made by Rex Malik in *And Tomorrow . . . the World* (London: Millington, 1975).

7. Paul Ceruzzi's 1980 doctoral dissertation gives us a most detailed account of Zuse's contributions to computer technology and places them in the proper context. Paul E. Ceruzzi, "The Prehistory of the Digital Computer, 1935–1945: A Cross-Cultural Study." Texas Tech University, 1980.

8. Zuse's own statement on his life and his computers (with many details of construction) appears in Konrad Zuse, *Der Computer—Mein Lebenswerk* (Berlin: Verlag Moderne Industrie, 1970). More recent reminiscences appear in Konrad Zuse, "Some Remarks on the History of Computers in Germany," in N. Metropolis, J. Howlett, and G. C Rota, eds., *A History of Computing in the Twentieth Century,* pp. 611–628.

9. John E. Savage, Susan Magidson, and Alex M. Stein, *The Mystical Machine,* pp. 25–26.

10. See Andrew Hodges, *Alan Turing: The Enigma.* Hodges's biography, now a standard reference on Turing's life, gives an original account of Turing's war-time computers.

11. For an engineering account of the Colossus project, see B. Randell, "The Colossus," reprinted in N. Metropolis, J. Howlett, and G. C Rota, eds., *A History of Computing in the Twentieth Century.*

12. An excellent set of brief biographies of computer pioneers, including one of Aiken, may be found in Robert Slater, *Portraits in Silicon.*

13. See Andrew Hodges, *Alan Turing: The Enigma.*

14. See Cuthbert Hurd, "Computer Development at IBM," in N. Metropolis, J. Howlett, and G. C. Rota, eds., *A History of Computing in the Twentieth Century,* pp. 389–418. IBM's role in the development of these early computers is covered in Charles Bashe et al., *IBM's Early Computers.* This detailed book is successful in showing how exhausting an intellectual and physical effort it was to construct computers.

15. *The History of Computing* (Framingham, Mass.: CW Communications, 1981), p. 52.

16. Grace Hopper is brought out as a strong, dedicated, and inspiring intellectual in Slater's biography in Robert Slater, *Portraits in Silicon.*

17. John E. Savage, Susan Magidson, and Alex M. Stein, *The Mystical Machine,* p. 30.

18. For a brief overview of the principles and construction of ENIAC and the lessons learned in the words of the designers themselves, see J. Presper Eckert, "The ENIAC," and John W. Mauchly, "The ENIAC." Both pieces appear in N. Metropolis, J. Howlett, and G. C Rota, eds., *A History of Computing in the Twentieth Century,* pp. 525–540, 541–550.

19. The court case brought out thousand of pages of material on early computers, valuable to the computer historian. Judge Larson's findings are recorded in E. R. Larson, "Findings of Fact, Conclusion of Law, and Order for Judgement," File no. 4-67, Civ. 138, Honeywell Inc. vs. Sperry Rand Corp. and Illinois Scientific Development, Inc., U.S. District Court, District of Minnesota, Fourth Division, October 19, 1973.

20. A description of the machine and its applications is given in J. V. Atanasoff, "Computing Machine for the Solution of Large Systems of Linear Algebraic Equations," Ames, Iowa: Iowa State College, 1940. Reprinted in Brian Randell, ed., *The Origins of Digital Computers: Selected Papers* (Berlin: Springer-Verlag, 1973), pp. 305–325.

21. The concept of a stored program has proved to be one of the most robust in computer science. For a history of its development and implementation, and also for a clear analysis of the ENIAC experience, see Arthur Burks, "From ENIAC to the Stored Program: Two Revolutions in Computers," in N. Metropolis, J. Howlett, G. C Rota, eds., *A History of Computing in the Twentieth Century*, pp. 311–344.

22. For a lucid explanation of the stored-program idea, see John E. Savage, Susan Magidson, and Alex M. Stein, *The Mystical Machine*, pp. 31–32, 58–62.

23. The excitement of these developments is skillfully captured in Wilkes's autobiography: Maurice Wilkes, *Memoirs of a Computer Pioneer* (Cambridge: MIT Press, 1981).

24. For the role of research and development in the rise of IBM, see Charles Bashe et al., *IBM's Early Computers*.

25. Alan M. Turing, "Computing Machinery and Intelligence," *Mind* 59 (1950): 433–460.

26. Pamela McCorduck, *Machines Who Think* (San Francisco: W. H. Freeman, 1979), pp. 93–102.

27. Von Neumann stressed the differences between the nervous system and the computer in "The General and Logical Theory of Automata," in L. A. Jeffress, ed., *Cerebral Mechanisms in Behavior* (New York: John Wiley & Sons, 1951). He fails to see how these two can be made to be functionally equivalent.

28. A book was published posthumously, however: J. von Neumann, *The Computer and the Brain* (New Haven: Yale University Press, 1958).

29. Norbert Wiener, *Cybernetics* (Cambridge: MIT Press, 1943).

30. Wiener is a delightful writer: the best biographies of him are perhaps his own. See Norbert Wiener, *Ex-Prodigy* (Cambridge: MIT Press, 1963) and Norbert Wiener, *I Am a Mathematician* (Boston: Houghton-Mifflin, 1964).

31. Wiener liked to believe that the medium underlying life was not energy but information. For an account of how this motivated many of Wiener's projects, see the excellent biography Steve Heims, *John von Neumann and Norbert Wiener: From Mathematics to the Technologies of Life and Death* (Cambridge: MIT Press, 1980).

32. Many of Fredkin's results come from studying his own model of computation, which explicitly reflects a number of fundamental principles of physics. See the classic Edward Fredkin and Tommaso Toffoli, "Conservative Logic," *International Journal of Theoretical Physics* 21, nos. 3–4 (1982).

33. A set of concerns about the physics of computation analytically similar to those of Fredkin's may be found in Norman Margolus, "Physics and Computation," Ph.D. thesis, MIT.

34. In his provocative book *The Coming of Postindustrial Society,* Harvard sociologist Daniel Bell introduces the idea that the codification of knowledge is becoming central to society. In *The Fifth Generation* (Reading, Mass.: Addison-Wesley, 1983), Edward Feigenbaum and Pamela McCorduck discuss the impending reality of such a society.

35. See Norbert Wiener, *Cybernetics.*

36. The Differential Analyzer and other such analog computing machines are described in chapter 5 of Michael Williams, *A History of Computing Technology* (Englewood Cliffs, N.J.: Prentice-Hall, 1985). Bush's own account of the computer is presented in "The Differential Analyzer," *Journal of the Franklin Institute* 212, no. 4 (1936): 447–488.

37. The drawbacks of analog computers are considered in chapter 5 of Michael Williams, *A History of Computing Technology* (Englewood Cliffs, N.J.: Prentice-Hall, 1985).

38. See Norbert Wiener, *Cybernetics.*

39. Such trends are fast paced. See Tom Forester, *High Tech Society* (Cambridge: MIT Press, 1987).

40. A clear account of the technology behind the compact disk appears in John J. Simon, "'From Sand to Circuits' and other Enquiries," Harvard University Office of Information Technology, 1986.

41. See John J. Simon, "'From Sand to Circuits' and Other Enquiries," Harvard University Office of Information Technology, 1986.

42. The structure of the transistor is explained in Stephen Senturia and Bruce Wedlock, *Electronic Circuits and Applications* (New York: McGraw-Hill, 1983).

43. See Claude Shannon and Warren Weaver, *The Mathematical Theory of Communication* (Urbana, Ill.: University of Illinois Press, 1964).

44. In recent years very interesting work has been done to find out how the brain processes perceptual inputs. For a sample of current thinking in the area, see Ellen Hildreth and Christof Koch, "The Analysis of Visual Motion: From Computational Theory to Neural Mechanisms," MIT Artificial Intelligence Laboratory, AI memo no. 919, 1986.

45. A clear and technically accurate piece on the revolution in music brought about by the representation of music in digital forms is presented in *Understanding Computers: Input, Output,* (Alexandria, Va.: Time-Life Books, 1986).

46. Haugeland clarifies many issues by attempting to formalize our intuitions. What does it mean when we say that the mind is a computer? asks Haugeland in *Artificial Intelligence: The Very Idea.*

47. Alan Turing, "Computing Machinery and Intelligence," *Mind* 59 (1950): 433–460 (reprinted in E. Feigenbaum and J. Feldman, *Computers and Thought*). Norbert Wiener, *Cybernetics, or Control and Communication in the Animal and Machine.* Warren McCulloch and Walter Pitts, "A Logical Calculus of the Ideas Immanent in Logical Activity," *Bulletin of Mathematical Biophysics*, 5 (1943): 115–137. Claude Shannon, "Programming a Digital Computer for Playing Chess," *Philosophy Magazine* 41 (1950): 356–375. A related paper, more amenable to the layperson, is "Automatic Chess Player," *Scientific American,* October 1950, p. 48.

48. See A. Newell, J. C. Shaw, and H. A. Simon, "Programming the Logic Theory Machine," *Proceedings of the Western Joint Computer Conference*, 1957, pp. 230–240.

49. See A. Newell, J. C. Shaw, and H. A. Simon, "Empirical Explorations of the Logic Theory Machine," *Proceedings of the Western Joint Computer Conference,* 1957, pp. 218–239.

50. The broad techniques of the Logic Theory Machine were generalized in GPS. This is described in A. Newell, J. C. Shaw, and H. A. Simon, "Report on a General Problem-Solving Program," reprinted in E. Feigenbaum and J. Feldman, eds., *Computers and Thought.* Newell and Simon continued their studies and summarized their results in *Human Problem Solving*, which placed less emphasis on the actual computer implementation of their ideas.

51. A. Newell and H. A. Simon, "Heuristic Problem Solving: The Next Advance in Operations Research," *Journal of the Operations Research Society of America* 6, no. 1 (1958), reprinted in Herbert Simon, *Models of Bounded Rationality,* vol. 1, *Economic Analysis and Public Policy* (Cambridge: MIT Press, 1982).

52. Notably the Dreyfus brothers. See Hubert Dreyfus, *What Computers Can't Do*, 2nd ed.

53. Indeed, the prediction about chess has not *yet* come true. The Fredkin Prize will go to the first computer to become world chess champion. Samuel's checker program was not written specifically as a game-playing program but as an exercise in machine learning. See Arthur L. Samuel, "Some Studies in Machine Learning Using the Game of Checkers," reprinted in E. A. Feigenbaum and J. Feldman, eds., *Computers and Thought*, pp. 279–293.

54. McCorduck's delightful book on the history of artificial intelligence, *Machines Who Think*, contains a chapter on the now famous Dartmouth Conference.

55. See Edward Feigenbaum's short reflection on twenty-five years of artificial intelligence: "AAAI President's Message," *AI Magazine*, Winter 1980–1981.

56. The version most referred to is Marvin Minsky, "Steps toward Artificial Intelligence," in E. A. Feigenbaum and J. Feldman, eds., *Computers and Thought*, pp. 406–450.

57. LISP was originally introduced in a set of memos at the MIT Artificial Intelligence Laboratory. Much of this found its way into formal publications. See John McCarthy, "Recursive Functions of Symbolic Expressions and Their Computation by Machine, Part I," *Communications of the ACM* 3, no. 4 (1960). The language soon became popular enough for McCarthy to publish a manual: John McCarthy, P. W. Abrahams, D. J. Edwards, T. P. Hart, and M. I. Levin, *LISP 1.5 Programmer's Manual* (Cambridge: MIT Press, 1962). See Pamela McCorduck, *Machines Who Think*, pp. 97–102.

58. Daniel Bobrow, "Natural Language Input for a Computer Problem Solving System," in Marvin Minsky, *Semantic Information Processing*, pp. 146–226.

59. Thomas Evans, "A Program for the Solution of Geometric-Analogy Intelligence Test Questions," in Marvin Minsky, *Semantic Information Processing,* pp. 271–353.

501

60. This work is described in R. Greenblatt, D. Eastlake, and S. Crocker, "The Greenblatt Chess Program," MIT Artificial Intelligence Laboratory, AI memo 174, 1968. The program defeated Hubert Dreyfus, who once strongly doubted that a chess program could match even an amateur human player.

61. The lessons of DENDRAL are recorded and analyzed in Robert Lindsay, Bruce Buchanan, Edward Feigenbaum, and Joshua Lederberg, *Applications of Artificial Intelligence for Chemical Inference: The DENDRAL Project* (New York: McGraw-Hill, 1980). A brief and clear explanation of the essential mechanisms behind DENDRAL is given in Patrick Winston, *Artificial Intelligence* (1984), pp. 163–164, 195–197.

62. Much has been written about ELIZA, but the clearest account on how ELIZA works is from Weizenbaum himself: "ELIZA—A Computer Program for the Study of Natural Language Communication between Man and Machine," *Communications of the ACM* 9 (1966): 36–45. ELIZA has, of course, attracted numerous criticisms, many of which were first voiced by Weizenbaum himself. See Hubert Dreyfus, *What Computers Can't Do.*

63. For many years SHRDLU was cited as a prominent accomplishment of artificial intelligence. Winograd's thesis has been published in book form: *Understanding Natural Language* (New York: Academic Press, 1972). A brief version appears as "A Procedural Model of Thought and Language," in Roger Schank and Kenneth Colby, eds., *Computer Models of Thought and Language* (San Francisco: W. H. Freeman, 1973).

64. Minsky and Papert point out that these toy examples offer many important abstractions for further analysis. See Marvin Minsky and Seymour Papert, "Artificial Intelligence Progress Report," MIT Artificial Intelligence Laboratory, AI memo 252, 1973.

65. Warren McCulloch and Walter Pitts, "A Logical Calculus of the Ideas Immanent in Logical Activity," *Bulletin of Mathematical Biophysics* 5 (1943): 115–137. Rosenblatt's classic work is *Principles of Neurodynamics* (New York: Spartan Books, 1962).

66. Minsky and Papert trace much of this controversy and history, with technical details, in the prologue and epilogue of the revised edition of their book, published in 1988.

67. This trend is explained and praised in Edward Feigenbaum, "The Art of Artificial Intelligence: Themes and Case Studies in Knowledge Engineering," *Fifth International Joint Conference on Artificial Intelligence,* 1977.

68. The approach was compelling in light of what it could do. See the papers in E. Feigenbaum and J. Feldman, *Computer and Thought.*

69. Knowledge representation was and continues to be an important area of artificial intelligence research. See R. Brachman and H. Levesque, eds., *Readings in Knowledge Representation* (Los Altos, Calif.: Morgan Kaufman, 1986).

70. The restaurant scene is a popular example of scripts as a means of representing knowledge. Scripts are brought out as a powerful scheme for reasoning in R. Schank and R. Abelson, *Scripts, Plans, Goals, and Understanding* (Hillsdale, N.J.: Lawrence Erlbaum Associates, 1977).

71. Minsky's work on frames is one of the most cited in AI. The most complete written form of the theory is Marvin Minsky, "A Framework for Representing Knowledge," MIT Artificial Intelligence Laboratory, AI memo 304, 1974.

72. See R. Schank and R. Abelson, *Scripts, Plans, Goals, and Understanding* (Hillsdale, N.J.: Lawrence Erlbaum Associates, 1977).

73. An excellent introduction to the technology and applications of expert systems is F. Hayes-Roth, D. A. Waterman, and D. B. Lenat, eds., *Building Expert Systems* (Reading, Mass.: Addison-Wesley, 1983).

74. Some famous expert systems are described by the creators themselves in F. Hayes-Roth, D. A. Waterman, and D. B. Lenat, eds., *Building Expert Systems* (Reading, Mass.: Addison-Wesley, 1983).

75. See Edward Feigenbaum and Pamela McCorduck, *The Fifth Generation.*

76. Artificial intelligence is beginning to have an important effect on the productivity of many organizations. This phenomena is explored in Edward Feigenbaum, Pamela McCorduck, and Penny Nii, *The Rise of the Expert Company* (Reading, Mass.: Addison-Wesley, 1989).

Pattern Recognition: The Search for Order

1. An excellent treatment of the role of imagery and "holistic" representations in cognition may be found in Ned Block, ed., *Imagery* (Cambridge: MIT Press, 1981).

2. See Newell and Simon's analysis of human chess playing in Allen Newell and Herbert Simon, *Human Problem Solving* (Englewood Cliffs, N.J.: Prentice-Hall, 1972).

3. An essay of special relevance to the discussion here is Zenon Pylyshyn, "Imagery and Artificial Intelligence," in C. W. Savage, ed., *Perception and Cognition: Issues in the Foundations of Psychology*, Minnesota Studies in the Philosophy of Science, vol. 9 (Minneapolis: University of Minnesota Press, 1978).

4. Imagination is a skill that we develop with age. Piaget's experiments show that to the infant (up to a certain age), an object that is not visible does not exist. See J. Piaget, *Play, Dreams, and Imitation in Childhood* (New York: W. W. Norton, 1951).

5. This technique is simple but surprisingly powerful and has been used extensively in AI programs. See Patrick H. Winston, *Artificial Intelligence*, pp. 159–167.

6. A clear introduction to the essential problems and procedures in machine vision appears in chapter 10 of the classic textbook Patrick H. Winston, *Artificial Intelligence*.

7. This and other techniques for identifying edges are reviewed in L. Davis, "A Survey of Edge Detection Techniques," *Computer Graphics and Image Processing* 4 (1975): 248–270. A more detailed review appears in Azriel Rosenfeld and Avinash Kak, *Digital Picture Processing* (New York: Academic Press, 1976). A more recent summary of results, including John Canny's work, is Ellen Hildreth, "Edge Detection," MIT Artificial Intelligence Laboratory, AI memo 858, 1985.

8. The use of zero crossings in stereo to isolate edges was introduced in David Marr and Tomaso Poggio, "A Theory of Human Stereo Vision," *Proceedings of the Royal Society of London* 204 (1979). The use of zero crossings was also addressed in Ellen Hildreth's work: "The Detection of Intensity Changes by Computer and Biological Vision Systems," *Computer Vision, Graphics, and Image Processing* 23 (1979). For efficiencies more recently incorporated, see John Canny, "Finding Edges and Lines in Images," MIT Artificial Intelligence Laboratory, technical report 720, 1983.

9. False hypothesis may be corrected also by some of the techniques detailed in L. S. Davis, "A Survey of Edge Detection Techniques," *Computer Graphics and Image Processing* 4 (1975): 248–270. Also see Ellen Hildreth, "Edge Detection," MIT Artificial Intelligence Laboratory, AI memo 858, 1985.

10. Hubel and Wiesel are responsible for many important aspects of our knowledge today about the biological mechanisms for vision. They conducted many imaginative experiments to reveal the structure and functional decomposition of the cortex. Notable is their discovery of the presence of edge-detection neurons. See D. H. Hubel and T. N. Wiesel, "Functional Architecture of Macaque Monkey Visual Cortex," *Journal of Physiology* 195 (1968): 215–242. A truly fascinating book written for the layperson as an introduction to the brain's vision processing is David Hubel, *Eye, Brain, and Vision*.

11. For details of the computational aspects of recovering details of surfaces from images by means of sombrero filtering and other related techniques, see W. Eric L. Grimson, *From Images to Surfaces* (Cambridge: MIT Press, 1981).

12. An illuminating article on the eye's computational capacities for image processing is Tomaso Poggio, "Vision by Man and Machine," *Scientific American*, April 1984.

13. See Tomaso Poggio, "Vision by Man and Machine," *Scientific American*, April 1984.

14. David Marr is brilliant at fusing studies from biology and machine vision. His highly influential classic, published posthumously, is *Vision*. A paper that excellently summarizes and demonstrates his computational approach to vision is D. Marr and H. K. Nishihara, "Visual Information Processing: Artificial Intelligence and the Sensorium of Sight," *Technology Review*, October 1978.

15. See Tomaso Poggio, "Vision by Man and Machine" *Scientific American*, April 1984.

16. The geometry of stereopsis and stereo vision is discussed well in S. T. Barnard and M. A. Fischler, "Computational Stereo from an IU Perspective," *Proceedings of the Image Understanding Workshop*, 1981.

17. Edges introduce constraints that greatly reduce the number of ways two images can be fused. Without such preprocessing, matching would be be extremely difficult. Consider, for example, the computational complexity of fusing random-dot stereograms. See David Marr, *Vision*, p. 9.

18. For the details of these techniques, see R. O. Duda and P. E. Hart, *Pattern Classification and Scene Analysis* (New York: Wiley, 1973).

19. See W. Eric L. Grimson, *From Images to Surfaces*. Object recognition and labeling is a hard problem. For the role of knowledge and preconceived models in this process, see Rodney Brooks, "Model-Based Three-Dimensional Interpretation of Two-Dimensional Images," *Proceedings of the Seventh International Joint Conference on Artificial Intelligence*, 1981. Generalized cylinders are frequently used as intermediate representations of objects. See D. Marr and H. K. Nishihara, "Visual Information Processing: Artificial Intelligence and the Sensorium of Sight," *Technology Review*, October 1978.

20. The parallel nature of the computational processes constituting early vision is examined in an excellent review article: Tomaso Poggio, Vincent Torre, and Christof Koch, "Computational Vision and Regularization Theory," *Nature,* September 26, 1985. The role of analog computations is also discussed there.

21. For some lessons that evolution offers for strategies in artificial intelligence, see Rodney Brooks, "Intelligence without Representation," *Artificial Intelligence,* 1989.

22. This point is brought out with particular elegance in Dana Ballard and Christopher Brown, "Vision: Biology Challenges Technology," *BYTE,* April 1985.

23. The structure of the Connection Machine is excellently described, along with some machine vision applications, in W. Daniel Hillis, "The Connection Machine," *Scientific American,* June 1987.

24. The role of analog computations in vision is discussed in Tomaso Poggio, Vincent Torre, and Christof Koch, "Computational Vision and Regularization Theory," *Nature,* September 26, 1985.

25. Neural networks and related mechanisms have been applied fairly successfully in vision problems. For work in early vision, see D. H. Ballard, "Parameter Nets: Toward a Theory of Low-Level Vision," *Artificial Intelligence Journal* 22 (1984): 235–267. For higher-level processes, see D. Sabbah, "Computing with Connections in Visual Recognition of Origami Objects," *Cognitive Science* 9 (1985): 25–50.

26. For instance, early neural networks failed to determine connectedness of drawings. The ability of more complex neural nets to determine connectedness remains controversial. See Marvin Minsky and Seymour Papert, *Perceptrons,* pp. 136–150.

27. The manifesto of the new connectionists is *Parallel Distributed Processing,* vols. 1 and 2, by David Rumelhart, James McClelland, and the PDP Research Group. Chapter 2 of this book describes the new neural-net structures.

28. Marvin Minsky and Seymour Papert, *Perceptrons,* revised ed., p. vii.

29. Distributed systems, whose mechanisms and memory are stored not centrally but over a large space, are less prone to catastrophic degradation. Neural networks are not only parallel but also distributed systems. See chapter 1 of D. E. Rumelhart, J. L. McClelland, and the PDP Research Group, *Parallel Distributed Processing: Explorations in the Microstructure of Cognition,* vol. 1.

30. An excellent study of skill acquisition with some implications for parallel distributed processing is D. E. Rumelhart and D. A. Norman, "Simulating a Skilled Typist: A Study of Skilled Cognitive-Motor Performance," Institute for Cognitive Science, technical report 8102, University of California, San Diego, 1981.

31. This objection is articulated in Hubert Dreyfus and Stuart Dreyfus, *Mind Over Machine: The Power of Human Intuition and Expertise in the Era of the Computer* (New York: The Free Press, 1986), pp. 101–121.

32. Daniel Hillis points out that for many physical systems that are inherently parallel, fluid flow, for example, it is simply not *convenient* to think in terms of sequential processes. Similarly, logic turns out to be inconvenient for the analysis of, say, early-vision processes. See W. Daniel Hillis, "The Connection Machine," *Scientific American,* June 1987.

33. This multilevel, multiparadigm approach is followed in the society theory of the mind. See Marvin Minsky, *The Society of Mind.*

34. Higher-level descriptions have a smaller *volume* of information, but they incorporate a larger number of constraints and require more extensive knowledge about the physical world. See chapter 1 in David Marr, *Vision.*

35. See the appendix of Marvin Minsky, *The Society of Mind.*

36. For recent developments in the design and fabrication of chips, see J. D. Meindl, "Chips for Advanced Computing," *Scientific American,* October 1987.

37. David Marr and Tomaso Poggio, "Cooperative Computation of Stereo Disparity," *Science* 194 (1976): 283–287.

38. See David Marr and Tomaso Poggio, "From Understanding Computation to Understanding Neural Circuitry," *Proceedings of the Royal Society of London,* 1977, pp. 470–488.

39. Daniel Hillis's thesis suggests areas where parallelism ought to be exploited. See W. Daniel Hillis, *The Connection Machine* (Cambridge: MIT Press, 1985).

40. David Marr is responsible for these important representations for vision processing. All three are clearly explained in D. Marr and H. K. Nishihara, "Visual Information Processing: Artificial Intelligence and the Sensorium of Sight," *Technology Review,* October 1978.

41. Segmentation was one of the chief concerns in the construction of the Hearsay speech-recognition system. The problem was resolved in part by using multiple knowledge sources and multiple experts. See L. Erman, F. Hayes-Roth, V. Lesser, and D. Raj Reddy, "The HEARSAY-II Speech Understanding System: Integrating Knowledge to Resolve Uncertainty," *Computing Surveys* 12, no. 2 (1980): 213–253.

42. See L. Erman, F. Hayes-Roth, V. Lesser, and D. Raj Reddy, "The HEARSAY-II Speech Understanding System: Integrating Knowledge to Resolve Uncertainty," *Computing Surveys* 12, no. 2 (1980): 213–253.

43. The early years of artificial intelligence saw a lot of work on character recognition. But researchers could not perform extensive experiments on their programs because of a lack of computer power. See W. W. Bledsoe and I. Browning, "Pattern Recognition and Reading by Machine," *Proceedings of the Eastern Joint Computer Conference*, 1959. A more general article is Oliver Selfridge and U. Neisser, "Pattern Recognition by Machine," *Scientific American*, March 1960, 60–68.

44. The Hearsay system has an interesting implementation of such a manager. See L. Erman, F. Hayes-Roth, V. Lesser, and D. Raj Reddy, "The HEARSAY-II Speech Understanding System: Integrating Knowledge to Resolve Uncertainty," *Computing Surveys* 12, no. 2 (1980): 213–253.

45. For some interesting points on the use of multiple experts, see Douglas Lenat, "Computer Software for Intelligent Systems," *Scientific American,* September 1984.

46. For basic techniques for template matching, see R. O. Duda and P. E. Hart, *Pattern Classification and Scene Analysis* (New York: Wiley, 1973).

47. A playful treatment of the nature of fonts and type styles is presented in chapter 13 of Douglas Hofstadter, *Metamagical Themas*.

48. This set of paradigms is successfully applied in the Hearsay system in the context of speech recognition. See L. Erman, F. Hayes-Roth, V. Lesser, and D. Raj Reddy, "The HEARSAY-II Speech Understanding System: Integrating Knowledge to Resolve Uncertainty," *Computing Surveys* 12, no. 2 (1980): 213–253.

49. For details of the project, see Tomaso Poggio and staff, "MIT Progress in Understanding Images," *Proceedings of the Image Understanding Workshop* (Cambridge, Mass., 1988), pp. 1–16.

50. The project tries to incorporate what we know about the nature of vision computation in the brain, an issue treated in Tomaso Poggio, Vincent Torre, and Christof Koch, "Computational Vision and Regularization Theory," *Nature,* September 26, 1985.

51. See T. Poggio, J. Little, et al., "The MIT Vision Machine," *Proceedings of the Image Understanding Workshop* (Cambridge, Mass., 1988), pp. 177–198.

52. For related work, see Anya Hurlbert and Tomaso Poggio, "Making Machines (and Artificial Intelligence)," *Daedalus,* Winter 1988.

53. The Terregator and some other projects of the robotics group at Carnegie-Mellon University are described in Eric Lerner, "Robotics: The Birth of a New Vision," *Science Digest,* July 1985.

54. An informative article on Carver Mead and his specialized chips for vision processing is: Andrew Pollack, "Chips that Emulate the Function of the Retina," *New York Times,* August 26, 1987, p. D6.

55. Harry Newquist, ed., *AI Trends '87: A Comprehensive Annual Report on the Artificial Intelligence Industry* (Scottsdale, Ariz.: DM Data, 1987).

56. See "Technology Aiding in Fingerprint Identification, U.S. Reports," *New York Times,* May 4, 1987, p. A20.

57. For a description of these new products, see Wesley Iversen, "Fingerprint Reader Restricts Access to Terminals and PCs," *Electronics,* June 11, 1987, p. 104.

58. A very good review paper on AI vision systems and their industrial applications is Michael Brady, "Intelligent Vision," in W. Eric Grimson and Ramesh Patil, eds., *AI in the 1980s and Beyond.*

59. Harry Newquist, ed., *AI Trends '87: A Comprehensive Annual Report on the Artificial Intelligence Industry* (Scottsdale, Ariz.: DM Data, 1987).

60. A substantive article on the role of intelligent systems in modern warfare is J. Franklin, Laura Davis, Randall Shumaker, and Paul Morawski, "Military Applications," in Stuart Shapiro ed., *Encyclopedia of Artificial Intelligence,* vol. 1 (New York: John Wiley & Sons, 1987).

61. The intelligence of remotely piloted aircraft offers great possibilities, as one can see from Peter Gwynne, "Remotely Piloted Vehicles Join the Service," *High Technology,* January 1987, pp. 38–43.

62. Expert systems, pattern recognition and other kinds of medical-information systems will become increasingly utilized in medicine. See Glenn Rennels and Edward Shortliffe, "Advanced Computing for Medicine," *Scientific American,* October 1987.

63. A beautifully illustrated article on medical imaging technology is Howard Sochurek, "Medicine's New Vision," *National Geographic,* January 1987, pp. 2–41.

64. Schwartz's proposal created excitement in the art world. Her research is described in Lillian Schwartz, "Leonardo's Mona Lisa," *Arts and Antiques,* January 1987. A briefer, more technical description appears in the following book on computers and art: Cynthia Goodman, *Digital Visions* (New York: H. N. Abrams, 1987), pp. 41–43.

65. To J. B. Watson, the founder of behaviorism in America, thinking was like talking to oneself. He attached great importance to the small movements of the tongue and larynx when one is thinking. See J. B. Watson, *Behaviorism* (New York: Norton, 1925).

66. Viewers of the film *My Fair Lady* will recall that the anatomy of speech production is an important topic for phoneticians. See M. Kenstowicz and C. Kissebereth, *Generative Phonology: Description and Theory* (New York: Academic Press, 1979) and P. Ladefoged, *A Course in Phonetics,* 2nd ed. (New York: Harcourt Brace Jovanovich, 1982).

67. The distribution of sound is particular to each language. An important study on English is N. Chomsky and M. Halle, *The Sound Pattern of English* (New York: Harper & Row, 1968).

68. Some problems and procedures for early auditory processing are presented in S. Seneff, "Pitch and Spectral Analysis of Speech Based on an Auditory Perspective," Ph.D. thesis, MIT Dept. of Electrical Engineering, 1985.

69. This issue is covered in J. S. Perkell and D. H. Klatt., eds., *Variability and Invariance in Speech Processes* (Hillsdale, N.J.: Erlbaum, Lawrence Associates, 1985).

70. H. Sakoe and S. Chita, "A Dynamic-Programming Approach to Continuous Speech Recognition," *Proceedings of the International Congress of Acoustics,* Budapest, Hungary, 1971, pp. 206–213.

71. This approach is faithfully followed in the construction of the Hearsay speech-recognition system. See L. Erman, F. Hayes-Roth, V. Lesser, and D. Raj Reddy, "The HEARSAY-II Speech Understanding System: Integrating Knowledge to Resolve Uncertainty," *Computing Surveys* 12, no. 2 (1980): 213–253.

72. A comprehensive review of ASR is Victor Zue, "Automated Speech Recognition," in W. Eric L. Grimson and Ramesh Patil, eds., *AI in the 1980s and Beyond.*

73. See Harry Newquist, ed., *AI Trends '87: A Comprehensive Annual Report on the Artificial Intelligence Industry* (Scottsdale, Ariz.: DM Data, 1987).

74. See the fascinating cover stories on computers and music in the June 1986 issue of *BYTE.*

The Search for Knowledge

1. These and other intriguing aspects of memory are discussed in chapter 8 in Marvin Minsky, *Society of Mind.*

2. The most complete written form of the frame theory is Marvin Minsky, "A Framework for Representing Knowledge," MIT Artificial Intelligence Laboratory, AI memo 306. Other, less technical versions have appeared since. See Marvin Minsky, "A Framework for Representing Knowledge," in John Haugeland, ed., *Mind Design.*

3. A brief description of the classification systems currently followed is given in *Classification: A Beginner's Guide to Some of the Systems of Biological Classification in Use Today,* British Museum (Natural History), London, 1983.

4. The successes and limitations of these systems are discussed in the excellent book Lynn Margulus and Karlene Schwartz, *Five Kingdoms: An Illustrated Guide to the Phyla of Life on Earth,* 2nd ed. (New York: W. H. Freeman, 1988).

5. Dewey first published his classic work anonymously under the title, "A Classification and Subject Title." Many editions have appeared since, because the Dewey system has grown to meet every challenge of the world's libraries. See Melvil Dewey, *Dewey Decimal Classification and Relative Index: Devised by Melvil Dewey,* 19th ed., edited under the direction of Benjamin Custer (Albany, N.Y.: Forest Press, 1979).

6. Ross Quillian is generally credited with developing semantic networks as a knowledge representation for AI systems. Although he introduced this representation as early as 1963, the standard reference for his work in this area is M. Ross Quillian, "Semantic Memory," in Marvin Minsky, *Semantic Information Processing* (1968).

7. See Patrick H. Winston, "Learning Structural Descriptions from Examples," in Patrick H. Winston, *The Psychology of Computer Vision* (New York: McGraw-Hill, 1975).

8. Some of the psychological realities behind semantic networks are discussed in M. Ross Quillian, "Semantic Memory," in Marvin Minsky, *Semantic Information Processing.*

9. Some interesting explanations of cognitive dissonance are given in Henry Gleitman, *Psychology,* 2nd ed. (New York: W. W. Norton & Co., 1986), pp. 374–376.

10. An excellent book on the influence of media on political thinking is Edwin Diamond and Stephen Bates, *The Spot: The Rise of Political Advertising on Television* (Cambridge: MIT Press, 1984).

11. A revealing book on the psychological aspects of advertising today is William Meyers, *The Image Makers: Power and Persuasion on Madison Avenue* (New York: Times Books, 1984).

12. Much research has been done in recent years on the mechanisms for computation and memory in the human brain, particularly since any new knowledge could contribute significantly to the debate on connectionism. An introductory account is in Paul M. Churchland, *Matter and Consciousness,* revised edition.

13. This last point is strongly brought out by Roger Schank and Peter Childers in *The Creative Attitude* (New York: Macmillan, 1988).

14. That computers can never be creative has long been an argument against the possibility of artificial intelligence. A short rebuttal and an examination of what it means to be creative appears as part of Marvin Minsky, "Why People Think Computers Can't" *AI Magazine* 3, no. 4 (Fall 1982).

15. D. Raj Reddy, *Foundations and Grand Challenges of Artificial Intelligence,* forthcoming. For a similar analysis of the brain's processing capabilities, see J. A. Feldman and D. H. Ballard, "Connectionist Models and Their Properties," *Cognitive Science* 6 (1982): 205–254.

16. Work is being done to allow intelligent systems to exploit past experiences instead of relying solely on the deep analysis of the current situation. For an example, see Craig Stanfill and David Waltz, "Toward Memory Based Reasoning," *Communications of the ACM* 29, no. 12 (1986).

17. See Craig Stanfill and David Waltz, "Toward Memory Based Reasoning," *Communications of the ACM* 29, no. 12 (1986).

18. Human chess-playing and computer chess are analyzed for similarities and differences in Eliot Hearst, "Man and Machine: Chess Achievements and Chess Thinking," in Peter Frey, ed., *Chess Skill in Man and Machine,* 2nd ed., 1983.

19. See Eliot Hearst, "Man and Machine."

20. Newell and his associates maintain that much of learning is reorganization of certain memories into efficient "chunks." See John E. Laird, P. Rosenbloom, and Allen Newell, "Towards Chunking as a General Learning Mechanism," *Proceedings of the National Conference of the American Association for Artificial Intelligence,* Austin, Tex, 1984.

21. To see how chunking fits into the SOAR view of cognition and intelligence, see John E. Laird, P. Rosenbloom, and Allen Newell, "SOAR: An Architecture for General Intelligence," *Artificial Intelligence Journal* 33 (1987): 1–64.

22. An excellent introductory book on the structure and design of expert systems, with contributions from many figures notable for their work in this area, is Frederick Hayes-Roth, D. A. Waterman, and D. B. Lenat, eds., *Building Expert Systems.*

23. XCON, once called R1, was jointly developed by Carnegie-Mellon University and Digital Equipment Corporation (DEC). See J. McDermott, "R1: A Rule-Based Configurer of Computer Systems," *Artificial Intelligence Journal* 19, no. 1 (1982).

24. For a DEC view of its experiences with XCON, see Arnold Kraft, "XCON: An Expert Configuration System at Digital Equipment Corporation," in Patrick Winston and Karen Prendergast, eds., *The AI Business* (Cambridge: MIT Press, 1984).

25. Many techniques were introduced to handle the uncertainty of propositions that an expert system is asked to deal with. Fuzzy logic is one such system. See Lofti Zadeh, "Fuzzy Logic and Approximate Reasoning," *Synthese* 30 (1975): 407–428. Zadeh's fuzzy logic has a number of limitations, and other systems for uncertainty have grown in popularity. See Edward Shortliffe and Bruce Buchanan, "A Model of Inexact Reasoning in Medicine," *Mathematical Biosciences* 23 (1975): 350–379.

26. The role of expert systems and knowledge-based systems in the economies of the future and the implications of the Japanese fifth-generation project, are discussed in Edward Feigenbaum and Pamela McCorduck, *The Fifth Generation.*

27. See Edward Feigenbaum, "The Art of Artificial Intelligence: Themes and Case Studies in Knowledge Engineering," *Fifth International Joint Conference on Artificial Intelligence*, Cambridge Mass., 1977.

28. The experiences and contributions of the DENDRAL experiments are recorded and analyzed in detail in R. Lindsay, B. G. Buchanan, E. A. Feigenbaum, and J. Lederberg, *DENDRAL: Artificial Intelligence and Chemistry* (New York: McGraw-Hill, 1980).

29. An excellent article reviewing the research on, and lessons from, the two systems is Bruce Buchanan and Edward Feigenbaum, "DENDRAL and Meta-DENDRAL: Their Applications Dimension" *Artificial Intelligence Journal* 11 (1978): 5–24.

30. Victor L. Yu, Lawrence M. Fagan, S. M. Wraith, William Clancey, A. Carlisle Scott, John Hannigan, Robert Blum, Bruce Buchanan, and Stanley Cohen, "Antimicrobial Selection by Computer: A Blinded Evaluation by Infectious Disease Experts," *Journal of the American Medical Association* 242, no. 12 (1979): 1279–1282.

31. The results of the MYCIN project at Stanford have been very influential on current thinking in artificial intelligence. They are presented and analyzed in Bruce Buchanan and Edward Shortliffe, eds., *Rule-Based Expert Systems: The MYCIN Experiments of the Stanford Heuristic Programming Project* (Reading, Mass.: Addison-Wesley, 1984).

32. The expert-system industry is a burgeoning one. See Paul Harmon and David King, *Expert Systems: Artificial Intelligence in Business*. The diversity of application areas for expert systems is remarkable. See Terri Walker and Richard Miller, *Expert Systems '87* (Madison, Ga.: SEAI Technical Publications, 1987).

33. Harry Newquist, ed., *AI Trends '87: A Comprehensive Annual Report on the Artificial Intelligence Industry* (Scottsdale, Ariz.: DM Data, 1987). Expert systems are changing the way problem solving is handled in corporations across the world. See Edward Feigenbaum, Pamela McCorduck, and Penny Nii, *The Rise of the Expert Company*.

34. See Edward Feigenbaum, "The Art of Artificial Intelligence: Themes and Case Studies in Knowledge Engineering," *Fifth International Joint Conference on Artificial Intelligence*, Cambridge Mass., 1977.

35. The MYCIN expert system originally appeared as Edward Shortliffe's doctoral dissertation in 1974. Other Stanford dissertations explored further the broad concepts behind MYCIN and produced some important tools and applications. Randall Davis's TEIRESIAS, an interactive tool to help the knowledge engineer structure expertise, is presented in Randall Davis, "Applications of Meta-Level Knowledge to the Construction, Maintenance, and Use of Large Knowledge Bases," Ph.D. dissertation, Stanford University, Artificial Intelligence Laboratory, 1976. William van Melle succeeded in showing that in keeping with the conceptual framework proposed earlier by Feigenbaum et al., the inference engine and the knowledge base could in fact be separated out. Van Melle's system, EMYCIN, represented the structure of inferences and reasoning in MYCIN. See W. van Melle, "A Domain-Independent System That Aids in Constructing Knowledge-Based Consultation Programs," Ph.D. dissertation, Stanford University, Computer Science Department, 1980.

36. EMYCIN was combined with a knowledge-base on pulmonary disorder diagnosis to produce PUFF. See Janice Aikens, John Kunz, Edward Shortliffe, and Robert Fallat, "PUFF: An Expert System for Interpretation of Pulmonary Function Data," in William Clancey and Edward Shortliffe, eds., *Readings in Medical Artificial Intelligence: The First Decade*.

37. William Clancey and Reed Letsinger, "NEOMYCIN: Reconfiguring a Rule-Based Expert System for Application to Teaching," in William Clancey and Edward Shortliffe, eds., *Readings in Medical Artificial Intelligence: The First Decade*; and E. H. Shortliffe, A. C. Scott, M. Bischoff, A. B. Campbell, W. van Melle, and C. Jacobs, "ONCOCIN: An Expert System for Oncology Protocol Management," in *Proceedings of the Seventh International Joint Conference on Artificial Intelligence* (Menlo Park, Calif.: American Association for Artificial Intelligence, 1981), pp. 876–881.

38. See Ramesh Patil, Peter Szolovits, and William Schwartz, "Causal Understanding of Patient Illness in Medical Diagnosis," in William Clancey and Edward Shortliffe, eds., *Readings in Medical Artificial Intelligence: The First Decade*.

39. Organization of knowledge is especially difficult when the domains are as broad as that of CADUCEUS, the system developed chiefly by Harry Pople and Jack Myers. See Harry Pople, "Heuristic Methods for Imposing Structure on Ill-Structured Problems: The Structure of Medical Diagnostics," in Peter Szolovits, ed., *Artificial Intelligence in Medicine* (Boulder, Col.: West View Press, 1982).

40. A short overview of the performance of CADUCEUS is Harry Pople, "CADUCEUS: An Experimental Expert System for Medical Diagnosis," in Patrick Winston and Karen Prendergast, eds., *The AI Business.*

41. A recent evaluation from the medical community of the performance and potential of medical artificial intelligence is William Schwartz, Ramesh Patil, and Peter Szolovits, "Artificial Intelligence in Medicine: Where Do We Stand?" *New England Journal of Medicine* 316 (1987): 685–688.

42. See William Schwartz, Ramesh Patil, and Peter Szolovits, "Artificial Intelligence in Medicine: Where Do We Stand?" *New England Journal of Medicine* 316 (1987): 685–688.

43. For applications of artificial intelligence in a wide variety of areas, including finance, see Wendy Rauch-Hindin, *Artificial Intelligence in Business, Science, and Industry.*

44. The structure of Prospector is explained in R. O. Duda, J. G. Gaschnig, and P. E. Hart, "Model Design in the PROSPECTOR Consultant System for Mineral Exploration," in D. Michie, ed., *Expert Systems in the Micro-Electronic Age* (Edinburgh: Edinburgh University Press, 1979). A report on Prospector's role in finding the molybdenum deposit in Washington is in A. N. Campbell, V. F. Hollister, R. O. Duda, and P. E. Hart, "Recognition of a Hidden Mineral Deposit by an Artificial Intelligence Program," *Science* 217, no. 3 (1982). Prospector is also discussed in Avron Barr, Edward Feigenbaum, and Paul Cohen, eds., *The Handbook of Artificial Intelligence* (Los Altos, Calif.: William Kaufman, 1981).

45. Digital Equipment Corporation's AI projects are described in Susan Scown, *The Artificial Intelligence Experience* (Maynard, Mass.: Digital Press, 1985).

46. Many of these expert-system products are described in Paul Harmon and David King, *Expert Systems: Artificial Intelligence in Business*, pp. 77–133

47. Two overviews of the goals and constituent projects of the Strategic Computing Initiative are Dwight Davis, "Assessing the Strategic Computing Initiative," *High Technology,* April 1985; and Karen McGraw, "Integrated Systems Development," *DS&E* (Defense Science and Electronics), December 1986.

48. The Pilot's Associate is assessed by two Air Force officers in Ronald Morishige and John Retelle, "Air Combat and Artificial Intelligence," *Air Force Magazine,* October 1985.

49. Solutions to some of the limitations of expert systems imposed by current architectures are discussed in Randall Davis, "Expert Systems: Where Are We? And Where Do We Go From Here?" MIT Artificial Intelligence Laboratory, AI memo 665, 1982.

50. Until recently, machine learning has been a neglected area within artificial intelligence, perhaps because of the many difficulties underlying the problem. An important collection of papers on machine learning is Ryszard Michalski, Jaime Carbonell, and Tom Mitchell, eds., *Machine Learning—An Artificial Intelligence Approach* (Palo Alto, Calif.: Tioga Publishing Company, 1983).

51. Douglas Lenat wrote AM (Automated Mathematician) as an experiment in causing machine learning by discovery, in the area of number theory. EURISKO is an improved discovery program. The systems are discussed in Douglas Lenat, "Why AM and EURISKO Appear to Work," *Artificial Intelligence Journal* 23 (1984): 269–294.

52. Robert Hink and David Woods, "How Humans Process Uncertain Knowledge," *AI Magazine,* Fall 1987. This paper is written primarily to assist knowledge engineers in structuring domain knowledge in a statistically accurate manner.

53. The cognitive and behavioral aspects of human decision making under uncertainty are considered in an important collection of papers: Daniel Kahneman, Paul Slovic, and Amos Tversky, eds., *Judgement under Uncertainty: Heuristics and Biases.* The essays in this volume assess intriguing aspects of the way people process and interpret information.

54. See Samuel Holtzmann, *Intelligent Decision Systems* (Reading, Mass.: Addison-Wesley, 1989).

55. This is not surprising, since language is a principle means of expressing thought. The entire field of psycholinguistics is devoted to studying the connection between language and thought. So strong is the appeal of this connection that some believe the Whorfian hypothesis, which, loosely stated, holds that there can be no thought without language. Others accept a much weaker form of the Whorfian hypothesis: that there has to be a language of thought, a language that is not necessarily the same as one's *spoken* language. See J. Fodor, T. Bever, and M. Garrett, *The Psychology of Language* (New York: McGraw-Hill, 1975); and Benjamin Whorf, *Language, Thought, and Reality: Selected Writings* (Cambridge, Mass.: MIT Press, 1956).

56. These and other theoretical aspects of computational linguistics are covered in Mary D. Harris, *Introduction to Natural Language Processing*.

57. Terry Winograd has cogently argued that natural languages assume an enormous quantity of background knowledge. A computer system that lacks this knowledge will not be able to understand language in the sense that the speaker would expect a human listener to. See Terry Winograd, "What Does It Mean to Understand Language," *Cognitive Science* 4 (1980).

58. Y. Bar-Hillel, "The Present Status of Automatic Translation of Languages," in F. L. Alt, ed., *Advances in Computers,* vol. 1 (New York: Academic Press, 1960).

59. An account of the impressive performance of Logos appears in Tim Johnson, *Natural Language Computing: The Commercial Applications* (London: Ovum, 1985), pp. 160–164.

60. There is more to what our statements mean than what we *actually* say. We are generally concerned with the practical *effects* of what we say. Some kinds of speech are actions, and such expressions are referred to as speech acts. See John Searle, *Speech Acts* (Cambridge: Cambridge University Press, 1969).

61. Metaphors and idioms are a powerful way to communicate. Lakoff argues that metaphors are not merely literary devices but permeate every aspect of everyday thought. See Mark Johnson and George Lakoff, *Metaphors We Live By.*

62. Terry Winograd, "What Does It Mean to Understand Language," *Cognitive Science* 4 (1980).

63. Much has been written about SHRDLU, since it demonstrates deep understanding and reasoning within its limited area of specialty. Winograd's 1970 thesis on SHRDLU is slightly modified and published as Terry Winograd, *Understanding Natural Language* (New York: Academic Press, 1972). A brief presentation of the main ideas appears as Terry Winograd, "A Procedural Model of Language Understanding," in Roger Schank and Kenneth Colby, eds., *Computer Models of Thought and Language* (San Fransisco: W. H. Freeman, 1973).

64. That toy worlds offer abstractions of significant value is argued by Marvin Minsky and Seymour Papert in "Artificial Intelligence Progress Report," MIT Artificial Intelligence Laboratory, AI memo 252, 1972.

65. A short article about Harris and Intellect is Barbara Buell, "The Professor Getting Straight *A*s on Route 128," *Business Week,* April 15, 1985.

66. Scripts appeared as early as 1973. See Robert Abelson, "The Structure of Belief Systems," in Roger Schank and Kenneth Colby, eds., *Computer Models of Thought and Language* (San Francisco: W. H. Freeman, 1973). But their use as a powerful mechanism for knowledge representation became sophisticated only a few years later. The standard reference on scripts is Roger Schank and Robert Abelson, *Scripts, Plans, Goals, and Understanding* (Hillsdale, N.J.: Erlbaum, Lawrence Associates, 1977).

67. Schank's efforts at Cognitive Systems are described by him in Frank Kedig, "A Conversation with Roger Schank," *Psychology Today,* April 1983. Roger Schank has since resigned all major roles at Cognitive Systems.

68. An excellent survey of the natural language business is Tim Johnson, *Natural Language Computing: The Commercial Applications* (London: Ovum, 1985).

69. Translating text by computer is a rapidly growing business. See Harry Newquist, ed., *AI Trends '87: A Comprehensive Annual Report on the Artificial Intelligence Industry* (Scottsdale, Ariz.: DM Data, 1987).

70. See Harry Newquist, ed., *AI Trends '87: A Comprehensive Annual Report on the Artificial Intelligence Industry* (Scottsdale, Ariz.: DM Data, 1987).

71. The production of *R.U.R.* and its implications for robots are discussed in Jasia Reichardt, *Robots: Fact, Fiction, and Prediction,* a delightful book on the history and future of robots.

72. Some of these early robots are described in Reichardt, *Robots: Fact, Fiction, and Prediction.*

73. This generation of robots and their role in factory automation is examined by Isaac Asimov with his usual scientific clarity in Isaac Asimov and Karen Frenkel, *Robots: Machines in Man's Image.*

74. See Harry Newquist, ed., *AI Trends '87: A Comprehensive Annual Report on the Artificial Intelligence Industry* (Scottsdale, Ariz.: DM Data, 1987).

75. Today the importance of robot programming is immense, since programming is the primary path to adaptive robots. See Tomas Lozano-Perez, "Robot Programming," MIT Artificial Intelligence Laboratory, memo 698, 1982.

76. Isaac Asimov and Karen Frenkel, *Robots: Machines in Man's Image.*

77. Fully automatic factories are unusual today. More common are plants whose organization and operation rely significantly on robotic machinery, while human workers handle other important operations. The structure of such production units is realistically described in Christopher Joyce, "Factories Will Measure As They Make," *New Scientist,* September 4, 1986.

78. What will the factory of the future be like? Some analyses are put forward in Philippe Villers, "Intelligent Robots: Moving Toward Megassembly," and Paul Russo, "Intelligent Robots: Myth or Reality." Both of these essays appear in Patrick Winston and Karen Prendergast eds., *The AI Business.* One writer speculates that fully automated factories will be moved away from earth, and we will soon be industrializing outer space. See Lelland A. C. Weaver, "Factories in Space," *The Futurist,* May–June, 1987.

79. Isaac Asimov and Karen Frenkel, *Robots: Machines in Man's Image.*

80. See Gene Bylinsky, "Invasion of the Service Robots," *Fortune,* September 14, 1987.

81. Gene Bylinsky, "Invasion of the Service Robots," *Fortune,* September 14, 1987.

82. For details on Odex and other robots being used to increase safety for human workers in nuclear plants, see Steve Handel, "AI Assists Nuclear Plant Safety," *Applied Artificial Intelligence Reporter,* June 1986. See "High Tech to the Rescue," a special report in *Business Week,* June 16, 1986 for a description of Allen Bradley's factory. Also see Gene Bylinsky, "Invasion of the Service Robots," *Fortune,* September 14, 1987.

83. Some of these new methodologies are described in the context of artificial legs in Marc H. Raibert and Ivan Sutherland, "Machines That Walk," *Scientific American,* January 1983.

84. Anderson's Ping-Pong player was an outcome of his doctoral work at the University of Pennsylvania. The design and construction of this robot are detailed in Russell Anderson, "A Robot Ping-Pong Player" (Cambridge: MIT Press, 1985).

85. The dexterity and versatility of some of today's robotic hands is certainly encouraging. A report, accompanied by some excellent photographs, appears in Daniel Edson, "Giving Robot Hands a Human Touch," *High Technology,* September 1985.

86. An informative article on what the voice-activated robots of Leifer and Michalowski could do for the disabled is Deborah Dakins, "Voice-Activated Robot Brings Independence to Disabled Patients," *California Physician,* August 1986. Studies in robotics are leading to an important industry: the eventual production of artificial limbs, hearts, and ears. See Sandra Atchison, "Meet the Campus Capitalists of Bionic Valley," *Business Week,* May 5, 1986.

87. The Waseda robotic musician is an interesting synthesis of a variety of technologies. There are two excellent references on Wabot-2. The performances aspects of the robot are covered in Curtis Roads, "The Tsukuba Musical Robot," *Computer Music Journal,* Summer 1986. The design and engineering aspects of the robot are covered in a set of articles authored by the Waseda team itself. These articles appear in a special issue of the university's research bulletin: "Special Issue on WABOT-2," *Bulletin of Science and Engineering Research Laboratory* (Waseda University) no. 112 (1985).

88. Paul McCready's unconventional experiments in aerodynamics are quite fascinating. One can meet him and his flying machines in Patrick Cooke, "The Man Who Launched a Dinosaur," *Science 86,* April 1986.

89. The Defense Department's Autonomous Land Vehicle project has produced at least two transportation "robots" that can be used in terrain that is not passable by conventional means. The Adaptive Suspension Vehicle, which was developed primarily at Ohio State University, is described in Kenneth Waldron, Vincent Vohnout, Arrie Perry, and Robert McGhee, "Configuration Designing of the Adaptive Suspension Vehicle," *International Robotics Research Journal,* Summer 1984. The Terregator (another vehicle) and other projects of robotics groups at Carnegie-Mellon University are described in Eric Lerner, "Robotics: The Birth of a New Vision," *Science Digest,* July 1985.

90. The intelligence of remotely piloted aircraft are described in Peter Gwynne, "Remotely Piloted Vehicles Join the Service," *High Technology,* January 1987, pp. 38–43.

91. The contribution of each these disciplines to the technology underlying robots is described in the important review article Michael Brady, "Artificial Intelligence and Robotics," MIT Artificial Intelligence Laboratory, AI memo no. 756, 1983.

92. That most robots today function in only organized or artificial environments has been a major concern to Rodney Brooks, an MIT roboticist whose mobile robots and artificial insects perform very

simple tasks in the dynamic environments we find ourselves in everyday. See Rodney Brooks, "Autonomous Mobile Robots," in W. Eric Grimson and Ramesh Patil, eds., *AI in the 1980s and Beyond.*

93. Noel Perrin, a professor at Dartmouth, argues that even though robots are not yet rampant in households, research in robotics has been successful enough to warrant a serious look at the impact robots will ultimately have on society. See Noel Perrin, "We Aren't Ready for the Robots," *Wall Street Journal,* editorial page, February 25, 1986.

94. Japan's Fifth Generation Project and the role of ICOT and MITI are presented in their technological, personal, and sociopolitical dimensions in the well-written book Edward Feigenbaum and Pamela McCorduck, *The Fifth Generation.* This provocative book served as a rallying cry for the American industry's efforts to respond to ICOT.

95. The first complete description of the the Japanese fifth-generation project is "Outline of Research and Development Plans for Fifth Generation Computer Systems," Institute for New Generation Computer Technology (ICOT), Tokyo, May 1982. Descriptions of work in progress are frequently released by ICOT through its periodicals, conference proceedings, and research reports. ICOT's primary journal is *ICOT Journal Digest.*

96. A brief but complete description of the American and European responses to the Japanese effort appears as chapter 7 in Susan J. Scown, *The Artificial Intelligence Experience: An Introduction* (Maynard, Mass.: Digital Press, 1985). Perhaps the most thorough coverage of these international efforts appears in *Fifth Generation Computers: A Report on Major International Research Projects and Cooperatives* (Madison, Ga.: SEAI Technical Publications, 1985).

97. See Edward Feigenbaum and Pamela McCorduck, *The Fifth Generation,* 1983, pp. 224–226, and also Susan J. Scown, *The Artificial Intelligence Experience: An Introduction* (Maynard, Mass.: Digital Press, 1985), pp. 150–152.

98. Antitrust laws remain a problem in the operation of MCC. See David Fishlock, "The West Picks Up on the Japanese Challenge: How US Is Rewriting Anti-Trust Laws," *Financial Times* (London), January 27, 1986.

99. Susan J. Scown, *The Artificial Intelligence Experience: An Introduction* (Maynard, Mass.: Digital Press, 1985), pp. 154–155.

100. Research funded and administered by Alvey is described in its publications. See "Alvey Programme Annual Report, 1987," Alvey Directorate, London, 1987.

101. Susan J. Scown, *The Artificial Intelligence Experience: An Introduction* (Maynard, Mass.: Digital Press, 1985), pp. 153–154.

102. See *Fifth Generation Computers: A Report on Major International Research Projects and Cooperatives* (Madison, Ga.: SEAI Technical Publications, 1985).

103. Not everyone is concerned about the future of Japan's fifth-generation computer systems. See J. Marshall Unger, *The Fifth Generation Fallacy: Why Japan Is Betting Its Future on Artificial Intelligence* (Oxford: Oxford University Press, 1987).

The Science of Art

1. See the articles published in the *Computer Music Journal,* where much of this revolution is documented. A selection of such articles may be found in Curtis Roads, *The Music Machine: Selected Readings from "Computer Music Journal."* Articles on computer music also appear in the journal *Computers and the Humanities.*

2. The capacities and limitations of digital technology are reviewed in parts 1 and 2 of Curtis Roads and John Strawn, eds., *Foundations of Computer Music.* On digital tone generation, see chapter 13 of Hal Chamberlin, *Musical Applications of Microprocessors.*

3. For a general introduction to the principles of music synthesis and a brief history, see chapter 1 of Chamberlin's *Musical Applications.* Chapter 18 describes music-synthesis software, and chapter 19 reviews a number of synthesizers.

4. MIDI is described in Chamberlin, *Musical Applications*, pp. 312–316. Chamberlin made the prediction that by 1990 a new music protocol would be developed "as the weaknesses of MIDI become apparent" (p. 789).

5. In *The Technology of Computer Music*, a text for composers, Max V. Mathews provides an appendix on psychoacoustics and music, because, he argued, no intuitions exist for the new sounds possible with computers.

6. See chapter 16 in Chamberlin's *Musical Applications*.

7. Hal Chamberlin's "A Sampling of Techniques for Computer Performance of Music," originally published in *Byte* magazine in September 1977, describes how to create four-part melodies on a personal computer. Stephen K. Roberts described his own polyphonic keyboard system in "Polyphony Made Easy," an article originally published in *Byte* in January 1979. Both articles were reprinted in Christopher P. Morgan, ed., *The "Byte" Book of Computer Music*; see pp. 47–64 and pp. 117–120, respectively.

8. In chapter 18 of *Musical Applications*, Chamberlin describes programming techniques for pro-grammed performance systems, and claims, "It is immaterial whether the synthesis is performed in real time or not, since the 'score' is definitely prepared outside of real time" (p. 639).

9. On the editing of sequences, see Chamberlin, *Musical Applications*, chapter 11.

10. Bateman discusses the role of the computer in composing in chapters 11 and 12 of *Introduction to Computer Music*. He relates the stochastic composition possible with the computer to the fact that Mozart once composed with the aid of a pair of dice, but he emphasizes the computer's subservience to the human composer's creativity. For a good review of the various selection techniques involved in AI composing programs, see C. Ames, "AI in Music," in Stuart C. Shapiro, ed., *Encyclopedia of Artificial Intelligence*, vol. 1, pp. 638–642.

11. See Ames, "AI in Music," in Shapiro, *Encyclopedia of Artificial Intelligence*, vol. 1 pp. 638–642. Also see S. Papert, "Computers in Education: Conceptual Issues," in Shapiro, *Encyclopedia of Artificial Intelligence*, vol. 1, p. 183. Papert points out that the difficulties of performance may be circumvented by use of the computer, and that students may begin to compose in the same way that they learn to draw when studying art or to write when studying literature.

12. Music systems for personal computers are described in C. Yavelow, "Music Software for the Apple Macintosh," *Computer Music Journal* 9 (1985): 52–67. See also C. Yavelow, "Personal Computers and Music," *Journal of the Audio Engineering Society* 35 (1987): 160–193.

13. A comprehensive review of computerized music notation, including a table of important systems and a useful bibliography, is found in N. P. Carter, R. A. Bacon, and T. Messenger, "The Acquisition, Representation, and Reconstruction of Printed Music by Computer: A Review," *Computers and the Humanities* 22 (1988): 117–136. Professional Composer is being used by Garland Press to produce editions of sixteenth-century music (p. 130).

14. Chamberlin discusses the use of synthesizers in music education on p. 710 of *Musical Applications*.

15. A brief assessment of the role of computers in art can be found in Philip J. Davis and Reuben Hersh, *Descartes' Dream: The World According to Mathematics*, pp. 43–53. Herbert W. Francke discusses the resistance computer art encountered in "Refractions of Science into Art," in H.-O. Peitgen and P. H. Richter, *The Beauty of Fractals: Images of Complex Dynamical Systems*, pp. 181–187.

16. Neal Weinstock, in *Computer Animation*, discusses some of the resolution limitations of home computers (see chapter 1). For an overview of graphics hardware, including output-only and display hardware, see chapter 2 in Weinstock, and chapter 3 in the standard text, J. D. Foley and A. Van Dam, *Fundamentals of Interactive Computer Graphics*.

17. Advances in computer graphics are occurring at a rapid rate, and the literature is vast. Several important sources of up-to-date information are the *ACM Transactions on Graphics*, *Computer Graphics, Quarterly Report of the ACM Special Interest Group of Graphics, Computer Graphics World*, and articles on computer graphics in *Byte*. Melvin L. Prueitt's *Art and the Computer* has dazzling pictures produced using a wide variety of computer-graphics techniques and includes a series of examples of art produced on personal computers (see pp. 29 and 191–194). A review of the early history of computer graphics, complete with illustrations, is provided by H. W. Francke in *Computer Graphics—Computer Art*, pp. 57–105. Examples of practical applications of computer graphics are found in Donald Greenberg, Aaron Marcus, Allen H. Schmidt, and Vernon Gorter, *The Computer Image: Applications of Computer Graphics*. The shift from fixed images to the modern transformable computer image has stimulated a new analytical approach to graphics, exemplified by Jacques Bertin, *Semiology of Graphics*, trans. William J. Berg.

18. Recent developments in color-graphics displays are described in H. John Durrett, ed., *Color and the Computer*. Chapter 12 reviews the available technology for color hard-copy devices, and there are also chapters on color in medical images, cartography, and education applications.

19. Many of these techniques are described and illustrated in Prueitt, *Art and the Computer*. Some of the extraordinary achievements in rendering reflection are illustrated on pp. 144–150, and an example of the synthesis of natural and artificial scenes can be found on p. 29. An excellent example of

distortion is provided by plates E to J of Foley and Van Dam, *Fundamentals of Interactive Computer Graphics*, which illustrate the mapping of images of a mandrill onto a series of different geometric shapes. Chapter 14 of that work provides a description of techniques being used to enhance the realism of computer imagery.

20. Those interested in the technical aspects of image transformation should consult chapter 8 of Foley and Van Dam, *Fundamentals of Interactive Computer Graphics*.

21. Computer artists active during the 1970s describe their relations to their chosen medium in Ruth Leavitt, *Artist and Computer*. When asked if his work could be done without the computer, computer artist Aldo Giorgini said, "Yes, in a fashion analogous to the one of carving marble with a sponge" (p. 12).

22. The game of life was invented by John Conway in 1970 and is one example of a cellular automaton. As Tommaso Toffoli and Norman Margolis point out, "A cellular automata machine is a universe synthesizer." See their *Cellular Automata Machines: A New Environment for Modeling*, p. 1. An entertaining explanation of games of life can be found in chapter 7 of Ivars Peterson, *The Mathematical Tourist: Snapshots of Modern Mathematics*. See also A. K. Dewdney, *The Armchair Universe*, "World Four: Life in Automata." Dewdney explores the concepts of one-dimensional computers and three-dimensional life. Chapter 25 in Elwyn R. Berlekamp, John H. Conway, and Richard K. Guy, *Winning Ways for Your Mathematical Plays*, is devoted to games of Life. On page 830 the authors describe how to make a Life computer: "Many computers have been programmed to play the game of Life. We shall now return the compliment by showing how to define Life patterns that can imitate computers." See, as well, William Poundstone, *The Recursive Universe: Cosmic Complexity and the Limits of Scientific Knowledge,* chapters 11 and 12 and the section "Life for Home Computers."

23. See Richard Dawkins's 1987 work *The Blind Watchmaker*. Dawkins devised a simple model for evolution; starting with a stick figure, his program produces more and more complex figures often resembling actual natural shapes, such as insects. Sixteen numbers function as "genes" and determine the resulting forms, or "biomorphs."

24. In Dawkins's scheme, the human observer provides the natural selection, choosing "mutations" that will "survive." An artist could use aesthetic criteria to determine the direction of "evolution." A. K. Dewdney describes Dawkins's program, which runs on the Mac, in "A Blind Watchmaker Surveys the Land of Biomorphs," *Scientific American,* February 1988, pp. 128–131.

25. For an excellent introduction to the concept of recursion, see Poundstone, *The Recursive Universe*.

26. An account of Mandelbrot's eclectic career and his discovery of the "geometry of nature" can be found in James Gleick, *Chaos: Making a New Science*, pp. 81–118. The bible of fractal geometry is Benoit Mandelbrot, *The Fractal Geometry of Nature* (1983). This work superseded Mandelbrot's earlier volume *Fractals: Form, Chance, and Dimension*. Images produced by fractals are described and illustrated in the classic work by H.-O. Peitgen and P. H. Richter, *The Beauty of Fractals: Images of Complex Dynamical Systems*. Peitgen and Richter devoted themselves to the study of the Mandelbrot set and produced spectacular pictures, which they published and displayed (see Gleick, *Chaos*, pp. 229 ff).

27. See pp. 213–240 in Gleick's *Chaos*. Chaotic-fractal evolutions are discussed in chapter 20 of Mandelbrot's *Fractal Geometry*.

28. Some of Mandelbrot's work on price change and scaling in economics can be found in *The Fractal Geometry of Nature*, pp. 334–340. For more insight into Mandelbrot's application of fractals in economics and biology, see Gleick, *Chaos*, pp. 81–118. On the properties of scaling in music, see *The Fractal Geometry of Nature*, pp. 374–375.

29. Peterson, *The Mathematical Tourist*, pp. 114–116. Also see Mandelbrot, *The Fractal Geometry of Nature*, chapter 5.

30. Peterson, *The Mathematical Tourist*, pp. 126–127. On modeling clouds with fractals, see Mandelbrot, *The Fractal Geometry of Nature*, p. 112.

31. "One should not be surprised that scaling fractals should be limited to providing first approximations of the natural shapes to be tackled. One must rather marvel that these first approximations are so strikingly reasonable" (Mandelbrot, *The Fractal Geometry of Nature*, p. 19.) In "The Computer as Microscope," in *The Mathematical Tourist*, Peterson points out that "natural fractals are often self-similar in a statistical sense" (p. 119). See also pp. 155–164.

32. "Computer graphics provides a convenient way of picturing and exploring fractal objects, and fractal geometry is a useful tool for creating computer images" (Peterson, *The Mathematical Tourist*, p. 123.)

33. Mandelbrot explores the application of fractal geometry to cosmology in *The Fractal Geometry of Nature*. See in particular chapter 9.

34. Mandelbrot's discussion of the etymology is in *The Fractal Geometry of Nature*, pp. 4–5.

35. The concept of dimensionality is central to an understanding of fractals and to an understanding of the structure of nature. See chapter 3 in Mandelbrot, *The Fractal Geometry of Nature*.

36. See Mandelbrot, "Index of Selected Dimensions," in *Fractals: Form, Chance, and Dimension,* p. 365, where the seacoast dimension is given as 1.25. Mandelbrot devotes chapter 6 of *The Fractal Geometry of Nature* to "Snowflakes and Other Koch Curves." In "The Koch Curve Tamed" he gives its fractal dimension as 1.2618 (p. 36). Peterson describes the Koch curve, created in 1904, in *The Mathematical Tourist*, pp. 116–119.

37. See chapter 10 of Mandelbrot, *The Fractal Geometry of Nature*, and the chapter "Strange Attractors" in Gleick, *Chaos*.

38. See Mandelbrot on fractal art, pp. 23–24 of *The Fractal Geometry of Nature*. He points out that the images created by fractals may be reminiscent of the work of M. C. Escher because Escher was influenced by hyperbolic tilings, which are related to fractal shapes (p. 23). Mandelbrot also suggests that the work of certain great artists of the past, when it illustrated nature, exemplified "issues tackled by fractal geometry": the examples are the frontispiece of *Bible moralisée illustrées,* Leonardo's *Deluge,* and Hokusai's *Great Wave* (see pp. C1, 2, 3, 16). Some striking examples of fractal images are described and illustrated in Prueitt's *Art and the Computer* (pp. 119, 121–124, 127, 166, 169). Alan Norton has produced beautiful and bizarre complex shapes by generating and displaying geometric fractals in three dimensions (see Prueitt, pp. 123–124). For images that resemble natural landscapes, see plates C9, C11, C13, and C15 in Mandelbrot's *Fractal Geometry of Nature*. Mandelbrot himself claims that these artificial landscapes are the fractal equivalent of the "complete synthesis of hemoglobin from the component atoms and (a great deal of) time and energy" (p. C8).

39. On sophisticated animation systems, see chapter 4, in Nadia Magenat-Thalman and Daniel Thalman, *Computer Animation: Theory and Practice*. On fractals and their use in generating images, see pp. 106–110.

40. Harold Cohen, "How to Draw Three People in a Botanical Garden," AAAI-88, *Proceedings of the Seventh National Conference on Artificial Intelligence*, 1988, pp. 846–855. Some of the implications of AARON are discussed in Pamela McCorduck, "Artificial Intelligence: An Aperçu," *Daedalus,* Winter 1988, pp. 65–83. This issue of *Daedalus*, devoted to AI, has been published in book form as Stephen R. Graubard, ed., *The Artificial Intelligence Debate: False Starts, Real Foundations*.

41. For a comparison between traditional animation procedures and new computer methods, see chapters 1 and 2 in Magenat-Thalman and Thalman, *Computer Animation*. See also Weinstock, *Computer Animation*.

42. Prueitt, *Art and the Computer*, p. 30. Indeed, Prueitt suggests that computer art "may be closer to the human mind and heart than other forms of art. That is, it is an art created by the mind rather than by the body" (pp. 2–3).

43. The most famous of these editors is EMACS, a real-time display editor that Stallman developed in 1974 from earlier systems, in particular, TECO, developed in 1962 by Richard Greenblatt et al. For a description of EMACS, see Richard M. Stallman, "EMACS: The Extensible, Customizable, Self-Documenting Display Editor," in David R. Barstow, Howard E. Shrobe, and Erik Sandewell, eds., *Interactive Programming Environments*, pp. 300–325.

44. For example the electronic *Oxford English Dictionary* (*OED*) enables scholars to answer questions that would have taken a lifetime of work in the recent past. See Cullen Murphy, "Computers: Caught in the Web of Bytes," *The Atlantic,* February 1989, pp. 68–70.

45. New techniques for accessing information (on-line searches) are described in Roy Davies, ed., *Intelligent Information Systems: Progress and Prospects*.

46. For a recent assessment of desktop publishing, see John R. Brockmann, "Desktop Publishing—Beyond GEE WHIZ: Part 1, A Critical Overview," and Brockmann, "Desktop Publishing—Beyond GEE WHIZ: Part 2, A Critical Bibliography of Materials," both in *IEEE Transactions on Professional Communication,* March 1988.

47. New tools for conceptual organization are described in Edward Barrett, *Text, Context, and Hypertext*.

48. In the Introduction to RACTER, *The Policeman's Beard is Half-Constructed*, William Chamberlain describes the process behind RACTER's prose: certain rules of English are entered into the computer, and what the computer produces is based upon the words it finds in its files, which are then combined according to "syntax directives." Chamberlain concludes that this process "seems to spin a thread of what might initially pass for coherent thinking throughout the computer-generated copy so that once

the program is run, its output is not only new and unknowable, it is apparently thoughtful. It is crazy 'thinking' I grant you, but 'thinking' that is expressed in perfect English." See the discussion by A. K. Dewdney, "Conversations with RACTER," in *The Armchair Universe*, pp. 77–88. Dewdney points out that RACTER is not artificially intelligent but "artificially insane" (p. 77).

49. For the history and assessment of various attempts at translation using computers, see Y. Wilks, "Machine Translation," in Shapiro, ed. *Encyclopedia of Artificial Intelligence*, vol. 1, pp. 564–571.

Visions

1. Douglas R. Hofstadter, *Metamagical Themas: Questing for the Essence of Mind and Pattern*, p.128.

2. David Waltz, "The Prospects for Building Truly Intelligent Machines," *Daedelus*, Winter 1988, p. 204.

3. The preface in Tom Forester's *Information Technology Revolution* examines similar issues.

4. In the fall of 1987 an entire issue of *Scientific American* was devoted to this topic. In particular, see Abraham Peled, "The Next Computer Revolution," *Scientific American,* October 1987, pp. 56–64.

5. See James D. Meindl, "Chips for Advanced Computing," *Scientific American,* October 1987, pp. 79–81 and 86–88.

6. See Mark H. Kryder, "Data-Storage Technologies for Advance Computing," *Scientific American,* October 1987, pp. 117–125.

7. Such as massively parallel processors based possibly on superconductors. See Peter J. Denning, "Massive Parallelism in the Future of Science," *American Scientist*, Jan.–Feb. 1989, p. 16.

8. Marvin Minsky discusses this problem in "Easy Things Are Hard," *Society of Mind*, p. 29.

9. Koji Kobayashi, *Computers and Communication: A Vision of C & C*, pp. 165–166.

10. See Marshall McLuhan, *Understanding Media*.

11. For a vision of an office system interfacing with a public communication network, see Koji Kobayashi, *Computers and Communication,* chapter 10. See also Roger Shank and Peter G. Childers, "The World of the Future," in *The Cognitive Computer*, pp. 227–230.

12. David N. L. Levy, *All about Chess and Computers*. See also M. M. Botvinnik, *Computers in Chess*.

13. An intriguing study of the relevance of comments made by master chess players during play can be found in Jacques Pitrat, "Evaluating Moves Rather than Positions," in Barbara Pernici and Mareo Somalvico, eds., *III Convegno Internazionale L'Intelligenza Artificiale ed il Gioco Degli Scacchi* (Federazione Scacchistico Italiana, Regione Lombardia, Politecnico di Milano, 1981).

14. Evidence of this are early board-game programs modeled on master players' strategies. The 1959 checkers program of Arthur Samuels, for example, had 53,000 board positions in memory. See Peter W. Frey, "Algorithmic Strategies for Improving the Performance of Game-Playing Programs," in *Evolution, Games, and Learning: Models for Adaptation in Machines and Nature,* Proceedings of the Fifth Annual International Conference of the Center for Nonlinear Studies at Los Alamos, N.M., May 20–24, 1985, p. 355.

15. Recursiveness and massive computational power allow for subtle (and hence enormously varied) solutions to algorithmic problems. See, for example, Gary Josin, "Neural Net Heuristics" *BYTE*, October 1987, pp. 183–192; and Douglas Lenat, "The Role of Heuristics in Learning by Discovery," in R. Z. Michalski, J. J. Carbonell, and T. M Mitchell, eds., *Machine Learning: An Artificial Intelligence Approach*. Also see Monroe Newborn, *Computer Chess*, pp. 8–15.

16. See John Hilusha's article, "Smart Roads Tested to Avoid Traffic Jams," *New York Times*, October 18, 1988.

17. Plans are already in place for the development and use of flying vehicles. See, for instance, "Simulation of an Air Cushion Vehicle Microform," final report for period January 1975–December 1976, Charles Stark Draper Laboratory, Cambridge, 1977.

18. For recent advances in computer and chip design, see James D. Meindl, "Chips for Advanced Computing," *Scientific American,* October 1987, pp. 78–88. An extensive but less current review of the technology may be found in Alan Burns, *The Microchip*.

19. See Stewart Brand, *The Media Lab: Inventing the Future at MIT*, pp. 83–91.

20. Although the Turing test has been discussed at length in chapters 2 and 3, the general reader may further appreciate a straightforward presentation of this famous test in Isaac Malitz, "The Turing Machine," *BYTE,* November 1987, pp. 348–358.

21. Research at the University of Illinois is a case in point. The Center for Superconducting Research and Development was established there in 1984 for the purpose of demonstrating that high-speed parallel processing is practical for a wide range of applications.

22. Considerable mention is given to this technology in B. Deaver and John Ruvalds, eds, *Advances in Superconductivity*. See especially A. Barone and G. Paternò, "Josephson Effects: Basic Concepts."

23. See M. A. Lusk, J. A. Lund, A. C. D. Chaklader, M. Burbank, A. A. Fife, S. Lee, B. Taylor, and J. Vrba, "The Fabrication of a Ceramic Superconducting Wire," *Superconductor Science and Technology* 1 (1988): 137–140.

24. For brief but informative article on the subject, see Robert Pool, "New Superconductors Answer Some Questions," *Science* 240 (April 8, 1988): 146–147.

25. See David Chaffee, *The Rewiring of America: The Fiber Optics Revolution*. Also, a reliable, technically informative account may be found in Robert G. Seippel, *Fiber Optics*.

26. A terse and brief account of the new technology that serves as the basis for these advances may be found in Tom Forester, *The Materials Revolution*, pp. 362–364.

27. It is interesting to compare the mentions made of molecular computing in Tom Forester's *High Tech Society*, p. 39, with those in his *Materials Revolution*, pp. 362–364.

The Impact On . . .

1. Seymour Papert makes a convincing argument for extensive use of computers in the classroom in "Computers and Computer Cultures," *Mindstorms*, pp. 19–37.

2. See notes 5 and 14 to the prolog of this book for sources for these statistics.

3. Wassily Leontief and Faye Duchin, eds., *The Future Impact of Automation on Workers*, p. 18. See also note 13 to the prolog of this volume.

4. Wassily Leontief and Faye Duchin, eds., *The Future Impact of Automation on Workers*, pp. 20–21.

5. Wassily Leontief and Faye Duchin, eds., *The Future Impact of Automation on Workers*, pp. 12–19. See also James Jacobs, "Training Needs of Small and Medium Size Firms in Advanced Manufacturing Technologies," in *1987 IEEE Conference on Management and Technology*, Atlanta, Georgia, October 27–30, 1987, pp. 117–123.

6. Wassily Leontief and Faye Duchin, eds., *The Future Impact of Automation on Workers*. pp. 25–26, 52.

7. Wassily Leontief, "The World Economy to the Year 2000," *Scientific American*, Sept. 1980, pp. 206–231.

8. Wassily Leontief and Faye Duchin, eds., *The Future Impact of Automation on Workers*, pp. 25–26, 92.

9. Tom Forester, *High Tech Society*, p. 181.

10. See "The Electronic Office," in Tom Forester, *High Tech Society*, pp. 195–217.

11. Indeed, floppy disks and CDs have popularly been called a "new papyrus."

12. See Ted H. Nelson, "Getting It out of Our System," in G. Schechter, ed., *Information Retrieval*, pp. 191–210. For a recent account that reveals changes and advances, see Mark Bernstein, "The Bookmark and the Compass: Orientation Tools for Hypertext Users," *SIG OIS Bulletin* 9 (1988): 34–45.

13. Note, for example, the considerable professional reshuffling in the labor force to accommodate burgeoning technological advances in the workplace. See S. Norman Feingold and Norma Reno Miller, *Emerging Careers: New Occupations for the Year 2000 and Beyond*, vol. 1.

14. For a discussion of children's psychological responses to computers, see "The Question of 'Really Alive,'" in Sherry Turkle, *The Second Self*, pp. 324–332.

15. For the sake of brevity I shall use the term "education" here in the conventional sense of education during the school years, but the the ideas expressed in this section pertain to education in general. See, for example, Elizabeth Gerver, "Computers and Informal Learning," in *Humanizing Technology: Computers in Community Use and Adult Education*; and Jean-Dominique Warnier, "The Teaching of Computing," in *Computers and Human Intelligence*, p. 113 ff.

16. There is a growing volume of literature on the subject of children and computers. See, for instance, Sherry Turkle, "Child Programmers," in *The Second Self*, pp. 93–136; Robert Yin and J. L. White, "Microcomputer Implementation in Schools," in Milton Chen and William Paisley, eds., *Children and*

Microcomputers, pp. 109–128; Seymour Papert, Daniel Watt, Andrea di Dessa, and Sylvia Weir, "Final Report of the Brookline LOGO Project," MIT AI memo no. 545, Sept. 1979; and R. D. Pea and D. M. Kurland, "On the Cognitive and Educational Benefits of Teaching Children Programming: A Critical Look," in *New Ideas in Psychology.*, vol. 1.

17. Debra Liberman, "Research and Microcomputers," in Milton Chen and William Paisley, eds., *Children and Microcomputers*, pp. 60–61.

18. See John Seely Brown, "Process versus Product," in Chen and Paisley, eds., *Children and Microcomputers*, pp. 248–266.

19. Functioning well right now are networked computerized card catalogs linking various university libraries. For a skeptical view of networking, see Theodore Roszak, "On-Line Communities: The Promise of Networking," in *The Cult of Information: The Folklore of Computers and the True Art of Thinking.*

20. Tom Forester swiftly chronicles the obstacles that have contributed to this situation in *High Tech Society*, pp. 165–169. These obstacles notwithstanding, from the fall of 1980 to the spring of 1982 the number of computers more than tripled in American schools. See also Jack Rochester and John Gantz, *The Naked Computer*, p. 104.

21. Edward Tenner, *Harvard Magazine* 90 (1988): 23–29.

22. Tenner, *Harvard Magazine* 90 (1988): 23–29.

23. For a dispassionate and informative presentation of the Strategic Defense Initiative in which a "flexible nuclear response" is examined, see Stephen J. Cimbala, "The Strategic Defense Initiative," in Stephen J. Andriole and Gerald W. Hople, eds., *Defense Applications of Artificial Intelligence*, pp. 263–291.

24. See Randolf Nikitta, "Artificial Intelligence and the Automated Tactical Battlefield," in Allan M. Din, ed., *Arms and Artificial Intelligence: Weapons and Arms Control of Applications of Advanced Computing*, pp. 100–134.

25. McGeorge Bundy, George F. Kennan, Robert S. McNamara, and Gerard Smith, "Nuclear Weapons and the Atlantic Alliance," *Foreign Affairs*, Spring 1982, pp. 753–768. Another thoughtful and succinct appraisal of the subject of nuclear deterrence is Leon Wieseltier's *Nuclear War, Nuclear Peace*.

26. See Edward C. Taylor, "Artificial Intelligence and Command and Control—What and When?" in Andriole and Hople, eds., *Defense Applications of Artificial Intelligence*, pp. 139–149. See also Alan Borning, "Computer System Reliability and Nuclear War," in *Communications of the ACM* 30 (1987): 124.

27. See Alan Borning, "Computer System Reliability and Nuclear War," *Communications of the ACM* 30 (1987): 112–131.

28. See P. R. Cohen, D. Day, J. DeLisio, M. Greenberg, R. Kjeldsen, D. Suthers, and P. Berman, "Management of Uncertainty in Medicine," *International Journal of Approximate Reasoning*, Sept. 1987, pp. 103–116.

29. See Tom Forester's discussion of recent innovations in biotechnology in his *Materials Revolution*, pp. 362–364.

30. For the well initiated, the excellent but highly technical journal *Biomaterials, Artificial Cells, and Artificial Organs: An International Journal* frequently publishes articles relevant to the subject.

31. See Glenn D. Rennels and Edward H. Shortliffe, "Advanced Computing for Medicine," *Scientific American*, October 1987, pp. 154–161. See also James S. Bennell, "ROGET: A Knowledge-Based System for Acquiring the Conceptual Structure of a Diagnostic Expert System," *Journal of Automated Reasoning* 1 (1985): 41–50.

32. For a clear overview of the vision challenge, see Michael Brady, "Intelligent Vision," in Grimson and Patil, eds., *AI in the 1980s and Beyond*, pp. 201–243.

33. While we are still far from this achievement, advances are being made in the field of music notation. See, for instance, John S. Gourlay, "A Language for Music Printing," *Communication of the ACM* 29 (1986): 388–401.

34. Of interest to the reader may be the anonymous publication "Vladimir Ussachevsy: In Celebration of his Seventy-Fifth Birthday," University of Utah, 1987, pp. 8–9.

35. See David Dickson, "Soviet Computer Lag," *Science*, August 1988, p. 1033. Some other interesting facts about Soviet restrictions are to be found in Rochester and Gantz, "How's Your CPU, Boris?" *The Naked Computer*.

Postcript

1. See pp. 677–678 of Douglas Hofstadter's *Gödel, Escher, Bach: An Eternal Golden Braid* (New York: Basic Books, 1979) for a fuller account of his concept of potential computer weaknesses.

2. Marvin Minsky, *Society of Mind*, pp. 186, 288.

3. The general reader will find pertinent to the topic Paul M. Churchland's philosophical and scientific examination throughout *Matter and Consciousness*.

4. See Einstein's letters of August 9, 1939, and December 22, 1950, to E. Schrödinger, in K. Przibram, ed., *Letters on Wave Mechanics*, pp. 35–36 and 39–40.

5. Admittedly, some disavow the applicability of subatomic metaphors to any other aspect of life. See Paul G. Hewitt, *Conceptual Physics,* 2nd ed., pp. 486–487.

6. A dense and pertinent discussion of the sister particle paradox may be found in Abner Himony, "Events and Processes in the Quantum World," in R. Penrose and C. J. Isham, eds., *Quantum Concepts in Space and Time*, pp. 182–196.

Bibliography and Suggested Readings

The Second Industrial Revolution

Antébi, Elizabeth. *Biotechnology: Strategies for Life*. Cambridge: MIT Press, 1986.

Bellin, David, and Gary Chapman, eds. *Computers in Battle—Will They Work?* Boston: Harcourt Brace Jovanovich, 1987.

Bluestone, Barry, and Bennett Harrison. *The Deindustrialization of America*. New York: Basic Books, 1982.

Bythell, Duncan. *The Handloom Weavers: A Study in the English Cotton Industry during the Industrial Revolution*. Cambridge: Cambridge University Press, 1969.

Cohen, S. S., and J. Zysman. *Manufacturing Matters*. New York: Basic Books, 1987.

Din, Allan M., ed., *Arms and Artificial Intelligence*. Oxford: Oxford University Press, 1987.

Feigenbaum, Edward A., and Pamela McCorduck. *The Fifth Generation: Artificial Intelligence and Japan's Computer Challenge to the World*. Reading Mass.: Addison-Wesley Publishing Co., 1983.

Forester, Tom. *High Tech Society: The Story of the Information Technology Revolution*. Cambridge: MIT Press, 1987.

Forester, Tom. *The Information Technology Revolution*. Cambridge: MIT Press, 1985.

Fishman, Katherine Davis. *The Computer Establishment*. New York: McGraw-Hill Book Co., 1981.

Greenberger, Martin, ed. *Computers and the World of the Future*. Cambridge: MIT Press, 1962.

Harrison, Ben, and Barry Bluestone. *The Great U-Turn*. New York: Basic Books, 1988.

Leontief, Wassily W. *The Impact of Automation on Employment, 1963–2000*. Institute for Economic Analysis, New York University, 1984.

Schank, Roger, [with Peter G. Childers]. *The Cognitive Computer: On Language, Learning, and Artificial Intelligence*. Reading, Mass.: Addison-Wesley, 1984.

Smith, Christopher A., et al. *Discovery '84: Technology for Disabled Persons*. Materials Development Center, Stout Vocational Rehabilitation Institute, University of Wisconsin at Stout, 1985.

Taylor, Phillip A., ed. *The Industrial Revolution in Britain: Triumph or Disaster?* Lexington, Mass.: Heath, 1970.

Thomis, Malcolm I. *The Luddites: Machine-Breaking in Regency England*. Hamden, Conn.: Archon Books. 1970.

U.S. Department of Commerce, Bureau of the Census. *Historical Statistics of the U. S.: Colonial Times to 1970*. Vol. 1. Washington, D.C.: U.S. Government Printing Office, 1975.

U.S. Department of Commerce, Bureau of the Census. *How We Live: Then and Now*. Washington, D.C.: Government Printing Office, 1986.

U.S. Department of Commerce, Bureau of the Census. *Statistical Abstract of the United States, 1986*. 106th ed. Washington, D.C.: Government Printing Office, 1986.

United Nations. *Population and Vital Statistics Report*. Series A, vol. 38, no. 3. United Nations, 1986.

Wattenberg, Ben J. *The Statistical History of the United States from Colonial Times to 1970*. New York: Basic Books, 1976.

Wattenberg, Ben J., ed. *The Statistical History of the United States from Colonial Times to the Present*. Stamford, Conn.: Fairfield Publishers, 1965.

Winner, Langdon. *Autonomous Technology*. Cambridge: MIT Press, 1977.

Zysman, J. *Manufacturing Matters*. New York: Basic Books, 1987.

What is AI, Anyway?

Alexander, S. *Art and Instinct*. Oxford: Folcroft Press, 1970. Originally published in 1927.

Baron, Jonathan. *Rationality and Intelligence*. Cambridge: Cambridge University Press, 1985.

Barrett, Paul H., ed. *The Collected Papers of Charles Darwin*. Vols. 1 and 2. Chicago: University of Chicago Press, 1977.

Bruner, Jerome S., Jacqueline J. Goodnow, and George A. Austin. *A Study of Thinking*. New York: Science Editions, 1965. Originally published in 1956.

Darwin, Charles. *The Origin of the Species*. New York and London: D. Appleton & Company, 1910. Originally published in 1859.

Dawkins, Richard. *The Blind Watchmaker: Why the Evidence of Evolution Reveals a Universe without Design*. New York: W. W. Norton & Co., 1987.

Dawkins, Richard. *The Extended Prototype: The Gene on the Unit of Selection*. Oxford: Freeman & Co., 1982.

Dawkins, Richard, *The Selfish Gene*. New York: Oxford University Press, 1976.

Dobzhansky, Theodosius. *Mankind Evolving: The Evolution of the Human Species*. New Haven: Yale University Press, 1962.

Elithorn, Alick, and Ranan Banerji, eds. *Artificial and Human Intelligence: Edited Review Papers Presented at the International NATO Symposium on Artificial and Human Intelligence*. Amsterdam: North-Holland Publishing Co., 1981.

Elithorn, A., and D. Jones. *Artificial and Human Thinking*. San Francisco: Jossey-Bass, 1973.

Eysenck, H. J., and Leon Kamin. *The Intelligence Controversy*. New York: John Wiley & Sons, 1981.

Feigenbaum, Edward. "The Art of Artificial Intelligence: Themes and Case Studies in Knowledge Engines," in *AFIPS Conference Proceedings of the 1978 National Computer Conference*. Vol. 47. Anaheim, California, 1978.

Fogel, Lawrence J., Alvin Owens, and Michael Walsh. *Artificial Intelligence through Simulated Evolution*. New York: John Wiley & Sons, 1966.

Freud, Sigmund. *The Basic Writings of Sigmund Freud*. New York: The Modern Library, 1938.

Freud, Sigmund. *Collected Papers*. London: Hogarth Press and the Institute of Psychoanalysis, 1950.

Furth, Hans. *Piaget and Knowledge*. Englewood Cliffs, N.J.: Prentice-Hall, 1969.

Gould, Stephen Jay. *The Panda's Thumb*. New York: W. W. Norton. & Co., 1980.

Gould, Stephen Jay. *The Mismeasure of Man*. New York: W. W. Norton & Co., 1981.

Grant, Verne. *The Origin of Adaptation*. New York: Columbia University Press, 1963.

Gray, Ada, ed. *Darwiniana*. Cambridge: Harvard University Press, 1963.

Greenberger, Martin, ed. *Computers and the World of the Future*. Cambridge: MIT Press, 1962.

Hitching, F. *The Neck of the Giraffe, or Where Darwin Went Wrong*. London: Pan Books, 1982.

Hoage, R. J., and Larry Goldman. *Animal Intelligence: Insights into the Animal Mind*. Washington, D.C.: Smithsonian Institution Press, 1986.

Hookway, Christopher, ed. *Minds, Machines and Evolution: Philosophical Studies*. Cambridge: Cambridge University Press, 1984.

Jacob, Francois. *The Logic of Life*. New York: Pantheon Books, 1973.

James, William. *The Varieties of Religious Experience*. New York: Collier Books, 1961.

Jung, Carl, et al. *Man and His Symbols*. Garden City, New York: Doubleday, 1964.

Jung, Carl. *Memories Dreams and Reflections*. Rev. ed. Ed. Aniela Jaffé and trans. Richard and Clara Winston. New York: Pantheon Books, 1961.

Kent, Ernest W. *The Brains of Men and Machines.* New York: McGraw-Hill Publications, 1981.

Klix, Friedhart, ed. *Human and Artificial Intelligence.* Amsterdam: North-Holland Publishing Co., 1979.

McCorduck, Pamela. *Machines Who Think.* San Francisco: Freeman Press, 1979.

Mayr, Ernst. *Animal Species and Evolution.* Cambridge: Harvard University Press, 1963.

Metropolis, N., J. Howlett, and Gian-Carlo Rota, eds. *A History of Computing in the Twentieth Century.* New York: Academic Press, 1980.

Minsky, Marvin. *Society of Mind.* New York: Simon & Schuster, 1985.

Morris, Desmond. *The Naked Ape: A Zoologist's Study of the Human Animal.* New York: McGraw-Hill, 1967.

Piaget, Jean. *The Psychology of Intelligence.* London: Routledge & Kegan Paul, 1967. Originally published in 1947.

Pratt, Vernon. *Thinking Machines: The Evolution of Artificial Intelligence.* Oxford: Basil Blackwell, 1987.

Schank, Roger. *The Cognitive Computer.* Reading, Mass.: Addison-Wesley, 1984.

Shackle, G. L. S. *Imagination and the Nature of Choice.* Edinburgh: University of Edinburgh Press, 1979.

Simpson, George Gaylord. *The Meaning of Evolution.* The New American Library of World Literature. New York: A Mentor Book, 1951. Originally published in 1949.

Singer, P. *Animal Liberation.* London: Cape Books, 1976.

Stahl, Franklin W. *The Mechanics of Inheritance.* Englewood Cliffs, N.J.: Prentice-Hall, 1969.

Sternberg, Robert J., ed. *Handbook of Human Intelligence.* Cambridge: Cambridge University Press, 1982.

Turkle, Sherry. *The Second Self: Computers and the Human Spirit.* New York: Simon and Schuster, 1984.

Von Neumann, John. *The Computer and the Brain.* New Haven: Yale University Press, 1958.

Warmier, Jean-Dominique. *Computers and Human Intelligence.* Englewood Cliffs, N.J.: Prentice-Hall, 1986.

Winner, Langdon. *Autonomous Technology: Technics-out-of-Control as a Theme in Political Thought.* Cambridge: MIT Press, 1977.

Zadeh, Lofti. *Information and Control.* Vol. 8. New York: Academic Press, 1974.

Philosophical Roots

Anton, John D. *Science and the Sciences in Plato.* New York: EIDOS, 1980.

Ayer, Alfred J. *The Foundations of Empirical Knowledge.* London: Macmillan and Co., 1964.

Ayer, J. *Language, Truth, and Logic.* New York: Dover Publications, n.d. Originally published in 1936.

Ayer, Alfred J., ed. *Logical Positivism.* New York: Macmillan Publishing Co., 1959.

Block, Irving, ed. *Perspectives on the Philosophy of Wittgenstein.* Cambridge: MIT Press, 1981.

Boden, Margaret. *Artificial Intelligence and Natural Man.* New York: Basic Books, 1977.

Brittan, Gordon G., Jr. *Kant's Theory of Science.* Princeton: Princeton University Press, 1978.

Brumbaugh, R. S. *Plato's Mathematical Imagination.* Bloomington: Indiana University Press, 1954.

Cassirer, Ernst. *The Philosophy of the Enlightenment.* Princeton: Princeton University Press, 1951.

Cherniak, Christopher. *Minimal Rationality.* Cambridge: MIT Press, 1986.

Chomsky, Noam. *Syntactic Structures.* The Hague: Mouton, 1957.

Churchland, Paul M. *Matter and Consciousness.* Cambridge: MIT Press, 1984.

Clocksin, W. F., and C. S. Mellish. *Programming in PROLOG.* Berlin: Springer-Verlag, 1981.

Cohen, I. Bernard. *The Newtonian Revolution.* Cambridge: Cambridge University Press, 1980.

Cornford, Francis M. *Plato's Cosmology.* London: Routledge and Kegan Paul, 1937.

Davis, Philip J., and Reuben Hersh. *Descartes' Dream: The World According to Mathematics.* San Diego: Harcourt Brace Jovanovich, 1986.

Dennett, Daniel C. *Brainstorms: Philosophical Essays on Mind and Psychology.* Cambridge: MIT Press, 1978.

Dennett, Daniel C. *Elbow Room: The Varieties of Free Will Worth Wanting.* Cambridge: MIT Press, 1984.

Descartes, René. *Discourse on Method, Optics, Geometry, and Meteorology.* Indianapolis: Bobbs-Merrill Co., 1956. Original, 1637.

Dodds, E. R. *The Greeks and the Irrational.* Berkeley: University of California Press, 1951.

Dreyfus, Hubert L., ed. *Husserl, Intentionality, and Cognitive Science.* Cambridge: MIT Press, 1982.

Dreyfus, Hubert L. "Philosophic Issues in Artificial Intelligence." Department of Humanities, MIT, 1967.

Dreyfus, Hubert L. *What Computers Can't Do: The Limits of Artificial Intelligence.* Rev. ed. New York: Harper and Row, 1979. Original, 1972.

Einstein, Albert. *Relativity: The Special and General Theory: A Popular Exposition.* New York: Crown Publishers, 1961.

Findlay, J. N. *Plato and Platonism: An Introduction.* New York: Times Books, 1978.

Fodor, Jerry A. *Representations: Philosophical Essays on the Foundations of Cognitive Science.* Cambridge: MIT Press, 1981.

Fowler, D. H. *The Mathematics of Plato's Academy.* Oxford: Clarendon Press, 1987.

Freud, Sigmund. *Jokes and Their Relation to the Unconscious.* Vol. 8 of *Standard Edition of the Complete Psychological Works of Sigmund Freud.* London: Hogarth Press, 1957. Original, 1905.

Gay, Peter. *The Enlightenment: An Interpretation.* Vol. 1, *The Rise of Modern Paganism.* New York: W. W. Norton and Co., 1966.

Gay, Peter. *The Enlightenment: An Interpretation.* Vol. 2, *The Science of Freedom.* New York: W. W. Norton and Co., 1969.

Gillispie, Charles. *The Edge of Objectivity.* Princeton: Princeton University Press, 1960.

Graubard, Stephen R., ed. *The Artificial Intelligence Debate: False Starts, Real Foundations.* Cambridge: MIT Press, 1988.

Grossman, Reinhardt. *Phenomenology and Existentialism: An Introduction.* London: Routledge and K. Paul, 1984.

Guthrie, W. K. C. *A History of Greek Philosophy.* 6 vols. Cambridge: Cambridge University Press, 1962–1981.

Hankins, Thomas L. *Science and the Enlightenment.* Cambridge: Cambridge University Press, 1985.

Harel, David. *Algorithmics: The Spirit of Computing.* Menlo Park: Addison-Wesley Publishing Co., 1987.

Haugeland, John, ed. *Mind Design.* Cambridge: MIT Press, 1981.

Heisenberg, Werner. *Physics and Beyond: Encounters and Conversations.* New York: Harper and Row, 1971.

Helleman, Alexander, and Bryan Bunch. *The Timetables of Science.* New York: Simon and Schuster, 1988.

Hofstadter, Douglas R. *Gödel, Escher, Bach: An Eternal Golden Braid.* New York: Basic Books, 1979.

Hume, David. *An Inquiry Concerning Human Understanding.* Indianapolis: Bobbs-Merrill Co., 1955. Original, 1748.

Jones, W. T. *Kant and the Nineteenth Century.* Vol. 4 of *A History of Western Philosophy*, 2nd ed. New York: Harcourt Brace Jovanovich, 1975.

Jones, W. T. *The Twentieth Century to Wittgenstein and Sartre.* Vol. 5 of *A History of Western Philosophy*, 2nd ed. New York: Harcourt Brace Jovanovich, 1975.

Kant, Immanuel. *Critique of Pure Reason.* New York: St. Martin's Press, 1929. Originally published in 1781.

Kant, Immanuel. *Prolegomena to Any Future Metaphysics.* Indianapolis: Bobbs-Merrill Co., 1950. Original, 1783.

Kirk, G. S., J. E. Raven, and M. Schofield. *The Presocratic Philosophers.* Cambridge: Cambridge University Press, 1983.

Knorr, Wilbur Richard. *The Ancient Tradition of Geometric Problems.* Boston: Birkhäuser, 1986.

Lasserre, Francois. *The Birth of Mathematics in the Age of Plato.* New York: World Publishing Co., 1964.

Leibniz, Gottfried Wilhelm. *Philosophical Writings*. Ed. G. H. R. Parkinson. London and Toronto: J. M. Dent and Sons, 1973.

Leibniz, Gottfried Wilhelm, and Samuel Clarke. *The Leibniz-Clarke Correspondence*. Ed. H. G. Alexander. Manchester: Manchester University Press, 1956.

Lloyd, G. E. R. *Aristotle: The Growth and Structure of His Thought*. Cambridge: Cambridge University Press, 1968.

Lloyd, G. E. R. *Early Greek Science: Thales to Aristotle*. New York: W.W. Norton and Co., 1970.

McCorduck, Pamela. *Machines Who Think*. San Francisco: W. H. Freeman and Co., 1979.

Malcolm, Norman. *Ludwig Wittgenstein: A Memoir, with a Biographical Sketch by Georg Henrik Von Wright*. Oxford: Oxford University Press, 1958.

Mamdani, E. H., and B. R. Gaines. *Fuzzy Reasoning and Its Applications*. London: Academic Press, 1981.

Mayr, Otto. *Authority, Liberty, and Automatic Machinery in Early Modern Europe*. Baltimore: Johns Hopkins University Press, 1986.

Mohr, Richard R. *The Platonic Cosmology*. Leiden: E. J. Brill, 1985.

Mumford, Lewis. *The Myth of the Machine: Technics and Human Development*. New York: Harcourt Brace and World, 1966–1967.

Newmeyer, Frederick J. *Linguistic Theory in America*. 2nd ed. Orlando: Academic Press, 1986.

Newton, Isaac. *Philosophiae Naturalis Principia Mathematica*. 3rd ed. Ed. Alexander Koyré, I. Bernard Cohen, and Anne Whitman. 2 vols. Cambridge: Harvard University Press, 1972. Original, 1726.

Nussbaum, Martha. *The Fragility of Goodness: Luck and Ethics in Greek Tragedy and Philosophy*. Cambridge: Cambridge University Press, 1986.

Plato. *Epinomis*. The Loeb Classical Library. Ed. W. R. M. Lamb. Vol. 8 New York: G. P. Putnam's Sons, 1927.

Plato. *Timaeus*. Indianapolis: Bobbs-Merrill Co., 1959.

Rée, Jonathan. *Descartes*. New York: Pica Press, 1974.

Ringle, Martin D., ed. *Philosophical Perspectives in Artificial Intelligence*. Brighton: Harvester Press, 1979.

Russell, Bertrand. *The ABC of Relativity*. 4th ed. London: Allen and Unwin, 1985. Original, 1925.

Russell, Bertrand. *The Problems of Philosophy*. New York: Oxford University Press, 1959.

Sambursky, S. *The Physical World of the Greeks*. London: Routledge and Kegan Paul, 1963. Original, 1956.

Shapiro, Stuart C., ed. *Encyclopedia of Artificial Intelligence*. 2 vols. New York: John Wiley and Sons, 1987.

Torrance, Steve, ed. *The Mind and the Machine: Philosophical Aspects of Artificial Intelligence*. Chichester, England: Ellis Horwood, 1984.

Turkle, Sherry. *The Second Self: Computers and the Human Spirit*. New York: Simon and Schuster, 1984.

Vaina, Lucia, and Jaakko Hintikka, ed. *Cognitive Constraints on Communication*. Dordrecht: Reidel, 1985.

Weizenbaum, Joseph. *Computer Power and Human Reason*. San Francisco: W. H. Freeman and Co., 1976.

Westfall, Richard. *Never at Rest: A Biography of Isaac Newton*. Cambridge: Cambridge University Press, 1980.

Wittgenstein, Ludwig. *Philosophical Investigations*. New York: Macmillan Co., 1953.

Wittgenstein, Ludwig. *Tractatus Logico-Philosophicus*. New York: Routledge and Kegan Paul, 1961. Original German published in 1921.

Zeller, Eduard. *Plato and the Older Academy*. Reprint ed. New York: Russell and Russell, 1962. Originally published in 1888.

Mathematical Roots

Beth, E. W. *Foundations of Mathematics*. Amsterdam: North-Holland Publishing Co., 1959.

Bolter, J. David. *Turing's Man: Western Culture in the Computer Age*. Chapel Hill: University of North Carolina Press, 1984.

Bowden, B. W., ed. *Faster than Thought*. London: Pitman, 1953.

Church, Alonzo. *Introduction to Mathematical Logic*. Vol. 1. Princeton: Princeton University Press, 1956.

Dreyfus, Hubert. *What Computers Can't Do*. New York: Harper and Row, 1971.

Feigenbaum, Edward, and J. Feldman, eds. *Computers and Thought*. New York: McGraw-Hill, 1963.

Feigenbaum, Edward, and Pamela McCorduck. *The Fifth Generation*. Reading, Mass.: Addison-Wesley, 1983.

Hamming, R. W. *Introduction to Applied Numerical Analysis*. New York: McGraw-Hill, 1971.

Hodges, Andrew. *Alan Turing: The Enigma*. New York: Simon & Schuster, 1983.

Hofstadter, Douglas. *Gödel, Escher, Bach: An Eternal Golden Braid*. New York: Basic Books, 1979.

Kleene, Stephen Cole. *Introduction to Metamathematics*. New York: D. Van Nostrand, 1952.

Metropolis, N., J. Howlett, G. C. Rota, eds. *A History of Computing in the Twentieth Century*. New York: Academic Press, 1980.

Minsky, Marvin. *Computation: Finite and Infinite Machines*. Englewood Cliffs: Prentice-Hall, 1967.

Russell, Bertrand. *The Autobiography of Bertrand Russell: 1872–1914*. New York: Bantam Books, 1956.

Russell, Bertrand. *The Autobiography of Bertrand Russell: The Middle Years 1914–1944*. New York: Bantam Books, 1956.

Russell, Bertrand. *Introduction to Mathematical Philosophy*. New York: Macmillan, 1919.

Russell, Bertrand. *Mysticism and Logic*. Garden City, N.Y.: Doubleday, 1957.

Russell, Bertrand. *Principles of Mathematics*. 2nd ed. Cambridge: Cambridge University Press, 1938. 1st ed., 1903.

Schilpp, P. A., ed. *The Philosophy of Bertrand Russell*. Chicago: University of Chicago Press, 1944.

Van Heijenoort, Jean, ed. *From Frege to Gödel*. Cambridge: Harvard University Press, 1967.

Whitehead, Alfred N., and Bertrand Russell. *Principia Mathematica*. 3 vols. 2nd ed. Cambridge: Cambridge University Press, 1925–1927.

The Formula for Intelligence

Antébi, Elizabeth, and David Fishlock. *Biotechnology: Strategies for Life*. Cambridge: MIT Press, 1986.

Atkins, P. W. *The Second Law*. New York: Scientific American Books, 1984.

Barrow, John D., and Frank J. Tipler. *The Anthropic Cosmological Principle*. Oxford: Oxford University Press, 1986.

Boole, George. *An Investigation of the Laws of Thought on Which Are Founded the Mathematical Theories of Logic and Probabilities*. Peru, Ill.: Open Court Publishing Co., 1952. Original published in 1854.

Botvinnik, M. M. *Computers in Chess*. New York: Springer-Verlag, 1984.

Carver, Mead, and Lynn Conway. *Introduction to VLSI Systems*. Reading, Mass.: Addison-Wesley, 1980.

Chaitin, Gregory J. *Algorithmic Information Theory*. Cambridge: Cambridge University Press, 1987.

Crease, Robert P., and Charles C. Mann, *The Second Creation*. New York: Macmillan, 1986.

Dreyfus, Hubert. *What Computers Can't Do*. 2nd ed. New York: Harper and Row, 1971.

Ebeling, Carl. *All the Right Moves*. Cambridge: MIT Press, 1987.

Edelman, G. M. *Neural Darwinism: The Theory of Neuronal Group Selection*. New York: Basic Books, 1987.

Einstein, Albert. *Relativity: The Special and the General Theory*. 17th ed. New York: Crown Publishers, 1961.

Fadiman, Clifton, ed. *Fantasia Mathematica: Being a Set of Stories, together with a Group of Oddments and Diversions, All Drawn from the Universe of Mathematics*. New York: Simon and Schuster, 1958.

Feigenbaum, E., and Avron Barr, eds. *The Handbook of Artificial Intelligence*. Vol 1. Los Altos, Calif.: William Kaufman, 1981.

Feigenbaum, E. A., and J. Feldman, eds. *Computers and Thought*. New York: McGraw-Hill, 1963.

Freudenthal, Hans. *Mathematics Observed*. Trans. Stephen Rudolfer and I. N. Baker. New York: McGraw-Hill Book Co., 1967.

Frey, Peter, ed. *Chess Skill in Man and Machine*. 2nd ed. New York: Springer-Verlag, 1983.

Gamow, George. *One, Two, Three, Infinity: Facts and Speculations of Science*. New York: Bantam Books, 1947.

Garey, Michael R., and David S. Johnson. *Computers and Intractability*. San Francisco: W. H. Freeman. 1979.

Greenblatt, R. D., et. al. *The Greenblatt Chess Program*. Proceedings of the fall joint computer conference. ACM, 1967.

Guillen, Michael. *Bridges to Infinity: The Human Side of Mathematics*. Los Angeles: Jeremy P. Tarcher, 1983.

Hawking, Stephen. *A Brief History of Time*. Toronto: Bantam Books, 1988.

Hildebrandt, Stefan, and Anthony Tromba. *Mathematics and Optimal Form*. New York: Scientific American Books, 1985.

Hillis, Daniel. *The Connection Machine*. Cambridge: MIT Press, 1985.

Hofstadter, Douglas R. *Gödel, Escher, Bach: An Eternal Golden Braid*. New York: Basic Books, 1979.

Hofstadter, Douglas R. *Metamagical Themas: Questing for the Essence of Mind and Pattern*. New York: Basic Books, 1985.

Hsu, F. *Two Designs of Functional Units for VLSI Based Chess Machines*. Technical report. Computer Science Department, Carnegie Mellon University, 1986.

Judson, Horace F. *The Eighth Day of Creation*. New York: Simon and Schuster, 1979.

Kasner, Edward, and James Newman. *Mathematics and the Imagination*. New York: Simon and Schuster, 1940.

Kline, Morris. *Mathematics and the Search for Knowledge*. Oxford: Oxford University Press, 1985.

Luce, R. D., and H. Raiffa. *Games and Decisions*. New York: John Wiley & Sons, 1957.

McCorduck, Pamela. *Machines Who Think*. San Francisco: W. H. Freeman, 1979.

McCulloch, Warren S. *Embodiments of Mind*. Cambridge: MIT Press, 1965.

Minsky, Marvin. *Society of Mind*. New York: Simon & Schuster, 1985.

Minsky, Marvin, and Seymour Papert. *Perceptrons*. Expanded edition. Cambridge: MIT Press, 1988.

Newell, A., and H. A. Simon. *Human Problem Solving*. Englewood Cliffs, N.J.: Prentice Hall, 1972.

Nilsson, Lennart. *The Body Victorious: The Illustrated Story of Our Immune System and other Defences of the Human Body*. Trans. Clare James. New York: Delacorte Press, 1985.

Pagels, Heinz R. *Perfect Symmetry*. New York: Simon & Schuster, 1985.

Rucker, Rudy. *The Five Levels of Mathematical Reality*. New York: Houghton-Mifflin, 1987.

Rumelhart, D. E., J. L. McClelland, and the PDP Research Group. *Parallel Distributed Processing*. Vols. 1 and 2. Cambridge: MIT Press, 1986.

Russell, Bertrand. *ABC of Relativity*. 4th ed. London: George Allen & Unwin, 1958.

Sagan, Carl. *The Dragons of Eden*. New York: Random House, 1977.

Waterman, D. A., and F. Hayes-Roth, eds. *Pattern-Directed Inference Systems*.

Watson, J. D. *The Double Helix*. New York: Atheneum Publishers, 1968.

Winograd, Terry, and Fernando Flores. *Understanding Computers and Cognition: A New Foundation for Design*. Norwood, N.J.: Ablex Publishing, 1985.

Winston, Patrick H. *Artificial Intelligence*. 2nd ed. Reading, Mass.: Addison-Wesley, 1984.

Winston, Patrick H., and K. A. Prendergast, eds. *The AI Business*. Cambridge: MIT Press, 1984.

Mechanical Roots

Augarten, Stan. *Bit by Bit: An Illustrated History of Computers*. New York: Ticknor and Fields, 1984.

Austrian, Geoffrey D. *Herman Hollerith: Forgotten Giant of Information Processing*. New York: Columbia University Press, 1982.

Babbage, Henry Prevost. *Babbage's Calculating Engines*. Charles Babbage Institute Reprint Series for the History of Computing, vol. 2. Los Angeles: Tomash Publishers, 1982. Originally published in 1889.

Bashe, Charles J., Lyle R. Johnson, John H. Palmer, and Emerson W. Pugh. *IBM's Early Computers*. Cambridge: MIT Press, 1986.

Baxandall, D. *Calculating Machines and Instruments*. Rev. ed. London: Science Museum, 1975. Originally published in 1926.

Bernstein, Jeremy. *The Analytical Engine: Computers—Past, Present, and Future*. Revised ed. New York: William Morrow and Co., 1981.

Bolter, J. David. *Turing's Man: Western Culture in the Computer Age*. Chapel Hill: University of North Carolina Press, 1984.

Buxton, H. W. *Memoirs of the Life and Labours of the Late Charles Babbage, Esq., F.R.S.* Ed. A. Hyman. Los Angeles: Tomash, 1988.

Chapuis, Alfred, and Edmond Droz. *Automata: A Historical and Technological Study*. Neuchatel and New York: Griffon, 1958.

Cipolla, Carlo M. *Clocks and Culture, 1300–1700*. London: Collins, 1967.

Cohen, John. *Human Robots in Myth and Science*. London: Allen and Unwin, 1966.

Dickinson, Henry W. *Sir Samuel Morland, Diplomat and Inventor, 1625–1695*. Cambridge: Heffer, 1970.

Drachman, A. G. *The Mechanical Technology of Greek and Roman Antiquity*. Madison: University of Wisconsin Press, 1963.

Eames, Charles, and Ray Eames. *A Computer Perspective*. Cambridge: Harvard University Press, 1973.

Forbes, R. J. *Studies in Ancient Technology*. 9 vols. Leiden: E. J. Brill, 1955–1965.

Goldstine, Herman. *The Computer from Pascal to von Neumann*. Princeton: Princeton University Press, 1972.

Hindle, Brooke, and Steven Lubar. *Engines of Change: The American Industrial Revolution, 1790–1860*. Washington, D.C.: Smithsonian Institution Press, 1986.

Horsburgh, Ellice Martin, ed. *Modern Instruments and Methods of Calculation: A Handbook of the Napier Tercentenary Celebration Exhibition*. London: G. Bell and Sons, 1914.

Hyman, Anthony. *Charles Babbage: Pioneer of the Computer*. Oxford: Oxford University Press, 1982.

Landes, David S. *Revolution in Time: Clocks and the Making of the Modern World*. Cambridge: Harvard University Press, 1983.

McCorduck, Pamela. *Machines Who Think*. San Francisco: W. H. Freeman and Co., 1979.

Macey, Samuel L. *Clocks and the Cosmos: Time in Western Life and Thought*. Hamden: Archon Books, 1980.

Mayr, Otto. *Authority, Liberty, and Automatic Machinery in Early Modern Europe*. Baltimore: Johns Hopkins University Press, 1986.

Metropolis, N., J. Howlett, and Gian-Carlo Rota, ed. *A History of Computing in the Twentieth Century*. New York: Academic Press, 1980.

Moon, Parry H. *The Abacus: Its History, Its Design, Its Possibilities in the Modern World*. New York: Gordon and Breach, 1971.

Needham, Joseph. *Science and Civilisation in China*. Vols. 2 and 4. Cambridge: Cambridge University Press, 1956, 1965.

Neuberger, A. P. *The Technical Arts and Sciences of the Ancients*. London: Methuen, 1930.

Pascal, Blaise. *Pensées*. New York: E. P. Dutton and Co., 1932. Originally published in 1670.

Price, Derek J. de Solla. *Gears from the Greeks: The Antikythera Mechanism—A Calendar Computer from circa 80 B.C.* New York: Science History Publications, 1975.

Pullan, J. M. *The History of the Abacus*. London: Hutchinson, 1968.

Randell, Brian, ed. *The Origins of Digital Computers: Selected Papers*. New York: Springer-Verlag, 1975.

Shurkin, Joel. *Engines of the Mind: A History of the Computer*. New York: W. W. Norton and Co., 1984.

Singer, C., E. J. Holmyard, A. R. Hall, and T. I. Williams, eds. *A History of Technology*. 5 vols. Oxford: Oxford University Press, 1954–1958.

Stein, Dorothy. *Ada, a Life and a Legacy*. Cambridge: MIT Press, 1985.

Truesdell, L. E. *The Development of Punch Card Tabulation in the Bureau of the Census, 1890–1940*. Washington, D.C.: Government Printing Office, 1965.

Usher, A. P. *A History of Mechanical Inventions*. 2nd ed. Cambridge: Harvard University Press, 1958.

White, K. D. *Greek and Roman Technology*. London: Thames and Hudson, 1984.

Electronic Roots

Barr, Avron, and Edward A. Feigenbaum, eds. *The Handbook of Artificial Intelligence*. Vols. 1–2. Los Altos, Calif.: William Kaufmann, 1981–1982.

Bashe, Charles J., Lyle R. Johnson, John H. Palmer, and Emerson W. Pugh. *IBM's Early Computers*. Cambridge: MIT Press, 1986.

Boole, George. *An Investigation of the Laws of Thought on Which Are Founded the Mathematical Theories of Logic and Probabilities*. Peru, Ill.: Open Court Publishing Co., 1952. Originally published in 1854.

Charniak, Eugene, and Drew McDermott. *Introduction to Artificial Intelligence*. Reading, Mass.: Addison-Wesley Publishing Company, 1985.

Cohen, Paul R., and Edward A. Feigenbaum, eds. *The Handbook of Artificial Intelligence*. Vol. 3. Los Altos, Calif.: William Kaufmann, 1982.

Dreyfus, Hubert L. *What Computers Can't Do: The Limits of Artificial Intelligence*. Rev. ed. New York: Harper and Row, 1979.

Elithorn, A., and D. Jones, eds. *Artificial and Human Thinking*. San Francisco: Josey Bass, 1973.

Feigenbaum, E. A., and J. Feldman, eds. *Computers and Thought*. New York: McGraw-Hill, 1963.

Feigenbaum, E. A., and P. McCorduck. *The Fifth Generation: Artificial Intelligence and Japan's Computer Challenge to the World*. Reading Mass.: Addison-Wesley Publishing Co., 1983.

Gardner, Howard. *The Mind's New Science: A History of the Cognitive Revolution*. New York: Basic Books, 1985.

Haugeland, John. *Artificial Intelligence: The Very Idea*. Cambridge: MIT Press, 1985.

Hodges, Andrew. *Alan Turing: The Enigma*. New York: Simon and Schuster, 1983.

Hofstadter, Douglas. *Gödel, Escher, Bach: An Eternal Golden Braid*. New York: Basic Books, 1979.

Hopper, Grace Murray, and Steven L. Mandell. *Understanding Computers*. 2nd ed. St. Paul: West Publishing Co., 1987.

Lammers, Susan. *Programmers at Work*. Redmond, Wash.: Microsoft Press, 1986.

Laurie, Peter. *The Joy of Computers*. Boston: Little, Brown and Co., 1983.

Levy, Steven. *Hackers: Heroes of the Computer Revolution*. New York: Dell, 1984.

Lundstrom, David E. *A Few Good Men from Univac*. Cambridge: MIT Press, 1987.

McCorduck, Pamela. *Machines Who Think: A Personal Inquiry into the History and Prospects of Artificial Intelligence*. San Francisco: W. H. Freeman and Co., 1979.

Metropolis, N., J. Howlett, and G. C. Rota, eds. *A History of Computing in the Twentieth Century*. New York: Academic Press, 1980.

Minsky, Marvin, ed. *Semantic Information Processing*. Cambridge: MIT Press, 1968.

Minsky, Marvin. *The Society of Mind*. New York: Simon and Schuster, 1985.

Morgan, B. *Total to Date: The Evolution of the Adding Machine*. London: Burroughs Machines, 1973.

Newell, Allen. *Intellectual Issues in the History of Artificial Intelligence*. Pittsburgh: Carnegie-Mellon University, 1982.

Newell, A., and H. A. Simon. *Human Problem Solving*. Englewood Cliffs, N.J.: Prentice Hall, 1972.

Nilsson, Nils J. *Principles of Artificial Intelligence*. Los Altos, Calif.: Morgan Kaufman Publishers, 1980.

Peat, F. David. *Artificial Intelligence: How Machines Think*. New York: Baen Enterprises, 1985.

Randell, Brian. *The Origins of Digital Computers*. Berlin: Springer-Verlag, 1973.

Rich, Elaine. *Artificial Intelligence*. New York: McGraw-Hill Book Co., 1983.

Rucker, Rudy. *Mind Tools: The Five Levels of Mathematical Reality*. Boston: Houghton Mifflin Co., 1987.

Russell, Bertrand. *Principles of Mathematics*. 2nd ed. Cambridge: Cambridge University Press, 1938.

Savage, John E., Susan Magidson, and Alex M. Stein. *The Mystical Machine*. Reading, Mass.: Addison-Wesley, 1986.

Scown, Susan J. *The Artificial Intelligence Experience: An Introduction*. Maynard, Mass.: Digital Equipment Corp., 1985.

Siekmann, Jorg, and Graham Wrightson. *Automation of Reasoning*. Vol. 1, *Classical Papers on Computational Logic, 1957–1966*. Berlin: Springer-Verlag, 1983.

Siekmann, Jorg, and Graham Wrightson. *Automation of Reasoning* Vol. 2, *Classical Papers on Computational Logic, 1967–1970*. Berlin: Springer-Verlag, 1983.

Simon, Herbert A. *The Sciences of the Artificial*. 2nd ed. Cambridge: MIT Press, 1981.

Simon, Herbert A., and L. Siklossy, eds. *Representation and Meaning: Experiments with Information Processing Systems*. Englewood Cliffs, N.J.: Prentice-Hall, 1972.

Slater, Robert. *Portraits in Silicon*. Cambridge: MIT Press, 1987.

Tanimoto, Steven L. *The Elements of Artificial Intelligence: An Introduction Using LISP*. Rockville, Md.: Computer Science Press, 1987.

Torrance, Steve, ed. *The Mind and the Machine: Philosophical Aspects of Artificial Intelligence*. Chichester, England: Ellis Horwood Limited, 1984.

Waldrop, M. Mitchell. *Man-Made Minds: The Promise of Artificial Intelligence*. New York: Walker and Co., 1987.

Webber, Bonnie Lynn, and Nils J. Nilsson, eds. *Readings in Artificial Intelligence*. Los Altos, Calif.: Morgan Kaufmann Publishers, 1981.

Wiener, Norbert. *Cybernetics, or Control and Communication in the Animal and the Machine*. 2nd ed. Cambridge: MIT Press, 1961.

Winston, Patrick Henry. *Artificial Intelligence*. 2nd ed. Reading, Mass.: Addison-Wesley Publishing Co., 1984.

Winston, Patrick Henry, and Richard Henry Brown. *Artificial Intelligence: An MIT Perspective*. Vol. 1, *Expert Problem Solving, Natural Language Understanding, Intelligent Computer Coaches, Representation, and Learning*. Cambridge: MIT Press, 1979.

Winston, Patrick Henry, and Richard Henry Brown. *Artificial Intelligence: An MIT Perspective*. Vol. 2, *Understanding Vision, Manipulation, Computer Design, Symbol Manipulation*. Cambridge: MIT Press, 1979.

Winston, Patrick H., and Karen A. Prendergast, eds. *The AI Business: The Commercial Uses of Artificial Intelligence*. Cambridge: MIT Press, 1984.

Pattern Recognition: The Search for Order

Barr, Avron, and Edward A. Feigenbaum, eds. *The Handbook of Artificial Intelligence*. Vols. 1 and 2. Los Altos, Calif.: William Kaufmann, 1981 and 1982.

Cater, John P. *Electronically Hearing: Computer Speech Recognition*. Indianapolis: Howard W. Sams and Co., 1984.

Cater, John P. *Electronically Speaking: Computer Speech Generation*. Indianapolis: Howard W. Sams and Co., 1983.

Church, Kenneth W. *Phonological Parsing in Speech Recognition*. Norwell, Mass.: Kluwer Academic Publishers, 1987.

Cohen, Paul R., and Edward A. Feigenbaum, eds. *The Handbook of Artificial Intelligence*. Vol. 3. Los Altos, Calif.: William Kaufmann, 1982.

Denes, Peter B., and Elliot N. Pinson. *The Speech Chain: The Physics and Biology of Spoken Language*. Bell Telephone Laboratories, 1963.

Fant, Gunnar. *Speech Sounds and Features*. Cambridge: MIT Press, 1973.

Fischler, Martin A., and Oscar Firschein. *Intelligence: The Eye, the Brain, and the Computer.* Reading, Mass.: Addison-Wesley Publishing Co., 1987.

Fischler, Martin A., and Oscar Firschein. *Readings in Computer Vision: Issues, Problems, Principles, and Paradigms.* Los Altos, Calif.: Morgan Kaufmann Publishers, 1987.

Flanagan, James L. *Speech Analysis Synthesis and Perception.* 2nd expanded ed. Berlin: Springer-Verlag, 1972.

Frauenfelder, Uli H., and Lorraine Komisarjevsky Tyler, eds. *Spoken Word Recognition.* Cambridge: MIT Press, 1987.

Geissler, Hans-Georg, et al. *Modern Issues in Perception* Amsterdam: North-Holland Publishing Co., 1983.

Grimson, W. Eric L., *From Images to Surfaces.* Cambridge: MIT Press, 1981.

Grimson, W. Eric L. and Ramesh Patil, eds. *AI in the 1980s and Beyond.* Cambridge: MIT Press, 1987.

Hillis, W. Daniel. *The Connection Machine.* Cambridge: MIT Press, 1985.

Hoel, Paul G., Sidney C. Port, and Charles J. Stone. *Introduction to Stochastic Processes.* Boston: Houghton Mifflin Co., 1972.

Hofstadter, Douglas. *Metamagical Themas.* New York: Basic Books, 1985.

Horn, Berthold Klaus Paul. *Robot Vision.* Cambridge: MIT Press, 1986.

Hubel, David. *Eye, Brain, and Vision.* New York: W. H. Freeman, 1988.

Jamieson, Leah H., Dennis Gannon, and Robert J. Douglass, eds. *The Characteristics of Parallel Algorithms.* Cambridge: MIT Press, 1987.

Kohonen, Teuvo. *Self-Organization and Associative Memory.* Berlin: Springer-Verlag, 1984.

Lea, Wayne A., ed. *Trends in Speech Recognition.* Englewood Cliffs, N.J.: Prentice-Hall, 1980.

Lim, Jae S., ed. *Speech Enhancement.* Englewood Cliffs, N.J.: Prentice-Hall, 1983.

McClelland, James, David Rumelhart, and the PDP Research Group. *Parallel Distributed Processing.* Vol. 2. Cambridge: MIT Press, 1986.

Markov, A. *A Theory of Algorithms.* National Academy of Sciences, USSR.

Marr, David. *Vision.* San Francisco: W. H. Freeman, 1982.

Massaro, Dominic W., et al. *Letter and Word Perception: Orthographic Structure and Visual Processing in Reading.* Amsterdam: North-Holland Publishing Co., 1980.

Meisel, William S. *Computer-Oriented Approaches to Pattern Recognition.* New York: Academic Press, 1972.

Miller, Richard K. *Parallel Processing: The Technology of Fifth Generation Computers.* Madison, Ga.: SEAI Technical Publications, 1985.

Minsky, Marvin, and Seymour Papert. *Perceptrons.* Revised ed. Cambridge: MIT Press, 1988.

Myers, Terry, John Laver, and John Anderson, eds. *The Cognitive Representation of Speech.* Amsterdam: North-Holland Publishing Co., 1981.

Potter, Jerry L., ed. *The Massively Parallel Processor.* Cambridge: MIT Press, 1985.

Rabiner, Lawrence R., and Ronald W. Schafer. *Digital Processing of Speech Signals.* Englewood Cliffs, N.J.: Prentice-Hall, 1978.

Radford, Andrew. *Transformational Syntax: A Student's Guide to Chomsky's Extended Standard Theory.* Cambridge: Cambridge University Press, 1981.

Rock, Irvin. *Perception.* New York: Scientific American Books, 1984.

Rumelhart, David, James McClelland, and the PDP Research Group. *Parallel Distributed Processing.* Vol. 1. Cambridge: MIT Press, 1986.

Sacks, Oliver. *The Man Who Mistook His Wife for a Hat and Other Clinical Tales.* New York: Harper and Row, 1985.

Ullman, Shimon. *The Interpretation of Visual Motion.* Cambridge: MIT Press, 1979.

Watanabe, Satosi. *Pattern Recognition: Human and Mechanical.* New York: John Wiley and Sons, 1985.

Winston, Patrick H. *Artificial Intelligence.* Reading, Mass.: Addison-Wesley, 1984.

Winston, Patrick H., ed. *The Psychology of Computer Vision.* New York: McGraw-Hill, 1975.

Zimmermann, Hans J. *Fuzzy Set Theory and Its Applications*. Hingham, Mass.: Kluwer-Nijhoff Publishing, 1985.

Zue, Victor W., Francine R Chen, and Lori Lamel. *Speech Spectrogram Reading: An Acoustic Study of English Words and Sentences*. MIT special summer course, 1982.

The Search for Knowledge

Asimov, Isaac, and Karen Frenkel. *Robots: Machines in Man's Image*. New York: Harmony Books, 1985.

Ayres, Robert U., et al. *Robotics and Flexible Manufacturing Technologies: Assessment, Impacts, and Forecast*. Park Ridge, N.J.: Noyes Publications, 1985.

Bara, Bruno G., and Giovanni Guida, eds. *Computational Models of Natural Language Processing*. Fundamental Studies in Computer Science, vol. 9. Amsterdam, The Netherlands: North-Holland Publishing Co., 1984.

Barr, Avron, and Edward A. Feigenbaum, eds. *The Handbook of Artificial Intelligence*. Vols. 1 and 2. Los Altos, Calif.: William Kaufmann, 1981 and 1982.

Beni, Gerardo, and Susan Hackwood, eds. *Recent Advances in Robotics*. New York: John Wiley and Sons, 1985.

Berwick, Robert C. *The Acquisition of Syntactic Knowledge*. Cambridge: MIT Press, 1985.

Bobrow, Daniel G., and A. Collins, eds. *Representation and Understanding*. New York: Academic Press, 1975.

Brachman, Ronald J., and Hector J. Levesque, eds. *Readings in Knowledge Representation*. Los Altos, Calif.: Morgan Kaufmann Publishers, 1985.

Brady, Michael, et al., eds. *Robot Motion: Planning and Control*. Cambridge: MIT Press, 1982.

Brady, Michael, Lester A. Gerhardt, and Harold F. Davidson, eds. *Robotics and Artificial Intelligence*. NATO ASI series. Series F, Computer and Systems Sciences, vol. 2. Berlin: Springer-Verlag, 1984.

Churchland, Paul M. *Matter and Consciousness*. Revised ed. Cambridge: MIT Press, 1988.

Clancey, William J., and Edward H. Shortliffe, eds. *Readings in Medical Artificial Intelligence: The First Decade*. Reading, Mass.: Addison-Wesley Publishing Co., 1984.

Cohen, Paul R., and Edward A. Feigenbaum, eds. *The Handbook of Artificial Intelligence*. Vol. 3. Los Altos, Calif.: William Kaufmann, 1982.

Critchlow, Arthur J. *Introduction to Robotics*. New York: Macmillan Publishing Co., 1985.

Davis, R., and D. B. Lenat. *Knowledge-Based Systems in Artificial Intelligence*. New York: McGraw-Hill, 1980.

DM Data. *The Artificial Intelligence Directory: A Comprehensive Listing of the Artificial Intelligence Companies*. Third annual edition. Scottsdale, Ariz.: DM Data, 1987.

Fahlman, Scott E. *NETL: A System for Representing and Using Real-World Knowledge*. Cambridge: MIT Press, 1979.

Feigenbaum, Edward, and Pamela McCorduck. *The Fifth Generation*. Reading, Mass.: Addison-Wesley, 1983.

Feigenbaum, Edward, Pamela McCorduck, and Penny Nii. *The Rise of the Expert Company*. Reading, Mass.: Addison-Wesley, 1988.

Frey, Peter, ed. *Chess Skill in Man and Machine*. 2nd ed. New York: Springer-Verlag, 1983.

Gardner, Anne von der Lieth. *An Artificial Intelligence Approach to Legal Reasoning*. Cambridge: MIT Press, 1987.

Genesereth, Michael R., and Nils J. Nilsson. *Logical Foundations of Artificial Intelligence*. Los Altos, Calif.: Morgan Kaufmann Publishers, 1987.

Grimson, W. Eric L., and Ramesh Patil, eds. *AI in the 1980s and Beyond*. Cambridge: MIT Press, 1987.

Harmon, Paul, and David King. *Expert Systems: Artificial Intelligence in Business*. New York: John Wiley & Sons, 1985.

Harris, Mary D. *Introduction to Natural Language Processing*. Reston, Va.: Reston Publishing Co., 1985.

Haugeland, John, ed. *Mind Design*. Cambridge: MIT Press, 1981.

Hayes-Roth, Frederick, D. A. Waterman, and D. B. Lenat, eds. *Building Expert Systems*. Reading, Mass.: Addison-Wesley, 1983.

Hewett, Julian, and Ron Sasson. *Expert Systems 1986*. Vol. 1, *USA and Canada*. London: Ovum, 1986.

Jackendoff, Ray. *Semantics and Cognition*. Cambridge: MIT Press, 1983.

Johnson, L., and E. T. Keravnou. *A Guide to Expert Systems Technology*. Abacus Press, 1984.

Johnson, Mark, and George Lakoff. *Metaphors We Live By*. Chicago: University of Chicago Press, 1980.

Johnson, Tim. *Natural Language Computing: The Commercial Applications*. London: Ovum, 1985.

Kahneman, Daniel, Paul Slovic, and Amos Tversky, eds. *Judgement under Uncertainty: Heuristics and Biases*. Cambridge: Cambridge University Press, 1982.

Kuno, Susumu. *Functional Syntax: Anaphora, Discourse, and Empathy*. Chicago: University of Chicago Press, 1987.

Kuno, Susumu. *The Structure of the Japanese Language*. Cambridge: MIT Press, 1973.

Li, Deyi. *A PROLOG Database System*. Letchworth, England: Research Studies Press, 1984.

Lindsay, R. K., et al. *Applications of Artificial Intelligence for Organic Chemistry: The Dendral Project*. New York: McGraw-Hill, 1980.

Marsh, Alton K. *Guide to Defense and Aerospace Expert Systems*. Arlington, Va.: Pasha Publications, 1986.

Martin, James, and Steven Oxman. *Building Expert Systems: A Tutorial*. Englewood Cliffs, N.J.: Prentice-Hall, 1988.

Mason, Matthew T., and J. Kenneth Salisbury, Jr. *Robot Hands and the Mechanics of Manipulation*. Cambridge: MIT Press, 1985.

Merrett, T. H. *Relational Information Systems*. Reston, Va.: Reston Publishing Co., 1984.

Michalski, Ryszard S., Jaime G. Carbonell, and Tom M. Mitchell, eds. *Machine Learning: An Artificial Intelligence Approach*. Vol. 2. Los Altos, Calif.: Morgan Kaufmann Publishers, 1986.

Miller, Richard K. *Computers for Artificial Intelligence: A Technology Assessment and Forecast*. Madison, Ga.: SEAI Technical Publications, 1986.

Minsky, Marvin, ed. *Semantic Information Processing*. Cambridge: MIT Press, 1968.

Minsky, Marvin. *Society of Mind*. New York: Simon & Schuster, 1986.

Newell, Allen. "Unified Theories of Cognition." The William James Lectures. Psychology Department, Harvard University, 1987.

Newquist, Harvey P., III, ed. *AI Trends '87: A Comprehensive Annual Report on the Artificial Intelligence Industry*. Scottsdale, Ariz.: DM Data, 1987.

Osherson, Daniel N., Michael Stob, and Scott Weinstein. *Systems That Learn: An Introduction to Learning Theory for Cognitive and Computer Scientists*. Cambridge: MIT Press, 1986.

Raibert, Marc H. *Legged Robots That Balance*. Cambridge: MIT Press, 1986.

Rauch-Hindin, Wendy. *Artificial Intelligence in Business, Science, and Industry* Englewood Cliffs, N.J.: Prentice-Hall, 1986.

Reichardt, Jasia. *Robots: Fact, Fiction, and Prediction*. Middlesex, England: Penguin Books, 1978.

Schank, Roger C. *Dynamic Memory: A Theory of Reminding and Learning in Computers and People*. Cambridge: Cambridge University Press, 1982.

Schank, Roger C., and Kenneth Mark Colby, eds. *Computer Models of Thought and Language*. San Francisco: W. H. Freeman and Co., 1973.

SEAI Technical Publications, *Fifth Generation Computers: A Report on Major International Research Projects and Cooperatives*. Madison, Ga.: SEAI Technical Publications, 1985.

Shortliffe, E. *MYCIN: Computer-Based Medical Consultations*. New York: American Elsevier, 1976.

Sterling, Leon, and Ehud Shapiro. *The Art of Prolog: Advanced Programming Techniques*. Cambridge: MIT Press, 1986.

Toepperwein, L. L., et al. *Robotics Applications for Industry: A Practical Guide*. Park Ridge, N.J.: Noyes Data Corporation, 1983.

Tomita, Masaru. *Efficient Parsing for Natural Language: A Fast Algorithm for Practical Systems*. Hingham, Mass.: Kluwer Academic Publishers, 1986.

Walker, Terri C., and Richard K. Miller. *Expert Systems 1986: An Assessment of Technology and Applications*. Madison, Ga.: SEAI Technical Publications, 1986.

Wallace, Mark. *Communicating with Databases in Natural Languages*. Chichester, England: Ellis Horwood, 1984.

Weiss, Sholom M., and Casimir A Kulikowski. *A Practical Guide to Designing Expert Systems*. Totowa, N.J.: Rowman and Allanheld, 1984.

Winograd, Terry. *Understanding Natural Language*. New York: Academic Press, 1973.

Winston, Patrick H., and Karen Prendergast, eds. *The AI Business*. Cambridge: MIT Press, 1984.

The Science of Art

Barrett, Edward. *Text, Context, and Hypertext*. Cambridge: MIT Press, 1988.

Barstow, David R., Howard E. Shrobe, and Erik Sandewell, ed. *Interactive Programming Environments*. New York: McGraw-Hill Company, 1984.

Bateman, Wayne. *Introduction to Computer Music*. New York: John Wiley and Sons, 1980.

Berlekamp, Elwyn R., John H. Conway, and Richard K. Guy. *Winning Ways for Your Mathematical Plays*. London: Academic Press, 1982.

Bertin, Jacques. *Semiology of Graphics: Diagrams, Networks, Maps*. Madison: University of Wisconsin Press, 1983.

Chamberlin, Hal. *Musical Applications of Microprocessors*. 2nd ed. Hasbrouck Heights, N.J.: Hatden Book Co., 1985.

Davies, Roy, ed. *Intelligent Information Systems: Progress and Prospects*. Chichester: Ellis Horwood, 1986.

Davis, Philip J., and Reuben Hersh. *Descartes' Dream: The World According to Mathematics*. San Diego: Harcourt Brace Jovanovich, 1986.

Dawkins, Richard. *The Blind Watchmaker: Why the Evidence of Evolution Reveals a Universe without Design*. New York: W. W. Norton & Company, 1987.

Dewdney, A. K. *The Armchair Universe: An Exploration of Computer Worlds*. New York: W. H. Freeman and Co., 1988.

Durrett, H. John, ed. *Color and the Computer*. Orlando, Fla.: Academic Press, 1987.

Enderle, G., K. Kansky, and G. Pfaff. *Computer Graphics Programming: GKS, the Graphics Standard*. Berlin: Springer-Verlag, 1984.

Foley, J. D., and A. Van Dam. *Fundamentals of Interactive Computer Graphics*. Reprint ed. Reading, Mass.: Addison-Wesley, 1984.

Franke, Herbert W. *Computer Graphics—Computer Art*. 1st ed. London: Phaidon Press, 1971. 2nd ed., Berlin: Springer-Verlag, 1985.

Glassner, Andrew S. *Computer Graphics User's Guide*. Indianapolis: Howard W. Sams and Co., 1984.

Gleick, James. *Chaos: Making a New Science*. New York: Viking Penguin, 1987.

Goodman, Cynthia. *Digital Visions: Computers and Art*. New York: Harry N. Abrams, 1987.

Graubard, Stephen R., ed. *The Artificial Intelligence Debate: False Starts, Real Foundations*. Cambridge: MIT Press, 1988.

Greenberg, Donald, Aaron Marcus, Allen H. Schmidt, and Vernon Gorter. *The Computer Image: Applications of Computer Graphics*. Reading, Mass.: Addison-Wesley Publishing Co., 1982.

Langley, Pat, et al. *Scientific Discovery: Computational Explorations of the Creative Processes*. Cambridge: MIT Press, 1987.

Leavitt, Ruth, ed. *Artist and Computer*. New York: Harmony Books, 1976.

Magnenat-Thalmann, Nadia, and Daniel Thalmann. *Computer Animation*. New York: Springer-Verlag, 1985.

Mandelbrot, Benoit B. *The Fractal Geometry of Nature*. New York: W. H. Freeman and Co., 1983.

Mandelbrot, Benoit B. *Fractals: Form, Chance, and Dimension*. San Francisco: W. H. Freeman and Co., 1977.

Markle, Sandra, and William Markle. *In Search of Graphics: Adventures in Computer Art*. New York: Lothrop, Lee and Shepard Books, 1985.

Mathews, Max V. *The Technology of Computer Music*. Cambridge: MIT Press, 1969.

Morgan, Christopher P., ed. *The "Byte" Book of Computer Music*. Peterborough, N.H.: Byte Books, 1979.

Nallin, Walter E. *The Musical Idea: A Consideration of Music and Its Ways*. New York: Macmillan Co., 1968.

Peitgen, H.-O., and P. H. Richter. *The Beauty of Fractals: Images of Complex Dynamical Systems*. Berlin: Springer-Verlag, 1986.

Peterson, Dale. *Genesis II: Creation and Recreation with Computers*. Reston, Va.: Reston Publishing Co., 1983.

Peterson, Ivars. *The Mathematical Tourist: Snapshots of Modern Mathematics*. San Francisco: W. H. Freeman, 1988.

Pierce, John R. *The Science of Musical Sound*. New York: Scientific American Books, 1983.

Poundstone, William. *The Recursive Universe: Cosmic Complexity and the Limits of Scientific Knowledge*. Chicago: Contemporary Books, 1985.

Prueitt, Melvin L. *Art and the Computer*. New York: McGraw-Hill Book Co., 1984.

RACTER. *The Policeman's Beard Is Half Constructed: Computer Prose and Poetry by RACTER*. New York: Warner Books, 1984.

Roads, Curtis, ed. *Composers and the Computer*. Los Altos, Calif.: William Kaufmann, 1985.

Roads, Curtis, ed. *The Music Machine: Selected Readings from "Computer Music Journal."* Cambridge: MIT Press, 1988.

Roads, Curtis, and John Strawn, ed. *Foundations of Computer Music*. Cambridge: MIT Press, 1985.

Schank, Roger. *The Creative Attitude: Learning to Ask and Answer the Right Questions*. New York: Macmillan Publishing Co., 1988.

Shapiro, Stuart C., ed. *Encyclopedia of Artificial Intelligence*. 2 vols. New York: John Wiley and Sons, 1987.

Time-Life Books editors. *Computer Images*. Alexandria, Va.: Time-Life Books, 1986.

Tjepkema, Sandra L. *A Bibliography of Computer Music: A Reference for Composers*. Iowa City: University of Iowa Press, 1981.

Toffoli, Tommaso, and Norman Margolis. *Cellular Automata Machines: A New Environment for Modeling*. Cambridge: MIT Press, 1987.

Wawrzynek, John. *VLSI Concurrent Computation for Music Synthesis*. California Institute of Technology, 1987.

Weinstock, Neal. *Computer Animation*. Reading, Mass.: Addison-Wesley Publishing Co., 1986.

Wilson, Mark. *Drawing with Computers: The Artist's Guide to Computer Graphics*. New York: Perigee Books, 1985.

Visions

Agha, Gul. *Actors*. Cambridge: MIT Press, 1987.

Asimov, Isaac. *Robots of Dawn*. New York: Doubleday & Co., 1983.

Botvinnik, M. M. *Computers in Chess: Solving Inexact Search Problems*. Trans. Arthur A. Brown. New York: Springer-Verlag, 1984.

Brand, Stewart. *The Media Lab: Inventing the Future at MIT*. New York: Viking Penguin.

Burns, Alan. *The Microchip: Appropriate or Inappropriate Technology?* New York: John Wiley & Sons, 1981.

Chaffee, David. *The Rewiring of America: The Fiber Optics Revolution*. Boston: Boston Academic Press, 1988.

Churchland, Paul M. *Matter and Consciousness: A Contemporary Introduction to the Philosophy of Mind*. Cambridge: MIT Press, 1988.

Deaver, B., and John Ruvalds., eds. *Advances in Superconductivity*. New York: Plenum Press, 1982.

Dreyfus, Hubert L. *What Computers Can't Do: A Critique of Artificial Reasoning*. New York: Harper & Row, 1972.

Evolution, Games, and Learning: Models for Adaptation in Machines and Nature. Proceedings of the Fifth Annual International Conference of the Center for Nonlinear Studies at Los Alamos, N.M., May 20–24, 1985. Amsterdam: North-Holland, 1986.

Fjermedal, Grant. *The Tomorrow Makers: A Brave New World of Living-Brain Machines*. New York: Macmillan Publishing Co., 1986.

Forester, Tom. *High-Tech Society: The Story of the Information Technology Revolution*. Cambridge: MIT Press, 1987.

Forester, Tom. *The Materials Revolution*. Cambridge: MIT Press, 1988.

Forester, Tom. *The Information Technology Revolution*. Cambridge: MIT Press, 1985.

Hazen, Robert M. *The Breakthrough: The Race for the Superconductor*. New York: Summit Books, 1988.

Hofstadter, Douglas R. *Metamagical Themas: Questing for the Essence of Mind and Pattern*. New York: Basic Books, 1985.

Hofstadter, Douglas, and Daniel C. Dennett. *The Mind's I: Fantasies and Reflections on Self and Soul*. New York: Basic Books, 1981.

Kobayashi, Koji. *Computers and Communication: A Vision of C&C*. Cambridge: MIT Press, 1986.

Lambert, Steve, and Suzanne Ropiequet, eds. *CD ROM, the New Papyrus: The Current and Future State of the Art*. Redmond, Wash.: Microsoft Press, 1986.

Levy, David N. L. *All about Chess and Computers*. Rockland, Md.: Computer Science Press, 1982.

Levy, David N. L. *Computer Games*. New York: Springer-Verlag, 1988.

Levy, Steven. *Hackers: Heroes of the Computer Revolution*. Garden City, N.Y.: Doubleday, Anchor Press, 1984.

Lord, Norman W. *Advanced Computers: Parallel and Biochip Processors*. Ann Arbor, Mich.: Ann Arbor Science, Butterworth Group, 1983.

McLuhan, Marshall. *Understanding Media: The Extension of Man*. New York: McGraw-Hill, 1964.

Michalski, R. Z., J. J. Carbonell, and T. M. Mitchell, eds. *Machine Learning: An Artificial Intelligence Approach*. Palo Alto: Tioga Publishing, 1983.

Minsky, Marvin. *Society of Mind*. New York: Simon & Schuster, 1985.

Newborn, Monroe. *Computer Chess*. New York: Academic Press, 1975.

Schank, Roger, and Peter G. Childers. *The Cognitive Computer: On Language, Learning, and Artificial Intelligence*. Reading, Mass.: Addison-Wesley, 1984.

Seippel, Robert G. *Fiber Optics*. Reston, Va.: Reston Publishing Co., 1984.

Simon, Randy, and Andrew Smith. *Superconductors: Conquering Technology's New Frontier*. New York: Plenum Press, 1988.

Smith, Donald N., and Peter Heytler, Jr. *Industrial Robots: Forecasts and Trends*. Dearborn, Mich.: Society of Manufacturing Engineers, 1985.

Winkler, Nels, and Iben Browning. *Robots on Your Doorstep: A Book about Thinking Machines*. Portland, Oregon: Robotics Press, 1978.

The Impact On . . .

Abelson, Harold, and Andrea diSessa. *Turtle Geometry: The Computer as a Medium for Exploring Mathematics*. Cambridge: MIT Press, 1980.

Andriole, Stephen J., and Gerald W. Hople, eds. *Defense Applications of Artificial Intelligence*. Lexington, Mass.: Lexington Books, 1988.

Bellin, David, and Gary Chapman, eds. *Computers in Battle—Will They Work?* Boston: Harcourt Brace Jovanovich, 1987.

Bernstein, Jeremy. *The Analytical Engine: Computers—Past, Present, and Future*. New York: Random House, 1963.

Brand, Stewart. *The Media Lab: Inventing the Future at MIT*. New York: Viking, 1987.

Chandler, Daniel. *Young Learners and the Microcomputer*. New York: Taylor and Francis, 1983.

Chen, Milton, and William Paisley, eds. *Children and Microcomputers: Research on the Newest Medium*. Beverly Hills: Sage Publications, 1985.

Cotellessa, Robert G., ed. *Identifying Research Areas in the Computer Industry in 1995*. Park Ridge, N.J.: Noyes Publications, 1984.

Deakon, Rose. *Women and Computing: The Golden Opportunity*. London: Macmillan Publishers, 1984.

Dertouzos, Michael, and Joel Moses, eds. *The Computer Age: A Twenty Year View*. Cambridge: MIT Press, 1979.

Din, Allan M., ed. *Arms and Artificial Intelligence: Weapons and Arms Control of Applications of Advanced Computing*. Oxford: Oxford University Press, 1987.

Feingold, S. Norman, and Norma Reno Miller. *Emerging Careers: New Occupations for the Year 2000 and Beyond*. Vol. 1. Garrett Park, Md.: Garrett Park Press, 1983.

Fjermedal, Grant. *The Tomorrow Makers: A Brave New World of Living Brain Machines*. New York: Macmillan Publishers, 1986.

Forester, Tom. *High-Tech Society: The Story of the Information Technology Revolution*. Cambridge: MIT Press, 1987.

Forester, Tom. *The Materials Revolution*. Cambridge: MIT Press, 1988.

Gerver, Elisabeth. *Humanizing Technology: Computers in Community Use and Adult Education*. New York: Plenum Press, 1986.

Gilder, George. *Microcosm*. New York: Simon & Schuster, 1989.

Goldenberg, E. Paul, and Wallace Feurzeig. *Exploring Language with Logo*. Cambridge: MIT Press, 1987.

Greenberger, Martin, ed. *Computers and the World of the Future*. Cambridge: MIT Press, 1962.

Grimson, W. Eric L., and Ramesh S. Patil, eds. *AI in the 1980s and Beyond: An MIT Survey*. Cambridge: MIT Press, 1987.

Haugeland, John. *Artificial Intelligence: The Very Idea*. Cambridge: MIT Press, 1985.

Hawkridge, David. *New Information Technology in Education*. London: Croom Helm, 1983.

Horn, Berthold. *Robot Vision*. Cambridge: MIT Press, 1986.

Inose, Hiroshi, and John R. Pierce. *Information Technology and Civilization*. New York: W. H. Freeman & Co., 1984.

Inose, Hiroshi, et al. *Road Traffic Control*. Tokyo: University of Tokyo Press, 1975.

Kearsley, Greg, ed. *Artificial Intelligence and Instruction: Applications and Methods*. Reading: Addison-Wesley Publishing Co., 1987.

Kidder, Tracy. *The Soul of a New Machine*. London: Allen Lane, 1982.

Lambert, Steve, and Suzanne Ropiequet, eds. *CD ROM, the New Papyrus*. Redmond, Wash.: Microsoft Press, 1986.

Langley, Pat, et al. *Scientific Discovery: Computational Explorations of the Creative Processes*. Cambridge: MIT Press, 1987.

Lapp, Ralph E. *The New Priesthood: The Scientific Elite and the Uses of Power*. New York: Harper & Row, 1985.

Laver, Murray. *Computers and Social Change*. Cambridge: Cambridge University Press, 1980.

Leontief, Wassily W. *The Structure of the American Economy, 1919–1939*. White Plains, N.Y.: International Arts & Sciences Press, 1941.

Leontief, Wassily W., and Faye Duchin, eds. *The Future Impact of Automation on Workers*. Oxford: Oxford University Press, 1986.

Man-Computer Interactive Research: MACINTER-I. Proceedings of the First Network Seminar of the International Union of Psychological Science on Man-Computer Interaction Research, Berlin, October 16–19, 1984. New York: Elsevier Science Pub. Co., 1986

Mason, Matthew T., and J. Kenneth Salisbury. *Robot Hands and the Mechanics of Manipulation*. Cambridge: MIT Press, 1985.

Megarry, Jacquetta. *Inside Information: Computers, Communications, and People*. London: British Broadcasting Corp., 1985.

Minsky, Marvin. *Society of Mind*. New York: Simon & Schuster, 1986.

Moreau, R. *The Computer Comes of Age: The People, the Hardware, and the Software*. Trans. J. Howlett. Cambridge: MIT Press, 1986.

Mowshowitz, Abbe, ed. *Inside Information: Computers in Fiction*. Reading, Mass.: Addison Wesley Pub. Co. 1977.

Newborn, Monroe. *Computer Chess*. New York: Academic Press, 1975.

Nova, Simon, and Alain Minc. *The Computerization of Society*. Cambridge: MIT Press, 1980.

Pea, R. D., and D. M. Kurland. *New Ideas in Psychology*. Vol. 1. Elmsford, N.Y.: Pergammon, 1983.

Papert, Seymour. *Mindstorms: Computers, Children, and Powerful Ideas*. New York: Basic Books, 1980.

Piaget, Jean. *The Psychology of Intelligence*. London: Routledge & Kegan Paul, 1967.

Pool, Ithiel de Sola. *Technologies of Freedom: On Free Speech in an Electronic Age*. Cambridge: Harvard University Press, 1983.

Rochester, Jack B., and John Gantz. *The Naked Computer: A Layperson's Almanac of Computer Lore, Wizardry, Personalities, Memorabilia, World Records, Mind Blowers, and Tomfoolery*. New York: William Morrow Co., 1983.

Rothchild, Jean, ed. *Machina ex Dea: Feminist Perspectives on Technology*. New York: Pergammon Press, 1982.

Roszak, Theodore. *The Cult of Information: The Folklore of Computers and the True Art of Thinking*. New York: Pantheon Books, 1986.

Schechler, G., ed. *Information Retrieval: A Critical Review*. Washington, D.C.: Thompson Books, 1967.

Shackle, G. L. S. *Imagination and the Nature of Choice*. Edinburgh: Edinburgh University Press, 1979.

Stern, Virginia W., and Martha Ross Redden. *Technology for Independent Living: Proceedings of the 1980 Workshops on Science and Technology for the Handicapped*. Washington, D.C.: American Association for the Advancement of Science, 1982.

Torrero, Edward A., ed. *Next-Generation Computers*. New York: IEEE Press, 1985.

Traub, Joseph F., ed. *Cohabiting with Computers*. Los Altos, Calif.: William Kaufmann, 1985.

Turkle, Sherry. *The Second Self*. New York: Simon & Schuster, 1984.

U.S. Defense Intelligence Agency. *Soviet Military Power, 1986*. Washington, D.C.: U.S. Government Printing Office, 1986.

Vallée, Jacques. *The Network Revolution: Confessions of a Computer Scientist*. Hammondsworth, England: Penguin Books, 1984.

Warnier, Jean-Dominique. *Computers and Human Intelligence*. Englewood Cliffs, N.J.: Prentice-Hall, 1986.

Weizenbaum, Joseph. *Computer Power and Human Reason: From Judgment to Calculation*. San Francisco: W. H. Freeman and Co., 1976.

Wieseltier, Leon. *Nuclear War, Nuclear Peace*. New York: Holt, Rinehart and Winston, 1983.

Winner, Langdon. *Autonomous Technology: Technics-out-of-Control as a Theme in Political Thought*. Cambridge: MIT Press, 1977.

Winston, Patrick H., and Karen A. Prendergast, eds. *The AI Business: Commercial Uses of Artificial Intelligence*. Cambridge: MIT Press, 1984.

Yazdani, Masoud, and Ajit Narayanan, eds. *Artificial Intelligence: Human Effects*. Chichester, England: Ellis Horwood, 1984.

Postscript

Belinfante, F. J. *Measurements and Time Reversal in Objective Quantum Theory*. Oxford: Pergamon Press, 1975.

Churchland, Paul M. *Matter and Consciousness*. Cambridge: MIT Press, 1988.

Cohen, I. Bernard. *The Birth of a New Physics*. New York: W. W. Norton & Co., 1985.

Dechert, Charles R., ed. *The Social Impact of Cybernetics*. New York: Simon & Schuster, 1966

Hewitt, Paul G. *Conceptual Physics*. 2nd ed. Boston: Little Brown & Co., 1974.

Hofstadter, Douglas. *Gödel, Escher, Bach: An Eternal Golden Braid*. New York: Basic Books, 1979.

Landau, L. D., and A. I. Kitaigorodsky. *Physical Bodies*. Trans. Martin Greendlinger. Moscow: Mir Publishers, 1980.

Landau, L. D., and A. I. Kitaigorodsky. *Physics for Everyone*. Trans. Martin Greendlinger. Moscow: Mir Publishers, 1978.

March, Robert H. *Physics for Poets*. New York: McGraw-Hill Book Co., 1970.

Minsky, Marvin. *Society of Mind*. New York: Simon & Schuster, 1985.

Penrose, R., and C. J. Isham, eds. *Quantum Concepts in Space and Time,* Oxford: Oxford University Press, 1986.

Przibram, K., ed. *Letters on Wave Mechanics*. Trans. Martin J. Klein. New York: Philosophical Library, 1967.

Glossary

Boldface words in an explanation cross-refer to an entry for that word.

Algorithm
A sequence of well-defined rules and instructions describing a procedure to solve a particular problem. A computer **program** expresses one or more algorithms in a manner understandable by a computer.

Analog
Pertaining to data measurable and representable through continuously variable physical quantities. An analog computer manipulates physical variables that are analogs of (physically analogous to) the quantities being computed.

Android
A robot similar to a human being in physical appearance.

Artificial intelligence
Broadly, the study of intelligence as a collection of information-processing tasks. Some other definitions are the following: (1) The field of research concerned with making machines do things that people consider to require intelligence. (2) The primary goal of AI is to make machines smarter; the secondary goals are to understand what intelligence is. (3) The study of the computational connection between action and perception.

Artificial life
A sequence of outputs produced from a computer **program** that are presented with an initial configuration of points (the "organism") and a set of rules (the "genetic code") to generate subsequent generations of the organism. Artificial life is modeled on evolution by natural selection. Certain initial configurations and rules can produce visually pleasing images. This is thus one technique for generating computer art.

ASIC (application-specific integrated circuit)
A **chip** that, unlike a normal computer **microprocessor**, is designed to execute a specialized function or procedure. ASICs may be viewed as chip implementations of programs.

ASR (automatic speech recognition)
Refers to the ability of a machine to recognize high-level patterns in human speech. In general, the goal of ASR is to identify the words spoken.

Backward chaining

A technique of "reasoning" for an **expert system** in which the system tries to verify a hypothesis by verifying all statements that imply (or lead to) that hypothesis.

Binary code

A representation (or encoding) of data that makes use of exactly two distinct characters (say 0 and 1). An encoding is a set of rules that specifies a correspondence between one set of symbols and another.

Bit

Binary digit. In a **binary code**, one of the two possible characters, usually 0 and 1. In information theory, the fundamental unit of information.

Byte

A sequence of eight adjacent **bits** operated on as a unit for the sake of convenience and frequently used as a measure of memory or information. A byte may correspond, for example, to a letter of the English alphabet.

CAD (computer-assisted design)

Computer technology used in many aspects of the design of a product. Users enter design criteria and create partial designs. The computer then suggests, tests, and modifies the design in keeping with industry standards and regulations.

CAI (computer-assisted instruction)

Education that uses computers to present tutorials and subsequently to test and monitor the user's learning.

CAT (computer-assisted translation)

Automation of all or part of the difficult task of accurately translating text from one **natural language** to another.

CCD (charge-coupled device)

A device that stores information by representing it as packets of minute electrical charges. Also used as sensors for scanning visual images.

Chip

A (possibly large) collection of related circuits designed to work together on a set of tasks. These circuits reside on a wafer of **semiconductor** material (typically silicon).

COBOL (Common Business Oriented Language)

A data-processing **computer language**, the de facto standard for business programming. It makes use of statements very similar to business English and was first used in 1960.

Combinatorial explosion

The rapid (exponential) growth in the number of possible ways of choosing distinct combinations of elements from a set as the number of elements in that set grows. Specifically, in **artificial intelligence**, the rapid growth in the number of alternatives to be be explored while performing a **search** for a solution to a problem.

Compiler

A program that produces a machine code from a source code originally written in a high-level problem-oriented language.

Complexity theory

The mathematical study of the difficulty of solving any well-stated problem in terms of resources (time and space) consumed. Complexity theory is used primarily to determine the effect of an increase in the *size* of a problem.

Computer language
A set of rules and specifications to describe a process on a computer.

Connection Machine
A **parallel-processing** computer that makes use of a large number of well-connected low-computation-power processors (currently up to 65,536).

Connectionism
An approach to studying intelligence based on storing problem-solving knowledge as a pattern of connections among a very large number of simple processing units operating in parallel. Connectionism is often contrasted with the manipulation of the large symbolic structures traditionally used to represent knowledge in **artificial intelligence**. It was inspired by the structure of synapses (connections) and neurons (processing units) in the human brain.

Constrained search
A **search** on possible alternatives carried out after discarding those alternatives that seem unlikely to lead up to a solution.

CPU (central processing unit)
The principal operating part of a computer, encompassing the electronic circuits that control the interpretation and execution of instructions. It includes the arithmetic and logic unit, the control unit, and possibly the primary memory.

Cybernetics
The comparative study of information handling mechanisms (control and communication) in animals and machines. Cybernetics is based on the theory that intelligent living beings adapt to their environments and accomplish objectives primarily by reacting to feedback from their surroundings.

Demon
A support mechanism that performs simple decision making and low-level information gathering to aid the main (intelligent) program execute its larger tasks. In an **expert system**, rules that watch out for exceptions, special conditions, and dangerous situations and suggest precautionary action.

Data base
An organized store of data made accessible to a computer, ordinarily designed in connection with an information-retrieval system. A database management system (DBMS) allows monitoring, updating, and interacting with the database.

Debugging
Discovery and rectification of errors (features leading to unwanted results) in a computer **program**.

Decision tree
A set of rules written in the form of a tree. At each node (branch point) a rule is examined, and a decision is made to take a particular branch, which in turn leads to the next node or to the end result.

DENDRAL
The first **expert system**. It was designed to determine structures of organic compounds using data from mass spectrometers and magnetic-resonance imaging (MRI).

Digital
Pertaining to the use of combinations of **bits** to represent all quantities that occur in a problem or computation. Compare with **analog**.

Domain specific

Applicable only to a particular domain of knowledge and expertise. Chemistry is a very large domain, but organic structural analysis is narrow enough to be handled by **DENDRAL**, a domain-specific **expert system**.

Dynamic programming

A procedure that works backward to solve a multistage decision problem by making an optimal decision at each stage on the assumption that an optimal decision has been made in the *previous* stage. The solution for the final stage thus gives the solution for the entire problem.

ENIAC (Electronic Numerical Integrator and Computer)

Completed in 1946 at the University of Pennsylvania, ENIAC was the first general-purpose programmable electronic **digital** computer. It was originally designed to produce ballistic tables for use in the Second World War.

Entropy

In thermodynamics, a measure of chaos and unavailable energy in a physical system. In other contexts (even in the social sciences), a term used by analogy to describe the extent of randomness and disorder of a system and consequent lack of knowledge or information about it.

Expert system

A computer **program**, based on various **artificial intelligence** techniques, performing a specialized difficult task at the level of a human expert. An expert system is frequently partitioned into a knowledge base, an inference engine, and (possibly) an explanation mechanism.

Floating-point number

A number expressed as a product of a bounded number and a scale factor (consisting of an integer power of a number base), for example, 2.3×10^2.

Floppy disk

A secondary data-storage device consisting of a thin flexible magnetic disk covered by a semirigid protective jacket.

Fractal geometry

A nascent branch of mathematics named with a Latin word meaning irregular. Fractal geometry explores a world of crinkly convoluted shapes far removed from the straight lines and smooth curves of traditional Euclidian geometry. Fractal curves, produced by computer **algorithms**, bear striking resemblance to naturally occurring shapes (coastlines, clouds, etc.) and hence are extensively used to produce realistic computer graphics. The term "fractal" is also an abbreviation for "fractional dimension": the dimensions of fractal curves are not limited to integers. These curves are used to model chaotic phenomena appearing in such diverse fields as music, financial markets, and natural topology.

Fuzzy logic

A branch of logic designed specifically to support human reasoning by allowing such linguistic labels as "fairly" and "very" so that statements may be made with varying degrees of certainty and precision. In traditional logic a statement may have one of only two values (true or false). Fuzzy-logic labels and operators allow statements to have *multiple* values.

Gaussian filtering

A process by which each **pixel** is replaced by one whose intensity (brightness) is the weighted sum of the intensities of adjacent pixels. The weight for a pixel is chosen according to the Gaussian normal function (the bell-shaped curve) of its distance from the central pixel. This is often a preliminary step to recognizing the edges of a picture.

General Problem Solver (GPS)

A procedure and **program** developed by Allen Newell, J. C. Shaw, and Herbert Simon that attains an objective by using rules to generate many alternatives at any current state and pursuing the alternatives that appear to be the closest to the objective. It has failed on some classes of problems due to the lack of sufficient rules and an adequate measure of closeness.

Goal-driven reasoning

Reasoning that focuses attention only on those pieces of knowledge that seem likely to lead to a goal. A generalization of **backward chaining**.

GOTO statement

An instruction in a computer **program** used to explicitly redirect the computer's current operation to another line of the same program.

Hard disk

A rigid plate with magnetic coating. A hard disk can handle greater amounts of data at a higher speed than a floppy disk.

Heuristic

A rule of thumb or a technique based on experience and for which our knowledge is incomplete. A heuristic rule works with useful regularity but not necessarily all the time. More generally, a heuristic is any knowledge that reduces the amount of **search**.

Heuristic programming

The programming of problem-solving systems to reason and search for solutions by means of organized collections of **heuristics**.

Holograph

An interference pattern, often using photographic media, that is encoded by laser beams and read by means of low-power laser beams. This interference pattern can reconstruct a three-dimensional image.

Holy Grail

Any objective of a long and difficult quest. In medieval lore, the Grail refers to the plate used by Christ at the Last Supper. It subsequently became the object of knights' quests.

Hypertext

An approach to information management in which data is stored in a network of *nodes* connected by *links*. The nodes, which may contain text and even audio or video elements, are meant to be viewed interactively. Links provide pathways to other nodes for exploring further relevant information.

Idiot savant

A system or person that is highly skilled in a small task area but impaired in other areas of functioning. The term is taken from psychiatry, where it refers to a person who exhibits brilliance in one very limited domain but is underdeveloped in common sense, knowledge, and competence. Idiot savants have been known, for example, to be capable of multiplying very large numbers in their heads, although they are otherwise mentally disabled.

Image processing

Performing computations on sets of visual signals to recognize and interpret high-level patterns and to resolve the image into meaningful components.

Image scanner

A device that converts a visual image into sets of electronic signals that may be subjected to **image processing**.

Josephson junction

An oxide barrier between two metals across which electrons may be forced to tunnel. When immersed in liquid helium, a circuit containing such a junction is able to switch at very high speeds with low power dissipation. It thus avoids the heat-transfer problems that arise from silicon VLSI devices and is one way to attain superconductivity.

Knowledge engineering

The art of designing and building **expert systems**, in particular, collecting knowledge and **heuristics** from human experts in their area of specialty and assembling them into a knowledge base or expert system.

Knowledge principle

A "principle" that emphasizes the important role played by sheer knowledge (as opposed to general reasoning mechanisms) in many forms of intelligent activity. It states that a system exhibits intelligence primarily because of the specific knowledge that it contains about its domain of knowledge.

Knowledge representation

A scheme for organizing human knowledge into a manipulable data structure flexible enough to allow one to express facts, rules, relationships, and common sense.

LISP (list processing)

An interpretive **computer language** developed for manipulating symbolic strings of instructions and data. The principal data structure is the list, a finite ordered sequence of symbols. Because the programs themselves are expressed as lists, LISP lends itself to sophisticated recursion, symbol manipulation, and self-modifying code. It is widely used for AI programming.

Logic gate

A device implementing any of the elementary logic (or Boolean) functions (for example, AND, OR, NOT, NOR, XOR). A logic gate is characterized by the relationship between its inputs and outputs and not by its internal mechanisms.

Luddite

One of a group of early nineteenth-century English workmen that destroyed labor-saving machinery in protest. Today the Luddites are a symbol of opposition to technology.

Machine language

The written representation of machine code, which is the operation code understood directly by a computer. More generally, it is the language used by a computer for communicating internally with its own subsystems.

Mainframe computer

An expensive, sophisticated, general-purpose computer that can be simultaneously accessed by many users and that usually has a wide range of peripherals. Mainframes are distinguished from **minicomputers** and **microcomputers** primarily by their computational power.

Microcomputer

A small computer designed for a single user, ordinarily used in homes and by individual business users. A microcomputer usually uses a single-chip **microprocessor**.

Microprocessor

The entire **CPU (central processing unit)** of a computer in the form of a large-scale integrated circuit built on a single **chip**.

MIDI (Musical Instrument Digital Interface)

Technology that allows communication of **digital** data (representing musical notes and other information) between musical instruments and thus allows different electronic musical instruments to control and interact with each other.

Mind-body problem

The philosophical question of how a *nonphysical* entity such as the mind may interact with and exert control over a *physical* thing such as the body.

Minicomputer

A computer similar to a **mainframe computer** in that it supports multiple users, but not as powerful.

Minimax procedure or theorem

A basic technique used in game-playing **programs**. An organized enumeration of possible moves, together with corresponding possible moves from the opponent, is constructed in the form of a tree. An evaluation of the final position of the tree's leaves that always chooses the minimum value on the opponent's levels and the maximum value on the player's levels is then passed back down the tree.

MIPS (millions of instructions per second)

A conventional measure of the speed of a computer in terms of the number of the steps it can perform per second.

Molecular computers

Computers based on **logic gates** that are constructed on principles of molecular mechanics (as opposed to principles of electronics) by appropriate arrangements of molecules. Since the size of each logic gate is only a few times that of a molecule, the resultant computer could be microscopic in size. Limitations on molecular computers arise only from the physics of atoms. Thus, molecular computers are theoretically the fastest possible computers.

Multiple experts

A group of intelligent **programs**, each highly skilled in its own area of specialization, organized together to achieve a broader and higher level of generality in performance in the hope that at least one will rise to a problem solution.

Music-notation processor

A program or system working on music notation in the functionally equivalent way that **word processors** work on text.

MYCIN

A successful **expert system** developed at Stanford University in the mid 1970s and designed to aid medical practitioners in prescribing an appropriate antibiotic by determining the exact identity of a blood infection.

Natural language

Ordinarily spoken or written language (e.g., English) governed by sets of rules and conventions sufficiently complex and subtle for there to be frequent ambiguity in syntax and meaning.

Neural networks

Machinery implementing the ideas of **connectionism** and consisting of processing units and their interconnections patterned after the structure of the human brain.

90-10 rule

Generally, with a given set of resources and objectives, solving 90 percent of a problem will consume only 10 percent of the resources, and solving the remaining 10 percent of the problem will consume the remaining 90 percent of the resources.

NOR gate

A **logic gate** whose output is logical 1 (true) only when all its inputs are logical 0 (false) and is logical 1 otherwise. It is a universal gate, since any logical or Boolean function can be realized with circuits consisting only of NOR gates.

Object code

The machine-code output of a compiler after translation of the source code. See **compiler**.

OCR (optical character recognition)

A process in which a machine scans, recognizes, and encodes printed (and possibly handwritten) characters into **digital** form for input into a computer.

Operating system

A large, complex body of **programs** that control and administer all other programs of a computer.

Optical computers

Computers processing information encoded in patterns of light beams, unlike today's conventional computers, in which information is represented in electronic circuitry or encoded on magnetic surfaces. Optical computers present the potential of computing at higher speeds and with a massive level of **parallel processing**.

Optical disks

A disk, typically of plastic, on whose surface information is etched as a sequence of pits, which are read by a low-power laser beam. Optical disks can potentially store large amounts of information (a billion **bytes** or more).

Organic circuits

Circuitry consisting of processing units that, under favorable conditions, are self-replicating and self-organizing.

Orthogonal invariances

The distribution of strengths of two **expert systems** in a way that the chance of solving a particular problem is greater when using both experts than when using either expert alone. The reason for the success of **multiple experts** is that the chance is high that at least one of the experts will rise to a problem solution.

Pandemonium selection

An electionlike decision-making procedure in which a decision is made according to the level of excitation or response generated from a group of sensory or information-gathering units (or **demons**) when presented with each possible solution.

Parallel processing

Simultaneous operation (rather than sequential operation) of two or more devices to perform independent tasks within an overall job. More than one particular process is active at any instant. Compare with **serial computer**.

Parser

A program resolving a string of characters (representing, for example, an English sentence or a **computer-language** statement) into its elemental parts (or parts of speech) as determined by the particular language.

Pattern recognition

Recognition of patterns with the goal of identifying, classifying, or categorizing inputs.

Perceptron

An early model for the processing units that may be used in **neural networks**. Perceptrons are noted for the simplicity of the function they perform on input.

Pixel

An abbreviation for picture element. One of the elements in a large array holding information that represents a picture. Pixels contain data giving brightness and possibly color at particular points in the picture.

Predicate logic

A system of logical inference based on set theory. Variants are used in **artificial intelligence** in the representation of knowledge.

Primal sketch

A representation of images that gives explicit information about brightness changes, textures, and orientations of surfaces.

Program

A sequence of written statements that conform to the specifications of a **computer language**, for use by a computer (or any intelligence system).

PROLOG

A nonprocedural programming language used in **artificial intelligence**. A PROLOG program contains descriptions of relevant relationships between entities in the problem and of the rules governing the solution of a problem but not of the *procedures* that are to be used to find those solutions.

Prospector

An **expert system** designed to aid geologists in interpreting mineral data and predicting locations of mineral deposits. It is famous for correctly pointing to a previously unknown extension of a molybdenum deposit.

Punch card

A rectangular card that typically records up to 80 characters of data in a **binary coded** format as a pattern of holes punched in it.

Pushdown stack

A list of information in which insertions, and removals of data are made at one end of the stack (the top), also called a LIFO stack for "last in, first out." Stacks are convenient structures in computer science because they facilitate **recursive** computations.

RAM (random-access memory)

A type of temporary internal memory in which all locations of data can be accessed with equal speed.

Recursion

The process of defining or expressing a function or procedure in terms of itself. Each level of a recursive-solution procedure produces a simpler (or possibly smaller) version of the problem than originally posed. This process continues until a subproblem whose answer is already known is obtained. A surprisingly large number of symbolic and numerical problems lend themselves to recursive formulations.

Reverse Polish notation

A notation for arithmetic operations on numbers, where each operator follows its operands. For example, $7 + 5$ is expressed as $7\ 5\ +$ and $1 + (2 \times 3)$ is expressed as $2\ 3 \times 1\ +$. The order of evaluation is uniquely defined, and such expressions are readily evaluated on a **pushdown stack**.

Robot

A programmable device consisting of machinery for sensory activity and mechanical manipulation and connected to (or including) a computer. Typically, these machines automatically perform some task normally done by human beings.

ROM (read only memory)

A permanent internal memory whose contents are built into the device during manufacture. ROM contains data or instructions that can be read quickly but cannot be altered.

Sea-of-logic machine

A machine model proposed in this book constructed only of **NOR gates**. The mechanisms that account for intelligent behavior can in theory be constructed as a sea-of-logic machine.

Search

A procedure in which an automatic problem solver seeks a solution by iteratively selecting from various possible alternatives as intermediate steps toward a solution.

Segmentation

Generally, the broad problem of separating a problem into parts. For example, a string of speech may be analyzed at many levels: in terms of phonemes, in terms of words, or in terms of complete sentences.

Self-modifying code

A **program** that causes changes in portions of the program itself. Self-modifying code can thus selectively store, destroy, and transform information within itself (for example, it can replace problems with simpler subproblems). This ability is the crux of intelligent adaptive behavior.

Semantic networks

A type of **knowledge representation** that uses nodes to denote concepts and labeled links to indicate the relationships among these concepts.

Semiconductors

A material commonly based on silicon or germanium with a conductivity midway between that of a good conductor and an insulator. Semiconductors are used to manufacture transistors, which are used to construct **logic gates**.

Serial computer

A computer that performs two or more computations one after another, not simultaneously (even if the computations are independent). Opposed to a **parallel processing** computer.

SHRDLU

A landmark **natural-language** program, completed in 1970, that integrates the previously independent functions of reasoning, syntax, and semantics. It performed remarkably well in its own small domain of children's blocks.

Silicon compiler

A system producing a description of a given procedure or **algorithm** at the level of **logic gates** so that this low-level detail may be used to specify the design of a chip to be fabricated.

Simulator

A special-purpose computer or **program** designed to imitate the behavior of some existing or intended system in order to study the performance and effects of that system. Simulators are often used to study complex natural systems, such as chemical interaction or fluid flow. Another common example is the flight simulator used to train pilots.

Smart weapons

Attack systems that exhibit intelligence and skill in identifying, locating, tracking, and destroying targets.

Society of mind

A theory of the mind proposed by Marvin Minsky in which intelligence is seen to be the result of proper *organization* of a very large number of simple mechanisms, each of which is by itself unintelligent.

Sombrero filter

A process whereby each **pixel** is replaced by one whose intensity is the weighted sum of the intensities of adjacent pixels. The weights are chosen according to a function of the distance of the adjacent pixel from the center pixel. The function is the Laplacian of a Gaussian convolver and has the shape of a Mexican sombrero hat.

Speaker independence

Refers to the fact that some features of a speech string are not dependent on who the speaker is. "Speaker independence" also refers to the ability of a system for **automatic speech recognition** to understand any speaker, irrespective of whether or not the system has previously sampled that speaker's speech.

Subroutine

A **program** or block of programs organizationally distinct from the main body of the program.

Supercomputer

The fastest and most powerful computers available at any given time. Supercomputers are used for computations demanding high speed and storage (e.g., analyzing weather data).

Superconductivity

The physical phenomenon whereby some materials exhibit zero electrical resistance at low temperatures. Superconductivity points to the possibility of great computational power with little or no heat dissipation (a limiting factor today).

SUR (Speech-Understanding Research) Project

A project funded by DARPA in the early 1970s with the goal of producing an **automatic speech-recognition** system with the capacity to understand 90 percent of continuous speech (as opposed to isolated words) about some limited subject matter and making use of a vocabulary of at least one thousand words.

Synthesizer

An electronic device (typically for musicians) for the production of a wide range of sounds, allowing significant control over the nature of these sounds.

Stored program

Refers to a computer in which the **program** is stored in memory along with the data to be operated on. A stored-program capacity is an important capability for systems of **artificial intelligence** in that **recursion** and **self-modifying code** are not possible without it.

Template matching

Comparing stored prototype image patterns with shapes derived from **digitized** input images.

Toy world

An artificially simplified system used for studying and testing of ideas and devoid of the complexities and constraints that are ordinarily present in real circumstances.

Turing test

A criterion proposed by Alan Turing that maintains that a system is intelligent if it can deceive a human interrogator into believing that it is human.

$2^1/_2$-D sketch

A representation of a visual scene that shows the depth and orientation of all visible surfaces.

UNIX

A multiprogramming **operating system** developed at Bell Laboratories and favored by computer scientists. One of the goals of UNIX is to provide a uniform environment in which a relatively small number of users may collaborate on a single system with a considerable degree of cooperation.

Vacuum tube

A device with electrodes in an evacuated glass tube for the the control of current flows in a electric circuit. Used for the construction of early **logic gates**.

VLSI (very large scale integration)

Fabrication technology that allows tens of thousands (and possibly up to millions) of **logic gates** to reside on a single **chip**.

Von Neumann architecture

The design of conventional computers, based on **stored programs** and **serial** processing.

Word processor

A **program** for creating, altering, viewing, storing, and printing text with maximum flexibility. The term was coined by IBM in the late 1960s.

XCON

An **expert system** developed to specify how all the components of a computer should be placed and connected. Developed by Carnegie-Mellon University and Digital Equipment Corporation (DEC) for use in configuring DEC's VAX series of computers.

Z-series machines

A series of machines designed and constructed by Konrad Zuse in Germany: Z-1 (nonprogrammable, mechanical), Z-2 (nonprogrammable, electromechanical), Z-3 (programmable, electromechanical), and Z-4 (an improved version of Z-3). The Z-3 was the first programmable computer.

Index